Lecture Notes in Computer Science   3309

Commenced Publication in 1973
Founding and Former Series Editors:
Gerhard Goos, Juris Hartmanis, and Jan van Leeuwen

T0223726

Chi-Hung Chi   Kwok-Yan Lam (Eds.)

Content Computing

Advanced Workshop on Content Computing, AWCC 2004
ZhenJiang, JiangSu, China, November 15-17, 2004
Proceedings

 Springer

Volume Editors

Chi-Hung Chi
National University of Singapore, School of Computing
3 Science Drive 2, Singapore 117543
E-mail: chich@comp.nus.edu.sg

Kwok-Yan Lam
Tsinghua University, School of Software
Teaching Building, Room 206, Beijing, 100084, PR China
E-mail: lamky@mail.tsinghua.edu.cn

Library of Congress Control Number: 2004114980

CR Subject Classification (1998): H.4, H.3, C.2, I.2, H.2.8, H.5.1

ISSN 0302-9743
ISBN 3-540-23898-0 Springer Berlin Heidelberg New York

Springer is a part of Springer Science+Business Media

springeronline.com

© Springer-Verlag Berlin Heidelberg 2004
Printed in Germany

Preface

Welcome to the Advanced Workshop on Content Computing 2004. The focus of this workshop was "Content Computing". It emphasized research areas that facilitate efficient, appropriate dissemination of content to users with the necessary access rights. We use the word "content" instead of "information" or "data" because we want to cover not only raw data but also presentation quality.

The fast growth of the Internet has already made it the key infrastructure for information dissemination, education, business and entertainment. While the client-server model has been the most widely adopted paradigm for the WWW, the desire to provide more value-added services in the delivery layer has led to the concept of an active network, where content-driven, intelligent computation will be performed to provide quality-of-service for content presentation and best-fit client demand. These value-added services typically aim to enhance information security, provide pervasive Internet access, and improve application robustness, system/network performance, knowledge extraction, etc. They are realized by incorporating sophisticated mechanisms at the delivery layer, which is transparent to the content providers and Web surfers. Consequently, the notion of "Content Computing" has emerged. Content computing is a new paradigm for coordinating distributed systems and intelligent networks, based on a peer-to-peer model and with value-added processing of the application-specific contents at the delivery layer. This paradigm is especially useful to pervasive lightweight client devices such as mobile and portable end-user terminals with a wide variation of hardware/software configurations.

This year, the workshop was held in Zhenjiang, Jiangsu, China. We received 194 high-quality papers from 11 regions, namely PR China, Korea, Singapore, Japan, United States, Canada, Australia, Germany, Taiwan, Italy, and Hong Kong. Totally, 62 papers were accepted and presented in the workshop. Among them, 26 papers (13.4%) were long ones and 36 (18.6%) were short ones. The topics covered include mobile code, agent technologies, content sharing, consistency management, networking infrastructures, content-aware security, multimedia content understanding, mining, knowledge extraction, Web services, content retrieval, ontologies, and knowledge conceptualization.

The great success of the workshop is indebted to the hard work of all program and organizing committee members. External helpers assisted in the paper review process so that we could finish on time. We would also like to take this opportunity to thank all who submitted papers to AWCC 2004 for their valued contribution. Last, but not least, we would like to thank Tsinghua University and JiangSu University for their sponsorship.

Chi-Hung Chi
Kwok-Yan Lam

AWCC 2004

Advenced Workshop on Content Computing 2004
ZhenJiang, JiangSu, China
November 15–17, 2004

Jointly Organized by
Tsinghua University, Beijing, PR China
and
University of Jiangsu, Zhenjiang, Jiangsu, PR China

Program Chairs

Chi-Hung Chi	National University of Singapore
Kwok-Yan Lam	Tsinghua University

Program Committee

Jiannong Cao	HK Polytechnic University
Chin-Chen Chang	Chung Cheng University
Mao Chen	Princeton University
Chi-Hung Chi	National University of Singapore
Siu-Leung Chung	Open University of Hong Kong
Chen Ding	Ryerson University
Zongming Fei	University of Kentucky
Li Gong	Sun Microsystems, Inc.
Ming Gu	Tsinghua University
Kwok-Yan Lam	Tsinghua University
Chen Li	University of California, Irvine
Vincent Tam	University of Hong Kong
Xiao-Dong Zhang	NSF and College of William & Mary

Executive Committee

Shi-guang Ju (Organizing Chair)	University of Jiangsu
Hua-ji Shi	University of Jiangsu
Xing-yi Li	University of Jiangsu
Xi-bin Zhao	University of Jiangsu

External Reviewers

Patrick Hung, Hartono Kurnio, Yi Mu, Hung-Min Sun, Hong-Wei Sun, Yan Wang, Willy Susilo, Hui Yang, Minjie Zhang, X-bin Zhao

Table of Contents

Session 3: Networking Infrastructure and Performance

Session 4: Content Aware Security (I)

Session 5: Content Aware Security (II)

Session 6: Multimedia Content

Session 7: Content Mining and Knowledge Extraction

Session 8: Web Services and Content Applications (I)

Session 9: Web Services and Content Applications (II)

Session 10: Content Retrieval and Management (I)

Session 11: Content Retrieval and Management (II)

Session 12: Ontology and Knowledge Conceptualization

Mobility Prediction-Based Wireless Resource Allocation and Reservation*

Xiaolong Yang[1,2], Qianbin Chen[1,2], Youju Mao[1], Keping Long[1,2], and Bin Ma[1]

[1] Chongqing Univ. of Post and Telecommunication, Chongqing 400065, China
[2] Univ. of Electronic Science and Technology, Chengdu 610054, China
yangxl@cqupt.edu.cn

Abstract. Due to the mobility uncertainty of mobile user, it is a real challenge for wireless network to efficiently allocate and reserve resource. Firstly, motivated from a rationale which a good data compressor should be a good predictor, this paper develops a mobility prediction algorithm based on the *Ziv-Lempel* algorithm, which is both theoretically optimal and good in practice. Theoretically, the prediction algorithm can predict not only to which cell a mobile user will handoff but also when the handoff will occur. Then, we propose an efficient resource allocation and reservation scheme, called predict-based *GC*, which integrates the prediction algorithm into the guard channels (*GC*) policy. The simulation results show that the time-complexity of our proposed scheme (i.e., predict-based *GC*) is worse, but it outperforms Fixed-percent and *ExpectedMax* in the QoS support effectiveness.

1 Introduction

Over the last decade there have been a rapid growth in portable computing devices such as notebook computers and personal digital assistants (PDA), as a result of which many applications, e.g., e-mail, news-on-demand, video-on-demand, www browsing, are being available to mobile or roving users. For most of these value-added applications to be provided successfully, it is very important to guarantee quality-of service (QoS) between the mobile user end-systems. Therefore, both the network service providers and users at the present time are rather concerned about the QoS issues. However, to support QoS in wireless networks is more difficult than that in the wired networks. On the one hand, the resource in wireless network is usually costly and rare. On the other hand, mobile users may frequently change cells during the lifetime of call, the availability of wireless network resources at the call setup time does not necessarily guarantee that wireless network resources are available throughout the lifetime of a connection. Thus, as a whole, the requirements of network resource are obviously time-variable due to mobile handoffs. If a resource allo-

---

* This work is supported by National Natural Science Foundation of China (No.90304004), National Hi-tech Research and Development Program of China (863 Program) (No.2003AA121540), the Ministry of Education (No. 204125), the Education Council of Chongqing (No. 050309), and the Science and Technology Council of Chongqing (No. 8061).

C.-H. Chi and K.-Y. Lam (Eds.): AWCC 2004, LNCS 3309, pp. 1–11, 2004.

cation and reservation scheme in wireless networks cannot efficiently process the handoff events and adapt to the time-variable characteristic, users may experience performance degradations, which may be magnified in the wireless micro/pico-cellular networks. Therefore, it is more important to appropriately integrate the mobility tracking or location management of mobile user with the resource allocation and reservation for the QoS support in wireless network.

Due to the strongest driving force for wireless value-added applications, i.e., the seamless and ubiquitous connectivity, the movement of the mobile users is greatly uncertain, which leads to the difficulty in providing the QoS support. Recently, some schemes based on resource reservation have been proposed, e.g., RSVP (Resource Reservation Protocol) and its mobility-extension versions: MRSVP (mobility-RSVP) and LRR (Linear Resource Reservation)[4], none of which is suitable for the uncertainty since all of them usually assume that the mobility of user be known in advance from its mobility specification.

Besides, the other schemes have been also proposed, which have considered the mobility uncertainty. For example, literatures [1]-[3] have proposed the guard channels policy, the fractional guard channels policy [2], and the distributed call admission control scheme, which can calculate the number of guard channels for handoffs according to the status of the local cell and/or the adjacent cells under a certain assumption (e.g., exponentially-distributed channel holding time, and uniformly cell handoff). However, their assumptions are unrealistic in real networks. In addition, literature [5] proposed the shadow cluster scheme, in which the adjacent cells mobile user likely to visit in the future are informed of its resource requirements. The scheme may improve the capacity of QoS support by reducing the call blocking probability. However, it lacks a mechanism to determine the shadow cluster in real networks, as it assumes either precise knowledge of user mobility or totally random user movements.

From the drawbacks of the mentioned schemes, we can know that the QoS support efficiency of schemes based on resource reservation highly depends on the processing the movement uncertainty of mobile users, i.e., the mobility prediction.

As known, a good method to quantitatively describe the uncertainty is the Shannon entropy in information theory, which can exactly scale what the information source can tell. In the same way, it can also scale the uncertainty of movement of mobile user. In the data compression process, a good data compressor means to be a good predictor. If the trajectory of movement of mobile user is regarded as a sequence of event, we can predict the next event by a certain data compression algorithm. Motivated by the theoretic bases and observations, this paper proposes a novel resource allocation and reservation scheme based on *Ziv-Lempel* algorithm, which is both theoretically optimal and good in practice.

The rest of this paper is organized as follows. Section 2 illustrated a more general model of wireless network and the representation of mobile user mobility pattern. Section 3 describes and analyzes the *Ziv-Lempel* based mobility prediction algorithm, and furthermore the resource allocation and reservation scheme based on the mobility prediction algorithm is proposed in Section 4. Its performance analysis and simulation results are presented and discussed in Section 5, where we evaluate the scheme from its effectiveness (including handoff dropping, new call blocking, reserved resource utilization and overall call blocking) and its time-complexity. Finally, concluding remarks are given in Section 6.

2 The Representation of User Mobility Patterns

As usual, structured graph models for a wireless cellular network have been quite popular among researchers engaged in solving the mobility prediction and resource reservation problems. Circular, hexagonal or square areas are often used to model the cells while various regular graph topologies such as rings, trees, one and two dimensional grids are used to model their interconnection. These structured and regular graphs are useful to simplify the network analyses and designing, but they over-simplify the uncertainty of movement of mobile user since these models do not accurately represent a real wireless cellular network.

Here, we use a generalized graph model to represent the actual cellular network (shown as Fig.1), where the cell shape and size may vary depending on many factors, such as the receiver sensitivity, the antenna radiation pattern of the base stations, and propagation environment, and the number of neighboring cells, which can be arbitrary but bounded and vary from cell to cell.

An actual network can be represented by a bounded-degree, connected graph $G = (V, E)$, where the vertex-set V represents pairs of cells and the edge-set E represents the adjacency between pairs of cells. The example network shown in Fig. 1 can be modeled by the vertex set $V=\{a,b,c,d,e,f,g,h\}$ and the edge set $E=\{(a,d),(a,b), (b,c),...,(e,g)\}$, and we get its adjacency matrix as follows

$$Adj = \begin{bmatrix} 0 & 1 & 0 & \cdots & 0 \\ 1 & 0 & 1 & \cdots & 0 \\ 0 & 1 & 0 & \cdots & 1 \\ \vdots & \vdots & \vdots & \ddots & \vdots \\ 0 & 0 & 1 & \cdots & 0 \end{bmatrix}_{8\times8} \tag{1}$$

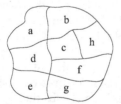
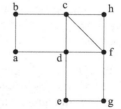
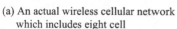

(a) An actual wireless cellular network   (b) Its general graph representation
which includes eight cell

Fig. 1. Modeling an actual wireless cellular network

In wireless networks, a call during its lifetime can be represented by a sequence of events $\{N\ H_1H_2SH_3H_nS...E\}$, where N denotes the event that a new call is admitted, H_n denotes the event of a mobile user nth handoff, S denotes the event of the call sojourning in the same cell and E denotes the call termination event. Note that in some cases, there are no handoff events during the lifetime of a call and thus no H_n in the sequence of events. According to the representation of the call events sequence, the trajectory of movement of mobile user can be also easily represented by a sequence of cells $\{v\}$, where $v(\ )$ denotes the cells users handoff to. In the example network shown in Fig. 1, the trajectory of movement of a certain mobile user may be the cells sequence $\{aabbbchfddedfch...\}$. For a mobile user, its current location and the trend of movement can be described through this two sequences.

3 Mobility Predictions and Location Update Based on Ziv-Lempel

For the mobility prediction processing, some literatures assume that the users independently handoff to its neighboring cells with equal probability, or assume that all of handoff events are independent and identically distributed. This two mobility patterns simplify the mobility prediction processing, but neither of them can exactly depict the actual movement of mobile user. Contrarily, the high-order Markov chain and the finite-context model are fairly reasonable. Of course, the order is higher, and the depictions of the actual movement can be more accurate, but we must note that the calculations of conditional probability and joint probability in practice are also more difficult. Based on the traditional information-theoretic definitions of entropy and conditional entropy in Ref. [9] and [10], the conditional entropy has a limit which equals to the per symbol entropy for a stationary stochastic process. So for each Markov chain and finite-context model, it is sure that there exists an appropriate order that depends on the actual mobility pattern. But its determination is a strenuous work.

From the viewpoint of the data coding technology, the drawbacks of the high-order Markov chain and the finite-context model result from the following factors. Firstly, its codeword is fixed-length because the conditional events of the N-order Markov chain are usually represented as $v_n|v_1v_2...v_{n-1}$, which is equivalent to N-symbol codeword. Secondly, the relationship in the context is simplex and independent, and does not vary with the input sequences. Hence, for the mobility prediction processing, only the model with variable-length codeword and adaptive-context is reasonable and practicable. According to the analyses of Ref. [11] and [12], the symbol-based version of the *Ziv-Lempel* algorithm can become the best candidate for the model because in actual data compression process, it is both theoretically optimal and good in practice.

Essentially, the *Ziv-Lempel* algorithm is universal variable-to-fixed coding scheme, which parses the input string S into block-to-variable distinct but the shortest substrings $\{s1, s2\ s3,...\}$ in a greedy manner. For each $j \geq 1$, substring s_j without its last character is equal to some previous substring s_i, where $j > i \geq 0$.

Example 1: Let the symbols be $\{a,b,c,d\}$, and given an input string $S = \{aaababbbbbaabccddcbaaaa...\}$, then the *Ziv-Lempel* encoder can parse it into the substrings $\{a,aa,b,ab,bb,bba,abc,c,d,dc,ba,aaa,...\}$.

The *Ziv-Lempel* coding process is interlaced with the learning process for the source characteristics. The key to the learning is a greedy de-correlating process, which implements by efficiently creating and looking up an explicit codeword dictionary, i.e., the decomposed substring derived from original string. Because of the Prefix Property, substring parsed so far can be efficiently maintained in a trie [12], which can store statistics information for contexts explored besides representing the codeword dictionary. Fig. 2 shows the trie formed by Example 1. Through the trie, a new codeword can be easily created by concatenating a single symbol v to a parsed codeword s_i. As the parsing process progresses along with the string extending, larger and larger codeword accumulate in the dictionary. At the same time, the trie will be updated. Consequently, the estimates of conditional probabilities for larger contexts can be built up. Moreover, the learning capacity of the trie can be boosted up, and its prediction is also more precise.

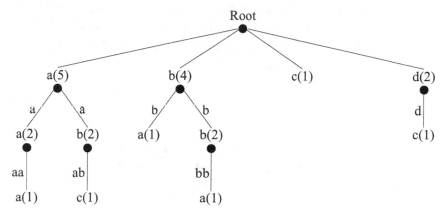

Fig. 2. The trie constructed in Example 1

For the sake of mobility prediction and location update, the trajectory of movement of mobile user is regarded as a substring in the symbol-based *Ziv-Lempel* algorithm. Similarly as shown in Fig. 3, we can also construct a mobility pattern predictor of the mobile user according to its mobility information base, which is equivalent to the trie. In natural, the predictor is a probability model based on *Ziv-Lempel* algorithm. When a new call is admitted, the predictor will set the current cell as a root of its mobility pattern, and update the probabilities of its possible events (including handoff and termination) during the call lifetime. When an event occurs in the sampling point, the predictor firstly judges whether it is the mobility pattern or not. If it is in the pattern, then the mobility pattern will be extended to the deeper layer, and be ready to the next prediction. Contrarily, a prediction fault is generated, and the mobility pattern and the context of current codeword are updated, as shown the red mark part in Fig. 3.

The performance of the predictor can be evaluated by two metrics, i.e., the prediction fault rate and the expected fault rate. The former is defined as the ratio of the total number of prediction faults to the total number of events, and the latter is defined as the best possible fault rate achievable by any prediction algorithm which makes its prediction based only on the past mobility pattern history. According to the analysis results shown in Ref. [12], the expected prediction fault rate of the predictor shown in Fig. 3 is proportional to $o(1/\sqrt{n})$ for stationary source, where n is the length of event sequence. The result implies that the predictor approaches optimality asymptotically for stationary sources. Therefore theoretically speaking, the predictor can predict not only to which cell a mobile user will handoff but also when the handoff will occur.

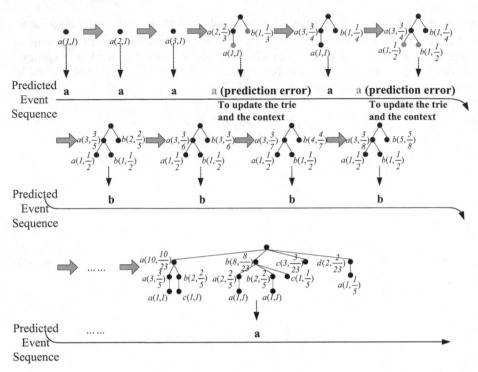

Fig. 3. The mobility prediction process of the symbol-based version of *Ziv-Lempel* encoder

4   The Dynamic Resource Allocation and Reservation Scheme

Since forced call terminations due to handoff blocking are generally more objection-able than new call blocking, the handoff of a call should be treated in higher priority than the admission of new call, which is a default rule for service provider, and is also the premise of our scheme in this paper. To improve the QoS capacity of wireless networks, we must address the resource allocation and reservation scheme, which critical evaluating factors usually include handoff dropping probability, new call blocking probability, and the reserved resource utilization.

Among many schemes, the guard channels (*GC*) policy [1] and its revisions (e.g., Fixed-percent, and Effective-Bandwidth expectation) are simple, but they cannot effectively satisfy the fluctuation of resource requirement due to the mobility of mo-bile user. However, their drawbacks can be overcome if their operations are based on the mobility predictor. Based on the clue, we can propose a scheme called as predic-tion-based *GC*.

Before the prediction-based *GC* puts into effect, the most likely *cell_j* (marked as *MLC*), which a mobile user may handoff to, must be firstly selected from the neighbor (marked as *Neighbor_Cell*) of current *Cell_i* based on the mobility predictor in section 3. *Neighbor_Cel(Cell_f)* can be obtained from the non-zero items in the adjacency matrix (1). Note that the two cell set meet the following relation:

$$Cell_j \in MLC(Cell_i) \subseteq Neighbor\_Cell(Cell_i) \tag{2}$$

Then we can pertinently allocate and reserve resource in $MLC(Cell_i)$ for the call during its lifetime.

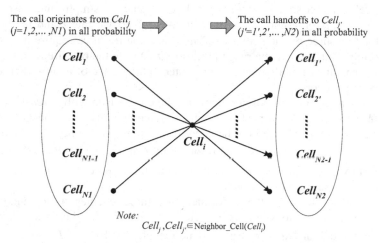

Fig. 4. The model of resource allocation and reservation during the call lifetime

As shown in Fig. 4, the call which handoffs to or originates from $Cell_i$ is our discussion objective in the proposed scheme. Assumed that the call comes from N_1 source neighbor cells, and possibly handoffs to N_2 target neighbor cells. There exist n_i and n_i calls in each source and target neighbor cells, respectively. According to the above mobility predictor, we can get the context (i.e., transition probability) of the handoff event from $Cell_j$ to $Cell_i$ (from $Cell_i$ to $Cell_{j'}$). The resource requirement in $Cell_i$ will fluctuate along with the calls continuously arrival at and departure from $Cell_i$. The fluctuation is represented by the following expression:

$$\Delta BW(N1,N2) = \sum_{l=1}^{N1} P_{l,i} \cdot \sum_{k=1}^{n_l} BW_k - \sum_{l'=1}^{N2} P_{i,l'} \cdot \sum_{k=1}^{n_{l'}} BW_k \qquad (3)$$

where BW_k denotes the effective-bandwidth 13.

When a new call arrives at $Cell_i$, which resource requirement is BW, its operation strategy is represented by the following expression:

$$Available\_BW\_of\_Cell_i > BW + \Delta BW \qquad (4)$$

If the expression (4) holds, then the scheme admits the call, or else rejects it.

When m calls handoff to $Cell_i$ while n calls terminate or handoff from $Cell_i$ to other cells, its strategy is represented by the following expression:

$$Available\_BW\_of\_Cell_i > BW_{Reserved} \qquad (5)$$

where $BW_{Reserved} = \Delta BW(N1+m, N2+n) - \Delta BW(N1, N2)$. If the expression (5) holds, then the scheme admits the calls handoffing to $Cell_i$, and reserves resources for them in advance, or else rejects the handoff requests.

5 Performance Analysis and Numerical Simulation

In this section, we construct a random Waxman-based 14 network with 100 nodes (i.e., 100 cells) as our simulation network. For the analysis simplifying, assumed the call creates in Poisson random process with average arrival rate λ and holding-time μ^{-1}, the total resource of each cell is 100 *unit*, and the resource requirement of each call uniformly distributes in the range [1, 20] *unit*. During the call lifetime, the trajectory of movement of mobile user is represented by the trace of a sub-graph of 100-node Waxman network.

Here, we evaluate our proposed scheme by the comparison with *Fixed-percent* and *ExpectedMax* 8 from two aspects, i.e., the time-complexity, and the QoS support effectiveness which is depicted by the handoff dropping probability P_{hd}, the new call blocking probability P_{nb}, the reserved resource utilization, and the overall call blocking probability. For *Fixed-percent*, assumed that the reserved resource for handoff occupies *8%* of total resource in each cell.

Fig.5(a) and (b) illustrates the performances of three schemes in the handoff dropping and the new call blocking. As expected, P_{hd} and P_{nb} for the three schemes increase with the call arrival rate. But, it is noticeable that both of P_{hd} and P_{nb} in our proposed scheme is the lowest. The gain benefits from the mobility prediction. Our proposed scheme considers the mobility of user during the resource reservation, and the reservation operations just aim at the predicted cells, i.e., $MLC(Cell_i)$. Obviously, the resource waste due to the useless reservations in each cell is greatly reduced. Therefore, P_{hd} and P_{nb} can be improved.

The reserved resource utilization is illustrated in Fig.5(c). When $\lambda<3.5$, it will rise sharply. But when $\lambda>3.5$, the distinctions among the three schemes will be more and more evident. In *Fixed-percent*, the reserved resource utilization will slowly rise and approach its limit *100%*. Contrarily in *Predict-based* and *ExpectedMax*, it will slightly decrease instead. The phenomena can be explained as follows. When λ increases, the constant resource reserved exclusively for the handoff process would be depleted, and cannot suffice the process of more handoff events. Hence, the utilization rate of its reserved resource certainly reaches *100%*. *Predict-based* and *ExpectedMax* reserve resource based on the mobility prediction. Moreover, these schemes exist some unavoidable prediction faults, which will appear frequently, and so incur much more invalid reservation operations when λ increases. Hence, it is impossible for *Predict-based* and *ExpectedMax* that the utilization rate is as high as *Fixed-percent*. As a whole, the utilization rate of *Predict-based* is better that of *ExpectedMax* When λ is high. The advantage comes from the better accuracy of mobility prediction based on Ziv-Lempel algorithm in *Predict-based*.

Obtained from the results in Ref. 15, the estimate of the overall call blocking probability in $Cell_i$ can be expressed as follows

$$P(Load_{Cell_i} \geq C) \leq \left(\frac{Load_{Cell_i}}{C} \right)^C \cdot e^{C-Load_{Cell_i}} \tag{6}$$

where *Load* consists of the actual resource used by the existing calls in $Cell_i$, and the reserved resource in $Cell_i$ for some arriving calls. In the comparison of Fig. 6, we take the upper bound. As illustrated by Fig. 5, when $\lambda > 3.5$, our proposed scheme distinctly outperforms *Fixed-percent* and *ExpectedMax*. Generally, the call arrival rate is more than *3.5-call/second* in actual wireless network. The result in Fig. 5 (d) shows that it is significant for our proposed scheme to improve the overall call blocking in a real wireless network.

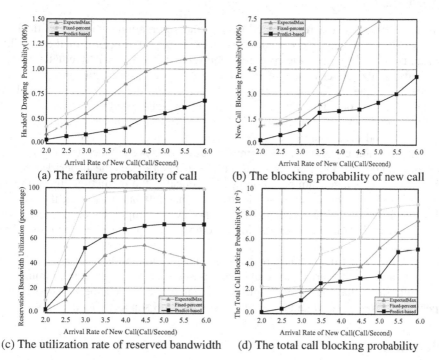

(a) The failure probability of call   (b) The blocking probability of new call

(c) The utilization rate of reserved bandwidth   (d) The total call blocking probability

Fig. 5. The QoS support effectiveness of our proposed scheme compared with other schemes

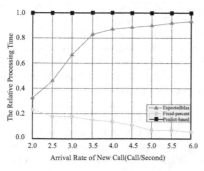

Fig. 6. The comparison of processing time, which of *Predict-based* acts as benchmark

As a whole, our proposed scheme will incur overhead as other schemes with mobility prediction. Here, we evaluate the overhead in terms of time-complexity. As shown by Fig. 6, the relative time-complexities of *Fixed-percent* and *ExpectedMax* are better than that of our proposed scheme. But when $\lambda > 3.5$, the distinction between *Predict-based* and *ExpectedMax* will be more and more blurring.

The above simulation results show that the integration mobility prediction into resource allocation and reservation can efficiently improve the QoS support capacity of wireless network, although it possibly incurs overhead of mobility prediction.

6 Conclusion

This paper discussed the resource allocation and reservation, which is critical for wireless network to improve the capacity of QoS support. Because of the mobility uncertainty of mobile user, the resource requirement in each cell fluctuates irregularly, and also the effectiveness of resource reservation is unsatisfactory, and much resource due to the useless reservations is wasted. Therefore, the process related the uncertainty has become the focus in the QoS support schemes. In this paper, we proposed the mobility prediction algorithm motivated from a rationale of data compression, i.e., a good data compressor should be a good predictor. In order to compress data well, the data compressor must predict future data well. Since the Ziv-Lempel algorithm is both theoretically optimal and good in practice, the paper develops a mobility prediction algorithm based on it. Theoretically, the prediction algorithm can predict not only to which cell a mobile user will handoff but also when the handoff will occur. Because the guard channels (GC) policy1 is simple, we proposed an efficient resource allocation and reservation scheme by integrating the prediction algorithm into GC.

Finally, we construct a random Waxman-based simulation network with 100 nodes, and analyze the performance of our proposed scheme by numerical simulation. The results show that the time-complexity of our proposed scheme is worse, but it outperforms *Fixed-percent* and *ExpectedMax* in the QoS support effectiveness.

References

1. E. C. Posner and R. Guerin, "Traffic policies in cellular radio that minimize blocking of handoff calls," Proc. of 11th Teletraffic Cong., Kyoto, Japan, Sept. 1985
2. R. Ramjee, R. Nagarajan and Don Towsley, "On optimal call admission control in cellular networks," Proc. of IEEE INFORCOM'96, San Francisco, CA, March 1996.
3. M. Naghshineh and M. Schwartz, "Distributed call admission control in mobile/wireless networks," IEEE J. Select. Areas Commun., vol. 14, No. 4, pp. 711-717, May 1996.
4. C.F.Koh, R.S.Chang, S.J.Leu and W.N.Yang, "Supporting QoS in Networks with Mobile Hosts" Journal of Computers, Vol. 12, No. 2, pp. 46-54, June 2000.
5. D.A.Levine, I.F.Akyldiz and M.Naghshineh, "The Shadow Cluster Concept for Resource Allocation and Call Admission in ATM-based Wireless Networks", Proc. of the 1st Annual International Conference on Mobile Computing and Networking, pp.62~74, Nov., 1995
6. K.C.Chua and S.Y.Choo, "Probabilistic Channel Reservation Scheme for Mobile Pico/ Microcellular Networks ", IEEE Communications Letters, Vol.2, No. 7, pp. 195~197, July 1998
7. W. Su, S-J.Lee and M. Gerla, "Mobility Prediction in Wireless Networks". Proc. of IEEE Milcom'2000, Vol.1, pp. 491-495, October 2000
8. P. Ramanathan, KM Sivalingam, P. Agrawal and S. Kishore, "Dynamic Resource Allocation Schemes During Handoff for Mobile Multimedia Wireless Networks", IEEE Journal on Selected Areas in Communications, vol. 17, no. 7, pp. 1270-1283, July 1999
9. Bhattacharya, S.K.Das, "LeZi-Update: An Information Theoretic Approach to Track Mobile Users in PCS Networks", Proc. of ACM/IEEE MobiCom'1999, pp.1-12, Aug. 1999.

10. Yixin Zhong, "The principle of information science" (the second edition), BUPT press, 1996
11. J. Ziv and A. Lempel, "Compression of individual sequences via variable-rate coding," IEEE Transaction on Information Theory, Vol.24, No.5, pp.530-536, Sep. 1978.
12. J. S. Vitter and P. Krishnan, "Optimal prefetching via data compression", Journal of the ACM, Vol.43, No.5, pp.771-793, September 1996.
13. Anwar I. Elwalid, Debasis Mitra, "Effective bandwidth of general Markovian traffic sources and admission control of high speed networks", IEEE/ACM Transactions on Networking, Vol.1, No. 3,pp.329-343, June 1993
14. Calvert K., M.Doar, E.Zegura, "Modeling Internet Topology", IEEE Communication Magazine, Vol. 35, No.6, pp.160-163, June 1997
15. Andras Farago, "Blocking Probability Estimation for General Traffic Under Incomplete Information", Proc. of ICCC'2000, pp.1547-1551, 2000.

An Agent-Enabled Content-Explicit Authorization Model for OGSA-Compliant Grid

Yunliang Jiang[1,2], Beishui Liao[2], Yong Liu[2], and Jun Hu[2]

[1] School of Information & Engineering,
Huzhou University, Huzhou 313000, China
[2] College of Computer Science,
Zhejiang University, Hangzhou 310027, China
jylsy@zju.edu.cn, cckaffe@yahoo.com.cn
{baiseliao,hujun_111}@zju.edu.cn

Abstract. Traditional methods for authorization within Grid computing have many shortcomings. Firstly, the enrolments of users and services into the server are done manually, which is not adaptable to the dynamic environment where the service providers and service consumers join or leave dynamically. Secondly, the authorization policy language is not expressive enough to represent more complex policies, and can't resolve the problem of semantic inconsistency between different parties who treat the same policy. This paper takes advantage of characteristics of intelligent agent such as autonomy, proactivity, and sociality, to treat with the authorization issues, including automated registrations and management of agents (service providers and service consumers), autonomous authentication and authorization based on policies, etc. On the other hand, an ontology-based content-explicit policy modeling framework is presented, which resolves the semantic inconsistency problem among different parties.

1 Introduction

When OGSA-compliant Grid[1] applications are developed, security is one of the most important problems to be dealt with. Security issues involve many aspects, including authentication, authorization, auditing, secure communication, availability and accountability, etc. In this paper, we focus on authorization management.

In large-scale, dynamic, heterogeneous, and cross-domain OGSA-compliant Grid, there are some issues related to authorization. Firstly, in the Grid, service providers and service consumers may join or leave dynamically, so the community memberships are not static. Secondly, the authorizations are difficult to be carried out centrally or unifiedly, but are managed and executed locally and independently instead. Thirdly, in the Grid environment, it is lack of flexibility and difficult to directly establish one-to-one trust relationships, so a trusted mediate mechanism is desirable for this purpose. Finally, how to represent the authorization policies to make them content-explicit is also a challenge. The simple ACL (Access Control list) is not powerful and expressive enough to meet all authorization requirements.

In recent years, many authorization solutions for the Grid have been developed, such as Akenti [2], Secure Virtual Enclaves [3], CAS [4], etc. Among them, CAS (Community Authorization Service), developed by the Globus security research

C.-H. Chi and K.-Y. Lam (Eds.): AWCC 2004, LNCS 3309, pp. 12–17, 2004.
© Springer-Verlag Berlin Heidelberg 2004

group, provides an intermediate layer that removes the requirement of a trust relationship between specific clients and services. This new approach for representation, maintenance, and enforcement of authorization policies has resolved the problems of scalability, flexibility, expressiveness, and policy hierarchy [4] that are brought about when expressing access policies in terms of direct trust relationships between providers and consumers.

However, there are some authorization problems that have not been resolved in CAS. First, the enrolments of users and services (resources) into the server are done manually, which is not adaptable to the dynamic environment where the service providers and service consumers join or leave dynamically. Second, the policy language adopted by CAS recently is a simple policy language consisting of a list of object names and a list of allowed actions on those objects, which is not expressive enough to express more detailed authorization requirements within VO environment, and may raise the problem of semantic inconsistency.

In this paper, we firstly propose an authorization model based on autonomous agents and content-explicit policies, which provides a new way to treat with the authorization problems listed above. Secondly, we address how to use an ontology language to represent the authorization policies, which resolves the problems of semantic inconsistencies among different participants of the VO and makes the policy content understandable to the machine (agents).

The remainder of this paper is as follows. In Section 2, the architecture of authorization model based on autonomous agents and content-explicit policies is introduced. In Section 3, we describe the authorization mechanism based on content-explicit policies. In section 4 conclusions are presented.

2 The Architecture of Authorization Model

On the top of OGSA-compliant Grid, we build an agent society, which is in charge of social interactions and security protections among various VO parties according to the high-level VO goals and policies. Each autonomous agent who encapsulates one or more grid services is a basic autonomic element (AE) [5]. A number of AEs may dynamically form a VO to implement specific goals of the VO. While the service composition by the AE, and the discovery, negotiation, service provisioning and monitoring among different AEs, are represented in [5,6], this paper focuses on authorization issues.

The architecture of authorization model based on autonomous agents and content-explicit policies is shown in figure 1. In this model, service provider (SP) is an autonomous agent (or an agent federation) who manage and control various grid services (or/and other agents); service consumer (SC) is an agent federation that is composed of a Federation Management Agent (FMA), several internal member agents (M_{ij}, $j \in \mathbb{N}$) and several external member agents (M_{ej}, $j \in \mathbb{N}$); community mediator (MedA) is an intermediate layer that bridges the gap of various partners. To each SC, MedA or SP, there is a policy service module (PSM) for policy specification and deployment (the PSM for SP is not presented in the figure). The process of trust relationship formation and authorization mainly consists of four steps, including VO participant enrolment organized by MedA, community-level authorization and local authorization.

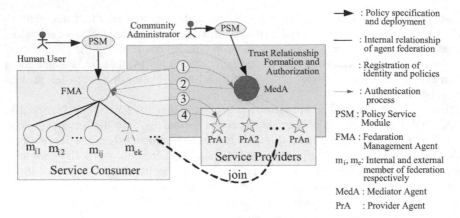

Fig. 1. Architecture of agent-enabled content-explicit authorization model for OGSA-compliant grid, in which, the authorization process is as follows. ①Service consumer (SC) makes a request to the MedA with its credential and the requirement policy; ②The MedA checks the credential and finds a service provider (SP) (if there is SP who satisfied the requirement), then returns the signed capability to the SC; ③The SC sends a request with this capability to the SP; ④ The SP checks the capability and returns a response to the SC (accepted if the local policies are satisfied, or rejected otherwise)

3 Authorization Mechanism Based on Content-Explicit Policies

As mentioned above, SPs and SCs are heterogeneous, dynamic entities. With the increasing number of them, it is difficult and not flexible to establish direct trust relationships among them. We adopt a third trusted party [4], MedA, to enroll and maintain the identities and policies (services providing or consuming policies), and take charge of community-level authorization. On the other hand, SPs allocate services in bulk to the MedA, and retain the final decision of service authorization based on their local authorization mechanisms. In this model, the SPs, SCs, and MedA are heterogeneous and autonomous agents, so the communication contents (identity, service providing policies, service consuming policies) should be explicit and machine-interpretable. In the following sub-sections, we first present the ontology-based policy specification. And second, the process of MedA mediated trust relationship formation is described. Then, we put forward the community-level authorization and local authorization, enabled by autonomous agents.

3.1 Content-Explicit Policy Specification

Considering the fact that in the heterogeneous environment, semantic inconsistency is obstructive to communication of different parties, we use the ontology language DCL (Domain Conceptualization Language)[7] to create application domain ontology.

Based on the DCL, we designed an ontology-based policy language for specific policy definition. The authorization policies specify the services providing strategies about what is shared, who is allowed to share, and conditions under which the sharing occurs. We use CPL (Conceptualization Policy Language) to define the service-providing policies. The CPL is described in the form of BNF in Definition 1.

Definition 1:

```
Grid-Service <Service-Name>{<Ontology-Name>}*
             <General-Information>
             <Application-Constraints>[<Owner>]
             [<Authorization-Constraints>]
             <Status> <Expiring-Time>
<General-Information>:= [<Description>]
             [<General-Classification>]
             [<Domain-Classification>]
<Application-Constraints>:=
             Constraints-Parameters:
                         {<Type><Parameter-Name>}+
         Constraints: <Condition-Expression>
<Authorization-Constraints> := {<User-Identity>
             <Permissive-Actions>}*
<User-Identity> := <User-Name>|<User-Category>
<Owner> := <Identity-of-Service-Provider>
<Status> := 'Active'| 'Inactive'
```

3.2 MedA Mediated Trust Relationship Formation

The MedA, as a trusted third party of SPs and SCs, is in charge of the enrolments of service providers and service consumers, the maintenance of memberships of a community, and the management and enforcement of community policies. The trust relationship between SP and SC is established by the bridging of MedA. The trust relationship formation mainly consists of there actions, i.e., registration, update, and revocation, of the identity and policies of SP or SC.

Registration. In order to participate in the cooperation and resource sharing in specific VOs, SP and SC should first register themselves to the MedA with their identities and policies signed by a certain certificate authority (CA). The policy is defined based on the CPL and DCL through policy service module (PSM in figure 1). The PSM is used to facilitate policy definition and deployment. The registration action is defined in the form of BNF as follows.

Definition 2:

```
registration <Type> <ID> [<Service-Providing-Policy>]
             {[<Role-Evaluation-Condition>]}*
<Type> := 'Service-Provider'| 'Service-Consumer'
```

In the definition 2, service consumer registers its ID and Role Evaluation Condition (REC) to the MedA, while service provider registers its ID, REC, and service providing policies. The REC is used to verify the properties (competence, reputation, functions, etc) of the SC or SP, and select proper role to SC or SP according to the community policies.

After registration, the MedA will maintain the registration information, and wait for update or revocation request from SC or SP.

Update and revocation. In the dynamic VO environment, SC or SP may leave a community dynamically, while the service providing policy may vary according to the

the high-level business strategy. So, the registration information may be updated or revoked at run-time. The update of service-providing policy of SP, and revocation of SP and SC, are defined in the form of BNF as follows.

Definition 3:

```
update <Type> <ID> <Data-Item> <Value>
<Data-Item> := <Status>|<Application-Constraints>
               |<Authorization-Constraints>
```

The status, application constraints, and authorization constraints are defined in the definition 1.

Definition 4:

```
revocation <Type> <ID>
```

By revocation, the registration information of SP or SC will be removed from the MedA of a community.

3.3 Community-Level Authorization and Local Authorization

In this model, the enforcement of authorization is localized and decentralized. MedA as a trusted third party undertakes the community-level authorization. The community-level authorization is defined in the form of BNF as follows.

Definition 5:

```
grant <Subject> <Action-List> <Target><Constraints>
<Subject> := <Service-Consumer-ID>
<Target>:= <Grid-Service-Name> ':' {<Operation>}
<Constraints> := <Condition-Expression>
```

When receiving a request from SC with its credential (identity and service requiring policy), the MedA authenticates the credential and chooses the available (active) services (SPs). Based on the service providing policies of SPs, the MedA automatically creates community-level authorization policy (capability of SC), and returns this policy with the credential of corresponding SP, to the SC.

Then, the SC checks the credential of SP presented by MedA (if pass) and makes a request to the SP with the capability.

On the other hand, local authorization is enforced by the specific service provider (SP). The policy engine of the SP takes charge of the authentication and authorization by three steps. First, in terms of local policies, it checks the credential of the MedA and the capability of the SC, from the request sent by the SC. Second, it checks the states of local resources (grid services). Third, if the local resources are available and the capability of the SC meets the local policies, then the SP schedule the resources for the SC and sends a notification message to the SC.

4 Conclusions

In this paper we have proposed a new approach for authorization of OGSA-compliant Grid On the basis of content-explicit policy and autonomous agents, this method is promising to solve the problems listed in section 1.

Acknowledgements

We gratefully acknowledge the support of Zhejiang Provincial Natural Science Foundation of China under grant M603169 and 602045, and Huzhou Natural Science Foundation of Zhejiang under grant 200415.

References

1. Foster, I., Kesselman, C., Nick, J. and Tuecke, S. The Physiology of the Grid: An Open Grid Services Architecture for Distributed Systems Integration. Globus Project, 2002, www.globus.org/research/papers/ogsa.pdf.
2. Thompson, M., et al., Certificate-based Access Control for Widely Distributed Resources, in Proc. 8th Usenix Security Symposium. 1999.
3. Shands, D., et al., Secure Virtual Enclaves: Supporting Coalition Use of Distributed Applications Technologies. ACM Transactions on Information and System Security, 2001. 4(2): p. 103-133.
4. L. Pearlman, et al. A Community Authorization Service for Group Collaboration, IEEE 3rd International Workshop on Policies for Distributed Systems and Networks, 2001.
5. Beishui Liao, et al. A model of Agent-Enabling Autonomic Grid Service System. to appear in the proceedings of GCC2004, Wuhan, China, Oct, 2004.
6. Beishui Liao, et al. A Federated Multi-agent System: Autonomic Control of Web Services. to appear in the proceedings of ICMLC2004, Shanghai, China, August, 2004.
7. Zhou Bin. The Systematism of Assistant Service for Agents (pp.31-33) [Thesis of Master degree].Hangzhou: Zhejiang University, 2004.

A Predictable Mobile Agent Computation Model and Its Fabric Architecture

Yong Liu, Congfu Xu, Zhaohui Wu, and Yunhe Pan

College of Computer Science, Zhejiang University
Hangzhou 310027, China
cckaffe@yahoo.com.cn

Abstract. Using the fabric of virtual organization architecture, a novel formalized mobile agent computation model is defined. In this model, all the actions (e.g. service, migration and communication etc.) of the mobile agents are treated as states. The process of the mobile agents' workflow is controlled by a finite-state-machine. This ensures the atomic action for each mobile agent to avoid the abnormal condition of communication mismatch. We propose a tolerance named service density of group, which will greatly decrease the probability of the mobile agent waiting for resource. It also can balance the service occupancy for the whole network.

1 Introduction

Mobile Agents are programs that can be migrated and executed between different network hosts. They locate for the appropriate computation resources, information resources and network resources, combining these resources in a certain host, to achieve the computing tasks. The more work that the mobile agents will proceed the larger the size of mobile agents will be. However, with the size decreasing, the intelligence of the mobile agents weakens. There is a conflict between the agent's size and the agent's intelligence. So there should be a compromise between sample and robust.

In fact, the Grid[3] technology has provided a powerful platform for the mobile agent. The WSDL[4] provides a web service description language for service disposing. How dose the service be composed together can be described by the WSFL[6]. And the UDDI (Universal Description, Discovery and Integration)[5] is used to enable online registry and the publishing and dynamic discovery of Web services offered by businesses. The RDF[7], which is recommended by W3C and can support a domain-independent metadata description, is used to describe the resources.

Fig. 1. shows hierarchy mobile agent architecture, the virtual organization can help the mobile agent to ignore the different OS problem and communication problem. Service layer is built upon the virtual organization layer, which provides the content of the proceeding. A service can be a sample operation or some combination of other services. The only thing that the mobile agents should do is discovering the service, managing the process of services' running. So the service

C.-H. Chi and K.-Y. Lam (Eds.): AWCC 2004, LNCS 3309, pp. 18–26, 2004.
© Springer-Verlag Berlin Heidelberg 2004

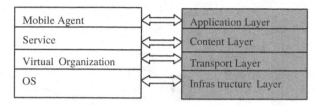

Fig. 1. Hierarchy Architecture of the Mobile Agent

layer can decrease the complexity of the mobile agent greatly. With the service disposing policy, the mobile agent can be more flexible and scalable: the service layer define and dispose the basic functions of the mobile agents, and mobile agents control and implement these meta-functions in practice applications.

2 Formally Definition of VO Based Fabric Architecture

Our computation model is established upon the virtual organization architecture, namely virtual organization (VO or group), which can greatly reduce the mobile agent size during migration, and this architecture can provide more intelligent support for mobile agent. The basic elements of virtual organization are nodes, which can be PC, PDA, laptop, and other devices connected by network. The nodes are grouped in virtual, and they can join and leave the group dynamically. The groups are virtually hierarchical, which means that the groups can be classified into root-layer, middle-layers and leaf virtual layers. The virtual group based fabric architecture is the platform of the mobile agent migration. By this way, the mobile agent can discovery and move more effective and it can also greatly decrease the mobile agent size during migration.

The VO based architecture mentioned in this paper is a structure similar to the fabric layer in [1]. Some definitions are given as the following:

Definition 1. Node, the minimized devices that can load and execute the mobile agents in network are denoted as R_i. Each node in VO can be a service provider or a service consumer.

Definition 2. Key Node is a kind of nodes that deals with the remote communications, denoted as R_i^0. Each group must contain a key node. And the key nodes are always positioned in two or more than tow groups. Normally the contiguity key nodes form a kernel group.

Definition 3. Group, the set includes one node or several nodes, denoted as $G_a^i = \{R_a^0, R_a^1, R_a^2, ..., R_a^n\}$, where a is the name of the group. Each group has a layer identifier i, which means that the group is the ith layer in VO. The node can join in more than one group in VO, which means that each node including key node can belong to two or more than two groups. R_j^i means that node belongs to group G_j. Group is a comparatively stable organization; the nodes belonging to certain group can leave this group and join in another group dynamically. The login and logout of nodes adopt the GGMP (Grid Group Management Protocol)[1], which is similar to the IGMP.

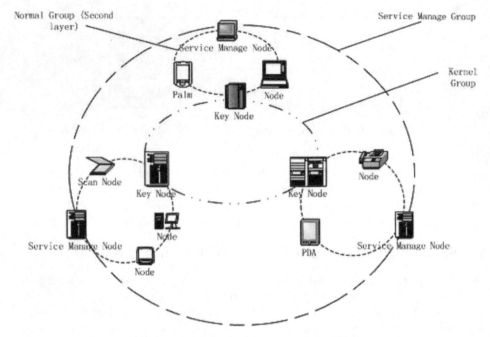

Fig. 2. Fabric Architecture of the VO

Definition 4. Service, in VO architecture, service is a kind of dealing process that provided by a certain nodes in VO. It can be formally defined as four-tuple: $S(GUIDS, Privilege, Content, Operation)$, where $GUIDS$ is the global unique ID of the service. And *privilege* is the privilege defined by the service provider, which include public and private privileges. *Content* is the process of service. *Operation* is a kind of special operations associated with service, which includes clone, serve, migration etc.

Definition 5. Service Management Node, is a kind of nodes that contains the services information of current group, denoted as R_s. Normally, all these contiguity service management nodes form a service management group automatically.

Definition 6. Virtual Organization, VO is a fabric structure that composed of nodes and is established by a serial of protocols. It is a hierarchical tree structure constituted by virtual groups. There exist a root group (denoted as RG, and it is the first layer) and other middle layer groups, denoted as G_j^i, i means that the group is the ith layer in the virtual organization. L is the leaf group, which is positioned at the bottom of the virtual tree. Normally, the group contains resembling and adjacent nodes. There is a key node R_i^0 in each group G_i. The functions of the key node in a group are similar to the gateway in a LAN, which communicates with other nodes outside the group. A protocol called GGMP (Grid Group Management Protocol)[2] has been used to determine the key node. Among all the nodes and groups, the key nodes constitute a virtual group called *kernel group*, G_k. It is the most important portion that serves for other nodes. It deals with communication and seeking etc. Among all of the nodes in virtual organization topology, the root (first layer) group in the tree structure of virtual organization is always chosen from one of the kernel groups.

Table 1. Privileges defined by the SSMP

Privilege Types	Privilege Sub-types	Notes
	Self private	The node, which releases the service, engrosses the service.
Private privileges	Group private	The service is privately belonged to the released node and its group.
	Below access	The service is public to the groups, which are the children of the original service released group.
Public privileges	Same level access	The service is public to the same layer group nodes in VO, which means the service released by the *ith* layer group node, and it can be cloned to the same *ith* layer group nodes.
	Full tree access	The service is public to all the tree nodes.
	Special level access	The service can specify the public layer from *ith* layer to *jth* layer, $i < j$.

3   Related Protocols

3.1   Safe Service Management Protocol

Service is disposed upon the virtual organization. Compared with the UDDI[5], the virtual organization based service is more dispersed. It is not necessary to establish a universal service information server in virtual organize, on the contrary, the service information is distributed in normal group, there is a service management node in each group. The available service information is stored in these service management nodes. For safe service management protocol, once the service has been released by the original node, it can be replicated to the same group nodes and others, and this operation is called *clone*. However, there may exist some services that would not share them with all the other nodes in VO. So the service disposed in the virtual organization has a privilege attribute. For the virtual tree is organized in hierarchy, the privilege of each layer is different, and in general the higher privilege is assigned to the higher layer group in VO. Table 1 lists the privileges that are defined by the SSMP. The privilege can be classified into two categories: private service and public service. This category division is based on the concept of the group, that is to say, whether the service is private or public to other groups. A farther category in private privilege can be classified into self-private and group-private, the difference between these two categories is whether the service can be cloned among the original group. There are four kinds of farther public privilege categories, they are below access, same level access, full tree access, and special level access respectively. This kind of public privilege category means that the services can be cloned out of their released groups, and the access degree out of the original groups is controlled by this privilege category.

3.2 Service Density

Before the service dispose protocol is presented, a tolerance named *Service Density* should be introduced firstly. It is one of the most important factors in our mobile agent computation model.

Definition 7. Service Density of Group, is a function, $f_s(A_{G_a^i}, N_{G_a^i})$, which symbolizes a certain available service in groups. Where s is the service name. $A_{G_a^i}$ is the number of nodes in group G_a^i, which contains available service of s. $N_{G_a^i}$ is the node number in group G_a^i.

In our mobile agent computation model, the service density of group (SDG) is defined as formulation (1). In SSMP, the service density of current group is stored in this service management node. Other groups can request for service density by sending message to this management node.

$$\eta_{G_a^i}^S = \frac{A_{G_a^i}}{N_{G_a^i}} \times 100\% \tag{1}$$

3.3 Description of Service

The service management node contains all the information of these services in current group, it also contains some service information of other groups, such as what kind of service, the service density of a certain service in other groups. There should be a meta-service description structure, which can offer sufficient service information storing in service management nodes. It will include the service identify information, position information and service density. Table 2 gives out the item structure of the service description information. This description information illustrates certain service's detail distribution information in a certain group. For example, there is service description information:

[File Search(2082-C000-0046), G_{AI}^3 , 50%, (R_{AI}^i, R_{AI}^j)]

Here service name is File Search, Service GUID is 2082-C000-0046, The name of the group that service lies at AI, The layer of the group that service lies at 3, The service density of File search in Group G_{AI}^3 is 50%, The file search service distributed nodes are R_{AI}^i, R_{AI}^j ($R_{AI}^i, R_{AI}^j \in G_{AI}^3$). The service management node saves its own service information, it also store some other groups' service information. The nodes in service management group can exchange the service description information when system is not too busy. In the message communication process, we use a XML based description file to give out the description

Table 2. Privileges defined by the SSMP

Service Information		Group Information		Other Information	
Service GUID	Service name	Group Layer	Group name	Service Density	Node List

information of each service, which can be parsed into the service description information structure in table 2.

4   Predictable Mobile Agent Computation Model

Definition 8. Predictable mobile agent computation model, is a six-tuple $MACM = (R, S, M, \phi, v, E)$, where, R is the node set, S is the finite state set of the mobile agent. S does not include the state of the agent migration Λ and the null state ε. Here, migration state Λ means that the mobile agent starts to move to another node to execute new state; null state means that the mobile agent does not perform any action (execution and migration).

$M \subset S$ is the set of all the message operation states for mobile agent. $M = \{M_s, M_a\}$, M_s is the state of sending message, and M_a is the state of receiving message.

$v \in R$ is the initial node that the mobile agent has been produced, a mobile agent's service firstly comes from the node v, and then cycles are driven by the finite states.

$E \subset R$ is the set of final node for the mobile agent, only in the final node the mobile agent can be destroyed and the service ends.

ϕ , the transition relation, is a finite subset of $(R \times (S \cup \{\Lambda, \varepsilon\})) \longrightarrow R$:

$\phi : (R \times (S \cup \{\Lambda, \varepsilon\})) \longrightarrow R$,Where

(1)To all the $R_i, R_j \in R$, if $\phi(R_i, \varepsilon) = R_j$, then $R_i = R_j$,

(2)To all the $R_i, R_j \in R$, if $\phi(R_i, \Lambda) = R_j$, then $R_i \neq R_j$,

(3)To all the $R_i, R_j \in R$, $S_k \in S$, if $\phi(R_i, S_k) = R_j$, then $R_i = R_j$,

(4)To all the $R_i \in R$, if $\phi(R_i, M_a) = R_i$, then the next transition state relation is $\phi(R_i, M_s) = R_i$,

(5)To $VO = \{G_{a_m}^n, n = 1, 2, 3, ..., m = 1, 2, 3, ...\}$, $\eta_{G_{a_m}^n}^{S_r}$ is the service S_r 's density of group $G_{a_m}^n$. When mobile agent begins to switch to S_r service, there will be:

$$\phi_{S_r}(R_i, \Lambda) = R_j$$

Here R_i is the current position node of the mobile agent. To the target node R_j, we have:

$$(R_j \in SN_{G_{a_k}^q}^{S_r}) \cap (SN_{G_{a_k}^q}^{S_r} \subseteq G_{a_k}^q) \cap (G_{a_k}^q \in G_{a_m}^n) \cap (\eta_{G_{a_k}^q}^{S_r} = max(\eta_{G_{a_m}^n}^{S_r}, n, m = 1, 2, 3, ...))$$

where $SN_{G_{a_k}^q}^{S_r}$ is the available service node in $G_{a_k}^q$ of service S_r.

(6)After the migration in (5) has finished, the service S_r's density of $G_{a_k}^q$ will change to:

$$\eta_{G_{a_k}^q}^{S_r} = \frac{A_{G_{a_k}^q}^{S_r} - 1}{N_{G_{a_k}^q}^{S_r}} \times 100\% \tag{2}$$

In this computation model, the migration state Λ is established by the communication of the nodes in VO. By adopting the service fabric communication protocol, mobile agent can move from the original node to the destination node efficiently. The state transition and message communication are all implemented by this protocol. The service density has been treated as an important tolerance to dispatch the mobile agent's migration.

5   A Case and Discussion

China ministry of education began to carry on a resource-sharing project among most of the top-ranked universities in China from 1999. The aim of this CSCR (Computer Support Cooperation Research) project is to fully utilize the device, data distributing in each university. One of the most difficult tasks is to establish a smart, high efficient, stable, and reliable CSCR platform. We implement the MACM in the platform. There are now 19 virtual organizers in this platform, each service for a special research domain. Each virtual organizer has average 6 nodes, which are located in universities or research institutes.

The division of the groups is based on the research field of the centers, the key nodes in each group are chosen, which constitute the kernel group. The services in this CSCR platform are deployed as mobile agents. Once a mobile agent gets enough resource, the service will be continued.

In this prototype, a typical service example is a literature discovery service, which released by the artificial intelligence (AI) group is positioned in the 2nd level. It can be cloned automatically to the resource nodes in different groups (it is full tree access). When a mobile agent wants to implement this service, it can easily find out this service in its near groups and then it can choose a proper target by the service density and the available service nodes list information which stores in the service management node of each group.

In this section, we will give an example to describe the work process of the MACM. To the topologic of collaborate research platform topologic , we can simplify the platform into a mobile agent computation model in fig. 3.

(1) There are seven nodes in this VO architecture, $R = \{R_0, R_1, R_2, ..., R_6\}$, where, R_0, R_1 R_2 belong to a group, R_3, R_4 belong to another group, R_5,R_6 belong to another group, supposing each node in the same group has the same resource. The number between nodes in fig. 3 represents the node distance.

(2) Finite state set $S = \{S_0, S_1, M_s, M_a\}$, where S_0 represents the born state of the mobile agent, S_1 represents service in a certain node state of the mobile agent, M_s represents the message sending state, M_a represents the message receiving state.

(3) All the message state set $M = \{M_s, M_a\}$.

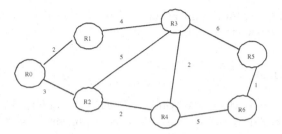

Fig. 3. MACM after Simplifying VO

(4) The initial agent born node $v = R_1$.
(5) The final node set $E = \{R_5, R_6\}$.
(6) Transition function ϕ is calculated by the minimal distance algorithm and the transition relation are given in table 3.

Table 3. State transition relation

$R_{original}$	**S**	R_{target}
R_0	S_0	R_0
R_0	Λ	R_4
R_4	M_a	R_4
R_4	M_s	R_4
R_4	S_1	R_4
R_4	Λ	R_6

From table 3, the mobile agent is born in node R_0, and move to the node R_4, after sending, receiving, serving in node R_4, it move to the R_6 and destroy in node R_6.

6   Conclusions

In this computation model, agent can use a tolerance defined as group service density to monitor the whole network service occupancy in groups, and this will balance the service's serving time, decrease the waiting list of service. This model integrates the advantages of the strong-migration agent and the weak-migration agent, so that it can provide a more intelligence and robust mobile agent computation model which can avoid much frequently data transmitting.

With the aid of the virtual organization architecture, this computation model can effectually avoid the communication invalidation problem.

Acknowledgements

This paper was supported by the Natural Science Foundation of China (No. 69973044) and the Advanced Research Project sponsored by China Defense Ministry (No. 413150804, 41101010207), and was partially supported by the Aerospace Research Foundation sponsored by China Aerospace Science and Industry Corporation (No. 2003-HT-ZJDX-13). Thanks for Dr. Zhang Qiong's advice to this paper.

References

1. Huang, L.C., Wu, Z.H., and Pan, Y.H.: Virtual and Dynamic Hierarchical Architecture for E-Science Grid. International Journal of High Performance Computing Applications, 17 (2003)329-350
2. Huang, L.C., Wu, Z.H., and Pan, Y.H.: A Scalable and Effective Architecture for Grid services' Discovery. First Workshop on Semantics in Peer-to-Peer and Grid Computing. Budapest, Hungary, 20 May 2003: 103-115
3. Foster, I., Kesselman, C., and Tuecke, S.: The Anatomy of the Grid: Enabling Scalable Virtual Organizations. International J. Supercomputer Applications, 15(3), 2001
4. Christensen, E., Curbera, F., Meredith, G. and Weerawarana., S.: Web Services Description Language (WSDL) 1.1. W3C, Note 15, 2001,
   http://www. w3. org /TR/wsdl
5. UDDI http://www.uddi.org/
6. Web Services Flow Language (WSFL) Version 1.0,
   http://www4.ibm.com/software/solutions/Webservices/pdf/WSFL.pdf
7. Brickley, D., and Guha,R. V.: Resource Description Framework (RDF) Schema Specification 1.0, W3C Candidate Recommendation 27 March 2000.

A Novel Reverse Rerouting Mechanism in Mobile Wireless Internet*

Xingwei Wang[1], Bo Song[1], Changqing Yuan[1], and Huang Min[2]

[1] Computing Center, Northeastern University, Shenyang, 110004, China
wangxw@mail.neu.edu.cn
[2] College of Information Science and Engineering, Northeastern University,
Shenyang, 110004, China

Abstract. In this paper, based on the analysis of existing partial and complete rerouting mechanisms, a novel reverse rerouting mechanism in mobile wireless Internet is presented, taking the characteristics of handover into account. It integrates a reverse rerouting algorithm with the resource handover and reservation mechanisms. Simulation results have shown that the signaling overhead for handover gets effective control, high resource utilization is achieved, and QoS (Quality of Service) guarantees are provided to mobile users to certain degree.

1 Introduction

Mobile wireless Internet (as shown in Fig.1) provides ubiquitous personalized information services [1]. However, due to user movements, handovers between neighboring cells often take place, which invalidates the original routes. To keep the continuous and smooth communication, rerouting should be put into use [2-4], the user QoS (Quality of Service) requirements should be guaranteed and the network resources should be utilized efficiently as much as possible [5,6,11].

There are mainly two kinds of existing rerouting mechanisms: PRR (Partial ReRouting) and CRR (Complete ReRouting) [7]. In the former, the original route is reserved as much as possible, only the varied parts are updated. One of its advantages is the smaller amount of processing time and overhead. However, the new route probably is not optimal, leading to inefficient network resource utilization, and the original QoS guarantees often being broken. In the latter, the original route is completely replaced with the newly generated one by default routing algorithm, which is usually optimal. One of its main disadvantages is the larger amount of processing time and overhead.

In [8], FHRP (Footprint Handover Rerouting Protocol) has been presented. It attempts to take advantage of both PRR and CRR. However, to some degree, it is only optimal to continuously moving user with frequent handovers within large region. For small region, PRR is used. Due to the majority of users often moving within small region, large amount of extended routes [7] will be generated, occupying large amount of network resources.

---

* This work was supported by the National High-Tech Research and Development Plan of China under Grant No.2001AA121064; the National Natural Science Foundation of China under Grant No.60003006 (jointly supported by Bell Lab Research China) and No.70101006; the Natural Science Foundation of Liaoning Province under Grant No.20032018 and No.20032019; the Modern Distance Education Engineering Project by China MoE.

C.-H. Chi and K.-Y. Lam (Eds.): AWCC 2004, LNCS 3309, pp. 27–32, 2004.
© Springer-Verlag Berlin Heidelberg 2004

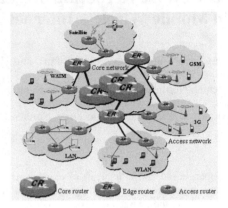

Fig. 1. Mobile wireless Internet

Taking features of CRR and PRR into account and based on the characteristics of mobile wireless Internet, a novel rerouting mechanism is proposed in this paper.

2   Reverse Rerouting Mechanism

In mobile wireless Internet, the handovers of users often take place between neighboring cells administrated by the same edge router. Most parts of the route are the same before and after handover. Based on this observation, a resource handover mechanism is adopted, the originally reserved resources along the same parts of the original and the new routes are used directly after handover. In addition, do resource reservation before initiating communication.

2.1   Reverse Rerouting

When a user handover will happen, the router that lead to the access router of the target cell with the lowest delay or the smallest hop count along the current route reversely is found, and then do resource reservation from that router to the access router of the target cell; for the same parts as those of the original route, just do resource handover. Thus, the route length of doing resource reservation has been reduced significantly; especially in the case of handover taking place between neighboring cells administered by the same edge router. Such kind of mechanism is called RRR(Reverse ReRouting).

For example, in Fig.2, R1, R2, R3, R4 and R5 are routers. R4 and R5 support wireless access. H0 is a static user or a mobile user with no handover. MH is a mobile user who will make handovers. When MH moved into cell of R4 from cell of R5, along the route from access router of H0 to router R5 reversely, H0 looks for the router that can reach R4 with the smallest hop count. Here, R3 is the access point with the shortest path. Thus, along the path from the access router of H0 to R3, just do resource handover; only for the path from R3 to R4, do resource reservation. For the original path from R3 to R5, after certain period of time has elapsed, if MH does not return, the original reserved resources will be released.

The resource handover is done through resource reservation marking. As shown in Fig.2, when the initial route is set up between H0 and MH, resources along the path

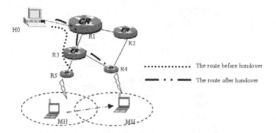

Fig. 2. The illustration of reverse rerouting

from H0 to MH will be marked "reserved by H0 and MH" before communication begins. The reserved resources by H0 and MH will not be released until the communication is over. When MH handovers, if RRR mechanism is used, reserved resources along the path H0-R1-R3 should be handed over. R3 just sets the R4 as its next hop to MH, and resources along the path H0-R1-R3 remain in the reserved state.

2.2   Comparison Among Reverse Rerouting, Partial Rerouting and Complete Rerouting

For simplicity, just the resource reservation signaling overhead is taken into account in this paper. Due to the same signaling packet size, use hop count of the resource reserved route to represent the overhead. In this sense, the overhead of PRR is lowest, and CRR highest.

The majority of handovers take place between neighboring cells administrated by the same edge router, the result of RRR and CRR is often the same. As shown in Fig.3, RRR gets the same result as CRR with the same signaling overhead as PRR. However, when handover takes place between the cells administered by different edge routers, RRR often gets different result than CRR, and consumes less network resources than PRR. As shown in Fig.4, for resource consumption RRR is the same as CRR, and for signaling overhead RRR is the same as PRR. Just like that in [8], when handover occurs, tradeoff between RRR and CRR is also needed in the proposed mechanism.

3   Reverse Rerouting Algorithm

Define some concepts at first. Reverse merging router (RMR) is the router that is found in the reverse direction with the smallest hop count to the access router that serves for the user after the handover. Reverse hop count is the number of the hops between the RMR and the access router that is serving for the user before the handover, denoted by tn. Access hop count is the number of the hops between the access router that is serving for the user before the handover and the access router that is serving for the user after the handover, denoted by tm. Minimum access hop count is the number of the hops between the RMR and the access router that is serving for the user after the handover, denoted by stm.

In general, tradeoff between CRR and RRR is based on the tn. Set constant K to be the threshold of tn, its value is determined according to actual networking situation. When $tn \leq K$, adopt RRR, otherwise adopt CRR.

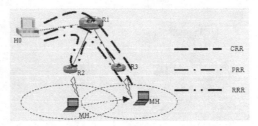

Fig. 3. Comparison of three kinds of rerouting mechanisms when handover occurs between cells administrated by the same edge router

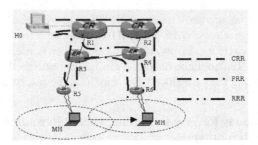

Fig. 4. Comparison of three kinds of rerouting mechanisms when handover occurs between cells administrated by different edge routers

The proposed RRR algorithm is described as follows:

Step 1: $tn = 0$, the RMR is set to be the access router that is serving for the user before handover, and the value of stm is set to be that of tm of the access router that is serving for the user before handover.

Step 2: Find the router of the previous hop in the reverse direction. $tn = tn + 1$.

Step 3: Compute the value of tm of the current router. If $tm \leq stm$, go to step 4; otherwise, go to step 5.

Step 4: If $tn \leq K$, the RMR is set to be the current router and the value of stm is set to be that of tm of the current router, go to step 5; otherwise, adopt CRR, using the default routing algorithm to find the new route, the algorithm ended.

Step 5: Check whether the router is the access router of the other end of communication, if so, go to step 6, otherwise, go to step 2.

Step 6: Perform resource handover by the RMR, and do resource reservation between the RMR and the access router that is serving for the user after handover, the algorithm ended.

4   Simulation Research and Discussion

The simulation has been done on NS2 (Network Simulator 2) platform over some actual network topologies (such as NSFNET and CERNET) and lattice topologies with self-developed modification under FreeBSD 4.7. One example lattice topology is shown in Fig.5. In Fig.5, the small point denotes the access router, the big point denotes the core or edge router. The default routing algorithm is the fuzzy-tower-based QoS unicast one [10].

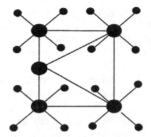

Fig. 5. One example topology used in simulation

Performance evaluation on RRR mechanism is done on the following two aspects: signaling overhead and optimal route similarity degree. In this paper, use the count of hops of the route that made resource reservation to denote the signaling overhead. The route generated by CRR is regarded as the optimal one according to the default routing algorithm [10]. Use the ratio of the number of the same nodes and edges in the two computed routes by RRR and CRR over the number of all nodes and edges in the optimal route to represent the optimal route similarity degree.

Use average statistical methods to do performance evaluations among RRR, PRR and CRR. The results are shown in Fig.6 and Fig.7. RRR can control signaling overhead effectively and approach the optimal result of CRR.

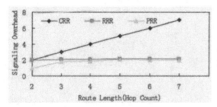 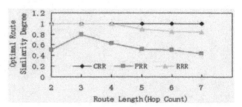

Fig. 6. Comparison of signaling overhead in three kinds of rerouting

Fig. 7. Comparison of optimal route similarity degree in three kinds of rerouting

5 Conclusions

Based on the analysis of PRR and CRR, a RRR mechanism is presented, with the characteristics of mobile wireless Internet and user mobility in mind. Simulation results have shown that it can solve the rerouting problem during handover, achieving the result similar to that of CRR with the overhead similar to that of PRR.

References

1. Jon, C.W., Cheng, C.W.: Intelligent Handover for Mobile Wireless Internet. Mobile Networks and Applications, vol.6, no.1. (2001)67-79
2. Waleed, S.A., Sridhar, R., Zheng, T.: Interaction of Wireless TCP Schemes and Rerouting: Analytical Models and Simulation. Proc. of ICDCSW'03. (2003)883-892
3. Krzysztof, M.W.: A Branch and Bound Algorithm for Primary Routes Assignment in Survivable Connection Oriented Networks. Computational Optimization and Applications, vol.27, no.2. (2004)149-171

4. Gueroui, A.: Quality of Service of a Rerouting Algorithm Using Stochastic Automata Networks. Proc. of ISCC'01. (2001)338-346
5. Wang, X.W., Zhang, Y.H., Liu, J.R., Li, H.T.: Research on Quality of Service Management Mechanisms in Distributed Multimedia Systems. Journal of Software, vol.9, no.2. (1998) 87-90 (in Chinese)
6. Nicole, K.B., Martin, K., Jens, S.: A Modular Approach to Mobile QoS Signaling: Motivation, Design & Implementation. Multimedia Tools and Applications, vol.22, no.2. (2004)117-135
7. Wang, L., Zhang, N.T.: Dynamic Probability Path Optimization Strategy for Satellite Handover in LEO Networks. Journal of China Institute of Communications, vol.23, no.9. (2002)8-15(in Chinese)
8. Uzunalioglu, H., Akyldizie, K., Yesha, Y.: Footprint Handover Rerouting Protocol for Low Earth Orbit Satellite Networks. Wireless Networks, vol.5, no.5. (1999)327-337
9. Zhang, L., Steve, D.: RSVP: A New Resource Reservation Protocol. IEEE Network Magazine, vol.31, no.9. (1993)8-18
10. Wang X.W., Yuan C.Q., Huang, M.: A Fuzzy-Tower-Based QoS Unicast Routing Algorithm. Proc. of EUC'04. (2004)923-930
11. Wang, X.W., Liu, J.R.: A Quality-of-Service-Based Point-to-Point Communication Routing Algorithm. Journal of Northeastern University(Natural Science), vol.21, no.2. (2000)132-135(in Chinese)

An Agents Based Grid Infrastructure
of Social Intelligence

Jun Hu, Ji Gao, Beishui Liao, and Jiujun Chen

Institute of Artificial Intelligence, Zhejiang University,
Hangzhou 310027, Zhejiang, China
hujun_111@zju.edu.cn

Abstract. The Grid and agent communities both develop concepts and mechanisms for open distributed systems, albeit from different perspectives. The Grid community has focused on infrastructure, tools and application for reliable and secure resource sharing within dynamic and geographically distributed virtual organizations. In contrast, the agents community has focused on autonomous problem solvers that can flexibly in uncertain and dynamic environments. Yet as the scale and ambition of both Grid and agent deployments increase, we see that multi-agent systems require robust infrastructure and Grid systems require autonomous, flexible behaviors. So, an Agent Based Grid Infrastructure of Social Intelligence (ABGISI) is presented in this paper. With multi-agents cooperation as main line, this paper expatiates on ABGISI from three aspects: agent information representation; the support system for agent social behavior, which includes agent mediate system and agent rational negotiation mechanism, and agent federation structure.

1 Introduction

In open distributed systems, independent components cooperate to achieve individual and shared goals. Both individual components and system as a whole are designed to cope with change and evolution in number and nature of the participating entities. The Grid and agent communities are both pursuing the development of such open distributed systems from different perspectives. The Grid community has focused on interoperable infrastructure and tools for secure and reliable resource sharing within dynamic and geographically distributed virtual organizations, and applications of the same to various resource federation scenarios. In contrast, those working on agents have focused on the development of concepts, methodologies, and algorithms for autonomous problem solvers that can act flexibly in uncertain and dynamic environments in order to achieve their aims and objectives. [1] So, we proposals a agent based grid infrastructure of social intelligence which, with multi-agent cooperation as controlling main line, aggregates advantages of multi-agent system and grid technique.

There are some projects that do similar research work with us. CoABS project [2], it realized cooperation among heterogeneous agents but it was not established on advance grid technique and web services that have became industry standard. [3] established an agent based computation grid, it realized unity management of computation resources by agent but it was only suit for computation work. An agent-based grid computing was proposed by [4], it established an agent-based grid computing

C.-H. Chi and K.-Y. Lam (Eds.): AWCC 2004, LNCS 3309, pp. 33–38, 2004.

environment but it did not make full use of negotiation and cooperation ability of agent.

This paper presents ABGISI: Agent Based Grid Infrastructure of Social Intelligence, which is based on our two previous works [5][6]. Target at Managing and Controlling social behavior of agents, our study focus on three fields, includes: agent information representation structure; the support system for agent social behavior, including agent mediate system and rational negotiation mechanism, agent federation structure. In following sections, this paper introduces the ABGISI architecture briefly, and then expatiates on the related essential element of ABGISI through three aspects that are mentioned above, then gives an evaluation and conclusion.

2   ABGISI Architecture

There are three levels of ABGISI architecture which shown in figure1.The bottom of ABGISI architecture is resources representation level. In this level, any resources are encapsulated as services which are organized to agent abilities. Services provided by agent ability are described with agent grid services specification and interoperation protocol suite. The middle of ABGISI architecture is agent support system for agent social behavior. This level provides the support system for application level, which main part is agent mediate system and agent rational negotiation mechanism. The top of ABGISI architecture is application level. In this level, agents are organized to agent federation and achieve application aims and objectives by agent cooperation.

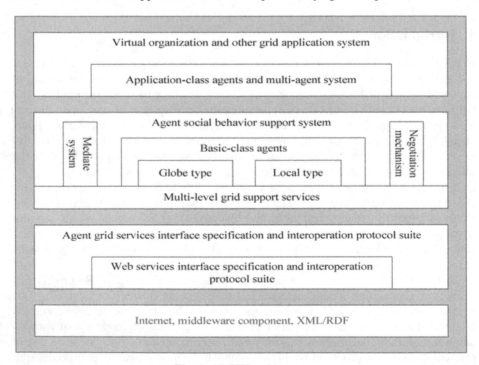

Fig. 1. ABGISI architecture

So, ABGISI system is described with a three-tuple as follows:
ABGISI= (IP, SS, AF), SS= (AS, NR)

- IP – the information representation, through based-ontologies modeling and expressing mechanism, make exchanging information contents of agents can be understood each other.
- SS – the support system for agent social behavior, including two parts as below:
  - AS – the agent mediate system, through establishing mediate system for agent sociality, it makes agent to accurately and conveniently gain the services at anytime and anywhere.
- NR – the agent rational negotiation mechanism, through integrating expression of negotiation contents and ratiocination into the negotiation process, agent can rationally boost negotiation process based on the agent social knowledge and negotiation mechanism to obtain higher negotiation intelligence.
- AF – the agent federation structure. Applying activity sharing oriented joint intention (ASOJI) [7] within nested agent federation, agents achieve application aims and objectives.

3 The Information Representation

ABGISI describes the semantics of information content with five-tuple as follows:
IP= (OKRL, OML, Mapping, ICMT, OAFM),

- OKRL – (Ontology Based Knowledge Representation Language) is used in inner part of agents, OKRL= (SDL, CDL, CPL);
- OML – (Ontology Based Markup Language), be used as the communication language among Agents;
- Mapping – mapping mechanism between OKRL with OML, Mapping: OKRL→OML;
- ICMT – Information Content Modeling Tools support modeling and conceptual description of information contents;
- OAFM – Ontology Automatic Form Mechanism, supports to automatic (or semi-automatic) establish domain term sets and classified system of terms.

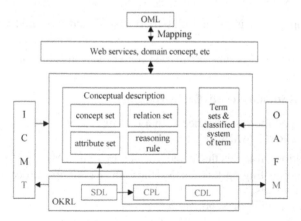

Fig. 2. ABGISI modeling framework

The modeling frame is shown in Figure 2. OKRL represents knowledge needed by agent when it launches social activity based on web services, from three aspects: Services Description Language (SDL); Concept Description Language (CDL); definition of restricted policy of agent behavior (CPL). Among them, SDL prescribes general descriptive format of services; CDL defines the domain conceptual description, and support domain term sets and to establish classified system of terms for supporting the services description; CPL is the descriptive format of the applied-area restricted agent behavior policy that is defined by CDL. By one to one mapping, OKRL is transited to OML which is limitary XML and contains descriptive ability of OKRL. OML is used as the communication language among Agents.

4   The Support System for Agent Social Behavior

4.1   The Agent Mediate System

The agent mediate system is composed of middle agent that provides mediate services for services provider and request. The middle agents collect agent ability advertisement and stored in the local services advertisement repository. When a services request asks middle agent whether it knows of services provider with desired capabilities, the middle agent matches the request against the stored advertisements and returns the result, a subset of the stored advertisements. This is a matchmaking process, which is the main part of mediate services. ABGISI provide three compatible matching strategies[8]:

- The classifying matching – according to the domain classified code of service, it located compatible classification service in services advertisement repository.
- The parameter matching – compatible matches with the input and output parameters of services request and provider.
- The constraint matching – compatible matches with the Pre-Condition, Post-Condition and Resource- Constraint of services request and provider.

In order to improve performance and efficacy of mediate service, it is necessary to establish classified system of services. Classified system (CS) is divided into two levels in ABGISI. $CS = CS_g \cup (CS_{d1} \cup CS_{d2} \ldots \cup CS_{dn})$.

- CS_g – the upper level is general classified system and is shared with all middle agents;
- CS^j_{di} – the lower level is sub-classified system of various domain.

4.2   The Agent Rational Negotiation Mechanism

Agent rational negotiation is described with a five-tuple as follows:
    NR = (NP, NE, RNC, MMA, IE)

- NP – Negotiation Protocols that be conformed by both parties,
- NE – Negotiation Engine that carries through negotiation process according to negotiation protocols;
- RNC – Representation of Negotiation Content.

- MMA – Mental Model of Agent, used to describe the agent social belief, domain knowledge, negotiation state information, and the reasoning knowledge related to negotiation behavior and contents.
- IE – Inference Engine, which is divided into three levels [9]: Evaluation, strategy and tactics, decides the agent negotiation behavior and contents.

Negotiation engine is designed as an enhanced type finite state automatic machine (Figure 3) that complies with specific negotiation protocol. As shown in figure 3, arcs between state nodes indicate the state transitions. The names of negotiation actions (*proposal, counterproposal, accept, and reject*) as labels of arc indicate the motivated factors that bring about the state transitions. The e*nhanced type* means that the state node can contain inference engine rather than only represents specific state.

Fig. 3. Agent negotiation process

The result of negotiation is a contract. A contract template can be defined as ontology at design-time. Values of some items of contract template are decided after negotiation at run-time. Once both parties of negotiation sign the contract, they should comply with it and will be monitored by supervision agents.

5 The Agent Federation Structure

Application-type agents are organized to agent federation in ABGISI. As shown in figure 4, agent federation is composed of one MA (manage agent) and some member's agents and some acquaintance's agents which are come from stranger agents by negotiation. One or more services are encapsulated and controlled by a member's agent. According to the goals of the specific agent federation, several member agents are recruited into an agent federation. For completing a certain service, MA can build dynamic agent federation by negotiating with other agents and signing the contract. This

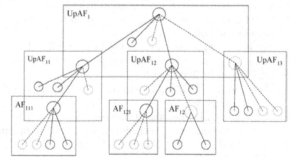

Fig. 4. A possible nested agent federation. (UpAF$_i$ indicates high-level federation, Af$_j$ indicates low-level federation, big circles indicate MAs, small circles indicate ordinary agents, and dotted circles indicate acquaintances, dotted line indicate dynamic joining and exiting agent federation)

dynamic federation can be dynamically established or canceled according requirement. Several AFs can join together to form a high-level agent federation (call upper agent federation, UpAF), then form nested structure. Theoretically, the agent federations can nest unlimitedly according to application requirements. Therefore, the whole agent federation has dynamic and flexible structure, which has good adaptability to the network environment. MA manages the whole process of agent cooperation by activity sharing oriented joint intention (ASOJI) which details could be found in [7].

6 Conclusion

This paper proposals agent based grid infrastructure of social intelligence (ABGISI), which regard agent social cooperation as the core, the architecture and running mechanism of ABGISI are described from three aspects: the agent information representation stucture, the support system for agent social behavior and the agent federation structure. Compare to the research of the same kind, such as CoABS[2],ACG[3], [4], The advantages of ABGISI is that it establish multi-agent social structure on current grid infrastructure and realize resource sharing and resource cooperation by multi-agent social cooperation. [2]only realize cooperation among heterogeneous agents, not make full use of current grid infrastructure and can not effectively achieve dynamic resources sharing and cooperation. [4]also apply multi-agent cooperation as controlling clue in grid, but it not make full use agent negotiation function. In a word, this paper presents agent based grid infrastructure of social intelligence, aggregating grid technique and multi-agent technique, providing a new ideal and way to realize agent based grid computing system.

References

1. Ian Foster, Nicholas R. Jennings, Carl Kesselman. "Brain Meets Brawn: Why Grid and Agents Need Each Other", The third international joint conference on autonomous agents & multi agent system, July 19-23,2004, New York city, USA.
2. Dylan Schmorrow. "Control of Agent-Based Systems"
   http://www.darpa.mil/ipto/programs/coabs/index.htm.
3. Li Chunlin, Li Layuan. "Agent framework to support the computational grid." The Journal of Systems and Software 70 (2004) 177-187.
4. Zhongzhi Shi, et al. "Agent-based Grid Computing". Keynote Speech, International Symposium on Distributed Computing and Applications to Business, Engineering and Science, Wuxi, Dec. 16-20, 2002.
5. Hu Jun, Gao Ji. "IMCAG:Infrastructure for Managing and Controlling Agent Grid". LNCS 3033, 161-165., 2004.
6. Hu Jun, Gao Ji, Liao Bei-shui, Chen Jiu-jun. "An Infrastructure for Managing and Controlling Agent Cooperation". Proceedings of The Eighth International Conference on CSCW in Design, May 26-28, 2004, Xiamen, PR China.
7. Gao Ji, Lin Donghao. "Agent Cooperation Based Control Integration by Activity-Sharing and Joint Intention." J.Comput. Sci. & Technol. 2002, 17(3),331-340..
8. Xu Fei. "Agent assistant services system." ZheJiang University Master's thesis, Mar 2003.
9. Liu Xin. "Content Modeling Based On Rational Negotiation". ZheJiang University Master's thesis, Mar 2003.

Agent Aided Workflow Modeling*

Jinlei Jiang and Meilin Shi

Department of Computer Science and Technology, Tsinghua University,
100084 Beijing, P.R. China
{jjlei,shi}@csnet4.cs.tsinghua.edu.cn

Abstract. Nowadays, workflow processes are mostly built out of the designers' experience, which is usually full of skills and tactics and the correctness of the resulting processes is hard to guarantee, especially for complex ones. To address this issue, a tool called AAWM (Agent Aided Workflow Modeler) is proposed. This paper details the design and implementation issues related to AAWM such as system architecture, user interface and so on.

1 Introduction

Workflow modeling plays an important role in building workflow systems because a workflow system runs a process under the direction of the model obtained during modeling phase. Though there are many literatures related to workflow modeling[2, 4, 6, 7, 9, 11], they mostly concentrate on how to describe a process by the supplied symbols/tools rather than to help people build workflow processes. At most time, workflow modeling is more like an art rather than a science[8]. Therefore, it is full of nondeterministic factors. On the other hand, tasks modeled in real world are so complex that persons can't carry it out without professional trainings. This, we think, cumbers the further application of workflow technology. To broaden the application of workflow technology, we believe a tool that assists people to identify the real world requirements and build the corresponding process with few errors introduced is significant. As an endeavor in this direction, a tool called AAWM (Agent Aided Workflow Modeler) is proposed in this paper. AAWM deploys agents to fully utilize the knowledge within an organization and to facilitate the communication between process designers. With the help of AAWM, even ordinary users can build a complex process quickly and accurately.

2 AAWM Overview

This section will show the foundation of AAWM and point out the aspects that agent may help.

2.1 System Foundation

The design of AAWM is based on the following observations related to workflow modeling.

---

* This work is co-supported by the National Natural Science Foundation of China under Grant No. 90412009, 60073011 and 985 Project of Tsinghua University.

1. The business process/task to model is divisible[3]. It usually includes a series of jobs(sub-tasks) and different users participate different jobs.
2. Roles hold a key position in improving workflow flexibility. With roles and their relations (Ref. to [5] for some basic role relations) identified, designers can then reason at a high abstract level and re-use previous design decisions.
3. Workflow modeling is also a cooperative process itself[3].
4. Modeling procedure can be divided into two phases[1], i.e., meeting phase and design phase. The main issues in meeting phase are defining objectives, decomposing the domain into smaller functions, defining boundaries and scope. In design phase, the users are asked to provide ever-increasing detail.
5. Object is exploited to guide an agent to achieve the goal specified. It plays a less important role in workflow modeling.

2.2 What Will Agent Help?

In AAWM, agents function in the following aspects.

- **Goal decomposition.** Here we emphasize that the decomposition is only done coarsely because workflow modeling is so complex a procedure that current technology can not fulfill all the work autonomously. Furthermore, even if it is possible, it is costly to develop such a system. Therefore, agent is only deployed as an aided approach in AAWM and designers are still needed to make final decisions based on the results got. In this way, the requirements on process designers and system development are both reduced.
- **Action coordination.** It mainly utilizes the social ability and pro-activeness of agents. Once operations from designers are received, they are checked for consistency. If conflict is found, agents will do some actions to reconcile them.
- **Interaction with users.** It mainly utilizes the reactivity of agents. In this scenario, agent will perceive users' operation and then collect and present related information to the users. Therefore, the requirements on process designers are reduced.

3 AAWM Details

This section will explain issues related to AAWM design and implementation.

3.1 System Architecture

The system architecture is illustrated in Fig. 1. According to the structure of the organization, the system is divided into many levels (only two levels are shown in Fig. 1). The whole system consists of multiple servers and clients. All servers have the same internal structure and can work independently. The only difference between enterprise-level server and department-level server is that tasks of the former are usually complex while those of the latter are relatively simpler. All servers should coordinate the behaviors of its clients. In addition, the top-level server should also coordinate the behaviors of the low-level servers.

The adoption of such architecture arises out of two reasons: 1) departments of an organization are usually formed according to their functionalities. Each department has its own familiar business. To allocate proper tasks to them will make the work

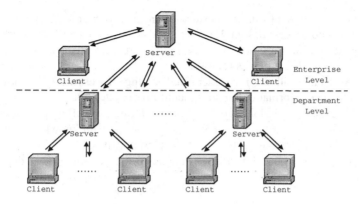

Fig. 1. AAWM Architecture

more efficient and effective, and 2) departments are autonomous. Besides taking part in the enterprise-wide tasks, they also have their own internal business processes. This architecture gives them the most freedom.

3.2 Server Structure

The main components of AAWM server are shown in Fig. 2. It consists of an agent and a set of databases.

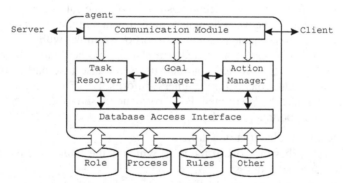

Fig. 2. Main Components of AAWM Server

Modules within agent are explained as follows.

- Communication Module is responsible for the interactions between servers and clients. In more details, it interacts with clients taking part in task decomposition during meeting phase while in design phase, it communicates with clients connected with it as well as the upper or lower servers.
- Task Resolver receives original task goal (from task decomposition tool) and decomposes it into sub-goals (Ref. to [10] for the methods), which are then handed to Goal Manager and sent back to clients involved.
- Goal Manager maintains both the original goals and the decomposed results. Besides, it records the status of each client or server involved in the process design.

- Action Manager is deployed to coordinate various operations related to task decomposition and process design. It is up to it to resolve the conflict occurring.
- Database Access Interface fulfills access to the underlying databases.
  Databases in Fig. 2 function as follows.
- Role base contains all the roles identified during process design. They can be used as reference information for subsequent process design.
- Process base contains various standard or user-defined workflow processes.
- Rules base contains various rules conducting business and knowledge needed for reasoning. They constitute the basis of task decomposition.
- Other base contains other information related to the system such as departments and users.

3.3 Client Tools

Corresponding to the two phases of workflow modeling, two client tools are provided and they are task decomposition tool and process design tool.

3.3.1 Task Decomposition Tool

Task decomposition tool is used to divide a complex task into a set of simpler ones. Its interface is shown in Fig. 3. From the figure, we can see that the whole interface is divided into three areas, i.e., decomposition result window, property window and chatting area. Decomposition result window displays decomposition result in tree view and chatting area provides a way for designers to communicate their ideas. This is one outstanding feature of task decomposition tool. The introduction of chatting makes the communication between designers more fluent and thus forms a well foundation for correct and reasonable decomposition. For example, with this tool two or more designers can easily determine whether a task should be divided into two ones through real-time discussion. In addition, end users can also take part in this procedure and raise their requirements for designers' information. Therefore, the structure of a process can be quickly determined. Property window shows the properties of the task specified. The important properties of task are as follows.

- Name is the unique identifier of a task.
- Description describes the goal of the task, which is the foundation of further decomposition or process design.
- Designer specifies who can handle the task.
  The interaction between task decomposition tool and the AAWM server is as follows: 1) One initial designer inputs the original task goal which is then sent to AAWM server; 2) Server agent decomposes the given goal according to the rules specified and sends the results back; 3) Based on the results presented, designers can do further modification and then submit the results to server.

3.3.2 Process Design Tool

After a complex task is decomposed, different users can then provide the details of sub-tasks got via process design tool. The internal structure of process design tool is illustrated in Fig. 4. It consists of an agent, an input interface and an output interface, where input interface accepts inputs from designers while output interface presents the related information to designers. Modules within agent are explained as follows.

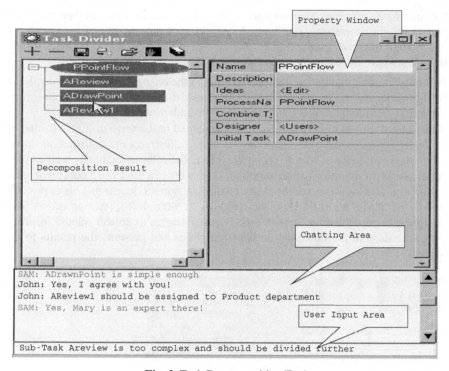

Fig. 3. Task Decomposition Tool

- Communication Module is responsible for information exchange with servers or peer clients. Communication between peer clients is mainly to negotiate activity interface or handle conflicts.
- Sensor is the driver of Info Handler. It is up to it to perceive actions of designer and to monitor notifications from server or peer clients.
- Task Goal contains the concrete task requirements and a set of constraints.
- Current Status records the specified properties of task till now.
- Info Handler is the core of design tool. It mainly does two things. That is, 1) handle the notification received, and 2) collect goal-related information according to designer's behavior and current status. In both cases, the result is presented to designer for their information.

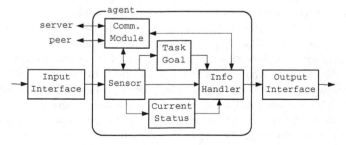

Fig. 4. Internal Structure of Process Design Tool

The interface, which is the only model-specific part of AAWM because each workflow system adopts only one workflow model, of process design tool is shown in Fig. 5. Here the model supported is Cova cooperation model[12]. To help designers build a process, the following steps are taken.

- Not only the task manipulated directly, but also the ones related to it are displayed in the working area. In other words, work context is supplied. With it, designers are apt to provide more precise details of tasks under modeling.
- Task related information is gathered and presented in the form of hint information to the designers in real time. For example, Fig. 5 illustrates the information shown when the mouse moves to role property. It lists the roles available as well as their relations. With the information supplied, designers can gain deep comprehension of the task and thus, it becomes easier to make a correct decision. This is possible due to the Sensor and Info Handler in Fig. 4. In more detail, once an action from designers is perceived by Sensor, Info Handler begins to collect related information according to the task goal and current status and presents the results to designers.

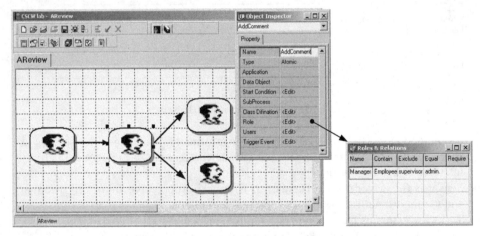

Fig. 5. Interface of Process Design Tool

4 Conclusions

Building workflow processes out of the designers' experience results in two problems: 1) it raises high requirements on process designers, and 2) it is hard to guarantee process correctness for this procedure is full of uncertainties. To address these issues, AAWM is developed bearing such experience in mind that one main reason for people to make wrong decisions is that they don't learn enough on the related information. The main contributions of AAWM to workflow modeling are 1) it firstly (to our best knowledge) introduces agent to help designers make correct decisions by gathering related information for them, and 2) it allows designers to define a workflow process collaboratively by exchanging their ideas synchronously. In this way, both the requirements on process designers and the uncertainties are reduced. In the end we should point out that AAWM is not limited to specific process model except the process design tool because only one model is adopted in each workflow system. In addition, AAWM can also be used to solve other problems, e.g., co-authoring a document and making a decision.

References

1. Carmel E., Whitaker R. D. and George J. F. PD and Joint Application Design: A Transatlantic comparison. Communications of the ACM, 1993, 36(4): 40-48
2. Davulcu H., Kifer M., Ramakrishnan C. R. and Ramakrishnan I. V. Logic Based Modeling and Analysis of Workflows. In: Proc of ACM PODS'98 (1998) 25~33
3. Hsieh Y. F., Yang G. X. and Shi M. L. CovaModeler: A Multi-user Tool for Modeling Cooperative Processes. International Journal of Computer Applications in Technology, 2003, 16(2/3): 67-72
4. Inamoto A. Agent oriented system approach for workflow automation. International Journal of Production Economics, 1999, 60-61(1-4): 327~335
5. Karageorgos A., Thompson M. and Mehandjiev N. Semi-Automatic Design of Agent Organisations. In: Proc of ACM SAC'02 (2002) 306-313
6. Knolmayer G., Endl R. and Pfahrer M. Modeling Processes and Workflows by Business Rules. In: Lecture Notes in Computer Science 1806, Springer-Verlag (2000) 16~29
7. Sadiq W. and Orlowska M. E. Analyzing Process Models Using Graph Reduction Techniques. Information Systems, 2000, 25(2): 117~134
8. Stohr E. A. and Zhao J. L. Workflow Automation: Overview and Research Issues. Information Systems Frontiers, 2001, 3(3): 281~296
9. van der Aalst W. The application of Petri Nets to workflow management. Journal of Circuits, Systems and Computers, 1998, 8(1):21~66
10. Weld D. S. Recent advances in AI planning. AI Magazine, 1999, 20(2): 55-68
11. Wirtz G., Weske M. and Giese H. The OCoN Approach to Workflow Modeling in Object-Oriented Systems. Information Systems Frontiers, 2001, 3(3): 357~376
12. Yang G. X. and Shi M. L. Cova: a Programming Language for Cooperative Applications. Science in China Series F, 2001, 44(1): 73-80

An Improved Hybrid Method
of Maintaining Content Consistency

Changming Ma and Daniel Cooke

Department of Computer Science, Texas Tech University, Lubbock, TX 79409, USA

Abstract. Content distribution networks use certain mechanisms to guarantee that the replicated documents are consistent with the original documents undergoing updates. In this paper, we present an improved hybrid consistency method based on an existing algorithm which dynamically combines server-side propagation and invalidation. A new threshold, in terms of the ratio of a document's request rate to its update rate, is established to determine which approach (invalidation or propagation) should be used. In addition, the improved algorithm makes consistency enhancement decisions based on request temporal locality and document size. Simulation results show that the improved algorithm reduces network traffic, achieves high request freshness rates, and introduces little extra response time when compared to other algorithms.

1 Introduction

Content distribution networks (or content delivery networks, CDNs) have been proposed to improve the performance of web applications, using a set of hosts located at different geographical locations across the World Wide Web. The contents on the origin server are replicated to surrogate servers, which are typically on the edge of the network. When appropriately deployed, CDNs also provide high availability and flexible scalability with reasonable costs and marginal extra maintenance efforts.

Although CDNs are mainly deployed for applications where the vast majority of documents are static data, they are increasingly used to deliver dynamic documents. As more and more documents are generated dynamically or updated frequently, content consistency management has been becoming one of the most important issues of CDNs. Applications raise different requirements of consistency levels. In [13], four levels of content consistency are identified, viz. strong consistency, delta consistency, weak consistency and mutual consistency. Certain mechanisms are required to realize these consistency levels.

The existing consistency methods can be categorized into one of the following three categories: 1) server-side mechanisms; 2) client-side mechanisms; and 3) explicit mechanisms [13]. Server propagation and invalidation fall into the first category. In the propagation scheme, an updated document is multicasted from the origin server to every surrogate server once the update is submitted. In the invalidation scheme, on the other hand, the origin server only sends a (usually very small) message to the surrogate servers to render the old document invalid.

C.-H. Chi and K.-Y. Lam (Eds.): AWCC 2004, LNCS 3309, pp. 46–57, 2004.
© Springer-Verlag Berlin Heidelberg 2004

The surrogate servers then download a new copy of the document from the origin server if they later receive requests for this document. Client-side mechanism involves client polling to determine the status of the document for every request received. While this mechanism requires less memory and computation overhead for document state information, it imposes substantial overhead for network traffic and results in extra response time. This mechanism is not so appealing as the others. The third mechanism, explicit mechanism, aims at trade-offs between state space and control messages. The origin server and the surrogate servers work cooperatively, trying to reach an optimistic (or near-optimistic) combination of state information and control messages. Examples of this mechanism include cooperative lease approach. The method proposed in this paper, based on the algorithm described in [9], can also be viewed as in this category.

The rest of the paper is organized as follows. Section II briefly reviews the related work. Section III presents our improved method. Section IV describes simulation results and compares the performances among various approaches. Section V concludes the paper.

2   Related Work

The studies of complex network topologies, particularly the Internet topologies, impose challenging difficulties. These problems are investigated in [3, 7, 8, 12, 17, 18]. For CDNs, study of [7] suggests a simple, yet intriguing and non-intuitive power law between the total number of the multicast links and that of the unicast links. This result is confirmed by [8] and [17]. Although [18] suggests a more sophisticated formula, the power law is accurate enough for the purpose of this paper. Using the similar notations as in [9], the relationship is expressed as $L_m/L_u = N^\epsilon$, where L_m is the total number of the multicast links, L_u is the total number of the unicast hops from the origin server to N surrogate servers, and ϵ (usually between -0.34 and -0.30) is the efficiency factor.

Web request characteristics are studied in [2, 4, 5]. It is widely accepted that web page requests follow Zipf-like distributions. These studies also suggest a weak correlation between the request frequency of a document and its size, as well as a weak correlation between a document's update rate and its request rate. On the other hand, web request exhibits strong temporal locality: the probability of the request to a document which is visited t time ago is proportional to $1/t$ [6].

As previously mentioned, a variety of consistency levels are provided by existing consistency schemes. Web applications require specific consistency schemes, depending on their requirements. WCIP has been proposed for delta consistency using server-side invalidation and application level multicasting [15]. Client-side polling method can guarantee strong consistency and the same is true for server-side propagation. The latter requires two-phase commit protocol for update transactions, resulting in longer update time observed at the origin server. Periodic polling, TTL based polling, lease, and volume lease are proposed to find good trade-offs between space information and control traffic overhead[11, 19].

A hybrid consistency mechanism, combining server-side propagation and invalidation, is described in [9]. The algorithm keeps track of the request rate and the update rate of every document and estimates the network traffic generated by propagation and invalidation. Using state information, it evaluates the costs of propagation and invalidation, in terms of network traffic introduced. When a document is modified, the origin server propagates the new document, or sends an invalidation message, whichever involves less cost. The simulations show that this hybrid mechanism effectively takes advantage of the delivery network, substantially reduces the traffic generated and improves freshness rate. But due to its simple assumptions, this algorithm overestimates the traffic introduced by invalidation. It also uses a uniform threshold to determine which mechanism (propagation or invalidation) is used, regardless of the document size. In addition, it does not explicitly take temporal locality into account. We believe this algorithm can be improved in these aspects. In the next section, we propose an improved algorithm.

3   The Improved Hybrid Algorithm

As in [9], the basic policy of our algorithm is to 1) use propagation when the ratio of request rate to update rate of a document exceeds a certain threshold; and 2) use invalidation otherwise.

First we evaluate the average number of the surrogate servers that receive at least one request of a document between two consecutive updates on this document. Based on this number, a new threshold for the request/update ratio is established. Then we describe how temporal locality and document size are modeled in the algorithm.

3.1   Preliminary

Let R be the overall request rate of a document, U be its update rate, $r = R/U$ be the ratio of the request rate to the update rate, N be the number of surrogate servers, and $\epsilon = -0.3$ be the network topology efficiency factor. In [9], the criterion determining which scheme (propagation or invalidation) should be used is expressed as

$$r \geq N^{1+\epsilon}, \text{use propagation};$$
$$r < N^{1+\epsilon}, \text{use invalidation}.$$

This is derived from comparing the network traffic generated by propagation and invalidation. However, the invalidate traffic is overestimated in [9]. In the invalidation mode, not every request introduces extra network traffic from the origin server to the surrogate serve. Between two succeeding updates of a document, if several requests of this document are received at a surrogate server, only the first request triggers the download of the latest document. A closer estimation of the invalidation traffic needs to compute the average number of the surrogate servers which receive at least one request between two consecutive updates.

We assume that the document requests are equally likely dispatched to every surrogate server. The probability that a request of a document is dispatched to a certain surrogate server, say server x, is

$$P = 1/N \ . \tag{1}$$

The probability that this request is dispatched to any other surrogate server y, $y \neq x$ is

$$\overline{P} = 1 - 1/N \ . \tag{2}$$

The ratio of the request rate to the update rate is $r = R/U$. In other word, r requests will be received on average between two consecutive updates of the document. These requests are served randomly by the surrogate servers. Because of the independence of the requests as assumed, the probability of none of these requests is served by surrogate server x is

$$P_n = \overline{P}^r = (1 - 1/N)^r \ . \tag{3}$$

That is, with probability P_n, surrogate server x serves no request for the document during this period of time. Thus the expectation of the total number of surrogate servers serving no request is

$$E_n = N \cdot (1 - 1/N)^r \ . \tag{4}$$

Now we can derive the average number of the surrogate servers that serve at least one request of the document between its two consecutive updates. We denote it as $E(N, r)$ to highlight the fact that it is a function of N and r.

$$E(N, r) = N \cdot (1 - (1 - 1/N)^r) \ . \tag{5}$$

Based on $E(N, r)$, we can compute the invalidation traffic more accurately and hence establish a more precise criterion.

3.2   The Refined Criterion

As in [9], we use the network traffic involved in propagation and invalidation to establish our criterion. Assume that a document of size S on the origin server has update rate U and request rate R. The multicast tree connecting N surrogate servers to the origin server has L_m total number of multicast links; the total hops of the unicast paths to all surrogate servers is L_u, $L_m/L_u = N^\epsilon$.

In propagation mode, a document is propagated to every surrogate server via the multicast tree whenever it is updated, generating a network traffic T_p

$$T_p = S \cdot L_m \ . \tag{6}$$

Between two consecutive updates of a document, the servers will receive $r = R/U$ requests of this document. As shown in the previous subsection,

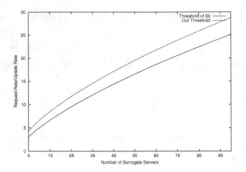

Fig. 1. Two thresholds

these requests are served by $E(N, r)$ surrogate servers on average. In invalidation mode, the number of downloading the updated document from the origin server to the surrogate servers during this period is $E(N, r)$. We assume that the average number of unicast hops from a surrogate server to the origin server is L_u/N; we also omit the traffic associated with document invalidation messages. The traffic incurred in invalidation mode is thus

$$T_i = S \cdot \frac{L_n}{N} \cdot E(N, r) \ . \tag{7}$$

The criterion is that using invalidation if $T_i/T_p < 1$, and propagation otherwise. From equations (5), (6), (7) and the power law $L_m/L_u = N^\epsilon$, the final criterion is

$$r \geq ln(1 - N^\epsilon)/ln(1 - 1/N), \text{ use propagation;}$$
$$r < ln(1 - N^\epsilon)/ln(1 - 1/N), \text{ use invalidation.}$$

As mentioned early, the threshold in [9] is based on an overestimated traffic of invalidate. It may result in that propagation is used for some documents while invalidation actually involves smaller traffic. Fig. 1 depicts two thresholds, $N^{1+\epsilon}$ of [9] and our $ln(1 - N^\epsilon)/ln(1 - 1/N)$, with the value of N ranging from 5 to 100 and an ϵ of -0.3. In this context, our threshold is significantly larger than that of [9]: ours exceeds it by 20% on average.

These two thresholds are asymptotically equivalent when N tends to infinity, that is

$$\lim_{N \to \infty} \frac{ln(1 - N^\epsilon)/ln(1 - 1/N)}{N^{1+\epsilon}} = 1 \ . \tag{8}$$

For realistic scenarios, however, our threshold more accurately captures the actual network traffic and provides a more precise threshold for the improved algorithm.

3.3   Modeling Temporal Locality

Certain patterns exist in web accesses as seen by surrogate servers [2]. The web access locality has long been observed, verified and analyzed [1, 4, 6]. The presence of web reference locality includes both geographical locality and temporal locality. The hierarchical data-collecting and decision-making scheme proposed in [9] handles uneven request distribution, effectively taking advantage of geographical locality. However, no measure is explicitly described in [9] to deal with temporal locality. We present a simple approach to capture the temporal locality of document requests in this subsection.

Temporal locality has been found in various web access traces, ranging from single-user traces, homogeneous user group traces to diverse user community traces. The study of [14] indicates that both long-term popularity and short-term temporal correlation contribute to the temporal locality. This implies that temporal localities of different documents exhibit at different time scales. An effective algorithm should be capable of modeling this property.

In our algorithm, the document request rates are periodically refreshed. Every document is associated with a refresh period. We evaluate an exponentially weighted moving average (EWMA) of the request rate. Let $R(i)$ be the request rate of a document at the end of the ith refresh period. During the $(i+1)^{th}$ period, suppose the document is requested R_{i+1} times and denote the new request rate at the end of the $(i+1)^{th}$ period as $R(i+1)$,

$$R(i+1) = \alpha \cdot R_{i+1} + (1-\alpha) \cdot R(i) \ . \tag{9}$$

α is a pre-defined smoothing constant, $0 < \alpha < 1$. In (9), the history request rate is updated with the latest data. The more remote the history information, the smaller the impact it contributes to the current value of request rate.

To avoid unnecessary updating of document request rates at the end of every period, we trade-off state space for smaller number of request rate updates. When a document receives at least one request, (9) is used to evaluate the new value. At the same time, the period order number is stored for this document. All the documents that are not requested during this period are skipped. Thus (9) is actually implemented as

$$R(j) = \alpha \cdot R_j + (1-\alpha)^{j-i} \cdot R(i) \ . \tag{10}$$

where i is the stored period order number when the request rate was last updated, j is the current period order number. Eqn. (10) is only applied to those documents with $R_j > 0$.

Documents exhibit diverse time scales of temporal localities. Requests of some documents may change dramatically in a relatively short period of time; other documents may receive steady rates of requests over a long period. To accommodate this time scale discrepancy, we use a series of update periods to refresh the request rates of different documents. The documents with fast changing request rates are associated with shorter update periods; those with slowly-changing request rates are associated with longer update periods. Typically, we use 8 to 32 periods ranging from 5 minutes to 5 hours as the update periods. The customization of these parameters can be one part of the management tasks of a CDN.

3.4   Modeling Document Sizes

Our algorithm is further improved by taking document size into account. Propagating a large document involves larger network traffic than propagating a small one does. The cost of a wrong decision depends on the document size as well. To reduce this cost, we use increasingly larger thresholds as the document size increases in a certain interval.

If a document size is smaller than the packet size of an invalidation message, this document should never be invalidated. In this case, the actual threshold should be 0. For the documents with sizes greater than a certain value S_r, we use the threshold established in subsection 3.2. For those documents in between, the threshold is increased from zero to r progressively. We call $r = ln(1-N^\epsilon)/ln(1-1/N)$ the nominal threshold. r is adjusted with the document size S to procure the final threshold r_f used in our algorithm. Let S_i be the invalidation message packet size; r_f is expressed as

$$
r_f = \begin{cases} r & \text{if } S \geq S_r \\ \frac{S-S_i}{S_r-S_i}r & \text{if } S_i < S < S_r \\ 0 & \text{if } S \leq S_i \end{cases} \tag{11}
$$

The value of S_r can be assigned according to the size distribution and network properties. Based on the simulation experiments, $S_r = min(20S_i, S_a/3)$ is believed to be a reasonable heuristic value for S_r, where S_a is the average document size.

3.5   The Implementation of the Improved Algorithm

In summary, the improved hybrid algorithm consists of two components. The first component is located at the origin server, collecting the document update rates, periodically polling the request rates and making the final decision. The second component is located at the surrogate servers, maintaining the request rates for every document and sending them to the origin server at its request.

4   Performance Evaluation

We present our simulation results and the comparisons among the improved algorithm and the other three approaches, viz., the propagation approach, the invalidation approach, and the approach of [9]. We first describe the simulation settings and then compare their network traffic and freshness ratios.

The simulations are performed on 10 artificially generated network topologies, among which 5 are generated in GT-ITM [10] and the rest are generated in BRITE [16]. Every topology has 1600 nodes. We simulate 10240 documents replicated from one origin server to 10, 60 and 110 surrogate servers. The documents have an average size of 15K bytes and the invalidation message is 0.1 Kbytes. The request follows a Zipf-like distribution. The probability of the ith

most popular document request is proportional to $\frac{1}{i^\alpha}$ and $\alpha = 0.75$. In the simulations, the total number of document requests ranges from 102400 to 10240000 times (i.e., the average request number per document is from 10 to 100). The update number of a document is uniformly distributed over $[1, 2U_{avg}]$, where U_{avg} is the average update number of a document, changing from 1 to 30. Due to the fact that the request distribution and the update distribution have different skewnesses, the resulting request-update ratio changes dramatically over a wide range.

We compare two performance measurements of the four methods: the network traffic generated and the freshness ratio. The traffic generated in various scenarios is depicted in Figs. 2(a)–(d); the freshness ratios of the four methods are illustrated in Figs. 3(a)–(d). In the following figures, "Hybrid 1" refers to the hybrid algorithm of [9] and "Hybrid 2" corresponds to our improved algorithm.

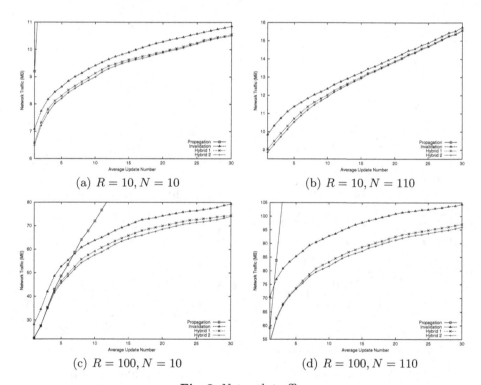

(a) $R = 10, N = 10$ (b) $R = 10, N = 110$

(c) $R = 100, N = 10$ (d) $R = 100, N = 110$

Fig. 2. Network traffic

In Fig. 2(a), the documents are replicated over 10 surrogate servers and the average request number is 10. When the average update number changes from 1 to 30, all the methods compared generate increasingly higher volume of network traffic. In this configuration, the propagation method generates substantially larger amount of traffic than the other methods do. In fact, the propagation traffic increases so rapidly that only the first data point of the propagation traffic is displayed in the figure. For both "Hybrid 1" and "Hybrid 2", the vast majority of the documents use invalidation method. The traffic of hybrid methods is less than that of invalidation. Our algorithm, "Hybrid 2", is also shown to have smaller amount of traffic than "Hybrid 1", the algorithm of [9].

Fig. 2(b) has 110 surrogate servers. The propagation traffic (not in the scope of the figure) increases speedily as it blindly propagates the new documents at every update. The invalidation, meanwhile, involves relatively smaller amount of traffic and it increases almost linearly when the update rates are greater than the request rates. This is reasonable, since most of the modified documents are not requested at all. The traffic introduced by invalidation messages, being proportional to the update rate, represents a large portion of the total traffic. Again, the hybrid methods introduce less traffic and our method generates the smallest volume of traffic.

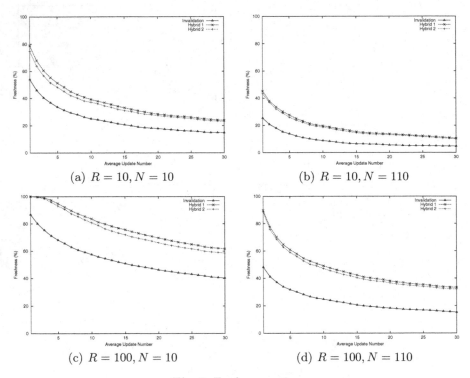

(a) $R = 10, N = 10$

(b) $R = 10, N = 110$

(c) $R = 100, N = 10$

(d) $R = 100, N = 110$

Fig. 3. Freshness ration

Similarly, Figs. 2(c) and 2(d) have 10 and 110 surrogate servers respectively; both have the average request numbers of 100. The general trends in these two figures are similar to those in Figs. 2(a) and 2(b). Traffic of propagation increases rapidly as the update number increases. When the average update number is small (<7 in Fig. 2(d) and <2 in Fig. 2(d)), the propagation traffic is less than the invalidation traffic. As illustrated in the figures, the hybrid methods generate less traffic than the other two methods (propagation and invalidation) do. The traffic of our method is also consistently smaller than that of "Hybrid 1" (quantitatively, the difference is 1.3MB in Fig. 2(c) and 1.1MB in Fig. 2(d) on average).

Figs. 3(a)–(d) demonstrate the freshness ratio comparisons. Since propagation always possesses a freshness ratio of 100%, it is not depicted in these figures. As the documents undergo more updates, the freshness ratios decrease consistently. It is shown that the hybrid methods produce substantially higher freshness ratios than invalidation does. In Fig. 3(b), the document requests are dispatched to a large pool of surrogate servers. When the update numbers are larger than the request numbers, the freshness ratio consistently keeps at a very low level. Since our algorithm uses a higher threshold (i.e., more documents will use invalidation), its freshness ratio is slightly smaller than that of "Hybrid 1". Owning to the fact that the overall high threshold is compensated by smaller threshold when the document size is small, the freshness ratio gap between these two hybrid methods is not so significant. This implies that our method reduces the network traffic without increasing response time considerably.

We also perform another set of simulations in which the request rates change over a certain interval and the update rates keep at fixed levels. Figs. 4–5 show the traffic and freshness ratio comparisons in these scenarios.

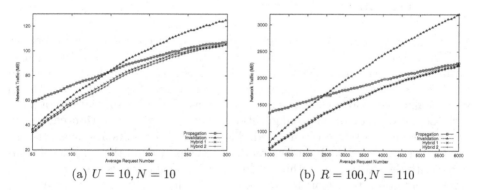

$$\text{(a) } U = 10, N = 10 \qquad\qquad \text{(b) } R = 100, N = 110$$

Fig. 4. Network traffic

Fig. 4(a) uses a fixed average update number of 10 and the average request number changes from 50 to 300. The propagation traffic is larger than that of invalidation when the average request number is less than 150; after that point, the invalidation traffic is greater than the propagation traffic. In this scenario, the traffic of propagation, with a fixed traffic volume corresponding to propagating updated documents, increases more slowly than the invalidation traffic does. Over the whole range of request rate, our method has the least amount of network traffic and it is on average 1.8MB less than that of "Hybrid 1". The same occurs

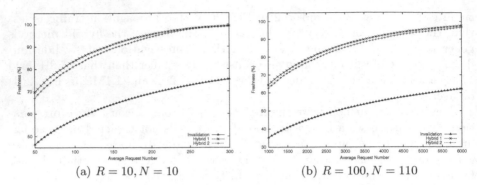

(a) $R = 10, N = 10$ (b) $R = 100, N = 110$

Fig. 5. Freshness ratio

in Fig. 4(b), where the traffic of our method is typically 20MB less than that of "Hybrid 1".

Figs. 5 are the freshness ratios corresponding to Figs. 4. Again, our method achieves freshness ratios that are very close to those of "Hybrid 1". Since the major concern of this paper is the network traffic and the primary purpose of the algorithm is to effectively reduce the traffic generated while keeping response time at about the same level, the minor freshness ratio difference is tolerable.

5 Conclusion

We have proposed an improved algorithm for content consistency maintenance in CDNs based on an existing hybrid method. A more accurate estimation of invalidation traffic is established and a refined threshold is found. The algorithm also takes account of temporal locality of document requests and document sizes when making consistency enhancement decisions. Extensive simulations over diverse scenarios and various configurations show that the algorithm effectively reduces the network traffic generated. The simulation results also suggest that the freshness ratio of the improved method remains around the same level compared with the existing algorithm. It does not significantly increase the response time. In addition, the algorithm introduces very little extra overhead and it is an implementation-friendly approach.

References

1. Almeida, V., Bestavros, A., Crovella M. and A. de Oliveira.: Characterizing Reference locality in the WWW. *Proceedings of PDIS*, December 1996.
2. Arlitt, M. and Williamson, C.: Web server workload characteristics: The search for invariants. *Proceedings of ACM SIGMETRICS*, May 1996.
3. Barabasi, A. and Albert, R.: Emergence of Scaling in Random Networks. *Science*, 286(5439)509-512, 15 October 1999.

4. Barford, P., Bestavros, A., Bradley, A., and Crovella, M.: Changes in Web client access patterns: Characteristics and caching implications. *World Wide Web*, 2(1):15-28, 1999.
5. Breslau, L., Cao, P., Fan, L., Phillips, G. and Shenker, S.: Web Caching and Zipf-like Distributions: Evidence and Implications. *Proceedings of IEEE INFOCOM 2000*, New York, NY, March 1999, pp. 126-134.
6. Cao, P. and Irani, S.: Cost-aware WWW proxy caching algorithms. *Proceedings USITS'97*, Monterey, California, December 1997.
7. Chung, J. and Sirbu, M.: Pricing Multicast Communication: A Cost-Based Approach. *Telecommunication Systems.* 17(3)281–297, 2001.
8. Faloutsos, M., Faloutsos, P., and Faloutsos, C.: On Power-Law Relationships of the Internet Topology. *ACM SIGCOMM*, 29(4), October 1999.
9. Fei, Z.: A new consistency algorithm for dynamic documents in content distribution networks. *Journal of Parallel and Distributed Computing*, 63(10)2003, pp. 916-926.
10. GT-ITM: Georgia Tech Internetwork Topology Models.
    http://www.cc.gatech.edu/projects/gtitm/
11. Gwertzman, J. and Seltzer, M. World-Wide Web Cache Consistency. *Proceedings of the 1996 USENIX Technical Conference*, January 1996.
12. Huberman, B. and Adamic, L.: Growth dynamics of the World-Wide Web. *Nature*, 401(6749)131, 9 September 1999.
13. Iyengar, A., Nahum, E., Shaikh, A., and Tewari, R.: Enhancing Web Performance. IFIP World Computer Congress (WCC), 2002.
14. Jin, S. and Bestavros, A.: Sources and Characteristics of Web Temporal Locality. *Proceedings MACOTS 2000*, San Francisco, California, Auguest,2000.
15. Li, D., Cao, P., and Dahlin, M.: WCIP: Web Cache Invalidation Protocol. *IETF Internet Draft*, November 2000.
16. Medina, A., Lakhina A., Matta, I., and Byers, J.: BRITE: An Approach to Universal Topology Generation. *Proceedings of MASCOTS 2001*, Cincinnati, Ohio, August 2001.
17. Medina, A., Matta, I., and Byers, J.: On the origin of Power Laws in Internet Topologies. *ACM Comp. Comm. Review*, April, 2000.
18. Phillips, G. and Shenker, S.: Scaling of Multicast Trees: Comments on the Chuang-Sirbu Scaling Law. *ACM SIGCOMM*, 29(4)41-51, October 1999.
19. Yin, J., Alvisi, L., Dahlin, M., and Lin, C.: Volume Leases for Consistency in Large-Scale Systems. *IEEE Transactions on Knowledge and Data Engineering*, January 1999.

Advanced Architecture for Distributed Systems with a Network Infrastructure Based on CAN and Internet for Content Distribution

Juan V. Capella, Alberto Bonastre, and Rafael Ors

Department of Computer Engineering, Technical University of Valencia,
46071 Valencia, Spain
{jcapella,bonastre,rors}@disca.upv.es

Abstract. A new layered architecture for the implementation of intelligent distributed control systems is proposed. This architecture distinguishes four levels in a distributed system. Upper layer consists of a digital control layer, where high level decisions are taken. This level is implemented by means of intelligent software agents and distributed expert systems that carry out the discrete control functions, system supervision as well as diagnosis and fault tolerance. Third layer deals with numeric values, performs analog operations and implement analog control loops. It is also in carry of the conversion from numerical variables values to evaluated expressions. This layer has been implemented by means of neural networks. Networking appears in the second layer, formed by CAN and Internet for content distribution. Finally, every node should implement a hardware interface with the process. Some interesting features provided by this architecture are its low-cost implementation, easy content distribution through the communication infrastructure, distributed execution in virtual generic nodes -with no hardware dependency-, bounded response time and fault tolerance mechanisms.

1 Introduction

Distributed systems offer several advantages when implementing control systems, such as scalability, fault tolerance, simplicity and power. Additionally, the advantages can be increased with the application of artificial intelligence techniques. In this line, an intelligent and distributed control architecture appropriate for multiple applications based on CAN and Internet networks is presented in this work.

A Distributed System (DS) can be defined as the one consisting of several physically dispersed nodes, each of them independent of the rest, but collaborating for the development of a common task. The collaboration implies the need of a communication network among the nodes, and the stating of a common communication protocol. The main difference between a DS and a networked one consists on transparency. From the user's point of view, all the nodes and network are abstracted in a single virtual centralized system. In this manner, the distribution of nodes is transparent to the user, relying on the system the nodes distribution solution.

Several problems arise when dealing with this approach. First of all, an automatic programming of each node must be performed by the system, distributing the variables and the program between possibly different nodes. No distribution of inputs and outputs is possible, because the node physically connected to a system variable must

C.-H. Chi and K.-Y. Lam (Eds.): AWCC 2004, LNCS 3309, pp. 58–69, 2004.
© Springer-Verlag Berlin Heidelberg 2004

handle it, but the subset of nodes related to every variable should know its current value. Also the complexity of using a programming language to the general public, as well as the necessity to know the complex functions that manages the protocols to control the network access, without forgetting the coherence problems due to the parallelism, etc.

In these systems the control response should take place in a deterministic amount of time. A too late action could be even worst than a wrong one or no action at all. In this sense, Real-Time capabilities of the control system must be considered.

Other main issue to study is the fault tolerance. It is necessary to know how the system will act if one node fall down, specially in systems with low maintenance possibility (i.e. remote control plants, spatial devices, ...)

In the proposed architecture several nodes, called control nodes (CN), collaborate to fulfill the control system task. Each CN reads its input variables from the system, by means of a A/D converter if the magnitude is reflected in analog values, or by means of digital inputs, and takes its output lines as actuator over the system (again, they can be analog or digital variables). Every node rule its own subset of the whole program, reading inputs and writing outputs and, if necessary, distributing its modified variables through the network. It can also take into account global variables, modified or obtained at other nodes.

The user interface resides at the programming and supervision node (PSN). This node, usually a PC, allows the user to interact with the control system, design and verify the control layers and, finally, performs the distribution of the same ones [1]. Also, the PSN has a web service, allowing the remote access by means of Internet to the system information. In this way, the users by means of a light-weight client devices such as mobile and portable end-user terminals have the information that they need from any place and in any moment.

2 Intelligent Software Agents

An intelligent agent [2] can be defined as a piece of software which performs a given task using information gleaned from its environment to act in a suitable manner so as to complete the task successfully. The software should be able to adapt itself based on changes occurring in its environment, so that a change in circumstances will still yield the intended result.

Perhaps the most general way in which the term agent is used, is to denote a hardware or (more usually) software-based computer system that owns the following properties:

- Autonomy: agents operate without the direct intervention of humans or others, and have some kind of control over their actions and internal state.
- Social ability: agents interact with other agents and (possibly) humans via some kind of agent communication language.
- Reactivity: agents perceive their environment (which may be the physical world, a user via a graphical user interface, a collection of other agents, the Internet, or perhaps all of these combined), and respond in a timely fashion to changes that occur in it. This may entail that an agent spends most of its time in a kind of sleep state from which it will awake if certain changes in its environment give rise to it.

- Proactivity: agents do not simply act in response to their environment, they are able to exhibit goal-directed behavior by taking the initiative
- Temporal continuity: agents are continuously running processes (either running active in the foreground or sleeping/passive in the background), not once-only computations or scripts that map a single input to a single output and then terminate.
- Goal oriented: an agent is capable of handling complex, high-level tasks. The decision how such a task is best split up in smaller sub-tasks, and in which order and in which way these sub-tasks should be best performed, should be made by the agent itself.

Thus, a simple way of conceptualizing an agent is as a kind of UNIX-like software process, that exhibits the properties listed above. A clear example of an agent that meets the weak notion of an agent is the so-called softbot ('software robot'). This is an agent that is active in a software environment (for instance the previously mentioned UNIX operating system).

For some researchers the term agent has a stronger and more specific meaning than that sketched out in the previous section, so that an agent can be a computer system that, in addition to having the properties as they were previously identified, is either conceptualized or implemented using concepts that are more usually applied to humans. For example, it is quite common in AI to characterize an agent using mentalistic notions, such as knowledge, belief, intention, and obligation.

Agents that fit the stronger notion of agent usually have one or more of the following characteristics :

- Mobility: the ability of an agent to move around an electronic network.
- Benevolence: is the assumption that agents do not have conflicting goals, and that every agent will therefore always try to do what is asked of it.
- Rationality: is (crudely) the assumption that an agent will act in order to achieve its goals and will not act in such a way as to prevent its goals being achieved - at least insofar as its beliefs permit.
- Adaptivity: an agent should be able to adjust itself to the habits, working methods and preferences of its user.
- Collaboration: an agent should not unthinkingly accept (and execute) instructions, but should take into account that the human user makes mistakes (e.g. give an order that contains conflicting goals), omits important information and/or provides ambiguous information. For instance, an agent should check things by asking questions to the user, or use a built-up user model to solve problems like these. An agent should even be allowed to refuse to execute certain tasks, because (for instance) they would put an unacceptable high load on the network resources or because it would cause damage to other users.

Although no single agent possesses all these abilities, there are several prototype agents that posses quite a lot of them.

The degree of autonomy and authority vested in the agent, is called its agency. It can be measured at least qualitatively by the nature of the interaction between the agent and other entities in the system in which it operates.

At a minimum, an agent must run a-synchronously. The degree of agency is enhanced if an agent represents a user in some way. This is one of the key values of agents. A more advanced agent can interact with other entities such as data, applications, or services. Further advanced agents collaborate and negotiate with other agents.

3 Distributed Expert Systems

An expert system can be defined as a computer program that behaves, as it a human expert would do in certain circumstances [3].

Another focus that we could really call distributed expert system, would be that in the one that the nodes that are part of the system are not limited to the acquisition of data, but rather they participate in the expert system execution. Evidently, this introduces a bigger complexity in the nodes design and in the communication protocols, but it offers significant advantages as the flexibility, the modularity, that allows to enlarge the system in an almost infinite way, and the hardware fault tolerance.

It can be seen how the expert system information it is distributed among the system nodes. Each one executes its corresponding part of the global reasoning, and diffuses the obtained results through the network. These data will be employed for some other nodes to continue its reasoning. This scheme corresponds to a truly distributed expert system.

Once mentioned the advantages of this system, let us pass to enumerate their inconveniences. Besides the biggest complexity in the nodes, already mentioned, serious problems arise, such as the nodes programming. This way, the programming easiness been able when using artificial intelligence techniques.

The true distributed system functionality would be obtained by means of a centralized programming system, where the expert system to use would be defined and tested in a single node. Later on, an automatic distribution of the rules among the nodes that belong to the system is required. This distribution would be carried out through the communications network, so that each node would obtain its part of the expert system to execute. It is possible to conceive several politicians of tasks distribution, as the traffic minimization or the rules redundancy in more than a node to offer fault tolerance.

A system complying with the features described above has been developed by the authors, and successful results having already been obtained.

3.1 Rule Nets

Basically, Rule Nets (RN) are a symbiosis between Expert Systems (based on rules) and Petri Nets (PN), in such a way that facts resemble places and rules are close to transitions. Similarly, a fact may be true or false; on the other hand, since a place may be marked or not, a rule (like a transition) may be sensitized or not. In the first case, it can be fired, thus changing the state of the system.

Like Petri Nets, RN admit a graphic representation as well as a matricial one; additionally, it also accepts a grammatical notation as a production rule, which drastically simplifies the design, thus avoiding the typical problems associated with PN.

3.2 Rule Nets Distribution

Given a distributed system formed by n nodes, it is possible to implement a control system through a Distributed RN (DRN), so that each one posses a part of the global reasoning, i.e., a part of the variables and the rules of the system. For this purpose, each node will handle a sub-set of variables and rules of the system.

After defining the set of all system variables, two cases may arise. Some variables will be used in more than one node and others only in one. Those variables required in more than one node are global variables (they will need a global variable identifier), whereas if they only affect one node will be known as local variables.

Obviously, a variable will be local if all the rules referring to it are in the corresponding node, whilst those appearing in rules of different nodes will necessarily be defined as global.

By minimizing the number of global variables, network traffic will be reduced. Besides, the variables referring to a physical input or output will necessarily be located in the node of the corresponding port. Taking this into account, an algorithm that permits the optimum assignment of variables and rules to each node has been developed. Optimal versions of this complex algorithm have been implemented successfully. It is possible to distribute the RN applying other criteria, such as fault tolerance approaches that allow several nodes to update any global variable.

Write-Through propagation mechanism guarantees that if the rule net meets a set of properties, once it is distributed and working on a broadcast network, the information will be coherent and the whole distributed system will run in a coordinated way.

4 Proposed Architecture

The architecture distinguishes four levels in a distributed system, as can be observed in figure 1. Upper layer consists of a digital control layer, where high level decisions are taken. This level should work with concepts i.e. the temperature is low rather than numbers: the temperature is 16°C.

The second layer deals with numeric values, performs analog operations and implement analog control loops. It is also in carry of the conversion from numerical variables values to evaluated expressions.

The communications infrastructure appears in the third layer. Network must perform the information share between nodes, offering to the upper layers a communication service. It should also be possible to access the system information in a remote way by means of Internet.

Finally, every node should implement a hardware interface with the process to control. It is implemented by means of A/D D/A converters prior to its transmission through the network.

Each of this layers is commented below in deep, also every layer must communicate with its upper and lower layer following a specified interface.

The system is controlled by means of a set of analog inputs and outputs. Hardware level converts these analog magnitudes into discrete (digitalized) data. These data can be transferred by means of the network to every node in this form (raw mode) or being evaluated by the analog level before its transmission. If the latter occurs, no analog data, but variable concepts expressions is transmitted. This feature increase the power of the architecture by reducing the bandwidth required (only elaborated and new concepts and transmitted, avoiding the transmission of repetitive or non-relevant data).

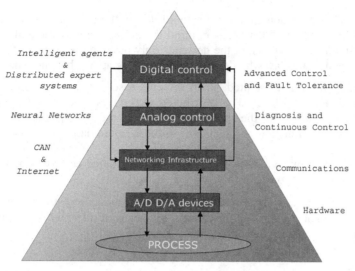

Fig. 1. Architecture levels

In this sense, network may transmit raw data or processed data (conceptual values), so both formats should be considered.

Analog level performs continuous control loops and is in charge of the numerical data interpretation to fit a conceptual value of each variable. These concepts must be the base of digital control and fault tolerance mechanism execution, given place to high abstraction level reasoning procedures in the intelligent agents. Comment finally that every layer must communicate with its upper and lower layer following a specified interface.

The detailed description of these levels and its suitable procedures is described in the following points.

The proposed architecture is the last advance in our research line, in which our group has developed and applied several intelligent systems [4] until obtaining the present architecture. With everything it is pursued to get a flexible architecture for the distributed and intelligent control systems implementation that facilitates in great way the designer's task.

4.1 Digital Level: Software Agents and Distributed Expert Systems

This layer implements the discrete control functions, system supervision as well as diagnosis and fault tolerance, making intelligent the whole control system.

The IA techniques to implement this level should complete the following requirements:

- Possibility to guarantee the design correction.
- Possibility to be executed in a distributed way.
- Abstraction of the distributed system, formed of diverse nodes, so that from the designer's point of view it behaves as a centralized system. This is the distributed systems methodology.
- Possibility to be executed in generic nodes, possibly very different between them.

- Possibility that even non-expert users could design the control system, by means of simple programming that keeps in mind the possible non sequential execution of the instructions. It is sought the designer only provide the basic system operation lines, and be this last who decides what rules are applicable and when.

Intelligent agents and distributed expert systems based on rule nets have been selected to implement this level. The distributed expert systems control the discrete variables of the process and the intelligent agents take decisions over the system, supervise the system function and diagnose failures, coordinating the whole distributed system.

This techniques provide a suitable base for the distributed control systems implementation by several reasons:

- Simplicity and power: Intelligent agents allows the complex control systems specification in an easy and intuitive way, by means of rules, without limiting for it the complexity of the control functions to implement [5].
- Analysis easiness.
- Compactness.
- Distribution: The intelligent agents are easily distributable units among the nodes of the control system as it is necessary. In the event of failure in some node, the agents will be relocated so that the system execution continues in a sure way. In the same way a distributed expert system is inherently distributable.
- Autonomy. Agents operate without direct intervention of human beings or other agents.
- Objective oriented. Agents are responsible for deciding where and when the proposed objectives are satisfied.
- Work in collaboration.
- Flexible. They carry out dynamically the election of what action they should invoke and in what sequence, in answer to the external state.
- Temporary continuity.
- Communication ability. An Agent can communicate with other agents, users, etc. to reach its objectives.
- Adaptability. An Agent automatically takes charge for itself of loading its user's preferences being based on previous experiences. It also adapts itself automatically to changes in the environment.
- Mobility. An Agent can be transported by itself from a node to other if it believes that is necessary.
- Persistence. Capacity that has an agent to reach or to achieve an objective.

4.2   Analogical Level: Neural Networks

Continuous and discrete control are not incompatible, but complementary, when dealing with complex systems. Combination of both techniques offers new possibilities, such as the implementation of hierarchical control systems. In this scheme, this level performs continuous control loops, diagnostics tasks and analog operations.

When dealing with a continuous control system implementation it was needed to decide the most accurate characteristics, such as:

- To be able to control any system almost with the same benefits that other control system already existent.
- Possibility that even non-expert users could design the control system, and even allowing the capacity for the self-learning of the system.
- Possibility to be executed in a distributed way.
- Easiness when being transmitted through the net for their execution in generic nodes (possibly very different between them).

After an exhaustive study of different continuous control techniques, the conclusion that Neural Networks meets all the previous conditions has been reached. Indeed, NN not only completes the first condition since they can deal successfully with any control system, but, far beyond, they are able to control systems where no other techniques can be applied.

It also fulfills perfectly the second condition due to their learning characteristics [6], making possible that even non-expert users in the control systems design can be capable, in a centralized way, to define the desired system behavior. NN are capable to learn in an automatic way thought the analysis of a group of samples that reflect the answers expected in real situations of execution. Even more, it is possible in the design phase the simulation of the system operation in front of hypothetical situations with the purpose of checking that it fulfils the desired specifications.

Since the NN are formed by perfectly detachable units (neurons), the distribution of these neurons in different nodes is not very difficult, so the results obtained by each neuron must be spread thought the interconnection network to be used as an input for any other neuron needing it.

Finally, it is possible to characterize a neural network as a group of neurons. All neurons present a common structure, and they are easily adapted in function of a parameters set. Therefore, it is possible to locate several generic neurons in the nodes and make a particularization of them in function of the desired control system by means of the transmission of these parameters.

4.3 Communications Infrastructure: CAN and Internet

One of the two main missions of this level is to offer the system information through Internet to the user. And the other mission, is to propitiate the information exchange among remote nodes, so that they can carry out its activity.

The first one, is carried out by means of a gateway node that is connected to both networks. This node stores locally all the information of the different system nodes, and through Internet offer this information to the user and even to receive orders from the system responsible (previous authentication).

Also, other value-added services have been added, mainly oriented to enhance information security, application robustness and network performance, being transparent to the web clients.

The SQL server system database is used to store all the generated information, so that it is simple its distribution by means of the web server through Internet, as well as the users administration [7][8].

This gateway node is a personal computer that has access on one hand to Internet and on the other hand has a CAN network card that connects it to the system backbone network (see figure 2). In this manner, the HTTP protocol can be used to access this information [9], in this way the operator can be connected from any computer connected to Internet and even from the modern mobile telephones or PDA's.

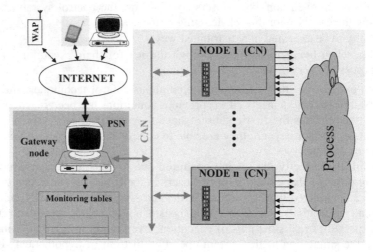

Fig. 2. System general structure

The second mission is carried out by means of a fieldbus. The industrial network to implement the information exchange among nodes should complete the following requirements:

- Diffusion network: Since this characteristic will minimize the traffic in the net, when not having to send for each node that needs certain information a different message.
- Priority schemes and the possibility to delimit the response time: Since to maintain limited in the whole system the response time, it should be delimited in all and each one of the levels.
- Fault tolerance characteristics.

A suitable network for this architecture is CAN (Controller Area Network) because of its particular characteristics [10]. First of all, CAN is a diffusion network, providing that all nodes that need a value produced by another node get the value with only one message. Even more, these messages are labeled (in the identifier field) with the generator that produced it, so avoiding any overload. Also, non-destructive contention allows a limited response time. Is it also possible to fix the priority of any messages, guaranteeing that values proceeding from latter entities will be sent before those from earlier ones. Finally, CAN offers several advantages, such as low cost, great variety of products, etc.

Over the network will need a protocol that provides the following characteristics. An HLP over CAN that meet this features has been implemented [11], the protocol is called ICCAL II. This features are the following:

Remote Identification of the Connected Devices. The proposed protocol is able to detect what system devices are really in operation, without necessity of carrying out the access to the net verification in an individualized way.

In all studied application protocols, the system designer should know all the existent nodes in the net and introduce this information in all the devices that require it. For the communication problems detection in a node, it is necessary to carry out explicit diagnoses (communication tests) on the same ones.

Net Virtualization. From the user's point of view, the whole net is contemplated as a centralized system in the PSN with all its inputs and outputs. It is transparent to the user the fact that these inputs and outputs don't reside in the PSN, rather they are distributed among the CNs. This is gotten thanks to the virtualization of each device in a series of inputs and outputs, the CN nodes identification to the PSN in a transparent way to the user and the CN programming interface. Also, this feature make possible to design general purpose nodes, generic and from different providers whose integration doesn't present problems.

None of the HLP over CAN contemplates the devices virtualization, although the nodes automatic identification is contemplated in CAN Open related with the defaulted profiles.

Centralized Programming. Once the user has all the system inputs and outputs in the PSN, he can proceed to the programming of the behavior wanted in the same one, without necessity of contemplating the details corresponding to the distribution. The programming in the PSN is carried out from an identical way to the corresponding to a centralized system. Thanks to this it is possible the off-line verification of the system operation, that is to say, without necessity of executing the program on the net, by means of the RN behavior simulation. Also, a tools series for the RN properties verification has been developed. These tools guarantee a correct behavior of the system (absence of blockades in the RN, absence of cycles, etc.). It is also possible to calculate the system states diagram, and over them verify the absence of not desired states. Once checked the system, the protocol takes charge of its distribution among the nodes.

Several studied protocols allow the transmission of data blocks that could contain program code. However, this code should be characteristic of the device implementation. None of this protocols contemplates the possibility of system behavior simulation, neither the properties analysis in order to guarantee the properly system operation

Fault Tolerance. This high layer protocol allows the implementation of several fault-tolerance techniques. All of them need the PSN to remain as a system watch dog, and the adoption of several actions to deal with failure events. In this case, PSN would send a WHO message periodically, which would be replied by means of an ALIVE message. If the ALIVE message does not arrive, and after several tries, the PSN will assume a failure in corresponding node.

More sophisticated methods are contemplated. PSN knows which rules and variables belong to each node and agent, so PSN can watch the network for variable updates. In this case, the PSN only would transmit a WHO message when no variable of a node has been updated for a fixed amount of time.

When the PSN notices that a node has fallen, several actions are available. PSN always will inform the user of the failure, but is also able to restart the system or that the agents are redistributed for degraded working mode.

Thanks to the centralized programming and to the identifiers assignment following the philosophy producer/consumer is possible to predict great part of the messages that will appear on the network in a given moment. Therefore, it is possible that several nodes arrive at the conclusion that a variable should change its state in a simultaneous way, and therefore to attempt the transmission of this upgrade. In none of the studied protocols the transmission of messages with the same identifier by different nodes is allowed. However, since it is possible to guarantee the system behavior a priori, it is allowed that several CN follows same or similar deduction lines to reach the same conclusions. So, in certain cases it is possible to carry out voting mechanisms among the conclusions of several nodes, also, in case of some CN falls down, another CN could follow the reasoning line and, therefore, it would minimize the effect of this failure. Of course, the node fall implies the impossibility of managing the inputs and outputs physically connected to the same one, but it doesn't impede the continuation of the reasonings based on the last well-known state of this variables, until the guardian node mechanism detects the failure and take the opportune measures.

5   Conclusions

A new generic architecture based on intelligent agents, distributed expert systems and neural networks, and a high layer protocol over CAN have been presented. Four levels can be distinguished: lower level implements a hardware interface with the process by means of A/D D/A devices, actuators, sensors and other acquisition systems. Second layer is the communications layer, indispensable in any distributed system. Third layer performs non-lineal control with the information obtained from lower layer by means of neural networks, and finally, on the upper level the distributed expert systems control the discrete variables of the process and the intelligent agents take decisions over the system, supervise the system function and diagnose failures, coordinating the whole distributed system.

This intelligent architecture is highly flexible due to its modularity. The changes or adjustments in one layer should not force the modification of the other layers. Also guarantees that the information will be coherent.

The proposed communications infrastructure provides the integration of the web server with the database server for a content-driven computation, in order to provide quality of service for content presentation. Another value-added services have been added, mainly oriented to enhance information security, application robustness and network performance.

Nowadays, this architecture is being applied to an experimental scale model of industrial plant, where NN implement the control loops and adaptable advanced features. To accomplish its mission, the NN takes into account the current values of several variables and magnitudes. On the other hand, the expert system based on rule nets implements the discrete control functions and over them a group of intelligent agents supervises the global system operation, under normal operation conditions and exceptional situations, in the last case the agents reconfigures the system to reach a safe-response in degraded mode. Very interesting results have been obtained, specially in fault tolerance capabilities, and the study of future developments is being carried out.

References

1. Verma, D.C.: Content distribution networks : an engineering approach. John Wiley & Sons, New York (2002)
2. Knapik, M., Johnson, J.: Developing intelligent agents for distributed systems: exploring architecture, technologies and applications. McGraw-Hill. New York (1998)
3. Liebowitz, J.: Introduction to Expert Systems. Mitchell Publishing, Inc. (1988)
4. Bonastre, A., Capella, J.V., Ors, R.: A new Hierarchical and Intelligent Control Architecture based on Distributed Neural Networks and Expert Systems applied to vehicle automation. Proceedings of the 2002 IEEE International Conference on Control and Automation, Xiamen, China (2002)
5. Alanis, A., Castillo, O., Rodríguez, A.: A method for multi-agents systems creation starting from an expert system. Proceedings of the 1st International Symposium of Intelligent Technologies, Instituto Tecnológico de Apizaco (1997)
6. Anthony, M., Bartlett, P.. Neural Network Learning: Theoretical Foundations. Cambridge University Press (1999)
7. http://www.mysql.com
8. Williams, H.E., Lane, D.: Web database applications with PHP and MySQL. O'Reilly, cop. Sebastopol (2002)
9. Comer, D.E.: Internetworking with TCP/IP. Prentice Hall (1996)
10. CAN specification version 2.0, Robert Bosch GmbH, Stuttgart (1991)
11. Bonastre, A., Ors, R., Capella, J.V., Herrero, J.: "Distribution of neural-based discrete control algorithms applied to home automation with CAN". Proceedings of the 8th International CAN Conference, Las Vegas, USA (2002)

Distributed Document Sharing with Text Classification over Content-Addressable Network

Tayfun Elmas and Oznur Ozkasap

Koc University
Department of Computer Engineering
Sariyer, 34450 Istanbul, Turkey
{telmas,oozkasap}@ku.edu.tr
http://www.ku.edu.tr

Abstract. Content-addressable network is a scalable and robust distributed hash table providing distributed applications to store and retrieve information in an efficient manner. We consider design and implementation issues of a document sharing system over a content-addressable overlay network. Improvements and their applicability on a document sharing system are discussed. We describe our system prototype in which a hierarchical text classification approach is proposed as an alternative hash function to decompose dimensionality into lower dimensional realities. Properties of hierarchical document categories are used to obtain probabilistic class labels which also improves searching accuracy.

1   Introduction

With increasing data storage capacity of the Internet, building information retrieval systems that will serve a wide range of purposes would be indispensable. Peer-to-peer (P2P) systems have become a popular alternative to build large-scale platforms for distributed information retrieval applications, as they provide a scalable, fault-tolerant and self-organizing operational environment. Several studies focus on network structures that make use of P2P organizations together with efficient decentralized and localized processing capabilities inherent to the P2P technology [2].

A key point in building P2P systems is organizing nodes in a distributed system to get maximum performance and speed from the overall structure. This can be accomplished by *semantic overlays*, which solve the problem of random distribution of documents among the nodes in the network [1]. With semantic overlays, documents are distributed among the nodes considering their semantic similarities so that the documents similar to each other would be located in a small region.

In addition to semantic issues, an organization scheme is needed to address the nodes, distribute both data and processing over these nodes and access them in an efficient manner. *Content-addressable networks (CAN)* [10] provide distributed hash tables which can be queried using a *key* to get the associated *object*. In the cartesian space, *object* is a point in the space representing queries or

C.-H. Chi and K.-Y. Lam (Eds.): AWCC 2004, LNCS 3309, pp. 70–81, 2004.

documents. Some recent search engines like *pSearch* [13] have used vector space model (VSM) and latent semantic indexing (LSI) that map each document into a term vector building a whole document-term matrix.

P2P networks are becoming increasingly popular since they offer benefits for efficient collaboration, information sharing, and real-time communication in large-scale systems. In such an environment, each peer has a collection of documents which represents the knowledge distributed by the peer. Moreover, each peer shares its information with the rest of the network through its neighbors, namely its *peers*. Each document can be associated with a unique id (e.g., generated by a hash function on the contents of the document) to uniquely identify the same documents located on different peers. A node searches for information by sending query messages to its peers. We can assume that a query is either a collection of keywords or a complete document containing the key information on the topic interested. A peer receiving a query message searches the documents locally among its collection of documents and also propagates the query to its neighbors if specified in searching policy. Most P2P systems use flooding, propagating the query along all neighbors until some threshold criteria is reached. If the search is successful, the peer generates a reply message to the querying peer.

In this study, we propose a distributed document sharing system that is capable of indexing and searching through a collection of documents. The system consists of peers that store indexes to documents and key vectors that identify each document uniquely, with capability of searching through them. Consequently, the amount of data each individual node stores is much less compared to the systems that store the actual contents of documents. In the proposed system, a machine-learning approach [6] is utilized to generate identifiers which uniquely locate a document. We use properties of hierarchical document categories to get probabilistic class (i.e. topic) labels which also improves searching accuracy.

The paper is organized as follows. Operation of CAN in document sharing system and basic protocols are explained in section 2. In section 3, design considerations and improvements are discussed with applications to our proposed system. Section 4 describes the system developed and results obtained. Related work is discussed in section 5. In Section 6, conclusions and future directions are stated.

2   Document Sharing on Content-Addressable Network

Content-addressable network (CAN) proposes a promising approach to organize a P2P overlay network and perform peer operations, transparent to most of the overlay. Each peer knows only a limited number of peers and each operation like joining or leaving can be established in a small fraction of time and in a limited region by not bothering the rest of the network.

CAN is a distributed hash table that maps *key* values to *object* values. *key* is a point in Cartesian space and the corresponding *object* is located in the network node. In a *cartesian coordinate system*, the coordinates of a point are its distances from a set of perpendicular lines that intersect at an origin. The upper limit of the space is specified as 1 in our system, thus a point can have coordinates as floating-point numbers between 0 and 1. In this space, each node has a corresponding *zone* in Cartesian space.

In the original definition, *reality* refers to multiple coordinate spaces with the same dimensionality. Further details on this concept are given in Section 3.2. In this study, we redefine the term reality. We use different dimensions for each reality where each reality corresponds to a topic group in topic hierarchy. In addition, we divide a key point into subkey points and perform routing and search to reach different subkey points of each reality for a single key. Therefore, the CAN space is decomposed into realities according to class hierarchy, and similarities were computed by separate realities for separate parts of class weight vector.

There are some fundamental operations in CAN networks, such as joining as a new node, publishing a document and searching through existing documents. All these operations require routing through the network to reach a desired node. In this section, these basic operations will be introduced considering our new reality definition and subkey concept.

2.1 Routing

Routing from a source node to a destination node on the overlay network is equivalent to routing from the zone of the source node to the destination zone in the Cartesian space, so that a message with key point is passed from the sender, through some other nodes, until it reaches the node whose zone surrounds that key point. The routing process here is established for a subkey in its associated reality. Since each node has direct connection to only its neighbors, a node uses its neighbors to redirect a message. Simple approach uses greedy choice. Once a node receives a message with a key point, it checks if its zone contains the point. If so, it handles the message according to its contents. Otherwise, it computes the distances between its neighbors and the key point, and chooses the neighbor with the smallest distance to the point. Then it passes the message to that neighbor.

2.2 Joining

The CAN space is divided amongst the nodes currently running in the system. To allow the CAN to grow incrementally, a new node that joins must be given its own portion of the coordinate space. This process is called the *join process* and a new node must join all realities defined in the CAN. The phases are as follows:

- A new node that wants to join the CAN space first discovers the IP host address of any node currently in the system. This address can be directly configured for the new node, which is actually done in this study, or can be retrieved through a bootstrapping mechanism as explained in [10].
- The new node randomly chooses a point P in the space and divides it into subkeys for each reality. Then it sends a join request message destined for each subkey of P through the associated reality. Each CAN node then uses

the routing process to forward the message in the reality. The destination node splits its zone in half and assigns one half to the new node. The split is done according to order of dimensions and the order decides along which dimension a zone is to be split, so that zones can remerge when a node leaves the CAN.

- Then there is some information exchange. First, information about the new zone is sent to the new node. After getting its zone in CAN space, the new node learns its neighbors set from the previous occupant. This set is a subset of the previous occupant's neighbors, plus that occupant itself. Similarly, the previous occupant updates its neighbor set to eliminate those nodes that are no longer neighbors. Finally, both the new and old nodes' neighbors are informed of this join operation.

The join of a new node affects only a small number of nodes ($O(d)$ where d is the number of dimensions) in a small region of the coordinate space. The number of neighbors of a node depends only on the dimensionality of the coordinate space, and is independent of the total number of nodes in the system.

2.3 Publishing

Publishing a document into the system requires some preprocessing to get *key* and *value* pair related to document which will be stored in CAN overlay. The original document is kept in the source machine whether this server is inside or outside CAN overlay, only URL address to that document needs to be stored. Once the URL of the document is obtained, accessing the original document is straightforward. Key generation process is performed by the *hierarchical Expectation Maximization (EM) algorithm* [6] that classifies a big number of documents which has no categorization information using a small number of categorized documents. Details of the EM algorithm implemented in this study are given in the Appendix. Once the classification finishes, the resulting class weight vectors are written in a file. The node publishing these documents reads the file and sends *(key,value)* pairs into the CAN overlay. Publishing process is depicted in Figure 1, and can be summarized as follows:

- Since class labels and thus class weights for most of the documents are not known, EM algorithm is used to assign probabilistic class labels to documents. After applying EM algorithm, the class weights along with the URL addresses are written to a file for the publishing application to read.
- The publishing application does not have to be inside the CAN system. It gets the IP address of any running bootstrap node in CAN and sends a message with *(key,value)* pairs. The communication between outside nodes and those in CAN is assumed to be secured.
- Once the inside node gets the *(key,value)* pair, it just sends this pair to the node which owns the zone containing the point represented by vector *key*.

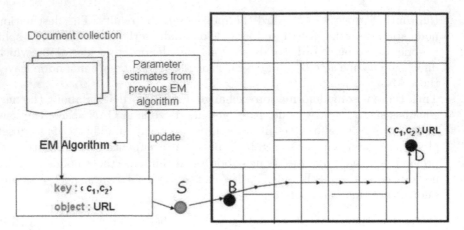

Fig. 1. Publish process for a collection of documents

2.4   Searching

Our system treats any expression, whether a keyword phrase or an ordinary document, given for search operation as the whole query document. Then the naive bayes classification algorithm [6] is used to classify the query document. It uses statistics on previously published documents and generates the vector whose elements are class labels of query document. Since naive bayes uses results of previous results of EM algorithm, it's assumed that most of the documents will be published from the same set of nodes. Naturally, it's common for usenet groups since usenet messages are stored in a fixed set of servers and can be classified on those servers. The search operation is as follows:

- The search operation can be initiated mostly by an outside node. As for publish process, the outside node contacts to a bootstrap node inside CAN and sends search request message with the query key-point.
- Once a node inside CAN gets the query point, it routes the search request message until the corresponding node that owns the surrounding zone is located. That node initiates the actual search process by flooding search messages through its neighbors. When a node gets the search message, it computes the similarity between its data and the query, and sends relevant document indices to the initiator node directly. It also computes the distance between its neighbors and the query point and if the distance does not exceed the threshold, sends the search message to its neighbors. If the document vector is X and the query vector is Y then the similarity measure is the cosine of the angle between these vectors as follows:

$$Cosine(X, Y) = \frac{X \odot Y}{|X| \cdot |Y|} = \sum_{i=1}^{l} X_i Y_i$$

- When a node determines that the distance from the query point exceeds the threshold, it stops the flooding process. The initiator node collects the results and delivers it to the user in a sorted format.

3   Improvements and Discussion

There are several improvements that contribute to the performance of operations on CAN overlays [10]. In this section, we discuss the set of improvements utilized in our prototype system implementation.

1. *Multidimensional Coordinate Space:* The system design does not put a limit on the dimensionality of the coordinate space. In fact, increasing dimensions of the CAN coordinate space reduces the routing path length, the number of nodes a message will pass through before reaching its destination. This in turn reduces the path latency only for a small increase in the size of the coordinate routing table of individual nodes. With this feature, since a node has more candidate next hop nodes, fault tolerance in routing mechanism also improves especcially in the case of some neighbor node crashes.

   In the classification scheme, we divide the class vectors into sub-vectors according to the class hierarchy, so the number of document classes in a branch of the topic hierarchy determines the dimensionality of its reality. An example is given in Figure 2. As the topic hierarchy grows and leaf classes increase, the dimensionality of realities and thus the system will increase and the routing mechanism will benefit from this. However, decomposing space according to the topic hierarchy reduces the total dimensionality, and computation cost in search operation, since most of the computation will take place only on a small number of realities.

2. *Using Realities:* Multiple coordinate spaces can be maintained, and each node in the system can be assigned to a different zone in each coordinate space which is called *reality*. Thus, if there exists r realities in a CAN, a single node is assigned to r coordinate zones, one on every reality and has r independent neighbor sets. This leads to the replication of information, namely document indices for every reality. The replication improves data availability and fault tolerance of routing process, because if a routing process fails on one of the realities, messages can continue to be routed over the other realities. Since the contents of the hash table are replicated on every reality, routing to a key point means reaching the given key on the nearest node on any reality. When forwarding a message, a node examines all its neighbors on each reality and selects the neighbor with coordinates closest to the destination.

   Hierarchical structure of classes makes weights of classes with common ancestors to be closer to each other facilitating to divide the whole space into lower dimensional realities, each reality representing an independent virtual space. If the class weight vectors resulting from classification are used as the only hash function, then those vectors are decomposed into lower dimension vectors. Each of these is associated with a common ancestor, so that class labels in vectors are close to each other. Then each reality represents a branch in hierarchy. This fact reduces computation and latency in parallel executions, since most of the computation will take place in realities associated with common branches.

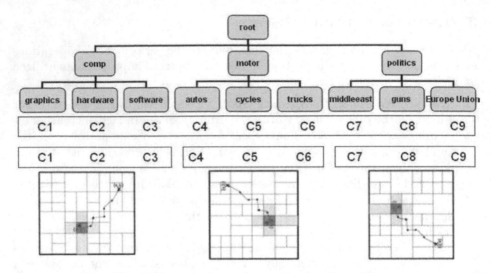

Fig. 2. Decomposing a class vector to sub-vectors

3. **Multiple Hash Functions:** Different hash functions can be used to map a single document onto different points in the coordinate space and accordingly replicate the data at distinct nodes in the system. Then, queries for a particular hash table entry could be distributed to all nodes in parallel, reducing the average query latency. This is possible at the cost of increasing the storage size and query traffic. Text classification brings an approach which uses leaf classes of a class hierarchy as dimensions of a space bounding from 0 to 1, and represents a document with probabilistic class labels in that space. Without decomposing whole class vectors to realities, classification can only be used as an additional hash function along with LSI since resulting vectors only cover a limited space. Note that the region comprising the classified documents will be $P(c_1|d_i) + P(c_2|d_i) + \cdots P(c_j|d_i) = 1$, where $P(c_j|d_i)$ is the probability of *class j* given *document i*. It can be used to improve searching performance since the zones to distribute a query can be easily determined and sent to only a small fraction of all neighbors of a node.

4   Prototype and Results

To see the effect of text classification on CAN performance, a prototype document sharing system was implemented in Java. In our system, each peer is capable of joining an existing CAN overlay, publishing documents and searching through them. The hierarchical EM algorithm was implemented as the classification module to generate key vectors for documents. The module writes its output into a file for peers to read and publish into the CAN. Using previous classifications, it also classifies query documents and generates query-key points to send as search message.

For evaluating classification performance of the algorithm, two collections of data were prepared. All documents and vocabulary were selected arbitrarily and without any assumption. No preprocessing were applied to documents. One of the test data sets consists of 8 leaf classes and an hierarchy of 3 levels. 4044 unlabeled and 576 labeled documents were downloaded from Microsoft's news site[1] and 828 of them were separated as unlabeled heldout data to update shrinkage weights. The vocabulary was build with 26411 words. Second test data set consists of 19 leaf classes and an hierarchy of up to 5 levels. 15658 unlabeled and 4788 labeled documents were downloaded from Microsoft's news site and Tom Mitchell's site[2], and 3420 of them were separated as unlabeled heldout data to update shrinkage weights. The vocabulary was build with 27907 words.

Some documents are exchanged between labeled-unlabeled-heldout collections, and results are collected on average. The algorithm converged at an accuracy of 30% for the first test set and at accuracy of 42% for the second test set. The basic EM algorithm used for the first data set converged at an accuracy of 20%. Note that increasing the number of labeled documents improves the performance. Number of labeled documents in the second data set was doubled and an accuracy of 55% was observed.

Some documents were selected arbitrarily and applied to get query key vectors. These query vectors were sent into CAN overlay and returned document indices were evaluated, detecting that the search latency and cost for computing similarities reduce compared to the results with only one reality. It can be stated that using class labels from classification of documents can be used efficiently along with proven techniques like LSI and VSM [3] as a hash function. Also, the closeness of labels with the existence of class hierarchy can be used to divide the overall CAN space into realities.

The documents stored in the system are collected from usenet news groups so that there is a hierarchy in which leafs of the hierarchy become the concrete classes. The hierarchical organization of documents relates documents in different leaf classes so that class labels of related classes with common ancestors will converge each other. This method deals with curse of dimensionality that appears in situations where documents are represented with high dimensionality vectors. If the classifier assigns class labels to documents correctly there will be no circumstance in which labels of classes that are unrelated and far from each other in dimensionality converge to each other.

There is a drawback that this approach classifies documents as a whole and does not take their individual parts in content into consideration, which LSI does. In effect, similarity between two documents is measured by the closeness of them to some topics, not by similarities of their contents to each other. Therefore, a big number of leaf classes are required to measure the similarity as relevant as the user expects. Nevertheless, the topic hierarchy in nowadays' usenet groups are extensive enough to differentiate two documents according to their topics.

---

[1] news.microsoft.com

[2] www-2.cs.cmu.edu/afs/cs/project/theo-11/www/naive-bayes.html

5   Related Work

pSearch system [13] is one of the distributed information retrieval systems that makes use of a variant of CAN called eCAN, which provides the semantic overlay. The system uses Latent semantic indexing (LSI) [3] to map document to semantic vectors in the space. LSI uses singular value decomposition, and includes semantic concerns like synonyms and uses conceptual vectors instead of single term weights. In vector space model (VSM) [5], the documents and queries are represented as vectors each of whose elements is the weight of the term in the document or the query. VSM uses the product of the frequency of the term and inverse document frequency.

In [8], a novel strategy for clustering peers that share similar properties, forming additional attractive links over the existing network to group similar peers, is proposed. In order to make use of clustered P2P network efficiently, a new query routing strategy called the Firework Query Model, is introduced, which aims to route the query intelligently to reduce the network traffic caused by query passing in the network.

Crespo and Molina [1] propose the semantic overlay network (SON) concept in which nodes are grouped by semantic relationships of documents they store. All nodes store information about the classification hierarchies, and routed queries accordingly. SON concept is devised especially for the creation of a network structure that improves query performance with flexibility and high node autonomy. They also propose creation of multiple overlay networks, in a P2P system, to improve search performance. They ignore the link structure within an overlay network and represented an overlay network just by the set of nodes in it.

Another study introduces Passive Distributed Indexing (PDI) [4], which is a general-purpose distributed search service for document exchange for mobile applications, and based on P2P technology. PDI defines a set of messages for transmission of queries and responses, and all those messages are exchanged using local broadcast transmission. PDI is intended to provide a general-purpose file search service to be used by different types of upper layer applications.

Similar to [13, 8, 1], our approach adopts the similarity relationship among the documents in the system in order to form a cartesian-space abstraction of the content distribution space. In contrast to these studies, we make use of a text classification technique and probabilistic closeness of documents to some classes to obtain the similarity information. We then map those information to a CAN overlay to access desired content efficiently.

Nakao, Peterson and Bavier [7] discuss that one common characteristic of overlay services is implementation of an application-specific routing strategy and propose a new architectural element, a routing underlay, that sits between overlay networks and the underlying Internet. Overlay networks query the routing underlay, which extracts and aggregates topology information from the underlying network, when making application-specific routing decisions. Their approach can be adapted to content-based overlays, like CAN, to reduce the tradeoff between the high-level content-based organization and the network layer topology of an overlay.

The Plaxton data structure [9], which is called a Plaxton mesh is novel that it allows messages to locate objects and route to them across an arbitrarily-sized network, while using a small constant-sized routing map at each hop. Additionally, it guarantees a delivery time within a small factor of the optimal delivery time, from any point in the network. The system makes the assumption that the Plaxton mesh is a static data structure, without node or object insertions and deletions. Objects and nodes have names independent of their location and semantic properties.

Pastry [11] is a scalable, fault resilient, and self-organizing P2P infrastructure. Each node in Pastry has a unique, uniform randomly assigned id in a circular 128-bit identifier space. Given a 128-bit key, Pastry routes an associated message towards the live node whose id is numerically closest to the key. Moreover, each Pastry node keeps track of its neighboring nodes in the namespace and notifies applications of changes in the neighbor set. Each node also maintains a leaf set, which ensures reliable message delivery and is used to store replicas of application objects.

Tapestry [14] provides location-independent routing of messages directly to the closest copy of an object or service using only point-to-point links and without centralized management. Similar to CAN architecture, Tapestry uses randomness to achieve both load distribution and routing locality. It is very similar to Pastry but differs in its approach to mapping keys to nodes in the sparsely populated id space, and how it manages replication. In Tapestry, there is no leaf set, and neighboring nodes in the namespace are not aware of each other.

Like Pastry, Chord uses a circular id space [12]. Unlike Pastry, Chord forwards messages only in clockwise direction in the circular id space. Instead of the prefix-based routing table in Pastry, Chord nodes maintain a finger table, consisting of pointers to other live nodes. Each node also maintains pointers to its predecessor and to its successors in the id space, which is called the successor list.

Each of those infrastructures [9, 11, 14, 12] for building and accessing overlays aim to exploit a structural organization in order to access desired nodes efficiently. CAN overlays have been devised for similar purposes, and they have also the advantage of providing a content-based organization. Moreover, they can fit well to content distribution frameworks to be leveraged in various operations.

6   Conclusions and Future Work

We demonstrate the basic aspects of a distributed document sharing system utilizing text classification techniques over a CAN, and the resultant prototype is assessed to be promising one to build detailed information retrieval systems. It favors availability of both data and processing by providing zone replication and fault-tolerant routing mechanism. In addition, the proposed text classification scheme to generate key vectors for documents provides an additional hash function that reduces the computation in search operation, limiting the search space.

It can also be used to decompose the key vector into lower dimensional vectors, separating overall space into multiple spaces.

There are some issues to be dealt with especially in search operation to make use of the reality decomposition as efficient as possible. In the existence of a huge hierarchical topic hierarchy, text classification would perform better, as long as optimal parameters like search and distance thresholds are supplied to the system. Another issue is constructing the overlay considering the underlying topology to have a better intuition on the effect of CAN message delivery mechanism.

Appendix

The EM algorithm [6] used in this study can be summarized as follows:

- Separate all data into three parts, *labeled, unlabeled and heldout* collections. Note that number of unlabeled documents are much bigger proportional to others.
- Prepare a vocabulary containing all words with some pruning irrelevant ones.
- Specify the class hierarchy with concrete classes at leaves. The hierarchy is defined within a configuration file and it's fed into the algorithm at the beginning.
- Build a naive bayes estimator at each leaf node of the class hierarchy using only labeled data owned by the leaf. Then, form the initial global estimator using the naive bayes estimators built at leaves.
- Classify all unlabeled documents using this naive bayes classifier built previously and place each unlabeled document into the document collection of resulting leaf class $argmax(c_j)$. This step can be considered as the *first E step* in EM algorithm.
- Iterate over the entire class hierarchy, until log likelihood of the global estimate, $\log P(\theta|D)$, converges:
  - **M Step:** Compute a naive bayes estimates at each node of the hierarchy starting from leaf nodes and going through until root. Documents used in an estimation at an ancestor node of c_j comprise documents owned by its children, except those used previously for the same class c_j. After all estimates finish, construct the global estimate using weighted sum of the estimates for each leaf class along the path from the leaf to the root.
  - **Weight Update:** Classify all heldout documents using the global classifier, and using the results of the classifications update weight of each node with respect to all leaf classes.
  - **E Step:** Using the global naive bayes estimator, reclassify all unlabeled documents and replace those whose resulting class changes.
- After finishing with EM algorithm, record the class vectors of documents consisting probabilistic class labels to a file for the publisher node to read and send into the overlay. In addition, record the parameters of the last global estimator to classify a given query document to get a key vector for searching later.

References

1. Arturo Crespo and Hector Garcia-Molina. Semantic overlay networks for p2p systems. Technical report, Computer Science Department, Stanford University, October 2002.
2. Zeinalipour-Yazti D. Information retrieval in peer-to-peer systems. *Master Thesis, Department of Computer Science University of California*, 2003.
3. Scott C. Deerwester, Susan T. Dumais, Thomas K. Landauer, George W. Furnas, and Richard A. Harshman. Indexing by latent semantic analysis. *Journal of the American Society of Information Science*, 41(6):391–407, 1990.
4. Christoph Lindemann and Oliver P. Waldhorst. A distributed search service for peer-to-peer file sharing in mobile applications. In *Proceedings of the Second International Conference on Peer-to-Peer Computing*, page 73. IEEE Computer Society, 2002.
5. Z. Drmac M. Berry and E. Jessup. Matrices, vector spaces and information retrieval. *SIAM Review*, 41(2):335–362, 1999.
6. A. McCallum and K. Nigam. Text classification by bootstrapping with keywords, em and shrinkage. In *ACL Workshop for Unsupervised Learning in Natural Language Processing*, 1999.
7. Akihiro Nakao, Larry Peterson, and Andy Bavier. A Routing Underlay for Overlay Networks. In *Proceedings of the ACM SIGCOMM Conference*, August 2003.
8. Cheuk-Hang Ng, Ka-Cheug Sia, and Irwing King. A novel strategy for information retrieval in the peer-to-peer network.
9. C. Greg Plaxton, Rajmohan Rajaraman, and Andrea W. Richa. Accessing nearby copies of replicated objects in a distributed environment. In *ACM Symposium on Parallel Algorithms and Architectures*, pages 311–320, 1997.
10. Sylvia Ratnasamy, Paul Francis, Mark Handley, Richard Karp, and Scott Shenker. A scalable content addressable network. In *Proceedings of ACM SIGCOMM 2001*, 2001.
11. Antony Rowstron and Peter Druschel. Pastry: Scalable, decentralized object location, and routing for large-scale peer-to-peer systems. *Lecture Notes in Computer Science*, 2218:329–350, 2001.
12. Ion Stoica, Robert Morris, David Karger, M. Frans Kaashoek, and Hari Balakrishnan. Chord: A scalable peer-to-peer lookup service for internet applications. In *Proceedings of ACM SIGCOMM*, pages 149–160. ACM Press, 2001.
13. Chunqiang Tang, Zhichen Xu, and Sandhya Dwarkadas. Peer-to-peer information retrieval using self-organizing semantic overlay networks. In *Proceedings of the 2003 conference on Applications, technologies, architectures, and protocols for computer communications*, pages 175–186. ACM Press, 2003.
14. B. Y. Zhao, J. D. Kubiatowicz, and A. D. Joseph. Tapestry: An infrastructure for fault-tolerant wide-area location and routing. Technical Report UCB/CSD-01-1141, UC Berkeley, April 2001.

Content Distribution Stochastic Fluid Models for Multi-regions P2P Networks

Zhiqun Deng[1], Dejun Mu[1], Guanzhong Dai[1], and Wanlin Zhu[2]

[1] Control & Networks Institute, College of Automation,
Northwestern Polytechnical University, Xi'an 710072, China
zhiqundeng@tom.com
[2] National Lab of Pattern Recognition,
Institute of Automation Chinese Academy of Sciences, Beijing 100080, China
wlzhu@nlpr.ia.ac.cn

Abstract. Region P2P networks (called RP2P), based on Chord protocol, are constructed by regions, but not the whole Internet as previous work. Nodes' joining and leaving, lookups and content forward algorithms are presented. To analyze the performance of the RP2P networks and study the dynamic content distribution process between RP2P networks, the stochastic fluid models as an important fluid-flow analytical model are adopted. The final results we got are as follows: the total number of RP2P networks has a more impact on the get probability of downloading content than the total number of nodes; and the content get probability will tend to be a stable value with the increase of nodes' number. These results demonstrate that the method of constructing RP2P networks is better than those of building the universal P2P network.

1 Introduction

Previous structured P2P overlay systems, such as Chord [1], are based on Distributed Hash Tables to provide an accurate search in the network. Such network is a global content distribution system and a universal P2P network. In [2], the multiple transport domains constructed is through bridge nodes, which have more than one network addresses. In [3], nearby hosts are constructed as groups that are connected each other. And information is completely shared among all the hosts within one group.

Region P2P Networks we proposed is based on the actual distance and bandwidth of networks. Each region network is organized into region P2P network (RP2P) based on the Chord protocol; and atop the RP2P networks, the multi-regions P2P network is constructed (see Fig. 1).

Now stochastic fluid models (SFM) have been successfully applied to study the performance of P2P cache in [4,5]. In these papers, the fluid flows mathematical models proposed are applied in analyzing the cache clusters and the Squirrel.

While our work is to apply SFM to a broader dynamical content distribution P2P network, but not just the cache clusters or P2P cache. Our system model is similar to

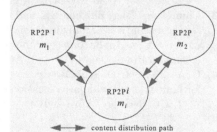

Fig. 1. Multi-regions P2P (RP2P) networks

that used in [5] with the following key difference that we apply SFM to the multi-regions P2P networks; and we do not consider expiration of objects in each node as

C.-H. Chi and K.-Y. Lam (Eds.): AWCC 2004, LNCS 3309, pp. 82–87, 2004.
© Springer-Verlag Berlin Heidelberg 2004

previous studies. And we got the results of the relation between the number of region P2P network, number of nodes and the download probability by SFM.

Our contributions are as follows. Firstly, RP2P network we proposed makes the content distribution in the local area network. Secondly, the stochastic fluid models are applied to the multi-regions P2P networks. Then we got the good performance parameters as follows: the total number of RP2P networks has a more impact on the get probability of downloading the content than the total number of nodes. These results show that the methods of constructing RP2P networks are superior to that of building a universal P2P network.

2 Multi-regions P2P Networks

2.1 Multi-regions P2P Networks Construct

As we all know that the spectrum of IP address is assigned to each country and area. For example, the range of IP addresses from 061.129.000.000 to 061.129.255.255 belongs to Shanghai city. In our prototype, we just select the former two numbers as the region number. Here we select (061.129) as the region number of Shanghai city. Then the region identifiers (R_{id}) are as follows:

R_{id} =Hash (the former two numbers of IP address).

Every node has a coordinate that is $(key, node, R_{id})$. Here *key* is the key identifier produced by hashing the original key words. And *node* is the node's identifier by hashing the node's IP address. *key* and *node* are the same as the ones of Chord.

Of course, the RP2P network identifier can be constructed by other methods.

2.2 Node Joins and Leaves

A new node belongs to the local area network, so the new node can only join the local region P2P network, because the new node has the same R_{id} with the local RP2P network. A host cannot determine which RP2P networks it belongs to. If the R_{id} is different, the latter operations will be different.

In the same RP2P network, all of the nodes have the same region number R_{id} and the node's operations like joins and leaves are the same as the Chord. But the nodes' number is m_i, not the total nodes' number. In Fig. 1, the nodes' number of each

$$RP2P \text{ is } m_i : 1 << m_i < N, N = \sum_{i=1}^{k} m_i .$$ Here, N is the nodes' number of all the RP2P

networks. And k is the total number of the RP2P networks and $k << N$. Indeed, the RP2P based on the Chord protocol can be implemented in the national scale. So the k value is not large. In the lab prototype we are implementing, k is equal to 128.

2.3 Lookups and Content Forward

Lookups in the RP2P network is the same as Chord protocol. Each RP2P network has m_i nodes. The lookups processes are as follows:

Firstly, the lookups proceed in the local RP2P network. The key location algorithm is the same as the scalable key location algorithm in Chord protocol. If the key is found in the local area, then the lookups stop. Else, the request will be forwarded to other RP2P networks. The other RP2P networks go on the same lookup process. If the key can be found, then the node identifier will be transmitted to the original request node according to the region identifier, else the lookups stop. The lookups maybe proceed in all the RP2P networks to the worst case.

3 Dynamic Content Distribution System

3.1 Microscopic Description of Multi-regions P2P Networks

In the dynamic content distribution P2P network, the parameters [5] of the P2P system are as follows.

N is the total number of nodes. The total number of objects of the system is c. Nodes go up and down independently of each other, the time until a given up (or down) node goes down (or up) is exponentially distributed with rate $\lambda > 0$ (or μ). Setting $\rho = \lambda / \mu$. $N(t)$ is the up nodes' number at time t. It is a birth-death process.

If there are i nodes that are up, there are x objects that are up. Here $i = 0, 1, \ldots, N$ and $x \in [0, c]$. So the get probability to download the content is G, which can be defined by $G = x / c$. The multi-regions P2P networks comprise k RP2P networks. Assume that the node can get the content with an equivalent probability and the downloading process is an independent and identical distribution (*i.i.d.*). The get probability function of each RP2P network is

$$G_i = \frac{x}{(\frac{c}{k})} = \frac{kx}{c}, \qquad\qquad kx << N < c. \tag{1}$$

Then the first successful get probability is

$$G = (1 - \frac{kx}{c})(1 - \frac{kx}{c})(1 - \frac{kx}{c}) \cdots (1 - \frac{kx}{c})\frac{kx}{c} = (1 - \frac{kx}{c})^{k-1}\frac{kx}{c}. \tag{2}$$

This function can be simplified to

$$G = (1 - \frac{kx}{c})^{k-1}\frac{kx}{c} = \frac{kx}{c} - (k-1)(\frac{kx}{c})^2 + o(\frac{kx}{c}) \approx \frac{kx}{c} - (k-1)(\frac{kx}{c})^2. \tag{3}$$

For the simplification, we just set the get probability function

$$G = \frac{kx}{c}. \tag{4}$$

The multi-regions P2P networks are based on the Chord protocol, so it can define the $\Delta_d(i) = (i-1)/i$, and $\Delta_u(i) = 1$ [5]. Each node launches a request for the content at a rate $\sigma > 0$, but $\sigma << c$.

For the objects expiration, we set the expiration rate zero. The reasons are as follows: firstly, the objects, whether new or old, are popular in the specific people group. Secondly, the old content may be popular again; finally, some content, such as books, will never expire with time. So the expiration rate of the content is set to be zero.

3.2 Stochastic Fluid Models for Multi-regions P2P Networks

The request process of each node is modeled by a fluid flow. The total amount of fluid in the network is $X(t) \in [0,c]$ at time t. $N(t) \in \{0,1,\ldots,N\}$ is the number of nodes that are up at time t. $0 \leq T_1 < T_2 < \cdots$ is the successive jump times of the process $\{N(t), t \geq 0\}$. The sample paths of $\{N(t), t \geq 0\}$ and $\{X(t), t \geq 0\}$ are left continuous.

In the paper [4], the following parameters were given:

$$E[X] = \frac{c}{(1+\rho)^N} \sum_{i=1}^{N} \binom{N}{i} \rho^i v_i \qquad (5)$$

Where the vector $\mathbf{v} = (v_1, \cdots, v_N)^T$ is the unique solution of the linear equation

$$Av = b. \qquad (6)$$

With $\mathbf{b} = (b_1, \cdots, b_N)^T$ a vector whose components are given by $b_i = \frac{\sigma}{\mu c} i$ for $1 \leq i \leq N$ and $A = [a_{i,j}]_{1 \leq i,j \leq N}$ is a $N \times N$ tridiagonal matrix whose non-zero elements are

$$
\begin{aligned}
a_{i,i} &= (\frac{\sigma}{\mu c} + 1)i + \rho(N - i), & 1 \leq i \leq N \\
a_{i,i-1} &= -i\Delta_u(i-1), & 2 \leq i \leq N \\
a_{i,i+1} &= -\rho(N-i)\Delta_d(i+1), & 1 \leq i \leq N-1
\end{aligned}
\qquad (7)
$$

Assume that for $i = 0, \cdots, N-1$, $0 \leq \Delta_u(i)\Delta_d(i+1) \leq 1$.

So the get probability of downloading the content is given by

$$G = k\frac{E[X]}{c} = \frac{k}{(1+\rho)^N} \sum_{i=1}^{N} \binom{N}{i} \rho^i v_i. \qquad (8)$$

4 Stochastic Fluid Models Analysis

For the multi-regions P2P networks, the parameters are as follows:

Table 1. Multi-regions P2P network parameters

N	Total number of nodes	k	Total number of RP2P networks
λ	Birth rate (up) of each node	μ	Death rate (down) of each node
$\Delta_d(i)$	$(i-1)/i$	$\Delta_u(i)$	1
G	Get probability	c	Total number of objects

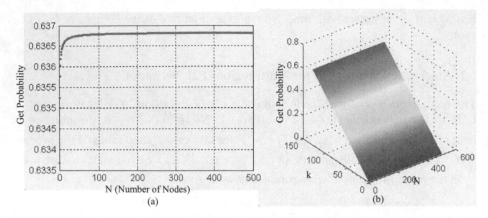

Fig. 2. (a) The impact number of nodes on the get probability (k =128); (b) Impacts of k and N value on the get probability (N is from 1 to 500; k is from 1 to 128)

In Fig. 2(a), we can get the conclusion that the get probability of downloading the content will get larger with the nodes joining, but more nodes' join do not increase the get probability, and the get probability eventually will tend to be a stable value.

In Fig. 2(b), we can see that joint impacts of k and N value on the get probability. The number of Nodes, N, has a less impact on the get probability than the number of P2P networks, k. In fact, from the equation (8), the get probability is mainly influenced by k. And the simulation results in Fig. 2(b) also prove this conclusion.

Though the get probability will be larger with the increase of k value, the probability will eventually be less than 1. In fact, $k \ll N$ and the get probability is much less than the simulation results. And, the function of get probability is simplified to the equation (4). Moreover, there is no consideration about the content expiration. If these were taken into account, the value of the get probability would be smaller.

So we can conclude that the multi-regions P2P networks have a higher get probability than that of the universal P2P network.

5   Conclusion and Future Work

In this paper, we have proposed that the multi-regions P2P networks based on the Chord protocol. We explore the stochastic fluid models to analyze P2P networks performance. We have got the good results as follows: the number of RP2P networks has a more impact on the get probability of downloading the content than the total number of nodes. We argued that the multi-regions P2P networks have a better performance than the universal P2P network in the previous work.

In the future research work, we will further extend the current work to construct the practical multi-regions P2P networks.

Acknowledgements

Our work has been supported by the Graduate Innovation Seed Foundation of Northwestern Polytechnical University under Grant No. Z20030051. The authors very much appreciate Ms. Florence Clévenot of INRIA in France and Mr. Daowu Zhou in University of Cambridge for their numerous useful and valuable help.

References

1. Stoica, R. Morris, D. Karger, F. Kaashoek, and H. Balakrishnan, Chord: A Peer-to-Peer Lookup Service for Internet Applications. In Proceedings of the ACM SIGCOMM Conference, San Diego, CA (September 2001)
2. Aaron Harwood and Minh Truong. Multi-space Distributed Hash Tables for Multiple Transport domains. In Proceedings of the IEEE International Conference on Networks, Sydney, Australia (2003) 283-287
3. Xin Yan Zhang, Qian Zhang, Zhensheng Zhang, and et al, A Construction of Locality-Aware Overlay Network: mOverlay and Its Performance. IEEE Journal on Selected Areas in Communications, Vol.22.No.1 (January 2004) 18-28
4. Florence Clévenot, Philippe Nain, Keith W. Ross. Stochastic Fluid Models for Cache Clusters. INRIA, Sophia Antipolis, Technical Report. Available at the website: http://www-sop.inria.fr/maestro/personnel/ Florence.Clevenot/peva_elsf.pdf. (2003)
5. Florence Clévenot, Philippe Nain. A Simple Fluid Model for the Analysis of the Squirrel P2P Caching System. In Proceedings of the IEEE INFOCOM 2004(March 2004)

Construct Campus Peer-to-Peer Networks

Zhiqun Deng, Guanzhong Dai, Dejun Mu, and Zhicong Liu

Control & Networks Institute, College of Automation,
Northwestern Polytechnical University, Xi'an 710072, China
zhiqundeng@tom.com

Abstract. The campus peer-to-peer networks, called CP2P networks, are proposed based on the existing Chord protocol. According to colleges' IP address ranges and users' interests, every college network constructs a CP2P network. The performance parameters we got are as follows: The average maximum lookup length of the first node in the CP2P network is $O(\log_2 N - \log_2 k)$. And other nodes' lookup lengths are $O(\log_2 m_i)$. Here N is the total number of nodes in the whole network; k is the total number of CP2P networks; m_i is nodes' number of each CP2P network. CP2P networks enable the transfer locally and reduce the traffic in the campus network backbone. Meanwhile, nodes join and leave only in the local CP2P network. Security problems such as DDOS can be traced back to the attackers' source colleges.

1 Introduction

In the past, the colleges or institutes in the university are independent to each other because the research fields are different. Nowadays the subjects mutually promote each other. So there urgently needs a uniform network services sharing environment to provide the users in the university with all kinds of resources.

The new emerging technology, peer-to-peer network (P2P), gives a good chance to advance the cooperation between colleges or institutes. The current structured P2P systems such as Chord [1], CAN [2], Pastry [3], and Tapestry [4] are based on Distributed Hash Tables (DHTs) to provide an accurate search in the network. All of the nodes as well as the key words are mapped into a virtual space with identifiers.

However, P2P networks based on the whole Internet do not consider different users' requirements or interests. Different users have different interests.

Additionally, the requested data might be stored in the nearby hosts (or in the local area networks) with the same interests, but for the fact that the data and the node is mapped randomly so that the data are transferred through a long distance or with a high latency, which results in the heavy traffic in the backbone.

So the methods that all of the nodes are mapped into a single virtual space may not be appropriate to the actual complex networks environment. While, the new scheme we proposed is based on the actual distance and users' interests. The campus network is partitioned into College P2P networks, called CP2P. And all of the CP2P networks form the whole campus P2P network (see Fig.1).

Our contributions in this paper are as follows:

Firstly, the CP2P network we proposed reduces the load of routers in the campus network backbone. Secondly, the users are organized into different interests groups according to the college. Thirdly, The average maximum lookup length of the nodes

C.-H. Chi and K.-Y. Lam (Eds.): AWCC 2004, LNCS 3309, pp. 88–93, 2004.

in the CP2P network is less than that of Chord protocol. Finally, security problems such as DDOS attacks can be traced back to the attackers' source colleges.

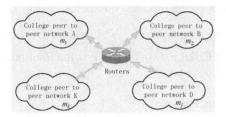

Fig. 1. College peer-to-peer (CP2P) networks

2 CP2P Networks' Architecture

2.1 CP2P Networks Construct

CP2P (see Fig.1) are based on the current work of structured P2P overlay networks, such as Chord, CAN. Our work is mainly based on the Chord protocol. But the ideas seem to apply a broader range of P2P protocols.

Firstly, we get the colleges identifiers. The IP address range of each college is assigned by the Campus Network Center, and it is deterministic. For example, the IP address range from 202.117.81.000 to 202.117.81.255 is assigned to the College of Automation. In our implementation, we just select the former three numbers as the colleges' numbers. Here we give a simple example, we select (202.117.81) as the college number of College of Automation. Then the college identifiers (C_{id}) are produced through hashing the college number:

C_{id} =Hash (the former three numbers of IP address).

Here, the *Hash* algorithm is the same as the consistent hashing algorithms [5]. Every node has a coordinate that is (key, node, C_{id}). Here the key is the key identifier produced by hashing the original key word. And the node is the node's identifier by hashing the node's IP address. In fact, the key and the node are the same as the ones in Chord protocol. Each college has a unique college identifier C_{id}.

How can we classify the users' interests and distance? Any user belongs to different colleges or institutes, which in fact belong to different research fields. The users' interests in the research field are roughly similar in the same college. And usually the distances between nodes in the same college are not far. So the users in the same college are organized into one group according to the distance and interests. Thus the users' interests can be classified according to the colleges, which they belong to. The college identifiers are the users' interests' identifiers. In the following, we will not differentiate the both.

2.2 Node Joins and Leaves

A node (or host, computer) belongs to the college network, so the new node can only join the local CP2P network. A host cannot determine which CP2P networks it belongs to. If the C_{id} is different, the latter operations will be different.

In the same CP2P network, all of the nodes have the same college identifier C_{id} and the node's operations like joins and leaves are the same as the Chord. But the nodes' number is m_i, not the total nodes' number N. In Fig.1, the nodes' number of each CP2P network is $m_i : 1 < m_i \leq N$, $N = \sum_{i=1}^{k} m_i$, $1 \leq k << N$. Here, N is the nodes' number of all the CP2P networks, and k is the total number of the CP2P networks, i.e. the number of colleges.

2.3 Lookup and Content Forward

Lookups are be implemented in the CP2P network, that is, are done by Chord protocol. The CP2P network has m_i nodes, while different CP2P networks may very well have the same key (content). The lookups algorithms are as following (see Fig. 2):

```
// Firstly lookup the key in the local CP2P network
if  C_id = the local CP2P identifier ,
    // t his is the lookup in the local CP2P network.
    { lookup (key); //call chord protocol lookup process;
      if the key is found, then return the location;
      else forward this request to other CP2P networks.}
else  //this is the lookup from other CP2P network request.
    Fo r  C_id (id = 1 to k - 1)
    { if  C_id ⊄ {C_id set that have accessed this CP2P network}
        lookup (key); //call chord protocol lookup process;
      else discard this request;
      if the key is found, then return the location;
      else tell the requester  the key was not been found. }
```

Fig. 2. The pseudo code of lookup algorithms

In our prototype, we adopt a simple algorithm. The lookups just proceed in a sequence of the college number. This algorithm may not be efficient but effective. The best lookup length is the one that lookups execute in the local (or first) CP2P network. It will take $O(\log_2 m_i)$ steps to find the key. While the worst case, with a low probability, is the case that the key is found in the last CP2P network, the lookup length is $\sum_{i=1}^{k} \log_2 m_i$. In this case, all of the nodes are searched. The average lookup length is $\mu_{aver} = O(\frac{1}{k}\sum_{i=1}^{k}\log_2 m_i) = O(\frac{1}{k}\log_2 \prod_{i=1}^{k} m_i)$, which is less than that in Chord protocol.

Proof (sketch).

$$\because m_1 + m_2 + ... + m_k = N, then \quad m_1 + m_2 + ... + m_k \geq k\sqrt[k]{\prod_{i=1}^{k} m_i}$$

$$\therefore \log_2(m_1 + m_2 + ... + m_k) \geq \frac{1}{k}\log_2 \prod_{i=1}^{k} m_i + \log_2 k$$

$$\therefore \mu_{aver} \leq \log_2 N - \log_2 k$$

The equal mark will come into existence iff $m_1 = m_2 = ... = m_k$. Here, $1 \leq k << N$. If $k = 1$, then the whole campus network is a uniform P2P network. Even if $k = N$, the average lookup length will be zero for there is no P2P network.

The average lookup length is just the lookup length of the first node initiating the lookup, not all of the nodes' lookup length. Once the first node find the content, other nodes in the same CP2P network having the same interest can just lookup in the local CP2P network and find the content.

Obviously, the first average maximum lookup length of CP2P network is $\mu^1_{averMax} = O(\log_2 N - \log_2 k)$. Here k is the total number of CP2P networks, not a large number. In our prototype, k is approximately equal to the number of colleges. We set it 2^4, i.e. 16. And the other nodes' lookup length is $O(\log_2 m_i)$. The lookup length of Chord protocol is $O(\log_2 N)$.

Apparently $\mu^1_{MaxAver} = O(\log_2 N - \log_2 k) < O(\log_2 N)$. If there also exists the first lookup operation in Chord protocol, the first lookup length is $O(\log_2 N)$. And other nodes lookup length is still $O(\log_2 N)$. Apparently $O(\log_2 m_i) < O(\log_2 N)$, so the lookup length of CP2P network is shorter than that of Chord protocol. The simulation result can be seen in Fig. 3. Here, k is from 1 to 128, and $N = 100,000$.

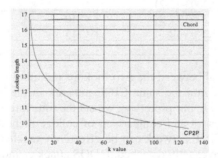

Fig. 3. Impact of k value on the average lookup length

3 Security Problems

The security problems in the CP2P network just occur in the local area network, but not globally as the Chord protocol. For example, once security problems, such as virus, come into being in the CP2P I network, the other CP2P networks can ban the content from this CP2P I network according to the college identifier C_i. And if users in a CP2P network attack the other CP2P networks, the attacked networks can shut down all the incoming messages from this CP2P network. Attacked networks can also appeal to the Campus Network Center to take measures against the attack behaviors, or notify the college directors where the attackers hide. So any attack can be traced back to the attackers' colleges.

How to handle attackers launching the loopy lookups across CP2P networks? And how to distinguish the correct lookups from the malicious lookups across different CP2P networks? Do there exist distributed denial of services (DDOS)? These similar problems embarrassing other P2P networks can be solved in CP2P networks.

Once the content are requested in CP2P network A by nodes in CP2P network B, the college's identifier will be recorded by nodes in the CP2P network A (in Fig. 4).

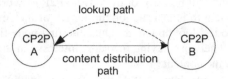

Fig. 4. Lookups in different CP2P networks

There is an access table in every node (see Table 1), which is updated periodically. Such table is encrypted and stored in each node so that the attackers cannot juggle the table. Of course, even if one node's access table is changed, the lookup still cannot execute in the next node. Because the next node still compares the foreign college's identifier to the local college's identifier in the access table. If the identifier is identical to one of college IDs of foreign access in the table, the lookup will be discarded.

Table 1. Access table recorded in every node

No.	Access time	CP2P ID of foreign access
1	15:39:09.22,2003-12-21	C-8
2	21:22:10.31,2003-12-21	C-10
3	21:35:00.82,2003-12-21	C-15
...	...	...

There is a time interval between the two lookups initiating by the same CP2P network with the same key into the same CP2P network in the lookup process across different CP2P networks. In our prototype, we set the time interval as 12 hours.

Through the time interval and comparison of college identifier, the loopy lookup attack across different CP2P network can be effectively tackled. And the correct and malicious lookups can be exactly detached. DDOS attack cannot impact on the whole P2P network.

4   Conclusion and Future Work

This paper proposes the college peer-to-peer networks, called CP2P networks, which partition the campus network according to the ranges of IP address of the colleges and users' interests. And every college network constructs a CP2P network.

In general, the CP2P network has the following good performance: The CP2P networks enable the transfer locally and reduce the traffic of the backbone on the campus network. Additionally, the maximum average lookup length of the first node is $O(\log_2 N - \log_2 k)$. And other nodes in the same CP2P network benefit from the first node' lookup, so their lookup length is $O(\log m_i)$. Here N is the total number of nodes in the whole network system, and k is the total number of colleges (CP2P networks); m_i is the nodes' number of each CP2P network. This performance is superior to that of Chord protocols. Finally, attacks can be traced back to attackers' colleges.

However, there are still some problems to be solved in our future work. The performance of actual content forward needs to be further explored. Security problems like in [6,7] will be further studied in CP2P networks. We need to further extend the current work to construct a practical P2P network (that is, CP2P network) in the campus network.

Acknowledgements

This work has been supported by the Graduate Innovation Seed Foundation of Northwestern Polytechnical University under contract Z20030051. We very much appreciate Mr. Daowu Zhou in University of Cambridge for his numerous useful comments and suggestions.

References

1. Stoica, R. Morris, D. Karger, F. Kaashoek, and H. Balakrishnan, Chord: A Peer-to-Peer Lookup Service for Internet Applications. In Proceedings of the ACM SIGCOMM Conference, San Diego, CA, (September 2001) 149-160
2. S. Ratnasamy, P. Francis, M. Handley, R. Karp, and S. Shenker, A scalable content-addressable network. Proceedings of the ACM SIGCOMM Conference, San Diego, CA, (Aug. 2001) 161-172
3. A. Rowstron and P. Druschel, Pastry: Scalable, distributed object location and routing for large-scale peer-to-peer systems. In Proceedings of International Conference on Distributed Systems Platforms, (Nov. 2001) 329–350
4. B.Y. Zhao, J. D. Kubiatowicz, et al, Tapestry: An infrastructure for fault-resilient wide-area location and routing. Technical Report UCB//CSD-01-1141, UC Berkeley (April 2001)
5. David Karger, Eric Lehman, et al, Consistent hashing and random trees: Distributed caching protocols for relieving hot spots on the World Wide Web. In Proceedings of the 29th Annual ACM Symposium on Theory of Computing, El Paso, TX, (1997) 654-663
6. John R.Douceur, The Sybil Attack. Proceeding of first international workshop on peer to peer systems (IPTPS 2002), Cambridge, MA, USA, (March 2002) 251-260
7. Emil sit and Rober Morris, Security Considerations for Peer-to-Peer Distributed Hash Tables. Proceeding of first international workshop on peer-to-peer systems (IPTPS 2002), Cambridge, MA, USA, (March 2002) 261-269

Fractional Gaussian Noise:
A Tool of Characterizing Traffic for Detection Purpose

Ming Li[1], Chi-Hung Chi[2], and Dongyang Long[3]

[1] School of Information Science & Technology, East China Normal University
Shanghai 200026, PR China
ming_lihk@yahoo.com, mli@ee.ecnu.edu.cn
[2] School of Computing, National University of Singapore, Lower Kent Ridge Road
Singapore 119260
chich@comp.nus.edu.sg
[3] Department of Computer Science, Zhongshan University, Guangzhou 510275, PR China
issldy@zsu.edu.cn

Abstract. Detecting signs of distributed denial-of-service (DDOS) flood attacks based on traffic time series analysis needs characterizing traffic series using a statistical model. The essential thing about this model should consistently characterize various types of traffic (such as TCP, UDP, IP, and OTHER) in the same order of magnitude of modeling accuracy. Our previous work [1] uses fractional Gaussian noise (FGN) as a tool for featuring traffic series for the purpose of reliable detection of signs of DDOS flood attacks. As a supplement of [1], this article gives experimental investigations to show that FGN can yet be used for modeling autocorrelation functions of various types network traffic (TCP, UDP, IP, OTHER) *consistently* in the sense that the modeling accuracy (expressed by mean square error) is in the order of magnitude of 10^{-3}.

1 Introduction

Detecting signs of DDOS flood attacks based on traffic time series analysis needs a statistical model to characterize traffic series. Our previous work uses FGN as a model of traffic for the detection purpose [1]. However, a technical issue concerned by researchers and engineers is whether or not FGN can characterize various types of traffic series consistently. By consistently, we mean that modeling accuracy is in the same order of magnitude. This paper experimentally investigates various types of traffic (TCP, UDP, IP, and OTHER). The experimental research presented in this paper exhibits that FGN can yet be used to consistently model various types of traffic with the modeling accuracy (expressed by mean square error) in the order of magnitude of 10^{-3}.

Time series with long-range dependence (LRD) has been widely studied in many fields of science and engineering, see for examples [2,3] and references therein. Experimentally exhibiting LRD property and correlation model of actual traffic series are beneficial in traffic modeling [4-9]. Though researchers have noticed the limitation of FGN in accurately modeling autocorrelation function (ACF) of real traffic [10,11], it may yet serve as an approximation model of traffic in traffic engineering, see e.g., [5,6,9-13]. Because the lack of experimental and quantitative evidence of the consistency regarding modeling various types of traffic by using FGN, this paper gives experimental investigations of modeling ACF of a type of time series called inter-arrival series using FGN.

C.-H. Chi and K.-Y. Lam (Eds.): AWCC 2004, LNCS 3309, pp. 94–103, 2004.

In the rest of paper, § 2 describes the preliminaries. Experimental investigations are given in § 3 and conclusions in § 4.

2 Preliminaries

2.1 Traffic Series (Inter-arrival Times)

Let $x[t(i)]$ be a computer network traffic (traffic for short) time series, indicating the number of bytes in the ith packet at the time $t(i)$, where $i \in I$ ($= 0, 1, 2, \ldots$). We call $t(i)$ timestamp series, implying the timestamp of the ith packet. Let the increment series of $t(i)$ be $s(i) = t(i + 1) - t(i)$. Then, $s(i)$ is called inter-arrival series of $x[t(i)]$.

2.2 FBM and FGN

Let $B(t)$, $t \in (0, \infty)$, be the Brownian motion. Let $B_H(t)$ be the fractional Brownian motion with $H \in (0, 1)$. Let $\Gamma(\cdot)$ be the Gamma function. Then,

$$B_H(t) - B_H(0) = \frac{1}{\Gamma(H + 1/2)} \left\{ \begin{array}{l} \int_{-\infty}^{0} [(t-u)^{H-0.5} - (-u)^{H-0.5}] dB(u) + \\ \int_{0}^{t} (t-u)^{H-0.5} dB(u) \end{array} \right\}. \tag{2.1}$$

Let the increment series of $B_H(t)$ be

$$G(t) = B_H(t+a) - B_H(t), \tag{2.2}$$

where a is a real number. Then, G is called FGN. The ACF of FGN is given by

$$\rho(\tau) = \frac{\sigma^2}{2} [(\tau+1)^{2H} - 2\tau^{2H} + (\tau-1)^{2H}]. \tag{2.3}$$

where $\sigma^2 = \dfrac{\Gamma(2-H)\cos(\pi H)}{\pi H(2H-1)}$. The normalized ACF of G is given by

$$R(\tau) = \frac{1}{2} [(\tau+1)^{2H} - 2\tau^{2H} + (\tau-1)^{2H}]. \tag{2.4}$$

Below, we use $R(k)$ (k is integer) to indicate ACF of FGN in the discrete case.

Note 2.1. A series is of LRD if its ACF is non-summable and it is of short-range dependence (SRD) if its ACF is summable [2]. □

Note 2.2. G for $H \in (0.5, 1)$ is of LRD while it is of SRD for $H \in (0, 0.5)$. □

2.3 *H* Estimation

H plays a vital role in time series with LRD. There are various methods for H estimation, see e.g., [2,3]. This paper uses the method introduced in [12].

A series measured in practical detection is of finite length. In fact, it is of finite length when numeric computation is involved. Let r be ACF of a real series s with LRD:

$$r(k) = \frac{E\{[s(i+k)-\mu][s(i)-\mu]\}}{\sigma^2} \sim ck^{2H-2} \ (k \to \infty), H \in (0.5, 1),$$

where $c > 0$ is a constant, $\mu = E(s)$ and $\sigma^2 = \text{Var}(s)$. Then, without losing generality, the maximum possible length of r is assumed to be N. Define the norm of r as inner product

$$\|r\| = \sqrt{<r,r>} = \sqrt{\sum_{k=0}^{N-1} |r|^2}, N \in I. \tag{2.5}$$

Then, the following

$$l_N^2 = \left\{ r; \sqrt{\sum_{k=0}^{N-1} |r|^2} < \infty \right\} \tag{2.6}$$

is an inner product space and moreover, Hilbert space [12,14].

Define the set $\mathcal{E}$ as

$$\mathcal{E} = \{R; R(k) = 0.5[(k+1)^{2H} - 2k^{2H} + (k-1)^{2H}], H \in (0.5, 1)\},$$

$$(k = 0, 1, \ldots, N-1), \tag{2.7}$$

Then,

$$\mathcal{E} \subseteq l_N^2. \tag{2.8}$$

According to the theorem of existence of a unique minimizing element in Hilbert space [14], for an ACF of a real series $r \in l_N^2$, there exists a unique $R \in \mathcal{E}$ such that

$$\|r - R\| = \inf_{a \in \mathcal{E}} \|r - a\|. \tag{2.9}$$

Let

$$J(H) = \frac{1}{N} \sum_k [r(k; H) - R(k; H)]^2. \tag{2.10}$$

Then, minimizing $J(H)$ yields an estimate

$$H_0 = \arg\min J(H). \tag{2.11}$$

The value of $J(H_0)$ is the minimum mean square error, which is denoted as $M^2(R) = E[(R - r)^2]$, where E is the mean operator.

3 Experimental Investigations

3.1 Real Data Used

Real data used in this paper consist of 28 series. They are 6 series of TCP traffic (Table 1), 10 series of UDP traffic (Tables 2.1-2.2), 6 of IP traffic (Table 3), and 6 of OTHER traffic (Table 4). The series with the prefix DEC were measured at Digital Equipment Corporation, those with Lbl were recoded at the Lawrence Berkeley Laboratory, and the series with NUS were collected at National University of Singapore. In Tables 1-4, the first column stands for series name, the second for record date, and the third for series length.

3.2 Demonstrations

3.2.1 Demonstration with DEC-pkt-1.TCP

The series $x[t(i)]$ of DEC-pkt-1.TCP is indicated in Fig. 1 (a) and timestamp series $t(i)$ is in Fig. 1 (b). The inter-arrival series $s(i)$ is in Fig. 2. The measured ACF of $s(i)$ is shown in Fig. 3 (a). Minimizing $J(H)$ yields $H_0 = 0.923$ with $M^2(R) = 2.264 \times 10^{-3}$. Therefore, we have modeled ACF $R(k)$ of $s(i)$ of DEC-pkt-1.TCP as indicated in Fig. 3 (b).

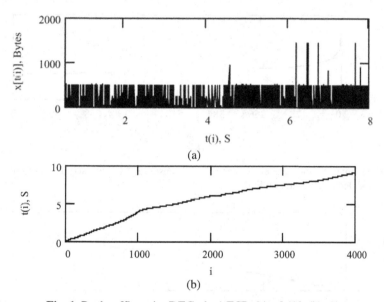

(a)

(b)

Fig. 1. Real traffic series DEC-pkt-1.TCP. (a). $x[t(i)]$. (b) $t(i)$

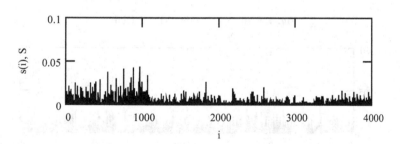

Fig. 2. Inter-arrival series $s(i)$ of DEC-pkt-1.TCP

3.2.2 Demonstration with NUS-1.UDP

Real series $t(i)$ for NUS-1.UDP is shown in Fig. 4 and $s(i)$ in Fig. 5. The measured ACF of s is shown in Fig. 6 (a). Minimizing J yields $H_0 = 0.935$ with $M^2(R) = 2.264 \times 10^{-3}$. Fig. 6 (c) indicates an ACF model of s of NUS-1.UDP using FGN.

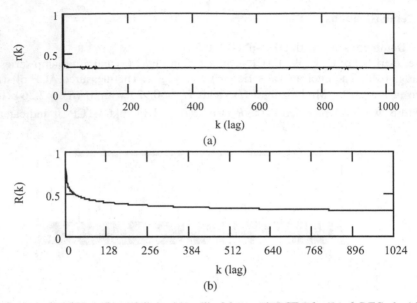

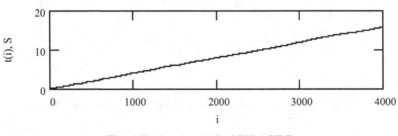

Fig. 3. H estimation and modeling. (a). $r(k)$: Measured ACF of $s(i)$ of DEC-pkt-1.TCP. (b). $R(k)$: Modeled ACF based on FGN

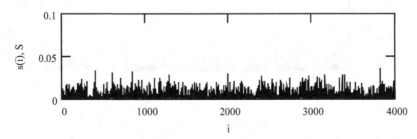

Fig. 4. Real series $t(i)$ for NUS-1.UDP

Fig. 5. Real series $s(i)$ for NUS-1.UDP

3.2.3 Demonstration with DEC-pkt-1.IP

Timestamp series for DEC-pkt-1.IP is plotted in Fig. 7 and $s(i)$ in Fig. 8. The measured ACF of $s(i)$ is in Fig. 9 (a). Minimizing J yields $H_0 = 0.955$ with $M^2(R) = 2.416 \times 10^{-3}$. Fig. 9 (b) indicates an ACF model of $s(i)$ of DEC-pkt-1.IP using FGN.

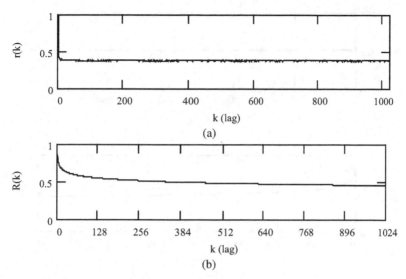

Fig. 6. *H* estimation and modeling. (a). Measured ACF of *s*(*i*) of NUS-1.UDP. (b). *R*(*k*): estimate of *r*(*k*) using FGN model

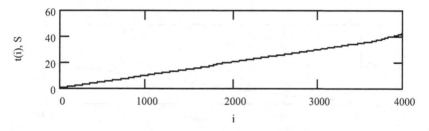

Fig. 7. Real series *t*(*i*) for DEC-pkt-1.IP

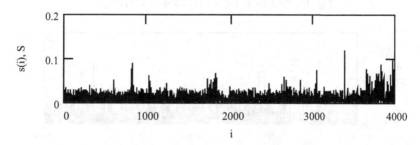

Fig. 8. Real series *t*(*i*) for DEC-pkt-1.IP

3.2.4 Demonstration with DEC-pkt-1.OTHER

The series *t*(*i*) of DEC-pkt-1.OTHER is indicated in Fig. 10 and *s*(*i*) in Fig. 11. The measured ACF of *s*(*i*) is in Fig. 12 (a). Minimizing *J* yields $H_0 = 0.931$ with $M^2(R) = 2.893 \times 10^{-3}$. Fig. 12 (b) indicates an ACF model of *s*(*i*) of DEC-pkt-1.OTHER using FGN.

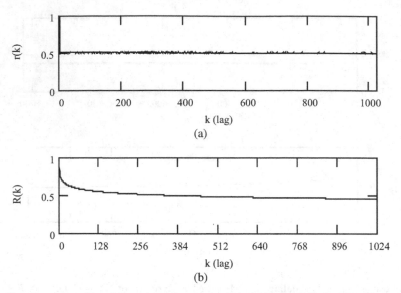

Fig. 9. *H* estimation and modeling. (a). Measured ACF of *s*(*i*) of DEC-pkt-1.IP. (b). *R*(*k*): estimate of *r*(*k*) using FGN model

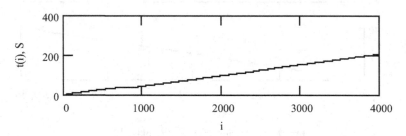

Fig. 10. Real series *t*(*i*) for DEC-pkt-1.OTHER

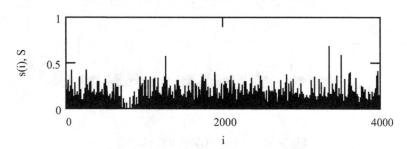

Fig. 11. Real series *s*(*i*) for DEC-pkt-1.OTHER

3.3 Summary

We summarize the experimental results for all 28 series in the columns 5-6 in Tables 1-4, where those in the fourth column are *H* estimates and the fifth $M^2(R)$s.

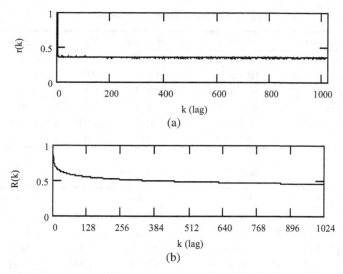

Fig. 12. *H* estimation and modeling. (a). Measured ACF of *s*(*i*) of DEC-pkt-1.OTHER. (b). *R*(*k*): estimate of *r*(*k*) using FGN model

Table 1. Six real series of TCP traffic

Series name	Record date	Series length	H_0	$M^2(R)$
DEC-pkt-1.TCP	08Mar95	3.3×10^6	0.923	2.264×10^{-3}
DEC-pkt-2.TCP	08Mar95	3.9×10^6	0.920	2.282×10^{-3}
DEC-pkt-3.TCP	08Mar95	4.3×10^6	0.925	2.270×10^{-3}
DEC-pkt-4.TCP	08Mar95	5.7×10^6	0.922	2.320×10^{-3}
Lbl-pkt-4.TCP	21Jan94	862946	0.930	2.208×10^{-3}
Lbl-pkt-5.TCP	28Jan94	710614	0.925	2.220×10^{-3}

Table 2.1. Four real series of UDP traffic in 2003

Series name	Record date	Series length	H_0	$M^2(R)$
NUS-1.UDP	24Mar03	1×10^6	0.920	3.654×10^{-3}
NUS-2.UDP	24Mar03	1×10^6	0.915	3.496×10^{-3}
NUS-3.UDP	26Mar03	1×10^6	0.915	3.415×10^{-3}
NUS-4.UDP	26Mar03	1×10^6	0.920	3.534×10^{-3}

Table 2.2. Six real series of UDP traffic in 1994 and 1995

Series name	Record date	Series length	H_0	$M^2(R)$
DEC-pkt-1.UDP	08Mar95	829759	0.935	7.729×10^{-3}
DEC-pkt-2.UDP	08Mar95	805802	0.935	2.881×10^{-3}
DEC-pkt-3.UDP	08Mar95	1035457	0.935	2.883×10^{-3}
DEC-pkt-4.UDP	08Mar95	1187454	0.935	2.886×10^{-3}
Lbl-pkt-4.UDP	21Jan94	33744	0.904	2.886×10^{-3}
Lbl-pkt-5.UDP	28Jan94	69358	0.875	2.182×10^{-3}

Table 3. Six real series of IP traffic

Series name	Record date	Series length	H_0	$M^2(R)$
DEC-pkt-1.IP	08Mar95	225237	0.955	2.416×10^{-3}
DEC-pkt-2.IP	08Mar95	335556	0.938	2.884×10^{-3}
DEC-pkt-3.IP	08Mar95	325833	0.900	2.517×10^{-3}
DEC-pkt-4.IP	08Mar95	511287	0.935	2.624×10^{-3}
Lbl-pkt-4.IP	21Jan94	303055	0.890	4.264×10^{-3}
Lbl-pkt-5.IP	28Jan94	195241	0.890	4.312×10^{-3}

Table 4. Six real series of OTHER traffic

Series name	Record date	Series length	H_0	$M^2(R)$
DEC-pkt-1.OTHER	08Mar95	74135	0.931	2.893×10^{-3}
DEC-pkt-2.OTHER	08Mar95	78021	0.931	3.040×10^{-3}
DEC-pkt-3.OTHER	08Mar95	105410	0.931	2.874×10^{-3}
DEC-pkt-4.OTHER	08Mar95	92361	0.931	2.662×10^{-3}
Lbl-pkt-4.OTHER	21Jan94	121140	0.878	1.105×10^{-3}
Lbl-pkt-5.OTHER	28Jan94	401231	0.890	2.012×10^{-3}

4 Conclusions

The results summarized in Tables 1-4 exhibit that $s(i)$ of traffic (TCP, UDP, IP, OTHER) is of LRD. This paper suggests that the accuracy of modeling ACF of $s(i)$ of real traffic by using FGN is consistent in the sense of $M^2(R)$ being in the order of magnitude of 10^{-3}. Therefore, FGN may yet serve as a simple LRD model for the purpose of detecting signs of DDOS flood attacks based on traffic series analysis.

Acknowledgements

The paper is partly sponsored by the Natural Science Foundation of China for the project number 60273062, Shanghai-AM Fund for the project number 0206, and SRF for ROCS, State Education Ministry, PRC.

References

1. M. Li, An approach for reliably identifying signs of DDOS flood attacks based on LRD traffic pattern recognition, 23 (6), *Computer & Security*, 2004.
2. B. B. Mandelbrot, *Gaussian Self-Affinity and Fractals*, Springer, 2001.
3. J. Beran, *Statistics for Long-Memory Processes*, Chapman & Hall, 1994.
4. W. Willinger, M. S. Taqqu, W. E. Leland, and D. V. Wilson, Self-similarity in high-speed packet traffic: analysis and modeling of Ethernet traffic measurements, *Statistical Science*, 10 (10), 1995, 67-85.
5. W. Willinger and V. Paxson, Where mathematics meets the Internet, *Notices of the American Mathematical Society*, 45 (8), 1998, 961-970.

6. A. Adas, Traffic models in broadband networks, *IEEE Communications Magazine*, 35 (7), 1997, 82-89.
7. M. Li, W. Jia, and W. Zhao, Correlation form of timestamp increment sequences of self-similar traffic on Ethernet, *Electronics Letters*, 36 (19), 2000, 1168-1169.
8. M. Li and C.-H. Chi, A correlation based computational model for synthesizing long-range dependent data, *J. Franklin Institute*, 340 (6-7), 2003, 503-514.
9. H. Michiel and K. Laevens, Teletraffic engineering in a broad-band era, *Proc. of the IEEE*, 85 (12), Dec. 1997, 2007-2033.
10. V. Paxson and S. Floyd, Wide area traffic: the failure of Poison modeling, *IEEE/ACM Trans. on Networking*, 3 (3), June 1995, 226-244.
11. B. Tsybakov and N. D. Georganas, Self-similar processes in communications networks, *IEEE Trans. on Information Theory*, 44 (5), Sep. 1998, 1713-1725.
12. M. Li, W. Zhao, D. Y. Long, and C.-H. Chi, Modeling autocorrelation functions of self-similar teletraffic in communication networks based on optimal approximation in Hilbert space, *Applied Mathematical Modelling*, 27 (3), 2003, 155-168.
13. V. Paxson, Fast, approximate synthesis of fractional Gaussian noise for generating self-similar network traffic, *Computer Comm. Review*, 27 (5), Oct. 1997, 5-18.
14. J. P. Aubin, *Applied Functional Analysis*, 2nd Edition, John Wiley & Sons, 2000.

Performance Analysis
of Virtual Time Optimistic Transaction Processing

Cong Liu[1], Wei Huang[2], and Zhiguo Zhang[1]

[1] Department of Computer Science, Information Science & Technology College,
Sun Yat-sen University, No. 135, Xingang Xi Road, Guangzhou, 510275, China
`gzcong@hotmail.com, lnszzg@zsu.edu.cn`
[2] Research center of software, Information Science & Technology College,
Sun Yat-sen University, No. 135, Xingang Xi Road, Guangzhou, 510275, China
`huangbodao@yahoo.com.cn`

Abstract. Aiming at solving the problems in the mobile computing environment such as low bandwidth, frequent disconnection and low battery capacity, we propose an improved optimistic transaction processing method – the virtual time optimistic transaction processing protocol. This protocol improves the performance of optimistic transaction processing by extending the concept of committability or, more specifically, by releasing the constraint of the total order relation between all transactions based on our analysis of the transaction processing approaches from a different angle. In this paper, we first explain and give the algorithm of the virtual time optimistic approach. Then we present and show the result of a simulation on the virtual time optimistic approach. Finally, we make comparison and performance analysis based on the simulation. The comparison and performance analysis show that the protocol has interesting performance gain in the metric of the number of abort.

1 Introduction

With the advent of third generation wireless infrastructure and the rapid growth of wireless communication technology such as Bluetooth and IEEE 802.11, mobile computing becomes possible. People with battery powered mobile devices can access various kinds of services at any time any place. However, existing wireless services are limited by the constraints of mobile environments such as narrow bandwidth, frequent disconnections, and limitations of the battery technology. Thus, approaches to efficiently process transactions have received considerable attention [1, 3, 4, 9, 10, 15, 17, 20].

The pessimistic approach successfully serializes all the transactions that have data dependency with each other [9]. However, it is the least efficient one in the mobile environment for the overhead of locking, waiting for locks and deadlock. The optimistic approach is therefore proposed and successfully address some of the above problems by the optimistically assuming that the data items accessed by a transaction would not likely to be updated before it commits [2, 5, 6, 7, 8, 11, 12, 13, 14, 16, 18, 19]. The virtual time optimistic approach, which is our contribution, allows that the imaginary time when a transaction performs all its operations and then commits to be a virtual time and consequently extends the concept of committability, and therefore offer an interesting performance gain.

The paper is structured as follows: Section 2 discusses from a different angle the way to handle concurrency control and show the advantage of the virtual time opti-

C.-H. Chi and K.-Y. Lam (Eds.): AWCC 2004, LNCS 3309, pp. 104–111, 2004.
© Springer-Verlag Berlin Heidelberg 2004

mistic transaction processing approach. Section 3 provides the algorithm and proof for the virtual time optimistic approach and some complementary algorithms. Section 4 provides an simulation to do experimental comparison and performance analysis to our approach and section 5 concludes the paper.

2 Motivating Analysis

If the relations between committed transactions could be represented by a directed acyclic graph in which each transaction is a vertex and each precedency relation is an edge, they are serializable because any directed acyclic graph has at least one topological order. But it seams that a transaction cannot easily be represented by a dot because transactions do not happen in instant but have durations of execution and might interleave with each other in time. However, if certain constraints are satisfied, it is possible to imagine transaction to be an instant action. If so, transaction processing could be implemented using a directed acyclic graph. Actually, some of the transaction processing approaches could be through of as trying to do that. For example, by making the data items visited by a transaction temporarily "invisible" to the other conflicting transactions, the Strict 2PL in [3] provides the illusion that a transaction only executes on the time it commits. As another example, the optimistic approach, such as the one proposed in [16], also provides the same illusion by facilitating the local cache and installing the data items modified by the transaction into the database only when it commits if the optimistic assumptions are satisfied. The later is obviously more desirable in the mobile computing environment because it eliminates the overhead on locking, waiting for lock holders and restarting when deadlock occurs. However, both of the above approaches have the dots corresponding to a real time, that's each dot is a spot in the time vector. Thus, the dependence relation between transactions is a total order relation. But it is possible to be a partial order because not all the transactions do have conflict operations. By not corresponding each dots of transactions to a real time, or using virtual time to represent the virtual execution instant of a transaction, we could extend the concept of committability and hence improve the overall efficiency of transaction processing.

The virtual time optimistic transaction processing approach is an extension to the traditional optimistic approach. In the traditional ones, such as in [16], timestamp is used to present the precedency relation between transactions, and the transaction commits earlier has a smaller timestamp than the transaction commits later. This constitutes a total order relation between all transactions, because any two transactions are comparable to each other in timestamp. This approach is effective, but it is not efficient however, because only those transactions have conflict operation is need to have a precedency relation between them in order to ensure valid executions and otherwise it is unnecessary. The virtual time optimistic transaction processing approach releases this constraint by presenting the partial order precedency relation between transactions in a directed acyclic graph.

3 The Virtual Time Optimistic Approach

For the purpose of simplifying the system model that our simulation is based on and for the consideration of the limitations of the mobile devices, we could make the assumptions that there is only one database server and the amount of data items that each transaction access is very small so that the limited amount of available local storage on the mobile devices can cache the data items they process and there are only short transactions. So, we use a very simple system model where there is only a single database and a number of mobile agents where transactions are running. Each data item records the number of the last transaction that updated it. Some information about the committed transaction is also maintained on the database, including the set of the data items red or written by the transaction and the directed acyclic graph used to hold the partial order precedency relation between transactions. We use the following denotation convention: $Ta <(>) Tb$ denotes an edge in the DAG which means The virtual execution time of transaction Ta is earlier(later) than that of transaction Tb.

Algorithm 1. This algorithm is executed in the respect of an executing transaction, and any transaction that is visible to the others is committed with their information sent to the database.

Each transaction T maintains a DAG in the local memory to hold part of the DAG in the database.

Add $T > Tewd$ in the local DAG if $Tewd$ updates a data item D (executes) before T read D.

Add $T < Tlwd$ in the local DAG if $Tlwd$ updates a data item D (executes) after T read D, that's $Tlwd > Tewd$.

Add $T > Trd$ in the local DAG if Trd read a data item D (executes) that T updates.

When T is prepared, try to add the local DAG into the global DAG in the database. If it constitutes a cycle in the global DAG, restart T. Otherwise, commit T.

When committing T, for each D updated by T, if $T < Twd$, where Twd is the last transaction updated D, ignore T's update on D. Otherwise install T's update on D in the database and add $T > Twd$ on the global DAG.

Theorem 1. The The virtual time optimistic approach generates serializable execution of transactions. Proof: Because the global DAG is acyclic, T and the rest of the transactions have a topological order on the precedency relation, therefore they are serializable.

The above algorithms should be combined with some other techniques in practical situations, including the technique to detect incommittable transactions before they prepare and the technique to delete something obsolete from the global DAG on the database periodically.

Algorithm 2. This algorithm uses *Invalidation Report* (*IR*) to earlier abort transactions that are impossible to commits successfully before they are prepared. When an *IR* containing the read-set and write-set of a committed transaction Tc is disseminated to T, the checking is perform in T's host agent as described in algorithm 1. If after the checking the local DAG is cyclic, restart T.

Algorithm 3. As time goes by, the DAG would occupy a great amount of disk space. This algorithm is used to delete the obsolete information. Any information represent a transaction has a life span (which is much larger than the general duration of a transaction), and the information is eliminate at the end of this time span. Using this algorithm, a change should be made to algorithm 1. That's, any prepared transaction trying to add an edge from a non-existed transaction in the global DAG should be restarted.

4   Simulation and Performance Evaluation

We use the aforementioned system model in our simulation in this section. This section consists of 3 parts. In the first part, we simulate the real execution of the transaction processing system to approximately testify the correctness of the virtual time optimistic transaction processing approach. In the second part, we compare the virtual time optimistic transaction processing approach with the optimistic transaction processing protocol in [16]. The third part is a performance analysis of the virtual time transaction processing approach.

The major experimental parameters are listed in the table below. In each of the performance analysis, one or two parameters vary to get the curve while the other values remain unchanged.

Table 1. Experimental parameters setting

Parameter Name	Value
Number of transaction	100
Transaction starting time	1~100
Number of data items	30
Number of mobile agents	20
Number of operation in a transaction	1~5
Percentage of write operation in a update transaction	30%
Offset of accessed data item in the subsequent operation.	1
Time to perform a read operation	3
Time to perform a mathematic operation	5~20
Time to perform invalidation checking	3
Time to transfer data	50
Time to restart a transaction	10

The method to testify the correctness of the virtual time optimistic transaction processing approach is described as follows: 1) randomly generate a number of transactions T and data items $D1$; 2) using the virtual time optimistic transaction processing approach to process all the above transactions T and get the DAG and the resulting values $D2$ of the data items; 3) restore the data item to value $D1$ and execute the transactions T again serially in a topological order of the above DAG and get the resulting values $D3$ of the data items; 4) compare to see if $D2$ and $D3$ are equal. If so, the virtual time transaction processing protocol is equal to a serial execution. We repeat this test for 100,000 times and found completely correct results, thus we testified approximately that the virtual time transaction processing approach generates serializable execution of transactions.

Next we will compare the virtual time optimistic transaction processing approach to the optimistic transaction processing protocol in [16]. The later is an optimistic transaction processing protocol designed to improve the overall throughput in the mobile environment. In the comparison, we use the number of abort as the metric to evaluate the performance of the different approaches. We assume all transaction would successful finished their execution if there is no other transactions. The transaction is aborted and restarted if it is found conflicting with any of the committed transaction (The DAG becomes cyclic if the transaction is committed).

Different from some of other optimistic transaction processing approaches, the virtual time optimistic transaction processing approach would not commit read only transaction autonomously, but if the last time when the transaction summits data access request to the database server can be pre-determined (for example, the transaction is summit with pre-declaration information provided by the compiler), the precommit request could be appended to that request and send to the server. However, the overhead to access the data through the wireless link is saved when the first operation to some data items is a write operation. More importantly, in other optimistic transaction processing approaches, a newly committed transaction must have a greater timestamp than those have committed, but in the virtual time optimistic transaction processing approach, a transaction is committable only if it keeps the DAG acyclic. So, the virtual time optimistic transaction processing approach releases the transaction from the stricter total order relation to a looser partial order relation in theory and enlarger the chance that a transaction is committable in practice. From figure 1, we can see that the virtual time optimistic transaction processing approach always has better performance than the optimistic transaction processing protocol in [16] as the number of transaction increasing from 20 to 100, and the performance remains tolerable even when the confliction on data items is relatively high (when the number of data items is 20 and the number of transactions is 100).

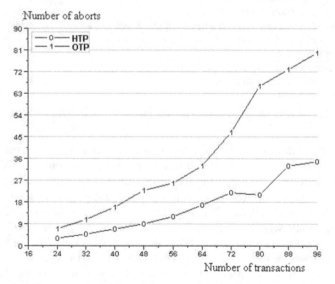

Fig. 1. The optimistic transaction processing protocol in [16] (OTP) vs. the virtual time optimistic transaction processing approach (HTP)

Finally, we will analyze the performance of the virtual time optimistic transaction processing approach using the experimental results showed in figure 2 and figure 3. As in the performance comparison, we also use as the metric of the number of aborts to evaluate the performance. There are 3 curves in each of these figures. In figure 2, these curves represents the system setting where the number of data items are different. The 3 curves in figure 2 represent 6, 12 and 18 data items respectively. In figure 3, each of these curves represents a kind of data access pattern which means the per-

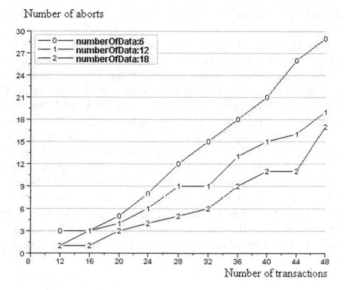

Fig. 2. Number of aborts vs. number of data items and number of transactions

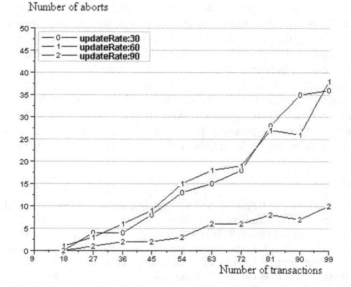

Fig. 3. Number of aborts vs. update rate and number of transactions

centage of write operations in an update transaction and is showed in these figures as update rate. The 3 curves in each of these figures represent the update rate of 30, 60 and 90 respectively.

In figure 2, we found as we expect that the number of aborts increase as the number of transactions increases and as the number of data items decreases. That is because the chance of confliction between transactions when accessing data items increases as the number of transaction increases and as the number of data items decreases.

In figure 3, readers maybe surprising to find that the number of aborts is not always increase as the update rate increases as would be seen in the results of the other transaction processing approaches where conflict occurs between read operation and write operation and between write operations. In the virtual time optimistic transaction processing protocol, precedency relation between the virtual execution times of the transactions does not correspond to that of the real execution times nor does it to that of the commit time. So, some of the conflicts between write operations would be avoided by adjusting the precedency relation between the virtual execution time. Observation shows that write conflicts rarely happen in this approach. In the virtual time optimistic transaction processing approach, the major conflict between transactions is read-write conflict. As is suggested in figure 3, the number of aborts does not increase as the update rate increases, but it reaches its maximum value when the update rate is between 30 and 60, which means that the overall performance become worst when the rate of read operation to write operations reaches a certain proportion but not in extremes.

5   Conclusion

In this paper, we have proposed an improved optimistic transaction processing method – the virtual time optimistic transaction processing protocol which improved the performance of optimistic transaction processing in the mobile computing environment by extending the concept of committability or by releasing the constraint of the total order relation between all transactions based on our analysis of transaction processing from a different angle. We have explained and given the algorithm of the virtual time optimistic approach, and presented and showed the result of a simulation on the virtual time optimistic approach. And finally, comparison and performance analysis based on the simulation was performed. Our next step is to make it richer and deeper on the theoretical side and also more practical than it is now.

References

1. S. Acharya, R. Alonso, M.J. Franklin and S.B. Zdonik: Broadcast Disks: Data Management for Asymmetric Communications Environments, in Proc. ACM SIGMOD International Conf. on Management of Data (1995) 199–210
2. D. Barbara: Certification Reports: Supporting Transactions in Wireless Systems, in Proc. IEEE International Conf. on Distributed Computing Systems (1997) 466–473
3. P.A. Bernstein, V. Hadzilacos, and N. Goodman: Concurrency Control and Recovery in Database Systems, Addison-Wesley, Massachusetts (1987)
4. B. Bhargava: Concurrency Control in Database Systems, IEEE Trans. on Knowledge and Data Engineering (1999) vol.11, no.1, 3–16
5. I. Chung, J. Ryu and C.-S. Hwang: Efficient Cache Management Protocol Based on Data Locality in Mobile DBMSs, in Current Issues in Databases and Information Systems, Proc. Conf. on Advances in Databases and Information Systems, Lecture Note in Computer Science, vol.1884, 51–64, Springer (2000)
6. J. Jing, A. Elmagarmid, A. Helal and A. Alonso: Bit Sequences: An Adaptive Cache Invalidation Method in Mobile Client/Server Environments, Mobile Networks and Applications (1997) vol.2, no.2, 115–127

7. A. Kahol, S. Khurana, S.K. Gupta and P.K. Srimani: An Ef.-cient Cache Maintenance Scheme for Mobile Environment, in Proc. International Conf. on Distributed Computing Systems (2000) 530–537
8. V.C.S. Lee and K.-W. Lam: Optimistic Concurrency Control in Broadcast Environments: Looking Forward at the Server and Backward at the Clients: in Proc. International Conf. on Mobile Data Access, Lecture Note in Computer Science, vol.1748, 97–106, Springer (1999)
9. S.K. Madria and B. Bhargava: A Transaction Model to Improve Data Availability in Mobile Computing, Distributed and Parallel Databases (2001) vol.10, no.2. 127–160
10. E. Pitoura and B. Bhargava: Data Consistency in Intermittently Connected Distributed Systems, IEEE Trans. On Knowledge and Data Engineering (1999) vol.11, no.6, 896–915
11. E. Pitoura and P.K. Chrysanthis: Exploiting Versions for Handling Updates in Broadcast Disks, in Proc. International Conf. on Very Large Databases (1999) 114–125
12. E. Pitoura and G. Samaras, Data Management for Mobile Computing, Kluwer, Boston, (1998)
13. M. Satyanarayanan: Mobile Information Access, IEEE Personal Communications (1996) vol.3, no.1, 26–33
14. J. Shanmugasundaram, A. Nithrakashyap and R. Sivasankaran: Efficient Concurrency Control for Broadcast Environments, in Proc. ACM SIGMOD International Conf. on Management of Data (1999) 85–96
15. K. Stathatos, N. Roussopoulos and J.S. Baras: Adaptive Data Broadcast in Hybrid Networks, in Proc. International Conf. on Very Large Data Bases (1997) 326–335
16. IlYoung Chung, Bharat Bhargava, Malika Mahoui, and Leszek Lilien: Autonomous Transaction Processing Using Data Dependency in Mobile Environments, in Proc. Workshop on Future Trends of Distributed Computing Systems (2003) 138-144
17. SangKeun Lee, SungSuk Kim: Performance Evaluation of a Predeclaration-based Transaction Processing in a Hybrid Data Delivery, in Proc. IEEE International Conference on Mobile Data Management (2004)
18. SangKeun Lee, Chong-Sun Hwang, Masaru Kitsuregawa: Using Predeclaration for Efficient Read-Only Transaction Processing in Wireless Data Broadcast, IEEE Transactions on knowledge and data engineering (2003) vol.15, no.6
19. Bettina Kemme, Fernando Pedone, Gustavo Alonso, Andre¡ä Schiper, Matthias Wiesmann: Using Optimistic Atomic Broadcast in Transaction Processing Systems, Transactions on knowledge and data engineering (2003) vol.15, no.4
20. Vasudevan Janarthanan, Purnendu Sinha: Modular Composition and Verification of Transaction Processing Protocols, Proc. the 23rd International Conference on Distributed Computing Systems, IEEE (2003)

A Measurement-Based TCP Congestion Control Scheme[*]

Lihua Song[1], Haitao Wang[2], and Ming Chen[1]

[1] Institute of Command Automation, PLA Univ. of Sci. & Tech., 210007 Nanjing, China
{Mingnihaha, Mingchen}@sina.com
[2] Institute of Communication Engineering, PLA Univ. of Sci. & Tech., 210007 Nanjing, China
Wht_slh_bao@sina.com

Abstract. TCP congestion control is being in a dilemma of if it should reckon on routers. Network measurement technology promises a different resolution. By analyzing several important schemes, a measurement-based TCP congestion control scheme basing on Fast is proposed. The basic idea is to introduce a macroscopical guidance layer upon end systems to determine for them appropriate parameter values according to the measured performance of network backbone. Simulation results indicate that this scheme can get a more steady *power* than Fast by having the bottleneck queue tend to a fixed length under no presumptions upon routers. Finally, the implemented measurement system is briefly introduced.

1 Introduction

Network measurement is some technology that collects traces of data or packets in networks to analyze the behavior of various applications. It is the foundation and preface for understanding and controlling Internet, which is becoming more and more complex. Today TCP congestion control is being in a dilemma of if it should reckon on routers. Routers are core of networks. Transferring some responsibility on routers, just as what AQM does, can make it easy to have user behavior accommodated to network states. But it also makes the routers heavy-burdened. On the other hand, it is difficult to take precise control actions by mostly depending on end systems. Because end systems might not be able to get complete network states due to their limiting location. Measurement provides a chance of different approach to this ambivalent problem.

2 Analyses and Comparison of Existing Schemes

The congestion control algorithm used by prevalent TCP Reno protocol was introduced by Jacobson in 1988 [1], which includes slow startup, additive-increase/multiplicative-decrease and fast-retransmit/fast-recovery mechanisms. These technologies play a crucial role in preventing Internet from collapse at its early age as well as in its evolutions. However, when it comes to Giga times and huge bandwidth-delay product becomes ordinary, Reno puts up low utilization and slow convergence. Many improvements have been proposed for it, among which Vegas [2] and Fast [3, 4] are two influential ones.

---

[*] Supported by the National Natural Foundation of China under Grant No. 90304016; the National High-Tech Research and Development Plan of China under Grant No. 2001AA112090.

C.-H. Chi and K.-Y. Lam (Eds.): AWCC 2004, LNCS 3309, pp. 112–119, 2004.
© Springer-Verlag Berlin Heidelberg 2004

2.1 Essentials of TCP Congestion Control

The objective of TCP congestion control is to find an optimal sending rate, or sending window, to get full utilization while keeping away from congestion. But the optimal window is a moving object because users joined and left. So an end system needs some indicator to show the difference between its actual window and the expected one as well as some algorithm by which adjusting its window approaching to the target. The indicator and algorithm, together with the response made to congestion (packet loss) form the essentials of TCP congestion control. There is an almost same response to loss in various schemes, which is window halving and timer doubling.

Effectiveness and fairness are two frequently examined criterions to know whether a congestion control scheme is good or not [5]. Effectiveness comprises metrics of throughput and delay. But in many circumstances increasing throughput also means increasing delay. So their ratio, referred to as *power*, is often used to evaluate a scheme's effectiveness.

2.2 Reno, Vegas vs Fast

Reno uses loss event as an indicator of difference between actual and expected windows. The corresponding adjustment algorithm is additive-increase/multiplicative-decrease. Loss is a binary signal. It only shows us that if the actual window is more than or less than the expected one. It can't make out how much the discrepancy is. Hence Reno has no way to regulate its window adjustment according to the distance from target. This weakness results in slow convergence and low utilization. In addition, using loss as indicator runs network at full utilization to detect loss. This will increase loss rate purposely and make the network oscillate. Fig. 1. (a) shows the window size, *power* and queue length curve of a Reno connection which is working on a path with *100Mbps* bottleneck bandwidth, where *power* is the ratio of the throughput and *RTT* this connection obtained. The sawtooth-like oscillation and periodical losses are obvious.

Vegas and Fast only regard loss as congestion signal. They convey from the optimal window objective to the optimal extra packets remaining in networks, and take the difference between actual and expected extra packets as an indicator. Moreover, *RTT* is involved in estimation of extra packets. *RTT* is a multi-bit signal. It carries queuing information along its path, with which appropriate actions could be taken before congestion practically occurred. In this sense Vegas and Fast are congestion avoidance mechanisms while Reno belongs to congestion control ones.

But Vegas doesn't take full advantage of obtained information because it copies a binary indicator. In fact, it does additive increase or additive decrease basing on actual extra packets being less than or more than the expected value, no matter how much the discrepancy is. Thus the problem of oscillating and slow convergence isn't resolved thoroughly. Fast goes farther. It adjusts its window in proportion to the distance between actual and expected extra packets. Adjustment is large when actual window far away from expected one and small when close. This enables the window converge quickly to and stabilize at an equilibrium point. Fig.1. (b), (c) gives the performance curves of Vegas and Fast under the same conditions as (a). A packet is dropped deliberately at *500s* for exhibitive purpose. In Fig.1., Fast is outstanding in stability, convergence rate and *power* aspects among three schemes. Besides, it is the fairest one, see [3].

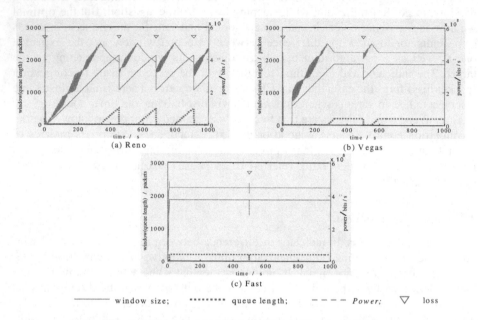

 ——— window size;   ········· queue length;   — — — — *Power*;   ▽ loss

Fig. 1. Performance Exhibition of Reno, Vegas and Fast

Unfortunately, even Fast has inevitable weakness. It concentrates on one single connection by keeping its extra packets around an expected value, and doesn't think of the aggregate impact on networks of competing connections. This leads to the difficulties in setting its parameter of expected extra packets, as revealed in Fig.4. (c), (d) (whose simulation settings can be found in Fig.3.). If it is set too large, as in (c), the delay will enlarge and the *power* will descend as new connections joining in. And if it too small, as in (d), the convergence rate will slow down. In fact, from the point of view of the whole network, to get high utilization together with low delay, the key lies in keeping bottleneck queue length constant, not in having every connection maintain constant packets in the buffer. This is also the idea of AQM. But AQM needs routers to play an important role, which is undesirable. Besides AQM, measurement technology also has the ability to fulfill this intention. For example, guiding end systems in setting appropriate parameter values by measuring network backbone's performance. The broadly deployed measurement infrastructure nowadays provides a good basis for this approach.

3   Measurement-Based Congestion Control Scheme

3.1   Elements

We suggest a measurement-based TCP congestion control scheme. Considering the maintenance of bottleneck queue length is aggregate-connection-oriented, its granularity should be coarser than the packet-level control. So the basic idea is to introduce a macroscopical guidance layer upon end systems to set for them appropriate parameter values according to the measured performance of network backbone. Fast mechanism is still used in end systems. But the value of expected extra packets is determined by the upper layer. The upper layer measures performance metrics such as bottleneck bandwidth and *RTT* of network backbone periodically. Measurement cycle may be tens of seconds or minutes. Upon measurement results it deduces the number of concurrent connections and computes an appropriate value of extra packets for end systems according to the expected queue length. Measurement is limited to backbone and its frequency is not high. So networks are unlikely to get much intrusion.

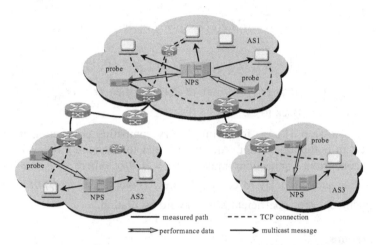

Fig. 2. An Implementation Frame of Measurement-Based TCP Congestion Control

Fig.2. shows a possible implementation frame of the suggested scheme. Measurement tools, such as bprobe and Ping, carry out measurement tasks at end points of backbone. The results are uploaded to NPSes (Network Performance Server). NPS is an intelligent component we introduced, which usually locates at the center of a network domain such as AS (Autonomous System). NPSes collectivity constitutes the core of the suggested frame. The task of a NPS is to collect and process measurement data from probes in its domain and communicate processing results to end systems. For example, in this frame, NPSes receive measurement samples uploaded by probes monitoring at backbone end points in their each domains. Basing on these samples and some historical data, they work out the value of expected extra packets for end systems in their domains and inform them by multicast. End systems join relevant multicast groups when connection established and leave when terminated, between which they reset their parameters periodically upon received multicast messages.

3.2 Algorithm

A simple iterative algorithm has been designed for NPS, as described below. α is the parameter of expected extra packets computed for end systems, with initial value α_0.

RTT_0 is the minimum RTT having been measured. It represents the propagation delay of the being measured path. q denotes the current queuing delay while $\widetilde{q}$, the ratio of expected queue length and bottleneck bandwidth, denotes the expected one.

Iterative algorithm for NPS:

1) $\alpha = \alpha_0$.
2) Wait. Until one of 3) or 4) happens.
3) Receive a request from end system. Return α Back to 2).
4) Receive RTT samples rtt_1, rtt_2, ... rtt_n from probe.

If $RTT_0 > \min_{1 \le i \le n}(rtt_i)$, then $RTT_0 = \min_{1 \le i \le n}(rtt_i)$.

$$\overline{rtt} = \frac{1}{n}\sum_{i=1}^{n} rtt_i, \quad q = \overline{rtt} - RTT_0 .$$

5) $$\alpha = (1-\mu)\cdot\alpha + \mu\cdot\alpha\cdot\widetilde{q}/q, \ \mu \in (0,1) . \tag{1}$$

If $\alpha \le \alpha_{\min}$, then $\alpha = \alpha_{\min}$; Else if $\alpha \ge \alpha_{\max}$, then $\alpha = \alpha_{\max}$.

6) Multicast new α. Back to 2).

Explanation to step 5) is as following. Every competing connection maintains α extra packets in bottleneck buffer. And the current total queuing delay is q. So the number of concurrent connections must be $m = q\,B/\alpha$, where B is the bottleneck bandwidth. For queuing delay to be $\widetilde{q}$, the new α would be $\widetilde{q}\cdot B/m = \alpha\cdot\widetilde{q}/q$. Averaging with old α on coefficient μ is to avoid oscillation.

3.3 Simulations

A set of simulation experiments is conducted in ns2 to explore the performance of the proposed scheme. Simulation settings are showed in Fig.3. Four TCP connections compete for bottleneck bandwidth of link R1R2. Connection i's end points are Si and Di, where $1 \le i \le 4$. Assume every connection has plentiful data to transit (FTP). Fast agent is used. Ping agents located at node P1 and P2 take charge of RTT measurement on path P1R1R2P2. NPS, which is located at node P1, functions upon the algorithm described above and informs end systems of results. Multicast is replaced with function invocation for simpleness purpose.

Fig.4. (a), (b) shows the simulation results, in which expected queue length is set to *600,000 bytes* while measurement cycle is set to *30 seconds* and *1 minute* severally. From left to right, the four charts are about window size, bottleneck queue length, *power* and fairness index respectively, where *power* is ratio of the aggregate throughput and forward delay of link R1R2. Fairness index's definition could be found in [5]. Simulation packet size is *1500 bytes*. Every time *10* samples are measured. $\mu = 0.8$, $\alpha_{\max} = 300$, $\alpha_{\min} = 10$. For comparison, Fig.4. (c), (d) gives the simulation results of Fast in same conditions (getting rid of Ping agents and NPS), whose expected extra packets is set to *200* and *50* respectively.

Fast converges quickly when the expected extra packets is set large (Fig.4. (c)). But along with new connections joining, bottleneck queue builds up and *power* decreases gradually. In even worse situations, the network will be congested and packets

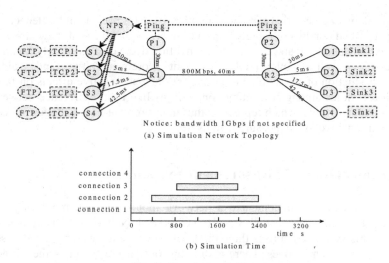

Notice: bandwidth 1Gbps if not specified

(a) Simulation Network Topology

(b) Simulation Time

Fig. 3. Simulation Settings

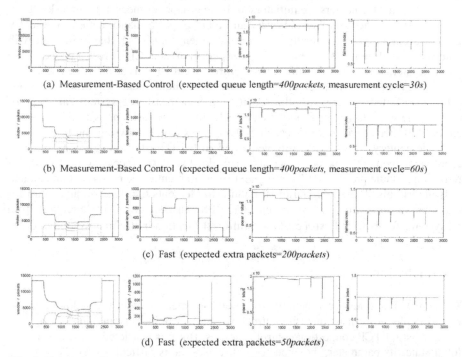

(a) Measurement-Based Control (expected queue length=*400packets*, measurement cycle=*30s*)

(b) Measurement-Based Control (expected queue length=*400packets*, measurement cycle=*60s*)

(c) Fast (expected extra packets=*200packets*)

(d) Fast (expected extra packets=*50packets*)

Fig. 4. Simulation Results of Measurement-Based TCP Congestion Control Scheme and Fast

will be dropped. When the expected extra packets is set small, as in (d), queue length is small too. However, convergence rate slows down meanwhile. And connections will not be able to respond to freed bandwidth rapidly. The two targets get balanced when measurement mechanism is introduced. In (a) and (b), end systems' parameters are accommodated to states of the bottleneck link. When there are a few concurrent connections, every connection remains a number of extra packets in bottleneck buffer to take over freed bandwidth rapidly and to converge quickly. With new connections joining, extra packets remained by every connection decrease accordingly, to have the queue length as well as *power* tend to constant. Moreover, fairness index indicates that the introduction of measurement mechanism has no negative effects on fairness. High fairness holds among competing connections like Fast. Difference between (a) and (b) is unperceivable, which represents that measurement-based congestion control scheme is insensitive to the measurement cycle.

4   Implementation of Measurement System

We have designed and implemented a network monitoring and measuring system following an architecture called UNMP (Universal Network Measurement Platform [6]). This system comprises three kinds of components, which are name server, monitoring centers and probes. There is one and only name server in the whole system. It is responsible for measurement resources assignment and working state maintenance. Monitoring centers are initiators and supervisors of measurement tasks. They also provide interfaces for users to query and analyze performance data. Probes carry out measurement tasks practically. Any measurement tool being able to interact with name server and monitoring centers by wrapped in an adapter will be a probe in the UNMP system. That is why this architecture is called universal. Three kinds of probes, NeTraMet, CoralReef and NP, have been implemented. Through various probes distributed in networks, the monitoring and measuring system can monitor passively network traffic of Ethernet and ATM in a flow fashion, as well as acquire actively E2E performance metrics such as delay, loss rate, bandwidth and jitter.

An elementary NPS has been implemented in the UNMP system environment. It accepts management of name server and provides two data processing modules. The prediction module predicts *RTT* for the next measurement cycle on median, mean and grads algorithms. The Alpha iteration module implements the iteration algorithm for parameter α in section 3.2. At present, the NPS can respond to single request from end systems for expected extra packets. Multicast function is still in development.

5   Conclusion

TCP congestion control can benefit from network measurement technology and the broadly deployed measurement infrastructure. Fast exhibits outstanding performance among existing TCP congestion control schemes. But it is restricted to the absence of global state. Its parameter, the expected extra packets, is difficult to set. Therefore a measurement-based TCP congestion control scheme is proposed, in which a macroscopical guidance layer is introduced to determine appropriate parameter values for end systems according to the measured performance of network backbone. Simulation results indicate that without presumption upon routers, this scheme could have the bottleneck queue length tend to constant. It obtains a more stable *power* than Fast while the fairness doesn't get affected.

References

1. Jacobson V., Karels M.: Congestion Avoidance and Control. Garcia L. Proc. of the ACM SIGCOMM '88 Conference. Stanford, California, USA (1988) 314-329
2. Brakmo L., Peterson L.: TCP Vegas: End to End Congestion Avoidance on a Global Internet. IEEE Journal on Selected Areas in Communication, Vol. 13. (1995) 1465-1480
3. Jin C., Wei D., Low S.: Fast TCP: Motivation, Architecture, Algorithms, Performance. Zhang Z. Proc. of IEEE InfoCom'2004. HongKong, China (2004)
4. Jin C., Wei D., Low S.: Fast TCP for High-Speed Long-Distance Networks. Internet Draft. http://netlab.caltech.edu/pub/papers/draft-jwl-tcp-fast-01.txt. (2003)
5. Peterson L., Davie B.: Computer Networks: A System Approach. Callifornia, USA: Morgan Kaufmann Publishers. (2000) 454-457
6. Chen M., Zhang R., Song L., (eds.): UNM: An Architecture of the Universal Policy-based Network Measurement System. Rouskas G. Proc. of IEEE LANMAN'2004. San Francisco, USA (2004)

BM-VF-SBD:
An Efficient Data Channel Scheduling Algorithm
to Support QoS for Optical Burst Switching Networks[*]

Xiaolong Yang[1,2], Demin Zhang[1], Qianbin Chen[1,2], Keping Long[1,2], and Lianghao Ji[1]

[1] Chongqing Univ. of Post & Telecommunication, Chongqing 400065, China
[2] Univ. of Electronic Science and Technology (UESTC), Chengdu 610054, China
yangxl@cqupt.edu.cn

Abstract. Currently optical burst switching (OBS) has been regarded as the most promising backbone networking technology for the next-generation Internet. In the OBS network, the data channel scheduling is one of key problems. Bandwidth efficiency and QoS support are its two concern focuses. However, the existing algorithms pay more attentions to bandwidth efficiency. In this paper, we develop an efficient data channel-scheduling algorithm, called *BM-VF-SBD*. It effectively integrates several mechanisms (i.e., *void filliing*, *burst migration* and *selective burst discard*) to reduce the bandwidth fragment and support QoS. Its basic idea is in that a new burst is scheduled by migrating some bursts to other channels if none of voids in any channels can accommodate it; otherwise repeating the above processes after selectively dropping some bursts. Meanwhile under an effective data structure, such as the balanced binary search tree, its computational complexity will be $o((2w+1)\log w)$ at most, and be close to LAUC-VF and ODBR. In the proposed algorithm, *burst migration* plays a key role in the improvement of bandwidth efficiency while *selective burst discard* has great effects on the two sides. The simulation results show that it performs much better than LAUC-VF and ODBR in burst loss probability (overall or individual) and bandwidth fragment ratio.

1 Introduction

Of all current high-speed transmission and switching technologies, optical burst switching (OBS) is the most promising ones since it combines the advantages of optical packet switching (OPS) and optical circuit switching (OCS) [1], [2]. In practice, OBS can not only be easily implemented because it effectively circumvents the buffering problem of OPS for which the technology is not yet mature, and also it can efficiently cope with the fluctuating traffic and the variable resource as OPS, which does not need to dedicate a wavelength for each end-to-end connection. Therefore, OBS is attracting more and more attentions of many researchers and institutes, and currently is regarded as a perfect backbone networking technology for the next-generation Internet.

---
[*] This work is supported by National Natural Science Foundation of China (No.90304004), National Hi-tech Research and Development Program of China (863 Program) (No.2003AA121540), the Ministry of Education (No. 204125), the Education Council of Chongqing (No. 050309), and the Science and Technology Council of Chongqing (No. 8061)

C.-H. Chi and K.-Y. Lam (Eds.): AWCC 2004, LNCS 3309, pp. 120–130, 2004.
© Springer-Verlag Berlin Heidelberg 2004

In OBS network, data is transmitted in the form of optical burst, which consists of burst header packets (BHP) and burst payload (BP). The wavelength channels are divided into two categories: data channel (DC) and control channel (CC) [4]. A data channel (DC) is used to carry BP while a control channel (CC) carries BHP and other control packets. Each BHP is transmitted ahead of its BP an offset time. During the offset time, each intermediate node in its transmission path must complete the electronic processing of BHP, and reserve enough resources for its arriving BP for a period of time equal to the burst length. If so, each BP can reach its destination along a transparent all-optical path. Otherwise, the burst will be dropped. A data channel-scheduling algorithm will play an important role in the resource reservation, which function is to assign an appropriate data channel for new arriving BP.

However, even though some burst assembly mechanisms (such as TQ-MAP in [5]) can effectively smooth the input traffic to alleviate its burstiness, the burst traffic injected into OBS network is still short-range dependent (SRD) and long-range dependent (LRD) [6]. Obviously, it causes that many bandwidth fragments so-called "void" are left in the data channel after the arriving BP being scheduled. Therefore, a data channel scheduling algorithm must concern bandwidth efficiency, i.e., how to reduce the void and improve the bandwidth utilization. Moreover, a scheduling algorithm must also concern QoS support in order to match the QoS requirements between high layer applications and OBS transmission.

In the early time, some scheduling algorithms such as horizon scheduling [3] or LAUC (latest available unused channel) [4] have been developed, which assign a burst to the latest available wavelength channel. But neither of them utilizes any voids between bursts. Therefore, the bandwidth efficiency will be lower. Naturally, some algorithms based on void filling (VF) mechanism, such as FF-VF (first fit with void filling) and LAUC-VF [4], are proposed. Evidently, the void filling mechanism can efficiently utilize voids to schedule bursts to data channels, and reduce the bandwidth fragment of data channel to some extent. Currently, VF has been widely integrated into many scheduling algorithms, e.g., *Iizuka* scheduling in [8], and Min-SV, Min-EV, and Best-fit in [10]. In the algorithms, voids in data channel can be utilized to the utmost extent through optimizing the starting or ending void interval, as illustrated in Fig. 1.

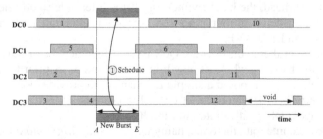

Fig. 1. The situation of time-domain algorithms (e.g., LAUC-VF) successfully scheduling

However, it is not enough for void filling to reduce bandwidth fragment in certain situations, where the new burst cannot be scheduled to any data channels even though some void intervals are wide enough to accommodate it, or FDL is used to buffer it, as illustrated in Fig. 2. In OBS network, contention resolution usually combines some methods of time domain (e.g., FDL buffering), wavelength domain (e.g., wavelength conversion) and space domain (e.g., deflect routing). Hence similarly, the effectiveness of algorithm must be limited if it only considers – VF or FDL buffering – this kind of time domain mechanisms. But if it also considers mechanisms from wavelength or space domain, its effectiveness can be greatly enhanced.

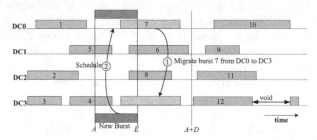

Fig. 2. The situation of time-domain algorithms failing while wavelength domain algorithms (e.g., ODBR and ABR [7]) being successful

Based on the above general idea, many scheduling algorithms have been developed, such as ODBR, ABR, DFMOC-VF, and SFMOC-VF [7],[9]. ODBR and ABR adopt a wavelength mechanism (i.e., burst rescheduling) to release the whole allocated bandwidth of a scheduled burst for new burst after migrating the scheduled burst to other available wavelength channel, as illustrated in Fig. 2. DFMOC-VF and SFMOC-VF use a space mechanism (i.e., burst segmentation) to distribute the bandwidth stress to several data channel by segmenting new burst into several parts (not concentrate to a single channel), and then each part is scheduled separately, as illustrated in Fig. 3(a).

However, the bandwidth efficiency of ODBR or ABR is worse than LAUC-VF because they migrate only the last scheduled burst of each data channel. It is interesting that their computational complexities are close to LAUC-VF. Hence, a wavelength mechanism derived from burst rescheduling, called as *burst migration*, will be used in our proposed algorithm. The mechanism can migrate any one scheduled bursts if one void can be filled by new burst after migration.

Due to high overhead, the burst segmenting [9] is infeasible to on-line scheduling, and cannot be considered by our proposed algorithm, although its bandwidth efficiency is better than LAUC-VF.

However, none of them concerns the QoS issue. When new burst fails to be scheduled, they simply discard a whole of new burst regardless of its priority. Hence in our proposed algorithm, we proposed a simple mechanism to provide QoS support, called as *selective burst discard*, which can effectively match the OBS transmission service with the high layer QoS, as illustrated in Fig. 3(b).

In this paper, we integrate three mechanisms, i.e., *void filling*, *burst migration*, and *selective burst discard*, and propose a data channel scheduling algorithm, called *BM-VF-SBD* (burst migration with void filling based on selective burst discard). Its two features are to support QoS and to reduce the bandwidth fragment. Meanwhile, it will be as efficient as ODBR and ABR. Its basic idea is in that a new burst is scheduled by migrating some scheduled bursts to other channels if none of voids in any channels can accommodate it, otherwise repeating the above processes after dropped selected

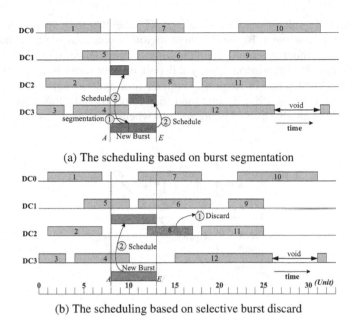

(a) The scheduling based on burst segmentation

(b) The scheduling based on selective burst discard

Fig. 3. The situation of time-domain and wavelength-domain algorithms failing while some algorithms (e.g., DFMOC-VF [9]) being successful

low priority bursts according to a selection rule. In order to quickly and accurately search a feasible scheduling solution, we present a simple method based on computational geometry [10]. Here, the void intervals are viewed as two-dimensional coordinates, where *x*-axis and *y*-axis respectively represent the starting and the ending time.

The rest of this paper is organized as follows. Section II depicts the proposed algorithms in detail. In the first part of Section II, the channel-scheduling problem is formulated and modeled by two-dimensional plane proposed by literature [10]. Then the solution to our proposed algorithm based on the model is given in the second part of Section II. Section III presents some numeric simulation results and analysis. And in the section IV, we conclude our work.

2 The Proposed Scheduling Algorithm

2.1 Problem Formulation and Modeling

Based on computational geometry, Ref.[10] maps the void intervals to points of a two-dimensional plane, where *x*-axis and *y*-axis represent the starting and the ending time of void respectively. In other words, the coordinate pair (s_i, e_i) denotes a void of *i*-th data channel. Similarly, the new burst can be denoted by a point (A, E), where A is the arrival time of new burst while E is its ending time, and they have the relation, i.e., $E=A+L_{burst}$, where L_{burst} is the length of new burst.

Due to the fact that the ending time of a void is not less than its starting time, the area below the line $s=e$, i.e., $s>e$, i.e., Region V, is an absolute non-schedulable area while other area above the line $s=e$, i.e., $s<e$, is schedulable area, which is subdivided into four regions by the arrival of new burst, i.e., by the two boundary lines $e=E$ and

s=A, as shown in Fig. 4. Here, Region I, II, and III mean that the voids are too short to accommodate the new burst. But in the three regions, some feasible scheduling solution can be found under a certain scheduling algorithm. Hence, they are conditional schedulable areas. But in Region I, only tail part of new burst is overlapping with other scheduled burst while in Region II both of font and tail part of new burst are overlapping with other scheduled burst, and in Region III only font part is overlapping. Region IV is an absolute schedulable area where new burst has no overlapping with other burst.

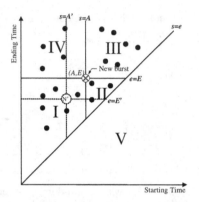

Fig. 4. The formulation and modeling of channel scheduling problem based on 2-D plane

Existing scheduling algorithms can be depicted by the shift operations of points in the 2-D plane. Some algorithms can directly use a certain region of the model plane. For example, LAUC-VF, Min-SV, and Best-fit can schedule the new burst if some points fall into Region IV. However, when there is no point in Region IV, how to efficiently adjust points from conditional schedulable areas to Region IV is what some scheduling algorithms concern. For example, ODBR and ABR [7] map the points in Region I to Region IV by moving some bursts overlapping with the font part of new burst to other data channels. But SFMOC-VF and DFMOC-VF adjust the point members of each region by several pairs of new boundary lines obtained from burst segmentation, each of which is corresponding to each burst segment respectively, e.g., the dash lines *e=E'* and *s=A'* as shown in Fig. 4.

A scheduled burst is called font-overlapping burst, short for *FB*, if it overlaps with the font of new burst. Likewise, it is called *TB* if it overlaps with the tail of new burst. Because the information of *FB* and *TB* will be useful to the scheduling decision, they should be also mapped to two-dimensional plane. The point distribution corresponding to Fig.2 and Fig.3 are shown by Fig.5 and Fig.6 respectively, where void is denoted by the solid point (marked as *V*) while the new burst by the cross point (marked as *NB*), the scheduled *TB* by the hollow point (marked as *TB*), and the scheduled *FB* by the shadow point (marked as *FB*). Obviously, the point distribution is close related with the arrival of new burst. Different arrival time and burst length establish different area partition, and result in different scheduling effect.

As the above examples do, we can design an efficient scheduling algorithm to support QoS based on a serial of operations in the two-dimensional plane, called *BM-VF-SBD*.

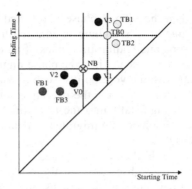

Fig. 5. The void points distribution corresponding to Fig.2

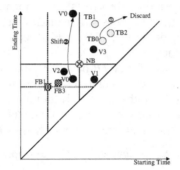

Fig. 6. The void point distribution corresponding to Fig.3

2.2   BM-VF-SBD: Burst Migration with Void Filling Based on Selective Burst Discard

Unlike existing channel scheduling algorithms, such as Best-fit, ODBR and SFMOC-VF, which give more emphasis to the computational complexity and burst loss probability, our algorithm also takes the QoS support into consideration. In our algorithm, the utilization efficiency of data channel is improved by two mechanisms, i.e., *void filling* and *burst migration* while QoS support is provided by *selective burst discard*.

BM-VF-SBD schedules the new burst as follows. When it cannot assign any voids at new burst arrival time, it attempts to be scheduled by migrating *TB* or *FB* to other channels. If migration fails, then it drops some low priority bursts, and repeats the above operations, i.e., searching available void and assigning void to new burst, migrating burst and re-assigning void to new burst.

According to the above processing idea, the algorithm works in three phases: *void filling*, *burst migrating* and *burst selective discarding*. The three phases are corresponding to different point distributions of the model plane.

The first phase is to search void point in region IV. If some void points have been searched, we choose a void point V_i by the channel selection criteria (such as Min-SV, Min-EV, and Best-fit [10]), and assign it to new burst.

If the first phase fails, then the second phase is invoked to complete two operations: searching and migrating. The searching is adjusted to the new region IV re-partitioned by the starting-time and ending-time lines of an overlapping burst FB_i or TB_i. If a void point V_j has been searched, then the phase migrates FB_i or TB_i to channel DC_j ($i \neq j$). After migration, some void points, such as V_i, will move to new positions. Then the phase will return to execute the operations of the first phase. For example, no point except V_3 in Fig.5 falls into the re-partitioned region IV of FB_0 or FB_2. Namely, burst 7 or 8 in Fig.2 can be migrated to data channel 3, and then new burst is scheduled to DC_0 or DC_2.

If the second phase fails, the third phase is invoked, including two operations, i.e., priority comparing and selectively discarding. If the priority of new burst is lower than that of FB_j or TB_j, then new burst is directly discarded, and the algorithm is terminated. Otherwise the low priority burst FB_j or TB_j should be discarded, then void point V_j will move to new positions. Hence, its region membership is changed. Likewise, the phase will return the first phase after discarding. For example, V_0 can be shifted upwards to V'_0 in region IV after TB_0 in Fig.6 is discarded, and so new burst can be scheduled to the channel DC_0.

However when more than one FB or TB have the same priority in the third phase, selective burst will be discarded according to a selection rule, by which the discard of the selected burst wastes the least channel bandwidth after other burst is migrated or scheduled to its channel. The bandwidth waste can be weighed by transmission efficiency η_{trans} and bandwidth fragment rate η_{frag}, which are simply defined by the ratio

$$\eta_{trans} = \frac{L_{burst}}{L_{burst} + L_{void}} \text{ and } \eta_{frag} = 1 - \eta_{trans} \text{ respectively. For example, assume that bursts 4, 7}$$

and 8 in Fig.3, which are corresponding to FB_3, TB_0 and TB_2 in Fig.6 respectively, have the same lower priority, burst 8 will be discarded because η_{trans} decreases the least and η_{frag} increases the least after new burst is scheduled to DC_2, as compared with that of other discard shown in Tab. 1.

Table 1. The transmission efficiency of overlapping burst discard (assumed $L_{new\_burst} = 5$ *unit*)

DC	L_{burst}	L_{void}	Before discard		After discard	
			η_{trans}	η_{viod}	η_{trans}	η_{viod}
DC0	TB_0: 7	V_0: 4	7/11	4/11	5/11	6/11
DC2	TB_2: 5	V_2: 5	5/10	5/10	5/10	5/10
DC3	FB_3: 6	V_3: 5	6/11	5/11	5/11	6/11

In the algorithm, it is crucial for its complexity to build an effective data structure. If not, *BM-VF-SBD* does not efficiently organize the information about the points in the model plane, and will have the worst-case complexity of $o(w^4)$ where w denotes the total number of data channel. But if its data structure is constructed as a balanced binary search tree presented in [10], then its main operation, i.e., searching, will run in $o(\log w)$, and not in $o(w)$. Hence its complexity will be $o((2w+1)\log w)$ at most. Therefore, *BM-VF-SBD* is close to ODBR and LAUC-VF in the computational complexity, but it is better than them in the bandwidth utilization and burst loss as shown in the following section.

3 Simulation Results

In this section, we present some simulations to evaluate the performance of the proposed algorithm *BM-VF-SBD*. Here, we compare it with ODBR and LAUC-VF from the aspects: the respective *BLP* (*burst loss probability*) for overall and different classes, and the bandwidth utilization. For simplicity, our focus here is the scheduling performance in the WDM link between an edge node and a core node in a simulation network, as shown in Fig. 7. Such simulation arrangement makes the scheduling at other link nontrivial. Assumed that the link is composed of 8 data channels and 1 control channel with transmission rate 1 Gbps, and there are three classes of bursts in the simulation network. Class-i burst have a priority higher than that of Class-j bursts if $i<j$ ($i, j=1, 2, 3$). Burst is assembled at edge node as a Poisson process with rate λ, which is measured as the number of burst arrived edge node per microsecond. Burst length is an exponential distribution with the same average L. In the total input load, each class burst contributes one third, respectively. For simplicity, all bursts have the same initial offset time τ, where L/τ is greater than the ratio of the number of data channel to that of control channel. Meanwhile, we focus on the burst loss due to the data channel congestion.

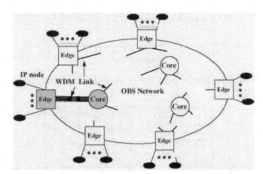

Fig. 7. Our focus simulated nodes and link in the simulated OBS network

We compare the performance of the proposed algorithm under several traffic load conditions. Fig. 8 shows the overall *BLP* without FDL. Obviously, the overall *BLP* increases as traffic load ρ increases, because it is more difficult to find available channel bandwidth for new arriving burst if traffic load is heavier. However, *BM-VF-SBD* performs better than LAUC-VF and ODBR in the overall *BLP*, as shown in Fig. 8. Moreover, this trend will become more obvious with the increasing traffic load. The reason is in that *BM-VF-SBD* has integrated migration and void filling, and so can give more successful scheduling chances to new arriving burst.

Next, we study the individual *BLP* under different traffic load conditions, and the same offset time for each class. In this simulation, we observe that the individual *BLPs* of *BM-VF-SBD* differ greatly from each other while the ones of LAUC-VF or ODBR are almost equal to each other. It shows that *BM-VF-SBD* can provide differentiated service while LAUC-VF and ODBR have not the capacity. For conciseness, Fig. 9 only plots *BLP* of Class-*1* in LAUC-VF and ODBR. As interestingly illustrated in Fig. 9, Class-*2 BLP* of *BM-VF-SBD* is much lower than Class-*1 BLP* of LAUC-VF and ODBR. Even for Class-*3 BLP* of *BM-VF-SBD*, it is also lower than Class-*1 BLP* of ODBR. This outstanding performance of *BM-VF-SBD* profits from the mechanism, i.e., selective burst discard. If some bursts are selectively discarded in the priority order during the data channel congestion, their allocated resources can be released, then reclaimed by scheduler, and re-allocated to the scheduled and new arriving bursts through migration and void filling. So, the new bursts can be scheduled with more chances after this resource adjustment. Therefore, from the above comparing results, we can easily conclude that *BM-VF-SBD* outperforms its two counterparts in overall and individual *BLP*.

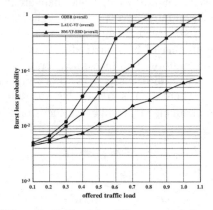

Fig. 8. The overall *BLP* vs. traffic load for different scheduling algorithm ($L/\tau = 10$)

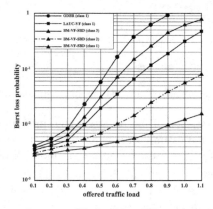

Fig. 9. The *BLP* for different class vs. traffic load for different scheduling algorithm ($L/\tau = 10$)

Lastly, we evaluate the effectiveness of bandwidth utilization, which is simply weighed by η_{trans} and η_{frag}. Here, it is enough to only use η_{frag} to evaluate the effectiveness because of the mathematical relation $\eta_{frag}=1-\eta_{trans}$. Based on the definition in previous section, it can be simply measured by the equation

$$\eta_{frag} = \frac{nT - \sum_m L_{burst_m}}{nT}$$

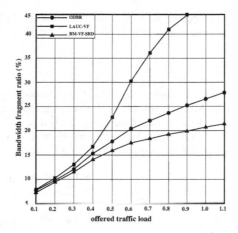

Fig. 10. η_{frag} vs. traffic load for different scheduling algorithm ($L/\tau = T/L = 10$)

where n denotes the number of data channel while m denotes the number of scheduled burst during an observation period T, which depicts the transmission capacity of data channel from the time axis if its channel bandwidth is constant. In the simulation, assumed that $L/\tau = T/L = 10$. Likewise, we compare the ratios among the three scheduling algorithms under different traffic load conditions. At low traffic load (less than *0.4*), they are nearly close. But when traffic load is more than *0.5*, their difference becomes more and more distinct. As a whole, it grows with the increasing traffic load in *BM-VF-SBD* much slower than in the counterpart algorithms, as shown in Fig. 11. In other words, *BM-VF-SBD* can schedule more bursts to data channel than other algorithms under the same conditions. Its lower fragment ratio results from the adjustment of void distribution by *selective burst discard* and *burst migration*. In the situations shown in Fig. 3(b) and Fig. 2 respectively, some void intervals would be wasted if neither of the two mechanisms were adopted, even though one of them can accommodate a whole burst. From the evident difference between the three curves $\eta_{frag} \sim \rho$ shown in Fig. 10, we can infer that *burst migration* is one of most important mechanisms to greatly improve the fragment ratio in the proposed algorithm *BM-VF-SBD*. Moreover, its combination with *selective burst discard* improves further the fragment ratio.

4 Conclusions

In this paper, we have proposed a new data channel-scheduling algorithm on the basis of the two existing algorithms LAUC-VF and ODBR, which is called as *BM-VF-SBD*. By the mechanisms *burst migration* and *selective burst discard*, the distribution of void intervals in data channels can be adjusted, and the voids are used to accommodate bursts as possible. The mechanisms are expected to obtain two aims. One is to reduce the bandwidth fragment, and improve the utilization of data channel; the other is to provide QoS support. As a whole, *BM-VF-SBD* works in three phases: void filling, burst migrating and burst selective discarding. If the information of voids and bursts is organized by an effective data structure, such as the balanced binary search tree, *BM-VF-SBD* will be as efficient as LAUC-VF and ODBR.

References

1. S. Verma, H. Chaskar, and R. Ravikanth: Optical burst switching:A viable solution for terabit IP backbone, *IEEE Network*, vol. 14, no. 6, (November/December 2000), pp. 48-53.
2. L. Xu, H. Perros, and G. Rouskas: Techniques for optical packet switching and optical burst switching, *IEEE Communications Magazine*, vol.39, no.1 (Jan. 2001), pp.136-142.
3. J.Turner: Terabit burst switching, *Journal High Speed Networks*, vol.8, no.1 (January 1999), pp.3-16.
4. Y. Xiong, M. Vandenhoute, and H. Cankaya: Control architecture in optical burst-switched WDM networks, *IEEE Journal on Selected Areas in Communications*, vol. 18, no. 10, (October 2000), pp. 1838-1851.
5. X. Yang, M. Dang, Y. Mao, and L. Li: A new burst assembly technique for supporting QoS in optical burst switching networks, to appear in *Chinese Optics Letters*, vol.1, no.5 (May, 2003)
6. X. Yu, Y. Chen and C. Qiao: A Study of Traffic Statistics of Assembled Burst Traffic in Optical Burst Switched Networks, *Proc. of SPIE Opticomm'02* (Boston, USA, July 2002), vol. 4874, pp. 149-159.
7. S. K. Tan, G. Mohan and K. C. Chua: Algorithms for burst rescheduling in WDM optical burst switching networks, *Computer Networks*, vol.41, no.1 (January 2003), pp. 41-55.
8. M. Iizuka, M. Sakuta, Y. Nishino and I. Sasase: A scheduling algorithm minimizing voids generated by arriving bursts in optical burst switched WDM network, *Proc. of IEEE Globecom'2002* (Taipei, Taiwan, November 2002), vol.3, pp. 2736- 2740.
9. V. M. Vokkarane, G. Thodime, V. Challagulla and J. P. Jue: Channel scheduling algorithms using burst segmentation and FDLs for optical burst-switched networks, *Proc. of IEEE ICC'2003* (Anchorage, USA. May 2003)
10. J. Xu, C. Qiao, J. Li and G. Xu: Efficient channel scheduling algorithms in optical burst switched networks, *Proc. of IEEE INFOCOM'2003* (San Francisco, USA, April 2003), vol. 4, pp. 2363-2367.

A Predictive Controller
for AQM Router Supporting TCP with ECN

Ruijun Zhu[1], Haitao Teng[1], and Weili Hu[2]

[1] College of Informatics and Electrical Engineering, Dalian Univ. of Technology,
116023 Dalian, China
zrj@rocketmail.com
[2] Department of Automation, Nanjing University of Science and Technology,
210094 Nanjing, China

Abstract. Although the P (Proportional) or PI(Proportional-Integral) controller for active queue management improves the stability. It is no systematic method in selecting the controller parameters to guarantee the transient performance, especially in rapidly changing environment. We use Generalized Predictive Control methods to propose a controller for AQM router supporting TCP with slightly modified ECN to enhance the robustness and transient performance of the P and PI controller. The simulation results demonstrated the effectiveness of the proposed controller.

1 Introduction

Two of the largest issues facing the Internet today are the problems of providing quality-of-service to applications that require some form of "guarantee" of bandwidth availability or end-to-end delay, and the problem of avoiding congestion between traditional best-effort flows. The Internet research community is promoting active queue management in routers as a means of addressing both of these issues. Active queue management (AQM) refers to managing the length of an outbound queue in a router by selectively dropping packets to bias the behavior and performance of connections transiting the router during times of congestion. Active queue management has become a key component of proposals for advanced congestion control and better-than-best-effort forwarding services.

Under Drop-Tail, packets are only dropped when the queue overflows. This leads to high queue sizes and high loss rates at congested links. As an improvement over Drop-tail[2], Random Early Detection (RED)[1] attempts to drop packets with a certain probability that is a function of the average queue size, when the incipient congestion is detected, that is, the average queue size exceeds a preset threshold. Amount of packet loss is roughly proportional to a connection's bandwidth utilization. There is no priori bias against bursty traffic. However, it is very difficult to tune RED parameters in order to perform well under different traffic conditions so that amount of variants[3–5] have been put forward.

C.-H. Chi and K.-Y. Lam (Eds.): AWCC 2004, LNCS 3309, pp. 131–136, 2004.
© Springer-Verlag Berlin Heidelberg 2004

Control systems are traditionally designed using either time domain techniques to meet time-domain specification such as closed-loop time constant, or frequency domain techniques to meet frequency domain specifications such as gain and phase margins and bandwidth. It is typical to measure the stability and robustness of the system in the frequency domain using gain and phase margins. Comparing with RED algorithm, although the P (Proportional) or PI (Proportional -Integral)[6] controller for AQM improves the stability, it is very difficulty in selecting the parameters for these controllers to guarantee the transient performance. The case is much worse especially in rapidly changing conditions, i.e., time-varying numbers of the users, the uncertain link utilization and heterogeneous delay etc. In this paper, we present a predictive controller of AQM for TCP with modified ECN[10] by generalized predictive control methods, which can improve the robustness and transient performance of the P,PI controller in changing environment. The simulation results show the effectiveness of the proposed method. The organization of the paper is as follows: Section two gives the linearization of the dynamical model of AQM router, The proposed controller design is presented in section three, and the realization of predictive controller with modified ECN is simply discussed in section four. Finally simulation is performed in section five.

2   Dynamical Model of AQM Router

Hollot et al.[6] have modeled the dynamic behavior of TCP/AQM as nonlinear differential equation, and obtain linearized model shown in Fig.1. Where $\Delta(s)$

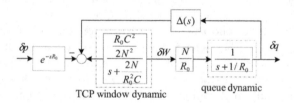

Fig. 1. Block-diagram of the linearized TCP connection

is high frequent component listed in (1) and $G(s, C, N, R_0)$ is open-loop transfer function from δp to δq given by (2).

$$\Delta(s) = \frac{2N^2 s}{R_0^2 C^3}(1 - e^{-sR_0})$$ (1)

$$G(s, C, N, R_0) = \frac{\frac{C^2}{2N}e^{-sR_0}}{(s + \frac{1}{R_0})(s + \frac{2N}{R_0^2 C})}$$ (2)

Where W is window size, q is queue length at a router, $R(t) = T_p + q(t)/C$ is round trip delay, C is link capacity, T_p is link delay, N is the number of TCP sessions, p is loss rate.

3   Predicitive Controller Design

The input-output model of (2) can be described by the following controlled auto-regressive and integrated moving average (CARIMA) model[7–9]

$$A(z^{-1})y(t) = B(z^{-1})u(t-1) + C(z^{-1})\omega(t)/\Delta \tag{3}$$

Where

$$
\begin{aligned}
A(z^{-1}) &= 1 + a_1 z^{-1} + a_2 z^{-2} \\
B(z^{-1}) &= b_0 + b_1 z^{-1} + ... + b_m z^{-m} \\
C(z^{-1}) &= c_0 + c_1 z^{-1} + ... + c_m z^{-m}
\end{aligned}
\tag{4}
$$

and $y(t)$ and $u(t)$ is the output and control input of the plant respectively, $\Delta = 1 - z^{-1}$ denotes the difference operator. Assume the known upper bounds of the round trip time is m.

Let the performance index take the following form

$$J = \varepsilon\{\sum_{j=1}^{N_u}[y(t+j) - y_r(t)]^2 + \sum_{j=1}^{N_u}Q_j(z^{-1})[\Delta u(t+j-1)]^2\} \tag{5}$$

Where N_u is the length of the prediction domain, and $Q_j(z^{-1})$ satisfying

$$
\begin{aligned}
Q_j(z^{-1}) &= q_0^1 + q_1^1 z^{-1} + ... + q_l^1 z^{-l} \\
Q_j(z^{-1}) &= q_0^j \quad (j = 2, 3, ..., N_u)
\end{aligned}
\tag{6}
$$

Introducing Diophantine equation as

$$
\begin{aligned}
1 &= E_j(z^{-1})A(z^{-1})\Delta + z^{-j}F_j(z^{-1}) \\
E_j(z^{-1})B(z^{-1}) &= G_j(z^{-1}) + z^{-j}H_j(z^{-1})
\end{aligned}
\tag{7}
$$

Where

$$
\begin{aligned}
E_j(z^{-1}) &= 1 + e_1(z^{-1}) + ... + e_{j-1}(z^{-j+1}) \\
F_j(z^{-1}) &= f_0^j + f_1^j(z^{-1}) + f_2^j(z^{-2}) \\
G_j(z^{-1}) &= g_0 + g_1(z^{-1}) + ... + g_{j-1}(z^{-j+1}) \\
H_j(z^{-1}) &= h_0^j + h_1^j(z^{-1}) + ... + f_{m-1}^j(z^{-m+1})
\end{aligned}
\tag{8}
$$

After simple manipulation, we can obtain

$$\mathbf{y} = \mathbf{G}u + \mathbf{F}y(t) + \mathbf{H}\Delta u(t-1) + \mathbf{E} \tag{9}$$

where

$$\mathbf{y} = [y(t+1), ..., y(t+N_u)]^T \tag{10}$$

$$\mathbf{u} = [\Delta u(t), ..., \Delta u(t+N_u-1)]^T \tag{11}$$

$$\mathbf{F} = [F_1, ..., F_{N_u}]^T \tag{12}$$

$$\mathbf{H} = [H_1, ..., H_{N_u}]^T \tag{13}$$

$$\mathbf{E} = [E_1\omega(t+1), ..., E_{N_u}\omega(t+1)]^T \tag{14}$$

$$
G = \begin{bmatrix} g_0 & & \mathbf{0} \\ g_1 & g_0 & \\ ... & & \\ g_{N_u-1} & g_{N_u-2} & \cdots & g_0 \end{bmatrix}
\tag{15}
$$

Define $\mathbf{y_r} = [y_r(t), ..., y_r(t)]^T$, and rewrite the performance index function as

$$J = \varepsilon[(\mathbf{y} - \mathbf{y_r})^T(\mathbf{y} - \mathbf{y_r}) + \mathbf{u}^T Q \mathbf{u}] \tag{16}$$

Where Q is $N_u \times N_u$ matrix given by

$$Q = diag\{Q_j(z^{-1})\} = Q_0 + Q_1(z^{-1}) + ... + Q_l(z^{-1}) \tag{17}$$

where $Q_0 = diag\{q_0^1, ..., q_0^{N_u}\}$ and $Q_i = diag\{q_i^1, ..., 0\}$ $i = 1, 2, ..., l$. Then the control law minimizing J is computed by

$$\mathbf{u} = (G^T G + Q_0)^{-1} G^T [\mathbf{y_r} - \mathbf{F}y(t) - \mathbf{H}\Delta u(t-1) + \sum_{i=1}^{l} Q_i z^{-i} \mathbf{u}] \tag{18}$$

Let $[p_1, ..., p_{N_u}]$ be the first row of $(G^T G + Q_0)^{-1} G^T$, then the GPC controller is represented by

$$u(t) = u(t-1) + \sum_{j=1}^{N_u} p_j y_r(t) - \sum_{j=1}^{N_u} p_j F_j(z^{-1})$$

$$- \sum_{j=1}^{N_u} p_j H_j(z^{-1})\Delta u(t-1) + p_1 \sum_{i=1}^{l} q_i^l \Delta u(t-i) \tag{19}$$

4 Implementation of the Predictive Controller

The Explicit Congestion Notification (ECN) option[10] allows active queue management mechanisms such as RED to probabilistically mark (rather than drop) packets when the average queue length lies between two thresholds, if both the sender and receiver are ECN-capable (determined at connection setup time). The algorithm uses 2 parameters α_{ECN} and β_{ECN} to indicate the required increase and decrease parameters. This algorithm exhibits the similar dynamic behavior of additive increase multiplex decrease (AIMD), but it is oscillated and too slow to response to the rapid change of the networks situation. We propose predictive controller by combining predictive controller with modified ECN to further improve the transient performance of the closed-loop systems and enhance the robustness to time-varying situation and nonlinear dynamics. The modified ECN is marked with 1 at the router when the queue length is greater than the upper bound q_{max}, and The modified ECN is marked with 0 at the router when the queue length is less great than the lower bound q_{min}, while the TCP sources will increase or decrease the window size to change their rates at the extreme cases, and ECN mark is closed when the queue length of the router enters into (q_{min}, q_{max}), and the predictive controller computes the drop probability and marks the packets at the routers by the probability calculated so that the TCP sources will regulate their sending rates to keep the queue tracking the desired value. From the above discussion, we can see that the modified ECN can make the queue keep in the interval (q_{min}, q_{max}), which reduces the queuing oscillation and enhances the transient performance of the controlled systems, while the predictive controller may drive the immediate queue tracking the queue setting point and further improve the steady-state response.

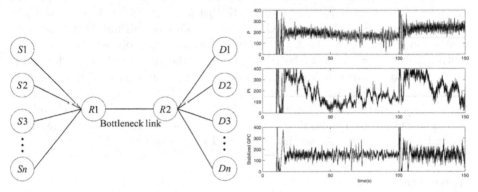

Fig. 2. Network topology   **Fig. 3.** Queue length in the router

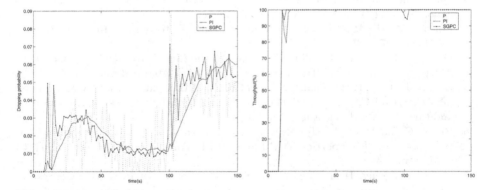

Fig. 4. Marking probability   **Fig. 5.** Link utilization

5   Simulation

In order to test the performance of the controller, we construct the simulation as follows. The network topology used here is shown in Fig. 2. It is a simple dumbbell topology based on a single bottleneck link of $15Mbps(3750packets/s)$ capacity. the sources are all persistent TCP flows supporting ECN with average packet size 500Bytes. the round trip time for the flows range uniformly between 40ms and 140ms. The buffer size on the routers is 400packets. At 10s, 180 users start to transfer data, and at 50s, 120 flows drop out, then the flows is increased to 360 at 100s. The queue setting value is 150 packets. There are also 360 users running http traffic in all the experiments. According to the parameters setting, we can choose the worst parameter setting as $C = 3750, N = 30, R = 0.14$, and prediction parameters as $N_u = 150, \lambda = 9 \times 10^{10}$. In fact, a great number of experiments suggested that the proposed controller works well when $N_u \geq 150, \lambda \geq 9 \times 10^{10}$, and the sample time is set to 0.00625s for all the experiments, For sake of simplicity, We choose $C = 3750 packets/s(15Mbps), N = 60, R_0 = 0.14s$, The drop probability of AQM router should be variant between 0 and 1. We also select $N_u = 200, \lambda = 9 \times 10^{15}$. We can easily obtain the predictive controller. In order to show the performance of the presented methods in this paper, we also perform the experiments on the same topology controlled by P[5], PI controller[6] with the following parameters: $P : K_p = 6.067 \times 10^{-4}, PI : K_p = 1.18189 \times 10^{-5}, K_i = 9.64 \times 10^{-6}$. The compared results are shown in Fig. 3~5, The simulation results illustrate that our methods have more stable queue dynamics and are superior to those of P and PI controller.

References

1. Floyd, S., Jacobson, V.: Random Early Detection Gateways for Congestion Avoidance. IEEE/ACM Trans. Networking **1** (1993) 397–413
2. Iannaccone, G., May, M., Diot, C.: Aggregate Traffic Performance with Active Queue Management and Drop From Tail. ACM SIGCOMM Computer Communication Rev **31(3)** (2001) 4–13
3. Lin, D., Morris, R.: Dynamics of Random Early Detection. in Proc. ACM SIGCOMM (1997) 127–137
4. Feng, W. C., Shin, K., Kandlur, D., Saha, D.: The Blue Active Queue Management Algorithms. IEEE/ACM Trans. Networking **10(4)** (2002) 513–528
5. Zhu, R. J., Teng, H. T., Chai, T. Y.: An Optimal PID Controller for AQM Supporting TCP with ECN. In: C.Y. Su(Eds): Advances in the Dynamics, Instrumentation and Control, World Scientific Press (2004)
6. Hollot, C. V., Misra, V., Towsley, D., Gong, W. B.: Analysis and Design of Controllers for AQM Supporting TCP Flows. IEEE Trans. Automatic Control **47(6)** (2002) 945–959
7. Zhu, R. J., Teng, H. T., Yin, F. L.: Simulation Study of Predictive Congestion Control Algorithm. in Proc. 7th Int. Conf. on Signal Processing. Beijing China (2004) 2616-2619
8. Zhu, R. J., Zhang, G. S., Teng, H. T.: Predictive Congestion Control in ATM Networks with Global Stability. in Proc. Int. Conf. on Complex Systems Control and Optimization. Shenyang China (2004)
9. Goodwin, G. Sin, K. S.: Adaptive Filtering, Prediction and Control. Englewood Cliffs, NJ: Prentice Hall (1984)
10. Floyd, S.: TCP and Explicit Congestion Notification. ACM Computer Communication Review **24(5)** (1994) 10–23
11. Ns Manumal. [Online]. Available: http://www.isi.edu/nsnam/ns/

Enhancing the Content of the Intrusion Alerts Using Logic Correlation

Liang-Min Wang[1,2], Jian-Feng Ma[1], and Yong-Zhao Zhan[2]

[1] The Key Laboratory of Computer Network and Information Security, Xidian University,
Ministry of Education, 710071 Xian, P.R. China
{liangminwang,ejfma}@hotmail.com
[2] The Computer School of Jiangsu Univ.
212013 Zhenjiang, P.R. China
{wanglm,yzzhan}@ujs.edu.cn

Abstract. To solve the problem of the alert flooding and information semantics in the existing IDS, the approach using the logic correction to enhance the content of the alerts is presented. The Chronicle based on time intervals is presented to describe the temporal time constrains among intrusion alerts, and the Chronicle patterns are designed to integrate the alerts of the sequence generated by an attacker into a high-level alert. Then the preparing relation between the high-level alerts is defined and the one-order logic algorithm is applied to correlate these high-level alerts with the preparing relationship. The attack scenario is constructed by drawing the attack graph. In the end an example is given to show the performance of this algorithm in decreasing the number and improving the information semantics of the intrusion alerts.

1 Introduction

Intrusion detection is regarded as the key technology to detect the malicious behaviors upon the network security. Unfortunately, the alerts generated by the existing IDSes(Intrusion Detection Systems) are low information semantic and big quantity which overwhelm the security operators [1,2]. Attacks are likely to generate multiple related alerts in a period of a time, but the current IDSes provide these reports individually, which needs the security experts to group and to recognize the true attacks. With the development of the net scales, the alerts generated from the large-scale distributed attacks make the alert flooding beyond the humans' working ability. The alert correlation technology, which combats this phenomenon by decreasing the number and enhancing the content of the alerts, attracts more and more researchers' attention.

This paper presents a two-layer correlation algorithm, which uses the Chronicle patterns to integrate some related alerts into a high-level alert, then constructs the attack scenarios by drawing the attack graph. Both these high-level alerts and the attack graph enhance the content of the IDS alerts and express the attack information in a gentle style.

2 Data Model of Alerts and the Chronicle Formalism

In recent years, some data models such as LAMBDA [9], M2D2 [15], and the IDMEF [16] of IETF, have been presented which made the interaction among the

C.-H. Chi and K.-Y. Lam (Eds.): AWCC 2004, LNCS 3309, pp. 137–142, 2004.
© Springer-Verlag Berlin Heidelberg 2004

information of alerts from heterogeneous sensors possible. In this section, we define a formal data model of alerts, then construct a Chronicle formalism based on this data model by introducing the time intervals to Dousson's chronicles [17].

2.1 Data Model of Alerts

Definition 1. The data model of alerts is a quadruplet, *Alert=(name, time, source, target)*, where *name* is the name of the alert; *time* is an ordered couple *time=(begin, end)*, *begin* and *end* denote the alert begin time and the end time of the attack respectively; *source* and *target* respectively denote the source and the target of the attack.

Our data model satisfies the definition of IDMEF of IETF, so it is suitable for large-scale deployment. In addition, the definition of this data model can be extended. For instance, the *source* in this definition can be regarded as a new quadruplet, *source=(node, user, process, service)*.

2.2 Chronicle Formalism Based on Time Intervals

Using reified temporal logic to track changes in the modeled system, Chronicle formalism provides a framework for modeling dynamic systems. The chronicle pattern is the temporal pattern that represents the possible evolution of the observed system. The instance of the chronicles is an event sequence completely fitted the chronicle pattern.

Morin [2] uses the classic Chronicle formalism [17] to correlate the alerts, in which time is considered as a linearly ordered discrete set of points and the attack an action finished on the time point. Otherwise, we assume that the attack be a continual behavior which generates plenty of same-name alerts on the most occasions. The definition of time interval is introduced in this paper. The denotation *(t1,t2)* is used to represent the time interval between *t1* and *t2*, and *(t, t)* the time point *t*. Then we can use a clause to represent the same-name alerts as *there is N alerts in the time interval between t1 and t2*, which decreases the alert number from *N* to *1*, then enhance the content of the alerts. Now we give the definition of the chronicle formalism based on the time interval as follows:

Definition 2. The chronicle model of alert correlation based on the time interval is a quintuple, *Chronicles=(Times, Constrains, P_Events, P_Assertions, Actions)*, where

- *Times* is a set of the pair *(begin, end)*, which denotes the time interval between two points *begin* and *end*;
- *Constrains* is a set of the constrains between the two time points in the pair of the element in the *Times* set, which determines the temporal time constrains among the alerts in a sequence and a deadline which is the invalidation mechanism of the chronicles;
- *P_Events* is the set of event patterns (alert sequence patterns) in a time interval of the *Times*, which represent relevant changes of the observed system for this chronicle:

$$P\_Events=\{\{Alert_k\ (name,\ time,\ source,\ target)\}\ ^m_{\ k\,=\,1}\}$$

- **P_Assertions** is a set of assertion patterns which represent the context of the occurrence of events;
- **Actions** is a set of external actions, which will be performed by the system when a chronicle is recognized.

Definition 3. The assertions of the Chronicles formalism in **P_Assertions** is the reifying predicates, such as *event, noevent* and *occur,* which are used to describe the time constrains among the elements in the set of **P_Events**. Their syntax and information semantics are list as follows:

- *event(P, (t₁, t₂))*: The alert P happened in the time interval [t_1, t_2];
- *noevent(P, (t_1, t_2))*: The chronicles would not be recognized if the alert P happened in the time interval [t_1, t_2];
- *occurs(n_1, n_2), P, (t_1, t_2))*: The alert P occurred exactly N times in the time interval [t_1, t_2], N belongs to (n_1, n_2) .

Where **P** belongs to **P_Events**, (t_1, t_2) belongs to **Times**.

Then we get the definition of the high-level alert.

Definition 4. The high-level alert has a form of the uniform alert data model, which is a quadruplet too, **Alert=(name, time, source, target)**, where name is the **name** of this high-level alert, **time, source** and **target** are defined in definition 1. This high-level alert is a sequence of many alerts which are from the same **source**, to the same **target** and recognized by a chronicle pattern.

3 *Preparing* Relationship and Attack Graph

In the proceeding section, the individual alerts are integrated to the high-level alert which represents a step of the attack. Now we will construct the attack scenarios by using of the one-order logic relationship between the high-level alerts.

3.1 *Preparing* Relationship Between Alerts

Obviously, most intrusions are not isolated, but related as different stages of attacks, with the early stages preparing for the later ones. The preparing relationship is formally defined in Definition 5.

Definition 5. Let two alerts (alert or high-level alert) *Alert1=(name1, time1, source1, target1)*, *Alert2=(name2, time2, source2, target2)*, satisfy two conditions as follows:

1) *source1= source2* or *target1= target2,* i.e. **Alert1** and **Alert2** are from the same source or attack the same target;
2) *time1_end< time2_begin,* i.e. the **Alert2** begins after the **Alert1** is ended;

Then the **Alert1** and the **Alert2** satisfy the preparing relationship, or the attack **name1** is preparing for the attack **name2**.

According to the definition of the high-level alert, Theorem1 is presented.

Theorem 1. *{Alert$_i$}$^n_{i=1}$* is the set of alerts(or high-level alerts), where all the **Alert$_i$,** have the same **source** or the **target**, i.e. all the **Alert$_i$** are from the same source or attack the same target. Then the preparing relationship between the two alerts in the set $\{Alert_j\}^n_{i=1}$ is a partial ordering relation.

Suppose three alert *Alert1*, *Alert2* and *Alert3* with the same source or the target, *Alert1* preparing for *Alert2*, and *Alert2* for *Alert3*, then we can determine *Alert1* for *Alert3* according to Therom1. Now we introduce the definition of the **directly preparing relationship** to simplify the preparing relationship:

Definition 7. All the alerts of the $\{Aler_j\}^n_{i=1}$ are from the same source or the same target, if the *Alert1* prepared for *Alert2*, and no other *Alert3* satisfies *time1_end<* *time2_begin* and *time2_end< time3_begin*, then *Alert1* is directly prepared for *Alert2*.

3.2 Correlation Algorithm Based on the Attack Graph

We present an algorithm to draw the attack graph to correlate the alerts and high-level alerts and provide the attack scenarios to the security operator.

From the Throem1, we can learn that the preparing relationship between the attacks which have the same source or target is partial ordering relation. Such that these attacks can be arrayed in an ordered line. And the drawing methods of the attack scenario are built as follows.

step1: use a knot X to denote the alert X;

step2: select an alert with the same source or target as the existing alert set {X} from the sequence in order. If the alert A prepare for X, then the knot A is set left of X; if the alert X is preparing for A, then put the knot A right of X;

step3: to the arbitrarily selected X from {X}, if X is directly prepared for the new knot A, then draw an oriented arc from X to A.

step4: go to step2, unless a deadline or the time constrain is achieved and no alerts satisfying are found in the input alert sequence.

This deadline is used to restrict the scale of the attack graph which is determined by the operator according to the existing security environment, such as the patience of the attack and the computing ability of the CPU.

4 Example of Semantic Improvement

Now we will show the performance of our approach. Suppose there is a series of attack behavior which use the tools traceroute to begin rout tracing, then the Superscan is used to scan the TCP port to avoid the ICMP blocked, and a vulnerable service of the ASP is found or the list privilege of IIS FTP anonymity service is gained to attempt a overflow attack, finally the program stream.c is used to exhaust the system. Fig.1 is report to the operator instead of plenty of general IDS alerts. For example, when we use the Snort to detect the ICMP Ping portscan. Three types of alerts a portscan_begin, one or many portscan_status and a portscan_end, will be generated. A high-level alert potscan integrate all these alerts. The high-level alerts and the attack graph decrease the alerts number and enhance the alert content. It is easy for us to catch the intentions of the intruder easily form Fig.1, thus it improves the information semantics of the alerts.

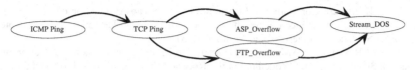

Fig. 1. The example of attack scenario

5 Related Works

There are some alert correlation techniques presented recently. The methods [7—9] based on the similarities aggregate the similar alerts from the heterogeneous sensors, which can decrease the number of the alerts but cannot improve the alert information semantics. The second-class methods [2, 3, 10] based on the known knowledge of the attack patterns correlate the alerts in a sequence generated in a certain stage. The third-class methods [1, 11–14] use one-order logic of the attacker to construct the attack scenarios, which make the intrusion intention easier to uncover.

Our work in this paper is closely related to the recent results in intrusion alert correlation based on the known attack pattern and the logic of the intruder. In particular, we introduce the idea of Ning [12,14] to integrate alerts into high-level alerts. We extend the chronicle modeling method [2] to get high-level alerts which is easier to understand than the hyper alerts presented by Ning [12]. The chronicle formalism presented in this paper is based on time interval and more appropriate to correlate intrusion alerts. Then we draw the attack graph to construct attack scenarios which enhance the content of the alert.

6 Conclusion and the Future Work

In this paper, we presented a series of methods to integrate high-level alerts and construct the attack scenario. Our approach integrates two correlation algorithm to enhance the content of the alert generated by IDS. When an attack is detected, an intuitionistic graph is provided to the security operator on line. In our future research, we plan to detect the attacks missed by IDSes and guess the future attacks which will possibly be launched by the attackers. And the methods based on the pattern recognition and heuristic learning are in our consideration.

Acknowledgement

The authors would like to acknowledge that this work is supported by the National Science Foundation under grant 90204012 and Hi-Tech Research and Development Program of China under grand 2002AA143021.

Reference

1. H. Debar, A. Wespi.: Aggregation and Correlation of Intrusion-Detection Alerts. In: Proceedings of the 4th International Symposium of Recent Advances in Intrusion Detection, Lecture Notes in Computer Science, Springer-Verlag :Berlin. (2001)

2. B. Morin, H. Debar.: Correlation of Intrusion Symptoms: an Application of Chronicles. In: 6th International Conference on Recent Advances in Intrusion Detection. Lecture Notes in Computer Science, Springer-Verlag :Berlin. (2003)
3. F. Cuppens, R. Ortalo.: LAMBDA: A Language to Model a Database for Detection of Attacks. In: 3th International Workshop on the Recent Advances in Intrusion Detection, Lecture Notes in Computer Science, Springer-Verlag :Berlin. (2000)
4. B. Moring, L. H. Debar, M. Ducassé, Me.: M2B2: A formal Data Model for IDS Alert Correlation. In: Proceedings of the 5th International Symposium on Recent Advances in Intrusion Detection,. Lecture Notes in Computer Science. Springer-Verlag:Berlin (2002)
5. D. Curry, H. Debar.: Intrusion Detection Message Exchange Format. http://www.ietf.org /internet-drafts/draft-ietf-idwg-idmef-xml-10.txt. August 2003.
6. C. Dousson.: Alarm Driven Supervision for Telecommunication Networks: Online Chronicle Recognition, Annales des Telecommunications, 51(1996): 501-508
7. S. Staniford, J. Hoagland, J. Mc Alerney.: Practical automated detection of stealthy portscans, Journal of Computer Security, 10(2002):105-136
8. A. Valdes, K. Skinner.: Probabilistic Alert Correlation. In: Proceedings of the 4th International Symposium of Recent Advances in Intrusion Detection, Lecture Notes in Computer Science, Springer-Verlag :Berlin. (2001)
9. F. Cuppens.: Managing alerts in multi-intrusion detection environments. In 17th Annual Computer Security Applications Conference. New-Oreans, (2001):74-94
10. O. Dain, R.Cuningham.: Fusing a heterogeneous alert stream into scenarios. In Proceeding of the ACM Workshop on Data Mining for Security Applications. (2001): 1-13
11. S. Templeton, K. Levit.: A requires/provides model for computer attacks. In Proceeding of New Security Paradigms Workshop, (2000): 31-39
12. P. Ning, Y. Cui, D. S. Reeves.: Constructing Attack Scenarios through Correlation of Intrusion Alerts, in Proceedings of the 9th ACM Conference on Computer & Communications Security, Washington,(2002):245-254
13. F. Cuppens, A. Miège.: Alert Correlation in a Cooperative Intrusion Detection Framework. In Proceedings of 2002 IEEE Symposium on Security and Privacy, (2002)
14. P. Ning, D. Xu, C. G. Healey, R. St. Amant.: Building Attack Scenarios through Integration of Complementary Alert Correlation Methods. In: the 11th Annual Network and Distributed System Security Symposium. (2004):97-111

Real-Time Emulation
of Intrusion Victim in HoneyFarm

Xing-Yun He[1], Kwok-Yan Lam[1], Siu-Leung Chung[2],
Chi-Hung Chi[3], and Jia-Guang Sun[1]

[1] School of Software, Tsinghua University, Beijing, P.R. China
{hexy02,lamky,sunjg}@tsinghua.edu.cn
[2] School of Business Administration, The Open University of Hong Kong
slchung@ouhk.edu.hk
[3] School of Computing, National University of Singapore
chich@comp.nus.edu.sg

Abstract. Security becomes increasingly important. However, existing security tools, almost all defensive, have many vulnerabilities which are hard to overcome because of the lack of information about hackers techniques or powerful tools to distinguish malicious traffic from the huge volume of production traffic. Although honeypots mainly aim at collecting information about hackers' behaviors, they are not very effective in that honeypot implementers tend to block or limit hackers' outbound connections to avoid harming non-honeypot systems, thus making honeypots easy to be fingerprinted. Additionally, the main concern is that if hackers were allowed outbound connections, they may attack the actual servers thus the honeypot could become a facilitator of the hacking crime. In this paper we present a new method to real-time emulate intrusion victims in a honeyfarm. When hackers request outbound connections, they are redirected to the intrusion victims which emulate the real targets. This method provides hackers with a less suspicious environment and reduces the risk of harming other systems.

Keywords: Honeypot, intrusion, interception proxy, reverse firewall

1 Introduction

Defensive security tools, such as firewall and intrusion detect system (IDS) may have difficulties in protecting organizations from intrusion. These tools only passively wait for hackers and a large volume of data is collected by firewall or IDS daily, they may fail to distinguish accurately malicious activities from production activities however. Also, we cannot observe the whole process of real attacks because hackers have attacked the target servers and run away before we see the logged data.

In order to overcome the vulnerabilities of existing security tools and secure our system, knowledge of the hackers' behavior is important. Hackers' behavior includes what hackers do before attacking, in the process of attacking and after attacking in cyberspace, such as actions which the hackers perform in computer

C.-H. Chi and K.-Y. Lam (Eds.): AWCC 2004, LNCS 3309, pp. 143–154, 2004.
© Springer-Verlag Berlin Heidelberg 2004

systems or networks, tools which the hackers use to attack others, targets which the hackers want to find, motivations that cause hackers to attack, tactics that the hackers take in order to compromise one system and avoid being prosecuted.

Understanding hackers' behavior requires the design of special tools. A honeypot, especially high-interaction honeypot, is an adaptive tool. Honeypots mainly aim at collecting information about hackers' behavior by providing an emulated environment that lures the hacker to attack. Honeypots and the data collected by honeypots can be of great value to improve overall security of the system.

However, nowadays nearly all honeypot designs limit hackers' outbound connections, many simple honeypots do not even allow any outbound connection. If hackers manage to penetrate into honeypots, they will soon realize that they can do nothing further. For example, hackers typically need to download tools from the Internet. If the honeypots do not allow them to do so, then they cannot proceed further and will run away. Thus, it is difficult to collect detailed information about their hacking techniques. Even if hackers are allowed outbound connections, these connections are also limited by the honeypot, and thus such honeypot is easy to be fingerprinted. If a honeypot is fingerprinted and hackers will bypass it, then the honeypot is of no security value. Furthermore, the risk of harming other systems exists if we permit hackers' connections to actual targets when the hackers compromise honeypots and want to connect to outside.

In this paper, we present a new honeypot design that can lure all levels of hackers (including high-skilled hackers) to do what they want, and at the same time largely reduce the risk of harming other systems. The proposed design is based on real-time emulation of intrusion victims in a honeyfarm. For example, if a hacker requests a connection to target website, we can provide an intrusion victim environment to simulate this website. The emulated intrusion victim looks like the actual target website, and thus hackers can hardly fingerprint it. To achieve this emulation, our method uses an interception proxy and a reverse firewall to control hackers' outbound connections and together with the website copying tools to real-time emulate intrusion victims. The rest of the paper is organized as follows. Section 2 introduces some basic concepts of honeypot. Our new design about real-time emulating intrusion victims in a honeyfarm is described in Section 3. Section 4 describes other issues pertinent to the real-time emulation of intrusion victims. Section 5 presents the analysis and evaluation of our method. We conclude the paper in Section 6 by summarizing the paper and pointing out further research directions.

2   Overview of Honeypot

Honeypot is an information system resource whose value lies in unauthorized or illicit use of that resource [1]. There is no production value in honeypots, so any connection to honeypots will be regarded as malicious activities. If the honeypots are never probed or attacked, then it has little or no value. Honeypots mainly aim at capturing hackers' behavior and can help other security tools by collecting data about hackers.

Honeypots have immense advantages. Firstly, usually data collected by honeypots is of higher value but in smaller amount. One of the challenges that the security community faces is to obtain valuable information from a large number of data. Organizations collect vast amounts of data every day, including firewall logs, system logs, and intrusion detection alerts. The sheer amount of data can be overwhelming, and makes it extremely difficult to derive any value from the data. Honeypots, on the other hand, collect very little data, but what they do collect is normally of high value. The honeypot concept of no expected production activity dramatically reduces the noise level. Instead of logging gigabytes of data every day, most honeypots collect several megabytes of data per day. Any logged data is most likely scan, probe, or attack information of high value. Secondly, honeypots can be used to study new attacks. New tools and methods come into being in hackers community at regular intervals. Traditional defensive security tools are almost based on rule, such as IDS (based on misuse detection) and firewall. They generally only detect or prevent known types of attack. Although IDS based on anomaly detection can find new attacks, it spends too much time building the normal behavior profile, and may have high false alarm rate. For honeypots, however, any traffic to and from them is suspicious and is all logged in detail. Thus we can analyze logs to find out the unknown attacks. Thirdly, honeypots can deal with hackers' encrypted packets. For example, honeypots can use kernel-based rootkits to capture the data in honeypot's kernel. There have been some tools available, such as SEBEK [3].

Honeypots do have disadvantages. For example, honeypots may give hosting organization more risks. All security technologies have certain level of risks. Firewalls have the risk of being penetrated, encryption has the risk of being broken, and IDS sensors have the risk of failing to detect attacks. Honeypots are no exception. Specifically, honeypots have the risk of being taken over and being used to harm other systems by the hackers.

According to the level of interaction afforded to attackers, honeypots can be classified as low-interaction honeypots and high-interaction honeypots [1].

Low-interaction honeypots [2] simply emulate a few services and are easy to install. A hacker is limited to interacting with these pre-designed services (such as fake ftp or http service). Thus low-interaction honeypots have a low level of risk, but only capture known behaviors and do not do well in interacting with or discovering unknown or unexpected behaviors or attacks. E.g. BOF, specter and honeyd [2] are low-interaction honeypots.

High-interaction honeypots [2], however, are systems with full-blown operating systems and applications. There is also a far greater level of risk compared with low-interaction honeypots. They can get a large amount of information about hackers and give insight into hackers and be proficient at discovering unknown attacks, thus being primarily used for research purposes. But high-interaction honeypots are extremely difficult and time-consuming to install and configure. Honeynets such as GEN I and GEN II [2] belong to the category of high-interaction honeypots.

From the view of users, honeypots can be categorized into production honeypots and research honeypots. When used for production purposes, honeypots can protect an organization or help mitigate risk. For example, helping organizations respond to an attack. Low-interaction honeypots are often used for production purposes. When used for research purposes, honeypots are used to collect information about hackers. High-interaction honeypots are often used for research purposes.

A honeyfarm [4, 5] (or a honeypot farm), a group of many honeypots deployed together in a single consolidated location. Hackers are redirected to the honeyfarm, regardless of what network they are on or probing. A redirector is needed to transport a hacker's probes to a honeypot within the honeyfarm, without the hacker ever knowing it. The hacker thinks he is interacting with a target victim, when in reality he has been transported to the honeyfarm. We can build and deploy a single centralized honeyfarm to simplify the deployment of distributed honeypots, instead of having individuals all over the world build, customize, deploy, and maintain a separate honeypot for every network (keeping in mind many organizations have thousands of networks). Updating and administering honeypots, especially high-interaction honeypots, also become far easier.

Honeypot is a new concept, and therefore research on emulating intrusion victims is also very little. At present, the systems emulated or run on honeypots do not aim at specific websites or hosts. That is, they emulate the common characters of many websites or hosts, but not a specific website or host.

If honeypots are compromised, hackers may connect to other networks from the honeypots. Until now, tactics of dealing with outbound connections has always been to block or limit them. Alternatively, honeypots may let hackers alone regardless of the risk. Both of these tactics are undesirable as they either cause honeypots to be figured out or put systems at excessive risk.

GEN I honeynets [2] take two available methods to limit outbound connections. One is to block whatever a hacker requests. The other is to set a limited number of outbound connections. When hackers' connections reach the limit, further connections will be blocked. It is obvious that experienced hackers can fingerprint them as "honeypot" by trying more connections. GEN II honeynets [2] modify or throttle outbound connections to non-honeynet systems. Likewise, if hackers compare their packets flowing through honeynet with the original, they will find the difference.

3   The New Design

The objective of the design is to give hackers a less suspicious environment just like the real targets for hackers to intrude, and reduce the risk of harming non-honeypot systems from compromised honeypots. An intrusion victim is the victim service or system or device intruded by hackers. Here, we real-time emulate the intrusion victim (the hackers' target) in a honeyfarm, and redirect hackers to the intrusion victim.

There are three requirements to be satisfied in order to real-time emulate intrusion victims in a honeyfarm.

– Real-time: the latency between hacker's request and the response to the hacker should be small enough to lure highly skilled hackers.

– Emulation: the emulated victim must be less suspicious, or at least looks like the real target server, thus is more difficult to fingerprint.
– Control of outbound connections of hackers: it includes transparent redirection and access restriction so as to prevent harming other systems.

After a hacker is attracted to a honeypot, the hacker may look for interesting data or further targets. In most situations, the hacker most likely requests outbound connections from the honeypot. This is what we want to deal with.

When a hacker requests the outbound connection from honeypot for the first time, we allow the connection in order to learn the hacker's target and then emulate the target victim. But access restriction must be imposed on the connection, such as limiting network bandwidth, thus making the hacker feel the target host or network is slow, rather than of suspecting the honeypot. The main advantage of access restriction is to slow down hacker's connection in order to earn time to emulate the intrusion victim and reduce the risk of harming non-honeypot systems. While we allow hacker's outbound connection, at the same time, we also set up the website copying tools to duplicate the target web pages at the local honeyfarm in order to real-time emulate the intrusion victim. When the hacker wants to connect to outside again, he is likely to request the next layer of the web page, so we can immediately redirect the hacker to the fake victim. Additionally, the access restriction does not totally block the hacker' request, but slow it down, so the hacker may not suspect the honeypot, and may think the target server is simply slow or overloaded. Even if he is impatient for the low traffic speed and runs away, he may still come back again in future. Thus we can also redirect the hacker to the emulated intrusion victim.

After intrusion victims are emulated in our honeyfarm, if hackers request outbound connections, we check whether their targets have been emulated in the honeyfarm. If the target servers have been emulated, we immediately redirect hackers to the corresponding intrusion victims. Otherwise, by following the same steps, the new intrusion victim is emulated.

Architecture of real-time emulating intrusion victims in a honeyfarm is illustrated in Figure 1. In this model, the interception proxy, including interceptor and cache, plays an important part in redirecting hackers' requests to the emulated intrusion victim in our honeyfarm and control the outbound requests together with a reverse firewall. A reverse firewall blocks known attacks and sets access restriction to outbound connections.

Honeyfarm is positioned close to the compromised honeypot. Thus if the target victim is accessed by the hacker, the response to the hacker's request will be very fast. In addition, today we have many existing website copying tools available, and the process of emulation is very simple, and the emulated intrusion victim can be made identical to the target server, at least on the surface, hence hackers may feel they are in actual targets. Finally, we select an interception proxy and a reverse firewall to help us control hackers' outbound connections.

An interception proxy [7–9], also known as transparent proxy, is located on the path of traffic. A proxy [6] is an application that sits somewhere between the client and the original server. It behaves like both a client and a server,

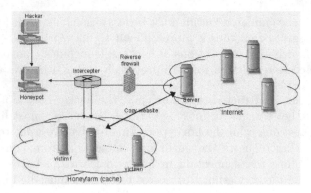

Fig. 1. Architecture of honeyfarm using interception proxy

that is, it acts like a server to clients, and like a client to servers. It receives and processes requests from clients, and then forwards those requests to original servers. A caching proxy [6, 8–11] is a proxy with a cache, and it is often referred to as "proxy cache" or simply "cache". It can alter the path of packets flowing through the network and split a web request into two separate TCP connections, one to the client and the other to the server. Transparent deployment [7] of a proxy relies on some network element (a switch or a router) to intercept all traffic from web clients to web servers and divert it to a cache instead of its actual destination. The cache pretends to be the original server. When the cache sends packets back to the client, the resource IP address is that of the original server. This tricks the client into thinking it's connected to the original server. For this reason, proxies deployed in this manner are called interception proxies. The network elements that intercept and divert packets to interception proxies are called intercepting elements or simply interceptors.

Since the proxy forwards requests to original servers, it hides the client's network address. The key feature of a caching proxy is its ability to store responses from the original servers for later use. When the requested data is found in the cache, we call it a hit. Similarly, referenced data that is not cached is known as a miss. The performance improvement that a cache provides is based mostly on the difference in service times for cache hits compared to misses. The percentage of all requests that are hits is called the hit ratio. Also, any system that utilizes caching must have mechanisms for maintaining cache consistency. This is the process by which cached copies are kept up-to-date with the originals. However, one of the most difficult aspects of operating a caching proxy is getting clients to use the service. For example, users might not configure their browsers correctly, and even they can disable the caching proxy.

Unlike a regular proxy, an interception proxy requires no browser configuration. They are transparent to the users, and most users are not even aware that their requests are going through or perhaps even served by an interception proxy. Even when the client has the IP address of the original servers it should contact, it might never reach it. Along the network path between the client and the server, there might be a network switch or router that directs all Web requests transparently to an interception proxy cache [8]. Thus administrators have greater control over the traffic sent to each cache, and users have no choice but to use interception proxy. However, the main limitation of interception proxies is that they can only work properly if all packets from a given client to a given destination flow through the same intercepting element [7]. In our method, you will see that this limitation becomes an advantage to deal with hackers.

In our design, we implement the honeyfarm as the cache in the interception proxy. When a hacker has compromised a honeypot and wants to connect to outside, all the hacker's requests must pass through an interceptor. The task of an interceptor is to divert hackers' requests to honeyfarm, regardless of HTTP or FTP requests. The interception proxy checks whether hacker's target website has been emulated in the honeyfarm (or cache). If not finding the fake target, that is, cache (honeyfarm) miss, the interception proxy will transmit the hacker's request to the original target server from the honeyfarm, as shown in Figure 2. Here only one honeypot is shown for simplifying, and in fact, all honeypots in an organization must connect to Internet through the interception proxy.

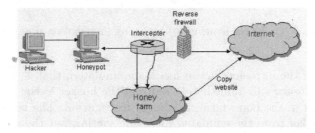

Fig. 2. Cache (or honeyfarm) miss using interception proxy

A reverse firewall is set in order to control the connection further. The reverse firewall filters the request and blocks a known attack, such as Denial of Service (DOS), Distributed Denial of Service (DDOS). Access restriction to the request will be set by the reverse firewall. For example, limiting the outbound bandwidth to a certain low value, like several bytes per second or tens of bytes per second, so that the hacker cannot do harm to other systems or fingerprint the honeypot.

The real response from the hacker's target is also redirected to the honeyfarm by the interceptor, and here the interception proxy can check the contents of response, and if necessary, it replaces the critical contents to avoid the risk of exposing information.

While we impose restrictions on the hackers' outbound connections, at the same time, we copy quickly the target web pages or services to the honeyfarm in order to build the intrusion victim. There are several tools available to copy website. For example, teleport pro is for windows systems; and wget is for both linux and windows. From Figure 2, we can see that the process of copying website does not pass through the interceptor and the reverse firewall. The purpose is to speed the copying of website to make the emulation of intrusion victim much faster, and make the reverse firewall deal with only hackers' requests thus simplifying the rules of the reverse firewall. However, the channel of copying websites must be protected. Additionally, we can set the number of layers of copying website for saving memory space because hackers generally only access very few web pages in a website. After the intrusion victim is completed, the interception proxy can redirect hackers to it. Unfortunately, if a hacker is impatient with the access restriction, he may run away. However, because the hacker may trust the honeypot and suspect the target is in question, he generally comes back to the honeypot again in the near future, and he has a high possibility to request the same target server.

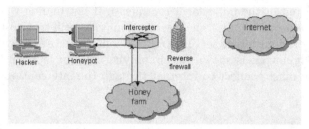

Fig. 3. Cache (or honeyfarm) hit using interception proxy

Otherwise, if the intrusion victim has been emulated, that is, cache (honeyfarm) hit, interceptor will immediately redirect the hacker to the corresponding intrusion victim in the honeyfarm, as shown in Figure 3. The response is sent back to the hacker from the emulated intrusion victim, but the source address of the response is that of the target server which the hacker requests. This tricks a hacker into thinking he is communicating with the actual target server.

4   Other Issues

In our method, there is a large difference between our interception proxy and a traditional interception proxy. It is the responses from original servers that the cache of a traditional proxy stores. However, the intrusion victim cannot be emulated, if we also wait for responses of the original server. So we must copy web pages much faster than hackers do, in order to real-time emulate the victim.

Besides, a traditional interception proxy generally only diverts HTTP requests. It assumes traffic from or to port 80 is HTTP. There is no need to distinguish HTTP from other traffic in our proxy. By the definition, all traffic from honeypot is malicious. What we need to do is only to divert all of them. Also, from the Figure 2, we can see that the interceptor will intercept all the responses from original servers to the honeyfarm (cache), and the responses will be sent to hackers from honeyfarm. Here, important content of responses can be identified replaced by useless data. It is important to reduce the risk of information exposure. In the process of real-time emulating intrusion victims, we can take the same measure to avoid exposing information. If the contents of files or pages are vital or critical (e.g. financial reports and credit card numbers), we can modify or replace them by fake data.

We take the means of prefetching [9] in order to enhance the hit ratio further. At the beginning of emulation, there is no intrusion victim in our honeyfarm. When hackers request outbound connections, the hit ratio of intrusion victims is very low. However, at first we can collect some information that is usually visited by hackers. According to the information, we can copy web pages and emulate some intrusion victims in our honeyfarm before hackers come to our honeypots.

The web pages in the original servers may have been changed. Therefore, the web pages in the honeyfarm may be old or stale. We need to maintain our intrusion victims consistency or keep them up-to-date with the original servers [9]. The honeyfarm can send requests to original servers to check whether the web pages have been changed since the last copy. However, because hackers are not authorized, we have no obligation to keep the victims fresh. Under the condition that hackers cannot fingerprint the honeypots, we may postpone the refreshing of web pages. Consequently, in order to simplify the process of emulating and reduce the latency responding to hackers' request, the refresh time span can be set longer, such as one day, even one week.

Additionally, hackers may request new targets continuously, and then there will be overloaded in the honeyfarm, that is to say, the cache is full. The new intrusion victim cannot be simulated any more. Here, we can take the replacement technique [11] just like those in operation system, such as First-In First-Out algorithm (FIFO) and Least Recently Used algorithm (LRU). When the space of honeyfarm is not big enough, some emulated intrusion victims will be deleted, and replaced by the new intrusion victim.

In our design, there may be legal and copyright issues. When we download other websites to emulate intrusion victims, we should also think about copyright issues. This is less of a technical issue nevertheless.

5   Analysis of the Real-Time Emulation of Intrusion Victim

In our design, an interception proxy is deployed close to the content consumer (consumer-oriented) [9]. When hackers request outbound connections through our honeypots, it can quickly redirect all requests to the honeyfarm, regardless of HTTP or FTP. Figure 4 [12] shows the comparison of latency between caching, redirection, direct and proxy (There are detailed definitions about caching latency, redirection latency, direct latency, and proxy latency in [12]). If the requested contents are in the cache, the latency is lowest. When caches miss, it has to get the contents from the original servers. The latency includes checking caches, transmitting the request to the original target, storing and returning response, so it has the highest latency.

Here, redirection means it has to transmit hackers' requests to the original servers. So the latency of an interception proxy should be the weighted average of cache and proxy latency. The hit ratio on caches can be up to furthest 50% [11] even if no other assistant techniques, such as profetching and replacement. The more the hit ratio, the less the latency. So, generally, with the reasonable hit ratio, we can make the latency lower. Moreover, by combining perfect caching and perfect prefetching between proxies and web servers, the proxy can at least reduce the client latency by 60% for high bandwidth clients [11]. In addition, the cache replacement technique can also enhance the hit ratio of interception proxy. So we conclude that the latency of interception proxy is also lower than that directing the requests to original servers.

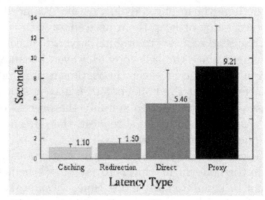

Fig. 4. The latency of caching, redirection, direct and proxy

If the hit ratio is higher than 46.2%, then the speed of real-time emulation is also quicker than that directing to original server. The following is the methods to enhance the hit ratio used in the paper.

- Prefetching: A central issue in prefetching is how to predict user future web-access patterns. There are many policies described in [10]. We take the prefetching technique between proxy and servers. Without prefetching, proxy caching with an unlimited cache size resulted in a 26% reduction in latency. However, with a basic prefetching strategy in place, that reduction in latency could be improved to 41%, and with a more sophisticated prefetching strategy, that number could be further improved to be 57% [13].
- Replacement: It is concerned with how to utilize the limited cache storage capacity to achieve the best caching performance. No known replacement policy can outperform others for all web access patterns [11], because the performance of replacement policies depends highly on the traffic characteristics of WWW accesses. Here, before knowing about hackers, we add only traditional replacement policies (E.g. LRU) to our interception proxy. Regardless of which policy, it may further improve the hit ratio of our honeyfarm.
- No delay of checking whether HTTP or FTP: All traffic from honeypots is malicious according to the definition of honeypot, so the interception proxy

can be configured to divert all of them. This is the difference between our interception proxy and traditional interception proxies, and such an implementation reduces the overload of interceptor. And the time wasted in distinguishing HTTP from others was saved.

- Website duplication: The special channel may improve the speed of responses to hackers' requests. If we used traditional interception proxy, there would be a challenge that we cannot real-time emulate intrusion victims, because the traditional interception proxy always wait for responses from original servers. The specific channel solves this problem. It not only fetches the currently requested web page, but also prefetches the next few layers of the web page. Since a hacker's request has a close correlation with the next request, thus the hit ratio also enhance, we may gain a much lower latency than the traditional interception proxy.

Compared with other honeypot designs, our method provides a more attractive environment for hackers. We duplicate target web pages to emulate hackers' destinations. It gives hackers a virtual websites or servers to intrude, in some sense, the environment is a replica, hackers can do everything just as in the actual one, but they cannot harm the targets. It not only real-time emulates a target server, but also real-time responds to a hacker's request.

6 Conclusion

At present, honeypots technology, especially high-interaction honeypots, has large risk of being taken over by hackers and being a facilitator to harm non-honeypot systems in that they allow hackers to connect to the actual target servers after they are compromised. In this paper, we have presented a new method to real-time emulate intrusion victims in a honeyfarm. When hackers compromise a honeypot and connect to Internet by the honeypot, they are secretly intercepted and redirected to a honeyfarm where intrusion victims were emulated.

This method provides hackers with an environment which is hard to be fingerprinted, and thus it may lure more advanced hackers compared with those honeypots which block or limit hackers' outbound connections or modify their packets. Also, when our honeyfarm responds to the hackers' requests, it replaces the source IP addresses of the response packets by the IP addresses of original servers, therefore further deceiving hackers to trust the emulated intrusion victims. More important, this design distracts the hackers' attention from the original servers, thus mitigating the risk of harming the real target websites or hosts. The information logged from the intrusion victims can be used to improve performance of existing security tools (E.g. IDS and firewall), and help us protect ourselves from attacks.

In future, we can design self-adapting emulation of intrusion victims. By analysis of the logs collected on existing intrusion victims, we may predict where hackers want to go next step. So we can emulate intrusion victims before the hackers request outbound connections, and the latency of real-time emulation will be reduced further. In addition, there may be many honeypots in the world, or even in one organization. Thus some distributed honeyfarms may be required and the caching structure of honeyfarm needs to be improved, because too many honeypots will bring much more traffic than before, and the honeyfarm may become a "bottleneck". Finally, caching dynamic web objects is another part that should be thought about to add to our method.

Acknowledgement

This research was partly funded by the National 863 Plan (Projects Numbers: 2003AA148020), P. R. China and the Internet Security project of PrivyLink International Limited (Singapore).

References

1. Lance Spitzner. Honeypots Definitions and Value of Honeypots, http://www.tracking-hackers.com/, May 29, 2003.
2. Lance Spitzner. Honeypots: Tracking Hackers. Addison-Wesley. Boston. 2002.
3. Lance Spitzner. Know Your Enemy: Sebek2 A kernel based data capture tool, http://www.honeynet.org/, Sept 13, 2003.
4. Lance Spitzner. Hitting the Sweet Spot, Jul 2003.
5. http://www.phrack.org/fakes/p62/p62-0x07.txt
6. Duane Wessels. Web Caching, the O'REILLY press, Nov 2002
7. M. Rabinovich and O. Spatscheck. Web Caching and Replication, Chapter 8. Reading, MA: Addison Wesley, 2002.
8. Brian D.Davison, Rurgers. A Web Caching Primer, IEEE Internet Computing, vol. 5, pp. 38-45, Jul/Aug 2001.
9. Greg Barish, Katia Obraczka. World Wide Web Caching: Trends and Techniques, IEEE Communications Magazine Internet Technology Series, May 2000.
10. Daniel Zeng, Fei-Yue Wang, and Mingkuan Liu. Efficient Web Content Delivery Using Proxy Caching Techniques, IEEE Transactions on Systems, Man, And Cybernetics—Part C: Applications and Reviews, VOL. 34, NO. 3, Aug 2004.
11. Jia Wang. A Survey of Web Caching Schemes for the Internet, ACM Computer Communication Review, vol. 29, no. 5, pp. 36-46, Oct 1999.
12. Radhika Malpani, Jacob Lorch, and David Berger. Making World Wide Web Caching Servers Cooperate, Proceedings of the 4th International WWW Conference, Boston, MA, Dec 1995
(http://www.w3.org/Conferences/WWW4/Papers/59/)
13. Thomas M. Kroeger, Darrell D. E. Long, Jeffrey C. Mogul. Exploring the Bounds of Web Latency Reduction from Caching and Prefetching, Proceedings of the Symposium on Internet Technologies and Systems, 1997.

On the Formal Characterization of Covert Channel

Shiguang Ju[1] and Xiaoyu Song[2]

[1] Jiangsu University, Zhenjiang, 212013, P.R. China
jushig@ujs.edu.cn
[2] Portland State University, Portland, OR 97207-0751, USA

Abstract. This paper presents a formal characterization model for covert channel. Some characteristic properties are proposed. The system characteristics are used to guide the development of covert channel identification and elimination algorithms. In addition, we audit a covert channel and evaluate the developed algorithms quantitatively with our formalism.

1 Introduction

In the late 1970s, the U.S. Department of Defense became aware that system acquisition personnel (users and buyers) were not in the best position to specify or evaluate trusted systems [1]. The department proposed a set of standards for computing systems with different levels of security requirements. The complete set of ratings from the lowest to the highest assurance is D, C1, C2, B1, B2, B3, and A1. They are classified in four categories: D, C1/C2/B1, B2, and B3/A1. Class D has no requirements. Class C1/C2/B1 requires security features that occur in many commercial operating systems. Class B2 requires a proof of security of the underlying model and a narrative specification of the trusted computing base. Class B3/A1 requires a precisely proven descriptive and formal design of the trusted computing base. Covert channel analysis and a formal security model become a basis for higher security systems.

Covert channel has been extensively addressed during the last twenty years. The proposed definitions can be classified into three categories:

(1) A communication channel is covert if it is neither designed nor intended to transfer information at all [2].
(2) A covert channel is a communication channel that allows a process to transfer information in a manner that violates the system's security policy.
(3) Given a nondiscretionary (e.g., mandatory) security policy model M and its interpretation I(M) in an operating system, any potential communication between two subjects $I(S_h)$ and $I(S_i)$ of I(M) is covert if and only if any communication between the corresponding subjects S_h and S_i of M is illegal in M[8].

The first definition has been used successfully in the security designs for new and retrofitted operating systems, as well as in general covert channel analysis. However, the definition does not reflect explicitly the fact that covert channels depend on the type of nondiscretionary access control (e.g., mandatory) policy being used and on the policy's implementation in a system design. The second definition underlines the consequence that a covert channel violates the security policy. However, it ignores the fact that the covert channel's operations are legal in system's security model. The third definition implies that, if a communication between the corresponding subjects S_h and S_i of M is illegal in M, the system does not allow to communicate, so the cov-

C.-H. Chi and K.-Y. Lam (Eds.): AWCC 2004, LNCS 3309, pp. 155–160, 2004.
© Springer-Verlag Berlin Heidelberg 2004

ert channel does not exist. The definition is not completely true. A covert channel violates the system's security policy, but the operations of a covert channel are legal in system's security model.

Although the above definitions have been used in various security designs for operating systems and covert channel analyses, however, none of them brings out explicitly the fact that covert channels depend on the type of nondiscretionary access control (e.g., mandatory) policy being used and on the policy's implementation within system designs. All the above definitions of a covert channel are important, to some extent, in understanding the relevance of covert channels for different access control policies[4,5,6]. However, they are insufficient to demonstrate generality and computability of a covert channel.

There is no general system with which we are able to use to develop, evaluate and compare various algorithms of identification, determination, handling and elimination of covert channels. There is no general description space about covert channels.

In this paper, we attempt to present a formal frame of covert channel. It will help develop, evaluate and compare various algorithms of identification, determination, handling and elimination of covert channels. The model addresses the relevance of covert channels under different access control policies.

2 Preliminaries

A security policy P is a set of security constraints. A security model M is a set of methods to implement a security policy. Let $S(M)$ be the maximum space covered by a model M. Let $S(P)$ be the security range determined by policy P. Clearly, $S(P) \subseteq S(M)$. A poetical security model M can realize security policy thoroughly.

The secure class is divided into n levels $< L_1, L_2, ..., L_n >$ with $L_i < L_i +1$. A secure level represents a distinct security constrained condition. A secure level is a set of security constraints. Let $\lambda(L_i)$ be the set of constraints of level L_i, $i = 1, 2, ..., n$. If Li $< L_i +1$, then $\lambda(L_i) \subseteq \lambda(L_i +1)$. The higher secure level is used, the more restrict secure constrained conditions are defined. Let S_1 and S_2 be two entities.

Definition 1. An information transmission transaction $T = <I, \beta, S_1 \rightarrow S_2, t>$ is an event such that information I is transferred from S_1 to S_2 via method β during time t.

Definition 2. A method β is a feasible transaction, denoted as $M |= \beta$, if it satisfies the constraints imposed by the security model M.

Definition 3. Let $T_1 = <I, \beta_1, S_1 \rightarrow S_2, t1>$ and $T_2 = <b1(I), \beta_2, S_2 \rightarrow S_3, t2>$ be two distinct transactions. The compositional operation is: $T_1 \oplus T_2 = < b1 \oplus b2(I), S_1 \rightarrow S_3, t3>$ where $t1 < t2 < t3$ and $b1 \oplus b2(I) = b2(b1(I))$.

Let $\Re$ be an non-empty set of all channels. Let Ψ be the set of all transmitted information elements. The compositional operation $\oplus$ is a function: $\Re \times \Psi \rightarrow \Psi$ where $\oplus = \{+, —, \%, \&\}$. Operation + is a transmission transaction with $\Delta(\epsilon) \subseteq \Delta(T_1 \oplus T_2) = \Delta(b1 \oplus b2(\epsilon))$. Operation - is a transmission transaction with $\Delta(\epsilon) \supseteq \Delta(T_1 \oplus T_2) = \Delta(b1 \oplus b2(\epsilon))$. Operation % is a transmission transaction with $\Delta(\epsilon) = \Delta(T_1 \oplus T_2) = \Delta(b1 \oplus b2(\epsilon))$.

3 A Formal Covert Channel Model

We model a covert channel as follows. Given three entities Ss, O and Sr, a covert channel is composed of three transactions T_1, T_2 and T_3. Transactions T_1 and T_2, which are legal in F(M), virtually form a communication channel ξ, modeled by an implicit transaction T_3, which is illegal in F(P). The covert channel ξ transmits hidden information I_3.

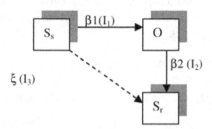

Fig. 1. Covert channel model

Due to the occurrences of T_1 and T_2, Sr gains information I_3. This realizes the virtual communication between Ss and Sr. A logical and hidden information implication T_3 by ξ is legal in system's security model M, but illegal in the security policy P. In fact, Sr can gain the information I3 by observing the change of O's values made by $\beta2$. Obviously, ξ infringes the secure constrained conditions.

Definition 4. A covert channel is composed of a series of transactions $T_1 = <I_1, \beta_1, S_s \rightarrow O, t1>$ where $M \models \beta1$ and $T_2 = <I_2, \beta_2, O \rightarrow Sr, t2>$ where $M \models \beta2$. If $\xi = \beta1 \oplus \beta2$ and $P \not\models \xi$, a covert channel occurs.

Lemma 1. There exist a sender and a receiver that access the same Shared resource in a covert channel. Formally, we have: $T_1 = <I_1, \beta_1, S_s \rightarrow O, t1>$ and $T_2 = <I_2, \beta_2, O \rightarrow Sr, t2>$.

Proof. If a covert channel exists in a secure system, an information transaction must happen so that Sr of a lower security level receives information from Ss of a higher security level. If the direct information conduction happens from Ss and Sr, that is, T3 = <I3, ξ, Ss $\rightarrow$ Sr, t2> occurs, it could not pass the check of security model M. So T3 cannot happen in a security system, and this hypothesis does not hold.

Assume that there are at least two information transactions between Ss and Sr : $T_1 = <I_1, \beta_1, S_i \rightarrow O, t1>$ and $T_2 = <I_2, \beta_2, O \rightarrow Sr, t2>$. If both T_1 and T_2 meet the security model M, then the medium of the two information transactions O must exist. The medium O Should be a Shared resource where two or more processes can access.

Lemma 2. The sender Ss of a higher security level can use method β to modify Shared attribute of object O. Formally, we have: $T_1 = <I_1, \beta_1, Ss \rightarrow O, t1>$ and $L(Ss) > L(O)$.

Proof. Suppose that sender Ss of a higher security level does not have a method β to modify the O's value in a covert channel, then the first information conduction $T_1 =$ $<I_1, \beta_1, Ss \to O, t1>$ cannot be formed. Since Ss cannot modify O's value, Sr does not observe the change of O, thus Ss does not send the information to Sr. As a result, $T_2 = <I_2, \beta_2, O \to Sr, t2>$ does not occur. Therefore, the system does not form a covert channel. So the hypothesis cannot hold.

Lemma 3. There exists a method β such that a receiver Sr of a lower security level can detect the change of object O's Shared attributes. Formally, we have: $T_2 = <I_2, \beta_2, O \to Sr, t2>$ and $L(O) > L(Sr)$.

Lemma 4. The communication between sender Ss and receiver Sr is ordered: t2>t1, where t1 and t2 are the occurrence times of T_1 and T_2, respectively.

From the above properties, we can summarize the main result in the following theorem.

Theorem 1. A covert channel is characterized by a 8-tuple $\Pi = <P, M, Ss, O, Sr, L, \beta1, \beta2>$ such that

a) $L(Ss) > L(Sr)$
b) An information delivery : $T_1 = <I_1, \beta_1, Ss \to O, t1> \wedge M \models \beta_1$.
c) An observation transaction: $T_2 = <I_2, \beta_2, O \to Sr, t2> \wedge M \models \beta_2$.
d) An implicit transaction: $T_3 = <I_3, \xi, Ss \to Sr, t2> \wedge M \models \xi \wedge P \not\models \xi$.
e) $I_3 \subseteq I_2 \subseteq I_1$
f) t2 > t1

4   An Example: Disk Scheduling Policy

We use the following example of disk-arm covert channels[7] to explain our model. Consider a multiprogramming environment where the operating system maintains a queue of requests for disk I/O system. For a single disk, there are I/O requests (reads and writes) from various processes in the queue. Suppose there are two processes: H and L. The security level of process L is lower than that of H. If sector access requests involve selection of tracks at random, then the disk I/O system does not perform effectively.

To reduce the average seeking time, consider a simple disk scheduling algorithm (SCAN). With SCAN, the arm is required to move in one direction only, satisfying all outstanding requests, until it reaches the last track or until there are no more requests in the direction.

For instance, process L sends a request Ll located in track 55. After sending the request, the process L puts off CPU possessed immediately and goes to waiting services. Then process H occupies CPU and sends a request H1 (information 0) located in track 53, or H2 (information 1) located in track 57. After sending the request, the process H puts off CPU possessed immediately and goes to waiting services. After the process L's request which located in track 55 is serviced, L sends other two requests immediately, one is that located in track 52, and another is that located in track 58.

According to the SCAN algorithm, if the CPU service order is path 1: Ll $(55) \rightarrow H1(53) \rightarrow L2(52) \rightarrow L3(58)$, where CPU serves L2 before L3. We say process H's request is H1. If the CPU serves order is path 2: Ll $(55) \rightarrow H2 (57) \rightarrow L3 (58) \rightarrow$ L2 (52), where CPU serves L3 before L2. We say process H's request is H2. Process L that has lower security level only accords the service order of its requests L2 and L3, it can get the information of what tracks requested from the process H that has higher security level. It is the higher security level process which leaks a bit information to the lower security level process.

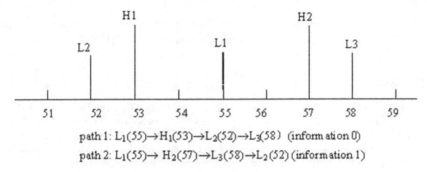

path 1: $L_1(55) \rightarrow H_1(53) \rightarrow L_2(52) \rightarrow L_3(58)$ (information 0)

path 2: $L_1(55) \rightarrow H_2(57) \rightarrow L_3(58) \rightarrow L_2(52)$ (information 1)

Fig. 2. Disk arm moving paths

In the example, the disk arm D is Shared by processes H and L, so D is a Shared object. H and L are two subjects. We construct the covert channel model as follows:

$T_1 = <I_1, \beta_1, H \rightarrow D, t1> \wedge M \models \beta_1.$

where I_1 is process H located in track 53, or location in track 57 ;

β_1 is path1 or path2 ;

t1 is the occurence time of CPU servicing process L;

$T_2 = < I_2, \beta_2, D \rightarrow L, t2> \wedge M \models \beta_2.$

where I_2 is process L located in track 52,or located in track 58;

β_2 is SCAN algorithm ;

t2 is the occurence time of CPU servicing process L;

$T = <I(0,1), \xi, H \rightarrow L, t2> \wedge M \models \xi \wedge P \not\models \xi.$

where $\xi = \beta_1 \oplus \beta_2 = $ (path1 or path2) $\oplus$ SCAN algorithm.

5   Concluding Remarks

We presented a formal characterization model for covert channel. Some characteristic properties have been identified. The system characteristics have been used to guide the development of covert channel searching and eliminating algorithms. In addition, we audit a covert channel and evaluate of the developed algorithms quantitatively with our formalism.

The future investigation is directed to developing the correlative identifying and eliminating algorithms. For example, we eliminate covert channel by breaking the necessary conditions. We limit the necessary condition of forming covert channels until the conduction information speed is lower than ρ. In addition, we audit a covert channel and evaluate the developed algorithms quantitatively. Based on the proposed model, it is interesting to destroy the conditions of forming a covert channel and find a trigger of a covert channel. Other open questions are to check the triggers of a covert channel and reduce the bandwidth of a covert channel to the safe level.

Acknowledgements

This work was supported by National Natural Science Foundation of China (No.60373069) and Jiangsu Nature Science foundation (No. BK200204).

References

1. Department of Defense Trusted Computer System Evaluation Criteria, December 1985.
2. J. C. Huskamp, Covert Communication Channels in TimeSharing Systems, Technical Report UCB-CS-78-02, Ph.D. Thesis, University of California, Berkeley, California, (1978).
3. Ford George G. Meade, A Guide to understanding covert channel analysis of trusted system, NCSC-TG-030 National computer security center, Maryland university, 1993
4. B. W. Lampson, "A Note on the Confinement Problem," Communications of the ACM, 16:10, pp. 613-615, October 1973.
5. Shiguang Ju, Hector J. Hernandez and Lan Zhang, A Security Access Control Mechanism for a Multi-layer Heterogeneous Storage Structure. Lecture Notes in Computer Science, Vol. 3033, 2004, pp907-912.
6. Changda Wang, Shiguang Ju, Guo Dianchun, Yang Zhen and Zheng Wenyi, Research on the methods of search and elimination in covert channels. Lecture Notes in Computer Science, Vol. 3033, 2004, pp988-991.
7. Wang Yuanzhen, Mao Zhongquan,Zhu Hong, Analysis and Research of the disk-arm covert channel, Computer Engineering, Vol.26, No.3,2000,pp.70-71.
8. C.-R. Tsai, V. D. Gligor, and C. S Chandersekaran, "A Formal Method for the Identification of Covert Storage Channels in Source Code," IEEE Transactions on Software Engineering, 16:6, pp. 569-580, 1990.
9. M. H. Kang and I. S. Moskowitz, A pump for rapid, reliable, secure communication. 1st ACM Conference on Computer and Communications Security, Fairfax,Virginia, November 1993, pp. 119-29.

Availability Analysis and Comparison
of Different Intrusion-Tolerant Systems

Chao Wang and Jian-Feng Ma

Key Laboratory of Computer Networks and Information Security, Xidian University,
Ministry of Education, 710071 Xi'an, P.R. China
{kevin020929,ejfma}@hotmail.com

Abstract. Based on the adopted redundancy techniques the intrusion-tolerant systems are classified into three kinds: resource redundancy based systems, complete information redundancy based systems, and partial information redundancy based systems. With the description of the generalized stochastic Petri net (GSPN) models, the availabilities of the three kinds of systems are analyzed and compared. The numerical results show that, for the most part, the partial information redundancy based systems have the highest availability and the resource redundancy based systems the lowest, the complete information redundancy based systems the intermediate. Also explained are the situations of the application of these different kinds of intrusion-tolerant systems.

1 Introduction

Intrusion tolerance is very useful in building server systems that withstand attacks, and intrusion-tolerant systems can provide services with much higher availability and integrity. Many research organizations present their own intrusion-tolerant systems, including Hierarchical Adaptive Control for QoS Intrusion Tolerance (HACQIT) [1], Intrusion Tolerance by Unpredictable Adaptation (ITUA) [2], Scalable Intrusion Tolerant Architecture (SITAR) [3], Intrusion Tolerance via Threshold Cryptography (ITTC) [4] and so on. Redundancy is the most important technique for these intrusion-tolerant systems in nature.

However, there have been few attempts at quantitative validation of the capability of intrusion-tolerant systems. Singh et al. evaluated the availability and reliability of the ITUA system [5]. Gupta et al. analyzed and compared the availability and throughput of intrusion-tolerant systems with different architectures [6].

In this paper, we analyze and compare the availability of the three kinds of intrusion-tolerant systems in probabilistic terms. Generalized Stochastic Petri net (GSPN) is used as the mathematical tool. Unambiguous information is obtained about the effects of the different redundancy techniques on the intrusion tolerance characteristics.

2 Classifying the Intrusion-Tolerant Systems

There are two major types of redundancies: resource redundancy and information redundancy. Resource redundancy means software and/or hardware replication. When a user request arrives, the system manager appoints a server to serve it [1]. Information redundancy means the information that users need is replicated repeatedly and

C.-H. Chi and K.-Y. Lam (Eds.): AWCC 2004, LNCS 3309, pp. 161–166, 2004.

distributed into different servers of the systems. Also information redundancy can be classified into two types: complete information redundancy and partial information redundancy. The difference lies in whether or not the replicas contain the complete information. For the systems that adopt the complete information redundancy technique, all the servers that hold the needed information take outputs when a user request arrives. A vote is taken based on the servers' outputs and its result is taken as the response of the system to the user request. This redundancy technique is widely used [2,3]. For the systems that adopt the partial information redundancy technique, the information that the users needed is partitioned into several shares and each share is settled in one server. It can be restored with the cooperation of some servers that hold the shares [4]. Any set of information shares whose cardinality is not less than the threshold can restore the information. So intrusion-tolerant systems can be classified into three kinds: resource redundancy based system, complete information redundancy based system, and partial information redundancy based system. Figure 1 shows their corresponding architectures. Some sensor components such as IDS are assumed to exist in the systems. Corrupt servers can be found by either the IDS, the voting process, or the information restoring process.

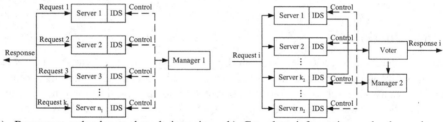

a) Resource redundancy based intrusion-tolerant systems

b) Complete information redundancy based intrusion-tolerant systems

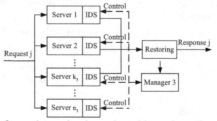

c) Partial information redundancy based intrusion-tolerant systems

Fig. 1. System architectures

3 GSPN Models

Among the various tools developed for performance and dependability modeling and analysis, Petri nets have been widely accepted because of their expressiveness and powerful solution techniques. Thus, GSPN are used here to model different types of intrusion-tolerant systems.

Figure 2 shows the GSPN models of the three types of intrusion-tolerant systems based on different redundancy techniques. The meaning of places and transitions

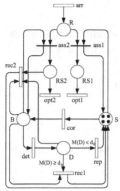

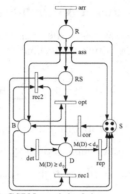

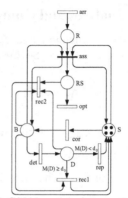

a) GSPN model of the resource redundancy based systems

b) GSPN model of the complete information redundancy based systems

c) GSPN model of the partial information redundancy based systems

Fig. 2. GSPN models

appear in figure 2 is illustrated as following: S is the "right server" place. When the place S holds tokens, the corresponding servers are right and available. B is the "corrupted and undetected server" place. When the place B holds tokens, the corresponding servers are corrupted but undetected. D is the "corrupted and detected" place. When the place D holds tokens, the corresponding servers are corrupted but detected. R is the place that models the "arrived request". RS, RS1, RS2 are the places that model the "arrived requests that are served by the system". arr is the "arrive" transition. When it fires, the user request arrives. cor is the "corrupt" transition. When it fires, some right server is corrupted. det is the "detect" transition. When it fires, some corrupted server is detected by the IDS component. rep is the "repair" transition. When it fires, some corrupted and detected server is repaired. ass, ass1, ass2 are the "assignment" transitions. When they fire, several servers are assigned to work for the arrived user request. opt, opt1, opt2 are the "output" transitions. When they fire, the system outputs a result to respond the user request. rec1, rec2 are the "reconfigurate" transitions. When they fire, the system returns to its initial state. The transition rec1 is enabled when the system is not dependable and the transition rec2 is enabled when the system can't correspond to the user requests.

Some assumptions are made as following:

1. The delay times of the timed transitions are exponentially distributed;
2. There exists a dependable threshold d_0. The firing predicates of the transition rep is $M(D) < d_0$ and that of the transition rec1 is $M(D) \geq d_0$.
3. In Figure 2 a), there is a conflict between the transitions ass1 and ass2, their firing probability distribution can be expressed as follows:

$$\begin{cases} \Pr(\text{ass1}) = \dfrac{M(S)}{M(S) + M(B)} \\ \Pr(\text{ass2}) = \dfrac{M(B)}{M(S) + M(B)} \end{cases} \qquad (1)$$

4 Analyses and Comparisons of Availabilities

For the resource redundancy based systems, their services are unreliable if there exists any corrupt server. So the availability of this kind of systems can be expressed as follows:

$$A_1 = \Pr(M(B) = 0 \wedge M(S) > n - d_0) = \sum_{i < d_0} \pi(n - i, 0, i) \tag{2}$$

Where $\pi_{(n-i,0,i)}$ is the stationary probability distribution of the state (n-i, 0, i).

For the complete information redundancy based systems, their services are always worthy of confidence if the numbers of the right servers are not less than $\left\lceil \dfrac{n+1}{2} \right\rceil$ so that the most commonly used majority votings can be adopted. So the availability of this kind of systems can be expressed as follows:

$$A_2 = \Pr\left(M(S) \geq \left\lceil \frac{n+1}{2} \right\rceil\right) = \sum_{i \geq \left\lceil \frac{n+1}{2} \right\rceil} \pi_{(i,j,k)} \tag{3}$$

Where $\pi_{(i,j,k)}$ is the stationary probability distribution of the state (i, j, k) when $i \geq \left\lceil \dfrac{n+1}{2} \right\rceil$.

For the partial information redundancy based systems, their services are always creditable if the numbers of the available information shares are not less than the threshold determined in advance. We used th to denote the dependable threshold, and then the availability of this kind of systems can be expressed as follows:

$$A_3 = \Pr(M(s) \geq th) = \sum_{i \geq th} \pi_{(i,j,k)} \tag{4}$$

Where $\pi_{(i,j,k)}$ is the stationary probability distribution of the state (i, j, k) when $i \geq th$.

We designed several studies to analyze and compare the availabilities of the various redundancy techniques based intrusion-tolerant systems. The parameters of the exponential distributions of the timed transitions cor, det, rep are set to 0.1, 0.2, 0.5 respectively. The parameters of the exponential distributions are set to 10 identically for the timed transitions arr, opt, opt1 and opt2 and set to 0.25 identically for the timed transitions rec1 and rec2. A corrupt server misbehaves or halts with the equal probability of 0.5. The total numbers of the servers in these systems are set to 7 and d_0 is set to 2. Generally speaking, the dependable threshold th of the secret sharing system satisfies $th \leq \dfrac{n-1}{2}$, so th is set to 3.

Figure 3 a) ~ d) shows the dependencies of the stationary availabilities of the three kinds of systems on different parameters, i.e. the failure rate of the server, the reconfiguration rate of the systems, the arrival rate of the user request, and the preset dependable threshold of the systems. Based on the results we can find that, for the most part, the partial information redundancy based systems keep the highest availability

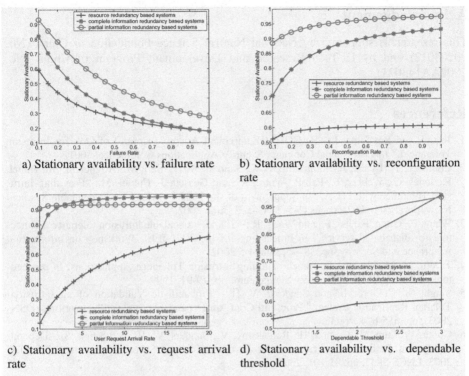

a) Stationary availability vs. failure rate

b) Stationary availability vs. reconfiguration rate

c) Stationary availability vs. request arrival rate

d) Stationary availability vs. dependable threshold

Fig. 3. Dependencies of the stationary availability vs. system parameters

while the resource redundancy based systems the worst; the availability of the complete information redundancy based systems is a little less than the highest one. So the resource redundancy based systems is rarely found [1] while the information redundancy based systems are much more familiar [2,3,4]. As to a specified user request, the availability of an intrusion-tolerant system is determined by that of the pointed server for a resource redundancy based system and is determined by that of several servers for an information redundancy based system. The more corrupt servers that the redundancy techniques can tolerate, the more available the intrusion-tolerant systems are.

5   Conclusions

The capability of the intrusion-tolerant systems to tolerate intrusion is a tradeoff between system performance and several properties such as availability, confidentiality, security and so on. So the choice of redundancy techniques must be made based on the user requirements and practical situations.

In this paper GSPN models are presented for different kinds of intrusion-tolerant systems, based on which the availability analyses are made. Our work aims at providing a method to analyze and compare the system. In fact, performance and other properties of these systems can be analyzed by the GSPN models presented with more detailed system parameters, too.

Acknowledgement

This research is supported by National Natural Science Foundation of China (No. 90204012) and by Hi-Tech Research and Development Program of China (No. 2002AA143021).

References

1. Just, J. and Reynolds, J.: "HACQIT (Hierarchical Adaptive Control of QoS for Intrusion Tolerance)," In 17th Annual Computer Security Applications Conference, 2001.
2. Courtney, T., Lyons, J., Ramasamy, H.V., Sanders, W.H., Seri, M., Atighetchi, M., Rubel, P., Jones, C., Webber, F., Pal, P., Watro, R., and Gossett, J., Cukier, M.: "Providing Intrusion Tolerance with ITUA," In Supplement of the 2002 Intl Conf. on Dependable Sys. and Networks (DSN-2002), pages C–5–1– C–5–3, June 2002.
3. Wang, F., Gong, F., Jou, F., and Wang, R.: "SITAR: A scalable intrusion tolerance architecture for distributed service," In Proceedings of the 2001 IEEE Workshop on Information Assurance and Security, pp. 38–45, June 4-5 2001.
4. T. Wu, M. Malkin, and D. Boneh. Building Intrusion Tolerance Applications. In proceedings of the 8th USENIX Security Symposium, pp. 79-91, 1999.
5. Singh, S., Cukier, M., and Sanders, W. H.: "Probabilistic Validation of an Intrusion-Tolerant Replication System," Proc. Intl Conf. on Dependable Sys. and Networking (DSN-2003), pp. 615-624, 2003.
6. Gupta, V., Lam, V., Govind, H., Ramasamy, V., Sanders, W. H., and Singh, S.: "Dependability and Performance Evaluation of Intrusion-Tolerant Server Architectures," LADC 2003, LNCS 2847, pp. 81-101, 2003.

Security Analysis
of User Efficient Blind Signatures

Tianjie Cao[1,2,3], Dongdai Lin[1], and Rui Xue[1]

[1] State Key Laboratory of Information Security of Institute of Software,
Chinese Academy of Sciences, Beijing 100080, China
{tjcao,ddlin,rxue}@is.iscas.ac.cn
[2] School of Computer Science and Technology,
China University of Mining and Technology, Xuzhou 221008, China
[3] Graduate School of Chinese Academy of Sciences, Beijing 100039, China

Abstract. Blind signature schemes allow a person to get a message signed by another party without revealing any information about the message to the other party. To believe the message contains a certain form, cut and choose protocol and partially blind signature protocol are used to prevent cheating. In electronic cash system, unconditional anonymity may be misused for criminal activities such as blackmailing and money laundering. Fair electronic cash schemes are introduced for preventing these fraudulent activities. In this paper, we point out a weakness in Fan and Lei's user efficient blind signatures. Utilizing this weakness, a user can cheat the signer in cut and choose protocol, and the user can also break Fan and Lei's low-computation partially blind signature scheme and Yu et al.'s user efficient fair e-cash scheme.

1 Introduction

The concept of blind signature scheme was first introduced by Chaum in 1982 [3]. Blind signatures can be used in cryptographic applications such as electronic voting (e-voting) systems and electronic cash (e-cash) systems.

In a blind signature scheme, the signer cannot learn the message he signs. To believe the message contains a certain form, there are two solutions: cut and choose protocol and partially blind signature protocol. In cryptographic protocols, cut and choose protocol is widely used to prevent cheating. Cut and choose was first used in Chaum, Fiat and Naor's original scheme in conjunction with blind signatures to prove that a signature had been correctly formed [4]. Partially blind signatures were introduced by Abe and Fujisaki [1] to allow the signer to explicitly include some agreed information in the blind signature. Using partially blind signatures in e-cash system, the bank can assure that each e-cash issued by it contains the information it desires, such as the date and the face value information.

In electronic cash scheme, von Solms and Naccache [11] discovered that unconditional anonymity might be misused for criminal activities such as blackmailing and money laundering. Fair blind signatures introduced by Stadler et

C.-H. Chi and K.-Y. Lam (Eds.): AWCC 2004, LNCS 3309, pp. 167–172, 2004.
© Springer-Verlag Berlin Heidelberg 2004

al. [12] provide a way to ensure that the anonymity of blind signatures is not abused by the criminal in society.

In 1998, Fan and Lei gave a user efficient blind signature scheme based on quadratic residues [6], and then they proposed a low-computation partially blind signature scheme [7]. Soon, Fan [5] found a weakness in this partially blind signature scheme, and he also proposed an improved scheme to avoid the weakness. But, Fan's improved scheme has the same weakness as the original one [9]. Based on user efficient blind signatures, Yu et al. proposed a user efficient fair e-cash scheme [13]. In [2], Cao et al. found a weakness in Yu et al.'s scheme. Recently, based on user efficient blind signatures, Fan and Lei also proposed a divisible blind signature scheme [8].

In this paper, we point out a weakness in Fan and Lei's user efficient blind signature scheme. Because of this weakness, the user efficient blind signature scheme [6] and the divisible blind signature scheme [8] cannot utilize cut and choose protocol to prevent cheating. As the same reason, Fan-Lei low-computation partially blind signature scheme does not meet partial blindness property, and Yu et al.'s user efficient fair e-cash scheme does not meet fair property.

2   Security Analysis of User Efficient Blind Signature Scheme

Fan-Lei user efficient blind signature scheme [6] is described as follows.

(1) Initialization. The signer randomly selects two distinct large primes p_1 and p_2 where $p_1 \equiv p_2 \equiv 3 (mod 4)$. The signer computes $n = p_1 p_2$ and publishes n. In addition, let H be a public one-way hash function.

(2) Blinding. To request a signature of a message m, a user chooses two random integers u, v, and computes $\alpha = H(m)(u^2 + v^2) \bmod n$. He then submits the integer α to the signer. The signer randomly selects x such that $(\alpha(x^2+1) \bmod n)$ is a quadratic residue (QR) in Z_n^*, and then sends x to the user, where Z_n^* is the set of all positive integers less than and relatively prime to n. After receiving x, the user randomly selects an integer b, and then computes $\delta = (b^2 \bmod n)$ and $\beta = (\delta(ux + v) \bmod n)$. The user submits β to the signer.

(3) Signing. After receiving β, the signer computes $\lambda = (\beta^{-1} \bmod n)$ and derives an integer t in Z_n^*, such that $t^4 \equiv \alpha(x^2+1)\lambda^2 (\bmod n)$. The signer sends the tuple (t, λ) to the user.

(4) Unblinding. After receiving (t, λ), the user computes $s = (bt \bmod n)$ and $c = (\delta\lambda(u - vx) \bmod n)$. The tuple (c, s) is the signer's signature on m.

(5) Verifying. To verify (c, s, m), one can examine if

$$s^4 \equiv H(m)(c^2 + 1) \bmod n$$

In blinding stage, the user need submit $\alpha = H(m)(u^2 + v^2)(\bmod n)$ to the signer. In theorem 1, we will show that the user can complete the protocol no matter what integer α he submits to the signer. Thus, the user submits α to the signer is redundancy in the user efficient blind signature scheme. From the point of security that is a highly dangerous thing.

Theorem 1. *Given* $\forall \alpha, x, \alpha' \in Z_n^*$, *the user can construct integers* λ *and* c *in polynomial time such that*

$$\alpha(x^2 + 1)\lambda^2 \equiv \alpha'(c^2 + 1)(\mathrm{mod}\, n)$$

Proof. Given $\forall \alpha, x, \alpha' \in Z_n^*$, the user can derive (f, g) in polynomial time such that

$$f^2 + g^2 \equiv \alpha(x^2 + 1)\alpha'^{-1}(\mathrm{mod}\, n)$$

through the method introduced by Pollard and Schnorr [10] without knowing the factorization of n. The user randomly selects an integer $w \in Z_n^*$ and computes $\lambda = (w^2+1)(2fw-g(w^2-1))^{-1}(\mathrm{mod}\, n)$ and $c = (f(w^2-1)+2gw)(2fw-g(w^2-1))^{-1}(\mathrm{mod}\, n)$. Now integers λ and c satisfy $\alpha(x^2+1)\lambda^2 \equiv \alpha'(c^2+1)(\mathrm{mod}\, n)$.   □

3   Security Analysis of Some Protocols Based on User Efficient Blind Signatures

In this section, we exam some protocols based on user efficient blind signatures.

3.1   Cut and Choose Protocol Based on User Efficient Signatures

When Fan-Lei user efficient blind signatures [6] are used to design e-cash scheme, in order to establish correctness in the blind signature protocol, cut and choose technique may be used.

To withdraw a coin with the amount W, the user prepares k messages $\{m_1, m_2, ..., m_k\}$ where k is a larger integer. Each message contains the amount W and a random serial number. The user chooses $2k$ random integers u_i, v_i, and computes $\alpha_i = H(m_i)(u_i^2 + v_i^2) \bmod n(1 \leq i \leq k)$. He then submits the integers $a_i(1 \leq i \leq k)$ to the bank.

The bank randomly selects $k - 1$ elements from the set $\{\alpha_1, \alpha_2, ..., \alpha_k\}$. We assume that the leaving integer is α_l. The user reveals m_i, u_i and $v_i(i \neq l)$. The bank checks that each element in the set $\{m_i : i \neq l\}$ contains the correct amount W.

The bank randomly selects x such that $(\alpha_l(x^2 + 1) \bmod n)$ is a QR in Z_n^*, and then sends x to the user. The user randomly selects an integer b, and then computes $\delta = (b^2 \bmod n)$ and $\beta = (\delta(u_l x + v_l) \bmod n)$. The user submits β to the bank.

After receiving β, the bank computes $\lambda = (\beta^{-1} \bmod n)$ and derives an integer t in Z_n^*, such that

$$t^4 \equiv \alpha_l(x^2 + 1)\lambda^2(\mathrm{mod}\, n)$$

The bank sends the tuple (t, λ) to the user.

After receiving (t, λ), the user computes $s = (bt \bmod n)$ and $c = (\delta\lambda(u_l - v_l x) \bmod n)$. The tuple (c, s, m_l) is a coin. To verify (c, s, m_l), one can examine if $s^4 \equiv H(m_l)(c^2 + 1) \bmod n$.

Here we show that the user can cheat the bank. After receiving x, the user can randomly choose an integer b and prepare a message m contained another amount $W' \neq W$. The use computes $\alpha' = b^{-4}H(m)(\bmod n)$. Utilizing Theorem 1, the user can construct integers λ and c in polynomial time such that

$$\alpha_l(x^2 + 1)\lambda^2 \equiv \alpha'(c^2 + 1)(\bmod n)$$

When the signer derives t such that $t^4 \equiv \alpha_l(x^2 + 1)\lambda^2(\bmod n)$, we have

$$t^4 \equiv \alpha_l(x^2 + 1)\lambda^2 \equiv \alpha'(c^2 + 1) \equiv b^{-4}H(m)(c^2 + 1)(\bmod n)$$

The user can form a coin (s, m, c) with $s = bt(\bmod n)$ such that $s^4 \equiv H(m)$ $(c^2+1)(\bmod n)$ where the message m contained another amount $W' \neq W$. Thus, Fan-Lei user efficient blind signature scheme cannot use cut and choose technique to design e-cash systems. Similarly, Fan-Lei divisible blind signature scheme [8] has the same disadvantage.

3.2   Fan-Lei Low-Computation Partially Blind Signature Scheme

Fan-Lei low-computation partially blind signature scheme [7] is based on user efficient blind signatures. The protocol is briefly described below.

A user prepares a common message a, a plaintext message m and two random integers u and v in Z_n^*. He computes $\alpha = H(m)(u^2 + v^2) \bmod n$ and then sends α and a to the signer.

After verifying that the string a is valid, the signer randomly selects x such that $H(a)(\alpha(x^2 + 1))^3 \bmod n$ is a QR in Z_n^*, and sends x to the user.

After receiving x, the user randomly selects an integer b, and then computes $\delta = (b^4 \bmod n)$ and $\beta = (\delta(u - vx) \bmod n)$. He then submits β to the signer.

After receiving β, the signer computes $\lambda = (\beta^{-1} \bmod n)$ and derives an integer t in Z_n^*, such that $t^8 \equiv H(a)(\alpha(x^2 + 1))^3\lambda^6(\bmod n)$. The bank sends the tuple (t, λ) to the user.

After receiving (t, λ), the user computes $s = (b^3 t \bmod n)$ and $c = (\delta\lambda(ux + v) \bmod n)$. To verify the signature (s, m, c, a), one can examine if $s^8 \equiv H(a)$ $(H(m)(c^2 + 1))^3 \bmod n$.

Here we show how the user cheats the signer. After receiving x, the user chooses b and a string $a' \neq a$, and prepares $\alpha' = b^{-8}H(m)H(a)^{-3}H(a')^3(\bmod n)$. Utilizing Theorem 1, the user can construct integers λ and c in polynomial time such that

$$\alpha(x^2 + 1)\lambda^2 \equiv \alpha'(c^2 + 1)(\bmod n)$$

When the signer derives t such that $t^8 \equiv H(a)(\alpha(x^2 + 1))^3\lambda^6(\bmod n)$. We have

$$
\begin{aligned}
t^8 &\equiv H(a)(\alpha(x^2 + 1))^3\lambda^6 \\
&\equiv H(a)(\alpha'(c^2 + 1))^3 \\
&\equiv H(a)(b^{-8}H(m)H(a)^{-3}H(a')^3(c^2 + 1))^3 \\
&\equiv (b^{-3}H(a)^{-1}H(a'))^8 H(a')(H(m)(c^2 + 1))^3
\end{aligned}
$$

Thus, the user can form a signature (s, m, c, a') with $s = b^3 H(a)H(a')^{-1}t(\bmod n)$ such that $s^8 \equiv H(a')(H(m)(c^2 + 1))^3 \bmod n$. The user can obtain a signature on m with the predefined-format information $a' \neq a$.

3.3   Yu et al.'s Fair e-Cash Scheme

Yu et al.'s fair e-cash scheme [13] is also based on user efficient blind signatures.

The bank publishes its public key $n = p_1p_2$ where $p_1 \equiv p_2 \equiv 3(\bmod 4)$ and a hash function H. The judge also publishes its public key $n' = p_3p_4 > n$ where $p_3 \equiv p_4 \equiv 3(\bmod 4)$ and a string ϖ. In addition, the judge selects a symmetric key K, and $E_K(m)$ denotes encrypting m with the secret key K.

After mutual authentication, the customer sends $H(m)$ to the judge, where m is the message to be signed. The judge randomly selects a bit string σ and forms an anonymous ID token $I = (\varpi || ID_{Customer} || \sigma)^2 \bmod n'$, where $ID_{Customer}$ is the customer's identity. The judge computes $I' = E_K(I)$. Next, the judge randomly selects u and v in Z_n^* and computes $\alpha = H(H(m), I)(u^2 + v^2) \bmod n$. Then the judge generates a signature on α, $ID_{Customer}$, and I' as follows: $S_{judge}(\alpha, ID_{Customer}, I') = (H(\alpha, ID_{Customer}, I'))^{1/2} \bmod n'$. The judge sends $(S_{judge}(\alpha, ID_{Customer}, I'), \alpha, I, I', u, v)$ to the customer in a secure manner.

The customer then requests the bank to sign m. The customer sends α, I', and $S_{judge}(\alpha, ID_{Customer}, I')$ to the bank. After mutual authenticating, the bank verifies the signature $S_{judge}(\alpha, ID_{Customer}, I')$ and then randomly selects an integer x in Z_n^* such that $\alpha(x^2 + 1) \bmod n$ is a QR in Z_n^*. Then the bank sends x to the customer.

The customer randomly selects an integer $b \in Z_n^*$ and computes $\delta = (b^2 \bmod n)$ and $\beta = (\delta(u - vx) \bmod n)$. Then he submits β to the bank. The bank computes $\lambda = (\beta^{-1} \bmod n)$ and derives an integer t in Z_n^* satisfying $t^4 \equiv \alpha(x^2 + 1)\lambda^2(\bmod n)$. Then he sends (t, λ) to the customer. The customer computes $s = bt(\bmod n)$ and $c = \delta\lambda(ux + v)(\bmod n)$ and verifies whether the coin (I, c, s, m) satisfies $s^4 \equiv H(H(m), I)(c^2 + 1) \bmod n$.

Coin tracing. The bank sends I' to the judge. The judge decrypts I' to recover the ID token I.

Owner tracing. The bank sends the coin (I, c, s, m) to the judge. The judge derives $ID_{Customer}$ from equation $(\varpi || ID_{Customer} || \sigma)^2 \bmod n' = I$. $ID_{Customer}$ is exactly the person who withdraw the coin.

When the user withdraws a coin, the user chooses an integer b and a string $F \neq I$, and prepares $\alpha' = b^{-4}H(H(m), F)(\bmod n)$. Utilizing Theorem 1, the user can construct integers λ and c in polynomial time such that

$$\alpha(x^2 + 1)\lambda^2 \equiv \alpha'(c^2 + 1)(\bmod n)$$

When the signer derives t such that $t^4 \equiv \alpha(x^2 + 1)\lambda^2(\bmod n)$, we have

$$t^4 \equiv \alpha(x^2 + 1)\lambda^2 \equiv \alpha'(c^2 + 1) \equiv b^{-4}H(H(m), F)(c^2 + 1)$$

Thus, the user can form a signature 4-tuple (s, m, c, F) with $s = bt(\bmod n)$ such that $s^4 \equiv H(H(m), F)(c^2 + 1) \bmod n$.

4   Conclusion

In this paper, we have showed a weakness in Fan-Lei user efficient blind signature scheme. Utilizing this weakness, the user can cheat the signer in cut and choose protocol based on Fan-Lei scheme, and the user can also break Fan-Lei partially blind signature scheme and Yu et al.'s user efficient fair e-cash scheme.

Acknowledgments

We thank the support of National Natural Science Foundation of China (NSFC 90204016, 60373048) and the National High Technology Development Program of China under Grant (863, No.2003AA144030).

References

1. Abe, M, Fujisaki, E.: How to date blind signatures, Advances in Cryptology - Asiacrypt'96, Lecture Notes in Computer Science, Vol. 1163, Springer-Verlag. (1996) 244–251
2. Cao, T., Lin, D., Xue, R.: Cryptanalysis of User Efficient Fair E-Cash Schemes, Proceedings of 16th International Conference on Computer Communication. (2004) 524–528
3. Chaum, D.: Blind signatures for untraceable payments, Advances in Cryptology - CRYPTO' 82, Plenum (1983) 199–203
4. Chaum D. Fiat A, Naor M.: Untraceable Electronic Cash, Advances in Cryptology - CRYPTO '88, Lecture Notes in Computer Science, Vol. 403, Springer-Verlag, (1990) 319–327
5. Fan C-I. Improved low-computation partially blind signatures, Applied Mathematics and Computation, Vol 145, Issues 2-3, (2003) 853–867
6. Fan C-I, Lei C-L. User efficient blind signatures, Electronics letters, vol. 34(6) (1998) 544–546
7. Fan C-I, Lei C-L. Low-Computation Partially Blind Signatures for Electronic Cash, IEICE Transactions on Fundamentals of Electronics, Communications and Computer Sciences, vol. E81-A, no. 5 (1998) 818–824
8. Fan C-I, Lei C-L. Divisible Blind Signatures Based on Hash Chains, International Journal of Computers and Application, Vol. 26(1), (2004) 202–210
9. Liao G-J. Presentation of improved low-computation partially blind signatures, (2003) http://140.134.25.71/~education/subgroup_2/031021.ppt.
10. Pollard JM, Schnorr CP. An efficient solution of the congruence $x^2 + ky^2 = m(\mod n)$, IEEE Transactions on Information Theory, vol. 33(5) (1987) 702–709
11. von Solms S, Naccache D. On blind signatures and perfect crimes, Computer & Security, vol. 11, (1992) 581–583
12. Stadler M, Piveteau JM, Camenisch J. Fair Blind Signatures, Proceedings of EUROCRYPT'95, Lecture Notes in Computer Science, Vol. 921, Springer-Verlag, (1995) 209–219
13. Yu P-L, Lei C-L, Chen H-J, Huang C-Y, User Efficient Fair Blind Signatures, The Second International Workshop for Asian Public Key Infrastructures, (2002) http://dsns.csie.nctu.edu.tw/iwap/proceedings/proceedings/sessionD/15.pdf.

A Novel DDoS Attack Detecting Algorithm
Based on the Continuous Wavelet Transform

Xinyu Yang, Yong Liu, Ming Zeng, and Yi Shi

Dept. of Computer Science and Technology, Xi'an Jiaotong University,
710049 Xi'an, P.R. China
yxyphd@mail.xjtu.edu.cn

Abstract. Distributed denial-of-service(DDoS) attacks have recently emerged as a major threat to the security and stability of the Internet. As we know, traffic bursts always go with DDoS attacks. Detecting the network traffic bursts accurately in real-time can catch such attacks as quickly as possible. In this paper, we categorize the traffic bursts into three kinds: Single-point-burst, Short-flat-burst and Long-flat-burst, and propose a network traffic burst detecting algorithm (BDA-CWT) based on the continuous wavelet transform. In this algorithm, we use a slip window to analyze the traffic data uninterruptedly to detect the Short-flat-burst or the Long-flat-burst, which always represents DDoS attacks. Our experiment has demonstrated that the proposed detection algorithm is responsive and effective in curbing DDoS attacks, in contrast with the discrete wavelet transform and traditional methods (N-point-average and gradient).

1 Introduction

DDoS (Distributed denial-of-service) attacks have recently emerged as a major threat to the security of network and the QoS (Quality of Service) of web sites. On October 21, 2002, the root DNS servers were flooded with DDoS attacks. Only five out of thirteen root DNS servers were able to withstand the attacks [1]. Previously, DDoS attacks had shut down several large Internet sites, such as Yahoo, eBay, Amazon and CNN etc [2].

To prevent a DDoS attack effectively and timely, it must be detected and handled at the beginning of its staging. Many methods have been proposed to solve the problem of DDoS detection, such as DDoS character analysis [3], packet trace analysis [4] and packet filtering [5,6] etc. Most of these methods focus on analyzing historical data of network traffic or modifying the structure of the network, so an efficient self-adaptive DDoS detecting algorithm is demanded.

A DDoS attack overwhelms a targeted host with an immense volume of useless traffic from distributed and coordinated attack sources[7]. So, when there is a DDoS attack, there will always be traffic bursts. Much research have been done to show that Wavelet-based scaling analysis can be used to characterize Internet traffic and the scaling properties of wavelets can be effectively tapped to capture the variations in behavior of network traffic during an attack. Mallat and his collaborators developed and perfected Grossmann's theory [8-11] after Grossmann proposed to detect the singularity of a signal using Wavelet Transform in 1986 [7]. Wavelets have been applied to nonstationary signal detection and character analysis area ever since then. In DDoS attack detecting area, Raymond C. Garcia proposed to analyze the traffic

C.-H. Chi and K.-Y. Lam (Eds.): AWCC 2004, LNCS 3309, pp. 173–181, 2004.
© Springer-Verlag Berlin Heidelberg 2004

with discrete wavelet transform and then identify if there are DDoS or other attacks [12]. David A. Nash proposed to detect DDoS attacks by using multiresolution wavelet analysis and the self-similarity of the network traffic [13]. These methods are helpful in Denial of Service Attack Detection, but they can't detect the attacks as quickly as possible. In this paper, we will attempt to use Continuous Wavelet Transform methods to detect a DDoS attack in real-time.

We organize the rest of this paper as follows. Section 2 briefly introduces the continuous wavelet transform and the reason we choose it. Section 3 categorizes bursts in the network traffic and describes our BDA-CWT (network traffic burst detecting algorithm based on the continuous wavelet transform) algorithm. In section 4, we perform an experiment to evaluate the effectiveness of the BDA-CWT algorithm in detecting traffic bursts. In section 5 we conclude this work with future work.

2 Introduction to Continuous Wavelet Transform

Wavelet Transform develops from the classic Fourier Transform. As a signal analysis tool, there is no information loss in the process of wavelet transform, and this feature assures the analytic validity in the transform fields. Wavelet transform can be categorized as continuous wavelet transform, discrete wavelet transform and orthogonal wavelet transform based on multi-resolution analysis. Continuous wavelet transform was proposed by Morlet and Grossmann [14].

Let $\psi(x)$ be a complex valued function. The function $\psi(x)$ is said to be a wavelet if and only if its Fourier transform $\hat{\psi}(x)$ satisfies

$$\int_{0}^{+\infty} \frac{|\hat{\psi}(\omega)|^2}{\omega} d\omega = \int_{-\infty}^{0} \frac{|\hat{\psi}(\omega)|^2}{|\omega|} d\omega = C_\psi < +\infty \tag{1}$$

This condition implies that

$$\int_{-\infty}^{+\infty} \psi(u) du = 0$$

For any function $f(x) \in L^2(R)$, its continuous wavelet transform is of form,

$$W_f(a,b) = <f, \Psi_{a,b}> = |a|^{-1/2} \int_{-\infty}^{+\infty} f(t) \overline{\Psi(\frac{t-b}{a})} dt \tag{2}$$

Its reverse transform is on form,

$$f(x) = \frac{1}{C_\Psi} \int_{0}^{+\infty} \int_{-\infty}^{+\infty} \frac{1}{a^2} W_f(a,b) \Psi(\frac{t-b}{a}) da db \tag{3}$$

Continuous wavelet transform has time-invariance and scale-continuum and its localization and approach character is very good. There is no information loss while analyzing transient or nonstationary signals with continuous wavelet transform. Therefore, in this paper, we select continuous wavelet transform as the base of the algorithm.

3 BDA-CWT

3.1 Categorization of Bursts in Network Traffic

If we measure the network traffic with a certain time interval and get that there is a long time persisting burst and a short time persisting burst in it. Then if we increase the time interval, the long time persisting burst will probably become a short time persisting burst correspondingly and the short time persisting burst will become very difficult to be detected. If we decrease the time interval, the long time persisting burst will become a group of bursts and the duration of the short time persisting burst will become long correspondingly. So we consider that traffic bursts could be classified by their duration if we adjust the time interval properly. For a certain window, on the assumption that there are W data points in it, if a burst's duration is a point, we call it a Single-point-burst; if a burst's duration is longer than 1 point and less or equal to $\left(\left\lceil \frac{W}{10^n} \right\rceil \times 10\right)$ points, we call it a Short-burst; and if the duration of a burst is longer than $\left(\left\lceil \frac{W}{10^n} \right\rceil \times 10\right)$ points, we call it a long-burst. Thus we categorizes bursts in the network traffic into three below:

1. Single-point-burst
2. Short-flat-burst
3. Long-flat-burst

If a single-point-burst we get in a certain time interval is really a DDoS attack traffic, it would become a short-flat-burst or a long-flat-burst when the time interval decreases. Contrarily, if it's still a single-point-burst in the decreasing time interval, it is really just a normal burst, not an attack burst, and wouldn't cause trouble in the network. So what we are concerned about is how to detect those two kinds of bursts in the network in real-time to catch the DDoS attacks as quickly as possible. We advise to measure the network traffic with several time scales and detect short-flat-bursts and long-flat-bursts in the traffic of different time scales. Because the three kinds of bursts are defined according to the measuring time scale, short-flat-bursts and single-point-bursts of large time scale may be long-flat-bursts of small time scale.

3.2 Description of BDA-CWT

As described above, what we are concerned about is flat-bursts (long-flat-bursts and short-flat-bursts) in the network traffic, so the main function of BDA-CWT is detecting flat-bursts in the traffic in real-time. In this algorithm, we analyze the traffic data by using a slip window uninterruptedly. When a flat-burst is detected in the window, its position is marked.

Description of BTA-CWA is as below:

1) Read some data S whose length is equal to the window size;
2) Select proper wavelet and character scale to transform S with continuous wavelet transform, then get a group of wavelet coefficient under different scales (In the experiment, we select DB3 and scale is 16);
3) Select proper character scale as detecting scale and select proper valve according to the traffic data, and then detect the wavelet coefficient with the detecting scale. Because the coefficient of transformed bursts is bigger, we can find positions of bursts, then mark them (the detection scale and valve must be adjusted by the traffic);
4) Slip the window forward n points, and update the data S, go to 2).

The flow of BDA-CWT shows as Fig.1.

4   Analysis of Experiment

4.1   Network Traffic Data Collection

The traffic record in our experiment is collected in our laboratory. Its length is 4000 seconds. We simulated the abnormity phenomenon by using SYNFlood software when DDoS attack emerged in the network. We calculated the record and get a time sequence of Packets/s. The main process is as below.

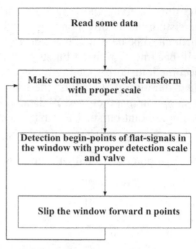

Fig. 1. Flow of BDA-CWT

1) We have a public FTP server A in our laboratory. There is a great deal of TCP traffic on the server.
2) Connect FTP server A with two other computers B and C, and get a LAN.
3) Run Sniffer Pro3.0 on computer B to measure the TCP traffic on FTP server A, the time interval is 1 second, and the total measure time is 4000 seconds.
4) Run SYNFlood software on computer C and attack FTP server A (the begin-point and duration are shown in Table 1). Now we get bursts in the traffic.
5) After above 4 steps, we get original traffic signal S0 including burst signals.

Begin-points, duration and average value of bursts in the original signal S0 show in Table 1, the shape of S0 shows as Fig. 2. From Table 1 and Fig. 2, we can find that the average value of those flat-bursts is smaller than the largest single-point-bursts.

Table 1. Begin-points, duration and average value of bursts in the original signal

Type of bursts	Begin-point	Duration	Average value
Long-flat-burst	3855	145seconds	398.21
Short-flat-burst A	341	3 seconds	400.13
Short-flat-burst B	2508	5 seconds	402.60
Short-flat-burst C	1428	3 seconds	357.67
Short-flat-burst D	2009	5 seconds	363.50
Single-point-burst A	229	1 seconds	495.00
Single-point-burst B	584	1 seconds	512.00
Single-point-burst C	2418	1 seconds	522.00
Single-point-burst D	2829	1 seconds	500.00

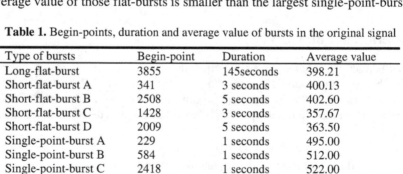

Fig. 2. Shape of original signal S0

4.2 Analysis of Experiment

A. Detect Results of BDA-CWT

In order to validate the result of BDA-CWT, we detect the flat-bursts in the original signal with different parameters. The detailed parameters we have used and the detected results are shown in Table 2 to Table 6 and Fig.3 to Fig.8. Fig.3 is the transformed result of the data in 11th window. There are 2 short-flat-bursts in 11th window and the wavelet coefficient of short-flat-bursts is larger than normal signals when we select parameters in Table 2. Table 2 to Table 6 show wavelets, window sizes, detecting scales, valves and steps we have selected. Fig.4 to Fig.7 show the begin-points of detected flat-bursts.

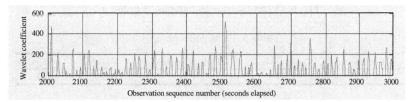

Fig. 3. Result of transformed data in 11th window

Table 2. Parameters group 1

Wavelet	Window size	Detect scale	Valve	Step
DB3	1000	11	400	10

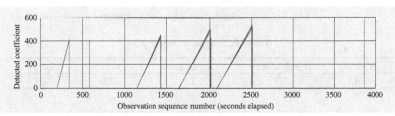

Fig. 4. Detect result with parameters group 1

Table 3. Parameters group 2

Wavelet	Window size	Detect scale	Valve	Step
DB3	500	11	400	10

Fig. 5. Detect result with parameters group 2

Table 4. Parameters group 3

Wavelet	Window size	Detect scale	Valve	Step
DB3	300	11	400	10

Fig. 6. Detect result with parameters group 3

Table 5. Parameters group 4

Wavelet	Window size	Detect scale	Valve	Step
DB3	150	11	400	10

Fig. 7. Detect result with parameters group 4

Table 6. Parameters group 5

Wavelet	Window size	Detect scale	Valve	Step
DB3	50	11	400	10

Fig. 8. Detect result with parameters group 5

From tables and figures above, we can find that BDA-CWT could detect all the flat-bursts caused by SYN Flood if the parameters are proper. The single-point-burst B is detected because its value is much larger than points beside it.

B. Comparison Between BDA-CWT and Other Methods

Traditional methods could detect flat signals generally, but the value of Short-bursts is small and the distinguishing rates of those methods are very low. In order to compare

BDA-CWT with traditional methods, we show detect results of traditional methods as Fig. 9 to Fig. 11 and the comparison is given in Table 7. We can find from those figures and tables that the detecting rate of BDA-CWT is not less than other three traditional methods and the correct rate of BDA-CWT is much higher.

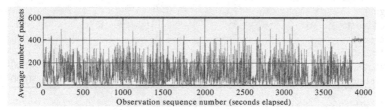

Fig. 9. Result of N-average

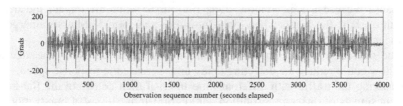

Fig. 10. Result of gradient

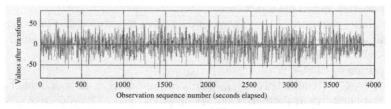

Fig. 11. Result of integration of gradient and N- average

As described in section 2, continuous wavelet transform is better than discrete wavelet transform in orientation. In order to compare those two methods, we transform the original signal by using discrete wavelet transform, but the result is not satisfactory. The comparison is given in Table 7. Fig.13 shows the 3rd decomposition coefficient of the original signal using DB3.

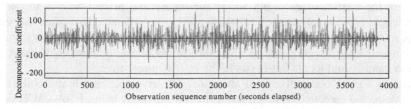

Fig. 12. Result of discrete wavelet transform

Table 7. Comparison of 4 methods (Detect rate=Correct detected bursts/All bursts, Correct rate=Correct detected bursts/Detected bursts)

Method	BDA-CWT	Discrete wavelet transform	N-point-average	Gradi-ent	Combine gradient with N-point-average
All bursts in the signal	5	5	5	5	5
Detected bursts	6	3	13	8	8
Correct de-tected bursts	5	3	5	1	4
Detect rate	100.00%	60.00%	100.00%	20.00%	80.00%
Correct rate	83.33%	100.00%	34.46%	12.50%	50.00%

C. Analysis of BDA-CWT

According to the results, we think that,

1) Because we use a slip window, long-flat-bursts wouldn't impact the detecting result of short-flat-bursts when long-flat-bursts and short-flat-bursts emerge in the same window.
2) If the operation doesn't impact the calculation speed, adjusting the size of the window could reduce the detecting delay and increase the response speed.
3) Measuring the traffic with different time interval then detecting the flat-bursts in traffic signals of different resolution could confirm positions of bursts more accurately
4) Because of characters of wavelet transform, there is small detection error, but the error doesn't impact the effect.
5) Essentially, our work is using wavelet transform to extrude the flat-bursts in the traffic signal, and then distinguish them. So if signals in the window are flat-burst, BDA-CWT couldn't identify them.
6) Adaptation of BDA-CWT
   [1] BDA-CWT could detect begin-points of flat-bursts in the signal that has long-flat-bursts, short-flat-bursts and single-point-bursts. Our objective is to detect the begin-points of flat-bursts, so BDA-CWT doesn't detect end-points of them.
   [2] BDA-CWT couldn't detect single-point-bursts effectively.

5   Conclusion

Bursts in the network traffic often have lots of important information about current status of the network. Intrusions of network, especially DDoS attacks, often result in bursts in the traffic, so detecting bursts accurately and in real-time in the network traffic could provide information for the security surveillance. This paper categorizes bursts in the network traffic into three categories (long-bursts, short-bursts and one-point bursts) and then proposes an algorithm based on the continuous wavelet transform to identify and locate flat-bursts in the traffic in real-time.

We use SYN Flood software to attack a FTP server in the lab and collected the traffic data, and detected the begin-points of flat-bursts by using BDA-CWT, discrete wavelet transform and traditional methods (N-point-average and gradient). Results of above show that the BDA-CWT is excellent in flat-bursts detecting. There is small error in the detection result using this algorithm because of the characteristics of wavelet transform. But our experiment proves that the error doesn't impact the detection result.

We use a slip window in BDA-CWT to detect the traffic signal. Because whether or not bursts will result in congestion and invalidation depends on degree of bursts, duration of bursts and network width etc, many factors need to be considered to decide best size of the slip window. That is also the next step of our research work.

References

1. Yaar, A.; Perrig, A.; Song, D.; Pi: a path identification mechanism to defend against DDoS attacks Security and Privacy, 2003. Proceedings. 2003 Symposium on, May 11-14, 2003, Pages:93 – 107
2. http://www.netscan.org/Guiding Against DDoS
3. Yaar, A.; Perrig, A.; Song, D.; Pi: a path identification mechanism to defend against DDoS attacks, Security and Privacy, 2003. Proceedings. 2003 Symposium on, May 11-14, 2003, Pages:93 – 107
4. Feinstein, L.; Schnackenberg, D.; Balupari, R.; Kindred, D.; Statistical approaches to ddos attack detection and response; DARPA Information Survivability Conference and Exposition, 2003. Proceedings, Volume: 1, April 22-24, 2003,Pages:303 - 314Scalable DDoS Protection Using Route-Based Filtering
5. Kihong Park; Scalable DDoS protection using route-based filtering, DARPA Information Survivability Conference and Exposition, 2003. Proceedings, Volume: 2, April 22-24, 2003, Pages:97 - 97
6. Yoohwan Kim; Ju-Yeon Jo; Chao, H.J.; Merat, F.; High-speed router filter for blocking TCP flooding under DDoS attack, Performance, Computing, and Communications Conference, 2003. Conference Proceedings of the 2003 IEEE International, 9-11 April 2003, Pages:183 – 190
7. CERT Coordination Center. Internet Denial of Service Attacks and the Federal Response, Feb.2000. http://www.cert.org/congressional_testimony/Fithen_testimony_Feb29.html
8. Grossmann A. Wavelet transform and edge detection, Stochastics processes in physics and engineering, Hazeaingke Meds., Dorecht,Reidel,1986.
9. Stephane Mallat and Wen Liang Hwang. Singularity Detection and Processing with Wavelets. IEEE Transactions on Information Theory, Vol.38, No.2, March 1992
10. Mallat S. Zero-crossing of wavelet transform, IEEE Trans. On Information Theory,1997,37(4),1019-1033
11. Mallat S, Zhong S F, Characterization of signals from multiscale edges. IEEE Trans. On Pattern Analysis and Machine Intelligence, 1992,14(u),710-732
12. S. Mallat and refs. Within, "A Theory for Multiresolution Signal Decomposition: the Wavelet Representation", IEEE Trans. On Pattern Anal. And Mach. Intell., Vol. 11, pp.674-693,1989
13. Garcia, R.C.; Sadiku, M.N.O.; Cannady, J.D.; WAID: wavelet analysis intrusion detection, Circuits and Systems, 2002. MWSCAS-2002. The 2002 45th Midwest Symposium on, Volume: 3, 4-7 Aug. 2002, Pages:III-688 - III-691 vol.3
14. Nash, D.A.; Ragsdale, D.J.; Simulation of self-similarity in network utilization patterns as a precursor to automated testing of intrusion detection systems, Systems, Man and Cybernetics, Part A, IEEE Transactions on, Volume: 31, Issue: 4, July 2001, Pages:327 – 331
15. A. Grossmann and J. Morlet, "Decomposition of Hardy functions into square integrable wavelets of constant shape" SIAM J. Math., vol.15, pp.723-736, 1984
16. A.V. Oppenheim, R.W. Sehafer. Digital Signal Processing. Englewood Cliffs, NJ Prentice-Hall 1975.

Enhancing the Scalability of the Community Authorization Service for Virtual Organizations

Jian-Ping Yong[1], Kwok-Yan Lam[2], Siu-Leung Chung[3],
Ming Gu[2], and Jia-Guang Sun[2]

[1] School of Comp Sci & Telecom Engrg, Jiangsu University, Zhenjiang, P.R. China
yjp@ujs.edu.cn
[2] School of Software, Tsinghua University, Beijing, P.R. China
{lamky,guming,sunjg}@tsinghua.edu.cn
[3] School of Business Administration, The Open University of Hong Kong
slchung@ouhk.edu.hk

Abstract. Grid computing has emerged as a special form of distributed computing and is distinguished from conventional distributed computing by its focus on dynamic, large-scale resource sharing over a wide geographic distribution. Grid Computing System (GCS) is a distributed system infrastructure over which distributed applications with cross-organization resource sharing are operated. Grid applications are modelled by the notion of virtual organization which is generally composed of participants from different organizations driven by specific tasks. In order to control participation and access to shared resource, authorization is essential in VO. Authorization in VO is challenging because of the dynamic and distributed nature of VO. A community authorization service (CAS) was proposed recently to meet the Grid challenges and to enforce fine-grained access control policies in the VO. However, the situation is aggravated when VO is used to model business application systems such as financial systems of commercial enterprises where security and accountability are of key concerns. The emphasis on separation of duties in business applications only make things worse. This paper aims to address these authorization issues when the GCS is used to support business applications. In this paper, we introduce the use of threshold closure as a tool for enhancing the CAS in order for the Grid to better support commercial VO.

Keywords: Grid organization tools, Virtual organization, Authorization service.

1 Introduction

The pervasive growth of the global Internet has created significant impact on the design of distributed computing systems. Starting in the $80s$ as a platform for sharing data and expensive equipment in a local area environment, distributed computing systems of today typically cover wide geographic areas and are used as a model for organizing and implementing large-scale business applications.

C.-H. Chi and K.-Y. Lam (Eds.): AWCC 2004, LNCS 3309, pp. 182–193, 2004.

More notably, in recent years, the Grid Computing System (GCS) has emerged as a special form of distributed computing and is distinguished from conventional distributed computing systems by its focus on dynamic and larger-scale resource sharing over a wide geographical distribution [1]. In contrast to conventional distributed computing systems, GCS may be viewed as a sophisticated distributed computing system with high-level abstractions and services to facilitate large-scale sharing of resources in a dynamic manner.

Resource sharing in GCS is built on the VO model [1]. VO is an abstraction for designing distributed systems that aims to provide a flexible abstraction for implementing distributed systems with complex inter-process relationships. The objectives of GCS are to facilitate coordinated resource sharing and problem solving in dynamic, multi-institutional VO. A key requirement of VO is the ability to negotiate resource-sharing arrangements among a set of parties and then use the resulting resource pool for achieving some application objectives. A set of participants defined by such sharing relationship/rules (also known as authorization policies) form a VO. The major issue in GCS is the provision of services and protocols that facilitate formation of VO and enforcement of the authorization policies of the VO.

The notion of VO has enabled GCS to support a wide variety of applications beyond scientific computing. In particular, recent development in e-commerce has made the concept of VO especially suitable for organizing and implementing distributed commercial applications. For example, financial applications in commercial enterprises typically require large-scale sharing of information resources (financial budget, capital expenses and man-day charges) by participating organizations.

The management of VO has become a critical issue in order for VO to be applied to business applications. The need to specify and enforce complex authorization policies is a key problem associated with the formation and operation of VO. Due to the dynamic and distributed nature of GCS, authorization policies of VO are difficult to manage. One needs to have mechanisms that are capable of expressing complex authorization policies involving a large number of participants. Worse yet, such policies are expected to be updated dynamically when participants join and leave the VO.

Besides, the enforcement of complex authorization policies incurs heavy processing overhead on resource managers which control access to shared resources. While resource providers most likely have their own access control mechanisms for enforcing authorization policies, fine-grained task-specific authorization policies are commonplaces for cross-organizational sharing. Such policies will introduce further burdens on the resource managers.

To allow enforcement of fine-grained authorization in a scalable manner, the notion of a community authorization service (CAS) was introduced [2]. The CAS implements VO-specific authorization policies which are represented in form of access control lists (ACL) at the CAS policy database.

However, the CAS has limitations for supporting Grid applications when ACL cannot efficiently represent complex authorization policies. As pointed out by [3], ACL cannot efficiently represent complex authorization policies that comply with control requirements of commercial enterprises such as separation of duties and dual control. This is especially so when enterprise financial applications are being modelled by VO. In the case of financial applications, the rights to modify a shared data may mean authority on some allocated budget for a specific task. Thus precise representation of access rights in form authorization policies on shared resources plays a key role in VO management. The crux of the problem being that commercial operations typically are governed by corporate policies which impose stringent control on financial systems. Accountability and liability protection measures such as separation of duties and dual control are always enforced when accessing financial resources. In these cases, access to resources almost invariably requires that access be authorized by a group of approved users from different organizations.

In this paper, we propose an enhancement to the CAS so as to facilitate support of business applications by GCS. The rest of the paper is organized as follows. The design of the community authorization service will be discussed in Section 2. This is followed by a discussion of the authorization issues when VO is applied to implement commercial applications. Section 4 reviews the concept of threshold closure as a basic mechanism for representing complex VO authorization policies. Section 5 proposes an enhancement to community authorization service based on the concept of threshold closure, it also explains the advantages of threshold closure in meeting the authorization needs of VO. Section 6 concludes the discussion of this paper.

2   The Community Authorization Service

Authorization service is one of the key system services of GCS. GCS is a system infrastructure for supporting distributed applications. VO is a model for building Grid applications that implement collaborative computing. VO is specified by the set of participants, the shared resources and the policies for using the resources. Such policies are called authorization policies and are specified as part of the VO description and enforced during the operations of VO. Authorization is therefore important for supporting VO formation and operations.

Specification of authorization policies is an integral part of VO management. A VO is composed of a set of participants sharing some allocated resources for accomplishing some specific task. The shared resources are owned and managed by their respective resource managers. Typically, a resource manager allocates certain resources for use by a VO. The use of the resources by the VO participants have to be regulated and controlled by the authorization policies specified by the resource managers. The proper functioning of the VO is largely affected by the correct and precise specification of the authorization policies. Therefore, authorization policies form an integral part of the VO definition and needs to be specified properly as part of the VO management efforts.

However, using a simple authorization approach as such will greatly affect the scalability of VO operations. In general, detailed descriptions of the control on use of shared resources are usually task-specific and are implemented as part of the program logic of the VO modules. The basic access control mechanisms implemented by resource managers may not be expressive enough to support task-specific policies. Furthermore, even if it is possible to specify such policies at the resource managers, the resource managers will most likely be overloaded if they are also responsible for the enforcement of such policies during the operations of the VO.

The introduction of fine-grained authorization at resource managers will greatly affect the scalability of the VO and GCS as an infrastructure for supporting VO. While fine-grained authorization policies are essential for ensuring proper functioning of VO and integrity of the resources, typical access control mechanisms implemented by resource managers usually do not support specification of fine-grained authorization policies. Even if they do, it is highly inefficient to enforce fine-grained policies at the resource manager because, in this case, the resource manager will have to go through the complex authorization policies during the processing of each VO operation.

To address this, the concept of Community Authorization Service (CAS) was introduced [2]. Though the Globus Toolkit implemented GSI protocols and APIs to address Grid security needs, it focus primarily on authentication and message protection. The GSI provides an implementation of security infrastructure in Globus that aims to meet the aforementioned requirements [4, 5]. GSI provides a number of services for Grid applications, including mutual authentication and single sign-on. GSI is based on public key infrastructure, X.509 certificates, and the Secure Socket Layer (SSL) communication protocol. The GSI provides a delegation capability, by extending the standard SSL protocol, to simplify the security interface to the Grid user. The delegation function is implemented using a new entity called "proxy". A proxy is created to represent the user, within a time limit, in a Grid application. The proxy's private key is a short-term key, thus has a less stringent security requirement as the owner's private key. The use of short-term digital certificate for implementing security that aims to balance risk and efficiency is discussed in [6]. The proxy also serves as the basis of the single sign-on implemented by Globus which provides a mechanism by which a process can authenticate to its user proxy or another process.

In recent efforts of Globus, the CAS has been added to the Globus Toolkit [2]. CAS augments the existing local mechanisms provided via GSI and enables community policies to be enforced based on the user's GSI identity, which is constant across resources. The architecture of CAS is shown in Figure 1 which shows that ACL is used as the basic authorization mechanism of CAS in Globus Tookit.

With this extension of the GSI, resources allocated to a VO are managed by the CAS. Authorization rights on the allocated resources are also granted by the resource manager to the CAS. The CAS in turn implements a fine-grained authorization policy that controls access to all shared resources by the VO participants. With the deployment of CAS as a system service, access to resources by the participants must be authorized by the CAS which implements an au-

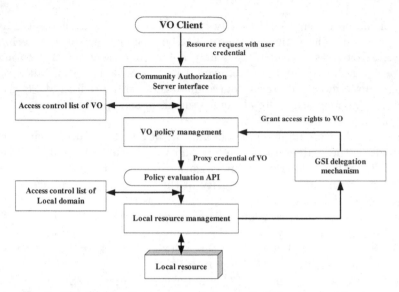

Fig. 1. The Globus Community Authorization Service Architecture

thorization database of fine-grained policies. The CAS must first check that it is authorized by the resource manager to access the resource and, if so, further checks against its policies database to ensure that such an access by the participant is authorized by the fine-grained policies specified during VO formation.

In the current design of CAS, ACL is being used as the underlying mechanism for specifying authorization policies. The use of ACL restricts the ability of CAS to handle complex policies as typical in VO. Due to the dynamic nature of sharing relationships in VO, security solutions for GCS must allow applications to coordinate diverse access control policies and to operate securely in heterogeneous environments. VO may grow and shrink dynamically, acquiring resources when solving a problem and releasing them when they not needed.

In the next section, we further discuss the authorization issues of VO when the concept is applied to commercial applications. Through this discussion, we suggest that ACL is insufficient for supporting authorization services for commercial VO. Thus we further propose the use of a new mechanism, namely the threshold closure, which is suitable for specifying complex authorization policies.

3 Authorization Issues for Commercial VO

Authorization is a critical service in GSI because of its important role in VO management. Authorization policy is important for controlling access to resources in GCS. GCS needs a flexible and scalable authorization service to support the management of complex VO structures.

The need for supporting commercial applications over the GCS introduces new research problems that need to be addressed in order to enhance the pervasiveness of GCS. While the CAS offers a sophisticated approach for implementing authorization service in Grid applications, in order to support complex policies typical in commercial applications, the existing approach needs to be enhanced in order to support the authorization needs of commercial VO efficiently.

In the case of financial applications for example, authorization policies needed will be much more complicated. Consider the situation that the rights to modify a shared data may mean authority on some allocated budget for a specific task. Thus precise representation of access rights in form authorization policies on shared resources plays a key role in VO management. This is because commercial operations typically are governed by corporate policies which impose stringent control on financial systems. Accountability and liability protection measures such as separation of duties and dual control are always enforced when accessing financial resources. In these cases, access to resources almost invariably requires that access be authorized by a group of approved users from different organizations.

Though ACL is used widely as a means for describing authorization policies in GCS, the limitations of ACL cannot be overlooked. Basically, ACL specifies the access rights a principal has on an object or resource. Firstly, the expressive power of ACL is very restrictive, it can only directly express policies such as "who can do what" and is a lot more clumsy to express complex access policies such as "any three of the five officers can authorize capital expenses chargeable to the budget". In this case, the ACL needs to be generalized to include groups in addition to individuals, and the "3 out of 5" policy is implemented by a number of group access rules. Secondly, when authorization policies change, a large number of ACL operations are needed to update the policy descriptions. For example, if the "3 out of 5" rule is changed and become "3 out of 6", then a lot of ACL operations will be needed in order to ensure that the ACL remains consistent with the security policy. Some other shortcomings of ACL are described in [7].

Despite its simplicity, systems using ACL cannot efficiently handle complex access control policies such as those described above. Since ACL cannot express these policies easily, the security administrator needs to analyze these policies and decides to create groups in order to facilitate description of complex policies. Obviously, it is inefficient to maintain the ACL in this manner. Besides, in order to cope with policy changes, the designer needs to analyze the policy rules and the corresponding ACL frequently. It is clear that the cost becomes huge when there is a large number of participants and resources. Thus, the authorization issues of VO are not straightforward even to implement such a simple policy in an efficient and effective manner.

Authorization of VO is not straightforward because of the complex and dynamic nature of authorization policies needed by VO. In the next section, we introduce a tool for enhancing the CAS in order for GCS to support commercial VO more efficiently. In essence, our scheme adopts the use of threshold closure [8], which is an optimal collection of threshold schemes [9], as the basis of the authorization service. The proposed approach is practical because it is possible to segregate the policy and mechanism aspects of threshold closure. With this approach, the complex and dynamic policies are specified by a threshold closure which allows the construction of a simple ACL efficiently. With the simplified ACL, enforcement of the policies may be achieved using the existing CAS mechanisms available from the GSI. In short, the enhanced community authorization service for VO proposed here will meet the following key requirements:

- Ability to represent complex and dynamic security policies efficiently.
- Can be implemented efficiently over existing security infrastructure of GCS.

4   Threshold Closure

In this section, we review the concept of threshold closure which is a new approach for implementing complex authorization policies. The proposed enhancement of CAS will be based on threshold closure. Threshold closure is a cryptographic scheme that facilitates implementation of the notion of access structure which is the most flexible structure for specifying authorization policies.

To allow efficient implementation of access structures and at the same time address the security management issues of threshold schemes, threshold closure was proposed by [8] as an efficient and flexible approach to secret sharing. A threshold closure is an efficient approach for representing an access structure by specifying a collection of threshold schemes. Besides, a threshold closure is an optimal collection of threshold schemes such that it uses the minimum number of threshold schemes to represent the policy rules of the original collection of threshold schemes. Therefore, complex authorization policies may be represented using an access structure (with each authorized set in the access structure represented by a threshold scheme) which is then translated to a threshold closure which in turn can be implemented efficiently using an optimal collection of threshold schemes.

In distributed computing systems such as the GCS, the authorized sets represented in an access structure will be excessively large due to the complex authorization policies and the large number of potential participants/users. Therefore the threshold closure algorithm is attractive for effectiveness and efficiency reasons. To facilitate discussion of the new authorization service, we briefly recap the concept of threshold closure. A threshold closure, denoted as ε, is a collection of (t, S)-threshold schemes (S is a set of l users such that $0 < t \leq |S|, S \subseteq P$ where P is the set of all potential participants/users), and satisfies the three conditions:

1. Redundant-free i.e. there do not exist two distinct $(t_1, S_1), (t_2, S_2) \in \varepsilon$ such that

$$S_1 \subseteq S_2 \text{ or } |S_1 \cap S_2| \geq \min\{t_1, t_2\}, t_1 \neq t_2.$$

2. Reduced i.e. there do not exist $(t, S_1), (t, S_2), \ldots, (t, S_m) \in \varepsilon$ such that

$$\bigcup_{i=1}^{m} [S_i]_t = [\bigcup_{i=1}^{m} S_i]_t.$$

where

$$[S]_t = \{S' : |S'| = t, S' \subseteq S\}.$$

3. Closed i.e. $\forall (t, S_1), (t, S_2), \ldots, (t, S_m) \in \varepsilon$ and $S'_1 \subseteq S_1, S'_2 \subseteq S_2, \ldots, S'_m \subseteq S_m$ ("=" cannot be held by all) if

$$\bigcup_{i=1}^{m} [S'_i]_t = [\bigcup_{i=1}^{m} S'_i]_t$$

then

$$(t, \bigcup_{i=1}^{m} S'_i) \in \varepsilon, \text{ or}$$

$$(t, \bigcup_{i=1}^{m} S'_i) \notin \varepsilon \text{ and } (\exists (t, S) \in \varepsilon) \bigcup_{i=1}^{m} S'_i \subset S.$$

It was proven in [8] that there exists a one-to-one correspondence between access structure Γ_0 and threshold closure ε. In addition, the $\min(\varepsilon)$ which is the minimal covering of threshold closure ε can be obtained. After implementing the algorithm of converting Γ_0 to ε, the number of the threshold schemes in the destination threshold closure is very much smaller than the number of the authorized sets in the access structure.

Besides, [8] also introduced four kinds of operation on Γ_0 and ε to allow authorization policies to be dynamically changed efficiently. The operations are:

1. Add (t, S) into ε.
2. Add S into Γ_0.
3. Delete (t, S) from ε.
4. Delete S from Γ.

The consistency between Γ_0 and ε can be maintained using these four operations. In fact, the authorization policies are changed frequently in real world scenarios. As such, the threshold closure also needs to be dynamic in order to correctly represent the access structure. By exploring these convenient operations, the threshold closure not only can expand and contract freely but also preserve its permanent consistency with the dynamic access structure. Therefore we can see that threshold closure has better efficiency and scalability while it keeps the high express power of other general access structure schemes.

5   Enhancing the Community Authorization Service

In this section, we propose enhancing the CAS with threshold closure as a mechanism for representing authorization policies. We study the rationale behind the use of threshold closure in the place of ACL in CAS. We then explain threshold closure may be integrated with existing CAS architecture smoothly.

ACL is one of the simplest approach for specifying authorization policies. Authorization of resource access is implemented by firstly specifying the identity of a user in the ACL maintained by the resource manager; and secondly requiring the user to authenticate himself/herself to the resource manager. Access is granted if the user's identity is listed in the ACL and the accessing party is the authentic user. ACL is simple to implement but usually inconvenient to use in real situations. Almost invariable, ACL is extended to include groups in addition to individual users. As such, the ACL is supplemented by some group membership mechanism.

Though ACL may support group access control in order to cater for more complex authorization policies, it is inefficient when describing security policies typical in commercial applications. For example, dual control and separation of duties are typical in business applications, and the security policies are typically of the form "access is allowed if any three of the five directors agree". In this connection, the threshold scheme was proposed for implementing access control [9]. With a (t, l) threshold scheme, a secret key needed for accessing the resource is split into l pieces such that any t (or more) of the l pieces are needed to reconstruct the secret, hence enabling access to the resource.

The beauty of the threshold scheme is that it is a simple mechanism for describing the "t out of l" authorization rules. More importantly, such rules can be directly implemented very efficiently using threshold cryptography [9]. Hence, a collection of threshold schemes may be used to efficiently implement the kind of security policies described before. The threshold scheme is attractive because it is computationally efficient and only involves the computation of a simple Lagrange interpolation. However, its expressive power is still very limited as it was proven that threshold schemes cannot express authorization policies in many cases [10]. For example, it cannot specify exactly which subset of participants is allowed to determine the secret and which is not. Therefore, the concept of access structure for representing complex secret sharing schemes was proposed by [11]. Unfortunately, access structures are difficult to implement. Furthermore, the use of threshold schemes will be tedious if the policies they represent are dynamic. For example, when more "t out of l" rules are added to the system, it is highly likely that the overall collection of threshold schemes are redundant, thus leading to serious security management problems [8].

To illustrate the advantages of threshold closure as an underlying mechanism for implementing authorization in VO, The following table compares the characteristics of the various schemes including ACL, threshold scheme, general access structure scheme and threshold closure.

Scheme	Easy to implement	Easy to manage	Performance efficiency	Good expressive power	Scalability
ACL	√	√	√		
Threshold Scheme	√	√			√
Genera Access Structure scheme				√	
Threshold closure	√	√	√	√	√

Although threshold closure is a desirable approach for specifying complex access control policies, there are practical constraints when they are implemented in a distributed computing system. For example, it is impossible to revoke a group once the secret shares are distributed to the group members unless the secret is changed. However, this will mean reconstructing and re-distributing the secret for all groups - an effort which is not practical in a large scale distributed environment. Besides, the implementation of threshold cryptography cannot leverage on the existing security infrastructure assumed by CAS. For example, the CAS of Globus is a ACL-based authorization service. In order to implement threshold closure in such a system, an additional security infrastructure based on threshold cryptography will be needed. This will be a serious concern for security practitioners, thus they are unlikely to adopt threshold closure for building a practical authorization service for GCS.

To this end, we make use of the result presented by [3] which addresses the implementation issues of threshold closure by segregating the policy and mechanism aspects of threshold schemes. It was noted by [3] that a threshold scheme is a simple security mechanism for enforcing a simple security policy of the form "access is allowed if any t or more out of l users make the request together". In other words, a threshold scheme implemented using threshold cryptography is both a security policy and a security mechanism. An access structure, however, is a complex security policy which is not easy to enforce due to the lack of suitable security mechanisms. The threshold closure was designed to be an efficient structure that represents the complex policies of an access structure using an optimal collection of threshold schemes. That means a threshold closure, like the threshold schemes, is both a security policy and a security mechanism.

To summarize, in this section, we studied the limitations of ACL as an underlying mechanism for building the authorization service of VO. We concluded that threshold closure is a most suitable approach for use in this scenario. However, threshold closure cannot be implemented directly using threshold cryptography for practical reasons. We suggest that the CAS service of Globus be enhanced by adopting the threshold closure as an approach for representing and managing authorization policies. However, the policies are not implemented using threshold cryptography. Instead, they are converted into an optimal collection of ACLs so that existing security infrastructure of distributed computing systems may be used to implement the enforcement mechanism.

With the enhanced CAS for VO, we adopt the threshold closure as a structure for representing and processing security policies while the enforcement is still achieved using the traditional ACL approach. In our proposed approach, the CAS server uses a threshold closure for representing authorization policies so that they can be manipulated as the VO participants/users change. However, the threshold closure, which is a collection of threshold schemes, is not implemented directly using threshold cryptography. Instead, the collection of (t, l) policies are stored explicitly at the authorization server. If a group of users need to access a shared resource, they need to authenticate themselves to the authorization server which in turn will check against the optimal set of (t, l) rules before deciding if the access should be granted.

The threshold closure is a pragmatic approach for implementing an effective, scalable and efficient community authorization service in a cost-efficient manner. This approach of authorization service for VO has the following advantages:

- It uses the rich expressive power of access structure and the scalability of threshold closure.
- It is implemented on simple and practical mechanisms available in typical security infrastructure i.e. ACL in CAS.

6   Conclusion

The notion of VO has enabled GCS to support a wide variety of applications beyond scientific computing. In particular, recent development in e-commerce has made the concept of VO especially suitable for organizing and implementing distributed commercial applications. For example, financial applications in commercial enterprises typically require large-scale sharing of information resources (financial budget, capital expenses and man-day charges) by participating organizations.

The management of VO has become a critical issue in order for VO to be applied to business applications. The need to specify and enforce complex authorization policies is a key problem associated with the formation and operation of VO. Besides, the enforcement of complex authorization policies incurs heavy processing overhead on resource managers which control access to shared resources. To allow enforcement of fine-grained authorization in a scalable manner, the notion of a community authorization service (CAS) was introduced. The CAS implements VO-specific authorization policies which are represented in form of access control lists (ACL) at the CAS policy database. However, the CAS has limitations for supporting Grid applications when ACL cannot efficiently represent complex authorization policies.

Authorization service is one of the key system services of GCS for supporting VO formation and operations. Specification of authorization policies is an integral part of VO management. The proper functioning of the VO is largely affected by the correct and precise specification of the authorization policies. However, using a simple authorization approach such as ACL will greatly affect the scalability of VO operations. The introduction of fine-grained authorization at resource managers will greatly affect the scalability of the VO and GCS as an infrastructure for supporting VO. To address this, the concept of Community Authorization Service (CAS) was introduced.

In recent efforts of Globus, the CAS has been added to the Globus Toolkit. CAS augments the existing local mechanisms provided via GSI and enables community policies to be enforced based on the user's GSI identity, which is constant across resources. In the current design of CAS, ACL is being used as the underlying mechanism for specifying authorization policies. The use of ACL restricts the ability of CAS to handle complex policies as typical in VO.

In this paper, we proposed an enhancement to the CAS so as to facilitate support of business applications by GCS. We reviewed the concept of threshold closure and analyzed the drawbacks of the existing CAS which uses ACL for representing authorization policies. We then identified threshold closure as a most suitable mechanism for specifying complex authorization policies typical in commercial VO. We conclude that the use of threshold closure can enhance the scalability of CAS and allow the Grid to better support commercial applications especially those that need to comply with financial control measures.

Acknowledgement

This research was partly funded by the National 863 Plan (Projects Numbers: 2003AA148020), P. R. China and the Grid Security project of PrivyLink International Limited (Singapore).

References

1. I. Foster, C. Kesselman, S. Tuecke. "The anatomy of the grid: enabling scalable virtual organizations", *Int. J. Supercomputer Applications*, Vol. 15, Issue 3, 2001, pp. 200-222.
2. L. Pearlman, V. Welch, I. Foster, C. Kesselman, S. Tuecke. "A Community Authorization Service for Group Collaboration". *Proceedings of the IEEE 3rd International Workshop on Policies for Distributed Systems and Networks*, 2002.
3. X.B. Zhao, K.Y. Lam, S.L. Chung, M. Gu and J.G. Sun. "Authorization Mechanisms for Virtual Organizations in Distributed Computing Systems", 9th Australasian Conference On Information Security and Privacy (ACISP'04), Sydney, Australia, July 13-15, 2004, Springer-Verlag LNCS 3108, pp 414-426.
4. K.Y. Lam, X.B. Zhao, S.L. Chung, M. Gu, J.G. Sun. "Enhancing Grid Security Infrastructure to Support Mobile Computing Nodes", 4th International Workshop on Information Security Applications (WISA 2003), Jeju Island, Korea, August 25-27, 2003, Springer-Verlag LNCS 2908, pp 42-54.
5. "Overview of the Grid Security Infrastructure" at http://www-fp.globus.org/security/overview.html.
6. J.Y. Zhou and K.Y. Lam. "Securing digital signatures for non-repudiation", *Journal of Computer Communications*, Vol. 22, No. 8, 1999, pp. 710–716.
7. S.V. Nagaraj. "Access control in distributed object systems: problems with access control lists". *Enabling Technologies: Infrastructure for Collaborative Enterprises, 2001. WET ICE 2001. Proceedings. Tenth IEEE International Workshops*, 2001.
8. C.R. Zhang, K.Y. Lam, S. Jajodia. "Scalable threshold closure". *Theoretical Computer Science*, 226(1999) 185-206.
9. A. Shamir. "How to share a secret", *Communications of the ACM*, Vol 22, No 11, 1979, pp. 612-613.
10. J.C. Benaloh, J. Leichter. "Generalized secret sharing and monotone functions". *Advances in Cryptology-CRYPTO'88, Lecture Notes in Computer Science*, vol.403, Springer, Berlin, 1989, pp27-35.
11. M. Ito, A. Saito, T. Nishizeki. "Secret sharing scheme realizing general access structure". in Globecom'87, Tokyo, Japan, 1987, pp.99-102.

Securing Multicast Groups in Ad Hoc Networks

Hartono Kurnio[1], Huaxiong Wang[1], Josef Pieprzyk[1], and Kris Gaj[2]

[1] Centre for Advanced Computing – Algorithms and Cryptography
Department of Computing, Macquarie University
Sydney, NSW 2109, Australia
{hkurnio,hwang,josef}@ics.mq.edu.au
[2] Electrical and Computer Engineering, George Mason University
4400 University Drive, Fairfax, VA 22030
kgaj@gmu.edu

Abstract. We propose a reliable and ubiquitous group key distribution scheme that is suitable for ad hoc networks. The scheme has *self-initialisation* and *self-securing* features. The former feature allows a cooperation of an arbitrary number of nodes to initialise the system, and it also allows node admission to be performed in a decentralised fashion. The latter feature allows a group member to determine the group key remotely while maintaining the system security.

We also consider a decentralised solution of establishing secure point-to-point communication. The solution allows a new node to establish a secure channel with every existing node if it has pre-existing secure channels with a threshold number of the existing nodes.

1 Introduction

An ad hoc network allows a collection of wireless devices or nodes to communicate each others without relying on any fixed infrastructure such as base stations. A node can establish direct communication with other nodes that are within its transmission range. The networking functions depend on the cooperation of the wireless nodes, where packet transmissions between two distant nodes are forwarded by a chain of intermediate nodes that is reachable by both. A multicast group consists of nodes communicating over a multicast channel. Multicasting is a popular media transmission for the group communication for its efficient mechanism of delivering packets from a source to a group of recipients. The sender only sends a copy of the message which will be replicated within the network and delivered to multiple recipients. The efficient bandwith requirement of multicast group is paramount in ad hoc networks that have limited resources. Note that several multicast routing mechanisms over ad hoc networks have been proposed in literature, see [14] for instance.

Wireless communications are usually implemented using broadcasting which is wide open to public access, and so multicast groups in ad hoc networks are prone to security attacks ranging from passive eavesdropping to active interfering. Securing group communication in ad hoc environments is important especially in military operations and rescue of hostages where communication among troops must be kept secret and authentic. Also, instantaneous conferences and classrooms need to ensure that only registered members can access the content.

C.-H. Chi and K.-Y. Lam (Eds.): AWCC 2004, LNCS 3309, pp. 194–207, 2004.
© Springer-Verlag Berlin Heidelberg 2004

A common way of securing multicast groups is to establish a cryptographic key known only to the group members. The group key will be used to provide secure and authentic communication within the group[1]. A multicast group is dynamic and at any time, some nodes may leave or some new nodes may join the group; the compromised nodes must be evicted from the group. To maintain security, the group key must be updated whenever the group membership changes. A group key distribution scheme provides algorithms to establish and maintain the group key. Each group member is required to hold an individual set of secret keys. When updating a group key, a rekeying message is multicast to the system and members of the new group use this information and their individual secret key sets to determine the new common key, while outsiders cannot do so. Consequently, when a new node joins the group, it needs to obtain an individual key set to be able to participate in the group operation.

Securing group communication in ad hoc networks is a challenging task since it must take into account the characteristics of the environments. An ideal group key distribution scheme for ad hoc networks will have the following basic properties:

(1) **Secure.** Wireless network is open to eavesdropping attack and wireless devices typically have low physical security (easy to be either stolen or compromised). A group key distribution system has to consider these vulnerabilities in the security assessments. That is, the designer of the system has to assume that the adversaries obtain access to all communications transmitted through the networks, including multicast messages for rekeying, and they also have the knowledge of some portion of individual secret key sets in the system. The system must satisfy the requirement of at any time, only group members, and no other nodes, knowing the common key of the group. The security goal normally includes three main security goals required in ad hoc group communication. They are:

- **Session secrecy:** Ensures that a collusion of nodes that leave a group cannot discover the common key of the new group. We may view the leaving nodes as revoked nodes of the particular session. The revocation is on temporary basis where the revoked nodes might be members of any future groups. This security goal is required in numerous scenarios, for example, delegates of the same organisation would like to have private discussion in the middle of an ad hoc meeting by temporarily revoking delegates from other organisations.
- **Forward secrecy:** Ensures that a collusion of nodes that leaves a group cannot discover the common keys of the group for all future communications[2]. The leaving nodes are permanently revoked from the system. Such nodes include compromised/corrupted nodes, crash nodes or nodes that are out of mission in a battlefield scenario and they must not access the communication during the rest of the system lifetime.

---

[1] Authenticity in this context is to ensure that the message is originated from a member of the group. Note that the authorship of the message may not be known to the other members.

[2] The leaving nodes might know all previous group keys.

- **Backward secrecy:** Ensures that a collusion of new nodes that join a group cannot discover the keys used by the group in the past. Joining the group allows the new nodes to participate in any current and future groups. This security goal is required in ad hoc admission where a node joins only for a certain time interval.

(2) **Decentralised.** Ad hoc networks usually involve mobile nodes that are subject to frequent changes of network topology. This dynamic behaviour is also influenced by group membership changes, node failures and channel errors. The group key distribution system should be able to function under these conditions. Relying on a single entity (trusted authority) to perform security operations has drawbacks such as (i) a single point of failure where the entity could be unavailable (because of congestion or DoS attacks such as *Smurf* at network layer and *SYN flooding* at transport layer) or unreachable by other nodes, and (ii) a single point of attack where compromising the entity means revealing all the system secrets. A decentralised model alleviates these problems by distributing the trust to all nodes in the network, and contributions from a number of nodes are required to perform security operations. This model allows the system to provide continuous and ubiquitous security services for mobile nodes despite the network condition. Also, the system is more resistant to attack where a single compromised node will not bring the entire system down.

(3) **Efficient.** A group key distribution system in ad hoc networks must require low amount of communication, computation and secure storage to perform security operations. These requirements are to accommodate the limited bandwidth in ad hoc networks and the limited energy and secure memory of mobile devices. A more efficient system implies a smaller response time, that is, the time elapsed between starting and completing a security operation. A smaller response time is important in ad hoc group applications since membership changes frequently and in short period of time, requiring fast key updates.

(4) **Scalable.** Another desired property of group key distribution systems is scalability for large groups *while preserving efficiency of the systems*. For example, in a battlefield scenario the system must work well for a small number of troop as well as for large numbers with hundreds or thousands of army troops.

In this paper we focus on the secure communication protocols for dynamic multicast groups in ad hoc networks, and assume the underlying wireless networks support multicast channel. We propose a group key distribution scheme that satisfies all of the basic properties described above. Our construction is based on Key Distribution Patters (KDPs) [12], and it has some desirable features such as self-initialisation and self-securing in which no trusted authority is required in system initialisation and key update, respectively[3].

We also consider a decentralised solution of establishing secure point-to-point communication. The solution allows a new node to establish a secure channel

---

[3] The terms *self-initialisation* and *self-securing* are also used in [10] and [11], respectively, but in different contexts.

with every existing node if it has pre-existing secure channels with a threshold number of the existing nodes. We use the idea of threshold cryptography and employ Blom key distribution scheme [2] in the construction.

Organisation of this paper. We first discuss several existing group key distribution systems and show their limitations in ad hoc environments in Section 2. Then we describe our proposed system that is suitable for ad hoc networks in Section 3, and give the construction in Section 4. We conclude this paper in Section 5.

2   Related Work and Drawbacks

Group key distribution schemes have been a popular research area and many schemes have been proposed, see for instance [20, 21, 4, 3, 16, 17, 1]. However, most of them consider traditional model of networking requiring wired and fixed infrastructure that is not suitable for ad hoc networks.

The schemes in [20, 21, 4] employ key hierarchy to implement an efficient key establishment for dynamic groups in multicast environments. In these schemes, each node in the tree corresponds to a key and each leaf corresponds to a user. A user's individual secret key set comprises of all keys along the path from his corresponding leaf to the root, and the individual secret key set has to be updated every time the group changes. Each scheme proposes different key generation and rekeying methods with the aim of reducing communication and storage costs. The authors of [13, 6] proposed revocation schemes in the context of broadcast encryption. They utilise binary tree structure to define a collection of user subsets and use a pseudo-random sequence generator to assign keys to the subsets. A user knows the keys corresponding to the subsets that contain him, but he only needs to store some fraction of the keys. In the revocation schemes, a sub-collection of disjoint subsets that partition all authorised users, but not contain any of the revoked users, needs to be found and the new group key is encrypted using the keys corresponding to the subsets. Although these solutions are secure, efficient and scalable for large groups, they are not suitable for ad hoc networks because of the requirement for a fixed trusted authority to perform all group operations.

The schemes in [7, 3, 16, 17] extend the two party Diffie-Hellman key exchange for multiple parties. The schemes are decentralised and require all parties to contribute for the initial group key establishment. The schemes in [7, 3] do not consider dynamic group membership and the update of group key is essentially equivalent to re-setup the system. The schemes in [16, 17] provide efficient protocols to update the group key. The work in [5] attempt to adapt the schemes in ad hoc networks. Nevertheless, they still involve excessive communication cost and computation cost in the system initialisation that are unbearable in most ad hoc applications.

The work in [22] and its extensions [8–10] consider security in ad hoc networks. Their approach is based on public key infrastructure (PKI) whereby any two entities might establish a secure and authentic channel using certificates carried by each of them. The schemes employ a t-out-of-n threshold secret sharing mechanism to distribute the certification authority function to n entities, in which each entity holds a secret share, and any t entities can collaboratively sign a public key. The scheme in [22] considers distribution of the function to n *special nodes* but it has a drawback that the special nodes may be multi-hop away or may move, so a reliable certification function is not guaranteed. The schemes in [9, 10] extend [22] to provide effective and ubiquitous certification service by enabling any t *local nodes* (one-hop away) to collaboratively perform the function. The PKI approach is suitable for secure point-to-point communication, but not for secure group communication (one-to-many, many-to-many, many-to-one). If the approach is used for group application, the sender needs to send a copy of the message to each node encrypted using the node's public key. This clearly results in high communication and computation costs. Therefore, the schemes, although have secure and decentralised solutions, they are only efficient for small groups.

3 Our Proposed System

We propose a group key distribution system using Key Distribution Patterns (KDPs). We consider a system of wireless ad hoc network with an upper bounded number of nodes, say n. Each node in the system has limited resource and it communicates with others via the bandwidth-constraint, error-prone, and insecure multicast channel. They may freely roam in the networks. Nodes in the system may form a secure group where all communication within the group is encrypted (symmetric encryption) using a group key. The number of nodes in the group may change over time because nodes temporarily or permanently leave, or new nodes join. A new group will have a new common key. Our security model tolerates a collusion of up to t adversaries to maintain session secrecy, forward secrecy or backward secrecy.

We assume each node P in the system has a globally unique identifier i, denoted by P_i. We also assume each node has a channel with other nodes for secure point-to-point communication. The secure channel can be realised by using a public-key based cryptosystem that is suitable for ad hoc networks such as [8], or as an alternative, private-key encryption in Section 4.3 can be employed for the purpose. We emphasize that secure point-to-point communication in our system is only for secure delivery of key information. Some desirable features of our system are as follows.

- *Self-initialisation* – It does not require a trusted authority to set up the system. Instead, a cooperation of ℓ, $\ell \leq n$, nodes can initilise the system and form a multicast group. First, they decide on mutually acceptable parameters of the underlying construction, i.e., key distribution patterns, that include the values of n and t [4]. Next, they cooperatively generate all system secrets and assist new nodes to join. When a new node joins the group, it obtains an individual secret key set from a subset of the existing nodes in the group,

---

[4] We do not consider the negotiation process in any detail and assume the initial nodes can reach a valid agreement.

called sponsors. The new joined node may be a sponsor for other new nodes. Note that this feature is desired in ad hoc networks where a group is usually formed in an ad hoc manner and node admission happens on the fly.

- *Self-securing* – Members of a new group can determine the common key by finding an appropriate combination of their secret keys, and no rekeying message is required in the key update. This implies a reliable and ubiquitous key update service since there is no transmission through unreliable wireless networks and all group members can compute the group key anywhere, anytime regarless the network topology. The key update method is also fault-tolerant as several faulty group members (node failures) will not affect the group key establishment at all (other group members still can determine the group key as if there is no faulty group members). The key update method is simple and very efficient since it requires (i) zero communication cost, and (ii) a group member to compute some elementary operations and to store a reasonable number of secret keys.

Distributed Establishment of Secure Channels

In ad hoc networks, the assumption that every pair of entities in the system can establish a secure channel using public key cryptosystem is not realistic, since it requires every entity in the system to hold a public-key certificate which is verifiable by all other entities. It is more realistic to assume that some, but not all, pre-existing point-to-point secure channels do exist.

We consider a scenario where any $t + 1$ nodes can cooperatively establish secure channels between a new node with other nodes assuming the new node has pre-existing secure channels with the $t + 1$ nodes. The channel between two nodes is secure against any collusion of at most t other nodes (an adversary must compromise $t+1$ nodes before she can listen to the private communication). The threshold t defines a tradeoff between service availability and security.

The secure channels are based on private-key setting where a symmetric encryption is used for secure communication. The system is more efficient than the system with public-key encryption since it requires less computation power compared to the public-key one. Also in a public-key encryption, allowing a node to have secure channels with all other nodes requires the node to store all public keys in the system, which consumes a large volume of memory.

4 Construction

We describe our architecture for the proposed group key distribution system. First we give some cryptographic primitives that will be employed in the construction. Later we will completely describe the protocols for the system.

4.1 Background

Key Distribution Patterns (KDPs). KDPs [12] are finite incidence structures that were originally designed to distribute keys between pairs of participants in a network in the absence of an online key distribution centre. A KDP is used to allocate a collection of subkeys to users in a system in such a way that any pair of users can compute a common key by finding an appropriate combinations of their subkeys. In general, a KDP can be defined as follows.

Definition 1. *Let $K = \{k_1, \ldots, k_v\}$ be a v-set and $\mathcal{B} = \{B_1, \ldots, B_n\}$ be a family of subsets of K. We call the set system $(K, \mathcal{B})$ a t-resilient (v, n, r) key distribution pattern (KDP) if the following condition holds: $\bigcap_{i \in \Delta} B_i \nsubseteq \bigcup_{j \in \Lambda} B_j$, where Δ and Λ are any disjoint subsets of $\{1, \ldots, n\}$ such that $|\Delta| = r$ and $|\Lambda| = t$.*

The KDP guarantees that for any r subsets, $\{B_{i_1}, \ldots, B_{i_r}\}$, and any t subsets, $\{B_{j_1}, \ldots, B_{j_t}\}$, where $\{B_{i_1}, \ldots, B_{i_r}\} \cap \{B_{j_1}, \ldots, B_{j_t}\} = \emptyset$, there exists at least an element k that belongs to the r subsets, but does not belong to the t subsets. This means, for a given r subsets or less, an arbitrary union of at most t other subsets cannot cover elements in the r subsets. A KDP with $|\Delta| = 2$ is considered in [12] and KDPs with more general size of Δ have been studied by Stinson et al (see for example [18, 19]).

Rationale. We may consider K is a set of keys and $\mathcal{B}$ is a collection of subsets of the keys. The KDP structure is public while keys of the KDP are secret. Therefore, given a t-resilient (v, n, r)-KDP, if we can distribute keys $K = \{k_1, \ldots, k_v\}$ to n nodes in such a way that each node P_i has a subset of keys B_i, then any r-subset $G = \{P_{i_1}, \ldots, P_{i_r}\}$ can come up with a common key without any interaction, that is $k_G = \bigoplus_{k \in \cap_{j=1}^{r} B_{i_j}} k$, where $\oplus$ denotes the exclusive-or operation (assuming that all the keys are strings of the same length). The common key k_G can be used to provide secure communication among nodes in G. For example, a node can send the ciphertext $E_{k_G}(m)$ of the plaintext m that can only be decrypted by other nodes in G. Any collusion of at most t nodes outside G cannot decrypt the plaintext m.

Observe that v corresponds to the number of keys in the system and naturally bounds the number of keys for each node P_i (the required secure memory to store keys in B_i). The trivial construction is to assign a key k to each d-subset of the n nodes, for all $d \leq r$, and every node obtains keys of subsets to which the node belongs. The construction is resilient to any number of colluders, however, observe that it has $v = \sum_{d=0}^{r} \binom{n}{d} = O(2^n)$ and every node has to store a huge number of keys.

An efficient KDP would be the one in which for given t, r, n the value v is as small as possible. An efficient KDP can achieve $v = O(\log n)$ that is shown in [19] as $v \geq 2c \frac{\binom{r+t}{r}}{\log(r+t)} \log n$, where the constant c is shown to be approximately $\frac{1}{8}$ in [15]. For example, given $t = 10, r = 5, n = 100$, and $c = \frac{1}{8}$, it gives $v \geq 1277$ keys. This number is very small compared to the trivial construction that gives $v = 79375495$ keys.

A lot of research has been done for efficient KDP construction with bounds on various parameters, such as in [18]. Note that the restriction on the collusion size is reasonable in most applications since it is unlikely that all unauthorised nodes are the colluders. In practice, a KDP must be designed with respect to the nature of group applications. For example, military applications require high collusion resistance in which case the underlying KDP will have a large t value.

The KDP structure can be represented as a $n \times v$ table $T = [e_{i,j}]$, where row i is indexed by $B_i \in \mathcal{B}$ and column j is indexed by $k_j \in K$, and where each entry $e_{i,j}$ is either 0 or 1 such that $e_{i,j} = 1$ if and only if $k_j \in B_i$. The entries can be represented as bits (there are $n \times v$ bits) and they are stored by each node.

Blom's Key Distribution Scheme. Blom's scheme [2] allows any pair of users in the network to compute a secret key without any interaction. The scheme is said to be t unconditional secure if, given a specified pair of users, any collusion of t or fewer users (disjoint from the two) cannot compute the secret key shared by the two. The scheme uses a symmetric polynomial $F(x, y)$ over a finite field $GF(q)$ in the construction. That is, $F(x, y) = \sum_{i=0}^{t} \sum_{j=0}^{t} h_{i,j} x^i y^j \bmod p$, where $h_{i,j} \in GF(q)(0 \leq i \leq t, 0 \leq j \leq t)$ and $h_{i,j} = h_{j,i}$ for all i, j. The polynomial $F(x, y)$ has a symmetry property, that is, $F(a, b) = F(b, a)$ for any $a, b \in GF(q)$. Blom's scheme requires a trusted authority to distribute the keys to the users. We will slighly modify the scheme to support decentralised setting.

Rationale. Given a symmetric polynomial $F(x, y)$, if we can distribute the polynomial $F(x, i)$ to every node P_i in the system, then any two nodes P_{i_1}, P_{i_2} can establish a secret key $F(i_1, i_2) = F(i_2, i_1)$, which can be used for secure communication. For example, P_{i_1} can send a ciphertext $E_{F(i_1,i_2)}(m)$ that can only be decrypted by P_{i_2}. Any collusion of at most t other nodes cannot learn the plaintext m.

The threshold t gives the balance between storage requirement and collusion resistance. An extreme case is to allow an arbitrary number of colluder that requires each pair of nodes to be independently assigned a secret key. This requires a total of $\binom{n}{2} \approx \frac{1}{2}n^2$ secret keys and each node must store $n - 1$ secret keys, which is unbearable if n is large. By using Blom's scheme, a node needs to store a polynomial of degree at most t, whereas at least $t+1$ nodes must collude (an adversary must break in at least $t + 1$ nodes) to discover the system secret $F(x, y)$. (In fact, t corrupted nodes will not reveal the secret key between any pair of other nodes.)

4.2   The Group Key Distribution Scheme

We assume each node has a secure channel with every other node in the system. If PKI is used to establish the secure channels, each node has to store certificates of all other nodes. As an alternative, the solution in Section 4.3 can be applied for the purpose in which each node is required to store a polynomial of degree at most t. A secure channel is for secure transmission of key information.

The straightforward scheme to establish a common key for each new created group is as follows. A selected node randomly generates a group key and sends it to all other nodes in the group through secure channels. The scheme has minimum secure memory requirement as each node holds just key information for the secure channel, and it is secure against an arbitrary number of colluders.

However, the scheme requires large amount of communication as the number of transmissions is equal to the number of nodes in the group. Ad hoc group applications require frequent group changes, and consequently, the total communication overhead required to establish all group keys will be prohibitively high. Also, the source may be unreachable by the recipients because of dynamic network topology, so the reliability of every key update cannot be guaranteed.

Our proposed scheme has several advantages over the straightforward scheme: (i) zero communication required to establish a group key, and (ii) *one time* system initialisation and *occasional* key refreshing that requires communication over secure channels to all nodes in the new created group. This minimizes the problem of unreachable source. It requires each node to store a reasonable number of keys and it is secure against a collusion of at most t adversaries.

Initialisation. Suppose initially there are ℓ nodes, $\{P_{i_1}, \ldots, P_{i_\ell}\}$, that form the ad hoc network. They agree on values for parameters (t, v, n, r) of a KDP satisfying $n \geq \ell$, and establish the $(K, \mathcal{B})$-KDP using some efficient construction. Every P_i corresponds to a block $B_i \in \mathcal{B}$. Next, the question is: how to distribute keys $K = \{k_1, \ldots, k_v\}$ to the nodes with respect to the KDP structure? We would like to have a decentralised fashion for key distribution. That is, generation and distribution of the v keys are cooperatively performed by the ℓ nodes.

We assume that the union of all blocks $\{B_{i_1}, \ldots, B_{i_\ell}\}$ corresponding to the ℓ nodes will cover K, that is, $B_{i_1} \cup \ldots \cup B_{i_\ell} = K$ (this can be easily achieved when designing the underlying KDP). The generation and distribution of the v keys is shown in Table 1. Recall that the KDP structure is public.

Table 1. Generation and distribution of system keys

$K' = K$, $z = \ell$
while $K' \neq \emptyset$ {
    P_{i_z} randomly generates keys for $B_{i_z} \cap K'$
    for $1 \leq u \leq z - 1$ {
        P_{i_z} sends to P_{i_u} the keys for $B_{i_z} \cap B_{i_u}$ over a secure channel
    }
    $K' = K' \setminus B_{i_z}$
    $z = z - 1$
}

Group Key Update. We consider three events that require key update: temporarily leaving nodes, permanently leaving nodes, and new joining nodes.

Temporarily Leaving Nodes

Suppose nodes $\{P_{j_1}, \ldots, P_{j_{t'}}\}$, $t' \leq t$, temporarily leave the group, and a node P_i of the remaining nodes $\{P_{i_1}, \ldots, P_{i_{r'}}\}$ wishes to securely send a message m to the the rest of nodes in the subgroup. Group key establishment is as follows, referring to the KDP description in Section 4.1.

1. If $r' \leq r$, clearly nodes in $\{P_{i_1}, \ldots, P_{i_{r'}}\}$ can establish the group key k_G that is known only by them. The node P_i uses the group key to encrypt the message m and multicasts the result to the subgroup.
2. If $r' > r$, the node P_i partitions $\{P_{i_1}, \ldots, P_{i_{r'}}\} \setminus \{P_i\}$ into subsets, each is of size at most $r - 1$, and adds itself as a member to each subset. Subsequently, the node P_i establishes the group key k_G with each of the subsets and encrypts the message m using the group key. The node P_i multicasts the ω encrypted messages to the subgroup, where ω is the number of partitions.

It is straightforward to see that the protocol satisfies session secrecy.

Permanently Leaving Nodes

Suppose nodes $\{P_{j_1}, \ldots, P_{j_{l'}}\}, l' \leq l$, permanently leave the system, and the remaining nodes are $\{P_{i_1}, \ldots, P_{i_{r'}}\}$. Secure communication within the new group can be done in the same way as temporarily leaving nodes. The permanently leaving nodes will not exist in all future groups, and so they naturally can be viewed as the nodes that will also leave all future groups. This requires the permanently leaving nodes to be consistently included in the set of temporarily leaving nodes in all future groups. Obviously, the permanently leaving nodes cannot find either the new group key or all future group keys. Nevertheless, this trivial method is not scalable since the total number of temporarily leaving nodes will grow over time, and they must not exceed t nodes.

We give a scalable method that requires some system keys to be replaced by fresh keys in order to maintain forward secrecy. That is, the keys in blocks $\{B_{j_1}, \ldots, B_{j_{l'}}\}$ that belong to nodes $\{P_{j_1}, \ldots, P_{j_{l'}}\}$ have to be refreshed in such a way that the permanently leaving nodes (even they collude) cannot learn the fresh keys. The fresh keys are collaboratively generated by nodes $\{P_{i_1}, \ldots, P_{i_{r'}}\}$ whose key blocks intersect with keys $B_{j_1} \cup \ldots \cup B_{j_{l'}}$, in the following way (see Table 2).

Table 2. Refreshing system keys

$K' = (B_{i_1} \cup \ldots \cup B_{i_{r'}}) \cap (B_{j_1} \cup \ldots \cup B_{j_{l'}}), z = r'$
while $K' \neq \emptyset$ {
P_{i_z} randomly generates fresh keys for $B_{i_z} \cap K'$
for $1 \leq u \leq z - 1$ {
P_{i_z} sends to P_{i_u} the fresh keys for $B_{i_z} \cap B_{i_u}$ over a secure channel
}
$K' = K' \setminus B_{i_z}$
$z = z - 1$
}
for $1 \leq u \leq r'$ {
P_{i_u} replaces the keys in $B_{i_u} \cap (B_{j_1} \cup \ldots \cup B_{j_{l'}})$ with the fresh keys
}

Observe that this method allows an arbitrary number of nodes to permanently leave the system. After key refreshment, the nodes $\{P_{i_1}, \ldots, P_{i_{r'}}\}$ can have secure communication by following the protocol of temporarily leaving nodes with none leaves.

None of the fresh keys is sent to the permanently leaving nodes so a collusion of them cannot learn the fresh keys. It is not necessary to include them in the set of temporarily leaving nodes in all future groups. Forward secrecy is satisfied because they hold outdated key information which is useless to find the new group key and all future group keys.

This method can be used in the conjunction with the trivial method to reduce the number of key refreshing operations. That is, the trivial method is normally used to update the group key, and the system keys are only refreshed each time the total number of temporarily leaving nodes reaches t nodes. Note that in a key refreshing operation, the permanently leaving nodes are those nodes that have permanently left the group since the previous key refreshment operation.

New Joining Nodes

Suppose the group contains nodes $\{P_{i_1}, \ldots, P_{i_{n'}}\}, n' \leq n$, that hold key blocks $\{B_{i_1}, \ldots, B_{i_{n'}}\}$, respectively. Observe that the system allows $n - n'$ new nodes to join during the rest of the system lifetime. If a new node $P_{i_{n'+1}}$ is going to join the group, it needs to obtain the key block $B_{i_{n'+1}}, B_{i_{n'+1}} \in \mathcal{B} \setminus \{B_{i_1}, \ldots, B_{i_{n'}}\}$. The new node can acquire the key block from some existing nodes, called sponsors, provided that the key blocks of the sponsors cover the key block of the new node (such sponsors can be found in a trivial way).

Node admission requires the group to do the following. First, the nodes $\{P_{i_1}, \ldots, P_{i_{n'}}\}$ establish a common key k_C by following the protocol of temporarily leaving nodes in which case no node leaves[5]. Each node P_i replaces every key $k \in B_i$ by a fresh key $k' = k + k_C$. Assuming the sponsors are $\{P_{g_1}, \ldots, P_{g_s}\} \subseteq \{P_{i_1}, \ldots, P_{i_{n'}}\}$, next, key distribution for the new node is as follows (see Table 3).

Table 3. Distributing system keys

$K' = B_{i_{n'+1}}, \ z = s$
while $K' \neq \emptyset$ {
    P_{g_z} sends to $P_{i_{n'+1}}$ the fresh keys for $B_{g_z} \cap B_{i_{n'+1}}$ over a secure channel
    $K' = K' \setminus B_{g_z}$
    $z = z - 1$
}

If multiple new nodes simultaneously join the group, the key replacement step above is carried out once only and each new node will obtain its key block by following the steps depicted in Table 3. Observe that if the keys are not refreshed, the new nodes may recover previous group keys. The key replacement

---

[5] If $n' \leq r$, $k_C = k_G$. If $n' > r$, a node takes the initiative to randomly generate k_C and securely communicate k_C to the group through a multicast channel.

step guarantees backward secrecy as it ensures the new nodes, that are unable to find k_C, hold a new version of keys which is useless to find the previous group keys.

After obtaining the key block, the new joined node might sponsor other new nodes. Also, the enlarged group can have secure communication by following the protocol of temporarily leaving nodes in which case no node leaves.

4.3   Distributed Establishment of Secure Channels

The model is as follows. If a new node has secure channels (trust relations) with some $t + 1$ existing nodes, then the secure channels (trust relations) can be used as a foundation to establish a secure channel between the new node with every existing node, with the absence of a trusted authority.

Suppose there are n' nodes $\{P_{i_1}, \ldots, P_{i_{n'}}\}$ in the group, and each node P_i has a secret polynomial $F(x, i)$, where $F(x, y)$ is a symmetric polynomial of variables x and y having degree at most t over a finite field $GF(q)$. (We will show a protocol whereby $\ell, \ell \leq n'$, nodes collectively generate $F(x, y)$ and distribute $F(x, i)$ to P_i – see Appendix A.) Also, suppose a new node $P_{i_{n'+1}}$ has secure channels (trust relations) with some $t+1$ nodes $\{P_{h_1}, \ldots, P_{h_{t+1}}\} \subset \{P_{i_1}, \ldots, P_{i_{n'}}\}$, but not with others. The new node $P_{i_{n'+1}}$ will be able to establish secure channels with all other nodes as follows.

1. For $1 \leq j \leq t + 1$, the node P_{h_j} whose secret polynomial is $F(x, h_j)$, sends $F(i_{n'+1}, h_j)$ to the new node $P_{i_{n'+1}}$ through the existing secure channel.
2. The new node $P_{i_{n'+1}}$ collects $t + 1$ points $F(i_{n'+1}, h_1), \ldots, F(i_{n'+1}, h_{t+1})$ and uses Langrange interpolation to compute a polynomial $f(x)$ of degree at most t such that $f(h_j) = F(i_{n'+1}, h_j)$, for $1 \leq j \leq t + 1$. That is, $f(x) = \sum_{h \in \Phi} F(i_{n'+1}, h) \times \psi(\Phi, h) \bmod q$, where $\Phi = \{h_1, \ldots, h_{t+1}\}$ and $\psi(\Phi, h) = \prod_{e \in \Phi, e \neq h} \frac{x - e}{h - e} \bmod q$. This gives $f(x) = F(x, i_{n'+1})$.

By referring to the description of Blom's key distribution in Section 4.1, the new node $P_{i_{n'+1}}$ shares a secret key $F(i_{n'+1}, i_j) = F(i_j, i_{n'+1})$ with each node P_{i_j}, for $1 \leq j \leq n'$. This shared key can be used for authentication and secure communication between the two nodes. In general, each node can establish a secure channel with every other node in the group using the secret key shared by the two nodes.

The decentralised solution is of high interest in ad hoc network. For example, node admission requires secure channels between the new node and its sponsors to be preserved. If they do not exist, the required secure channels can be created by some $t + 1$ other nodes provided that secure point-to-point communication is possible between the new node and the $t + 1$ nodes. In this case, each sponsor P_g encrypts key information using $F(g, i_{n'+1})$ and sends the result to the new node $P_{i_{n'+1}}$ through a public channel. Only the node who claims to be $P_{i_{n'+1}}$ can decrypt the ciphertext to get the key information. The proposed solution is also essential for a system that provides ubiquitous authentication services, such as [22, 8, 10].

5   Conclusion

We have proposed a group key distribution scheme that is suitable for ad hoc networks. Neither system setup nor key update in the scheme requires a trusted authority, instead, the group operations are performed by nodes in the system. We have shown that the proposed scheme is secure and efficient, and it provides reliable and ubiquitous security services.

We have also proposed a method to establish secure channels in a distributed way. The method, which is based on private-key encryption, allows each pair of nodes in the system to securely and efficiently form a secure channel.

References

1. G. Ateniese, M. Steiner, and G. Tsudik. Authenticated group key agreement and friends, *Proceedings of ACM CCS '98*, pages 17-26, 1998.
2. R. Blom. An optimal class of symmetric key generation systems, *Advances in Cryptology – EUROCRYPT '84, LNCS 209*, pages 335-338, 1985.
3. M. Burmester and Y. Desmedt. A secure and efficient conference key distribution system, *Advances in Cryptology – EUROCRYPT '94, LNCS 950*, pages 275-286, 1995.
4. R. Canetti, J. Garay, G. Itkis, D. Micciancio, M. Naor and B. Pinkas. Issues in multicast security: a taxonomy and efficient constructions, *Proceedings of INFOCOM '99*, pages 708-716, 1999.
5. T. C. Chiang and Y. M. Huang. Group keys and the multicast security in ad hoc networks, *First International Workshop on Wireless Security and Privacy (WiSPr'03)*, 2003.
6. D. Halevy and A. Shamir. The LSD broadcast encryption scheme, *Advances in Cryptology – CRYPTO 2002, LNCS 2442*, pages 47-60, 2002.
7. I. Ingemarsson, D. Tang and C. Wong. A conference key distribution scheme, *IEEE Transactions on Information Theory, IT-28, 5, September 1982*, pages 714-720.
8. A. Khalili, J. Katz and W. A. Arbaugh. Toward secure key distribution in truly ad-hoc networks, *Symposium on Applications and the Internet Workshops (SAINT'03 Workshops)*, pages 342-346, 2003.
9. J. Kong, H. Luo, K. Xu, D. L. Gu, M. Gerla and S. Lu. Adaptive security for multi-layer ad-hoc networks, *John Wiley InterScience Press Journal : Special Issue of Wireless Communications and Mobile Computing*, 2002.
10. J. Kong, P. Zerfos, H. Luo, S. Lu and L. Zhang. Providing robust and ubiquitous security support for mobile ad-hoc networks, *IEEE Ninth International Conference on Network Protocols (ICNP'01)*, pages 251-260, 2001.
    Efficient revocation schemes for secure multicast. pages
11. H. Luo, J. Kong, P. Zerfos, S. Lu and L. Zhang. Self-securing ad hoc wireless networks, *IEEE Symposium on Computers and Communications (ISCC'02)*, 2000.
12. C. J. Mitchell and F. C. Piper. Key storage in secure networks, *Discrete Applied Mathematics* **21** (1988), 215-228.
13. D. Naor, M. Naor and J. Lotspiech. Revocation and tracing schemes for stateless receivers, *Advances in Cryptology – CRYPTO 2001, LNCS 2139*, pages 41-62, 2001.
14. K. Obraczka and G. Tsudik. Multicast routing issues in ad hoc networks, *IEEE International Conference on Universal Personal Communication (ICUPC'98)*, 1998.

15. M. Ruszinkó. On the upper bound of the size of the r-cover-free families, *Journal of Combinatorial Theory A* **66** (1994), 302-310.
16. M. Steiner, G. Tsudik, and M. Waidner, Diffie-Hellman key distribution extended to group communication, *Proceedings of ACM CCS '96*, pages 31-37, 1996.
17. M. Steiner, G. Tsudik and M. Waidner. Key agreement in dynamic peer groups. *IEEE Transactions on Parallel and Distributed Systems* **11** no. 8 (2000), 769-780.
18. D. R. Stinson, T. van Trung and R. Wei, Secure frameproof codes, key distribution patterns, group testing algorithms and related structures, *J. Statist. Plan. Infer.*, **86** (2000), 595-617.
19. D. S. Stinson, R. Wei and L. Zhu. Some new bounds for cover-free families, *Journal of Combinatorial Theory A* **90** (2000), 224-234.
20. D. M. Wallner, E. C. Harder, and R. C. Agee. Key management for multicast: issues and architectures, *Internet Draft, ftp://ftp.ietf.org/internet-drafts/draft-wallner-key-arch-01.txt*, 1998.
21. C. K. Wong, M.Gouda, and S.S. Lam. Secure group communications using key graphs, *Proceedings of SIGCOMM '98*, pages 68-79, 2000.
22. L. Zhou and Z. Haas. Securing ad hoc networks, *IEEE Network* **13 6** (1999), 24-30. A revocation scheme with minimal storage at receivers, pages 433-450, 2002.

A   Generation of Symmetric Polynomial $F(x, y)$

The group consists of nodes $\{P_{i_1}, \ldots, P_{i_{n'}}\}$. Without loss of generality, we assume the ℓ, $\ell \leq n'$, nodes are $\{P_{i_1}, \ldots P_{i_\ell}\}$ and a secure channel exists between every pair of the nodes. The ℓ nodes collectively generate the symmetric polynomial $F(x, y)$ as follows.

1. For $1 \leq j \leq \ell$, the node P_{i_j} randomly generates a symmetric polynomial $F_{i_j}(x, y)$ of variables x and y having degree at most t over a finite field $GF(q)$, independently sends the polynomial $F_{i_j}(x, i_g)$ to the node P_{i_g}, for $1 \leq g \leq \ell$ and $g \neq j$, through the existing secure channels.
2. For $1 \leq j \leq \ell$, the node P_{i_j}, after receiving the polynomials $F_{i_g}(x, i_j)$, for $1 \leq g \leq \ell, g \neq j$, computes a polynomial $f_{i_j}(x) = \sum_{g=1}^{\ell} F_{i_g}(x, i_j) \bmod q$.
3. For $1 \leq j \leq \ell$, observe that $f_{i_j}(x) = F(x, i_j)$ where $F(x, y) = \sum_{g=1}^{\ell} F_{i_g}(x, y)$ $\bmod q$. Therefore, the symmetric polynomial $F(x, y)$ is implicitly generated by the ℓ nodes and each node P_{i_j} has $F(x, i_j)$ of $F(x, y)$.

Subsequently, the ℓ nodes can distribute $F(x, i_j)$ to every remaining node P_{i_j}, for $\ell + 1 \leq j \leq n'$, in the group as follows.

If $\ell \leq t$: For $1 \leq g \leq \ell$, the node P_{i_g} sends the polynomial $F_{i_g}(x, i_j)$ to the remaining node P_{i_j} through the existing secure channel. The node P_{i_j}, after receiving the polynomials $F_{i_g}(x, i_j)$, for $1 \leq g \leq \ell$, computes a polynomial $f_{i_j}(x) = \sum_{g=1}^{\ell} F_{i_g}(x, i_j) \bmod q = F(x, i_j)$.

If $\ell > t$: Any $t + 1$ of the ℓ nodes perform the steps described in Section 4.3.

Improved Privacy-Protecting Proxy Signature Scheme

Tianjie Cao[1,2,3], Dongdai Lin[1], and Rui Xue[1]

[1] State Key Laboratory of Information Security of Institute of Software,
Chinese Academy of Sciences, Beijing 100080, China
{tjcao,ddlin,rxue}@is.iscas.ac.cn
[2] School of Computer Science and Technology,
China University of Mining and Technology, Xuzhou 221008, China
[3] Graduate School of Chinese Academy of Sciences, Beijing 100039, China

Abstract. The proxy signature allows a proxy signer to sign on behalf of an original signer and can be verified by anyone with access to the original signer's public key. Recently, Dai et al. proposed a privacy-protecting proxy signature scheme. In this scheme, the messages the original signer entrust to the proxy signer to sign on behalf of him are kept secret from the proxy signer during the generation of the proxy signature except the receiver designated by the original signer. Therefore, the privacy of the original signer is protected. Unfortunately, Dai et al.'s scheme is insecure and inefficient. Particularly, the receiver can cheat the proxy signer and obtain a proxy signature on any message. To eliminate these weaknesses, we propose an improved scheme based on Nyberg-Rueppel signature.

1 Introduction

The proxy signature allows a designated person, called a proxy signer, to sign on behalf of an original signer. The proxy signer can compute a proxy signature that can be verified by anyone with access to the original signer's public key. After Mambo, Usuda and Okamoto firstly introduced the concept of proxy signature [9], many variant schemes have been proposed to achieve the varied specific requirements. Proxy signatures can be used in numerous practical applications, particularly in distributed computing where delegation of rights is quite common. Examples include distributed systems [10], Grid computing [6], mobile agent applications [7], distributed shared object systems [8], global distribution networks [1], mobile communications [13], and electronic commerce [3].

Recently, a privacy-protecting proxy signature scheme is proposed [4]. In this scheme, the messages the original signer entrust to the proxy signer to sign on behalf of him are kept secret from the proxy signer during the generation of the proxy signature except the receiver designated by the original signer. Therefore, the privacy of the original signer is protected. Unfortunately, Dai et al.'s privacy-protecting proxy signature scheme is insecure and inefficient. Particularly, in Dai et al.'s scheme the receiver can cheat the proxy signer and obtain a proxy signature on any message. To eliminate this weaknesses, we propose an improved scheme based on Nyberg-Rueppel signature [11].

C.-H. Chi and K.-Y. Lam (Eds.): AWCC 2004, LNCS 3309, pp. 208–213, 2004.
© Springer-Verlag Berlin Heidelberg 2004

2 Security Analysis
of Dai et al.'s Privacy-Protecting Proxy Signature

Dai et al.'s privacy-protecting proxy signature scheme is based on ElGamal public-key cryptosystem [5], Schnorr signature scheme [12] and blind Nyberg-Rueppel signature scheme [2].

System Parameters: The system parameters are follows.

p, q : two large prime numbers , $q|p-1$

g : g is a generator for Z_p^*

x_A , x_B , x_C : Original signer Alice, proxy signer Bob and receiver Cindy's private key

y_A: $y_A = g^{x_A} \bmod p$: Alice's public key

y_B: $y_B = g^{x_B} \bmod p$: Bob's public key

y_C: $y_C = g^{x_C} \bmod p$: Cindy's public key

m : Message

$h()$: Secure one-way hash function

Generation of Delegating Parameters: Original signer Alice selects $k \in Z_q^*$ at random and computes the following.

$$a = g^k \bmod p$$
$$b = m y_C^k \bmod p$$
$$s_A = x_A h(a, b, y_C) + k \bmod q$$

(a, b, y_C, y_A, s_A) is the delegating parameters of Alice and it is sent to proxy signer Bob secretly. The receiver Cindy is designated by Alice through the form of receiver's public key y_C in the delegating parameters.

Delivery and Verification of Delegating Parameters: Alice sends (a, b, y_C, y_A, s_A) to Bob in a secret manner. Bob checks whether $g^{s_A} \equiv y_A^{h(a,b,y_C)} a \bmod p$. If (a, b, y_C, y_A, s_A) passes the congruence, Bob accepts it. Otherwise, he rejects it and requests a valid one.

Signing by the Proxy Signer: The proxy signer Bob computes

$$x_P = s_A + x_B \bmod q$$
$$y_P = g^{x_P} = y_A^{h(a,b,y_C)} a y_B \bmod p$$

x_P is proxy private key, y_P is corresponding proxy public key, then Bob generates proxy signature by using x_P and blind Nyberg-Rueppel signature as follows.

1. Bob picks at random $\tilde{k} \in Z_q^*$ and computes $\tilde{r} = g^{\tilde{k}} \bmod p$. Bob sends $(a, b, y_A, y_B, \tilde{r})$ to Cindy.

2. a) Cindy decrypts the message m from a and b by using her private key x_C as follows.

$$\frac{b}{a^{x_C}} = \frac{mg^{x_Ck}}{g^{x_Ck}} = m \bmod p$$

   b) Cindy randomly selects $\alpha \in Z_q^*$ and $\beta \in Z_q^*$, computes $r = mg^\alpha \tilde{r}^\beta \bmod p$ and $\tilde{m} = r\beta^{-1} \bmod q$.

   c) Cindy checks whether $\tilde{m} \in Z_q^*$. If this is not the case, she goes back to step b). Otherwise, she sends $\tilde{m}$ to Bob.

3. Bob computes $\tilde{s} = \tilde{m}x_P + \tilde{k} \bmod q$ and sends $\tilde{s}$ to Cindy.

4. Cindy computes $s = \tilde{s}\beta + \alpha \bmod q$. (a, b, y_A, y_B, r, s) is the proxy signature of message m generated by proxy signer Bob on behalf of original signer Alice.

Verification of the Proxy Signature: Cindy verifies the proxy signature by checking if the equality of the following verifying equation holds or not:

$$g^{-s}y_P^r r = g^{-s}\left(y_A^{h(a,b,y_C)} a y_B\right)^r r = m \bmod p$$

If the equality of the above verifying equation holds, receiver Cindy accepts as a valid proxy signature. Otherwise Cindy rejects it.

Unfortunately, Dai et al.'s scheme is insecure. Cindy can obtain a proxy signature on any message. After Cindy decrypts the message m from a and b, Cindy can request a blind signature on any message $m' \neq m$ from Bob, then we have:

$$g^{-s}y_P^r r = g^{-s}\left(y_A^{h(a,b,y_C)} a y_B\right)^r r = m' \bmod p$$

(a, b, y_A, y_B, r, s) is the proxy signature on message m'. In addition, Bob can dishonestly forward (a, b, y_C, y_A, s_A) to other party Eve, then Eve becomes a proxy signer by setting her proxy key pair. Finally, in Dai et al.'s scheme, Alice needs a secure channel to transfer (a, b, y_C, y_A, s_A) and when Bob generates proxy signature Cindy needs be on-line. Obviously, these are undesirable in practice.

3   Improved Privacy-Protecting Proxy Signature Scheme

In this section, we propose an improved privacy-protecting proxy signature scheme to prevent the above weaknesses.

System Parameters: System parameters are same as the original scheme.

Generation of Delegating Parameters: Original signer Alice selects $k \in Z_q^*$ at random and computes the following.

$$a = g^k \bmod p$$
$$b = my_C^k \bmod p$$
$$\tilde{m} = h(m)$$
$$s_A = x_A h(a, b, \tilde{m}, y_B, y_C) + k \bmod q$$

$(a, b, \tilde{m}, y_A, y_B, y_C, s_A)$ is the delegating parameters of original signer Alice and it is sent to proxy signer Bob. The receiver Cindy is designated by Alice through the form of receiver's public key y_C in the delegating parameters.

Delivery and Verification of Delegating Parameters: Proxy signer Bob checks the following equation.

$$g^{s_A} \equiv y_A^{h(a,b,\tilde{m},y_B,y_C)} a \bmod p$$

If $(a, b, \tilde{m}, y_A, y_B, y_C, s_A)$ passes the congruence, Bob accepts it as a valid delegating parameters. Otherwise, he rejects it and requests a valid one.

Signing by the Proxy Signer: The proxy signer Bob generates proxy signature key pairs as follows.

$$x_P = s_A + x_B \bmod q$$
$$y_P = g^{x_P} = y_A^{h(a,b,\tilde{m},y_B,y_C)} a y_B \bmod p$$

x_P is proxy private key, y_P is corresponding proxy public key. Proxy signer Bob can generate proxy signature on behalf of original signer by using x_P and Nyberg-Rueppel signature scheme [11] as follows.

The proxy signer Bob picks at random $\tilde{k} \in Z_q^*$ and computes

$$r = \tilde{m}g^{-\tilde{k}} \bmod p$$
$$\tilde{r} = r \bmod q$$
$$s = \tilde{k} - \tilde{r}x_P \bmod q$$

Bob sends $(a, b, \tilde{m}, y_A, y_B, r, s)$ to Cindy.

Verification of the Proxy Signature: Cindy decrypts the message m from a and b by using her private key x_C as follows:

$$\frac{b}{a^{x_C}} = \frac{mg^{x_C k}}{g^{x_C k}} = m \bmod p$$

$(a, b, y_A, y_B, y_C, r, s)$ is the proxy signature of message m generated by proxy signer Bob on behalf of original signer Alice.

Cindy verifies the proxy signature by checking if the equality of the following verifying equation holds or not:

$$g^s y_P^{\tilde{r}} r = g^s (y_A^{h(a,b,\tilde{m},y_B,y_C)} a y_B)^{\tilde{r}} r = \tilde{m} \bmod p$$

where $\tilde{r} = r \bmod q$ and $\tilde{m} = h(m)$.

If the equality of the above verifying equation holds, receiver Cindy accepts $(a, b, y_A, y_B, y_C, r, s)$ as a valid proxy signature of message m. Otherwise Cindy rejects it.

4 Security Analysis of the Improved Privacy-Protecting Proxy Signature Scheme

Our privacy-protecting proxy signature not only satisfies the security requirements proposed by Mambo et al. [9], but also satisfies the requirements of privacy-protecting proxy signature [4].

Verifiability. The original signer's delegation on the signed message is verifiable using publicly available parameters. If $(a, b, y_A, y_B, y_C, r, s)$ is a proxy signature of a message m produced by the improved privacy-protecting proxy signature scheme, then $g^s (y_A^{h(a,b,\tilde{m},y_B,y_C)} a y_B)^{\tilde{r}} r = \tilde{m} (\bmod p)$ where $\tilde{r} = r (\bmod q)$ and $\tilde{m} = h(m)$.

Unforgeability. It is difficult to forge a specific proxy's signature, even by the original signer. In the original signer's delegating parameters $(a, b, \tilde{m}, y_A, y_B, y_C, s_A)$ the original signer designates the proxy signer and the valid receiver. The proxy private key is created as $x_P = s_A + x_B (\bmod q)$, in which x_B is secret key of proxy signer, so only the proxy signer can create valid proxy signature by himself.

Undeniability. It is difficult for a proxy signer to repudiate its signatures against any verifier. Once a proxy signer generates a valid proxy signature on behalf of original signer using proxy private key, he cannot disavow his signature creation against anyone because the proxy private key contains his private key x_B.

Identifiability. A proxy signer's identity can be determined from a proxy signature. The proxy signer's identity is included explicitly in a valid proxy signature $(a, b, y_A, y_B, y_C, r, s)$ as a form of public key y_B. Anyone can determine from a proxy signature the identity of the corresponding proxy signer.

Original signer's undeniability. Original signer designates proxy signer and receiver through the form of proxy signer and receiver's public keys y_B, y_C. If the original signer disavows her designation, the corresponding proxy signer can verify the delegating parameters given by the original signer as follows:

$$g^{s_A} \equiv y_A^{h(a,b,\tilde{m},y_B,y_C)} a \bmod p$$

if the delegating parameters $(a, b, \tilde{m}, y_A, y_B, y_C, s_A)$ passes the congruence, then original signer can not deny her designation.

Confidentiality. No one knows the message m except the valid receiver designated by the original signer. The message m is entrusted to the proxy signer to sign on behalf of the original signer after it is encrypted by ElGamal public-key cryptosystem .The proxy signer can not decrypt the ciphertext without the private key x_C.

5 Conclusion

In this paper, we have showed some weaknesses in Dai et al.'s privacy-protecting proxy signature scheme. To eliminate these weaknesses, we proposed an improved scheme based on Nyberg-Rueppel signature.

Acknowledgments

We thank the support of National Natural Science Foundation of China (NSFC 90204016, NSFC 60373048) and the National High Technology Development Program of China under Grant (863, No.2003AA144030).

References

1. Bakker, A., Steen, M., Tanenbaum, A. S.: A law-abiding peer-to-peer network for free-software distribution. In IEEE International Symposium on Network Computing and Applications (2001)
2. Camenisch, L.J., Pivctoau, M.J., Stadler, A.M.: Blind signatures based on the discrete logarithm problem. Advances in Cryptology' 92, Springer-Verlag (1995) 428–432
3. Dai, J.-Z., Yang, X.-H., Dong, J.-X.: Designated-receiver proxy signature scheme for electronic commerce. Proceedings of IEEE International Conference on Systems, Man and Cybernetics, Vol. 1. (2003) 384–389
4. Dai, J.-Z., Yang, X.-H., Dong, J.-X.: A privacy-protecting proxy signature scheme and its application. ACM Southeast Regional Conference, Proceedings of the 42nd annual Southeast regional conference (2004) 203–206
5. ElGamal, T.: A public-key cryptosystem and a signature scheme based on discrete logarithms. Advances in Cryptology'84. Springer-Verlag. (1985) 10–18
6. Foster, I., Kesselman, C., Tsudik, G., Tuecke, S.: A security architecture for computational grids. In Fifth ACM Conference on Computers and Communications Security (1998)
7. Lee, B., Kim, H., Kim, K.: Secure mobile agent using strong non-designated proxy signature. Proceedings of ACISP. Lecture Notes in Computer Science, Vol. 2119, Springer-Verlag, Berlin Heidelberg New York (2001) 474–486
8. Leiwo, J., Hanle, C., Homburg, P., Tanenbaum,A.S.: Disallowing unauthorized state changes of distributed shared objects. In SEC 2000 (2000) 381–390.
9. Mambo, M., Usuda, K., Okamoto, E.: Proxy signatures for delegating signing operation. Proceedings 3rd ACM Conference on Computer and Communications Security, ACM Press New York (1996) 48–57
10. Neuman, B.C.: Proxy based authorization and accounting for distributed systems. Proceedings of the 13th International Conference on Distributed Computing Systems (1993) 283–291
11. Nyberg, K. Rueppel, R.: Message recovery for signature schemes based on the discrete logarithm problem. Advances in Cryptology-EuroCrypt'94. Lecture Notes in Computer Science, Vol. 950, Springer-Verlag, Berlin Heidelberg New York (1995) 182–193.
12. Schnorr, C.P.: Efficient identification and signatures for smart cards. Advances in cryptology-crypto'89. Lecture Notes in Computer Science, Vol. 435,Springer-verlag (1990) 239–252.
13. Zhang, J., Wu, Q., Wang, J., Wang, Y.: An Improved Nominative Proxy Signature Scheme for Mobile Communication, 18th International Conference on Advanced Information Networking and Applications, Vol. 2 (2004) 23–26

Improving Security Architecture Development Based on Multiple Criteria Decision Making

Fang Liu, Kui Dai, and Zhiying Wang

Department of Computer Science and Technology,
National University of Defense Technology, Changsha 410073, P.R. China
liufang_nudt@yahoo.com.cn

Abstract. This paper describes an effort to improve security architecture development of information systems based on the multiple criteria decision making (MCDM) techniques. First, we introduce the fundamental of MCDM, describe how the security architecture is developed and analyze the main problems in the development. Finally, this paper shows how the MCDM techniques were applied to solve two problems in security architecture development. And an approach which could assist in prioritizing threats and selecting security technologies is illustrated. The practices indicate that MCDM techniques are valuable in formulating and solving problems in security architecture development.

Keywords: Security Architecture, Development, Multiple Criteria Decision Making, Risk Assessment, Security Technology

1 Introduction

Taking correct security architecture design decisions becomes essential for the survival of information system. Our work is to assess the information system security and examine alternative security technologies for incorporation into security architecture and how they relate to the risks and expected outcomes of diverse risks. This examination was done from a cost-benefit perspective using MCDM theory.

2 Multiple Criteria Decision Making Theory

Everyone is interested in making decisions that have good outcomes. We always compare, rank, and order the objects with respect to "multiple criteria of choice". Only in very simple cases can we think that a "single criterion of choice" is satisfactory. The MCDM theory is attractive in security architecture development because it provides a systematic way to consider tradeoffs among attributes and to deal with the uncertainty and multi-objective nature of these decisions. In the MCDM context, the selection is facilitated by evaluating and comparing each available security technology which represents a decision alternative on the set of criteria [1]. Decision maker's preferences with respect to evaluation criteria are expressed in terms of weights. The weights express relative importance of the evaluation criteria under consideration. Figure 1 outlines the steps of decision process in the MCDM approach [2].

C.-H. Chi and K.-Y. Lam (Eds.): AWCC 2004, LNCS 3309, pp. 214–218, 2004.

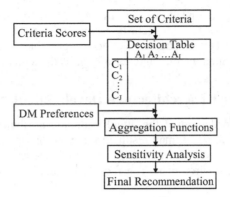

Fig. 1. Steps of decision process in MCDM approach

3   Security Architecture Development

Security Architecture Development means an assessment of current security policies, procedures and technologies; organization of security policies, procedures, and technologies into a meaningful framework; development of communication, audit and monitoring processes to assure security architecture compliance. The following figure illustrates the correlations in the security architecture development.

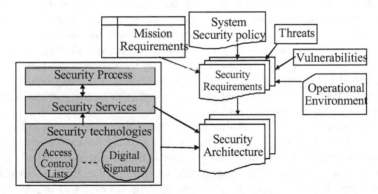

Fig. 2. Correlations in the security architecture development

How does an organization go about developing security architecture? Security architecture development follows three phases [3]. Development begins with a risk assessment, which analyzes the expected threats and outcomes. Analysis and selection of risk mitigation strategies or countermeasures follows the risk assessment. Finally, integrating the selected countermeasures into the system and configuring the security technologies to enforce organizational security policies. The development process is revisited periodically to ensure that the security architecture is up to date with changes in the threat environment.

There are two key problems in the process of developing security architecture. The first is the uncertainty about the outcome of attack. For example, once an attacker has access to the system, there are many possibilities. Furthermore, different attacks may result in different outcomes and at different magnitudes. The other problem is how to make the appropriate choices from security technologies to stop attacks, or mitigate the consequences of successful attacks as much as possible. Frequently, the tension among performance, maintainability and security adds difficulty of the selection.

4 Improving Security Architecture Development with MCDM

The first problem is to determine the attack outcome attributes. In an operational information system, each attack may result in different or similar outcome. And the outcome attributes of an attack is likely to be unpredictable as a result of the dynamic changes of the security environment. The fact adds complexity to the application of MCDM techniques.

There are some significant possibilities with which we should be concerned, such as lost productivity, lost revenue and damage to corporate image. We define an initial outcome attributes set X ($\{X_1, X_2, \cdots X_n\}$ = {lost productivity, lost revenue, $\cdots$}). In the multi-attribute risk assessment, the actual outcome attribute damage from an attack is the attribute's value x_i. Therefore, the outcome from each attack can be described as a vector of attribute values $\bar{O}_a = [x_1, x_2, \cdots, x_n]$. And we tried to determine the consistent weights of every outcome attributes by calculating the normalized principal eigenvector to reflect relative preferences for outcomes over the relevant range. Our method is focused on comparing the relative impact of the same type attributes rather than the net value to reflect the relative severity of each type of attack. Since the relative impact value is a non-dimensional unit, the indications of relative damage on the information system could reduce subjective influence on decisions. More specifically, the relative value analysis allows the different outcomes attributes to be expressed in different terms, which is useful when describing outcomes attributes that are difficult to be expressed in same term, such as the potential damage to corporate image and the lost productivity.

Then we can use the additive value model combining attack frequencies and the analyzed outcome attributes values to determine a ranking for each threat, instead of the security engineer's estimation. Though there is little reliable statistical data about attack since so few organizations report incidents, if threat data becomes available we could get better selection decisions and results from the effort to improve security architecture development with the MCDM techniques.

Another significant problem in security architecture development is selecting the security technologies. The security architecture should identify the appropriate security mechanisms to fulfill the security requirements related to the existed information system architecture and fit the risk environment. Clearly, the sound selection should evaluate and compare each security technology on a set of criteria and make tradeoffs among those criteria.

The first set of criteria to be considered is the existing information system's security architecture. Researchers at Carnegie Mellon University have been using decision theory techniques to develop a selection method [3] for the security technology selection problem. This led to the Security Attribute Evaluation Method (SAEM), which identifies the most effective security technologies for an organization. Although the security analysis in their method ultimately showed a high positive correlation, the case study showed that it would have been more useful if the security analyses were used to evaluate security technologies in the context of the organization's security architecture, not independent of the security architecture [4]. Since no single technology can provide absolute security for an information system, a typical security architecture is composed of multiple layers of controls with different capabilities. The value of a security control at any level depends on other controls surrounding it as they may substitute or complement other [5]. These characteristics require that an organization simultaneously develop all layers of security technologies and use multiple complementary security technologies, so that a failure in one does not mean total insecurity. We construct four defensive layers: 1) protection, 2) detection, 3) reaction, and 4) recovery, different from the three layers coverage model in the SEAM [3]. It provides a structured way and system level perspective to analyze security and develop security architecture. We propose the layered security architecture and the existing technologies should be analyzed before selecting the security technologies to get a "clear view" of what is missing and reveal significant gaps or weaknesses.

Then, we should determine the benefit of a security technology. The ranking of threats determined in the risk assessment based on MCDM can be thought of as one of the decision criteria. The effectiveness of security technologies is determined by the expected reduction percentages of the frequency or outcome of attacks. And the security technologies are weighted based on their overall contribution to mitigating outcomes. Similarly, we rank the security technology on its relative effectiveness when compared to other technologies to reduce subjective influence on decisions.

Third, although the benefit analysis determines which security technologies are the most effective in mitigating threats, there are some other factors, such as purchase cost, that should be considered before selecting a technology for inclusion in the security architecture [6]. It is important to remember that we do not want to implement "security at any cost". In fact, the security manager often considers purchase cost or maintenance to be more important than the effectiveness of the technology [7]. We could compare security technologies using multiple criteria decision making techniques to rank each security technology according the system's decision objectives.

5 Conclusion and Future Work

We presented preliminary ideas on using multiple criteria decision analytical techniques to help make decisions during the development or update of the information system security architecture. Specifically, it is a flexible, systematic, and repeatable process that prioritizes threats and helps select countermeasures to make clear the best investments for the organization's objectives.

Potential future work includes evaluating security of information system quantitatively and conducting sensitivity analysis to show how sensitive the security decisions are to the analyzed data and models. We would like to expand our approach to integrate a fuzzy MCDM model [8] and a structured group decision making process to improve the quality of the security decisions. Finally, we hope that our work will be of service to the growing population of security architecture developers.

Acknowledgements

The research reported here has been supported by the National Natural Science Foundation of China (No.90104025). And the authors would like to acknowledge Dr. Shawn A. Butler for her help and encouragement.

References

1. Yoon, K. Paul and Hwang, Ching-Lai.: Multiple Attribute Decision Making: An Introduction. Sage Publications (1995)
2. Malczewski, J.: GIS and Multicriteria Decision Analysis. John Wiley & Sons, Inc. ISBN 0-471-32944-4 (1999)
3. Shawn A. Butler.: Security Attribute Evaluation Method. Carnegie Mellon University, Doctoral Thesis. May (2003)
4. Shawn A. Butler: Improving Security Technology Selections with Decision Theory. Third Workshop on Economics-Driven Software Engineering Research (EDSER-3) (2001)
5. Shawn A. Butler: Security Issues in the Architecture of the Global Command and Control. TC2 First Working IFIP Conference on Software Architecture (WICSA1), 22-24 February (1999) San Antonio, Texas, pp. 407-421
6. Christopher M. King, Curtis E. Dalton and T. Ertem Osmanoglu.: Security Architecture: Design Deployment and Operations. Osborne/McGraw-Hill ISBN: 0072133856 July (2001)
7. Kazman, R., J. Asundi, et al.: Quantifying the Costs and Benefits of Architectural Decisions. International Conference on Software Engineering-22, IEEE (2000)
8. Lootsma FA: Fuzzy logic for planning and decision making. Kluwer Academic Publishers. (1997)

A LSB Substitution Oriented Image Hiding Strategy Using Genetic Algorithms

Ming-Ni Wu[1], Min-Hui Lin[2], and Chin-Chen Chang[1]

[1] Department of Computer Science and Information Engineering
National Chung Cheng University, Chaiyi, Taiwan 621, R.O.C.
{mnwu,ccc}@cs.ccu.edu.tw
[2] Department of Computer Science and Information Management
Providence University, Taichung, Taiwan 433, R.O.C.
mhlin3@pu.edu.tw

Abstract. Image hiding is an important technique in information security field. The simplest method is the least significant bit (LSB) substitution method that embeds a secret image in the least significant bits of the pixels of a host image. The embedding idea is simple, but the embedding process may degrade the host image quality so much that a hacker's suspicion may be raised. To improve the image quality of the stego-image, we applied the LSB substitution and genetic algorithm (GA) to develop two different optimal substitution strategies: one is the global optimal substitution strategy and the other is the local optimal substitution strategy. The experimental results confirm that our methods can provide better image quality than the simple LSB and Wang et al.'s method do while provide large hiding capacity.

Keywords: image hiding, LSB substitution, genetic algorithm

1 Introduction

Image hiding [1, 2, 3] is a technique used to embed secret data in an image, i.e., data is hidden in a publishable image, but the hiding process does not damage the original image. The image in which the secret data is hidden is called a stego-image. The stego-image will not attract suspicion so that attacks can be prevented. But an intended receiver can successfully decode the secret data hidden in the stego-image.

The simplest method for hiding data is the least significant bit (LSB) method. It hides data in the least significant bit of each image pixel. Because the variation between the original pixel value and the embedded pixel value is small, the image quality is often not bad even after the hiding process is completed. Many image-hiding techniques based on LSB have been proposed [4, 5, 6, 7]. For example, Wang et al. [4] proposed a method that uses the genetic algorithm (GA) to search for the nearest optimal replacement of LSB to enhance image quality. Recently, several papers utilized the dynamic programming and the greedy method to improve time efficiency [8, 9].

In this paper, we propose two image hiding methods to improve the image quality of the stego-image and to provide large hiding capacity. The first method is called global method, which explores all blocks' attributes of the secret image and host image. The second method is called local method, which explores each block's attribute of the secret image and host image. This paper is organized as follows. First, the introduction of the LSB method and Wang et al.'s method is given in the second sec-

C.-H. Chi and K.-Y. Lam (Eds.): AWCC 2004, LNCS 3309, pp. 219–229, 2004.

tion. Then, a new method is proposed in the third section. The fourth section gives the experimental results and discussions. Finally, the conclusion is given in the fifth section.

2 Relative Works

2.1 Image Hiding by Simple LSB Substitution

The LSB substitution method for hiding images is a very simple and easy method to implement. Fig. 1 is a flowchart showing the embedding process using LSB substitution. S is the secret image which is to be hidden in the host image H. Both are grayscale images with each pixel having n bits.

Suppose we want to embed S in the rightmost k bits of each pixel in H. First, S will be converted to S'. In this process, we decompose each pixel of S into several small k-bit units to form the k-bit image S'. For example, H is a 256×256, 8-bit grayscale image, S is an 8-bit gray scale image with a size of 128×128. For the secret image S to be embedded in the rightmost two bits of each pixel in the host image H, let n be 8 and let k be 2. So S' is a 2-bit image with a size of 256×256.

In the LSB extraction process, we retrieve the rightmost k bits of each pixel of the host image H to form a k-bit gray-scale residual image R. The leftmost $(n-k)$ bits of each pixel of the host image H are retrieved to form a $(n-k)$ bit gray-scale left-most image L in the MSB extraction process. In the replacement process, we replace R by S' pixel by pixel and call it the embedded temporary image T. Finally, we merge L and T pixel by pixel to form the embedded result Z.

For example, if R is an image of size 256×256 with 2-bits per pixel and L is an image of size 256×256 with 6-bits per pixel, then Z will be an image of size 256×256 with 8-bits per pixel when T and L are merged.

2.2 Image Hiding Using Wang et al.'s Optimal LSB Substitution Method

Wang et al.'s method is based on simple LSB substitution and GA [10]. Wang et al.'s process is illustrated in Fig.2. It has two key points that are different from the LSB substitution method. First, in the LSB substitution method, interceptors can extract a secret image from Z easily because the hidden secret image is regularly distributed in the stego-image. To eliminate this drawback, Wang et al.'s method uses a transform function to convert each location x in S' to a new location in the meaningless image ES'. The transform function used in Wang et al.'s method is $f(x) = (k_0 + k_1 \times x) \bmod p$, where k_0 and k_1 are the key constants for recovering the hidden secret image from ES' and p is the image size of the deconstructed image S'.

Second, a significant difference between the LSB substitution method and Wang's method is that Wang's substitution is optimal substitution rather than simple substitution. In Wang's method, each pixel value i in ES' will be converted to another value j in ES^*, where $0 \le i < 2^{k-1}$ and $0 \le j < 2^{k-1}$. The mapping strategy is based on a substitution matrix $M = \{m_{ij}\}$. If $m_{ij} = 1$ then the gray value i is replaced with the gray value j. If $m_{ij} = 0$, then nothing is done. There is only one m_{ij} equal to 1 in each row and each column. There are $(2^k)!$ substitution matrices in this method and only one matrix is selected that can provide the least distortion between the embedded resulting image Z and the host image H.

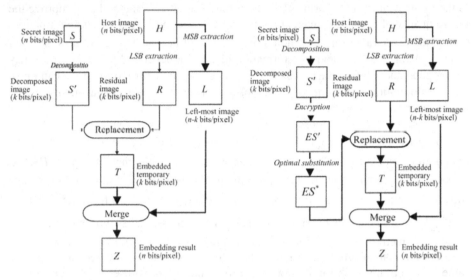

Fig. 1. The flowchart of the embedding process in the simple LSB substitution method

Fig. 2. The flowchart of the embedding process using Wang et al.'s optimal LSB substitution method

An example is given in Fig. 3. Suppose ES' is a 2-bits secret image with a size of 4×4. We can find a matrix M, as in Fig. 3(b), that is an optimal substitution matrix. The pixel value 0 in ES' will be replaced with the gray value 3 according to the M matrix, the pixel value 1 in ES' will be replaced with the gray value 2, and so on. Finally, the optimal substitution image ES' is generated. In the previous example, since $k=2$, there are only $(2^2)!= 24$ substitution matrices. But when k increases, for example, $k=4$, the number of matrices will be $(2^4)!$. It is time consuming to find the optimal substitution matrix that can generate the largest $PSNR$. To increase the efficiency in choosing the optimal substitution matrix, Wang et al. used the GA to reduce the search time and find the near optimal result.

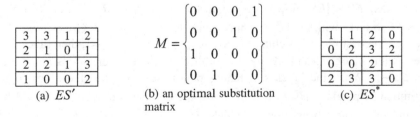

(a) ES'

$$M = \begin{cases} 0 & 0 & 0 & 1 \\ 0 & 0 & 1 & 0 \\ 1 & 0 & 0 & 0 \\ 0 & 1 & 0 & 0 \end{cases}$$

(b) an optimal substitution matrix

(c) ES^*

Fig. 3. An example of optimal substitution from ES' to ES^*

3   The Proposed Method

For the simple LSB method, a pixel value i in R is replaced by secret data j. However, for the optimal substitution in Wang et al.'s method, j is transformed to u, according to the optimal substitution principle. Although Wang et al.'s method can improve the image quality of the stego-image, the optimal substitution is a global transformation; that is, the pixel value i in the whole image ES' will be transformed to u in ES^*. In general, Wang et al.'s global transformation idea is not beneficial for all pixels. It may not be good enough for some areas of the image ES'. In other words, if we can make the transformation according to the block characteristics, the image quality of the stego-image should be better.

The flowchart of our proposed method is shown in Fig. 4. In our method, ES' will first be partitioned into $\{ES'_0, ES'_1, \cdots, ES'_{x-1}\}$, totaling x blocks. R will also be partitioned into x blocks, $\{R_0, R_1, \cdots, R_{x-1}\}$. Then we search for the matching pairs ES_i and R_j. Since they are the most similar, they have the best similarity. In this pair, we use a substitution matrix M to substitute the pixel values of ES'_i and to form ES^*_i. Therefore, ES^*_i and R_j have better similarity than other matched pairs. In this research, we use the GA method to search for optimal matching pairs. In addition, we propose two different optimal substitution strategies for different scenarios: one scenario uses the same substitution matrix for all blocks, and the other scenario uses a different substitution matrix for each block. In the first optimal substitution strategy, called global optimal substitution strategy, only one substitution matrix is required; therefore, fewer data is recorded. In the second optimal substitution strategy, called local optimal substitution strategy, more substitution matrices are required; however, better image quality of stego-image is provided. We call the method based on the global optimal substitution strategy as global method, and the method based on local optimal substitution strategy as local method. The detailed descriptions of these two strategies are presented as in the following subsections.

3.1   The Global Optimal Substitution Strategy

The significant difference between Wang et al.'s method and ours is the block matching and optimal substitution, therefore, the following is a detailed description of the procedure for transforming ES' to ES^*.

In this procedure for transforming ES' to ES^*, we partition both ES' and R into x blocks, i.e., $ES' = \{ES'_0, ES'_1, \cdots, ES'_{x-1}\}$ and $R = \{R_0, R_1, \cdots, R_{x-1}\}$. ES'_i will be hidden in R_j, so there will be $(x)!$ matching pairs. Here, we use the GA method [10] to search for the best block matching matrix, $B = \{b_{ij}\}$, where if $b_{ij}=1$, then block i is replaced with block j, and if $b_{ij}=0$, nothing is done. Here, $0 \leq i \leq x-1$ and $0 \leq j \leq x-1$. When the block's matching pair is searched for, the global optimal substitution of pixels is also found by using the GA method to search for all block matching pairs. The process flow by which ES' is transformed to ES^* is provided in Fig. 5.

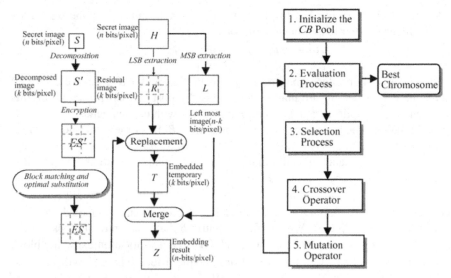

Fig. 4. The flowchart of the proposed method   **Fig. 5.** The proposed flowchart

The process whereby ES' is transformed to ES^* is detailed as follows.

Step 1: Prepare the initial chromosome pool. Divide ES' and R to x blocks $ES' = \{ES_0', ES_1', \cdots, ES_{x-1}'\}$ and $R = \{R_0, R_1, \cdots, R_{x-1}\}$. A chromosome CB_l consisting of x genes is one expression of the block matching matrix B_l, $CB_l = cb_0, cb_1, \cdots, cb_{x-1}$, where cb_o represents the position of row 0 in B_l that has a value of 1, cb_1 represents the position of row 1 in B_l that has a value 1, and so on. $0 \le cb_i \le x-1$, and any gene pair (cb_i, cb_j) that has the property $i \ne j$ implies that $cb_i \ne cb_j$. Q chromosomes CB_0, CB_1, ..., and CB_{Q-1} are produced by a random function generator to initialize the chromosome pool.

Step 2: Evaluation process.

Step 2.1 For every chromosome CB_l, we can produce ES'' from ES' by CB_l mapping, where $0 \le l \le Q-1$. We generate the global optimal substitution matrix from ES'' in the same way as Wang et al.'s method does. A common substitution matrix M is used to produce ES^* for all blocks in ES''.

Step 2.2 Apply the fitness function to calculate the MSE between Z and H.

$$F(G) = \sum_{i=0}^{N-1} (z_i - h_i)^2 ,$$

where z_i is the ith pixel value of Z, h_i is the ith pixel value of H, and N is the number of pixels H.

Step 2.3 If the number of loops has reached the default threshold, the best chromosome in the pool will be selected as the winning chromosome, and all other processes stop.

Step 3: Selection process. For all $F_i(G)$ in the CB_l pool after Step 2, we preserve the better chromosomes and drop the worse chromosomes.

Step 4: Crossover process. Choose any two chromosomes: $CB_i = p_0 p_1 \cdots p_{x-1}$, and $CB_j = q_0 q_1 \cdots q_{x-1}$. A random number z is produced, where $0 < z < x-1$. We split

CB_1 and CB_2 into left hand and right hand sides using z and replace the right hand sides with each other to get the new offspring.

$$CB'_i = p_0 p_1 \cdots p_{z-1} q_z q_{z+1} \cdots q_{x-1},$$
$$CB'_j = q_0 q_1 \cdots q_{z-1} p_z p_{z+1} \cdots p_{x-1}.$$

This process may produce non-unique genes in CB'_i and CB'_j. To make sure all genes in CB'_i and CB'_j are unique, we can add a post process phase before this step to remove duplicate genes and replacing them with unused genes.

Step 5: Mutation process. Select one chromosome CB_l from the pool and two random numbers y and z between 0 and x-1. Let $CB_l = cb_0 \cdots cb_y \cdots cb_z \cdots cb_{x-1}$. We select the genes cb_y and cb_z and replace their values with each other. The result is $CB_l = cb_0 \cdots cb_z \cdots cb_y \cdots cb_{x-1}$. Go to Step 2.

Consider the example shown in Fig. 6. Suppose ES' in Fig. 6(a) is a 2-bits/pixel secret image with a size of 4×4, is divided into 4 blocks, and is labeled Block 0, Block 1, Block 2, and Block 3. We can find a matrix B that is an optimal block matching matrix and transform the block location of ES' to a new location using the block matching matrix B, as shown in Fig. 6(b). For example, Block 0 in ES' will be transformed to the Block 1 location in ES'', and Block 1 in ES' will be transformed to the Block 0 location in ES'', and so on. The transformation result is shown in Fig. 6(c). At the same time, we transform the pixel values of Fig. 6(c) into ES^* (shown in Fig. 6(e)) according to the M matrix shown in Fig. 6(d).

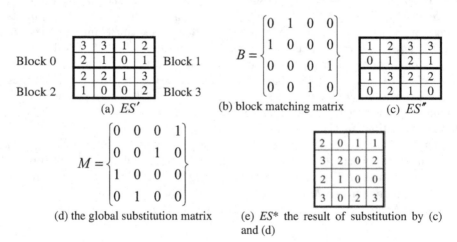

(a) ES' (b) block matching matrix   (c) ES''

(d) the global substitution matrix   (e) ES^* the result of substitution by (c) and (d)

Fig. 6. An example of the proposed global optimal substitution strategy

3.2 The Local Optimal Substitution Strategy

Here, we propose the other choice for the selection of the substitution matrix. The pixel values of each individual block in the secret image and those of the corresponding block in the host image are examined to determine the corresponding substitution matrix. This is called the local optimal substitution strategy.

The procedure for this strategy is the same as the global optimal substitution strategy, but the difference is the number of substitution matrices in Step 2.1 presented in

Subsection 3.1. There are x substitution matrices $\ulcorner$ for each block of ES'' used to produce ES^* in the local optimal substitution method, and only one common substitution matrix is used to produce ES^* for all blocks of ES'' in the global optimal substitution method.

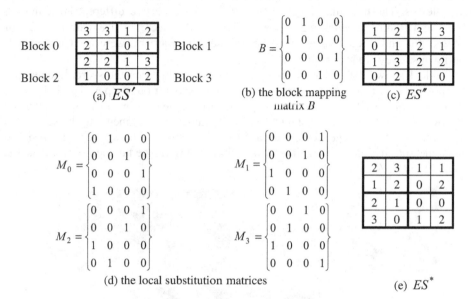

Block 0

3	3	1	2
2	1	0	1

Block 1

Block 2

2	2	1	3
1	0	0	2

Block 3

(a) ES'

$$B = \begin{cases} 0 & 1 & 0 & 0 \\ 1 & 0 & 0 & 0 \\ 0 & 0 & 0 & 1 \\ 0 & 0 & 1 & 0 \end{cases}$$

(b) the block mapping matrix B

1	2	3	3
0	1	2	1
1	3	2	2
0	2	1	0

(c) ES''

$$M_0 = \begin{cases} 0 & 1 & 0 & 0 \\ 0 & 0 & 1 & 0 \\ 0 & 0 & 0 & 1 \\ 1 & 0 & 0 & 0 \end{cases}$$

$$M_1 = \begin{cases} 0 & 0 & 0 & 1 \\ 0 & 0 & 1 & 0 \\ 1 & 0 & 0 & 0 \\ 0 & 1 & 0 & 0 \end{cases}$$

$$M_2 = \begin{cases} 0 & 0 & 0 & 1 \\ 0 & 0 & 1 & 0 \\ 1 & 0 & 0 & 0 \\ 0 & 1 & 0 & 0 \end{cases}$$

$$M_3 = \begin{cases} 0 & 0 & 1 & 0 \\ 0 & 1 & 0 & 0 \\ 1 & 0 & 0 & 0 \\ 0 & 0 & 0 & 1 \end{cases}$$

2	3	1	1
1	2	0	2
2	1	0	0
3	0	1	2

(d) the local substitution matrices

(e) ES^*

Fig. 7. An example of the proposed local optimal substitution

Consider the example, as shown in Fig. 7. The process shown in Fig. 7(a) to Fig. 7(c) is the same as the process shown in Fig. 6(a) to Fig. 6(c). In Fig. 7(d), there are 4 matrices, M_0, M_1, M_2, and M_3, for each block. Block 0 in Fig. 7(c) is substituted with matrix M_0 to produce Block 0 in ES^*, Block 1 in Fig. 7(c) is substituted with matrix M_1 to produce Block 1 in ES^*, and so on.

(a)   (b)

Fig. 8. The two test images with size of 512×512 that were used as the host images: (a)Lena, (b) Baboon

4 Experimental Results

This section presents and discusses the experimental results of the proposed method. All the programs were written in Borland C++ Builder and were run on a personal computer with a Windows XP operating system. The CPU was a Pentium 4 with 256 MB of main memory. In our experimental tests, all images were 8 bit images with 256 gray levels. The host images were 512×512. We used two different host images, Lena and Bamboo, which are shown in Fig. 8. The secret image with the size of 512×256, and three images, Airplane, Pepper and Barbara, were used for our experiments. They are shown in Fig. 9.

Table 1 shows the *PSNR* values resulting from embedding the secret images into the host image Lena with a different number of blocks for our proposed global substitution strategy. Table 1 shows that the greater the number of blocks is, the higher the *PSNR* value will be. Table 2 shows the *PSNR* values from embedding the secret images into the host image Lena, with a different number of blocks for our proposed local method. In this table, the inference is that the higher the number of blocks is, the higher the *PSNR* value will be.

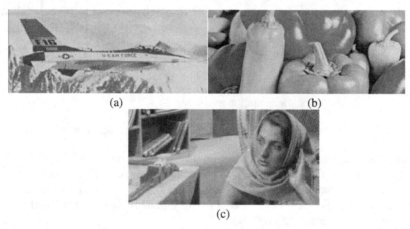

(a)   (b)

(c)

Fig. 9. The three images with size of 512×256 that were used as the secret data: (a) Airplane (b) Peppers (c) Barbara

Table 1. The results from embedding secret images into the host image Lena with different numbers of blocks in our proposed global method

Secret images	Number of Blocks				
	4	16	64	256	1024
Airplane	33.0310	33.1669	33.1843	33.2084	33.3795
Pepper	32.5493	32.6748	32.6971	32.7835	32.9667
Barbara	32.8981	32.9873	32.9910	33.0257	33.1048

To evaluate the image equality provided by our proposed local and global optimal substitution strategies, we also simulated the simple LSB and Wang et al.'s methods. In this experiment, we used the rightmost 4 bits of each pixel in the host image to hide the secret image. The test results are shown in Tables 3 and 4. The *PSNR* values of the four methods, the LSB substitution method, Wang et al.'s optimal LSB substitution method, our global method, and our local method, are listed in Table 3 for Lena as the host image and in Table 4 for Baboon as the host image. Fig. 10 shows the results from embedding the secret image Airplane into the host image Lena using the four methods. In these experiments, images were divided into 16 blocks for our global method and local method, which require lower storage space and provide reasonable *PSNR* values.

Table 2. The results from embedding secret images into the host image Lena with different numbers of blocks in our proposed local method

Secret images	Number of Blocks				
	4	16	64	256	1024
Airplane	34.4832	34.5349	34.6493	34.7370	34.9460
Pepper	34.1693	34.3667	34.4569	34.5843	34.7795
Barbara	34.1761	34.3948	34.5603	34.7236.	34.7692

Table 3. The results from embedding secret images into the host image Lena

Secret images	Host image is "Lena"			
	Simple LSB	Wang et al.'s method	Our global method	Our local method
Airplane	32.4303	33.0296	33.1669	34.5349
Pepper	32.2898	32.5453	32.6748	34.3667
Barbara	32.4479	32.8824	32.9873	34.3948

Table 4. The results from embedding secret images into the host image Baboon

Secret images	Host image is "Baboon"			
	Simple LSB	Wang et al.'s method	Our global method	Our local method
Airplane	32.3642	32.8717	33.0109	34.2259
Pepper	32.2065	32.8512	32.9987	34.1418
Barbara	32.3552	32.7586	33.0010	34.2859

From the results listed in Tables 3 and 4, we can see a comparison of the four methods. The *PSNR* of our global method was higher than that of the simple LSB substitution method and a little higher than the *PSNR* of Wang et al.'s optimal LSB method. However, the difference between our local method and Wang et al.'s method is significant because the local attribute was explored.

Since the generated block mapping matrix requires additional storage space in our two methods, the required storage space is also studied. Let the number of blocks be x, and let R be k-bits/pixel. In Wang et al.'s method, the additional information is one substitution matrix M. Then, their matrix M needs $2^k \times k$ bits space. Let k be 4. Wang et al.'s total amount of space is 64 bits. For our proposed global method, we need another additional storage space for one common block mapping matrix B. The matrix B needs $\lceil x \times \log x$ bits space. Let x be 16. Then the amount of the additional space is

64 bits. In this case, it takes 64+64=128 bits storage space for our global method because one substitution matrix and one block mapping matrix are needed. In our local substitution method, each block needs a corresponding substitution matrix. Here x blocks hold $x \times 2^k \times k$ bits space. The total space for our local optimal substitution strategy is $x \times \log x + x \times 2^k \times k$. Let x be 16 and k be 4. In this case, our proposed method thus takes 1028 bits of storage space. Therefore, we spent extra space in storing the mapping matrix that identifies the embedded message. This is an extra expense. However, the experiments also present that the *PSNR* can be significantly improved by our proposed global and local methods.

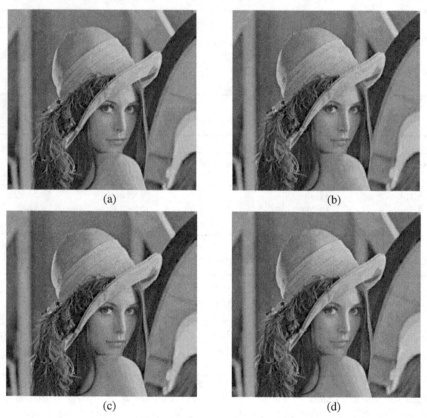

Fig. 10. The embedding results from the secret image Airplane and the host image Lena which were obtained using the four methods: (a)LSB substitution method, (b)Wang et al.'s method, (c) our global method, (d) our local method

5 Conclusions

In this paper, two methods considering the LSB optimal substitution of image pixel distributive characteristics are proposed. One is the global optimal substitution method, which uses one substitution matrix for all blocks. The other method is the local optimal substitution method, which uses separate substitution matrices for every block. The experimental results have shown that both local optimal substitution strategy and global optimal substitution strategy can enhance image quality. The *PSNR* values of stego-images are higher than those of the LSB substitution method and Wang et al.'s method. Of course, there is more extra-recorded information to be considered for local optimal substitution. Thus, we provide more choices between local optimal substitution and global optimal substitution depending on real life application requirements.

Reference

1. H. K. Pan, Y. Y. Chen, and Y. C. Tseng, "A Secure Data Hiding Scheme for Two-color Images," *Proceedings of the Fifth IEEE Symposium on Computers and Communications*, Antibes-Juan les Pins, France, July, 2000, pp. 750-755.
2. F. Petitcolas, R. Anderson, and M. Kuhn, "Information Hiding – A Survey," *Proceedings of the IEEE*, vol. 87, no. 7, July 1999, pp. 1062–78.
3. W. Bender, D. Gruhl, N. Morimoto, A. Lu, "Techniques for Data Hiding," *IBM Systems Journal*, Vol. 35, No. 3&4, 1996, pp. 313-336.
4. R. Z. Wang, C. F. Lin, and J. C. Lin, "Image Hiding by Optimal LSB Substitution and Genetic Algorithm," *Pattern Recognition*, Vol. 34, 2001, pp. 671-683.
5. S. Dumitrescu, X. Wu, and N. Memon, "On Steganalysis of Random LSB Embedding in Continuous-tone Images", *IEEE International Conference on Image Processing*, Vol. 3, Rochester, New York, USA, September, 2002, pp. 641-644.
6. J. Fridrich, M. Goljan, and R. Du, "Detecting LSB Steganography in Color and Gray-Scale Images," *IEEE Multimedia*, Oct-Dec, 2002, pp. 22-28.
7. T. Zhang, and X. Ping, "A New Approach to Reliable Detection of LSB Steganography in Natural Images," *Signal Processing*, Vol. 83, 2003, pp. 2085-2093.
8. C. C. Chang, J. Y. Hsiao, and C. S. Chan, "Finding Optimal Least-Significant-Bit Substitution in Image Hiding by Dynamic Programming Strategy," *Pattern Recognition*, Vol. 36, 2003, pp. 1583-1593.
9. C. C. Chang, M. H. Lin, and Y. C. Hu, "A Fast Secure Image Hiding Scheme Based on LSB Substitution," *International Journal of Pattern Recognition and Artificial Intelligence*, Vol.16, No. 4, 2002, pp. 399-416.
10. D. Goldberg, "Genetic Algorithms in Search, Optimization, and Machine Learning," *Addison-Wesley*, Reading, MA, 1989.

A Prediction Scheme for Image Vector Quantization Based on Mining Association Rules

Chih-Yang Lin and Chin-Chen Chang

Institute of Computer Science and Information Engineering
National Chung Cheng University
Chiayi, Taiwan, 621, R.O.C.
{gary,ccc}@cs.ccu.edu.tw

Abstract. Vector Quantization (VQ) is an efficient method for image compression. Many conventional VQ algorithms for lower bit rates, such as SMVQ, consider only adjacent neighbors in determining a codeword. This leads to awful distortion. In this paper, we propose an efficient association rules mining method inspired by an approach widely adopted in data mining, for predicting image blocks based on the spatial correlation. The proposed method is divided into two parts. First, it generates dominant vertical, horizontal, and diagonal association rules of training images. Then it searches for a suitable replacement according to the matched rules. The rule-based method for prediction is more efficient than conventional VQ since finding the matched rules is easier than calculating the distances between codewords. The experimental results show that our method is excellent in the performance in terms of both image quality and compression rate.

1 Introduction

In recent years, many image compression schemes have been proposed for multimedia applications to facilitate more effective storage and transmission. One of the most powerful methods is Vector Quantization (VQ). This lossy compression, proposed in 1984 by Gray [9], uses a codebook to represent images. Its principal features are effective compression and simple implementation by both software and hardware. When an image is to be indexed by the VQ system, it is first partitioned into non-overlapping blocks, each mapped to the closest codeword of the codebook and denoted by the index of the codeword. If each block contains sixteen pixels of a gray level image and the codebook size contains 256 codewords, the compression rate of the traditional VQ system is 1/16 (about 6%). In other words, the bit rate (**b**it **per p**ixel) of the traditional VQ system is 0.5, since sixteen pixels are represented by eight bits.

Although the traditional VQ system is very simple, the compression rate (or bit rate) is still not ideal since it never considers the relationship of neighboring blocks. Therefore, finite state vector quantization (FSVQ) [7] and side match vector quantization (SMVQ) [12] are proposed. FSVQ trains a finite state machine to represent the relationship of blocks. Each state dynamically contains a smaller codebook called state codebook from the master codebook. For example, when an input block comes in, the new state is determined by a transition function of the previous state and the input block. Besides, the transition function selects a proper state codebook from the master codebook for best fitting with the input block. Since the size of the state codebook is smaller than the master codebook, the bit rate is further reduced. However, the finite

C.-H. Chi and K.-Y. Lam (Eds.): AWCC 2004, LNCS 3309, pp. 230–240, 2004.
© Springer-Verlag Berlin Heidelberg 2004

state machine and the transition function are not easy to design, so SMVQ was devised. SMVQ predicts an input block by the adjacent borders of its upper and left blocks. The values of the borders are used to select some similar codewords out of the master codebook to form the state codebook for the input block. Therefore, SMVQ performs well not only in compression rate but in eliminating the block effect caused by the traditional VQ. Nevertheless, SMVQ may result in high distortion when border values of the input block are not similar to its neighbors. And even worse, a bad predicted codeword for an image block may cause worse selection of codewords for successive blocks. This is the *derailment problem*.

Although many methods, such as CSMVQ [4] and PSMVQ [3], have been proposed to solve the serious distortion problem in SMVQ, their prediction efficiencies are not desirable. In 2004, Chen proposed a highly efficient fuzzy prediction algorithm (FPVQ) [6] for image vector quantization to infer the unknown index values. However, the accurate fuzzy rules are not easily designed so the serious distortion may still occur. For better evaluation of rules, image quality, efficiency, and compression rate, we propose an alternative prediction method.

Based on the observation that the correlation of blocks exists not only on adjacent pixels, we employ an association rules mining method to generate the prediction rules that consider a greater range of nearby blocks. The prediction rules are used to predict the closest index value of a block, called the *base index*, and then the best-matched index is determined by searching the neighborhood of the base index in the sorted codebook, in which similar blocks are relocated close together. Since the candidates resulted from the prediction are sorted by their weight function values, our method serves as a systematic way to approach the fittest codeword. The decoding process of the proposed method is just a series of rule look-ups, which is more efficient than computing Euclidean distances, as in SMVQ. The experimental results show that the proposed method has better performance in terms of both image quality and compression rate.

The rest of this paper is organized as below. First, we briefly review the related works of Apriori and SMVQ in Section 2. Then our proposed scheme will be detailed in Section 3. Empirical results are demonstrated in Section 4. Finally, some concluding remarks are stated in Section 5.

2 Related Works

In this section, we first briefly review the Apriori mining algorithm. Then, the VQ and SMVQ algorithms are described.

2.1 Apriori

Apriori [1] is designed to discover the association rules between items in a large database, usually called transaction database. Finding association rules can be divided into two steps. Firstly, find all *frequent itemsets*, or *large itemsets*, whose *counts*, or *frequencies*, are greater than or equal to a pre-defined threshold. Secondly, generate all association rules from the frequent itemsets. Let $L = \{i_1, i_2, i_3, ..., i_m\}$ be a set of items of a given database. An association rule is an implication of the form $X \rightarrow Y$ with confidence c, where $X \subset L$, $Y \subset L$, and $X \cap Y = \varnothing$. The confidence c is the percentage of transactions in the given database containing X that also contain Y, namely the conditional probability $P(Y|X)$. If the confidence of an association rule is greater than or equal to a pre-defined threshold, or *minimum confidence*, the rule is called a strong rule.

Finding all strong association rules requires finding all frequent itemsets beforehand. Apriori uses a level-wise approach to obtain the large itemsets by deriving the k-itemsets from large $(k-1)$-itemsets. We illustrate with an example in Figure 1, assuming the minimum support is 2. In database D, there are four transactions with five distinguishable data items (i.e., A, B, C, D, E). In the first iteration, Apriori simply scans all the transactions to count the number of occurrences of each distinguishable data item, or *candidate 1-itemset*, denoted by C_1. The large 1-itemsets, denoted by L_1, can then be determined from C_1 by retaining only those whose counts are greater or equal to the minimum support. After that, C_2 can be obtained by applying the *join* operation [1] to L_1; the database is scanned again to generate L_2 from C_2 as was done in the previous iteration. The process is repeated until no candidate itemsets can be generated from the previous large itemsets.

After generating the large itemsets, the strong mining association rules can be determined in a straightforward manner. For example, if the minimum confidence is set 90%, the rule BC→E is strong since $P(E|BC)$ is 100%.

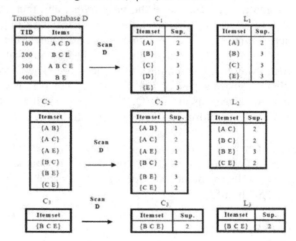

Fig. 1. Generation of large itemsets with Apriori

2.2   SMVQ

The main idea of VQ is to search the best-matching codewords from the codebook to replace the blocks of image as shown in Figure 2. The source image is divided into non-overlapping blocks with size $l \times m$. Each block, also called an image vector, is represented (and is thereby compressed) by the index whose corresponding codeword is closest to the block. After encoding, the image is represented by an index table. The decoding, or the reconstruction, of the image is just a codebook look-up procedure.

SMVQ (side match vector quantization) [12] is a variation of VQ. It also uses codebook indices to compress an image. However, SMVQ further considers the relationships among the image blocks to improve the compression bit-rate. Consider the image blocks shown in Figure 3, where U and L are image blocks reconstructed by VQ and X is an image block to be encoded. The aim of SMVQ is to predict the unknown block as accurately as possible. The prediction process of SMVQ is as follows. Assume the size of the master codebook is n. First, the border values of X are temporarily assigned by its upper and left neighbor blocks U and L, such as $x_1=(u_{13}+\ell_4)/2$, $x_2=u_{14}$, $x_3=u_{15}$, $x_4=u_{16}$, $x_5=\ell_8$, $x_9=\ell_{12}$, $x_{13}=\ell_{16}$. Then, the assigned values are used to search the master codebook to pick up m closest codewords as the state codebook that will be used to get the best codeword for the unknown block X. Therefore, since the state codebook is smaller than the master codebook, the bit rate of the unknown block is reduced from $\log_2 n$ to $\log_2 m$. Besides, the state codebooks can be generated dynamically from the master codebook, so these state codebooks need not be stored for reconstructing the original image.

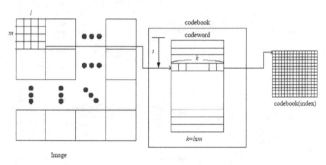

Fig. 2. Sketch of the VQ encoding scheme

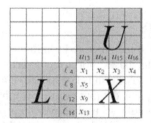

Fig. 3. The prediction process of SMVQ

3 The Proposed Prediction Scheme

In this section, we propose our prediction scheme for VQ. Figure 4 shows the framework of our method, which is divided into two phases: training and encoding. In training phase, the goal is to generate association rules of VQ images. These rules are used in encoding phase for prediction of unknown indices. In the following subsections, the steps of training and encoding phases will be detailed.

3.1 Preprocessing of the Codebook

The first step of our prediction scheme is reordering the codebook. The purpose of the preprocessing procedure is to efficiently find a similar codeword in the neighborhood of a given index of the reordered codebook, instead of searching the whole codebook. To achieve this goal, we apply the principal component analysis algorithm (PCA) to the codebook. PCA is a widely used method in data and signal analysis [10, 11, 13], such as multimedia coding and recognition. The power of PCA is projecting a high dimension input vector onto a lower-dimensional space while still preserving the maximal variances of the input vectors on the new coordinate axes. In our scheme, each codeword with sixteen dimensions is projected onto a one-dimensional space, resulting in its first principal component value, according to which the codewords are sorted.

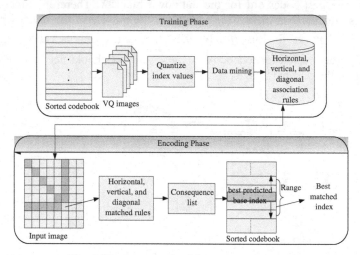

Fig. 4. The framework of the proposed method

3.2   Mining Predictive Rules

To generate the prediction rules, each indexed training image (using a sorted codebook) is regarded as three kinds of databases: horizontal, vertical, and diagonal databases. In the horizontal database, each transaction is composed of a row of indices of the indexed image. The vertical and diagonal databases are composed in a similar fashion and undergo the mining process as follows to discover their own association rules.

Before mining, these databases should be quantized again to avoid generating too complicated and specific rules. The quantized method is described in Formula (1), where v is the index value of a given block and v' is the quantized value.

$$v' = \lfloor v/10 \rfloor. \tag{1}$$

After quantization, the databases are processed by a revised Apriori algorithm to generate horizontal, vertical, and diagonal large itemsets. Note that, since the original Apriori algorithm doesn't discriminate the order of items in the transactions, the algorithm should be modified to discriminate the order and demand the itemsets in the resulting association rules be consecutive. Mining association rules with these restrictions are usually called mining traversal patterns [2, 5, 16]. When the large itemsets are generated, the association rules can be determined in a straightforward manner.

In our scheme, the form of the association rules is confined to $X \rightarrow y$, where X is a set of five or fewer items, but y is only an item. Our scheme also requires each rule in a rule set R be maximal. That is, if "$X \rightarrow y$" $\in R$, there is no such rule "$X' \rightarrow y'$" in R, where $X' \subset X$ and $y' = y$. For convenience of description, we define R_H as the rule set containing the horizontal association rules; rule sets R_V and R_D are defined similarly.

3.3 Determining the Predicted Index

In our scheme, the top three rows and left three columns of blocks of an image are obtained by full-search VQ. The rest are predicted according to the existing values. The prediction is computed based on quantized values by Formula (1). Therefore, the top three rows and left three columns should be quantized in the beginning. After that, the index value of block at the x-th row and the y-th column, denoted as $G(x, y)$, is predicted from three directions: horizontal, vertical, and diagonal. All the addresses in the following text are 0-based.

Figure 5 shows the prediction strategy for $G(x, y)$. We define the horizontal *look-back k-itemset*, denoted by $H_{x,y}$, as

$$H_{x,y} = \begin{cases} G(x, y-1) \| G(x, y-2) \| \cdots \| G(x, y-k), & \text{if } y \geq k, \\ G(x, y-1) \| \cdots \| G(x, 0), & \text{if } y < k. \end{cases}$$

Here $\|$ denotes the concatenation of itemsets (quantized index values); k is set to 5 according to our experiments. The vertical and diagonal look-back k-itemsets are defined in a similar fashion.

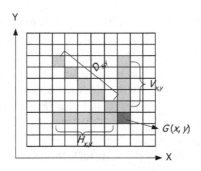

Fig. 5. The prediction strategy for $G(x, y)$

Afterward, each look-back k-itemset is used to match against the left-hand sides, or *antecedents*, of the rules from the corresponding rule set. For example, if $V_{x,y}$ = {4, 2, 3, 3, 1} and R_V = { (4, 2, 3, 3, 7 $\rightarrow$ 5), (4, 2, 3 $\rightarrow$ 1), (4, 2, 3, 3 $\rightarrow$ 15)}, there are three matching vertical rules: (4, 2, 3, 3 $\rightarrow$ 5), (4, 2, 3 $\rightarrow$ 1), and (4, 2, 3 $\rightarrow$ 15).

The sets of matching rules for $G(x, y)$ in the three directions are denoted by $M^v_{(x,y)}$, $M^h_{(x,y)}$, and $M^d_{(x,y)}$, respectively. Besides, the *consequence list* $C_{(x,y)}$ is defined as the set of right-hand items of matching rules from $M^v_{(x,y)}$, $M^h_{(x,y)}$, and $M^d_{(x,y)}$ collectively. The items in $C_{(x,y)}$ are sorted in descending order of their *weight function* (defined as follows) values.

$$w(c) = \{ |l_c^v| * conf_v + |l_c^h| * conf_h + |l_c^d| * conf_d \},$$ (2)

where c: an item in $C_{(x,y)}$; l_c^v, l_c^h, l_c^d: the antecedents of c in $M_{(x,y)}^v$, $M_{(x,y)}^h$, and $M_{(x,y)}^d$, respectively; $conf_v$, $conf_h$, $conf_d$: the corresponding confidences.

For example, if $M_{(x,y)}^v$ is $\{(4, 2, 3, 3 \rightarrow 5, conf_v = 90\%), (4, 2, 3 \rightarrow 1, conf_v = 85\%)\}\}$, $M_{(x,y)}^h$ is $\{(12, 12, 1, 3 \rightarrow 5, conf_h = 90\%), (12, 12 \rightarrow 1, conf_h = 95\%)\}$, and $M_{(x,y)}^d$ is $\{(6, 4, 2, 2, 3 \rightarrow 5, conf_d = 100\%), (6, 4, 2 \rightarrow 10, conf_d = 75\%)\}$, the consequence list $C_{(x,y)}$ is $(5, 1, 10)$ since the weight of 5 is 12.2 ($4*90\%+4*90\%+5*100\%$), the weight of 1 is 4.45, and the weight of 10 is 2.25.

After generating the consequence list $C_{(x,y)}$, a number, denoted by n_1, of the first items of $C_{(x,y)}$ are selected as candidates for predicting $G(x,y)$. If the size of $C_{(x,y)}$ is too small ($< n_1$), more matched rules are selected from R_V, R_H, and R_D according to the Euclidean distance compared with $V_{x,y}$, $H_{x,y}$, and, $D_{x,y}$. The smaller the Euclidean distance is, the higher the priority of the rule to be selected will be. In the following subsection, we will elaborate on the encoding scheme for best-matched index of $G(x, y)$.

3.4   Finding and Encoding the Best-Matched Index

When the first n_1 candidates are selected from $C_{(x,y)}$ for $G(x, y)$, they are de-quantized and distances from each of their corresponding codewords to the codeword resulting from application of full-search VQ on block (x, y). If the distances are all greater than a user-defined threshold δ, the full-search VQ result of $G(x, y)$ is adopted to avoid the derailment problem of SMVQ [4]. On the other hand, if there exist distances less than or equal to δ, the index with the smallest distance is the best predicted base index, and the best-matching index of $G(x, y)$ is selected from the preset range, denoted by n_2, centered at the predicted base index.

These factors n_1 and n_2 have opposite effect on the compression ratio and image quality: larger number of candidates from $C_{(x,y)}$ and larger offset result in higher quality of image but worse bit rate, or compression rate. Therefore, it's a tradeoff between image quality and compression rate. Fortunately, based on the benefits of PCA and association rules, the proposed method can predict well in most cases, even when the ranges of $C_{(x,y)}$ and offset are small.

The encoded binary string for $G(x, y)$ by the proposed method is composed of two parts: the base position k_1 and the offset k_2. The base position k_1 refers to the item in $C_{(x,y)}$ selected as the predicted base index; the offset k_2 is the distance of the best-matching index from the base position. The best-matching index is represented by $\lceil \log_2 (n_1 + 1) \rceil + \lceil \log_2 (n_2 + 1) \rceil$ bits. Note that whether the encoded values of a block is an index of association rules or a full-search VQ result need to be recorded by a bit. This bitmap can be suitably compressed by Run-Length-Encoding [8].

The decoding of the proposed method is quite straightforward. The decoder first decodes the bitmap. If the predicted index is replaced by the original index value, the corresponding codeword is directly fetched from the codebook. On the other hand, if the predictive index is according to the mining association rules, fetch $\lceil \log_2(n_1+1) \rceil + \lceil \log_2(n_2+1) \rceil$ bits to reconstruct the best-matched index. The $\lceil \log_2(n_1+1) \rceil$ bits indicate the best predicted base index from the three directional association rules. The $\lceil \log_2(n_2+1) \rceil$ bits indicate the offset of the de-quantized base index. Since the decoding scheme just searches for rules, instead of calculating Euclidean distance to generate state codebook in SMVQ, the proposed method is more efficient than the SMVQ.

We summarize the encoding and decoding algorithms as follows:

The Proposed Encoding Algorithm

Input: An image with top three rows and left three columns encoded by full-search VQ, a sorted codebook, vertical, horizontal, diagonal association rules (R_V , R_H , R_D), and a user-defined threshold δ.

Output: An encoded image and the corresponding bitmap.

Step 1: Quantize the values of the encoded part of the input image by Formula (1).

Step 2: Fetch the look-back k-itemsets of $G(x, y)$ from horizontal, vertical, and diagonal directions and search for the matching rules $M^v_{(x,y)}$, $M^h_{(x,y)}$, and $M^d_{(x,y)}$ from R_V , R_H , R_D .

Step 3: Generate the consequence list $C_{(x,y)}$ from $M^v_{(x,y)}$, $M^h_{(x,y)}$, $M^d_{(x,y)}$ and then reorder the elements of $C_{(x,y)}$ with the weight function in Formula (2).

Step 4: Select the subset of the first n_1 elements, $C'_{(x,y)}$, of $C_{(x,y)}$ and de-quantize the elements of $C'_{(x,y)}$. Later calculate $\min_{i=0}^{n_1-1}\{\|cw(c_i)-cw(x)\|\}$, where c_i belongs to $C'_{(x,y)}$, x is the index value of $G(x, y)$ resulting from full-search VQ, $cw(c_i)$ and $cw(x)$ are the corresponding codewords of c_i and x, respectively.

Step 5: If $\min_{i=0}^{n_1-1}\{\|cw(c_i)-cw(x)\|\} > \delta$, $G(x, y)$ is encoded as the full-search VQ result and the corresponding bitmap value is set to 1.

Step 6: If $\min_{i=0}^{n_1-1}\{\|cw(c_i)-cw(x)\|\} \le \delta$, search the best-matching codeword for $G(x, y)$ through the $(c_j-n_2/2)$-th to the $(c_j+n_2/2-1)$-th entries in the sorted codebook, where j satisfies $\|cw(c_j)-cw(x)\| = \min_{i=0}^{n_1-1}\{\|cw(c_i)-cw(x)\|\}$. The encoded index of $G(x, y)$ is the concatenation of the binary strings of k_1, the (0-based) index of c_j in $C'_{(x,y)}$ and the offset of the best-matching codeword from the base index (k_2). Besides, the corresponding bitmap value is set to 0.

Step 7: Repeat Steps 1 to 6 until all unknown indices are encoded.

The Proposed Decoding Algorithm
Input: An encoded image, the corresponding bitmap, and a sorted codebook with size m.
Output: A predicted index image.
Step 1: Decode the image sequentially from left to right, top to down.
Step 2: If the bitmap value is 1, fetch $\log_2 m$ bits from the encoding image as the codeword index of the sorted codebook.
Step 3: If the bitmap value is 0, generate and reorder the consequence list $C'_{(x,y)}$, as in the encoding algorithm. Then, fetch $\lceil \log_2(n_1+1) \rceil + \lceil \log_2(n_2+1) \rceil$ bits from the encoding image. The former $\lceil \log_2(n_1+1) \rceil$ bits is k_1, which indicate the position of selected item, denoted by c of $C'_{(x,y)}$ and the latter $\lceil \log_2(n_2+1) \rceil$ bits represent the offset value k_2. Therefore, the predicted index of $G(x, y)$ is the de-quantization of c offset by k_2, namely $10c+k_2$.
Step 4: Repeat Steps 2 to 3 until all indices are decoded.

4   Experiments

In this section, we conduct some experiments to evaluate the performance of our proposed method. Several standard gray level images of sizes 512×512 pixels, including "Lena", "Baboon", "Peppers", and "F16" as shown in Figure 6, are used for training the codebook by the LBG algorithm [14] and generating the association rules by the modified Apriori algorithm [5]. In the experiments, images are partitioned into non-overlapping 4×4 blocks, and the trained codebook contains 256 codewords. Besides, the minimum confidence is set to 60% and the threshold δ is set to 35.

Lena   Baboon   Peppers   F16

Fig. 6. The test images

Figure 7 shows the correlation between the PSNR and the support threshold for image "Lena" encoded with the codebook of 256 codewords. The bit-length of the prediction base index (k_1) is set to 2, and 3 bits, respectively, while the bit-length of offset (k_2) is fixed at 3 bits. The curves initially increase with the decline of the support threshold. The PSNR value rises to maximum when we decrease the support threshold to 10%, but it slightly deteriorates due to the overfitting problem [15] if the support threshold declines further.

The comparisons of various methods are shown in Table 1. Our method has lower bit rate than full-search VQ and higher PSNR than SMVQ. Selection of the size of k_1

depends on the tradeoff between compression rate and image quality. Our suggested length of k_1 is 3 bits (i.e., $n_1 = 8$) based on our experimental results.

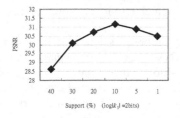
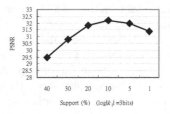

Support (%) (log$|k_1|$ =2bits)   Support (%) (log$|k_1|$ =3bits)

Fig. 7. The correlation between PSNR and support threshold

Figure 8 shows the comparisons between the images reconstructed with VQ and the proposed method with bit-length of k_1 equal to 3. It is very difficult for human eyes to differentiate these images since the distortion is quite small.

Table 1. The performance comparisons on various methods

	Performance	Lena	Pepper	F16
Full-search VQ	PSNR (dB)	32.25	31.41	31.58
	Bit-rate (bpp)	0.5	0.5	0.5
SMVQ	PSNR (dB)	28.57	28.04	27.94
	Bit-rate (bpp)	0.33	0.32	0.33
Our Scheme (k_1: 2bits)	PSNR (dB)	30.64	30.05	29.74
	Bit-rate (bpp)	0.33	0.32	0.34
Our Scheme (k_1: 3bits)	PSNR (dB)	32.16	31.33	31.45
	Bit-rate (bpp)	0.38	0.38	0.39

(a) Reconstructed image by full-search VQ   (b) Reconstructed image by the proposed method

Fig. 8. The comparison of the original image and the reconstructed image

5   Conclusions

In this paper, an efficient image block prediction scheme has been proposed. The proposed technique utilizes a data mining approach to generate association rules representing the correlations between blocks. It is mainly different from SMVQ in three ways. First, the proposed method predicts a block value based on a broader spatial correlation, instead of by only adjacent pixels. Second, the prediction accuracy of the proposed method is independent of the block size, but that of SMVQ is not. Third, the decoding process of the proposed method is just matching of association rules. This is more efficient than that of SMVQ, in which each block requires a search of the closest codewords from the codebook.

The experiments show the advantage of the proposed scheme. It has better performance than others in terms of bit rate and PSNR. Therefore, the spatial association rules is more suitable for prediction of image blocks than conventional prediction methods, which considers only the adjacency blocks. It can be concluded that association rules mining is a good tool to predict and compress images. In future work, we will investigate the benefit of association rules mining on image retrieval systems.

References

1. R. Agrawal and R. Srikant.: Fast Algorithms for Mining Association Rules in Large Databases. Proceedings of the 20th International Conference on Very Large Data Bases, Santiago de Chile, Chile, (1994) 487-499.
2. R. Agrawal and R. Srikant.: Mining Sequential Patterns. Proceedings of the Eleventh International Conference on Data Engineering, Taipei, Taiwan, (1995) 3-14.
3. C. C. Chang, F. C. Shine, and T. S. Chen.: Pattern-based Side Match Vector Quantization for Image Quantization. Imaging Science Journal, 48, (2000) 63-76.
4. R. F. Chang and W. T. Chen.: Image Coding Using Variable-Rate Side-Match Finite-State Vector Quantization. IEEE Transactions on Image Processing, 38(4), (1993) 591-598.
5. M. S. Chen, J. S. Park, and P. S. Yu.: Efficient Data Mining for Path Traversal Patterns. IEEE Transactions on Knowledge and Data Engineering, 10(2), (1998) 209-221.
6. P. Y. Chen.: An Efficient Prediction Algorithm for Image Vector Quantization. IEEE Transactions on Systems, Man, and Cybernetics – Part B: Cybernetics, 34(1), (2004) 740-746.
7. A. Gersho and R. M. Gray.: Vector Quantization and Signal Compression. Kluwer Academic Publishers (1992).
8. R. C. Gonzalez and R. E. Woods.: Digital Image Processing. Addison-Wesley (2002).
9. R. M. Gray.: Vector Quantization. IEEE ASSP Magazine, (1984) 4-29.
10. A. Hyvarinen, J. Karhunen, and E. Oja.: Independent Component Analysis. John Wiley & Sons (2001) 125-146.
11. R. A. Johnson and D. W. Wichern.: Applied Multivariate Statistical Analysis. Prentice Hall (2002).
12. T. Kim.: Side Match and Overlap Match Vector Quantizers for Images. IEEE Transactions on Image Processing, 1(2), (1992) 170-185.
13. R. C. T. Lee, Y. H. Chin, and S. C. Chang.: Application of Principal Component Analysis to Multikey Searching. IEEE Transactions on Software Engineering, SE-2(3), (1976) 185-193.
14. Y. Linde, A. Buzo, and R. M. Gary.: An Algorithm for Vector Quantization Design. IEEE Transactions on Communications, 28, (1980) 84-95.
15. S. J. Russell and P. Norvig.: Artificial Intelligence: A Modern Approach. Prentice Hall (2002).
16. Y. Xiao and M. H. Dunham.: Efficient Mining of Traversal Patterns. Data & Knowledge Engineering, 39(2), (2001) 191-214.

Fuzzy Logic-Based Image Retrieval

Xiaoling Wang and Kanglin Xie

Dept. of Computer and Engineering, Shanghai JiaoTong University, Shanghai 200030, China
jgbdos@sohu.com, klxie@mail.cs.sjtu.edu.cn

Abstract. Classical mathematic method adopts the rigid logic to measure the similarity of images, and therefore cannot deal with the uncertainty and imprecision exist in the human's thoughts. This paper imports fuzzy logic method into image retrieval to simulate these properties of human's thoughts. Different from other researches that also adopt the fuzzy logic method, we emphasis on the followings: (1) adopting the fuzzy language variables to describe the similarity degree of image features, not the features themselves. In this way, we can simulate the nonlinear property of human's judgments of the image similarity. (2) Making use of the fuzzy inference to instruct the weights assignment among various image features. The fuzzy rules that embed the users' general perceive of an object guarantee their good robustness to the images of various fields. On the other hand, the user's subjective intentions can be expressed by the fuzzy rules perfectly. In this paper, we propose a novel shape description method called Minimum Statistical Sum Direction Code (MSSDC). The experiment demonstrates the efficiency and feasibility of our proposed algorithms.

1 Introduction

Due to the development of computer network and the low cost of large storage device, the visual information is widely used in many fields. How to retrieve the information efficiently has led to the rise of interest in techniques for retrieving images through the image databases. Image Retrieval (IR) aims to retrieve similar or relevant images to the query image by the image features or the keywords related with the query image. In the past, various approaches to the image retrieval were proposed, most of which were Content-Based Image Retrieval (CBIR) that derives the image features such as color, texture and shape or any combination of them. However, CBIR has the following problems which degrade its' efficiency:

(1) The semantic gap between the high-level semantic expressed by the image and the low-level features of an image Human is accustomed to retrieve images according to the "semantic " or "concept " embedded in the images such as "animal" or "scenery". However, CBIR depends on the absolute distance of image features to retrieve the similar images. Research has concealed that the relation between the high-level semantics and the low-level features is nonlinear. For instance, an image may be regarded as similar (semantic) although its' color and shape (low-level features) are not quite similar to the query image. The classical mathematic method adopts the rigid logic to measure the similarity between two images and therefore cannot deal with the uncertainty and imprecision exist in the human's judgments. We should notice that "similar" is a fuzzy concept itself.

(2) Integration of various features Multi features outperform the single feature in image retrieval. Currently, the weight assignment of variuous features is

C.-H. Chi and K.-Y. Lam (Eds.): AWCC 2004, LNCS 3309, pp. 241–250, 2004.
© Springer-Verlag Berlin Heidelberg 2004

conducted in a linear manner according to the experience such as [1]. For example, if a user thinks that the color is important twice as the shape feature, he (she) assigns 2/3 to the color weight and 1/3 shape weight. Such precisie and fixed assignment of weights dosen't consist with the human's thoughts and consequently can not reflect the semantic of the image and the users' requiemnts. An effieient method to solve this problem is the famous User Relevance Feedback (URF) [2]. The deficiency of URF is that it makes the interface complex and heavy the users' burden in retrieval.

(3) The users' subjective intentions in image retrieval Different user under different circumstance may have different perceive of a same image, which refers to the users' subjective intentions. The research of how to apply and reflect it in the image retrieval is rather few.

In a word, any image retrieval system should be recognized by human ultimately, which requires the computer to simulate the human's thoughts in image retrieval and not depend on the rigid logic measure to decide the similarity. Fuzzy mathematic is a powerful tool to realize this goal.

Fuzzy logic has been widely used in image retrieval. Most researches adopt the fuzzy set to describe the properties of image features such as texture coarse [3][4] and edge thickness [5]. Different from the previous works, we emphasis on the followings: (1) adopting the fuzzy language variables to describe the similarity degree of image features, not the features themselves. In this way, we can simulate the nonlinear property of human's judgments of the image similarity. (2) Making use of the fuzzy inference to instruct the weight assignment among various image features. The fuzzy rules that embed the users' general perceive of an object guarantee their good robustness to images of various fields. On the other hand, the user's subjective intentions can be expressed by the fuzzy rules perfectly. In this paper, we propose a novel shape description method called MSSDC (Minimum Statistical Sum Direction Code). The experiment demonstrates the efficiency and feasibility of our proposed algorithms.

2 The Fuzzy Logic-Based IR

In this paper, we propose a fuzzy logic-based image retrieval system illustrated in figure 1. The fuzzy inference scheme is applied to decide the similarity of two images. As we know, color and shape features are of importance to the image retrieval. Therefore we take the difference of color and shape features of the images as two inputs and the similarity of them output. The system is composed of the following 4 parts:

(1) Feature Extraction The color feature C is represented by HSV histogram. We adopt a novel shape description method called MSSDC (Minimum Statistical Sum Direction Code) to extract the shape feature S. Suppose the query image is Q and image from the image database is I. The color distance $D_C(C_Q, C_I)$ and shape distance $D_S(S_Q, S_I)$ between Q and I are two inputs of the fuzzy image retrieval system.

(2) Fuzzifier 3 fuzzy variables including "very similar", "similar" and "not similar" are used to describe the feature difference $D_C(C_Q, C_I)$ and $D_S(S_Q, S_I)$ of image Q and I. By such description, we can infer the similarity of images in the same way as human.

(3) Fuzzy Inference According to the general knowledge of an object and the retrieval requirements of the user, a fuzzy rule base including 9 rules is created. The output of the fuzzy system S is the similarity of two images and it is also described by 3 fuzzy variables including "very similar", "similar" and "not similar".

(4) Defuzzifier We adopt the Center Of Gravity (COG) method to defuzzy the output S.

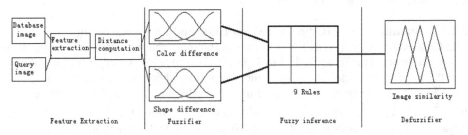

Fig. 1. Fuzzy logic-based IR

3 Feature Extractions

The color and shape representations and measurement methods are introduced in the following section.

3.1 HSV Color Histogram

Color is one of the most salient and commonly used features in the image retrieval. The color histogram is more popular for its' effectiveness and efficiency [6]. We select the color histogram in the HSV color space for its consistence to the human's perceives of color. The details of conversion form RGB to HSV can be found in [7]. Given a color space C, the conventional histogram H of image I is defined as Enq. (1).

$$H_C(I) = \{N(I_i, C_i) \mid i \in [1, ..., n]\} .\tag{1}$$

Where $N(I_i, C_i)$ is the number of pixels of I fall into cell C_i in the color space C and i is the gray level. $H_C(I)$ shows the proportion of pixels of each color within the image. One of the most commonly used matching techniques is called histogram intersection [6]:

$$D_C(C_Q, C_I)) = \sum_{i=1}^{n} \min(H(I_i) - H(Q_i)) .\tag{2}$$

3.2 Shape Fature Description

Shape is one of the key visual features used by human to distinguish images. In general, shape representation can be categorized into either boundary-based or region-based [8]. The former uses only the outer boundary characteristics of the entities while the latter uses the entire region. Well known methods include Fourier descriptors and moment invariants [9]. Chain code [10] has been widely used to encode the boundary lines for its simplicity and low storage requirement [11]. One problem with the Chain code is that an object can be recognized only when it is viewed from a predetermined angle and viewpoint, which limited its use in image retrieval. To solve this problem, in this paper, we propose a novel contour encode called Minimum Sum Statistical Direction Code (MSSDC). This encode has the advantages of being invariant to translation, rotation and proportional to scaling of the image.

3.2.1 Minimize Sum Statistical Direction Code and Shape Encoding

The Chain code is defined as follows: for one pixel on the boundary of the object, it has 8 neighbors, numbered from 0 to 7. Fig 2 illustrates an object with its boundary and the 8-direction code. The even number represents horizontal or vertical line and the odd number represents the diagonal line. If the length of the horizontal or vertical line is d, then the length of the diagonal line is $\sqrt{2}d$. Along the clockwise direction, beginning from the start point illustrated in figure 2, the 8-direction chain code is: 00002223312124444444455544667070070. Evidently, the traditional boundary chain code is not invariant to the scaling and rotation of the image contents.

Fig. 2. Boundary direction chain code

However, shape representation is normally required to be invariant to translation, rotation and scaling of the image contents. To solve this problem, in this paper, we propose a novel boundary chain code called Minimum Sum Statistical Direction Code (MSSDC). First, we give the definition of Statistical Direction Code (SDC) (in the direction of clockwise):

$$X = (x_0 \quad x_1 \quad x_2 \quad x_3 \quad x_4 \quad x_5 \quad x_6 \quad x_7) . \tag{3}$$

Where $x_i (i = 0....,7)$ counts the number of pixels on the boundary with direction number i. Assumed that the chain code is always created in the direction of clockwise, and then SDC has nothing to do with the start point. The definition of the direction number vector is as Enq. (4):

$$D = (0 \quad 1 \quad 2 \quad 3 \quad 4 \quad 5 \quad 6 \quad 7)^T . \tag{4}$$

Let $X_0 = (x_0 \quad x_1 \quad x_2 \quad x_3 \quad x_4 \quad x_5 \quad x_6 \quad x_7)$ be the initial SDC of an object. As the image rotates in the direction of clockwise $45° * i$ ($i = 0, ..., 7$) in turn, the SDC varies as follows:

$$X_i = \{x_{(i+0)\oplus 8} \quad x_{(i+1)\oplus 8} \quad x_{(i+2)\oplus 8} \quad x_{(i+3)\oplus 8} \quad x_{(i+4)\oplus 8}$$
$$x_{(i+5)\oplus 8} \quad x_{(i+6)\oplus 8} \quad x_{(i+7)\oplus 8} \mid i = 0,1...7\}$$
(5)

$\oplus$ is the modulus computation. The periodicity of the image rotation is 8. Evidently, if the image rotates, the boundary of an object will have different SDC as shown in Enq. (5). To overcome this drawback, we design a code named Minimum Sum Statistical Direction Code (MSSDC) to describe the boundary of an object:

$$D_{\min} = Min\{X_i \cdot D \mid i = 0,....,7\} .$$
(6)

Through the minimum sum restriction, one of the 8 directions is definitely selected to describe the boundary of an object. If more than one SDC satisfies the Enq. (6), we select the first one we meet in the direction of clockwise. Obviously, when the object rotates or translates in the image, there exists a unique MSSDC corresponding to it. Now, for an object, it can be viewed from the same angle and viewpoint by MSSDC representation. When the object scale changes (zooms in or zooms out λ), suppose P and P_λ are the boundary perimeter before and after the image scale changes, then:

$$P = \sqrt{2}x_i + x_j \ (i = 1,3,5,7, j = 0,2,4,6) .$$
(7)

Accordingly,

$$P_\lambda = \lambda P = \sqrt{2}(\lambda x_i) + \lambda x_j .$$
(8)

If X and X_λ are the respective MSSDC before and after the scaling, then according to the definition of SDC and Enq. (8):

$$X_\lambda = \lambda X .$$
(9)

If $\lambda > 1$, image zooms in while $\lambda < 1$ zooms out. It is reasonable to assume that for the similar images which have similar boundary, they should have similar MSSDC encoding. In the direction determined by MSSDC, similar images will rotate to similar angle or viewpoint, which ensures the effectiveness of the following retrieval.

3.2.2 Similarity Measure: Direction Entropy (DE)

The encoding of an object's contour has carried enough information of the shape, so it is suitable to estimate the boundary information with entropy. In this paper, we design a novel similarity measure called Direction Entropy (DE) E_D to measure the shape information embedded in the MSSDC:

$$E_D = \sum_{i=0}^{7} e_i .$$
(10)

Where

$$e_i = -p_i \log_2 p_i .$$
(11)

$$p_i = \frac{x_i}{\sum_{i=0}^{7} x_i} .$$
(12)

p_i is the occurrence probability of the ith direction of the pixels on the boundary. Obviously, according to Enq. (9) and Enq. (12), we obtain:

$$p_i(x) = p_i(x_\lambda) .$$ (13)

$$E_D(X) = E_D(X_\lambda) .$$ (14)

The shape distance $D_S(S_Q, S_I)$ between the query image Q and the image I from the image database is defined as Enq. (15):

$$D_S(S_Q, S_I) = \sum_{i=0}^{7} [(e_{Qi} - e_{Ii})^2]^{\frac{1}{2}} .$$ (15)

Figure 3 gives the entropy distributions of the 8 directions of the figure (a), (b), (c) and (d) before and after MSSDC. The variance trend of the entropy distributions becomes similar after MSSDC. It verifies that the MSSDC arranges the images into a similar viewpoint.

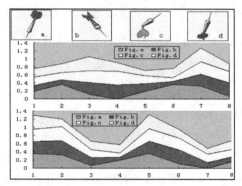

Fig. 3. The DE distributions following the 8 directions before and after MSSDC

4 Fuzzy Logic-Based Image Similarity Matching

4.1 Data Normalization

See Enq. (2) in section 3.1, if $D_C(C_Q, C_I)$ is close to 1, it indicates that the two images Q and I have strongly similar color. However, in the fuzzy inference, we assume that the feature distance which closes to 1 means "not similar". So we must convert $D(C_Q, C_I)$ through Enq. (16):

$$D_C(C_Q, C_I) = \|D_C(C_Q, C_I) - 1\| .$$ (16)

Before the fuzzy inference, the shape difference $D_S(S_Q, S_I)$ needs to be transformed into range [0,1] with the Gauss-normalization method [12].

$$D_S' = (\frac{D_S - m_{D_S}}{3\sigma_{D_S}} + 1)/2 .$$ (17)

Enq. (17) guarantees that 99 percents of $D's$ belong to the range [0,1]. m_D and σ_D are the mean value and standard deviation of D_s respectively.

4.2 The Fuzzy Inference of Image Similarity

In general, human use the following experiences to retrieve images: if the feature difference is no more than 20%, the two images are very similar, between 40%-50% similar, between 70%-90% not similar. The Membership Grade Function (MGF) of color and shape features difference is built according to the above experiences.

3 fuzzy variables including "very similar", "similar" and "not similar" are used to describe the two inputs. Their respective MGF are: Gauss MGF, Union Gauss MGF and Gauss MGF. The output of the fuzzy image retrieval system is the similarity of images, which is also described by 3 fuzzy variables: "very similar", "similar" and "not similar". Their respective MGF are: Gauss MGF, Union Gauss MGF and Gauss MGF. Figure 4 shows the MGFs of the two inputs and one outputs of the fuzzy image retrieval system.

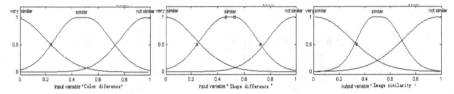

Fig. 4. Membership functions of the two inputs and one output of the system

Once we acquire the fuzzy descriptions of the color difference and shape difference of the two images, the rule base including 9 rules can be built to make an inference of their similarity. The fuzzy relation matrix R is computed in Enq. (18). The inference can be conducted by R.

$$R = \bigcup (D_C \times D_S) \times S . \tag{18}$$

These rules are consistent with the user's requirements and what his (her) perceive of the object. The weight of a rule reflects the user's confidence of it. For one user named A, he wants to retrieve all the flower images with different color and shape to the query image 5.jpg. So he assumes that two images with similar color and very similar shape maybe similar. According to his requirements, the rules are shown in table 1. For another user named B, he just retrieves the flower images with strongly similar color to 5.jpg. So he may thinks that two images with similar color and very similar shape are not similar. The rules related to his requirements are shown in table 2. The difference of the two rule bases is illustrated in bold in table 1 and table 2. The two corresponding output surfaces are illustrated in figure 5. Figure 6 shows their respective retrieval result (the top is for user A and the bottom user B). Obviously, the retrieval results satisfy the two users' initial requirements. The 9 rules altogether deal with the weight assignments perfectly. For the fuzzy inference processes the 9 cases parallel and makes a reasonable decision synthetically, the weight assignments are consistent with the users' perceive in a nonlinear manner.

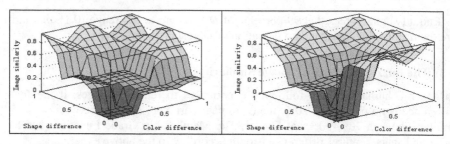

Fig. 5. The output surface of the fuzzy inference according to table 1 and table 2

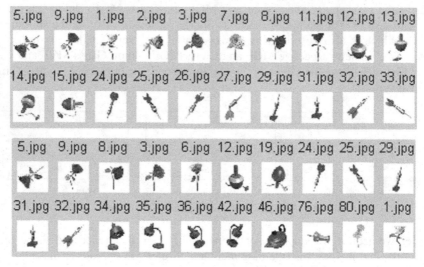

Fig. 6. The retrieval results for user A and B

If the user's requirements are similar, the fuzzy retrieval system has a good robustness to the images of different fields because the rules embed the user's general not the particular perceive of the objects. Each rule accompanying with its' weight indicates the possible variance scope of the color and shape features. Meanwhile, they altogether can express the subjective intentions of a particular user.

Table 1. The fuzzy rules for the user A

Rules	Input		Output	Weight
	D_C	D_S	S	
1	Very similar	Very similar	Very similar	1
2	**Very similar**	**Similar**	**Similar**	**1**
3	Very similar	Not similar	Not similar	1
4	**Similar**	**Very similar**	**Similar**	**0.3**
5	Similar	Similar	Similar	0.5
6	Similar	Not similar	Not similar	1
7	**Not similar**	**Very similar**	**Similar**	**0.5**
8	Not similar	Similar	Not similar	1
9	Not similar	Not similar	Not similar	1

Table 2. The fuzzy rules for the user B

Rules	Input		Output	Weight
	D_C	D_S	S	
1	Very similar	Very similar	Very similar	1
2	**Very similar**	**Similar**	**Similar**	**0.5**
3	Very similar	Not similar	Not similar	1
4	**Similar**	**Very similar**	**Not similar**	**1**
5	Similar	Similar	Similar	0.6
6	Similar	Not similar	Not similar	1
7	**Not similar**	**Very similar**	**Not similar**	**1**
8	Not similar	Similar	Not similar	1
9	Not similar	Not similar	Not similar	1

5   Experiments

5.1   Image Preprocessing

Before experiment, the color images, which have 256^3 levels in the RGB color system, are converted into the HSV color space. In order to apply the shape representation method proposed in this paper, the whole boundary of the object is needed. We make use of the edge detection and the basic morphological operator to obtain the object boundary as follows: firstly, detect the edges with the Sobel operator, then dilate the image with line structure element, fill the hole inside the object. Finally erode the image with the diamond structure element to smooth the boundary.

5.2   Retrieval Performance

There are two principals to evaluate a retrieval system: the precision and the recall. The precision of the result is the fraction of retrieved images that is truly relevant to the query while the recall is the fraction of relevant images that are actually retrieved. Figure 7 illustrates the precision-recall of our proposed algorithm.

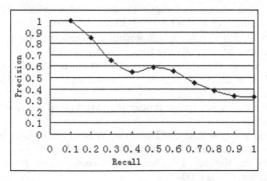

Fig. 7. The precision-recall of the fuzzy retrieval system

For the images with large different appearance such as lamp, flower and knap, our proposed method has an average precision of above 41% vs. the top 20 images, which means that the fuzzy retrieval method has a good robustness to the image categories.

6 Conclusions

In this paper, a fuzzy logic-based image retrieval system based on color and shape features is presented. A novel shape description method called Minimize Statistical Sum Direction Code (MSSDC) is proposed. The experiments demonstrate the efficiency and robustness of our algorithm, which owes to the following reasons:

(1) We adopt the fuzzy scheme not the absolute distance measure to match the image, which consists with the human's perceive.
(2) The fuzzy inference rules integrate various features perfectly and reflect the user's subjective requirements in image retrieval.

If we apply this method for field-related image retrieval and embed the users' retrieval requirements into the fuzzy rules, we have reason to believe that the image retrieval performance will be improved.

References

1. Bao, P., Xisnjun Zhang: Image Retrieval Based on Multi-scale Edge Model. ICME (2002) 417-420
2. Rui Y, Huang TS: Mehrotra S. Content-based Image Retrieval With Relevance Feedback in MARS. ICIP (1997) 815-818
3. Kulkami, S., Verma, B.: Fuzzy Logic Based Texture Queries for CBIR. Fifth International Conference on Computational Intelligence and Multimedia Applications, (2003) 223-228
4. Chih-Yi Chiu, Hsin-Chin Lin, Shi-Nine Yang: A Fuzzy Logic CBIR System. The 12th IEEE International Conference on Fuzzy Systems, (2003) 1171-1176
5. Banerjee, M., Kundu, M.K: Content Based Image Retrieval With Fuzzy Geometrical Features. The 12th IEEE International Conference on Fuzzy Systems, (2003) 932-937
6. Swain, M. J. and Ballard, D. H.: Color Indexing. International Journal of Computer Vision, Vol.7 (1), (1991) 11-32
7. Ardizzone, M. Cascia, Automatic Video Database Indexing and Retrieval. Multimedia Tools and Applications, Vol.4 (1), (1997) 29-56
8. Safar, M. Shahabi, C. and Sun, X.: Image Retrieval by Shape: A Comparative Study. International Conference on Multimedia and Expo, (2000) 141-144
9. Ezer, N., Anarim E., Sankur, B.: A Comparative Study of Moment Variants and Fourier Descriptors in Planar Shape Recognition. Proceedings of 7th Mediterranean Electro technical Conference, (1994) 242-245
10. Kennrth R. Castleman: Digital Image Processing [M], Publishing House of Electronics Industry, Beijing, China (1996)
11. D.L.Neuhoff, K.G.Castor: A Rate and Distortion Analysis of Chain Codes for Line Drawings. IEEE Trans. Information Theory. Vol. IT (31), (1985) 53-68
12. Jiawei Han, Micheline Kamber: Data Mining Conception And Technology [M]. Mechanism industry, Beijing, China (2001)

Deriving Facial Patterns for Specifying Korean Young Men's 3D Virtual Face from Muscle Based Features

Seongah Chin[1] and Seongdong Kim[2]

[1] Division of Multimedia, Sungkyul University, Anyang-City, Korea
solideo@sungkyul.edu
[2] Department of Gameware, Kaywon School of Art and Design, Uiwang-City, Korea
sdkim@kaywon.ac.kr

Abstract. In the work approached here we derive facial patterns defined by shape descriptors for making the feature of the Korean young men's 3D virtual face. The clustering algorithms calculated on the feature vertices are employed to bring out the canonical facial model from the reference model. Shape descriptors are specified with respect to convexity of the facial components such as eyebrows, eyes, nose mouth and facial shape. By the comparison, we have shown considerable dissimilarity of the facial shape descriptors between clustering algorithms.

1 Introduction

Formulating face models for animation and recognition has been remarkably interesting topics in computer graphics and computer vision. Geometric descriptions tend to be obviously complex and considerably dissimilar between individual faces due to variations of facial components [1, 3–9]. Lots of researches in facial animation have been contributed in modeling and animating facial motions. However specifying the canonical facial patterns between ethnic faces has been less challenged. It seems that they have paid attention to the facial animation only for the specific model. Obviously different geometric features and varying proportions of individual faces between ethnic groups are thought of as critical clues to derive facial patterns defined by shape descriptors. The facial models should be formulated not in just showing static models but in supporting facial animation. The feature points can be utilized in facial animation as well as facial recognition.

In the proposed approach, facial patterns computed and analyzed by shape descriptors are determined by 42 facial points, which frame 18 muscles for facial animation defined by Parke [1] and FACS (Facial Action Coding System) [2]. Facial muscles can be interpreted as the crucial components in anatomy highly influencing on the facial movement. The method begins with aligning 3D facial feature vertices of the reference model with the corresponding feature points in the sample images from young Korean men. Finally K means (KM), Fuzzy c-means (FCM) and Subtractive clustering algorithms have been applied to derive the canonical facial models [12–19]. Shape descriptors are defined in order to show dissimilarity of the facial components between models.

C.-H. Chi and K.-Y. Lam (Eds.): AWCC 2004, LNCS 3309, pp. 251–257, 2004.
© Springer-Verlag Berlin Heidelberg 2004

2   The Proposed Approach

2.1   Alignment of the Facial Feature Vertices

The dominant models are based on polygonal models. In our method we select 42 facial points enabling 18 muscles to be manipulated for facial animation defined by Parke. Facial muscles can be thought of as the crucial components in anatomy highly influencing on the facial movement. In particular the eyes and the mouth are astonishingly expressive regions in the face. Facial muscles are the organs of facial expressions created by their contractions and relaxations [1].

Once gathering sample images taken from young Korean men, Feature points on the sample images should be aligned with corresponding feature vertices on the reference mesh models. First, our 3D reference mesh model has been manipulated into a transparent model simply by switching opacity.

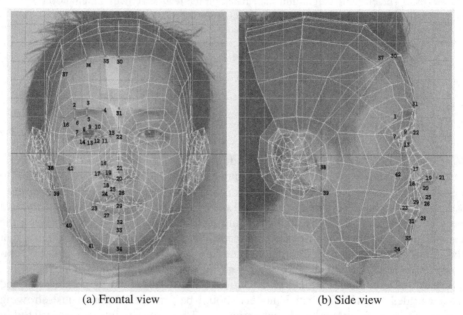

(a) Frontal view   (b) Side view

Fig. 1. 42 facial feature points in the image overlapped with facial feature vertices in the 3D reference mesh model

We locate the sample images in the back so that it is possible to adjust feature vertices in the 3D reference mesh model to feature points in a sample image by moving feature vertices as shown in Figure 1. Coloring of the specific polygon enable us to avoid ambiguous decision when selecting vertices. In Figure 1, our 3D reference mesh model is displayed conveying its index of the feature vertices in the front along with a sample image in the back.

2.2   Facial Shape Descriptors

At first comparative facial metrics must be defined in order to show dissimilarity between derived models. Shape descriptors [20] are useful to compute and analyze individual shape components such as facial shape, eyebrows, eyes, nose and mouth. Eccentricity is calculated by the ratio of major and minor axes of an object. Compactness independent of linear transformations is computed by the square of the length of the border divided by the area of the object. It is natural for eyebrows and nose to be eccentricity due to concavity and for facial shape, eyes and mouth to be compactness due to convexity as shown in Figure 2.

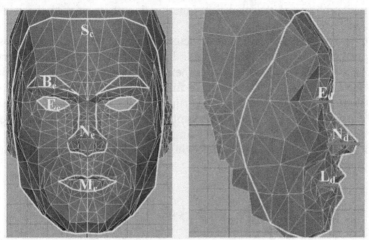

[Notation] S_c: shape compactness, E_c: eye compactness, M_c: mouth compactness, B_e: eyebrow eccentricity, N_e: nose eccentricity, E_d: eye depth, N_d: nose depth, L_d: lip depth

Fig. 2. Facial patterns defined by shape descriptors

The aim of comparisons with four mesh models is to represent relative dissimilarity with respect to comparative metric as shown in Figure 4 and Table 1. Prior to comparison, normalization has been conducted by adjusting size of mesh models.

2.3 Comparative Clustering Algorithms on Feature Vertices

K-Means Algorithm
The aim of the K-means (KM) clustering technique [11] is to divide N sample vectors in M dimensional space into C clusters so that the within-cluster sum of squares is minimized. The general process is to search for C clusters corresponding to locally minimal within-cluster sum of squares by moving data from one cluster to another.

Fuzzy C-Means Algorithm
The Fuzzy C-means (FCM) algorithm found by Bezdek consists in the iteration of the given Eq. (1)(2). It is a commonly used clustering approach. It is a natural generalization of the K-means algorithm allowing for soft clusters based on fuzzy set theory. To classify a data set of N data items into C classes FCM can formulated as a minimization problem of the objective function J with respect to the membership function u and centroid c, where J is given by

$$J = \sum_{k=1}^{C} \sum_{i=1}^{N} u_{ki}^{m} d_{ki}^{2}$$

and it is subject to

$$u_{ki} \in [0,1], \sum_{k=1}^{C} u_{ki} = 1, 0 < \sum_{k=1}^{N} u_{ki} < N,$$
$$1 \le i \le N, 1 \le K \le C \tag{1}$$

To classify a data set of N sample vectors into C clusters FCM can formulated as a minimization problem of the objective function J with respect to the membership function u and centroid c.

Here m (>1) is control parameter of determining the amount of fuzziness of the clustering results. $d_{ki} = ||v_i - c_k||$ is the Euclidean distance between the observed data v_i and the class centroid c_k and u_k is the membership value reflecting the degree of similarity between v_i and c_k. The objective function J is minimized when high membership values are assigned to feature vertices whose coordinates are close to the centroid of its particular class, and low membership vales are assigned to them when the vertices are far from the centriod. Taking the first derivative of J in Eq. (1) with respect to u_{kj}, c_k we can obtain the following necessary conditions to minimize the objective function J:

$$u_{ki} = \frac{(d_{ki})^{-2/(m-1)}}{\sum_{l=1}^{C} (d_{li})^{-2/(m-1)}}, c_k = \frac{\sum_{i=1}^{N} u_{ki}^{m} v_i}{\sum_{i=1}^{N} u_{ki}^{m}} \tag{2}$$
$$1 \le i \le N, 1 \le K \le C$$

After initialization of the centroids, u_{ki} and c_k are iteratively calculated until some stop criteria are reached. Finally the clustering can be obtained by the principle of maximum membership.

In Figure 3, we have shown the clustering centers of the left eye whose feature point indices are 7(leftmost), 8, 9, 10, 11, 12, 13, and 14 in a clockwise direction in (d). Corresponding clustering centers of the eye are displayed in (a) from FCM clustering i, KM clustering in (b) and Subtractive clustering in (c). We can recognize that FCM algorithm is better than Subtractive or KM clustering algorithm because it distributes equably.

Subtractive Algorithm
The subtractive clustering method was first introduced in the context of extracting fuzzy rules for function approximation. The method is based on the density of the feature vertices [12],[13]. Let us consider n vertex vectors specified by m-dimensional vectors. Because each vertex vector is a potential cluster center, the density J_i at vertex v_i is defined as:

$$J_i = \sum_{j=1}^{n} \exp \left[\frac{-||v_i - v_j||^2}{\left(r_a/2\right)^2} \right] \tag{3}$$

where r_a is a positive number and $|| . ||$ denotes the Euclidean distance. Obviously a vertex has the highest density value if the vertex is surround by more vertices. A radius defines a neighbor area. The vertex with the highest density is chosen as the first clustering center c_1 associating with its density J_{c1}. The following Eq. (4) computes the next clustering center.

$$J_i' = J_i - J_{c1} \exp\left[\frac{-\|v_i - c_1\|^2}{\left(r_b/2\right)^2}\right] \tag{4}$$

where r_b is a positive number generally larger than r_a.

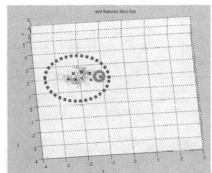

(a) C_7=(-2.5380, 1.2410, 4.4440) marked by the red circle in FCM

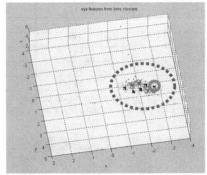

(b) C_7=(-2.6390 1.3190 4.3660) marked by the red circle in KM

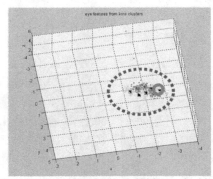

(c) C_7=(-2.4400 1.3150 4.4200) marked by the red circle in Subtractive

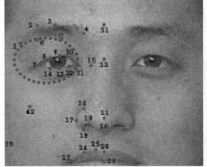

(d) Eye image marked by the blue dotted circle and index 7 marked by the red circle

Fig. 3. Clustering centers of the eye in (a): FCM, (b): KM and (c): Subtractive

3   Results and Discussion

Clustering center vertices acquired from KM, Subtractive and FCM represent feature vertices of our proposed 3D facial mesh model. Given clustering center vertices, we derive our proposed 3D facial mesh models.

Let f_c be the clustering center vector such that f_c=($c_1, c_2, c_3, \ldots c_N$) = ($c_{11}, c_{12}, c_{13}, c_{21}, c_{22}, c_{23} \ldots c_{N1}, c_{N2}, c_{N3}$) $\in R^{3N}$ where N=42. Each clustering center vertex is represented by three coordinates x, y and z sequentially. Let v_i be a reference feature vertex and c_i be a clustering center vertex such that $v_i=(x(u_1), y(u_1), z(u_1))$, $c_i=(x(u_2), y(u_2), z(u_2))$ then the length between v_i and c_i is calculated in order to move reference vertices by the displacement, which enable us to build the clustering models as shown in Figure 4.

Table 1. Comparison among models (in pixels)

Shape descriptor	Reference model	KM	Subtractive	FCM
S_c	14.783	14.012	13.087	15.757
E_c	5.000	8.167	9.800	8.000
M_c	16.333	13.066	14.000	10.286
B_e	2.555	3.333	2.667	2.714
N_e	1.353	1.263	1.278	1.211
E_d	23	25	24	22
N_d	58	57	56	58
L_d	49	33	42	52

[Notation] S_c: shape compactness, E_c: eye compactness, M_c: mouth compactness, B_e: eyebrow eccentricity, N_e: nose eccentricity, Ed: eye depth, N_d: nose depth, L_d: lip depth

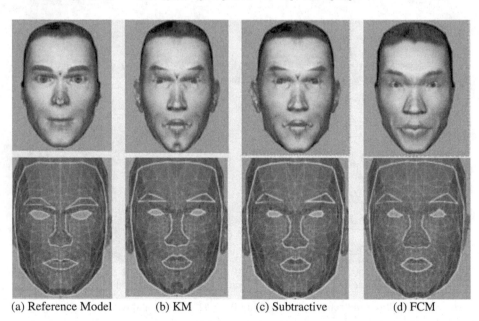

(a) Reference Model   (b) KM   (c) Subtractive   (d) FCM

Fig. 4. Clustering models after texture mapping along with mesh models

We can recognize that FCM algorithm is better than Subtractive or KM clustering algorithm because it distributes equably in Figure 3. Also we applied to compare clustering models with respect to shape descriptors. The model result of FCM was more distinctive than other methods as shown in Figure 4. Table 1 represents dissimilarity with respect to shape descriptors. FCM holds the strongest in S_c while E_c, M_c, and N_e are the least among clustering models.

4 Conclusions

In this paper, we present facial patterns for Korean young men's 3D virtual face defined by shape descriptors. KM, Subtractive and FCM clustering algorithms are computed on 3D feature vertices to derive canonical face models for young Korean men. Experimental results are displayed along with mapping models. In the future we plan to transform the canonical models for young Korean men into an arbitrarily model.

References

1. Parke , F. I. , Waters, K: Computer Facial Animation. A K Peters. (1996)
2. Ekman, P., Friesen W.V: Manual for the Facial Action Coding System. Consulting Psychologist Press, Palo Alto. (1978)
3. Guenter, B Grimm, C., Wood, D., Malvar, H. Pighin F..:Making Faces. Proc. ACM SIGGRAPH98 Conf. (1998)
4. Lee, W.S., Thalmann, N. :Fast head modeling for animation. Journal Image and Vision Computing, Volume 18. Number 4. Elsevier, 1 March. (2000) 355-364
5. Pantic, M., Rothkrantz, L.J.M.:Automatic Analysis of Facial Expressions: The State of the Art. IEEE Pattern Analysis and Machine Intelligence, Vol. 22. (2000) 1424-1445
6. Lee, Y, Terzopoulos, D., Waters, K. :Realistic modeling for facial animation. Proc. ACM SIGGRAPH95 Conf. (1995) 55-62
7. Guenter,B., Grimm, C., Wood,D., Malvar,H., Pighin, F.: Making Faces. Proc. ACM SIGGRAPH98 Conf. (1998)
8. Kshirsagar, S., Garachery, S., Sannier, G., Thalmann, N.M.: Synthetic Faces:Analysis and Applications. International Journal of Images Systems & Technology. Vol. 13. (2003) 65-73
9. Hsu, R.L., Mottaleb, M-A., Jain, A.K.:Face Detection in Color Images.. IEEE Pattern Analysis and Machine Intelligence. Vol. 24. (2002) 696-706
10. Zhang, Y., Prakash, E.C, Sung, E.: Constructing a realistic face model of an individual for expression animation. International Journal of Information Technology. Vol.8. (2002)
11. Theodoridis, S., Koutroumbas, K:Pattern Recognition. Academic Press. (1999)
12. Stphen Chiu: Method and software fro extracting fuzzy classification rules by subtractive clustering. Proc. of IEEE International Fuzzy system (1996)
13. J.S Jang, C.T. SUN and E.Mizutani, Neuro-Fuzzy and Soft Computing. Prentice Hall. New Jersey, 1997
14. Hsu, R. L. and Jain, A. K.:Face Modeling for Recognition. IEEE International Conference Image Processing. Vol.2. (2001) 693-696
15. Shan, Y., Liu, A. and Ahang, Z.: Model-Based Bundle Adjustment with Application to Face Modeling. Proc. of the 8th ICCV01 Vol.2. (2001) 644-651
16. Lanitis, A., Taylor, C. J., and Cootes, T. F.: Automatic Interpretation and Coding of Face Images Using Flexible Models. IEEE Pattern Analysis and Machine Intelligence. Vol. 19. (1997) 743-756
17. Masulli, F, Schenone, A., and Massone, A.M.:Fuzzy clustering methods for the segmentation of multimodal medical images. Fuzzy Systems in Medicine. Springer-Verlag. (2000) 335-350
18. Zhu, C. and Jiang, T.:NeuroImage. Vol.18. (2003) 685-696
19. Wang, J., Tang, W.J., and Acharya, R.:Color Clustering Techniques for Color-Content-Based Image Retrieval from Image Databased. Proc. of ICMCS97. (1997) 442-449
20. Sonka, M., Hlavac, V. and Boyle Roger. Image Processing, Analysis, and Machine Vision 2nd edition. PWS Publishing (1999)

A Content-Based Fragile Watermarking Scheme
for Image Authentication

Mi-Ae Kim and Won-Hyung Lee

Department of Image Engineering,
Graduate School of Advanced Imaging Science, Multimedia & Film,
Chung-Ang University, #10112, Art Center, 221 Hukseok-Dong,
Dongjak-Gu, Seoul, Korea, 156-756
kimma@dreamwiz.com, whlee@cau.ac.kr

Abstract. In this paper, we present an effective image authentication scheme that can tolerate incidental distortions but that indicates tampered regions in cases of malicious manipulation. After having divided an image into blocks in the spatial domain and having obtained the average of each block's pixel values, we represent the size relationship among three random blocks in a binary tree and use it as a fragile watermark. We insert the watermark, which has been extracted based on content, into the DCT block, which is the frequency domain of the image. The experimental results show that this is an effective technique of image authentication.

1 Introduction

Image authentication plays an extremely important role in the digital age, as it allows one to verify the originality of an image. Using digital imaging software, individuals can easily modify an image for malicious purposes. Therefore, if an image carries important information, its authenticity should be ensured. Due to constraints on space and bandwidth, images are often compressed for purposes of storage and transmission. In addition, in many applications, images are filtered or sharpened for specific purposes. Thus, an image authentication system should tolerate acceptable manipulations such as image compression, sharpening and/or filtering while detecting malicious manipulations (e.g., image replacement). In this paper, we present an image authentication scheme that meets these criteria.

Two main approaches have been taken to the authentication of images: the digital signature-based method and the watermark-based method. The former, which uses a digital signature, is a cryptographic method of multimedia authentication. In this method, extracted multimedia data digest is encoded using a hash function and then transmits them to a receiver along with data. If the hash values correspond, the integrity of the multimedia data is confirmed. This approach does not permit even a single bit change. Therefore, it is not appropriate to apply this method to an image authentication system, as images must often be compressed and/or quality enhanced. Different from digesting of data as described above, there is the digital signature approach, which is based on the features of an image [1-4]. In this approach, which is used frequently for image authentication, the features of an image that are resistant to common image processing (including compression) are extracted and are used as a digital signature. The digital signature is stored (or transmitted) separately from the

C.-H. Chi and K.-Y. Lam (Eds.): AWCC 2004, LNCS 3309, pp. 258–265, 2004.
© Springer-Verlag Berlin Heidelberg 2004

image. Thus, the original image is not modified; however, it is cumbersome to manage digital signature separately from images.

In the watermark-based approach, authentication information is inserted imperceptibly into the original image [5-8]. If the image is manipulated, it should be possible to detect the tampered area through the fragility of the hidden authentication information (watermark). Ideally, the embedded watermark should only be disrupted by malicious modifications; it should survive acceptable modifications such as compression.

The scheme proposed by Chun-Shin Lu and Hong-Yuan Mark Liao [4] relies on the fact that the interscale relationship is difficult to destroy with incidental modification but is hard to preserve in cases of malicious manipulation. However, the image authentication scheme is verified by having the sender store the digital signature.

Kundur and Hatzinakos [5] designed a wavelet-based quantization process that is sensitive to modification. The main disadvantages are that their method cannot resist incidental modifications and the tampering detection results are very unstable.

Zou et al. [9] embedded a verification tag into the spatial domain of the image after having extracted it using a DSA (digital signature algorithm) on the DCT (discrete cosine transform) block. However, their image authentication system can only tolerate JPEG-quality factors greater than or equal to 80, and the algorithm requires extensive computation.

In this paper, we propose an image authentication scheme that is robust to image content-preserving manipulations (i.e., compression, filtering and/or sharpening) and fragile against image content-changing manipulations (e.g., image objects replacement). This scheme accurately indicates tampered regions of an image. After dividing an image into blocks in the spatial domain and obtaining the average of each block's pixel values, we represent the size relationship among three random bocks in a binary tree and use this relationship as a fragile watermark. We insert the watermark, which has been extracted based on content, into the DCT block, which is the frequency domain of the image.

The most significant advantage of the proposed authentication scheme is that it can easily extract authentication information robust to common image processing from the spatial domain and insert it into the host image through a very simple method.

The remainder of this paper is organized as follows. The proposed authentication system is explained in Sec. 2. Sub sections of Sec. 2 describe the generation of the content-based watermark, the insertion procedure, and the verification procedure. Experimental results and conclusions are given in Sec. 3 and Sec. 4, respectively.

2 Proposed Authentication System

2.1 Basic Description of the System

The basic purpose of the system is to extract from the spatial domain the main features of the image that can resist acceptable manipulation. These features are then inserted into the frequency domain.

We divide an image into a set of non-overlapping blocks and then calculate the average gray scale for each block. By calculating the average of three blocks, we capture the relationship among them. This relationship is presented in a binary tree structure. At this point, three blocks are selected at random; in other words, random numbers generated by the seed determine the ordering of all blocks, or three blocks are selected in a series according to random permutation of the images divided into blocks. The watermark obtained this way is inserted into the frequency domain of the image. After translating an image into DCT in an 8 x 8 block, we randomly select three groups from the middle band of the DCT block. We modify each coefficient value so that the size relationship of the sum of each group coefficient has the same binary tree structure as that obtained from the spatial domain of the corresponding block. The watermark is inserted in the middle band of the DCT domain to achieve the perceptual invisibility of the image.

Possible relationships among the blocks fall into six types. One by one, each block becomes a root-node. The blocks located in the front (left) and back (right) become child-nodes. At this point, if the average of the front block is less than that of the root-node, it is determined to be a left-child node. If the average is greater than that of the root-node, it is determined to be a right-child node. The position of the rear block is determined by comparing the rear block to root node and to its child-node.

Fig. 1 shows the possible relationship types for three blocks. Fig.1 (a) shows the case in which the block to the left of the selected block is less than the root-node block and the block to the right is greater than the root-node. The form is a full binary tree. Fig.1 (b) represents the case in which the block to the left of the selected block is less than the root-node block and the block to the right is less than the root-node and greater than the block on the left. In Fig.1 (c), the block to the left of the selected block is less than the root-node; as expected, the block to the right is less than the block to the left. Thus, the form is a skewed binary tree. The tree structure is determined in the same manner for (d), (e) and (f). The binary tree structure constructed this way is directly reflected in the DCT coefficients of the image.

To verify the authenticity of an image, we extract the authentication information from the candidate image with the same method we used to generate it from the original image. Then, after translating the image into DCT, we capture the watermark from the middle band of the DCT block and compare it with the authentication information extracted from the spatial domain.

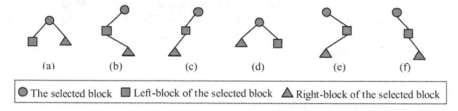

| (a) | (b) | (c) | (d) | (e) | (f) |

● The selected block   ■ Left-block of the selected block   ▲ Right-block of the selected block

Fig. 1. Types of relationship among three blocks

If the authentication information matches, the image is considered authentic; otherwise, it is considered inauthentic. Here, each block is compared three times because the type of relationship among blocks is determined by comparing two selected blocks (one in the front and the other in the rear) when we are composing a tree that represents the relationship among the blocks. Each and every block is determined to have been tampered with only if the type of relationship among blocks in the spatial domain and that of the DCT coefficients are determined to be different in all three comparisons.

The general steps for generating content-based watermark and embedding, with verification scheme can be seen in Fig. 2.

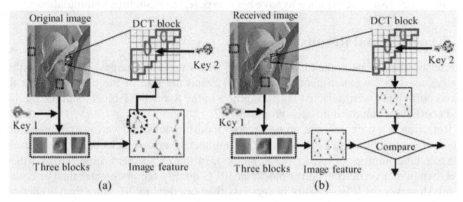

Fig. 2. (a) Generating and embedding watermark, (b) Verification scheme

The content-based authentication watermark proposed for image authentication is preserved in common image processing, but it is fragile in cases of malicious manipulation and can indicate tampered regions. Performance analysis is given, and experimental results are presented.

2.2   Generation of Content-Based Watermark and Insertion Procedure

The steps used to generate and embed a fragile watermark are as follows:

1) Divide the original image into *8* by *8* blocks. For each block, compute the average of pixel values.
2) Order the blocks in a manner defined by a pseudo-random number generator (PRNG) using a previously defined seed (Key_1).
3) For each block, determine the appropriate type within the binary tree and the type of relationship among three blocks by comparing the averages of two neighboring blocks according to the order determined in step 2.
4) Translate the image into DCT in *8* by *8* blocks.
5) Select three groups from the middle band of the DCT domain with a pseudo-random number generator (PRNG) using a previously defined seed (Key_2). Calculate the sum of the coefficients in each group.
6) Modify the coefficients to make the relation among the sums of the three groups identical to the binary tree type obtained in step 3.
7) Perform inverse DCT for each DCT block.

2.3   Verification Procedure

The process of verifying a received image is described below.

1) Identically apply the watermark generation and embedding processes (as described in steps 1 through 5 above) to the transmitted image.

2) For all the blocks, compare the watermark extracted from the spatial domain to the relation among the sums of the coefficients in the DCT domain. If the type of relationship among blocks for a block (B_i) differs, and if the type of relationship among blocks for each of the neighboring two blocks $(B_{i-1}$ and $B_{i+1})$ also differs, the block (B_i) is determined to have been exposed to malicious manipulation.

3   Experimental Results

We tested our image authentication scheme with over 100 images. The size of the images used in the experiment was 512 x 512, and the size of the block was 8 x 8. Two coefficients were selected for each group in the 8 x 8 DCT block, and the modified coefficient value within each group was 27.

Referring to an experiment on acceptable modifications and various compression ratios of several images, Table 1 shows the number of error blocks detected for each image's total number of blocks (4096 blocks). In the experiment, images had either less than two or no detected error blocks in JPEG-quality factors greater than or equal to 60. However, in JPEG-quality factors less than or equal to 30, more than 40 detection errors appeared.

Table 1. Number of error blocks against JPEG lossy compression and other acceptable modifications

Acceptable Modifications	Image					
	Lena	Barbara	Baboon	Bridge	Goldhill	Girl
JPEG (QF = 70%)	0	0	0	0	0	0
JPEG (QF = 60%)	1	2	1	0	1	0
JPEG (QF = 50%)	3	3	1	1	2	2
JPEG (QF = 40%)	5	13	7	2	6	6
JPEG (QF = 30%)	27	40	25	17	31	29
median filtering (3 x 3)	25	104	93	53	37	6
scaling	7	7	14	6	8	1
sharpening (3 x 3)	14	100	20	23	13	7
Gaussian filtering (3 x 3)	28	57	112	45	57	14

Fig. 3 shows the result for acceptable manipulation of the "Goldhill" image. Detected error blocks for acceptable manipulations (including JPEG compression) appear throughout the image; they are not concentrated in one part of the image. This pattern, as seen in Fig. 4(f), differs from the result of malicious manipulation, in which detected error blocks appear in a particular area of the image. Based on the experimental results, we have concluded that our image authentication scheme can be practically applied in an authentication application.

Fig. 4 shows the detection results for a manipulated image. The original image is shown in Fig. 4(a), and Fig. 4(b) shows the watermarked image, for which the PSNR is 37.21dB. Fig. 4(c) shows the JPEG-compressed image (QF = 40%), and Fig. 4(d) shows the manipulated watermarked image. In Fig. 4(d), the replaced part of the image is the flower attached to the Lena's hat. Fig. 4(e) shows the detection result when the attack is object placement only, and Fig. 4(f) is the detection result of the JPEG-compressed image (QF = 40%) after being manipulated. Except for the manipulated flower of the hat, scattered white blocks in the rest of the image are detection error blocks, and they consist of detection error blocks due to JPEG (QF = 40%) compression and a few tamper detection error blocks (there are 11 in this case). As can be seen from the experiment results, tampered regions are sufficiently identifiable although the tampered shape might not be indicated in detail and detection error blocks might appear.

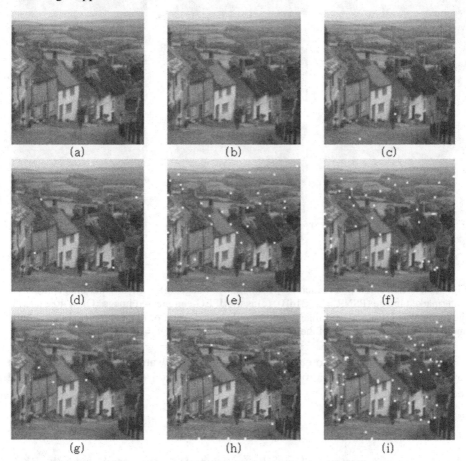

Fig. 3. Detection result for an incidentally distorted image. (a) is the original image, (b) is the watermarked image (PSNR = 36.54dB), (c) is the JPEG-compressed image (QF = 50%), (d) is the JPEG-compressed image (QF = 40%), (e) is the JPEG-compressed image (QF = 30%), (f) is the median-filtered image, (g) is the scaled image, (h) is the sharpened image, and (i) is the Gaussian-filtered image

4   Conclusions

In this paper, a new image authentication scheme--which involves simply extracting an image feature that is robust to acceptable manipulation from the spatial domain of the image and then inserting it into the frequency domain--has been proposed. The watermark, which is extracted from the content base and embedded into the DCT block, is resistant to incidental distortions (including JPEG compression) but is fragile to malicious manipulation.

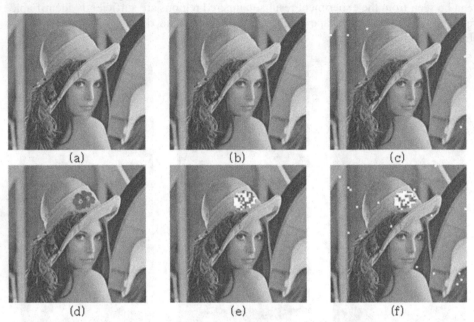

Fig. 4. Detection result of a maliciously manipulated image. (a) is the original image, (b) is the watermarked image (PSNR = 37.21dB), (c) is the JPEG-compressed image (QF = 40%), (d) is the manipulated watermarked image, (e) is the detection result of the manipulated image only, and (f) is the detection result of the JPEG-compressed image (QF = 40%) after manipulation

Future work is needed to ensure that the embedded watermark remains robust in low JPEG compression quality factors and that detection of tampering is indicated more specifically.

Acknowledgements

The Ministry of Education in Seoul, Korea, supported this research under the BK21 project. The Industry Research Consortium, an organization affiliated with the Small and Medium Business Administration, also supported this project.

References

1. M.Schneider, S.F.Chang: A robust content based digital signature for image authentication. In Proc. IEEE ICIP (1996) 227-230
2. C.Y.Lin, S.F.Chang: A robust image authentication method surviving JPEG lossy compression. In Proc. SPIE Storage and Retrieval of Image/Video Database, San Jose (1998)
3. S.Bhattacharjee, M.Kutter: Compression tolerant image authentication. In Proc. IEEE Int. Conf. on Image Processing (1998) 435-439

4. C.S.Lu, H.M.Liao: Structural Digital Signature for Image Authentication: An Incidental Distortion Resistant Scheme. Proc. ACM Multimedia and Security Workshop at the 8th ACM Int. Conf. on Multimedia, Los Angeles, California, USA (2000) 115-118
5. D.Kundur, D.Hatzinakos: Digital watermarking for telltale tamper proofing and authentication. In Proc. IEEE ICIP (1997) 1167-1180
6. M.Yeung, F.Mintzer: An invisible watermarking technique for image verification. In Proc. IEEE Int. Conf. on Image Processing (1997) 680-683
7. M.Wu, B.Liu: Watermarking for image authentication. In Proc. IEEE Int. Conf. on Image Processing (1998) 437-441
8. P.W.Wong: A public key watermark for image verification and authentication. In Proc. IEEE Int. Conf. on Image Processing (1998) 455-459
9. D.Zou, C.W.Wu, G.Xuan, Y.Q.Shi: A content-based image authentication system with lossless data hiding. In Proc. ICME Int. Conf. on Multimedia and Expo (2003) 213-216

A New FP-Tree Algorithm for Mining Frequent Itemsets

Yu-Chiang Li and Chin-Chen Chang

Department of Computer Science and Information Engineering,
National Chung Cheng University, Chiayi 621, Taiwan, ROC
{lyc,ccc}@cs.ccu.edu.tw

Abstract. Data mining has become an important field and has been applied extensively across many areas. Mining frequent itemsets in a transaction database is critical for mining association rules. Many investigations have established that pattern-growth method outperforms the method of Apriori-like candidate generation. The performance of the pattern-growth method depends on the number of tree nodes. Accordingly, this work presents a new FP-tree structure (NFP-tree) and develops an efficient approach for mining frequent itemsets, based on an NFP-tree, called the NFP-growth approach. NFP-tree employs two counters in a tree node to reduce the number of tree nodes. Additionally, the header table of the NFP-tree is smaller than that of the FP-tree. Therefore, the total number of nodes of all conditional trees can be reduced. Simulation results reveal that the NFP-growth algorithm is superior to the FP-growth algorithm for dense datasets and real datasets.

1 Introduction

During the past few decades, the development of information science focused on treating a surprisingly rapid accumulation of data. Therefore, the needs for new techniques for managing massive bodies of data, discovering useful information, and making correct decisions, are urgent [5]. Newly developed data mining techniques have made possible the formerly impossible tasks of discovering and extracting hidden but potentially useful information from data in a data warehouse.

Mining association rules constitutes one of the most important data mining problems. The mining of association rules can be decomposed into two subproblems (1) identifying all *frequent* (*large*) *itemsets* that arise more often than a minimum support requirement, and (2) using these frequent itemsets to generate association rules. The corresponding association rules can be straightforwardly derived from the frequent itemsets. Accordingly, the first subproblem plays an essential role in mining associations [2, 3].

Numerous methods have been developed for mining frequent itemsets efficiently. These existing algorithms can be categorized into two classes according to whether candidates are generated. The first class includes the methods that generate candidates. Apriori [2, 3] is the most famous algorithm of this class. Apriori and subsequent Apriori-like algorithms apply the downward closure property to reduce the number of candidates generated [4, 11, 13]. However, for long frequent itemsets, they require a huge space to store the candidates. For instance, if the length of the longest frequent itemsets is 50, at least 2^{50} candidates must be generated. Additionally, the number of times the database is scanned equals to the length of the longest candidate itemsets.

The other class comprises pattern-growth methods. Over the past few years, several pattern-growth methods have been presented, such as FP-growth [7, 8], Tree-projection

C.-H. Chi and K.-Y. Lam (Eds.): AWCC 2004, LNCS 3309, pp. 266–277, 2004.
© Springer-Verlag Berlin Heidelberg 2004

[1] and H-mine [12], among others [6, 9, 10, 14], to prevent the storage overhead associated with candidate generation and reduce the frequency of the scanning of the database. A pattern-growth algorithm partitions the database and stores the projected or conditional database in the main memory. Rather than generating candidates, it assembles pattern fragment into longer fragments. Various pattern-growth methods have been established significantly to outperform the Apriori-like candidate generation method, especially on dense database [1, 7, 8, 10, 12, 14].

This work proposes a new frequent patterns structure, called the NFP-tree, to improve on the performance of FP-growth. NFP-growth reduces the number of tree nodes by adding a second counter to each node. Then, NFP-growth applies a smaller tree and header table to discover efficiently frequent itemsets.

This paper is organized as follows. Section 2 introduces the background and some work on association rules. Then, Section 3 describes the proposed new FP-growth method (NFP-growth). Section 4 provides experimental results and evaluates the performance of the proposed algorithm. Section 5 finally draws conclusions.

2 Background and Related Work

Agrawal *et al.* first presented a model to address the problem of mining association rules in 1993 [2]. Given a transaction database, the definition of mining association rules is to discover the important rules that apply to *items*. Let $DB = \{T_1, T_2, ..., T_n\}$ represent the transaction database, which comprises set of transactions of variable length. Let $I = \{i_1, i_2, ..., i_m\}$ be a set of items (*itemset*). Each transaction T constitutes a subset of I. The associated unique identifier of each transaction is called its *TID*. Let X be an itemset; $X \subseteq T$ means that transaction T contains X. The form $X \Rightarrow Y$ indicates an association rule, where $X \subseteq I$, $Y \subseteq I$ and $X \cup Y = \phi$. For instance, $I=\{ABCDE\}$, $X=\{AD\}$, $Y=\{BE\}$. An association rule $X \Rightarrow Y$ accompanies two characteristic values, *support* and *confidence*. If the percentage $s\%$ of transactions in DB contains $X \cup Y$, than the support is $s\%$. The confidence is $c\%$ when $c\%$ of transactions in DB that contain X also contain Y. Confidence is formally expressed as confidence$(X \Rightarrow Y)$ = support$(X \cup Y)$/support(X). The problem of mining association rules is to discover all association rules for which support and conference are not below a user-specified minimum support (*minSup*) and the minimum conference (*minConf*) thresholds, respectively. An itemset (or a pattern) is called a large itemset (or a frequent itemset) when its support exceeds or equals the minSup threshold; otherwise, it is called a *small itemset* (or an infrequent itemset).

2.1 Apriori Algorithm

Given a user-specified minSup, the Apriori process makes multiple passes over the database to find all frequent itemsets. In the first pass, Apriori scans the transaction database to evaluate the support of each item and identify the frequent 1-itemsets. In a subsequent kth pass, Apriori establishes a candidate set of frequent k-itemsets (which are itemsets of length k) from frequent $(k-1)$-itemsets. Two arbitrary frequent $(k-1)$-itemsets join each other when their first $k-1$ items are identical. Then, the downward closure property is applied to reduce the number of candidates. This property refers to the fact that any subset of a frequent itemset must be frequent; otherwise, the itemset is small. Therefore, the process deletes all the k-itemsets whose subsets with length k-1 are small. Next, the algorithm scans the entire transaction database to check whether each candidate k-itemset is frequent.

2.2 FP-Growth Algorithm

Apriori-like algorithms expensively handle a great number of candidates. Additionally, it repeated scanning of the database is tedious. Therefore, Han *et al.* developed an efficient FP-tree based method, FP-growth, for mining frequent itemsets without generating candidates; this approach scans the database only twice [7, 8].

FP-growth first discovers all frequent 1-itemsets and then establishes a compact tree structure, called an FP-tree (frequent-pattern tree). The FP-tree is a prefix-tree structure that stores information about each frequent 1-itemset, in which the items are arranged in order of decreasing support value. Then, the mining process is transformed to mine the FP-tree.

Example 2.1. Consider the transaction database in Table 1 with a minimum support threshold of 40%. First, FP-growth scans the database to discover all frequent 1-itemsets and sorts these 1-itemsets in order of descending frequency of occurrence. The order is "*CABD*" and their support values are 5, 4, 4 and 4, respectively. The frequent 1-itemsets in each transaction are ordered as in the list of all frequent 1-itemsets. The last column of Table 1 lists the results. Then, FP-growth stores the entire frequent 1-itemsets of each transaction in an FP-tree structure, to eliminate the need to scan the database iteratively. The root of the tree is created first, and labeled with "NULL". Next, the database is scanned again. The first transaction is employed to establish the first branch $\{C(1), A(1), B(1), D(1)\}$ (where the numbers in parentheses represents the values of support) of the tree as depicted in Fig. 1 (a). The common prefix 2-itemset $\{C, A\}$ is shared across the second and third transactions, and the count of each common prefix node is increased by one, as shown in Fig. 1 (b) and Fig. 1 (c). In Fig. 1 (d), for the forth transaction, the count of the common prefix node $\{C(3)\}$ is increased by one; the new node $\{B(1)\}$ is generated as a child of $\{C(4)\}$, and the new node $\{D(1)\}$ is then created as a child of $\{B(1)\}$. The fifth transaction is inserted into the FP-tree to generate the second branch, as shown in Fig. 1 (e). In Fig. 1 (f), the final transaction involves the common prefix 3-itemset $\{C, B, D\}$, and the count of each common prefix node is increased by one.

FP-growth applies a header table, which lists all frequent 1-itemsets to improve the performance of the tree traversal. Each item in the header table relies on a side-link to points to its occurrence in the tree. The dotted lines in Figs. 1 (a)-(f) represent side-links. FP-growth recursively generates the conditional FP-tree to mine frequent itemsets.

Table 1. Example of a transaction database

TID	Transaction	Frequent 1-itemsets (sorted)
001	A B C D	C A B D
002	A C E F	C A
003	A C E	C A
004	B C D F	C B D
005	A B D	A B D
006	B C D	C B D

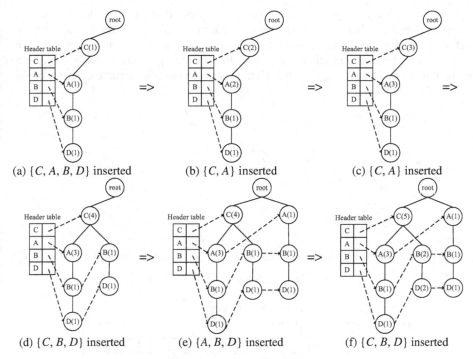

Fig. 1. Construction of FP-tree

Example 2.2. Consider the example in Table 1 and minSup = 40%. Figure 1 (f) presents the corresponding FP-tree. The mining process begins from the bottom of the header table, and moves toward the top. For the D_node, $\{D\}$ is a frequent itemsets and the FP-tree has three paths that contain D (*CABD*, *CBD*, and *ABD*). The three paths appear once, twice and once in the database, respectively as shown in Fig. 2 (a). Although "*CA*" appears thrice, it appears only once with "*D*". In Fig. 2 (b), the prefix paths of "*D*" are employed to form a single branch "*CB*" and the node "*A*" is omitted because the path "*AD*" arises infrequently. Therefore, the frequent 2-itemsets $\{C, D\}$ and $\{B, D\}$ can be generated. Then FP-growth constructs a *BD'* conditional FP-tree that yields only one frequent 3-itemsets $\{C, B, D\}$. Figure 2 (c) presents the conditional FP-tree of "*BD*". No more frequent itemsets can be generated in this conditional FP-tree. Hence, the process of generating the conditional FP-tree associated with "*D*" terminates. The recursive mining of a conditional FP-tree yields all the combinations of the items in the path. For the next B_node in the header table, $\{B\}$ is a frequent itemsets and its conditional FP-tree includes only one node $\{C\}$. For A_node, it is similar to B_node. The conditional FP-trees of "*B*" and "*A*" are identical with Fig. 2 (c) in this example. The two frequent itemsets $\{C, B\}$ and $\{C, A\}$ can be generated from the "*B*" and "*A*" conditional trees, respectively. All frequent itemsets are listed in Table 2.

2.3 Other Algorithms

Pei *et al.* described the H-mine algorithm [12], which applies a hyper-linked data structure, an H-struct on transactions and dynamically adjusts links to mine frequent itemsets. The H-mine algorithm is efficient on sparse datasets. For dense datasets, however, H-mine switches the data structure from H-struct to FP-tree to improve the performance. Wang *et al.* developed a top-down traversal strategy for FP-tree [14]. Liu *et al.* presented the opportunistic project method, which projects datasets to grow a frequent itemsets tree and adaptively switches between two data structures array-based and tree-based [10].

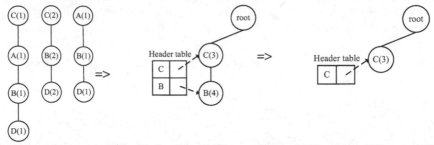

(a) Three paths contain "*D*"   (b) Conditional FP-tree of "*D*"   (c) Conditional FP-tree of "*BD*"

Fig. 2. Conditional FP-tree

Table 2. Frequent itemsets

L_1		L_2		L_3	
Itemset	Support	Itemset	Support	Itemset	Support
{A}	4	{AC}	3	{BCD}	3
{B}	4	{BC}	3		
{C}	5	{BD}	4		
{D}	4	{CD}	3		

3   NFP-Growth Algorithm

3.1   NFP-Tree Construction

A typical structure of an FP-tree node comprises one node label, one counter and four node-links, as shown in Fig. 3 (a). The node label stores the unique identifier of the frequent 1-itemset. The counter records the number of occurrences of this tree path from the root to the node. The parent-link, the child-link and the sibling-link point to the node's parent node, the child node and the right sibling node, respectively. The side-link points to the next node with an identical label. In Figs. 1 (a)-(f), the dotted lines represent side-links.

The tree structure of the NFP-growth (NFP-tree) can be considered as extracting the subtree *MF* (*MF* denotes the most frequent 1-itemset) from the FP-tree. Other subtrees of the root are merged with the *MF* subtree. Additionally, the *MF* node becomes the root of the NFP-tree. Therefore, the nodes in the NFP-tree are fewer than those of the FP-tree. Each node of the NFP-tree depends on the addition of a second counter to elucidate all frequent itemsets. Figure 3 (b) depicts the structure of an NFP-tree node. When a transaction involves *MF*, the two counters are each increased by one. If the transaction does not include *MF*, then only the second counter is increased by one. Consequently, the first counters of the NFP-tree record the same information as the counters of the *MF* subtree of the FP-tree. The FP-growth's pattern-growth algorithm can be applied to the second counters of the NFP-tree, to generate all frequent itemsets that do not include *MF*. Obviously, recursively applying the pattern-growth algorithm to the NFP-tree twice, generates all frequent itemsets. It first traverses the NFP-tree involving the first counters. The second traversal concerns the second counters.

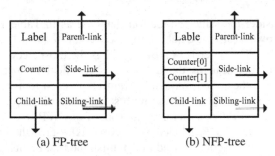

(a) FP-tree   (b) NFP-tree

Fig. 3. Structure of a node

An NFP-tree can be constructed as follows.

Algorithm 1 (NFP-tree construction)
Input: (1) *DB*: a transaction database, and (2) minSup: minimum support threshold
Output: NFP-tree
Procedure:

1. Scan *DB* once. Store all the frequent 1-itemsets *F* and their individual support values. Sort *F* in order of decreasing support value to generate a list of frequent 1-itemsets *L*.
2. Select the most frequent 1-itemset (*MF*) to generate the root node of the NFP-tree, labeled *MF*.
3. For each transaction $T \subset DB$, perform the following;
   3.1. Select the frequent 1-itemsets in *T* and sort them in order of *L*. Let the frequent 1-itemsets list in *T* be $\{p_1, p_2, ..., p_n\}$.
   3.2. If $p_1 == MF$, call function Insert_node(p_2, root); else call function Insert_node(p_1, root).

The pseudo code of the function Insert_node(p, *N*) is as follows.

```
Function Insert_node(p, N)
1.    if p₁== MF {
2.          for each child Ch of N {
3.                if exist N'∈ Ch such that N'.label == p {
4.                      N'.counter[0]++;   N'.counter[1]++;
5.                      Insert_node(pᵢ₊₁, N'); }
6.          else {
7.                create a new node N';
8.                N'.counter[0] = 1;
9.          N'.counter[1] = 1;
10.               Insert_node(pᵢ₊₁, N'); }    }
11.  else {
12.         for each child Ch of N {
13.               if exist N'∈ Ch such that N'.label == p {
```

```
14.                 N'.counter[1]++;
15.                 Insert_node(p_{i+1}, N'); }
16.             else {
17.                 create a new node N';
18.                 N'.counter[0] = 0;      N'.counter[1] = 1;
19.                 Insert_node(p_{i+1}, N'); }      }
```

Example 3.1. Consider the same transaction database as in Table 1 with minSup = 40%. First, NFP-growth scans the database to discover all frequent 1-itemsets, and then sorts these 1-itemsets. The order is "*CABD*". {*C*} is the most frequent 1-itemset *MF*. The process of the first scan of the database is identical to that associated with FP-growth. Therefore, the sorted frequent 1-itemsets in each transaction are listed in the last column of Table 1. Then, NFP-growth stores the entire frequent 1-itemsets of each transaction in an NFP-tree structure. The root of the NFP-tree is created first and stores the support value of *MF*, labeled "*C*". Next, NFP-growth scans the database second time. The first transaction is used to establish the first branch {$A(1, 1)$, $B(1, 1)$, $D(1, 1)$} (where the two numbers in parentheses represent the values of the support of the two counters, respectively) of the tree, as shown in Fig. 4 (a). The support value of *MF* is known in advance, so the process skips *MF* to create NFP-tree. The second and third transactions share the common prefix 1-itemset {*A*}, and the count of the common prefix node is increased by one, as shown in Figs. 4 (b) and (c), respectively. In Fig. 4 (d), the fourth transaction is inserted into the NFP-tree to form the second branch {$B(1, 1)$, $D(1, 1)$}. The fifth transaction does not include *MF* and the common prefix 3-itemset {A, B, D} is shared, so the second counters of these common prefix nodes are increased by one, as shown in Fig. 4 (e). In Fig. 4 (f), the last transaction shares the common prefix 2-itemset {B, D}, and the two counters of each common prefix node are each increased by one. The FP-tree in the example in Table 1 requires ten nodes, unlike the NFP-tree, which include only six nodes. Additionally, the size of the header table of the NFP-tree is less than that of the FP-tree.

3.2 Mining Frequent Itemsets Using NFP-Tree

A simple method for discovering all frequent itemsets is recursively to traverse the NFP-tree twice using the pattern-growth algorithm, but it is not efficient. This work develops the NFP-growth algorithm, which is also a pattern-growth algorithm, to improve the performance efficiently. NFP-growth recursively traverses the NFP-tree only once. The following algorithm uses the NFP-tree for mining frequent itemsets.

Algorithm 2 (NFP-growth)
Input: (1) NFP-tree: constructed based on Algorithm 1, (2) minSup: minimum support threshold, and (3) *MF*: most frequent 1-itemset
Output: The complete set of frequent itemsets *FI*
Procedure:

```
NFP-growth(Tree, m) {
1.    FI = MF;
2.    if Tree contains a single path P {  // single path
3.    for each m ∈ Combination(P) {
4.        FI = FI + m;
5.        if m.counter[0] ≥ minSup {
```

```
6.                m' = MF catenates m
7.                FI = FI + m'; }        }        }
8.    else {    // multiple paths
9.          for each mᵢ in the header table of Tree {
10.         m = m catenates mᵢ;
11.         FI = FI + m;
12.         if m.counter[0] ≥ minSup {
13.                m' = MF catenates m;
14.                FI = FI + m'; }
15.         construct conditional NFP-tree Treeₘ with base m;
16.         if Treeₘ != ∅ {
17.                NFP-growth(Treeₘ, m);  }        }        }
18.    Output FI;
```

In Line 1, MF is also a frequent itemset. In Line 3, the function Combination(P) enumerates all the combinations of the sub-paths of P. In Lines 4 and 11, the algorithm recursively visits the NFP-tree and checks the second counter of each node, to yield all frequent itemsets, except MF and its superset. In Lines 5-7 and 12-14, instead of re-traversing the NFP-tree second time, this algorithm individually catenates MF with each frequent itemset and examines the first counter to determine whether the superset of MF is frequent. Therefore, NFP-growth correctly discovers the complete set of frequent itemsets.

Example 3.2. Consider the same transaction database as in Table 1 with a minimum support threshold of 40%. Figure 4 (f) presents the corresponding NFP-tree. The header table of the NFP-tree includes three items $\{A\}$, $\{B\}$ and $\{D\}$. The mining process starts from the bottom of the header table and heads toward the top. First, the first frequent itemset $\{C\}$ is output. For the D_node of the header table, the NFP-tree has two paths that contain D (ABD and BD), as shown in Fig. 5 (a). The second counter of D_node reveals that the two paths both appear twice. The D' prefix paths are employed to form only one branch "B", as shown in Fig. 5 (b). $\{D(3, 4)\}$ is the base of the conditional NFP-tree. The frequent itemset $\{D\}$ is output. Then, the algorithm catenates MF with $\{D\}$ and checks the first counter of D_node in the conditional tree. Hence, $\{C, D\}$ is also a frequent itemset. NFP-growth visits the conditional tree recursively and generates the frequent itemsets $\{B, D\}$ and $\{C, B, D\}$. No more frequent itemsets can be generated in this conditional NFP-tree. Hence, the process of generating the conditional NFP-tree associated with D_node terminates. Recursive mining of a single path NFP-tree can yield all of the combinations of the items in the path. For the next node $\{B\}$ in the header table, no conditional NPF-tree can be constructed. NFP-growth outputs the frequent itemset $\{B\}$ and joins it to MF. The 2-itemset $\{C, B\}$ is also a frequent itemset. Similarly, for the next C_node of the header table, NFP-growth outputs the frequent itemsets $\{A\}$ and $\{C, A\}$. Table 2 lists all frequent itemsets.

4 Experimental Results

The performance of NFP-growth is compared with that of FP-growth using a 1.5GHz Pentium IV PC with 1GB of main memory, running Windows 2000 professional. All algorithms are coded in Visual C++ 6.0, and applied to process several real-world and artificial datasets. The first scan of the dataset for FP-growth is identical to that for

NFP-growth. Therefore, the running time excludes the execution time of the first scan dataset. The whole frequent itemsets are output to main memory to reduce the effect of disk writing.

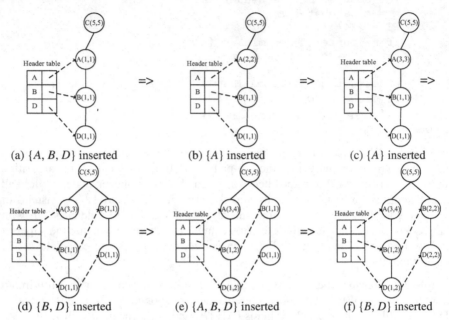

(a) {A, B, D} inserted   (b) {A} inserted   (c) {A} inserted

(d) {B, D} inserted   (e) {A, B, D} inserted   (f) {B, D} inserted

Fig. 4. Construction of NFP-tree skips *MF*

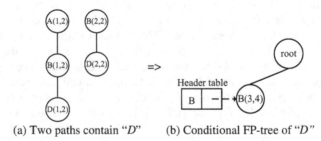

(a) Two paths contain "*D*"   (b) Conditional FP-tree of "*D*"

Fig. 5. Conditional NFP-tree

BMS-WebView-1 and BMS-WebView-2 are two real-world datasets of several months' click stream data from two e-commerce web sites [15]. They are sparse datasets. The Connect-4 dataset is from the UCI Machine Learning Repository [18]. Each transaction in the dataset includes legal 8-ply positions in a game of connect-4, which has not yet been won, and in which the next move is not forced. The dataset is very dense. Table 3 lists the characteristics of the three datasets.

Figures 6 and 7 plot the performance curves associated with the two algorithms applied to BMS-WebView-1 and BMS-WebView-2 datasets, respectively. The *x*-axis represents the several distinct minimum support thresholds, and the *y*-axis represents the running time. In Fig. 6, the minSup is between 0.056% and 0.066%. At a higher minSup value, the curves of the two methods are very close. When minSup = 0.056%,

NFP-growth outperforms FP-growth 13.8%. In Fig. 7, the minSup threshold is decreased from 0.032% to 0.008%. At minSup = 0.02%, NFP-growth outperforms FP-growth by 11.2%. When minSup is as low as 0.008%, the difference in performance is increased to 24.5%. Figure 8 demonstrates that NFP-growth outperforms FP-growth by between 35.7% (minSup = 75%) and 45.9% (minSup = 57%) when applied to the Connect-4 dataset.

Table 3. Characteristics of three real-world datasets

Dataset	Transaction number	Distinct items	Mean size of transactions	Max size of transactions
BMS-WebView-1	59602	497	2.5	267
BMS-WebView-2	77512	3340	5	161
Connect-4	67557	129	43	43

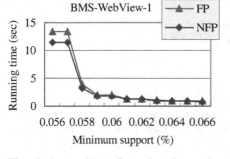

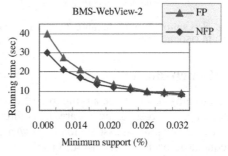

Fig. 6. Comparison of running time using BMS-WebView-1

Fig. 7. Comparison of running time using BMS-WebView-2

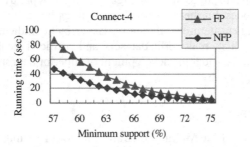

Fig. 8. Comparison of running time using Connect-4

The IBM artificial datasets are generated using a synthetic data generator [16]. The VC++ version of the data generator is obtained from [17]. Table 4 lists the parameters of the synthetic data generation program. The notation Tx.Iy.Dz.Lm denotes a dataset, where $|T| = x$, $|I| = y$, $|D| = z$ and $|L| = m$. Figure 9 compares the performance of NFP-growth with that of FP-growth applied to T10.I6.D500k.L10k, where $N = 1,000$. The performance of each approach for this dataset is very close. The parameter $|L|$ is reduced to 50 to generate the dense dataset T10.I6.D500k.L50. For the dense datasets in Fig. 10, NFP-tree outperforms FP-tree.

Table 4. Parameters

$|D|$	Number of transactions in DB
$|T|$	Mean size of the transactions
$|I|$	Mean size of the maximal potentially frequent itemsets
$|L|$	Number of maximal potentially frequent itemsets
N	Number of items

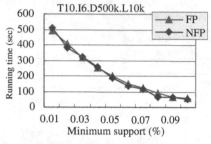

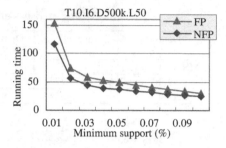

Fig. 9. Comparison of running time using T10.I6.D500k.L10k

Fig. 10. Comparison of running time using T10.I6.D500k.L50

5   Conclusions

Data mining has become an important field of research and has found a wide range of applications across to various areas. Mining frequent itemsets in a transaction database is critical for mining association rules. An efficient method for discovering complete frequent itemsets is very useful in solving many mining problems. This investigation presented a new method, NFP-growth, for mining frequent itemsets. NFP-growth applies the NFP-tree structure and develops an efficient mining frequent itemsets approach based on the NFP-tree. NFP-tree uses two counters per tree node to reduce the number of the tree nodes. Furthermore, NFP-growth applies a smaller tree and header table to discover frequent itemsets efficiently. Experiments indicate that NFP-growth outperforms FP-growth in real-world datasets and artificial dense datasets. In the future, the authors will consider the development of superior data structures and extend the pattern-growth approach.

Acknowledgements

We would like to thanks Blue Martini Software, Inc. for providing the BMS datasets.

References

1. R. C. Agarwal, C. C. Aggarwal, and V. V. V. Prasad: A tree projection algorithm for generation of frequent itemsets. *J. of Parallel and Distributed Computing* **61** (2001) 350-361
2. R. Agrawal, T. Imielinski, and A. Swami: Mining association rules between sets of items in large databases. In *Proc. ACM SIGMOD Intl. Conf.* (1993) 207-216
3. R. Agrawal and R. Srikant: Fast algorithms for mining association rules. In *Proc. VLDB Intl. Conf.* (1994) 487-499
4. S. Brin, R. Motwani, J. D. Ullman, and S. Tsur: Dynamic itemset counting and implication rules for market basket data. In *Proc. ACM SIGMOD Intl. Conf.* (1997) 255-264

5. M. S. Chen, J. Han, and P. S. Yu: Data mining: An overview from a database perspective. *IEEE Trans. Knowledge Data Engineering* **8** (1996) 866-883
6. G. Grahne and J. Zhu: Efficiently using prefix-tree in mining frequent itemsets. In *Proc. IEEE ICDM Workshop on FIMI* (2003)
7. J. Han, J. Pei, and Y. Yin: Mining frequent patterns without candidate generation. In *Proc. ACM-SIGMOD Intl. Conf.* (2000) 1-12
8. J. Han, J. Pei, Y. Yin, and R. Mao: Mining frequent patterns without candidate generation: A frequent pattern tree approach. *Data Mining and Knowledge Discovery* **8** (2004) 53-87
9. G. Liu, H. Lu, Y. Xu, and J. X. Yu: Ascending frequency ordered prefix-tree: Efficient mining of frequent patterns. In *Proc. DASFAA Intl. Conf.* (2003) 65-72
10. J. Liu, Y. Pan, K. Wang, and J. Han: Mining frequent item sets by opportunistic projection. In *Proc. ACM-SIGKDD Intl. Conf.* (2002) 229-238
11. J. S. Park, M. S. Chen, and P. S. Yu: An effective hash-based algorithm for mining association rules. In *Proc. ACM-SIGMOD Intl. Conf.* (1995) 175-186
12. J. Pei, J. Han, H. Lu, S. Nishio, S. Tang, and D. Yang: H-mine: Hyper-structure mining of frequent patterns in large databases. In *Proc. IEEE ICDM Intl. Conf.* (2001) 441-448
13. A. Savasere, E. Omiecinski, and S. Navathe: An efficient algorithm for mining association rules in large databases. In *Proc. VLDB Intl. Conf.* (1995) 432-444
14. K. Wang, L. Tang. J. Han, and J. Liu: Top down FP-growth for association rule mining. In *Proc. PAKDD Pacific-Asia Conf.* (2002) pp. 334-340
15. Z. Zheng, R. Kohavi, and L. Mason: Real world performance of association rule algorithm. In *Proc. ACM-SIGKDD Intl. Conf.* (2001) 401-406
16. http://alme1.almaden.ibm.com/software/quest/Resources/datasets/syndata.html
17. http://www.cse.cuhk.edu.hk/~kdd/data/IBM_VC++.zip
18. http://www.ics.uci.edu/~mlearn/MLRepository.html

Evaluation Incompleteness of Knowledge in Data Mining

Qiang Li, Jianhua Li, Xiang Li, and Shenghong Li

Modern Communication Research Department, Shanghai Jiaotong Univ.,
Shanghai 200030, China
liqiang@sjtu.edu.cn

Abstract. In this paper, we prove that using rough degree of rough set in classic rough sets to measure of uncertainty of knowledge is not comprehensive. Then we define a new measure named rough entropy of rough set, and we prove it is a more comprehensive measure of incompleteness of knowledge about rough set X. At the same time, the research suggests the rough degree of rough set X about knowledge R, the rough entropy of knowledge R, and the rough entropy of rough set X about knowledge R in classic rough sets decrease monotonously as the granularity of information become smaller through finer partitions. These results will be very help for understanding the essence of concept approximation and measure of incompleteness in rough sets.

1 Introduction

The classic rough sets theory [1-2] developed by Professor Pawlak in 1982 has made a great success in machine learning, data mining, intelligent data analysis in recent years [3 etc]. Pawlak's rough sets provide a systematic approach for classification of objects through an indiscernibility relation. For example, when a universe of objects is described by a family of attributes, the indiscernibility of the objects can be based on the attribute values of these objects. When two objects have the same value over a certain group of attributes, we say they are indiscernible with respect to this group of attributes. Objects of the same description consist of an equivalent class and all equivalent classes form a partition of the universe. With this partition, the rough set theory approximates any subset of objects of the universe by the lower and upper approximations.

In paper [2], the roughness is used to measure rough degree of a rough set. But by our research it is not comprehensive in measuring the incompleteness of some rough sets, so a new measure is needed. Fortunately, the entropy of a system as defined by Shannon [4] gives a measure of uncertainty about its actual structure, and its variants are used to measure uncertainty in rough set theory by several authors [5-6]. Paper [5] introduced the concepts of information entropy, rough entropy and knowledge granulation, and established the relationships among those concepts, but they do not give an application in real-life. Paper [6] gave some examples about measurement of uncertainty in rough sets, and got some conclusions. In this paper, we combine rough degree and rough entropy of knowledge to introduce a new measure of uncertainty of knowledge named rough entropy of rough set. This measure is more comprehensive than the measure rough degree and rough entropy of knowledge respectively.

C.-H. Chi and K.-Y. Lam (Eds.): AWCC 2004, LNCS 3309, pp. 278–284, 2004.
© Springer-Verlag Berlin Heidelberg 2004

2 Pawlak's Rough Sets Model

In 1982, Pawlak created rough sets theory, which can be described by equivalence relation.

Definition 2.1. Suppose A is an approximation space $A = (U, R)$, $X \subseteq U$, where U is a finite nonempty set and R is an equivalence relation on U. $[x]_R$ denotes equivalence class of object x ($x \in U$). Then the lower and upper approximations of equivalence relation about X is defined by

$$R_-(X) = \{x \mid x \in U, [x]_R \subseteq X\}, \ R^-(X) = \{x \mid x \in U, [x]_R \cap X \neq \Phi\} \tag{1}$$

When X can be denoted by R equivalence class $[x]_R$, we say X is R-definable, otherwise X is not R-definable, namely R rough sets. If X is R-definable, then $R_-(X) = R^-(X)$. This time $X = \bigcup\limits_{[x]_R \subseteq X} [x]_R$.

Example 2.1. Let the universe set U={1,2,3,4,5} and take an equivalence relation,
    R={(1,1), (2,2), (2,3), (2,4), (3,2), (3,3), (3, 4), (4,2), (4,3), (4,4), (5,5)}
Thus,

$$[1]_{R = \{1\}}, \ [2]_R = [3]_R = [4]_{R = \{2,3,4\}}, \ [5]_{R = \{5\}}$$

Now, if we take an arbitrary set X={2,3}, then $R_-(X) = \Phi$, $R^-(X) =$ {2,3,4}.

We can see that both lower and upper approximations are unions of some equivalence class. More precisely, the lower approximation is the union of those equivalence classes, which are subsets of X. The upper approximation is the union of those equivalence classes, which have a nonempty intersection with X. So we also can describe the approximations based on partition in definition 2.2

Definition 2.2. Suppose A is an approximation space $A = (U, R)$, $X \subseteq U$. Let R is a partition on U, that is $R = \{R_1, R_2, \cdots, R_m\}$, then the lower and upper approximations of equivalence relation about X is defined by

$$R_-(X) = \bigcup\{R_i \mid R_i \in R, R_i \subset X\}$$
$$R^-(X) = \bigcup\{R_i \mid R_i \in R, R_i \cap X \neq \Phi\} \tag{2}$$

Example 2.2. Let the universe set U={1,2,3,4,5} and take an equivalence relation,
    R={(1,1), (2,2), (2,3), (2,4), (3,2), (3,3), (3, 4), (4,2), (4,3), (4,4), (5,5)}
Thus, the partition R on U is:

$$R = \{\{1\}, \{2,3,4\}, \{5\}\}$$

Now, if we take an arbitrary set X={2,3}, then $R_-(X) = \Phi$, $R^-(X) =$ {2,3,4}.

3 Measure of Uncertainty in Rough Sets

First, we define a partial order on all subsets of U. Let P and Q be two partitions of a finite set U, and we define the partition Q is coarser than the partition P (or P is strictly finer than Q), $P \preceq Q$, between partitions by

$$P \preceq Q \Leftrightarrow \forall P_i \in P, \exists Q_j \in Q \rightarrow P_i \subseteq Q_j .$$

If $P \preceq Q$ and $P \neq Q$, then we say that Q is strictly coarser than P (or P is strictly finer than Q) and write $P \prec Q$.

3.1 Rough Entropy of Knowledge

Definition 3.1. [5] Suppose A is an approximation space $A = (U, R)$, $X \subseteq U$. Let R is a partition of U. The rough entropy $E(R)$ of knowledge R is defined by

$$E(R) = -\sum_{i=1}^{m} \frac{|R_i|}{|U|} \log_2 \frac{1}{|R_i|} \tag{3}$$

If $R = \{\{x\} \mid x \in U\}$, then the rough entropy of knowledge R achieves minimum value 0.

If $R = \{U\}$, then the rough entropy of knowledge R achieves maximum value $\log_2 |U|$.

Proposition 3.1. [5] Let P and Q be two partition of finite set U. If $P \prec Q$, then

$$E(P) < E(Q) \tag{4}$$

Proposition 3.1 states that the entropy of knowledge R in classic rough sets decreases monotonously as the granularity of information become smaller through finer partitions.

3.2 Rough Entropy of Rough Set

We know from paper [2] the roughness of a rough set can be measured by its rough degree.

Definition 3.2. Suppose A is an approximation space $A = (U, R)$. Let R is a partition of U. The rough degree of subset X ($X \subseteq U$) about knowledge R is defined by

$$\rho_R(X) = 1 - \frac{|R_-(X)|}{|R^-(X)|} \tag{5}$$

where $R_-(X)$, $R^-(X)$ denote respectively the lower and upper approximation sets of X about knowledge R.

If $R = \{\{x\} \mid x \in U\}$, then for any X ($X \subset U$), the rough degree of rough set X about knowledge R achieves minimum value 0, namely, X is R-definable.

If $R = \{U\}$, then for any X ($X \subset U$), the rough degree of rough set X about knowledge R achieves maximum value 1. Namely, X is totally not R-definable.

Proposition 3.2. Let P and Q be two partitions of finite set U. $P = \{P_{11}, P_{12}, \cdots, P_{1p}\}$, $Q = \{Q_{21}, Q_{22}, \cdots, Q_{2q}\}$, If $P \stackrel{-}{\prec} Q$, $X \subseteq U$ then

$$\rho_P(X) \le \rho_Q(X) \tag{6}$$

Proof. $\forall x \in Q_-(X)$, $\exists C_{2i} \in Q$ ($1 \le i \le q$), and $x \in C_{2i} \subseteq X$, for $P \succsim Q$, $\exists C_{1j} \in P$ ($1 \le j \le p$), and $x \in C_{1j} \subseteq C_{2i} \subseteq X$, so $x \in P_-(X)$, thus $Q_-(X) \subseteq P_-(X)$. On the other hand, $\forall x \in P^-(X)$, $\exists C_{1j} \in P$ ($1 \le j \le p$), and $x \in C_{1j} \cap X \ne \Phi$, for $P \prec Q$, $\exists C_{2i} \in Q$ ($1 \le i \le q$), $C_{1j} \subseteq C_{2i}$ and $x \in C_{2i} \cap X \ne \Phi$, so $P^-(X) \subseteq Q^-(X)$. Then

$$\frac{|P_-(X)|}{|P^-(X)|} \ge \frac{|Q_-(X)|}{|Q^-(X)|}, \quad 1 - \frac{|P_-(X)|}{|P^-(X)|} \le 1 - \frac{|Q_-(X)|}{|Q^-(X)|}$$

Namely, $\rho_P(X) \le \rho_Q(X)$.

Proposition 3.2 states that the rough degree of rough set X about knowledge R in classic rough sets decreases monotonously as the granularity of information become smaller through finer partitions.

The rough degree of rough set X about different knowledge sometimes have the same value, so it is necessary to introduce a new measure for rough set X about some knowledge.

Example 3.1. Let P and Q be two partition of finite set U, $X \subseteq U$.

If $\quad P = \{\{1\}, \{2\}, \{3\}, \{4,5\}\}$ and $Q = \{\{1,2\}, \{3\}, \{4,5\}\}$,

So $\quad\quad\quad\quad P \prec Q$.

If we let $\quad\quad X = \{1,2,3,4\}$,

Then $\quad P_-(X) = Q_-(X) = \{1,2,3\}$, $P^-(X) = Q^-(X) = \{1,2,3,4,5\}$,

but $\quad\quad\quad\quad \rho_P(X) = \rho_Q(X) = 2/5$.

Example 3.2. Let P and Q be two partition of finite set U.

If $\quad P = \{\{1\}, \{2\}, \{3\}, \{4,5\}\}$ and $Q = \{\{1,2\}, \{3\}, \{4,5\}\}$,

So $\quad\quad\quad\quad P \prec Q$.

If we let $X = \{3,4\}$ $X \subseteq U$,

Then $\quad P_-(X) = Q_-(X) = \{3\}$, $P^-(X) = Q^-(X) = \{3,4,5\}$,

but $\quad\quad\quad\quad \rho_P(X) = \rho_Q(X) = 2/3$.

We can see from examples above that the rough degrees of different knowledge have equal value, so the rough degree does not completely measure the uncertainty related to the granularity of the indiscernibility relation, such as for those values which are totally included (Example 3.1) or totally not included (Example 3.2) in the lower approximation region. So we introduce the rough entropy of rough set to solve this trouble.

Definition 3.3. Suppose A is an approximation space $A = (U, R)$, $X \subseteq U$. Let R is a partition of U. The rough entropy $E_R(X)$ of subset X ($X \subseteq U$) about knowledge R is defined by

$$E_R(X) = \rho_R(X)E(R) \tag{7}$$

If $R = \{\{x\} \mid x \in U\}$, then for any X ($X \subset U$), the rough entropy of rough set X about knowledge R achieves minimum value 0.

If $R = \{U\}$, then for any X ($X \subset U$), the rough degree of rough set X about knowledge R achieves maximum value $\log_2 |U|$

Proposition 3.3. Let P and Q be two partition of finite set U. If $P \prec Q$, $X \subseteq U$ then

$$E_P(X) < E_Q(X) \tag{8}$$

Proof. From Proposition 3.1 and Proposition 3.2, we can see it is true.

The rough entropy of rough set about knowledge R more accurately denotes the incompleteness of rough set X about knowledge R.

Proposition 3.3 states that the rough entropy of rough set X about knowledge R induced from classic rough sets decreases monotonously as the granularity of information become smaller through finer partitions.

Example 3.3. In Example 3.1, the rough entropy of rough set X about knowledge P and Q are calculated as follows:

$E(P) = -[(1/5)\log(1)+ (1/5)\log(1)+ (1/5)\log(1)+ (1/5)\log(1)+ (2/5)\log(1/2)] = 2/5.$

$$E(Q) = -[(2/5)\log(1/2)+ (1/5)\log(1)+ (2/5)\log(1/2)] = 4/5$$

and $\qquad\qquad \rho_P(X) = \rho_Q(X) = 2/5$,

so $\qquad \rho_P(X)E(X) = (2/5)*(2/5) = 4/25, \qquad \rho_Q(X)E(Q) = (2/5)*(4/5) = 8/25$

namely $\qquad\qquad E_P(X) < E_Q(X).$

4 An Illustration

An example is presented in detail in this section. Data are often presented as a table, columns of which are labeled by attributes, rows by objects of interest and entries of the table are attribute values. Such tables are known as information systems. An example of information system is shown in Table 1. In Table 1, $U = \{1,2,3,4,5\}$, attributes Headache, Muscle-pain, Temperature and Night sweat are condition attributes, whereas the attribute Flu is a decision attribute. We use H, M, T, N stand for Headache, Muscle-pain, Temperature and Night sweat respectively.

Table 1. An application example

Objects	Headache	Muscle	Temperature	Night sweat	Flu
1	Yes	Yes	Very high	No	Yes
2	Yes	No	Very high	Yes	Yes
3	No	Yes	Very high	Yes	Yes
4	No	No	High	Yes	Yes
5	No	No	High	No	No

We consider the following partitions:

U/(T)={{1, 2, 3}, {4, 5}}, we denotes this knowledge as *P1*.

U/(H,T)={{1, 2}, {3}, {4, 5}}, we denotes this knowledge as *P2*.

U/(H,M,T)={{1}, {2}, {3}, {4,5}}, we denotes this knowledge as *P3*.

U/(flu)={{1, 2, 3, 4}, {5}}.

Next if we let $X = \{1,2,3,4\}$, we get the rough degree of above knowledge as follows:

$$\rho_{P1}(X) = \rho_{P2}(X) = \rho_{P3}(X) = 2/5,$$

and

$$E(P1) = (3\log(3)+2)/5,$$
$$E(P2) = 4/5$$
$$E(P3) = 2/5$$

while

$$E_{P1}(X) = 2(3\log(3)+2)/25$$
$$E_{P2}(X) = 8/25$$
$$E_{P2}(X) = 4/25$$

so we have

$$E_{P1}(X) > E_{P2}(X) > E_{P3}(X)$$

Thus we can see the knowledge *P3* more accurately implicates the incompleteness of
rough set X than knowledge *P2* and *P1*.

5 Conclusion

In this paper, we combine rough degree and rough entropy of knowledge to introduce
a new measure of uncertainty of knowledge named rough entropy of rough set. This
measure is more comprehensive than the measure rough degree and rough entropy of
knowledge respectively. The research denotes the rough degree of rough set X about
knowledge R in classic rough sets decreases monotonously as the granularity of information become smaller through finer partitions, the rough entropy of knowledge R
in classic rough sets decreases monotonously as the granularity of information become smaller through finer partitions, and the rough entropy of rough set X about
knowledge R in classic rough sets decreases monotonously as the granularity of information become smaller through finer partitions, too. In the future work, we will
continue to study the measure of uncertainty of knowledge in Generalized rough sets.

Acknowledgements

This research is supported by 863 Foundation of P. R. China, NO.2003AA142160,
And Foundation of Shanghai Science Committee, NO. 035115015

References

1. Z.Pawlak, Rough Sets, Int J Comput Inform Sci 11 (1982), pp341-356.
2. Z.Pawlak, Rough Sets: Theoretical Aspects of Reasoning About Data, Klwer Acadamic
   Publishers, Norwell, MA, 1991

3. Tsumoto, S.;Automated discovery of positive and negative knowledge in clinical data-bases,Engineering in Medicine and Biology Magazine, IEEE, Volume: 19, Issue: 4, July-Aug. 2000 Pages:56 – 62
4. C.E. Shannon, "The mathematical theory of communication", The Bell System Technical Journal 27 (3 and 4) (1948), pp373-423.
5. Liang Jiye, Shi Zhongzhi, The information entropy, rough entropy and knowledge granulation in rough set theory,International Journal of Uncertainty, Fuzziness and Knowlege-Based Systems, v12, n 1, February, 2004, pp 37-46
6. T.Beaubouef, F.E.Petry, G.Arora, Information-theoretic measures of uncertainty for rough sets and rough relational databases, Information Sciences 109(1998) pp 535-563.

The Variable Precision Rough Set Model for Data Mining in Inconsistent Information System

Qingmin Zhou[1,3], Chenbo Yin[2,4], and Yongsheng Li[4]

[1] Institute of Computer Application in Planning and Design, University of Karlsruhe,
76128 Karlsruhe, Germany
zhou@rpk.uni-karlsruhe.de

[2] Institute of Product Development, University of Karlsruhe, 76128 Karlsruhe, Germany
yin@ipek.uni-karlsruhe.de

[3] College of Information Science and Engineering, Nanjing University of Technology,
210009 Nanjing, P.R. China

[4] College of Mechanical and Power Engineering, Nanjing University of Technology,
210009 Nanjing, P.R. China

Abstract. The variable precision rough set (VPRS) model is an extension of original rough set model. For inconsistent information system, the VPRS model allows a flexible approximation boundary region by a precision variable. This paper is focused on data mining in inconsistent information system using the VPRS model. A method based on VPRS model is proposed to apply to data mining for inconsistent information system. By our method the deterministic and probabilistic classification rules are acquired from the inconsistent information system. An example is given to show that the method of data mining for inconsistent information system is effective.

1 Introduction

Rough set theory was first introduced by Pawlak in 1982 and it has been applied to machine learning, data mining, decision analysis, and pattern recognition etc.[1],[2]. However, the strict definition of the approximation boundary limits the usage of original rough sets theory to the situations that inconsistent data is included. As an extension of original rough set model, the variable precision rough set (VPRS) model is defined by W. Ziarko [3], [4]. The VPRS model presents the concept of the majority inclusion relation. For inconsistent information system, it allows a flexible region of lower approximations by the precision level β. Rules are acquired by β reduction. The rules that are supported by majority objects can be acquired with the VPRS model.

In this paper, a method based on VPRS model is proposed to apply to data mining for inconsistent information system. By selecting proper precision level β and using knowledge reduction, the deterministic and probabilistic classification rules are acquired from the inconsistent information system. An example is given to show that the method of data mining for inconsistent information system is effective.

C.-H. Chi and K.-Y. Lam (Eds.): AWCC 2004, LNCS 3309, pp. 285–290, 2004.

2   The Variable Precision Rough Set Model

2.1 Rough Approximation Analysis

Suppose an information system $S = (U, A)$, in which U is a finite non-empty universe; $A = C \cup D$, $C \cap D = \phi$; C is a set of condition attributes; D is a set of decision attributes. This kind of information system is also called decision table. *E1* and *E2* are two equivalence classes of condition attributes C. Q is an equivalence class of decision attributes D. For instance, there are 100 objects in *E1*, *E2* respectively. For equivalent class Q, only an object in *E1* belongs to Q, and only an object in *E2* does not belong to Q. Based on approximation sets of original rough set model, *E1* and *E2* belong to same boundary region of Q. That is to say, it is difficult to make a judgment for two results. Thus in the approximation sets of original rough set model, the date classification of 99% consistent and 1% inconsistent can not be distinguished.

The VPRS model extends the original rough set model by relaxing its strict definition of the approximation boundary using a precision variable. Hence some boundary regions are included in the positive region. It uses *majority inclusion* relations for classification rather than *equivalence relation* of original rough set [5]. Therefore, the VPRS model enhances discovery capabilities of the original rough set model and tolerates the inconsistent data of information system.

2.2 The VPRS Model

In the VPRS model, for a given information system $S = (U, A)$, $X \subseteq U$, $B \subseteq A$, the lower approximation and the upper approximation are defined with precision level β. The value β denotes the proportion of correct classifications [7], in this case, the domain of β is $0.5 < \beta \le 1$.

$$\underline{B}^{\beta}(X) = \bigcup \left\{ [x]_B : P(X / [x]_B) \ge \beta \right\} \tag{1}$$

$$\overline{B}^{\beta}(X) = \bigcup \left\{ [x]_B : P(X / [x]_B) > 1 - \beta \right\} . \tag{2}$$

$\underline{B}^{\beta}(X)$ and $\overline{B}^{\beta}(X)$ are respectively called the lower and upper approximation of X with precision level β. Here, $[x]_B$ is the equivalence class, $x \in U$. $P(X / [x]_B)$ is referred as conditional probability function [3], [5], [6].

$$P(X / [x]_B) = |X \cap [x]_B| / |[x]_B| . \tag{3}$$

Where $|X|$ is the cardinality of the set X.

The β-positive, β-negative and β-boundary regions are respectively defined by

$$POS_B^{\beta}(X) = \bigcup \left\{ [x]_B : P(X / [x]_B) \ge \beta \right\} \tag{4}$$

$$NEG_B^{\beta}(X) = \bigcup \left\{ [x]_B : P(X / [x]_B) \le 1 - \beta \right\} \tag{5}$$

$$BN_B^{\beta}(X) = \overline{B}^{\beta}(X) - \underline{B}^{\beta}(X) = \bigcup \left\{ [x]_B : P(X / [x]_B) \in (1 - \beta, \beta) \right\} . \tag{6}$$

As β decreases, the boundary region of the VPRS model becomes narrower. That is to say, the size of the uncertain region is reduced. We can say that the VPRS model is an extension of the original rough set model. When $\beta = 1$, the VPRS model can come back to the original rough set model.

3 Data Mining Method for Inconsistent Information System

3.1 On the Data Mining for Inconsistent Information System

In information system $S = (U, C \cup D)$, R_C and R_D are equivalence relation of C and D respectively. If $R_C \subseteq R_D$, then the information system is consistent. Otherwise, the information system is inconsistent. That is to say, the inconsistent information system contains inconsistent (conflicting) decision rules. There are the objects that have same condition attributes but different decision attributes in an inconsistent information system [10]. In practice, many information systems are inconsistent with probabilistic certainty factors. The inconsistency of an information system may be caused by many factors such as insufficiency of condition attributes, errors in measuring process and mistakes in recording process [9].

In recent years, more attention has been paid to data mining in inconsistent information systems. Many methods on this area had been reported and useful results were obtained. However in those methods for data mining from inconsistent information systems, if the inconsistency degree is weak, a non-deterministic rule is considered as a deterministic one. In this case, the little inconsistent rule is believed to be caused due to some noises mixed in the given information system. If the inconsistency degree is strong, the certain rule can not be generated from inconsistent information systems. The corresponding rule is treated as a random rule. So the classification method may interfere with the acquisition of important and valuable rules.

Handling these inconsistencies is of crucial importance for data mining. They can not be simply considered as noise or error to be eliminated from data, or amalgamated with consistent data by some averaging operators. These inconsistencies should be identified and expressed as uncertain patterns. The deterministic and probabilistic classification rules should be efficiently acquired from inconsistent information system. In this paper, we propose a method to compute a probabilistic degree of decisions or predictions in the inconsistent information system by using VPRS model. Those rules with probabilistic degree is very important for data mining.

3.2 Approximate Reduction and Rules Acquisition Using VPRS Model

For a given information system $S = (U, C \cup D)$, $X \subseteq U$, $B \subseteq C$. The measure of classification quality in VPRS model is defined by β-dependability of knowledge as follows:

$$\gamma^{\beta}(B,D) = \left| \bigcup \left\{ [x]_B : \frac{|X \cap [x]_B|}{|[x]_B|} \geq \beta \right\} \right| \Big/ |U| \,. \tag{7}$$

The value $\gamma^{\beta}(B,D)$ measures the proportion of objects in the non-empty universe U, where the classification is possible at the specified value of β [3], [6].

In VPRS model, the knowledge reduction is to select the minimum attribute subsets of C which don't change the quality of classification with the precision level β. We assume that $red^\beta(C,D)$ is β approximate reduction (β-reduction), then

$$\gamma^\beta(C,D) = \gamma^\beta\left(red^\beta(C,D),D\right) \ . \tag{8}$$

No proper subset of $red^\beta(C,D)$ at the same β value can also give the same quality of classification. In other words, if any one of attributes from $red^\beta(C,D)$ is eliminated, the formula (8) will be not valid.

Rules acquisition is one of the most important tasks in data mining. Supposing the decision attribute $D = \{d\}$, $V_d = \{1,2,...,n\}$, and $U/D = \{Y_1, Y_2, ...Y_n\}$, the decision class Y_j is $\{x \in U, d(x) = j\}$ [10], [11]. In VPRS model, for each $x \in \underline{B}_C^\beta(Y_j)$ a rule may be acquired from information system as follows:

$$\bigwedge_{r \in C}(r, r(x)) \rightarrow d = j \ . \tag{9}$$

3.3   The Method of Data Mining for Inconsistent Information System

For a given inconsistent information system $S = (U, C \cup D)$, $D = \{d\}$, the method of data mining in inconsistent information system can be expressed as following steps:

Step 1 Computing respectively all equivalence classes for condition attribute C and decision attribute D, $U/C = \{X_1, X_2, ..., X_m\}$, $U/D = \{Y_1, Y_2, ...Y_n\}$.

Step 2 For inconsistent equivalence class X_i, computing respectively conditional probability function $P(Y_j / X_i)$.

Step 3 For a given β, computing $POS_C^\beta(Y_j)$, $NEG_C^\beta(Y_j)$ and $BN_C^\beta(Y_j)$.

Step 4 Computing quality of classification $\gamma^\beta(C,D)$ with the precision level β.

Step 5 Computing β approximate reduction $red^\beta(C,D)$, where the quality of classification $\gamma^\beta(C,D)$ is not changed.

Step 6 For each $x \in POS_C^\beta(Y_j)$, acquiring the rule by $\bigwedge_{r \in C}(r, r(x)) \rightarrow d$.

Step 7 Synthesizing the corresponding deterministic and probabilistic classification rules.

4   An Example

Here, we give an example to show the process of rule acquisition for an inconsistent information system based on VPRS model. Table1 is an inconsistent decision table. $C = \{c_1, c_2, c_3, c_4\}$ is condition attribute set, $D = \{d\}$ is decision attribute. Obviously, the decision table1 is inconsistent because objects O_2, O_3 and O_5 are inconsistent.

In table1, U is divided into the equivalence classes $U/C = \{X_1, X_2, X_3, X_4\}$, where $X_1 = \{O_1\}$, $X_2 = \{O_2, O_3, O_5\}$, $X_3 = \{O_4\}$ and $X_4 = \{O_6\}$. Objects O_2, O_3 and O_5 in X_2 have the same condition attribute values, but different decision attributes. Hence that is an inconsistent decision table. The equivalence classes for the decision attribute are $U/D = \{Y_1, Y_2\}$, $Y_1 = \{O_1, O_2, O_3\}$ and $Y_2 = \{O_4, O_5, O_6\}$. Here the conditional probability function is $P(Y_1 / X_2) = |Y_1 \cap X_2| / |X_2| = 2/3 = 0.67$. The measurement of VPRS model is based on ratios of elements contained in various sets. That is to say, $X_2 = \{O_2, O_3, O_5\}$ have a majority inclusion in Y_1. Hence when $\beta = 0.6$, X_2 belong to positive region $POS_C^{0.6}(Y_1)$, then $POS_C^{0.6}(Y_1) = \{O_1, O_2, O_3, O_5\}$ and $NEG_C^{0.6}(Y_1) = \{O_4, O_6\}$. Thus, the boundary region is $BN_C^{0.6}(Y_1) = \{\phi\}$. Similarly for decision class Y_2, $POS_C^{0.6}(Y_2) = \{O_4, O_6\}$, $NEG_C^{0.6}(Y_2) = \{O_1, O_2, O_3, O_5\}$, and $BN_C^{0.6}(Y_2) = \{\phi\}$. If $\beta = 0.7$, then X_2 is not in the $POS_C^{0.7}(Y_1)$, since its upper bound on β is 0.67.

The β-reduction and quality of classification $\gamma^\beta(C, D)$ are computed by using the same method as above-mentioned. The some results of β-reduction are shown in table2. Table3 provides the minimal rules associated with β-reduction $\{c_2, c_4\}$.

Table 1. An inconsistent decision table

U	c_1	c_2	c_3	c_4	d
O_1	1	2	2	2	1
O_2	2	1	2	2	1
O_3	2	1	2	2	1
O_4	2	1	1	1	2
O_5	2	1	2	2	2
O_6	2	1	2	1	2

Table 2. Some results of β-reduction

β	β-reduction	Quality of classification
0.60	$\{c_3\}$	1.0
0.67	$\{c_1, c_4\}$	1.0
0.67	$\{c_2, c_4\}$	1.0
1.0	$\{c_1, c_2, c_4\}$	0.5

Table 3. Rules Acquisition for the β-reduction $\{c_2, c_4\}$

Rules	Support	Degree of confidence
$c_2 = 2 \wedge c_4 = 2 \xrightarrow{100\%} d_1$	1	1.0
$c_2 = 1 \wedge c_4 = 1 \xrightarrow{100\%} d_2$	2	1.0
$c_2 = 1 \wedge c_4 = 2 \xrightarrow{67\%} d_1$	3	0.67

5 Conclude Remarks

This paper is focused on the data mining in inconsistent information system based on VPRS model. Rough approximation of original rough set model is analyzed. The analysis result shows that VPRS model extends the original one by a predefined precision level β. A method based on VPRS model is proposed to apply to data mining for inconsistent information system. By selecting proper precision level β and using knowledge reduction, the deterministic and probabilistic classification rules are acquired from the inconsistent information system.

An inconsistent information system may have many β- reductions. People always pay attention to the reduction that have the least attributes–minimal reduction sets, because the minimal rule sets of the information system can be obtained through the minimal reduction sets. However, it has been proved that the minimal reductions of the information system are the NP-hard [8]. In further research, for the decrease of the computation cost a method of selecting an appropriate β-reduction is being developed.

References

1. Pawlak, Z.: Rough Sets. International Journal of Computer and Information Sciences, 11(5) (1982) 341-356
2. Pawlak, Z.: Rough Sets - Theoretical Aspects of Reasoning about Data. Kluwer Academic Publishers, London (1991)
3. Ziarko, W.: Analysis of Uncertain Information in the Framework of Variable Precision Rough Sets. Foundations of Computing and Decision Sciences, 18(3-4) (1993) 381-396
4. Katzberg, J.D. Ziarko, W.: Variable Precision Extension of Rough Sets. Fundamental Informatics 27 (1996) 155-168
5. Beynon, M.: An Investigation of β-reduct Selection within the Variable Precision Rough Sets Model. In: Ziarko W. and Yao Y. (Eds.) Proceedings of RSCTC 2000, LNAI 2005. Springer-Verlag, Berlin Heidelberg (2001) 114-122
6. Beynon, M.: Reducts within the Variable Precision Rough Set Model: A Further Investigation. European Journal of Operational Research, 134 (2001) 592-605
7. An, A., Shan, N., Chan, C., Cercone, N., Ziarko, W.: Discovering Rules for Water Demand Prediction: An Enhanced Rough-set Approach. Engineering Applications in Artificial Intelligence, 9(6) (1996) 645-653
8. Skowron, A., Rauszer, C.: The Discernibility Matrices and Functions in Information Systems. Intelligent decision support-handbook of applications and advances of the rough sets theory, Kluwer Academic Publishers, (1992) 331-362
9. Wang, G.Y., Liu, F.: The Inconsistency in Rough Set Based Rule Generation. In: Ziarko, W. and Yao, Y. (Eds.) Proceedings of RSCTC 2000, LNAI 2005. Springer-Verlag, Berlin Heidelberg (2001) 370-377
10. Zhang, W.X., Wu, W.Z., Liang, J.Y.: Rough Set Theory and its Method. Science Press, Beijing (2001) (In Chinese)
11. Mi, J.S., Wu, W.Z., Zhang, W.X.: Approaches to Knowledge Reduction based on Variable Precision Rough Set Model. Information Sciences, 159 (2004) 255-272

Rule Discovery
with Particle Swarm Optimization

Yu Liu[1], Zheng Qin[1,2], Zhewen Shi[1], and Junying Chen[1]

[1] Department of Computer Science, Xian JiaoTong University,
Xian 710049, P.R. China
liuyu@mailst.xjtu.edu.cn
http://www.psodream.net
[2] School of Software, Tsinghua University, Beijing 100084, P.R. China

Abstract. This paper proposes Particle Swarm Optimization (PSO) algorithm to discover classification rules. The potential IF-THEN rules are encoded into real-valued particles that contain all types of attributes in data sets. Rule discovery task is formulized into an optimization problem with the objective to get the high accuracy, generalization performance, and comprehensibility, and then PSO algorithm is employed to resolve it. The advantage of the proposed approach is that it can be applied on both categorical data and continuous data. The experiments are conducted on two benchmark data sets: Zoo data set, in which all attributes are categorical, and Wine data set, in which all attributes except for the classification attribute are continuous. The results show that there is on average the small number of conditions per rule and a few rules per rule set, and also show that the rules have good performance of predictive accuracy and generalization ability.

1 Introduction

There has been a great interest in the area of data mining, in which the general goal is to discover knowledge that is not only correct, but also comprehensible and interesting for the user [1]. Hence, the user can understand the results produced by the system and combine them with their own knowledge to make a well-informed decision, rather than blindly trusting on results produced by system. Classification is an important topic in data mining research. The knowledge in classification is often expressed as a set of rules. IF-THEN rules are high-level symbolic knowledge representations and have the advantage of being intuitively comprehensible for users. Evolutionary approaches like genetic algorithms (GA) and genetic programming (GP) have been applied to discover classification rules. Examples of GA for rule discovery can be found in [2-3], and examples of GP for rule discovery can be found in [4-6]. Recently, Particle Swarm Optimizer (PSO) has attracted researchers in optimization field. But using Swarm Intelligence in data mining is a fairly new research area and needs much more work to do. So using PSO for rule discovery is a quite new and challenging research area. Tiago Sousa et al. in [7-8] proposed a binary-encoding way to discover classification

C.-H. Chi and K.-Y. Lam (Eds.): AWCC 2004, LNCS 3309, pp. 291–296, 2004.
© Springer-Verlag Berlin Heidelberg 2004

rules with PSO for categorical data. However, our PSO algorithm of rule discovery adopts a real-encoding way, which can be applied to both categorical and continuous attributes, as demonstrated in the experiment on Zoo (categorical attributes) and Wine (continuous attributes) data sets.

2　Rule Discovery with PSO

Particle Swarm Optimization (PSO), a new population-based evolutionary computation technique inspired by social behavior simulation, was first introduced in 1995 by Eberhart and Kennedy [9]. PSO is an efficient and effective global optimization algorithm, which has been widely applied to nonlinear function optimization, neural network training, and pattern recognition. In PSO, a swarm consists of N particles moving around in a D-dimensional search space. The position of the i-th particle at the t-th iteration is represented by $X_i^{(t)} = (x_{i1}, x_{i2}, \ldots, x_{iD})$ that are used to evaluate the quality of the particle. During the search process the particle successively adjusts its position toward the global optimum according to the two factors: the best position encountered by itself (*pbest*) denoted as $P_i = (p_{i1}, p_{i2}, \ldots, p_{iD})$ and the best position encountered by the whole swarm (*gbest*) denoted as $P_g = (p_{g1}, p_{g2}, \ldots, p_{gD})$. Its velocity at the t-th iteration is represented by $V_i^{(t)} = (v_{i1}, v_{i2}, \ldots, v_{iD})$. The position at next iteration is calculated according to the following equations:

$$V_i^{(t)} = \lambda(\omega * V_i^{(t-1)} + c_1 * rand() * (P_i - X_i^{(t-1)}) + c_2 * rand() * (P_g - X_i^{(t-1)})) \quad (1)$$

$$X_i^{(t)} = X_i^{(t-1)} + V_i^{(t)} \quad (2)$$

where c_1 and c_2 are two positive constants, called cognitive learning rate and social learning rate respectively; $rand()$ is a random function in the range $[0, 1]$; w is $inertia factor$; and λ is $constriction factor$. In addition, the velocities of the particles are confined within $[Vmin, Vmax]^D$. If an element of velocities exceeds the threshold $Vmin$ or $Vmax$, it is set equal to the corresponding threshold.

In this paper, our PSO algorithm for rule discovery follows Michigan approach where an individual encodes a single prediction rule. Each run only one rule can be discovered. In order to get a set of rules, the algorithm must be run several times. All possible values of classification attributes are assigned one by one to PSO algorithm. Each run of PSO algorithm has a fixed value of classification attribute. So to get a rule set, the algorithm must be run at least K times if we want to predict K different classes.

2.1　Rule Presentation

The particle is concatenation of real-valued elements in the range $[0, 1]$, which is divided into three parts as shown in Figure 1. If there are m decision attributes, each part has m elements respectively. So the size of a particle is $3m$. In order to form a rule according to a particle, three parts are translated into the original

| Attribute-existence-array | Operator-array | Attribute-array |

Fig. 1. Structure of a particle

information: (1) presence of attributes, (2) operators between attributes and their values, and (3) original values of attributes based on their types in the data set. If the i-th elements in *Attribute-existence-array* is greater than 0, then the i-th attribute is present in rule antecedent, else the i-th attribute is absent. Attributes in data mining tasks are often of several types: categorical or continuous types. So PSO algorithm for rule discovery must provide a way to encode these two types of attributes. For *Operator-array*, first the types of attributes must be considered. When the attribute is continuous, if the i-th elements in *Operator-array* is great than 0, then the operator is '$\geq$' else it is '$<$'; when the attribute is categorical (integer or nominal), if the i-th element is greater than 0, then the operator is '$=$' else it is '$! =$'. While the translation of *Attribute-array* is relatively complex because the different types of the attributes must be considered.

– For integer type, the translation is as follows:

$$V_{org}[i] = ceil(v_i * (V_i max - V_i min) + V_i min) \tag{3}$$

– For real type, the translation is as follows:

$$V_{org}[i] = v_i * (V_i max - V_i min) + V_i min \tag{4}$$

– For nominal type, the translation is as follows:

$$V_{org}[i] = ValArr_i(ceil(v_i * Count_i)) \tag{5}$$

Where $V_{org}[i]$ means the value translated from the particle for the i-th attribute, v_i is the i-th value in the particle which is a real value. In Equations (3) and (4), the type of the i-th attribute is of integer or real, here $V_i max$ means the maximum of the i-th attribute, and $V_i min$ the minimum. In Equation (5), the type of the i-th attribute is nominal, here $ValArr_i$ means the array that stored every different nominal values of the i-th attribute and $Count_i$ means the total number of different values of the i-th attribute. $ceil()$ is a function that returns the value round towards plus infinity.

2.2   Rule Evaluation (Fitness Function Design)

Let a rule be of such form: IF A THEN C

Where A is a rule antecedent, which is a conjunction of conditions, and C is a rule consequent which is the prediction class. The accuracy of classification rule is defined in Equation (6) to measure the degree of confidence for rules. The coverage of a rule is defined in Equation (7) to interpret the proportion of the examples that satisfy the rule in all examples that are of C class.

$$Accuracy = TP/(TP + FP) \tag{6}$$

$$Coverage = TP/(TP + FN) \qquad (7)$$

TP = Number of examples satisfying A and C
FP = Number of examples satisfying A but not C.
FN = Number of examples not satisfying A but satisfying C.
TN = Number of examples not satisfying A nor C.

The comprehensibility of a rule set is often presented by less number of conditions in the rule antecedent and less rules in the rule set. In the process of rule discovery, we use Equation (8) to assure the shortness of a rule at the same time.

$$Succinctness = 1 - (countAnt - 1)/attributeCount \qquad (8)$$

Where $countAnt$ means the number of the conditions in the rule antecedent, $attributeCount$ means the number of decision attributes in the data set. To present the three criterions, as a result, we define our fitness function as follows:

$$Fitness = w_1*(Accuracy*Coverage)+w_2*Succinctness+w_3*Interesting \quad (9)$$

Where w_1, w_2, and w_3 are constants used to balance the weights of the three criterions in the rule discovery process. Since $Interesting$ is highly dependent on users, in this paper we did not consider this criterion. In our experiment, w_1, w_2, and w_3 were set to 0.8, 0.2, and 0, respectively.

3   Experiments

3.1   Data Sets and Experiments Setup

The data sets, Zoo and Wine, were obtained from UCI repository of Machine Learning databases [10]. The Zoo data set with 18 categorical attributes was divided into 7 classes. The Wine data set with 13 continuous attributes was divided into 3 classes. To evaluate both the accuracy and generalization of the discovered rules, two different kinds of experiments were conducted on each data set. In the first kind of experiment, the data set was divided into two parts: 2/3 as training set and 1/3 as test set. The division was randomly generated. The experiment was run 5 times, each time on a different division. Then the average results were generated based on the 5 independent runs. The purpose of the first kind of experiment was to evaluate the generalization ability, measured as the classification accuracy on test set. In the second kind of experiment, the full data set was used to discover the final rules reported to users. The purpose of this experiment was to evaluate the classification accuracy and comprehensibility by the number of rules in the data set, and the average number of rule conditions per rule. Here, Linearly Decreasing Weight PSO (LDW-PSO) [11] was employed, where a weight w decreased linearly between 0.9 and 0.4; $\lambda = 1$; $Vmin = Xmin = 0$; $Vmax = Xmax = 1$. The learning rates were $c1 = c2 = 2$.

3.2   Results and Discussion

The results in the first kind of experiment were as follows. The accuracy values averaged over 5 runs on training set for 7 classes were 1, 1, 1, 1, 1, 1, 0.9131, while corresponding accuracy values on test set were 0.9548, 1, 0.6000, 0.9667, 0.7000, 0.7150, 0.8767. For Wine, the accuracy values on training set for 3 classes were 0.9705, 0.9448, 0.9707, while corresponding accuracy values on test set were 0.9378, 0.6559, 1. From the results, it seems that the algorithm has good performance of predictive accuracy and generalization ability not only on categorical attributes of Zoo data set but also continuous attributes of Wine data set. In the second kind of experiment, the final rules discovered from full Zoo and Wine data sets were listed in Tables 1 and 2 respectively. The best rules for each class, the number of examples covered by rule antecedent $| A |$, and the number of correctly predicted examples $| A\&C |$ were showed in the tables. The results indicate that not only the predictive accuracy is pretty good, but also the number of rule conditions is relatively short and there are a small number of rules in the rule set, so the rules are competitively comprehensible.

Table 1. The results of learning from the full Zoo data set (rules with less coverage are removed from the table)

Class	Rule	$| A\&C |$	$| A |$
1	if $milk = 1$ then $type = 1$	41	41
2	if $feathers = 1$ $toothed = 0$ then $type = 2$	20	20
3	if $hair = 0$ $feathers = 0$ $aquatic = 0$ $backbone = 1$ $legs! = 8$ then $type = 3$	4	4
4	if $milk = 0$ $fins = 1$ then $type = 4$	13	13
5	if $milk = 0$ $aquatic = 1$ $breathes = 1$ legs $!=2$ catsize $=0$ then $type = 5$	4	4
6	if $aquatic = 0$ $legs = 6$ then $type = 6$	8	8
7	if $airborne = 0$ $backbone = 0$ then $type = 7$	10	12

Table 2. The results of learning from the full Wine data set (rules with less coverage are removed from the table)

Class	Rule	$| A\&C |$	$| A |$
1	If $A7 \geq 2.29$ $A13 \geq 723$ then $Class = 1$	57	58
2	If $A1 < 12.81$ $A12 \geq 1.81$ then $Class = 2$	60	62
2	If $A2 < 2.35$ $A11 \geq 0.81$ $A13 < 758$ then $Class = 2$	8	8
3	If $A7 < 1.51$ $A10 \geq 3.97$ then $Class = 3$	46	47

4   Conclusions

We proposed a real-encoding way for rule discovery using PSO algorithm. The experiments show that this encoding way is effective and efficient. The rules discovered in the two datasets are generally with high accuracy, generalization and comprehensibility. Furthermore, the real-encoding way is competitive in discovering rules not only from categorical data, but also from continuous data. The results on the Wine data set show that our approach has good performance for rule discovery on continuous data.

References

1. Fayyad, U., Piatetsky-Shapiro, G., Smyth, P.: From data mining to knowledge discovery in databases: An overview. Advances in Knowledge Discovery and Data Mining (1996) 1–34
2. Noda, E., Freitas, A.A., Lopes, H.S.: Discovering interesting prediction rules with a genetic algorithm. In Angeline, P.J., Michalewicz, Z., Schoenauer, M., Yao, X., Zalzala, A., eds.: Proceedings of the Congress on Evolutionary Computation. Volume 2., Mayflower Hotel, Washington D.C., USA, IEEE Press (1999) 1322–1329
3. Jong, K.A.D., Spears, W.M., Gordon, G.: Using genetic algorithms for concept learning. Machine Learning **13** (1993) 161–188
4. Bojarczuk, C.C., Lopes, H.S., Freitas, F.: Discovering comprehensible classification rules using genetic programming: a cas study in a medical domain. In Banzhaf, W., Daida, J., Eiben, A.E., Garzon, M.H., Honavar, V., Jakiela, M., Smith, R.E., eds.: Proc. of the Genetic and Evolutionary Computation Conf. GECCO-99, San Francisco, CA, Morgan Kaufmann (1999) 953–958
5. Freitas, A.A.: A genetic programming framework for two data mining tasks: Classification and generalized rule induction. In Koza, J.R., Deb, K., Dorigo, M., Fogel, D.B., Garzon, M., Iba, H., Riolo, R.L., eds.: Genetic Programming 1997: Proceedings of the Second Annual Conference, Stanford University, CA, USA, Morgan Kaufmann (1997) 96–101
6. De Falco, I., Della Cioppa, A., Tarantino, E.: Discovering interesting classification rules with genetic programming. Applied Soft Computing **1** (2001) 257–269
7. Sousa, T., Neves, A., Silva, A.: Swarm optimisation as a new tool for data mining. In: 17th International Parallel and Distributed Processing Symposium (IPDPS-2003), Los Alamitos, CA, IEEE Computer Society (2003) 144–144
8. Sousa, T., Neves, A., Silva, A.: A particle swarm data miner. In: 11th Portuguese Conference on Artificial Intelligence, Workshop on Artificial Life and Evolutionary Algorithms. (2003) 43–53
9. Kennedy, J., Eberhart, R.C.: Particle swarm optimization. In: Proceeding of IEEE International Conference on Neural Networks (ICNN'95). Volume 4., Perth, Western Australia, IEEE (1995) 1942–1947
10. Blake, C., Merz, C.J.: UCI repository of machine learning databases, http://www.ics.uci.edu/~mlearn/MLRepository.html (1998)
11. Shi, Y., Eberhart, R.C.: A modified particle swarm optimizer. In: IEEE Congress on Evolutionary Computation (CEC 1998), Piscataway, NJ, IEEE (1998) 69–73

Data Mining Service Based on MDA*

Yiqun Chen[1], Chi-Hung Chi[2], and Jian Yin[1,3]

[1] Zhongshan University, Guangdong 510275, P.R. China
[2] National University of Singapore, Singapore
[3] State Key Laboratory for Novel Software Technology, Nanjing University,
Nanjing 210093, P.R. China
issjyin@zsu.edu.cn

Abstract. Data Mining is a helpful tool for business decision support. The adaptability, reusability and flexibility of Data Mining System is still a big challenge and in great need, for requirement and platform changes are inescapable. The idea is to make business layer, technology layer and realization layer become more independent to each other. In this paper, we describe the Model-Driven Architecture(MDA) foundation for Data Mining Service, including store metadata in desired way for users to define operation level and build Metadata-Driven Tools, enrich UDDI specification for application components publish service inside system, also we discuss the benefits of using it and its future work.

1 Introduction

Data Mining(DM) is widely used for analysis purpose, as a helpful tool for business decision support. To reach best decision support effect, new requirement and adaption are inescapable. New platforms and applications must interoperate with legacy systems. The idea is to design a architecture that can be easily adapted to new business and platform requirement.

Combines ideas from two exiting standards for metadata representation and exchange in the area of data warehousing (OIM and CWM), researchers bring out M^4, which is the metamodel used by Mining Mart, a system for supporting data preprocessing for data mining[1]. M^4 can be logically divided into two main parts, one managing information with regard to data modelling and the other one regarding case modelling. M^4 only presents a metamodel for a metadata-driven software package performing preprocessing for data mining. Our system persents a design for a metadata-driven software package performing overall procedure for data mining based on DW. We also make a further development to confirm the adaptability, reusability and flexibility of our systems, which will be explained in section 3. Our design contributes the following:

* This work is supported by the National Natural Science Foundation of China (60205007), Natural Science Foundation of Guangdong Province (001264, 031558), Research Foundation of Science and Technology Plan Project in Guangdong Province(2003C50118) and Research Foundation of Science and Technology Plan Project in Guangzhou City(2002Z3-E0017).

C.-H. Chi and K.-Y. Lam (Eds.): AWCC 2004, LNCS 3309, pp. 297–302, 2004.
© Springer-Verlag Berlin Heidelberg 2004

1. Web Service technology is used to publish the application components inside our system as service provider by enriching the Universal Description, Discovery and Integration (UDDI) specification.
2. A metadata depository is used to store metadata in a desired way so that we can make full use of them.
3. Further use of metadata is extended for end user by building a Query System in our system.

2   System Overview

Data Mining Service architecture is depicted in Figure 1.

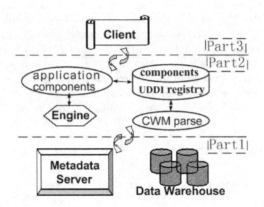

Fig. 1. System Architecture

2.1   Data Repository and Management

Part 1 is the data repository level including Metadata Server and Data Warehouse. In DW, metadata(data about data) is a general notion that captures all kind of information necessary to support the management, query, consistent use and understanding of data. It may be any information related to schema definitions and configuration specifications, physical storage, and access rights, but also end-user-specific documentation, business concepts, terminology, and details about user reports.

Additionally, considering a DM task, the data mining process may uncover thousands of rules, many of which are uninteresting to the user. In the Constraint-based Data Mining, mining is performed under the guidance of various kinds of constraints provided by the users. These constraints, including knowledge type constraints, data constraints, dimension/level constraints, interestingness constraints, rule constraints and so on, allow users to specify the rules to be mined according to their intention, thereby making the data mining process more effective. All these metedata should be recorded in a desired way so that system can access. Follow the idea of an XML DTD for CWM in a CWM supporting

DW platform, we defined an XML DTD for preprocessing for data mining, an XML DTD for data mining task control information. An example of an XML file for data mining task control information is shown on table 1.

Table 1. XML document abstract for DM task

```
<DM task>
  <summary>
    <department>Market of South China</department>
    <title>Price Trend</title>
    <date>10-12-2004</date>
    <requestorID>mark0323534</requestorID>
    <description>...</description>
    ......
  </summary>
  <detail>
    <table>Food</table>
    ......
    <dimension>
      <time>day</time>
      ......
    </dimension>
    <rule format>.....</rule format>
    ......
  </detail>
</DM task>
```

In a DW platform that support CWM, such as Oracle, IBM DB2, etc, there are tools inside for exporting and importing CWM metamodel instance and also a XML Document Type Definition (DTD) for CWM. A CWM instance is stored as an XML file, containing metadata mentioned aboved. System will build up a CWM metamodel instance object as reference for users or application components inside system, according to the CWM metamodel instance from DW. In the DW environment that hasn't CWM-supporting tools, we can insert a metadata translation layer to settle the communication between DW and upper level application. Thus, we can also build up a CWM metamodel instance object in system, achieving platform independence.

2.2   CWM Parser

As the common specification to share metadata, CWM takes an important role in our system. MOF is an extensible model driven integration framework for defining, manipulating and integrating metadata and data in a platform independent manner. UML notation is used for representing metamodel and models.

The XMI specification defines technology mappings from MOF metamodel to XML DTD and XML documents. These mappings can be used to define an interchange format for metadata conforming to a given MOF metamodel.

The CWM metamodel instance may be a reference in the procedure shown in Figure 2. Firstly, a XML Parser will parser the XML document of CWM metamodel instance according to CWM DTD or MOF DTD. Secondly, system will build the CWM metamodel instance object according the information it got from the XML document. Thirdly, we can procedure many tasks such as querying according to this object.

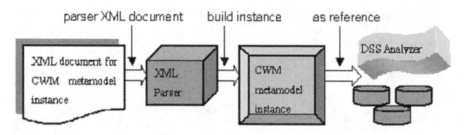

Fig. 2. System Architecture

2.3   UDDI Registry for Components

The UDDI project encourages the inter operability and adoption of Web services. A UDDI registry contains programmatically accessible descriptions of businesses and the services they support. It also contains references to industry-specific specifications that a Web service might support, taxonomy definitions (used for meaningful categorization of businesses and services), and identification systems (used for meaningful identification of businesses). UDDI provides a programming model and schema, which define the rules for communicating with the registry.

UDDI is based on existing standards XML and Simple Object Access Protocol (SOAP), integration and communication among application components is predigested on higher abstract level. XML provide data organization and exchange method in a platform and programming language independent manner. SOAP defines a simple information package method in a platform-independent manner, based on XML. Changes inside and outside system and component are considered, the implementation is transparent between upper and lower level, service provider and requestor.

The UDDI specification is imported and enriched in our design. After the enrichment, the UDDI specification is not only applicable to Web services, but also applicable to the description, discovery and integration of applications component in the application system. Application components, particularly the DM components, as service provider register in UDDI registry for components. At the same time, other application components also as service providers publish their service. All the components may be a service requestor to another. Due to such special architecture, our system enforces flexibility, reusability and adaptability of software and allows the integration of additional tools, such as DM components.

2.4 Metadata-Driven Tools

Metadata for Data mining task and other applications in DW is mentioned above. These metadata in application components are abstracted to store in Metadata Server, outside of applications and programs.

Engine is responsible for building the connection between metadata server and application components. At run time, metadata is read by Engine, is dynamically bound into the engine software, then Engine brings out the resulting application. The resulting application then can be executed and also publish its service in UDDI registry for components inside our system.

It is obvious that the metadata determines the behavior of the application components. Application components semantics is simply distributed between the repository and the engine and is pieced together at runtime only. One of the main benefits expected from metadata-driven software is reusability and flexibility. On the one hand, objects encapsulating control information are stored in the repository (instead of being hidden in scripts and programs) and may be reused in different contexts and applications. On the other hand, the engines running on top of the repository may be used for all metadata instances fitting the given metadata structure. This results in improved flexibility. The system may be extended and adapted without difficulty since metadata instances may be sassily changed without affecting the clients (i.e., engines) sharing it. Thus, maintenance is easier.

2.5 Query System

Grasp information as much as possible is a great help to decision support analyzer and system operator in their work. In this motivation, we bring out a Query system.

As a data mining system based on data warehousing, there is amount of information stored Data Warehouse and Metadata Server as mentioned above. All may be a reference for decision support analyzer. RDBMS provide full text index tools for text column in database tables such as Oracle Text. Free form keyword search over RDBMS has attracted recent research interest[2]. Given a query, the system will return the join tuples include the words in query.

As we know, most metadata are stored as a XML document. system can parses XML documents to generate and load inverted file information into a relational database[5]. The rest procedure is the same with keyword search in RDBMS. Thus implement query over XML document.

Given a query, we will carry out parellel search on XML document and information in RDBMS, we omit the detail due to limited space.

2.6 Client

As the platform to connect client and server,**Client** provides tools for system user to hand in query request; read metadata such as table design and business logic in DW to decide DM task's business logic and direction; learn about DM arithmetic and DW information through Query System; point out the constraints of DM task; specify metadata instance for DM components, etc.

3 Conclusion

This paper presents MDA foundation architecture for Data Mining Service, based on CWM, Metadata-driven Tools and Web Services technology. This flexible architecture allows to easily extending when additional tools, new business requirement or new data sources are added to the system, without platform limited. MDA improve long-term productivity by minimizing the sensitivity of primary software artifacts to change and maximize the useful lifetime of key software development assets, as a way to fetch up the shortcoming of DM tools: lack of adaptability, reusability and flexibility, with a limited lifecycle. However, there is still some future work for the MDA foundation architecture, and the flexibility and adaptability could be only partially solved with the actual solution.

References

1. Anca Vaduva, Jorg-Uwe Kietz, Regina Zcker. M4: a metamodel for data preprocessing. Proceedings of the fourth ACM international workshop on Data warehousing and OLAP. Atlanta, Georgia, USA, Sept 2001 Page(s): 85-92
2. Vagelis Hristidis, Luis Gravano and Yannis Papakonstantinou. Efficient IR-Style Keyword Search over Relational Databases. Proceedings of the 29th VLDB Conference. Berlin, Germany. 2003.
3. Colin Atkinson, Thomas Khne. The Role of Metamodeling in MDA. International Workshop in Software Model Engineering (in conjunction with UML '02), Dresden, Germany, October 2002 http://www.metamodel.com/wisme-2002/
4. Colin Atkinson, Thomas Khne. Model-driven development: a metamodeling foundation. Software, IEEE, Volume: 20 Issue: 5, Sept.-Oct. 2003 Page(s): 36 -41
5. D. Florescu, I. Manolescu, Integrating Keyword Search into XML Query Processing, 9th WWW Conf., 2000
6. John D. Poole. Model-Driven Architecture: Vision, Standards And Emerging Technologies. Position Paper Submitted to ECOOP 2001 Workshop on Metamodeling and Adaptive Object Models, April 2001
7. J. Mukerji and J. Miller, eds. Model Driven Architecture. http://www.omg.org/cgi-bin/doc?ormsc/2001-07-01.
8. Vaduva and K. R. Dittrich. Metadata management for data warehousing: Between vision and reality. In International Database Engineering δ Applications Symposium, IDEAS'O1, Grenoble, France, July 2001 Page(s): 129-135

Web Service Composition Based on BPWS-Net*

Jian Sun and Changjun Jiang

Dept. of Computer Sci. and Eng.,Tongji University, 200092 Shanghai, China
simbasun@msn.com, cjjiang@online.sh.cn

Abstract. Web Service is a more efficient and economical framework for distributed computing. However, it's an important challenge to integrate Web Services provided by different enterprises or organizations into a new value-added Web Service. BPEL4WS (Business Process Execution Language for Web Services) is such a procedure language for Web Service composition. An approach to model BPEL4WS described process based on a kind of Service-Oriented Petri Net, BPWS-net, is proposed in this paper. Both the basic activities and structured activities of BPEL4WS are discussed using BPWS-Net. By means of this approach, not only the formal semantics of Web Service and its composition can be definitely described, but also the control flow of BPEL4WS process can be graphically modeled. Furthermore, this approach can be used to validate the correctness or soundness of Web Service composition.

1 Introduction

Web Service is a kind of new framework for distributed computing, which provides a uniform interface for access to all kinds of heterogeneous resources on the World-Wide-Web.

As the capability of an individual Web Service is limited, it is necessary to create new functionalities with existing Web Services in the form of processes or flows. Web Service composition is the ability to take existing services (or building blocks) and combine them to form new services. Though WSDL has provided a model of synchronous or asynchronous interactions for Web Service composition, the real application of Web Service composition is more complex than it.

BPEL4WS [1] is a complex procedure language for Web Service composition, which is on the top of the stack of WSDL [2], SOAP [3], UDDI. It uses XML to describe the process of Web Service composition, and also can map the process into Web Service described by WSDL. [4] has proposed an approach to Web Service composition based on Petri net. By means of this approach, formal semantic of Web Service composition is given, which ensures reliable control flow model of Web Service composition. However, a formal definition and validation for BPEL4WS has not been defined [5].

In this paper, an approach to BPEL4WS process modeling based on a high level Petri net, named BPWS-net, is proposed. The BPWS-Net can express the semantic of

---

* This research is supported by projects of National Natural Science Foundation (No. 60125205, 90412013), Foundation for the University Key Teacher by the Ministry of Education of China, Shanghai Science & Technology Research Plan (03DZ15029, 03JC14071), and 973 Project of China (No. 2003CB316902).

C.-H. Chi and K.-Y. Lam (Eds.): AWCC 2004, LNCS 3309, pp. 303–313, 2004.

composition Web Service described by BPEL4WS. And because BPWS-Net is a graphical and formal modeling language, it facilitates the correctness verification of the model. Furthermore, process described by BPEL4WS can be mapped into BPWS-Net model directly, so BPEL4WS process modeling based on this approach is valuable for engineering application.

In the following sections, we will first give an overview of Petri Net and BPEL4WS in Section 2. Then, Section 3 presents several mapping rules between Petri Net and BPEL4WS, in which a set of Activity-Net Definitions to represent elements in BPEL4WS is defined. In Section 4, a real work example will be presented to illustrate the application of our BPWS-Net-based approach to BPEL4WS process. Section 5 discusses briefly the analysis and verification of BPEL4WS process. Finally, we will present a conclusion in Section 6.

2 Backgrounds

In this section, we will give an overview of BPEL4WS and Petri Net. We will first introduce BPEL4WS briefly and show it's two categories of elements, which we will analyze one by one in the next section. We will then quickly review the informal definitions of Petri nets.

2.1 Overview of BPEL4WS

The composition of Web services consists of providing logic around a set of interactions between the composition and the Web services that participate in it. These interactions are simply invocations to the operations offered by the services in play. One approach to providing the control and data logic is the use of workflow.

BPEL4WS is a workflow-based composition language for Web services. It introduces several types of basic activities: to allow for interaction with the applications being composed (invoke, reply and receive activities), wait for some time (the wait activity), copy data from one place to another (the assign activity), indicate error conditions (the throw activity), terminate the entire composition instance (the terminate activity), or to do nothing (the empty activity). Data is available in global containers.

These basic activities can be combined into more complex algorithms using structured activities. These are the ability to define an ordered sequence of steps (the sequence activity), the ability to have branching using the now common "case-statement" approach (the switch activity), the ability to define a loop (the while activity), the ability to execute one of several alternative paths (the pick activity), and finally the ability to indicate that a collection of steps should be executed in parallel (the flow activity). Within activities executing in parallel, one can indicate execution order constraints by using links.

2.2 Overview of Petri Net

A Petri net is a five-tuple $PN=(P,T,F,W,M0)$, where P is the set of places of PN, T is the set of transitions of PN, $P \cap T=\varnothing$, $F \subseteq (P \times T) \cup (T \times P)$ the edges (flow relations) of PN, $W:F \to N$ the weight function of PN (N is used to denoted the set $\{1,2,\dots\}$), and

M0: P→N∪{0} is called the initial marking of PN. R(M0) represents the set of all markings reachable from M0. For ∀M∈R(M0), M(p) denotes the number of tokens in p∈P at M. We use the following symbols for the pre-set and post-set of a node x∈P∪T: •x={y| (y,x) ∈F}, x•={y| (x,y) ∈F}.

Places are graphically drawn as circles, transitions as bars. The flow relations between the nodes (i.e. places and transitions) are represented as directed arcs, and the tokens of the making as dots inside places. Weight function W is annotated close to its corresponding directed arc. But ∀t∈T, ∀p∈P, if W(p,t)=1 or W(t,p)=1, weight function W is graphically omitted for the sake of simplicity. A transition t is enabled when its each input place p∈•t has at least W(p,t) tokens. When an enabled transition t is fired, for ∀p∈•t W(p,t) tokens are removed from p, and for ∀p∈t• W(t,p) tokens are added to p; this results in a new marking M' (notation M[t>M').

3 Mapping Rules Between BPEL4WS and Petri Net

In this section, we will present several mapping rules between BPEL4WS and Petri Net, which focus on how to represent activities in BPEL4WS using the Petri Net approach. Several specific Activity-Nets, which are pre-defined Petri Net model used to describe specific control flows, will be introduced in order to describe the structural control elements in BPEL4WS.

The "suppressJoinFailure" attribute determines whether the "joinFailure" fault will be suppressed for all activities in the process. For convenience, we assume all the suppressJoinFailure attributes are "yes" in this paper.

3.1 Activities

Each BPEL4WS activity has optional nested standard elements <source> and <target>. The use of these elements is required for establishing synchronization relationships through links. Each <source> element may optionally specify a transition condition that functions as a guard for following this specified link. If the transition condition is omitted, it is deemed to be present with the constant value true.

We map all the BPEL4WS activities to Activity-Nets.

Definition 1. Activity-Net
An Activity-Net is a Petri net, i.e., a 3-tuple Activity-Net = {P, T, TA, F}, where:

(1) P = {p_s, p_e}.
(2) T = {t_s, t_e, empty}, t_s/ t_e is the start/end transition of the Activity-Net, empty is a transition representing an bypass of the activity.
(3) TA is a transition (for basic activity) or a sub-net (for structured activity) representing the execution of the activity.
(4) F = {(t_s, p_s), (p_s, empty), (p_s, TA), (empty, p_e), (TA, p_e), (p_e, t_e)}.

Fig. 1 shows an Activity-Net of an activity (basic activity or structured activity), the activity has one <source> element "Link_c" and two <target> elements, "Link_a" and "Link_b". When one of the transition conditions ("Link_a" or "Link_b") is true, the TA transition will be executed. Otherwise, the empty transition will be executed which means the execution of TA is skipped.

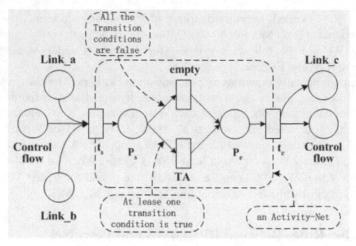

Fig. 1. An Activity-Net

If an activity has no target element which means the "empty" transition will never be executed, the corresponding Activity-Net can be rendered in a simpler style, i.e., simply a transition.

An Activity-Net = {P, T, F} represents an activity with no source elements, where:

(1) P = ∅.

(2) T = {TA}, TA is a transition representing the execution of the activity.

(3) F = ∅.

All the BPEL4WS basic activities are mapped into Activity-Nets where the TAs of the Activity-Nets is simply a transition. And all the BPEL4WS structured activities are mapped into Activity-Nets where the TAs of the Activity-Nets is a sub-net. For each structured activity, the TA (sub-net) has different structure. The following of this section will describe the sub-nets of all the BPEL4WS structured activities.

3.2 Sequence

A sequence activity contains one or more activities that are executed sequentially, in the order in which they are listed within the <sequence> element, that is, in lexical order. The sequence activity completes when the final activity in the sequence has completed.

We map the sequence element to Sequence-Net which will be the TA of its Activity-Net. The activities contained in the sequence structure will be treated as a sub-net (or transition) of Sequence-Net.

Definition 2. Sequence-Net

A Sequence-Net is an Activity-Net, i.e., a 5-tuple Sequence-Net = {t_s, t_e, T, P, F}, where:

(1) t_s is the start transition of the Sequence-Net.

(2) t_e is the end transition of the Sequence-Net.

(3) T = {T_i }, i = 1, 2,...,n, is a finite set of sub-net representing the children activities of the sequence structure;

(4) P = {P_i}, i = 1, 2,...,n, n+1, is a finite set of Place.

(5) F = (t_s, P_1) ∪{ (P_i, T_i) }∪ (T_n, P_{n+1})∪ ∪·(P_{n+1}, t_e), i = 1, 2,...,n, is a set of directed arcs.

Fig. 2 shows a Sequence-Net representing a sequence structure contains two children activities.

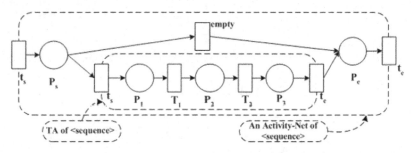

Fig. 2. A Sequence-Net

3.3 Flow

The flow construct provides concurrency and synchronization. A flow completes when all of the activities in the flow have completed. The link construct is used to express these synchronization dependencies, and every link declared within a flow activity MUST have exactly one activity within the flow as its source and exactly one activity within the flow as its target.

We map the flow element to Flow-Net which will be the TA of its Activity-Net. The activities contained in the flow structure will be treated as a sub-net (or transition) of Flow-Net.

Definition 3. Flow-Net

A Flow-Net is an Activity-Net, i.e., a 8-tuple Flow-Net = {t_s, t_e, T, LS, LT, LINKS, P, F}, where:

(1) t_s is the start transition of the Flow-Net.

(2) t_e is the end transition of the Flow-Net.

(3) T = {T_i }, i = 1, 2,...,n, is a finite set of sub-net representing the children activities of the flow structure;

(4) P = {PA_i, PB_i}, i = 1, 2,..., n, is a finite set of Place.

(5) LINKS = {L_j }, j = 1, 2,...,m, is a set of Place representing the Links of the flow.

(6) LS = {LS_j} ⊆ T, j = 1, 2,..., m, is a set of sub-net representing the activities which has the source link property. LS_j is a set of sub-net representing the jth Link's source activities.

(7) LT = {LT_j} ⊆ T, j = 1, 2,..., m, is a set of sub-net representing the activities which has the target link property. LT_j is a set of sub-net representing the jth Link's target activities.

(8) F = {(t_s, PA_i), (PA_i, T_i), (T_i, PB_i), (PB_i, t_e)} ∪(LS_j×Lj) ∪ (Lj×LT_j), i = 1, 2,...,n, j = 1, 2, .., m, is a set of directed arcs.

Fig. 3 shows a Flow-Net representing a flow structure contains three children activities. L_1 represents the Link element of the flow structure which is the source of T_1 and target of T_2.

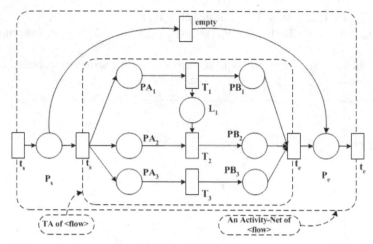

Fig. 3. A Flow-Net

3.4 Switch and Pick

The switch structured activity supports conditional behavior in a pattern that occurs quite often. The activity consists of an ordered list of one or more conditional branches defined by case elements, followed optionally by an otherwise branch.

The pick activity awaits the occurrence of one of a set of events and then executes the activity associated with the event that occurred. The occurrence of the events is often mutually exclusive.

We map both the switch and pick elements to Choice-Net which will be the TA of its Activity-Net. The activities contained in the switch or pick structure will be treated as a sub-net (or transition) of Choice-Net.

Definition 4. Choice-Net

A Choice-Net is an Activity-Net, i.e., a 5-tuple Choice-Net = $\{t_s, t_e, T, P, F\}$, where:
(1) t_s is the start transition of the Choice-Net.
(2) t_e is the end transition of the Choice-Net.
(3) $T = \{T_i\}$, i = 1, 2,…,n, is a finite set of sub-net representing the children activities of the switch or pick structure;
(4) P = {pa, pb}, is a finite set of Place.
(5) $F = (t_s, pa) \cup \{ (pa, T_i), (T_i, pb) \} \cup (pb, t_e)$, i = 1, 2,…,n, is a set of directed arcs.

Fig. 4 shows a Choice-Net representing a switch or pick structure contains three children activities.

3.5 While

The while activity supports repeated execution of a specified iterative activity. The iterative activity is executed until the given Boolean while condition no longer holds true.

We map the while element to While-Net which will be the TA of its Activity-Net. The activities contained in the while structure will be treated as a sub-net (or transition) of While-Net.

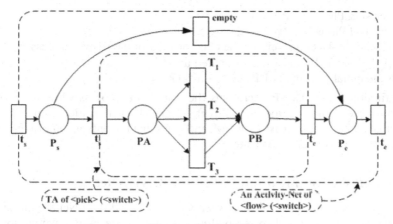

Fig. 4. A Choice-Net

Definition 5. While-Net

A While-Net is an Activity-Net, i.e., a 5-tuple While-Net = {t_s, t_e, T, P, F }, where:

(1) t_s is the start transition of the While-Net.

(2) t_e is the end transition of the While-Net.

(3) T is a sub-net representing the child activity of the While structure;

(4) P = {pw}, is a finite set of Place.

(5) F = {(t_s, pw), (pw, T), (T, pw), (pw, t_e)} is a set of directed arcs.

Fig. 5 shows a While-Net representing a while structure. The transition T represents the child activity of while structure.

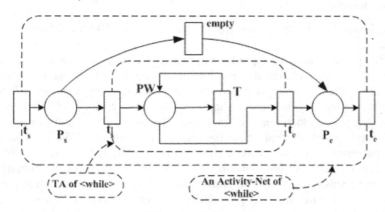

Fig. 5. A While-Net

3.6 Definition of BPWS-Net

As for the <process> element, there should be only one child activity included. So, we map the entire process to the BPWS-Net defined as follow:

Definition 6. BPWS-Net

A BPWS-Net is a Petri Net, i.e., a 5-tuple BPWS-Net = {P_i, P_o, T, F, M_0}, where:

(1) P_i is the start Place of BPWS-Net;
(2) P_o is the end Place of BPWS-Net;
(3) T is an Activity-Net representing the child activity of the BPWS process;
(4) $F = \{(P_i , T), (T, P_o)\}$ is a set of directed arcs.
(5) M_0 is the initial marking of BPWS-Net, $M_0 (P_i) = 1$.

In Definition 6, the place P_i represents the start of the process while the place P_o represents the end of the process. Sub-net T, may be a transition, represents the unique child activity the process owns. M_0 indicates that the only token of BPWS-Net belongs to P_i on the initialization state.

4   Web Service Composition Based on BPWS-Net

In section 3, a set of mapping rules between BPEL4WS and Petri Net are introduced. With these mapping rules and corresponding Activity-Net definition, we propose our BPWS-Net-based approach to Web Service composition. The approach could be divided into a two steps: First, we use the BPWS-Net to describe the process according to definition 6. Second, let all the structured Activity-Nets are refined recursively according to the definitions introduced in Section 3. After all Activity-Nets are refined, the process's Petri Net model is created.

In the rest of this section, we will present an example to illustrate how BPWS-Net-based approach to Web Service composition is used in practice. Though the example is rather simple, it is sufficient to illustrate the expressive power of our BPWS-Net-based approach.

4.1   Case Description

The loan approval example is taken from [1] in which the BPEL4WS document can be found.

The example considers a simple loan approval Web Service that provides a port where customers can send their requests for loans. Customers of the service send their loan requests, including personal information and amount being requested. Using this information, the loan service runs a simple process that results in either a "loan approved" message or a "loan rejected" message. The approval decision can be reached in two different ways, depending on the amount requested and the risk associated with the requester. For low amounts (less than $10,000) and low-risk individuals, approval is automatic. For high amounts or medium and high-risk individuals, each credit request needs to be studied in greater detail. Thus, to process each request, the loan service uses the functionality provided by two other services. In the streamlined processing available for low-amount loans, a "risk assessment" service is used to obtain a quick evaluation of the risk associated with the requesting individual. A full-fledged "loan approval" service (possibly requiring direct involvement of a loan expert) is used to obtain in-depth assessments of requests when the streamlined approval process does not apply.

4.2   The BPWS-Net of Loan Approval Process

According to definition 6, we illustrate the BPWS-Net in Fig. 6.

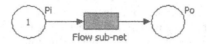

Fig. 6. The BPWS-Net of Loan Approval Process

4.3 Refinement of the Activity-Net

After the BPWS-Net was created, we now refine the "Flow sub-net" to get more detailed Petri Net model. According to Definition 3, we got the refined BPWS-Net shown in fig. 7. The diagram shown in fig. 7 was automatically created from the BPEL4WS document by the "SimPetri" Eclipse Plug-in – a Petri Net and BPEL4WS tool we developed.

In fig. 7, there are 5 Activity-Nets named "receive", "invoke assess", "assign", "invoke approval" and "reply" respectively. These 5 Activity-Nets represent the 5 activities that the flow structure contains. Moreover, there are 6 places named "receive-to-assess", "receive-to-approval", "approval-to-reply", "assess-to-setMessage", "setMessage-to-reply" and "assess-to-approval" respectively which represent the <Links> elements defined in the flow structure. The arcs from and to these places indicate the dependence of the 5 Activity-Nets.

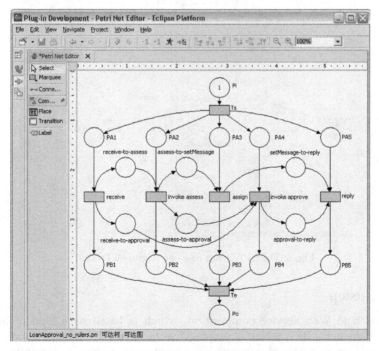

Fig. 7. The BPWS-Net of Loan Approval Process

5 System Analysis

A composite Web Service contains several Web Services. These services are often autonomous, heterogeneous, and independent units. Once integrated into one system, they will interact with each other for a desired task. Since interactions among services are loosely coupled, it's very important to verify the business logic of the composite service. By means of the feature of Petri net, analyzing the behavioral feature of the control flow modeled by BPWS-Net can be used to verify the business logic.

As for BPWS-Net, if the last reachable state is that place P_o owns one token and all the other places own none, we say the process works properly. With the help of reachability diagram of Petri net, the business logic of the composite service can be verified, and in the meanwhile, the soundness of the model can be checked.

Fig. 8 shows a reachability diagram of the BPWS-Net created above. This diagram was automatically created by "SimPetri" Eclipse plug-in. The reachability diagram shown in fig. 8 represents all the reachable states and execution steps of the BPWS-Net. Whether an activity is skipped or executed will be decided on the runtime according to the <Link> element's transition condition. Although the execution of an Activity-Net does not indicate this information in the diagram, we can deduce that the Loan Approval process is sound and works properly.

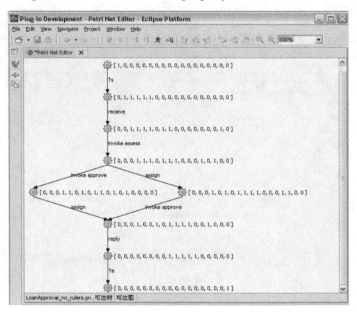

Fig. 8. The BPWS-Net of Loan Approval Process

6 Conclusion

An approach to Web Service composition, which is based on a kind of Service-Oriented Petri net – BPWS-Net, is proposed in the paper. This method can capture the not only the semantic of composition, but also the necessary semantic of Web Service. And because BPWS-Net is a graphical and formal modeling language, it's easy to verify correctness of the model. Furthermore, a business process described by BPEL4WS can be mapped into BPWS-Net directly, so Web Service composition based on this approach is valuable for engineering application. Future work is to deal with some issues about exception handling and services coordination.

References

1. Tony Andrews, Francisco Curbera, Hitesh Dholakia,etc., Specification: Business Process Execution Language for Web Services Version 1.1, 05 May 2003, http://www-106.ibm.com/developerworks/library/ws-bpel/
2. Roberto Chinnici, Martin Gudgin, Jean-Jacques Moreau, Sanjiva Weerawarana, Web Services Description Language (WSDL) Version 1.2 Part 1: Core Language, W3C Working Draft 11 June 2003,http://www.w3.org/TR/wsdl12/#Service
3. Martin Gudgin, Marc Hadley, Noah Mendelsohn, Jean-Jacques Moreau, Henrik Frystyk Nielsen,SOAP Version 1.2 Part 1: Messaging Framework, W3C Recommendation 24 June 2003, http://www.w3.org/TR/2003/REC-soap12-part1-20030624/
4. Hamadi, R. and Benatallah, B. (2003). A Petri Net-based Model for Web Service Composition. In Proc. Fourteenth Australasian Database Conference (ADC2003), Adelaide, Australia. Conferences in Research and Practice in Information Technology, 17. Schewe, K.-D. and Zhou, X., Eds., ACS. 191-200.
5. Rania Khalaf, Nirmal Mukhi and Sanjiva Weerawarana, Service-Oriented Composition in BPEL4WS, WWW2003,2003

Testing Web Services
Using Progressive Group Testing

Wei-Tek Tsai[1], Yinong Chen[1], Zhibin Cao[1], Xiaoying Bai[2],
Hai Huang[1], and Ray Paul[3]

[1] Department of Computer Science and Engineering, Arizona State University,
Tempe, AZ 85287-8809, USA
[2] Tsinghua University, Beijing, China
[3] Department of Defence, Washington DC, USA

Abstract. This paper proposes progressive group testing techniques to
test large number of Web services (WS) available on Internet. At the unit
testing level, the WS with the same functionality are tested in group using progressively increasing number of test cases. A small number of WS
that scored best will be integrated into the real environment for operational testing. At the integration testing level, many composite services
will be constructed and tested by group integration testing. The results of
group testing at both unit and integration levels are verified by weighted
majority voting mechanisms. The weights are based on the reliability
history of the WS under test. A case study is designed and implemented,
where the dependency among the test cases in WS is analyzed and used
to generate progressive layers of test cases.

Keywords: Web Services, Service-Oriented Architecture, Verification
and Validation, Web testing.

1   Introduction

Numerous approaches are possible to generate unit testing for Web services
(WS) [4], e.g., generate test scripts based on functional description, based on
process description (such as the process description proposed by DAML-S [11],
OWL-S Web Ontology Language or the ACDATE scenario model [8], based
on various coverage criteria (object methods, sequence, decision and condition
coverage), or based on sequence constraints such as MtSS and MgSS [1] The
issue for WS is that in most cases, only the service providers have the full access
to the WS white-box specification, while service brokers and service clients have
access to WS description only such as WSDL or OWL-S description. In [5], it
was suggested that WSDL should include some of these information so that test
cases/scripts can be automatically generated. The group testing scheme that we
proposed in [1] is powerful and efficient, yet its improvement over the individual
sequential testing is a linear function of the number available computers. It may
not cope with the possible exponential growth of WS available over the internet.
This paper presents a modified and more aggressive group testing scheme to
combat this problem.

C.-H. Chi and K.-Y. Lam (Eds.): AWCC 2004, LNCS 3309, pp. 314–322, 2004.
© Springer-Verlag Berlin Heidelberg 2004

In [2], Bloomberg suggested to develop WS testing technologies in three phases. In phase one, WS are mainly tested like the ordinary software. In phase two (2003-2005), the following features should be included in testing: WS, the publishing, finding, and binding capabilities, the asynchronous capabilities of WS, the SOAP intermediary capability, and the Quality of services. In phase three (2004 and beyond), dynamic runtime capabilities, WS orchestration testing and WS versioning should be tested.

WS-I (Web Services Interoperability Organization), an industry organization chartered to promote WS interoperability across platforms, released a WS testing tool in March 2004 [http://www.ws-i.org]. The tool consists of two components: WS-I monitor and WS-I analyzer. The WS-I monitor can be placed between the client and the WS. It logs all messages, requests and responses, as they go back and forth. The WS-I analyzer then goes through every message in the log and analyzes them against all the interoperability requirements.

In the past few years, we developed in the past few years techniques related to testing and verification of WS. In [6], a variety of test generation techniques are proposed to test WS in an enhanced UDDI-based service broker. These test scripts can be arranged hierarchically to test domains of related WS. An early form of WS check-in and check-out processes are also proposed to increase the confidence of WS used. In [1, 7, 9], rapid testing techniques were developed, including group testing, regression testing, and pattern-based verification. In [7], WS scenarios are developed in stages, the first stage the individual service scenarios are developed, in the second stage, interaction among WS are modeled, and finally the overall scenarios are developed combining previously developed scenarios. These scenarios are then translated into test scripts to be performed by organized distributed agents. In [5], an enhanced WSDL interface was developed to include dependency information, functional description, invoking, and concurrent sequence specifications so that test cases/scripts can be generated based on WSDL descriptions.

This paper proposes progressive group testing techniques to test possible large number of WS available on online, at both unit testing and integration testing levels. The sequence constraint concept is used to generate the progressive sets of test cases. The rest of the paper is organized as follows. Section 2 outlines the trustworthy computing model on WS. Section presents group testing for at unit test level and section 4 extend the testing scheme to integration test. Section 5 study the description of WS, the test case generation, and the test case partitioning based on their dependencies. Section 6 concludes the paper.

2   Progressive Group Unit Testing

WS-based computing has an open platform that allows service providers and requestors freely adding and accessing the available services. As a result, huge amount of check-in, check-out, and acceptance testing need to be performed. Progressive group unit testing and group integration testing are designed to address this problem. Group testing technique was originally developed for testing large samples of blood [3] and this paper uses it to test large number of WS submitted to the trustworthy service provider at runtime. It tests the "contamination" of an entire group of services by applying one test. The principles of this new testing scheme include:

- The platform is open and everyone can submit WS for consideration;
- Testing must be completed within available time frame, possibly to meet a real-time deadline;
- WS are evaluated and competed based on objective measures;
- Only the best WS will be accepted.

2.1 Prescreening

At the beginning, fast testing process is applied to immediately eliminate the unlikely-to-win candidates. The sophistication of testing increases progressively and the final winners will be tested rigorously. The system will pick up multiple winners with ranking. The reasons to accept multiple services with the same functionality are (1) Fault tolerance: When a service is unavailable, a backup spare can replace it; (2) Parallel processing: When the demand is high, multiple services will be used to process the same kinds of requests; (3) The ranks of services could be linked to the price. To implement this scheme, we organize our rigorous unit testing scripts into a hierarchy according to the dependency relationship among test cases. We define a dependency relationship R on a set of test cases T as a binary tuple (u, v) which means that test case u fails implies that test case v will fail. Examples for such dependency will be provided later for both unit testing and integration testing. Assume no cyclic dependency, the graph of R on T is a directed acyclic graph (dag) and a topological sorting will define the hierarchy (a leveled graph). The hierarchy may save tremendous cost on testing since when a WS fails a test case u, we know for sure that the WS will fail all test case v such that (u, v) R. Hence we will apply test cases on a WS in the order defined by the hierarchy. Multiple strategies are feasible to rule out a WS:

1. Based on the number of test cases a WS fails in one level of the hierarchy
2. Based on the criticality of test cases a WS fails in one level of the hierarchy
3. Based on the weight of test cases a WS fails in one level of the hierarchy.

For each strategy, there are different levels of tolerance. For example, in strategy 1, the strictest tolerance is that if a WS fails one test case, it will be dropped. The least strict tolerance is that the WS fails all test cases. We can also have a predefined threshold M so that we only drop a WS if it fails more than M test cases. The level of each strategy is depicted in the following table. One important factor that affects the tolerance is the competitiveness. If many service vendors provide a same WS, then the tolerance should be strict and vice versa.

We would like to remark that a WS fails M test cases in one level does not necessarily imply that it will fail more than or equal to M test cases in the next level. This is because test cases may have different number of descendants. For a

	Strictest	Moderate	Least Strict
# of test cases	1 test case fail	# of failures is greater than M	All fail
Criticality	1 critical test case fail	# of critical test case failures is greater than M	All critical fail
Weight	positive weight fail	# of weight failures is greater than M	Total weight fail

test case u, define its descendants as a set of test cases D(u) such that v D(u) if (u, v) R or there exists a test case w, such that (w, v) R. A good weight function for test cases could be the number (total weight) of test cases in its descendants. The number of test cases applied on a WS increases as it passes more levels in the hierarchy as shown in Figure 1. The rank of a WS is defined as the number (or weight) of test cases it fails so far. The rank serves as an additional criterion to rule out extra WS. The basic algorithm is as follows: The "not applying descendants test cases" in step 4 will further reduce the cost of the testing, in addition to the ruling out of WS at each level. In the prescreening process, voting mechanism can be used to determine if an atomic WS has performed the desired service.

1. Identify dependency among test cases
2. Do topological sorting on test cases and form the hierarchy
3. Starting from level 1 in the hierarchy, for each level
4. Apply all test cases in the current level on all survivors WS, except those in the descendants of some test case u that the WS fails before.
5. Rule out some WS
6. Rule out extra WS according to their ranks if too many WS survive
7. end

2.2   Runtime Group Testing

The best candidates identified in prescreening step will be integrated into the live system and further tested in runtime.

Figure 2 illustrates the part of the system in the trustworthy service broker that performs runtime group testing. Assume CSn is a composite service consisting of n services S1, S2, ..., Sn, where Si can be an atomic service or a composite service. While CSn is performing services, many atomic services could be registered. Assume services S11, S12, ..., S1m are functionally equivalent to the service S1 in SCn. We can forward (broadcast) the input to S1 to S11, S12, ..., S1m, as shown in Figure 2. The results from all services, including that from S1, are voted by a voting service. The voting is weighted based on the current reliabilities of the services under test. The voting service can set the initial weight of each incoming service to zero while the exiting service S1's weight to the reliability R(S1). The voting service detects faults by comparing the output of each service with the weighted majority output. A disagreement indicates a fault.

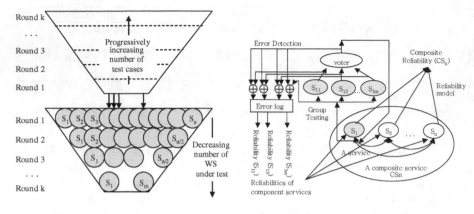

Fig. 1. Progressive group testing   **Fig. 2.** Group testing scheme

Based on the failure log generated by group testing, the reliabilities individual services under test can be evaluated [10].

The novelty and features of the group integration testing include:

- One of the tough problems in software testing is to construct an oracle that can determine if a failure has occurred. In this group integration testing scheme, the voting service serves as the oracle according to the majority principle.
- Another advantage is that testing is done while performing the normal operations. In other words, the WS under test are actually integrated into the real operational environment without a separate testing phase at no extra time, provided that sufficient computing power is available. A remote test agent can take spare computers on the Internet to perform distributed testing was proposed to address this problem [1].

Both prescreening and runtime testing applied the group testing principle. The major difference is the test cases applied. The former applied the progressive test cases designed for testing while the latter apply the runtime environment to drive the unit under test.

There is a possibility that the majority voting may fail to choose the best service, if a malicious service provider submit thousand of the WS to gain the majority. This potential problem is addressed as follows:

- All service provider must register and be certified. The submission of a WS must append the digital signature of the service provider.
- The voting is weighted. The WS that have a known oracle or a track record of producing reliable output will be given higher weights. The newly submitted WS will be assigned an initial weight of zero, which mean it's output will not be used to form the majority output. When the output of a WS agrees with the majority, its weight is increased.
- The reliability of each service is stored in a database together with the profile of the service.

– For some test inputs, it is relatively easy to obtain the expected outputs. During the prescreening or group testing (in either group unit testing or group integration testing), run those test cases first. This will identify some of the malicious code.

If a component WS, e.g., S1, has not gone through unit testing, the unit testing voter can check their outputs to make sure they are correct. The outputs of the composite services are sent to the integration testing voter for error detection.

3   A Case Study

This section defines two banking systems to illustrate the service compositions and test case generation for progressive unit and integration testing, respectively.

3.1   Atomic Service and Unit Testing

Before a WS and a composite WS are integrated in the actually system, we need to generate test cases to drive testing and we need to divide the test cases into layers for progressive testing. We first define a simplified bank system that offers a single service and use this service as an example for unit test. The functions of the service are listed Table 1. As unit test, we designed 35 test cases, named TC1, TC2, ..., TC35, to test the functions in Table 1.

Table 1. The functions of a banking service

Service Name	Function Description
Login	Provide authentication function for the ATM system. Many other operations are based on user's correct login.
Check Balance	Check the balance and return the result to the client.
Update Account	Update the account information in the database
Check Account	Check if the account ID or other information exits in the database
Delete Account	Delete the account and process other necessary functions, such as withdraw all remaining money.
Create Account	Create a new account
Withdraw Money	Withdraw money from the account. Require login correctly
Deposit Money	Deposit the money into account. Request to login correctly
Get Account Information	Get all information for an account, such as the balance and interest

In order to perform progressive testing, we need to divide the test cases into progressive layers. We divide the tests cases based on the dependencies among the functions. For example, WithdrawMoney function in Table 1 depends on the success of Login function. Based on the dependencies among the functions, we can obtain the dependencies among the test cases as follows: A test case

TCj depends on TCi, if the failure of the test applying TCi will lead to the failure of the test applying TCj. The dependencies among the functions must be assigned manually while the dependencies among the test cases can be computed automatically based on the functions dependencies.

Figure 3 shows the automatically generated dependency diagram among the 35 test cases. Once we obtained the dependency diagram, we can automatically obtain the progressive layer of each test case. Table 2 divides the 35 test cases into four layers for progressive testing, i.e., layers 1, 2, 3, and 4 will be tested in four different rounds.

Table 2. Layers of test cases for unit test

Layer	Test Case Number
1	TC1, TC2, TC3, TC4, TC5, TC6, TC7, TC8, TC9
2	TC10, TC11, TC14, TC15, TC16, TC17 TC18, TC19, TC20, TC21, TC22
3	TC12, TC13, TC32, TC33, TC34, TC35
4	TC23, TC24, TC25, TC26, TC27, TC28, TC29, TC30

Table 3. Layers of test cases for integration test

Layer	Test Case Number
1	TC1, TC4, TC11
2	TC2, TC8, TC10
3	TC6, TC9, TC7, TC3
4	TC5, TC12, TC13

For testing the integrated service, we use MfSS specification [?] to describe the test cases. Each test case use at least two services' functions. These functions are the integrations of different service.

In this example, there is some functional dependence which must be specified manually. And the ranking of all other test cases will be effected. For example: GetAccountInformation gets the information related to an account, including the current balance information which is also provided by the function CheckBalance. The function CreateAccount depends on the function CheckAccountID, since if CheckAccountID failed, system can not process CreateAccount. From the MfSS specification of TC1 and TC2, we can see that the only difference between TC1 and TC2 is that TC1 uses CheckAccountID and TC2 uses the

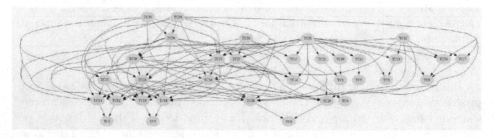

Fig. 3. Dependencies among test cases

CreateAccount. Thus in our ranking algorithm, TC1 belongs to the first layer, and TC2 is the second layer. According the dependency relationship, we can define the layers of test cases for progressive testing. Table 3 divides the 13 test cases into four layers.

3.2 Composite Service and Integration Testing

Then we define more complex system with three services that offer different sub-functions. Tables 4 and 5 show the two composite services examples, respectively. The following two composite services are used to form another larger composite service: the banking service. They are used to design the integration test cases in this case study.

Table 4. WS1: ATM Service

Service Name	Code	Service Description
Check Balance	m11	Check the balance for the user and return the number to the client.
Withdraw Money	m12	Withdraw the money from the account. Request to login correctly
Deposit Money	m13	Deposit the money into account. Request to login correctly
Get Account Information	m14	Get all information for an account, such as the balance and interest

Table 5. WS2: Authentication Service

Service Name	Code	Service Description
Login	m21	Provide the authentication function for the ATM system. Many other operations need user to login correctly at the first.
Update Account	m22	Update the account information in the database.
Check Account	m23	Check if the account ID or other information is not already used in the database.
Delete Account	m24	Delete the account and process other necessary functions, such as withdraw all left money.
Create Account	m25	Create a new account.

4   Conclusion

We proposed progressive group testing techniques for unit and integration testing of WS. The techniques are designed to test large number of WS available on the Internet rigorously and at runtime. The major contributions of the paper are threefold: Progressive test case generation, group testing with majority voting, and weighting the reliability history of WS. The definition and the efficient selection algorithm of progressive test cases ensure that WS are tested by applying an optimal sequence of test cases. Group testing ensure that WS are test in parallel and their results are verified by weighted majority voting. The WS that have proven history of reliable behavior will have a higher weight while the new WS will start their initial weight from zero, which means they have no influence to the majority output at the beginning. The weights of WS increase dynamically when their outputs agree with the majority outputs.

References

1. X. Bai, W. T. Tsai, T. Shen, B. Li, and R. Paul, "Distributed End-to-End Testing Management", EDOC 2001: 140-151
2. J. Bloomberg, "Web Services Testing: Beyond SOAP", ZapThink LLC, Sep 2002, http://www.zapthink.com
3. D. Z. Du and F. Hwang, "Combinatorial Group Testing And Its Applications", World Scientific, 2nd edition, 2000
4. A. D. Gordon and R. Pucella, "Validating a Web Service Security Abstraction by Typing", Microsoft MSR-TR-2002-108, December 2002
5. W. T. Tsai, R. Paul, Y. Wang, C. Fan, and D. Wang, "Extending WSDL to Facilitate Web Services Testing", Proc. of IEEE HASE, 2002, pp. 171-172
6. W. T. Tsai, R. Paul, Z. Cao, L. Yu, A. Saimi, and B. Xiao, "Verification of Web Services Using an Enhanced UDDI Server", Proc. of IEEE WORDS, 2003, pp. 131-138
7. W. T. Tsai, Lian Yu, Feng Zhu, and R. Paul, "Rapid Verification of Embedded Systems Using Patterns", Proc. of IEEE COMPSAC 2003, pp. 466-471
8. W. T. Tsai, R. Paul, L. Yu, A. Saimi, and Z. Cao, "Scenario-Based Web Service Testing with Distributed Agents", IEICE Transactions on Information and Systems, 2003, Vol. E86-D, No. 10, 2003, pp. 2130-2144
9. W.T. Tsai, N. Liao, H. Huang, and R. Paul, "Application of Group Testing in Verification of Dynamic Composite Web Services", in Workshop on Quality Assurance and Testing of Web-Based Applications, in conjunction with COMPSAC, September 2004, pp. 28-30
10. W. T. Tsai, D. Zhang, Y. Chen, H. Huang, Ray Paul, and N. Liao, "A Software Reliability Model for Web Services", submitted to the 8th IASTED International Conference on software engineering and applications, Cambridge, MA, November, 2004
11. D. Wu, et al., Automating DAML-S Web Services Composition Using SHOP2, http://www.mindswap.org/papers/ISWC03-SHOP2.pdf

XFCM – XML Based on Fuzzy Clustering and Merging – Method for Personalized User Profile Based on Recommendation System of Category and Product

JinHong Kim and EunSeok Lee

School of Information and Communication Engineering, SungKyunKwan University
300 Chunchun Jangahn Suwon, 440-746, Korea
{ziromirado,eslee}@ece.skku.ac.kr

Abstract. In data mining, to access a large amount of data sets for the purpose of predictive data does not guarantee a good method. Even, the size of Real data is unlimited in Mobile commerce. Hereupon, in addition to searching expected Products for Users, it becomes necessary to develop a recommendation service based on XML Technology. In this paper, we design the optimized XML Recommended products data. Efficient XML data preprocessing is required in include of formatting, structural, attribute of representation with dependent on User Profile Information. Our goal is to find a relationship among user interested products and E-Commerce from M-Commerce to XDB. First, analyzing user profiles information. In the result creating clusters with user profile analyzed such as with set of sex, age, job. Second, it is clustering XML data, which are associative objects, classified from user profile in shopping mall. Third, after composing categories and Products in which associative Products exist from the first clustering, it represent categories and Products in shopping mall and optimized clustering XML data which are personalized products. The proposed personalizing user profile clustering method is designed and simulated to demonstrate the efficiency of the system.

1 Introduction

Now days, concerning a large amount of various data available on the Internet and E-Commerce, there are existing websites and shopping mall, which provide recommended service for users to search interest data. For text and image data in web pages, the websites providing user log files, URL-based navigation, keyword-based searching and e-mail service or recommendation are developed, such as the recommendation system of Amazon, content-based filtering system of Web Watcher, personalization recommendation system ACRNews and search engine of Yahoo! (Yahoo shopping mall)[4][5]. In Recommendations system, however, the shopping malls providing such kinds of services are still limited. To solve the problem, i) Develop on structural shopping mall, that is, most of them are on the XML built for E-Commerce and M-Commerce. ii) Creating a XFCM Algorithm based on optimized recommendation data. iii) Having User Profile Information create cluster group, create user profile data based on created cluster group K-means Algorithm by Apriori. Clustering group compose re-group with XFC (XML based on Fuzzy Clustering) algorithm method in filtering. As Re-grouped structural XML data of cluster, recommend products data for users. In this paper, we propose about clustering method to be personalized to cate-

C.-H. Chi and K.-Y. Lam (Eds.): AWCC 2004, LNCS 3309, pp. 323–330, 2004.

gory and product data based on structural pattern.[13] The paper is organized as follows: Section 2 described clustering algorithm. Section 3 described cluster creation and composition based on FCM algorithm as proposal system. Section 4 presented the results on implementation and simulation using the XFCM applied user profile of patterns. Section 5 we proposed conclusion.

2 Related Work

Until present, most recommended systems that operate in web-based divide by three classifications; Manual Decision Rule System, Collaborative Filtering System, and Content-based Filtering Agent System are come hereupon. Manual Decision Rule System describe rule base that web site operator are collecting static profile, user session history through user's registration instruction. Representative example of this system is Broad vision. Broad vision provides an array of business solutions that is Content Management Solutions, Personalization Solutions, Commerce Solutions, and Enterprise Portal Solutions and so on, to meet your greatest challenges, from the power of personalization to robust content management to leading edge applications and enterprise portals [1],[3],[7],[14]. In this way, Rules are influence in contents that offered to particular users. Collaborative Filtering System provide predicted information's that suitable with user's preference degree through correlation engine based on clarified information that equipped user's estimation or type of preference degree. Representative example is Net Perceptions[12],[13]. Content-based Filtering such as Web Watchers puts weight from user by express or in content similarity of web document about getting individual Profile allusively[6],[11]. Shown as Fig 1.

Fig. 1. Broad Vision: One – to – One Package and Net Perception: Group Lens Recommendation System

2.1 ISODATA and Fuzzy Clustering Algorithm

This algorithm based on the k-means algorithm, and employs processes of eliminating, splitting, and clustering. The algorithm described as following.

1. Start with K_{init} (initial number of clusters) which is user-given. Assign the first K_{init} samples as cluster centers.
2. Assign all samples to the clusters by minimum distance principle.
3. Eliminate clusters that contain less than n_{min} feature vectors and reassign those vectors to other clusters to yield K clusters.
4. Compute a new cluster center as the average of all feature vectors in each cluster.
5. For each kth cluster, compute the mean-squared error $\sigma_n^2(k)$ of each nth component x_n over that cluster and find the maximum $\sigma_{n*}^2(k)$ component mean-squared error over within cluster k for over n = 1, ..., N, where the index n* is for the maximum component.

6. If there are not enough clusters ($K_{init} < K/2$) and this is not the last iteration, then if $\sigma_{max}(k) > \sigma_{split}$ for any cluster k, split that cluster into two.

7. If this is an even iteration and $K_{init} > 2K$, then compute all distances between cluster and centers. Merge the clusters that are close than a given value.

The advantages of the ISODATA are its self-organizing capability, its flexibility in eliminating clusters that are too small, its ability to divide clusters that are too dissimilar, and its ability to merge sufficiently similar clusters[8]. However, there is some disadvantages such as, i) multiple parameters must be given by user even they are not known as priori. ii) a considerable amount of experimentation may required to get a reasonable values. iii) the clusters are ball shaped determined by the distance function, iv) the value determined for K depends on the parameters given by the user and is not necessarily the best value, and v) a cluster average is often not the best prototype for a cluster[9]. Fuzzy clustering plays an important role in solving problems in the areas of pattern recognition and fuzzy model identification. A variety of fuzzy clustering methods was proposed, and most of them were base upon distance criteria. One widely used algorithm is the fuzzy c-means (FCM) algorithm[2][10]. It uses reciprocal distance to compute fuzzy weights. A more efficient algorithm is the new XFCM. It computes the cluster center using Gaussian weights, uses large initial prototypes, and adds processes of eliminating, clustering and merging after filtering in user clusters. In the following section, we propose and simulation XML based on Fuzzy Clustering and Merging Method (XFCM).

3   Proposed System

3.1   System Architecture

The proposed system intended to support all the purchasing activities, range from product search to payment, for E-Commerce and M-Commerce on the World Wide Web. In this paper, we propose Clustering Module based on User Profile. *Clustering Module:* Clusters group based on the similarity of personal data of users. XFCM (XML based on fuzzy Clustering and Merging) algorithm is used for clustering users by FCM algorithm. The XFCM algorithm has efficient recommender product with structural cluster grouping that can solve the multiple parameters must be given by the user. Although they are unknown K-means, a considerable amount of experimentation may be required to get reasonable values. The clusters are ball shaped as determined by the distance function, the value determined for K depends on the parameters given by the user and is not necessarily the best value, and a cluster average often not the best prototype for a cluster. Therefore, it can organize by itself, and control the intensity of classification through the vigilance parameter.

3.2   XFCM Algorithm Applied FCM

XFCM Clustering is new cluster merging or eliminating from small cluster filtering part and cluster's central distance and similarity. This algorithm measures user propensity from user profile information, action, etc., and provide personalized recommends product rely on this measurement. Small cluster filtering part measure that rating of entire data and clustered data, similarity of other cluster. Measured small cluster except from merging step (Phase3-step2), improve efficiency of merging step.

Merging Part based on the i) most closer central distance (similarity of cluster), ii) after selected 1 part, iii) performed using clustering validity between clusters. This clustering solved the Xie-Beni Validity. The Xie-Beni Validity result on compactness and separatio measurement by prototype. XFCM Algorithm use user's cluster group structural method by XML. XML is Data Independence, Improved domain knowledge, Improved data searches, Extension data. This algorithm relies on XML Pattern Matching to analyze structured user profile pattern. The concept of this algorithm is as follow: i) match the root element information (match= "Age, Sex, Job") that is selected via match = "/, *, |, @" pattern of four cases attribute to xsl : template by user profile. ii) The select= attribute of the xsl : value - of element works almost identically.

3.3 Proposal Module

Database Module: This Module composes Product Data, Action Data, Product and Action Data, Recommendation Data (New product, Event product, and so on). Database keeps information on product that gathered by the Shopping Mall Data (Product Data, Action Data) including user's personal information, transaction information, basket placement (the placement of the product in the shopping basket).

Clustering Module: This module is base on the similarity of User Profile Information. User profile compose Age, Sex, Job that is three terms resolve root, element of each node and each data inside database with user profile create clusters. Created clusters merge and filter, Result of optimized clusters reflected Mining Sequential XML Patterns Model. K- means algorithm is used for clustering users by Apriori. The K-means algorithm has the Characteristics that Classification, precedence work for estimate are use in various analysis such as loss value processing work as many as error value in addition to throng analysis. It uses data about purchase information of customers who are in the same cluster.

Mining Sequential XML Based on Structural Pattern Module: This Module selects the recommendation products by using XFCM algorithm based on FCM. It uses data about purchase information of users who are in the optimized cluster. This data is clustered by Clustering Module. This Module has three data types. i) Product data composed category products in shopping mall, ii) Action data composed purchase action, shopping basket, click stream, and so on., Product and Action data composed common and similar products data. On the basis of above three types of data, this algorithm relies on Structural method based on association rule to analyze the sequential user action patterns.

4   Evaluation

The implementation environment is as follows: we employed IIS Web Server based on Windows 2000 and MS SQL 2000 for server side, XML, Weka Tool as simulator for client side.

4.1 System Implementation

We simulated using three algorithms based on cluster module. With K-means algorithm, utilized each to product data, action data, product and action data using user set = {Sex, Age, Job}. We result that experiment with K-means by Apriori Algorithm, Product data Clustering (PC), Action data Clustering (AC), Product and Action data Clustering (PAC) and all the experiment done by using WEKA Tool base on K-means by Apriori algorithm. The result is shows as following on Figure 2.

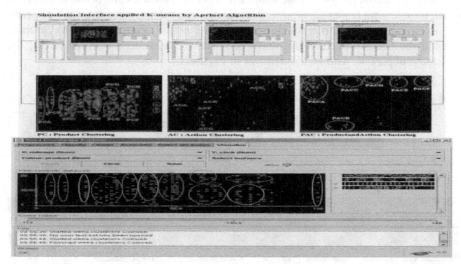

Fig. 2. Simulation Interface applied K-means by Apriori Algorithm and Result on entire simulation with Weka Tool

Based on K-means by Apriori algorithm and WEKA Tool, We create clustering groups. This clustering groups recommended product data user's personalization each of clustering groups can be express to set and type of set is as followed.

Product Data
Ps = {Age}, {Job} : Clustering 1
Result : {PCA}, {PCB}, {PCC}, {PCD}, {PCG}, {PCH}, {PSC}

Action Data
As = {Age}, {Job} : Clustering 1
Result : {ACA}, {ACB}, {ACC}, {ACD}, {ACE}, {ACF}, {ACG}

Product and Action Data
PAs = {Age}, {Job} : Clustering 1
Result : {PACA}, {PACB}, {PACD}, {PACE}, {PACF}

Structural Category: Create structural Shopping Mall (large-scale portal sites) of data that is Product Data, Action Data, Product and Action Data for E-Commerce and M-Commerce formatted and Category of each data. Then it present category information on products of structural shop, such as Great Classification, Bisection Kind, Subdivision Kind that include IDs(GC, BK, SK), Product Names. There were some patterns and differences as result that experiment structured category with XML. Firstly, if examine about some patterns, <product-category>, <action-category>, <productandaction-category> with relationship high position root name and <product-data>, <action-data>, <productandaction-data> with relationship sub element name could be seen in two patterns : i) <template match="category"> that is matches the first category name, ii) <template match="data"> that is matches the first data name. In addition, each classification is a same structure according to category depth and appeared sequentially. Secondly, if examine about differences, product categories, action categories, product and action categories. We can see that category depth for the end page that user monitoring is different. We examined the first cluster result. We propose examine the second (Refiltering) and third cluster (Optimized XFCM). Also, We Implement of XFCM with FCM as shown in Figure 3.

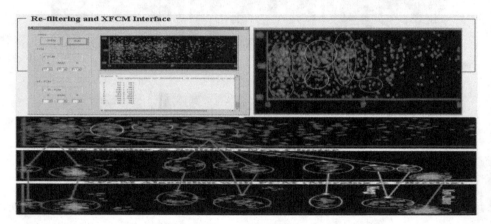

Fig. 3. Re-Filtering and XFCM Interface

XML Transformations User Profile {Age, Sex, Job} and Data {Ps, As, PAs} show the detailed information of products and present structural. Finally, The Categories of product reorganized through the standard category by XFCM.

4.2 System Evaluation

We create structural user profile, personalization and recommendation data, structured shopping mall as result at recommend algorithm based on user inclination. We create structural user profile, personalization and recommendation data, structured shopping mall as result at recommend algorithm based on user inclination. We applied on three categories (Product Data, Action Data, Product and Action Data) with Chair Data of Sex based on three algorithms (K-means, FCM, XFCM). The combination of three algorithms and clusters is composing by using nine cells with number of Man, Woman, Neutral cluster. I proposed that i) apply on each of nine cells that selected Chair data, standard category number, Products include of GC, BK, SK. ii) result in product data cluster with K-means algorithm by Apriori is same initial declaration. iii)

The result in data cluster with XFCM algorithm by FCM is well-done personalized recommend product.

5 Conclusion

Recommendation Algorithm provides an effective XML form of targeted E-Commerce and M-Commerce by creating personalized products and categories. In this paper presents an approach for structural data analysis step with the user profile structure patterns discovery in data. In this paper, we proposed a recommended system with personalized user profile for E-Commerce and M-Commerce. Advantage of this paper is as following. First, with structural User Profile, Recommend products data efficiently. Second, it is easy to apply on M-commerce with XML format. Third, create structured shopping mall directory. Fourth, efficient products and category recommend creating cluster group, which is structural and optimized that XML based. Final, even if user inclination changes, Cluster group regeneration is possible and apply easily to M-Commerce. We have actually simulated the recommendation algorithm and evaluated effectiveness partially in practice. In further study, More efficient E-Commerce and M-Commerce is expected to be possible by that apply for Agent System in real world.

References

1. http://www.Broadvision.com/OneToOne/SessionMgr/home_page.
2. J.C.Bezdk: Pattern Recognition with Fuzzy Objective Function Algorithms, Plenun Press, N.Y., 1981.
3. Resnick, P., et al. Group Lens: An Open Architecture for Collaborative Filtering of Net-news. In Proceedings of ACM CSCW'94 Conference on Computer-Supported Cooperative Work, pages 175-186. 1994.
4. Paul Resnick and Hal R. Varian, Guest Editor: Recommender Systems, Communication of the ACM, Vol. 40, No. 3, March 1997.
5. Hirsh, H., Basu, C., and Davison, B. D.: (2000) Learning to Personalize. Communications of the ACM, 43, 8, 102-106.
6. Jermann, P., Soller, A., and Muehlenbrock, M.:(2001) From Mirroring to Guiding: A Review of State of the Art Technology for Supporting Collaborative Learning. Proceedings of the Computer Support for Collaborative Learning(CSCL) 2000, 324-331.
7. Basu, C., H. Haym, and W. W. Cohen: Recommendation as classification: Using social and content-based information in recommendation, Proceedings of International Conference on User Modeling, June 1999.
8. G. H. Ball and D. J. Hall: ISODATA: an interactive method of multivariable analysis and pattern classification, Proc. IEEE Int. Communications Conf., 1996.
9. M.J.Sabin: Convergence and Consistency of Fuzzy c-means / ISODATA Algorithms, IEEE Trans. Pattern Anal. Machine Intell., September 1987.
10. Liyan Zhang: Camparison of Fuzzy c-means Algorithm and New Fuzzy Clustering and Fuzzy Merging Algorithm, May 2001 Univ. Nevada, Reno.
11. Mikael Sollenborn and Peter Funk: Category-Based Filtering in Recommender Systems for Improved Performance in Dynamic Domains. P. De Bra, P. Brusilovsky, and R. Conejo (Eds.): AH 2002, LNCS 2347, pp 436–439. Springer-Verlag Berlin Heidelberg 2002

12. Konstan, J.A., Miller, B.N., Maltz, D., Herlocker, J.L., et. al.: GroupLens: Applying collaborative filtering to usenet news. Communications of the ACM 40 (1997) 3:77-87
13. Funakoshi, K., Ohguro, T.: A content-based collaborative recommender system with detailed use of evaluations. In Proceedings of 4th International Conference on Knowledge-Based Intelligent Engineering Systems and Allied Technologies, Volume 1 (2000) 253-256
14. Hayes, C., Cunningham, P., Smyth, B.: A Case-Based Reasoning View of Automated Collaborative Filtering. In Proceedings of 4th International Conference on Case-Based Reasoning, ICCBR2001 (2001) 243-248

Analyzing Web Interfaces of Databases for Retrieving Web Information

Jeong-Oog Lee[1], Myeong-Cheol Ko[1], Jinsoo Kim[1],
Chang-Joo Moon[2], Young-Gab Kim[3], and Hoh Peter In[3]

[1] Dept. of Computer Science, Konkuk University,
322 Danwol-dong, Chungju-si, Chungcheongbuk-do, 380-701, Korea
{ljo,cheol,jinsoo}@kku.ac.kr
[2] Center for Information Security Technologies(CIST), Korea University,
1, 5-ka, Anam-dong, Sungbuk-gu, Seoul, 136-701, Korea
mcjmhj@korea.ac.kr
[3] Dept. of Computer Science & Engineering, Korea University,
1, 5-ka, Anam-dong, Sungbuk-gu, Seoul, 136-701, Korea
ygkim@software.korea.ac.kr, hoh_in@korea.ac.kr

Abstract. Much of the information on the web is indeed dynamic content provided through linkups with databases. However, due to heterogeneity of databases, it is difficult to provide an integrated information retrieval. Meanwhile, information on web databases can be easily provided to users through web interfaces. In analyzing web interfaces, therefore, an information integration system can integrate web databases without concerning the database structures. This paper presents a solution to semantic heterogeneity through the analysis of web interfaces and the building of semantic networks.

1 Introduction

The sharp increase in the number of the world's internet users is driving the tremendous growth of the content production industry. With contents on the web increasing, information search services are booming. It should also be noted that majority of the information on the web is indeed dynamic content provided through linkups with databases. Today, search engines such as Google, Yahoo and Altavista are providing web search services through the logical classification system, the large volume indexing technique, and the web agent technique. Since these search engines search only static contents, they cannot access all information on the web, including dynamic contents.

Many web documents, multimedia, and databases have been built or are being built to provide quality information services. Their search functions are still insufficient, however, due to their heterogeneity. It makes it difficult to enjoy a total integrated search. Therefore, we need an integrated information retrieval system that can effectively combine and access a vast resource of dynamic web contents linked with databases. Meanwhile, information on web databases can be easily provided to users through web interfaces. In analyzing web interfaces,

C.-H. Chi and K.-Y. Lam (Eds.): AWCC 2004, LNCS 3309, pp. 331–336, 2004.

therefore, an information integration system can integrate web databases without concerning the database structures. This paper presents a solution to semantic heterogeneity through the analysis of web interfaces and the building of semantic networks.

The rest of this paper is organized as follows. Section 2 describes the importance of web interface analysis for web information integration, and the building of a global semantic network to solve the semantic heterogeneity issue. Section 3 introduces the semantic query language and illustrates the process of handling semantic queries, with examples. Finally, in section 4, we offer our conclusions.

2   Analyzing Web Interfaces for Database Integration

2.1   Databases and Web Interfaces

Generally, a web site that provides information via databases is implemented in two phases. First, a database for information on the web site is designed. Then the web interface (or the template) for retrieving information from the database is constructed. A user's query can be delivered to the query processor of the database through the web interface. Fig. 1 shows a web interface for a plant-related database, the CalFlora database. In analyzing web interfaces, an information integration system can integrate web databases without concerning the database structures. The basic idea is to create virtual database tables for the databases using the fields in the web interfaces, which provides an easy mechanism for integration regardless of the database models, DBMSs, and so forth. For example, *CalFlora(name, county, lifeform, community, ...)* can be a virtual database schema for the CalFlora database. The integration system for web databases can integrate web databases easily using these virtual database tables, without needing to know all the actual database schema information.

2.2   Semantic Networks Using WordNet

An ontology is an explicit specification of a conceptualization[1]. Ontologies can be applied for inter-operability among systems, communication between human beings and systems, increasing system reusability, and so forth. There are several endeavors within the industrial and academic communities that address the problem of implementing ontologies, such as TOP, WordNet, Ontolingua, Cyc, Frame Ontology, PANGLOSS, MikroKosmos, SENSUS, EngMath, PhysSys, TOVE, and CHEMICALS[2][3]. WordNet, one of those efforts, is a digital vocabulary system[4].

To explore and solve the semantic heterogeneity issue between component databases, this paper proposes the building of semantic networks, which present the relationship between the concept that information has and the schema using WordNet. Fig. 2 shows part of the semantic network for the CalFlora database in Fig. 1. In WordNet, each synset is granted a unique concept number. In the *Concept* field in Fig. 3, the entity concept and the attribute concept are combined and

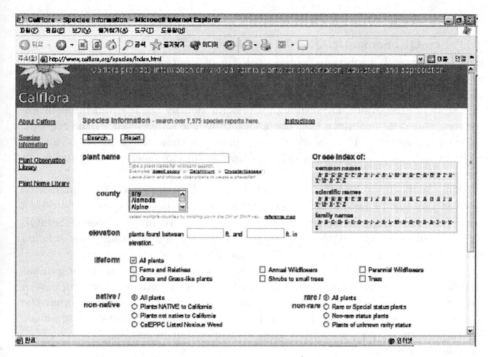

Fig. 1. A plant-related database, the CalFlora database

expressed in $< EntityConcept.AttributeConcept >$. In the *WNConcept* field, the concept numbers are combined into $< EntityConceptNumber.Attribute ConceptNumber >$. The *Entity* field expresses the database object corresponding to the entity concept, while the *Attribute* filed expresses the database object corresponding to the attribute concept.

ConceptID	Concept	WNConcept	Entity	Attribute
1	flora.name	00008864.04778525	CalFlora	where-name soup
2	flora.community	00008864.06104982	CalFlora	where-pretty_plantcomm

Fig. 2. Part of the semantic network for the CalFlora database

The global semantic network is built by combining the semantic networks for individual component databases. The global semantic network provides the *access knowledge* necessary to identify component databases that have information on the query and the *semantic knowledge* needed to determine what objects, attributes, attribute values of each component database meet the connoted meaning of the query.

3   Semantic Query Processing

3.1   SemQL: Semantic Query Language

One of the possible solutions to the problem of locating and integrating information is to allow users to access all relevant information sources themselves.
Sometimes, however, users are even ignorant of whether the relevant information sources exist or not. Even though users can identify the relevant information
sources, this does not mean that the users know the schemas of all the relevant
information sources. This solution forces users to know the schemas of all the
relevant information sources, which will impose an extremely heavy burden on
them.

One of the more effective approaches is to allow users to issue queries to
a large number of autonomous and heterogeneous databases with their own
concepts. This frees users from learning schemas. We have proposed SemQL
as a semantic query language for users for issuing queries using not schema
information but concepts that the users know[5].

The SemQL clauses specify not the entity or attribute names in component
database schemas but concepts about what users want. For example, suppose a
user wants to find those plants that live in wetland habitats. Assuming that the
user is familiar with SQL but knows neither of the component database schemas,
he might issue a query in SemQL using concepts that he knows:
SELECT plant.name
WHERE plant.habitat = "wetland"

Another user might issue a query as follows based on his concepts:
SELECT flora.name
WHERE flora.habitat = "wetland"

Although in the above two queries, *"plant"* and *"flora"* are different in terms
of their point of word forms, the two queries are semantically equivalent.

3.2   Procedure of Semantic Query Processing

The following example describes the process of handling the semantic queries.
Fig. 3 is an example of entering a query to find out the "names of the plants
whose habitat is wetland" The unit terms are extracted from the entered query.
The extracted unit terms are mapped to the WordNet concept number.

SELECT plant.name
WHERE plant.habitat = "wetland"
⇩
{<Plant>, <name>, <habitat>, <wetland>}

Fig. 3. Unit terms extracted from query

The original query is converted to concept numbers and the query terms in
the SELECT and WHERE sentences are extracted. The original query in Fig. 3
are converted as follows:

SELECT 00008864.04778525
WHERE 00008864.06325667 = "06787418"

When the concepts in the original query have been converted to the concept numbers, the global semantic network is used to explore and solve the semantic heterogeneity. The query terms included in the query are identified using global semantic network and the entities and attributes of each component database for the query terms are extracted. Fig. 4 illustrates that the semantic heterogeneity of the query in Fig. 3 is solved and the information needed to create the sub-queries is produced.

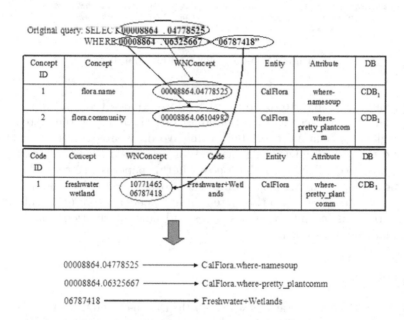

Fig. 4. The semantic heterogeneity is solved by using the global semantic network

The sub-queries can be created with the information obtained in the process of solving the semantic heterogeneity. Fig. 5 illustrates that the results shown in Fig. 4 are used to show the results of producing a sub-query for the CalFlora database. The produced sub-queries are readjusted according to the web interfaces. The sub-queries are delivered to and processed in each component database.

4   Conclusions

The virtual database tables produced through the web interface analysis on information sources provide an easier mechanism for integration across different data model and DBMSs. The integrated web information system uses these

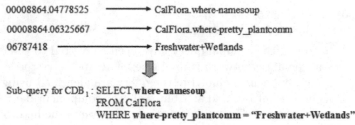

Fig. 5. Sub-query for CalFlora database

virtual database tables to integrate web information without needing to know the actual database schemas of all databases participating in the system.

The global semantic network built using WordNet provides the access knowledge and the semantic knowledge needed for integrated access to individual information sources. The approach proposed in this paper is also very adaptable to dynamic and open environments. Since the process of an individual information source being integrated into the system is independent from other information sources, the existing information sources and new information sources can be easily modified and added.

References

1. Thomas R.Gruber, "Toward Principles for the Design of Ontologies Used for Knowledge Sharing", International Journal of Human-Computer Studies, 1995.
2. Maurizio Panti, Luca Spalazzi, Alberto Giretti, "A Case-Based Approach to Information Integration" , Proceedings of the 26th VLDB conference, 2000.
3. J. Hammer, H. H. Garcia-Molina, K. Ireland, Y. Papakonstantinou, J. Ullman, J. Widom, "Information translation, mediation, and mosaic-based browsing in the tsimmis system", In Proceedings of the ACM SIGMOD International Conference on Management of Data, 1995.
4. G. A. Miller, R. Beckwith, C. Fellbaum, D.Gross, and K. Miller: Five Papers on WordNet, CSL Reort 43, Cognitive Systems Laboratory, Priceton Univ., 1990.
5. J. O. Lee, D. K. Baik, "SemQL: A Semantic Query Language for Multidatabase Systems", Proc. 8th International Conf. on Information and Knowledge Management (CIKM-99), 1999.

A New Universally Verifiable and Receipt-Free Electronic Voting Scheme Using One-Way Untappable Channels*

Sangjin Kim[1] and Heekuck Oh[2]

[1] Korea Univ. of Technology and Education, School of Internet Media Eng.,
Byeoncheonmyeon, Cheonan, Chungnam, Republic of Korea
sangjin@kut.ac.kr
http://infosec.kut.ac.kr/sangjin/
[2] Hanyang University, Department of Computer Science and Engineering,
Sa-1-dong 1271, Ansan, Kyunggi, Republic of Korea
hkoh@cse.hanyang.ac.kr
http://infosec.hanyang.ac.kr/~hkoh/

Abstract. Electronic voting schemes must provide universal verifiability and receipt-freeness. However, since their objectives are mutually contradictory, providing both properties are difficult. To date, most electronic voting schemes provide only one of these properties and those few which provide both properties are not practical due to heavy computational requirements. In this paper, we present an efficient electronic voting scheme that provides both properties. The proposed scheme uses a trusted third party called HS (Honest Shuffler) and requires only one-way untappable channels from HSs to voters. Currently, this is the weakest physical assumption required for receipt-freeness. Among the schemes which assume only one-way untappable channels and provide both properties, our scheme requires the least amount of computation.

1 Introduction

Electronic voting schemes must satisfy basic properties such as privacy and eligibility to replace the current offline voting schemes. Providing these basic requirements have been successful. However, more sophisticated requirements such as universally verifiability and receipt-freeness have not been that successful. Earlier systems only provided individual verifiability, meaning that only voters can verify whether their votes were properly counted. Sako and Kilian [1] argued that other interested parties, independent of their participation, should be able to verify the correctness of the election results. Sako and Kilian called this property universal verifiability and currently this has become a mandatory requirement. Another problem with electronic voting is the possibility of vote buying and selling. Current offline voting takes place inside a voting booth which conceals

---

* This work was supported by Korea Research Foundation Grant (KRF-2003-003-D00445).

C.-H. Chi and K.-Y. Lam (Eds.): AWCC 2004, LNCS 3309, pp. 337–345, 2004.

the voters' actions. However, in electronic voting, voters can store all the data used during the voting and use it as a proof of voting for a specific candidate. These proofs allow voters to sell their vote and allow vote-buyers to buy votes in return for these proof. To prevent this, it must be impossible for a voter to convince a buyer that he/she has voted for a specific candidate. A system which satisfies this is called receipt-free.

Providing both universal verifiability and receipt-freeness is difficult because they have contrary meanings. In other words, there must exist a proof of correctness to satisfy universal verifiability while, to satisfy receipt-freeness, one should not be able to construct a proof. Most of the current electronic voting schemes provide only one of the properties [2, 3], and those few that provide both properties are not practical due to heavy computational requirements [1, 4].

In this paper, we propose a new electronic voting scheme based on homomorphic encryption that provides both universal verifiability and receipt-freeness. This scheme uses a third trusted party called HS (Honest Shuffler) and assumes the existence of one-way untappable channels from HSs to voters. When the election begins, a voter contacts a HS of his/her choice. The HS encrypts the votes representing each candidate and post these encrypted votes in a random order on the voter's area of the bulletin board. The HS also posts proofs of the validness of encrypted votes. HS then tells the order to the voter using a designated verifier proof through an untappable channel from itself to the voter. The voter chooses one of the encrypted votes and re-encrypts it and publish the final vote on the board. He/she also posts a proof of the validness of the final vote. Among the schemes that assume only one-way untappable channels and provide both properties, our scheme requires the least amount of computation.

2   Previous Work

Lee and Kim [5] proposed a scheme based on homomorphic encryption that provides both universal verifiability and receipt freeness. They used a trusted third party called HV (Honest Verifier). In this scheme, a voter first encrypts his/her vote and then re-encrypts it with a pair of random values, given by the HV, to construct the final vote. The protocol between a voter and the HV must be done through a physically secure bi-directional channel. HV proves the correctness of the pair of values using a plain zero-knowledge proof of equality of discrete logarithms. Hirt [3] found that if the buyer coerced the voter to fix the challenge in this interactive proof, the voter cannot make false transcripts to deceive the buyer.

Hirt [3] proposed a scheme similar to Lee and Kim's [5] that does not provide universal verifiability but provides receipt-freeness. This scheme also uses a trusted third party called HR (Honest Randomizer), which plays a similar role to that of HV in Lee and Kim's scheme. In this scheme, when the voter sends his/her vote to a HR through an untappable channel, the HR does not return a pair of values needed for encryption. Instead, HR itself encrypts the vote and posts it on the bulletin board on behalf of the voter. HR also proves the

$$
\begin{array}{ll}
\text{Prover } \mathcal{P} & \text{Verifier } \mathcal{V} \\
a_1, \ldots, a_K, b_1, \ldots, b_K \in_R \mathbb{Z}_q & \\
A_i = \left(\frac{X_i}{X}\right)^{a_i} g_A^{b_i} & \\
B_i = \left(\frac{Y_i}{Y}\right)^{a_i} y_A^{b_i} & \xrightarrow{\;(A_1, B_1), \ldots, (A_K, B_K)\;} \quad c \in_R \mathbb{Z}_q \\
a_j' = c - \sum_{i \neq j}^{K} a_i & \xleftarrow{\qquad c \qquad} \\
b_j' = \beta a_j + b_j - \beta a_j' & \\
a_j = a_j', \; b_j = b_j' & \xrightarrow{\;(a_1, b_1), \ldots, (a_K, b_K)\;} \quad c \stackrel{?}{=} \sum a_i \\
& A_i \stackrel{?}{=} \left(\frac{X_i}{X}\right)^{a_i} g_A^{b_i} \\
& B_i \stackrel{?}{=} \left(\frac{Y_i}{Y}\right)^{a_i} y_A^{b_i}
\end{array}
$$

Fig. 1. ZKProof($\log_{g_A} \frac{X_1}{X} = \log_{y_A} \frac{Y_1}{Y} \lor \cdots \lor \log_{g_A} \frac{X_K}{X} = \log_{y_A} \frac{Y_K}{Y}$)

validness of the final vote to the voter using a designated verifier proof through an untappable channel. Therefore, this scheme also requires a physically secure bi-directional channel between a voter and a HR.

Hirt and Sako [4] proposed a scheme based on mix-net that provides both universal verifiability and receipt-freeness. This scheme, contrast to the above schemes, uses a weaker physical assumption. They only require a physically secure one-way untappable channel from the authorities to the voters. Although they have improved the efficiency of the system significantly compared to previous mix-net based schemes, it is still not practical due to the heavy computational and communication load during the mixing procedure.

3   Building Blocks

In this paper, all operations are performed in a subgroup G_q of order q in $\mathbb{Z}_p^*$, where p and q are some large prime numbers such that $q|(p-1)$. We omit the modulus of operations when illustrating protocols or proofs, since it can easily be determined from the context. In our scheme, we use homomorphic ElGamal encryption, threshold ElGamal encryption, and some witness indistinguishable proofs. In this section, we will only discuss the proofs we use in our system. Although we show interactive version of these proofs, all these proofs can be converted to non-interactive proofs using the Fiat-Shamir heuristics. We use non-interactive versions in our voting scheme.

3.1   1-out-of-K and K-out-of-1 Re-encryption Proof

A witness indistinguishable proof that proves that there is a re-encryption of (X, Y) among K re-encrypted ciphertexts (X_1, Y_1), ..., (X_K, Y_K) is depicted in Fig 1 [4]. This protocol is used in our voting scheme to prove the validness of encrypted votes published by the HS. In Fig 1, we assume that $(X_j, Y_j) = (g_A^\beta X, y_A^\beta Y)$ is the re-encryption of (X, Y). Recently, more efficient shuffling protocols have been proposed [6]. We can also use these protocols instead of this

Prover $\mathcal{P}$ Verifier$\mathcal{V}$

$a_1, \ldots, a_K, b_1, \ldots, b_K \in_R \mathbb{Z}_q$

$A_i = \left(\frac{X_F}{X_i}\right)^{a_i} g_A^{b_i}$

$B_i = \left(\frac{Y_F}{Y_i}\right)^{a_i} y_A^{b_i}$ $\quad\quad \xrightarrow{\;(A_1, B_1), \ldots, (A_K, B_K)\;}$ $c \in_R \mathbb{Z}_q$

$a_k' = c - \sum_{i \neq j}^{K} a_i$

$b_k' = \beta a_k + b_k - \beta a_k'$ $\quad\quad \xleftarrow{\quad\quad c \quad\quad}$

$a_k = a_k', \; b_k = b_k'$ $\quad\quad \xrightarrow{\;(a_1, b_1), \ldots, (a_K, b_K)\;}$ $c \overset{?}{=} \sum a_i$

$A_i \overset{?}{=} \left(\frac{X_F}{X_i}\right)^{a_i} g_A^{b_i}$

$B_i \overset{?}{=} \left(\frac{Y_F}{Y_i}\right)^{a_i} y_A^{b_i}$

Fig. 2. ZKProof($\log_{g_A} \frac{X_F}{X_1} = \log_{y_A} \frac{Y_F}{Y_1} \vee \cdots \vee \log_{g_A} \frac{X_F}{X_K} = \log_{y_A} \frac{Y_F}{Y_K}$)

protocol. This protocol can be modified into a proof that proves (X_F, Y_F) is a re-encryption of one of K ciphertexts (X_1, Y_1), ..., (X_K, Y_K) [4]. This protocol is given in Fig 2. In this protocol, $(X_F, Y_F) = (g_A^\beta X_k, y_A^\beta Y_k)$ is a re-encryption of (X_k, Y_k). This protocol is used in our voting scheme to prove the validness of the final vote posted by individual voters. For more detail on these proofs, refer to [4]. The following assumptions are later used in the analysis of our scheme.

Assumption 1. We assume that it is computationally infeasible for the prover i) to prove that there is a re-encryption of (X', Y') among K re-encrypted ciphertexts (X_1, Y_1), ..., (X_K, Y_K) using the proof given in Fig 1 when actually there is not a re-encryption of (X', Y') among K ciphertexts, ii) to prove that there is a re-encryption (X, Y) without knowing the corresponding ciphertext and the randomness used to encrypt (X, Y).

Assumption 2. We assume that it is computationally infeasible for the prover i) to prove that (X_F', Y_F') is a re-encryption of one of K ciphertexts (X_1, Y_1), ..., (X_K, Y_K) using the proof given in Fig 2 when actually (X_F', Y_F') is not a re-encryption of one of K ciphertexts, ii) to prove that (X_F', Y_F') is a re-encryption of one of K ciphertexts without knowing the corresponding plaintext and the randomness used in the encryption.

3.2   Designated Verifier Proof of Knowledge of Equality of DLs

To provide universal verifiability, we need proofs of validness of encrypted votes published by HS that do not reveal the permutation. However, for a voter to cast a vote, the permutation must be conveyed to the voter in a way that prevents him/her from making a receipt. To achieve this, we use a designated verifier proof. Designated verifier proof that proves $(X_j, Y_j) = (g_A^\beta X, y_A^\beta Y)$ is a re-encryption of (X, Y) is given in Fig 3 [3]. In this proof, the private key of the verifier is $x_V \in \mathbb{Z}_q$ and the corresponding public key is $y_V = g_V^{x_V}$, where g_V is a generator of G_q.

$$
\begin{array}{ll}
\text{Prover } \mathcal{P} & \text{Designated Verifier } \mathcal{V} \\
w, s_2, c_2 \in_R \mathbb{Z}_q & \\
A = g_A^w, B = y_A^w, D = g_V^{s_2}/y_V^{c_2} \quad \underrightarrow{A, B, D} \quad c \in_R \mathbb{Z}_q & \\
c_1 = c - c_2 & \underleftarrow{\quad c \quad} \\
s_1 = w + \beta c_1 & \underrightarrow{c_1, c_2, s_1, s_2} \quad c \stackrel{?}{=} c_1 + c_2 \\
& g_A^{s_1} \stackrel{?}{=} \left(\frac{X_j}{X}\right)^{c_1} A, \; y_A^{s_1} \stackrel{?}{=} \left(\frac{Y_j}{Y}\right)^{c_1} B \\
& g_V^{s_2} \stackrel{?}{=} y_V^{c_2} D
\end{array}
$$

Fig. 3. DVZKProof($\log_{g_A} \frac{X_j}{X} - \log_{y_A} \frac{Y_j}{Y}$)

Table 1. An Area on the Bulletin Board Designated to a Voter

Field	Posting Entity	Size
final vote	voter	$2|p|$
a proof of validation of the final vote	voter	$2K|p| + (2K+1)|q|$
list of encrypted votes	HS	$2K|p|$
proofs of validation of encrypted votes	HS	$K(2K|p| + (2K+1)|q|)$

Note: p and q are system parameters used in construction of $\mathbb{Z}_p^*$ and its subgroup G_q.

In the following, for any (X_k, Y_k), we will show how the verifier can make a valid transcript of a proof that proves it is a re-encryption of (X, Y). The verifier randomly selects $\tilde{c}_1, \tilde{s}_1, \tilde{s}_2 \in \mathbb{Z}_q$ and computes the following:

$$
\tilde{A} = g_A^{\tilde{s}_1}(X_k/X)^{-\tilde{c}_1}, \quad \tilde{B} = y_A^{\tilde{s}_1}(Y_k/Y)^{-\tilde{c}_1}, \quad \tilde{c}_2 = \tilde{c} - \tilde{c}_1, \quad \text{and} \quad \tilde{D} = g_V^{\tilde{s}_2 - x_V \tilde{c}_2}.
$$

We can easily see that this proof passes the verification process of Fig 3.

4 Our Proposed Scheme

4.1 System Model

Participants. Our model consists of N authorities $A_1, \ldots, A_N$, L voters $V_1, \ldots, V_L$, M HSs, and K candidates. A voter interacts with only one HS, but we use M HSs for fault-tolerance reasons and to prevent too many voters from flooding one HS. A threshold t denotes the least number of authorities that must remain honest during the voting process. If more than t authorities cooperate, they can decrypt individual votes.

Communication. We use a bulletin board to post data relevant to voting. This board is publicly readable and every eligible voter has his/her own area where only they can append to, but nobody can delete from. This area is again divided into the four fields shown in Table 1. To control access rights to each area and each field of that area, we assume the use of digital signatures. A HS must have an authorization certificate issued by the voter in order to gain access to the portion of the voter's area.

We assume the existence of one-way untappable channels from the HSs to the voters. These channels are regarded as the weakest physical assumption needed to provide receipt-freeness [4]. The following definition of an one-way untappable channel is from [2] with slight modification.

Definition 1. *An one-way untappable channel is a physically secure channel that guarantees the following properties: i) only the sender can send messages to the receiver, ii) the receiver cannot prove what he received through the channel, and iii) nobody can eavesdrop on this channel.*

4.2   System Setup

The authorities first select a subgroup G_q of order q in $\mathbb{Z}_p^*$ by choosing two large primes p and q such that $q|(p-1)$. These authorities also select three generators g_A, g_C, and g_V of G_q in random and publish them. g_A is used to generate authorities' public key, g_C is used to encode votes, and g_V is used to generate voter's public key. They also calculate $g_i = g_C^{L^{i-1}}$, $i = 1, \ldots, K$, which will represent each candidate i. This encoding was first suggested by Cramer et al. [7]. The initial vote of each candidate i is $(1, g_i)$. The authorities execute the key generation protocol of (t, N) threshold ElGamal encryption to obtain a share $x_j \in \mathbb{Z}_q$ of the private key $x_A \in \mathbb{Z}_q$. Each authority commits to their share by publishing $y_j = g_A^{x_j}$. They also publish the public key $y_A = g_A^{x_A}$.

During registration, each voter submits their public key $y_V = g_V^{x_V}$ to an authority, where $x_V \in \mathbb{Z}_q$ is the corresponding private key. This key is used in authenticating voters before allowing access to the bulletin board. It is also used in designated verifier proof which is used to prove the order of encrypted votes.

4.3   Voting Procedure

When the election gets started, a voter contacts a HS and gives it an authorization certificate. This certificate grants access to some fields of voter's area of the bulletin board to the HS. The HS constructs encrypted votes $(X_i, Y_i) = (g_A^{\alpha_i}, y_A^{\alpha_i} g_i)$ for each candidate i by encrypting each candidate's initial vote. The HS then posts the list of encrypted votes $(X_1, Y_2), \ldots, (X_K, Y_K)$ in random order on the voter's area of the bulletin board. The HS also proves the validness of these encrypted votes by proving that there is a re-encryption of $(1, g_i)$ among K encrypted votes for each $(1, g_i)$. This is done using the proof depicted in Fig 1. Therefore, K non-interactive version of the proofs must be posted along with the list. Through this proof, anyone can verify that there is no duplication, invalid, and missing votes in the list. The voter does not have to verify these proofs.

The HS then proves to the voter which vote corresponds to which candidate using the proof depicted in Fig 3. Thus, it sends K non-interactive proofs to the voter through a one-way untappable channel from it to the voter. The voter does not have to verify all the proofs. The voter is only required to verify one of the proofs which proves the validness of the encrypted vote representing the voter's choice.

The voter then selects his choice. Let's assume the voter chose $(X_k, Y_k) = (g_A^{\alpha_j}, y_A^{\alpha_j} g_j)$, meaning that the voter chose the candidate j and k-th vote on the encrypted list represents the candidate j. The voter re-encrypts it to hide his/her selection. The final vote is $(X_F, Y_F) = (g_A^\beta X_k, y_A^\beta Y_k)$. The voter posts this final vote on the designated field of his/her area on the board. The voter also posts a proof of validness of the final vote which proves that (X_F, Y_F) is a re-encryption of one of the votes on the encrypted list posted by the HS on his/her area of the board. This is done using a non-interactive version of the proof depicted in Fig 2. Anyone can verify that a voter has cast a valid vote without knowing who the voter voted for by verifying the proofs on the voter's area of the board.

4.4 Tallying Procedure

Our scheme uses the encoding method suggested by Cramer et al. [7]. In this encoding, each candidate i is represented by $g_i^{L^{i-1}}$, where L is the total number of voters. When the voting closes, the authorities collect valid votes and compute $(X_T, Y_T) = \left(\prod_{i=1}^l X_{F,i}, \prod_{i=1}^l Y_{F,i}\right)$, where $l \le L$ denotes the total number of valid votes. Since these valid votes are posted on the board, anyone can compute (X_T, Y_T). The authorities perform the decryption protocol of threshold ElGamal encryption to obtain $W = Y_T / X_T^{x_A}$. At least t authorities must participate in the decryption process to obtain $W = g_1^{T_1} g_2^{T_2} \cdots g_K^{T_K} = g_C^T$, where T_i denotes the final tally for candidate i and $T = T_1 + T_2 L + T_3 L^2 + \cdots + T_K L^{K-1}$. L is used in this encoding to limit T_i's range to $[1, L-1]$. One can easily determine the exact number of cast votes for each candidate, if one can compute $\log_{g_C} W = T$. The computation of $\log_{g_C} W$ is generally considered as a computationally hard problem. Although we can use the fact that T's range is $[l, lL^{k-1}]$ to speed up the computation, it is only feasible for reasonable values of l and K. Moreover, as stated by Cramer et al. [7], using this encoding bounds the number of candidates K to approximately $\log_L q$.

5 System Analysis

5.1 Security Analysis

In this subsection, due to space limitation, we only discuss how our scheme satisfies the universal verifiability and receipt freeness.

Theorem 1 (Universal Verifiability). *Anyone, independent of participation, can verify the validness of individual votes and the final tally of the election.*

Proof. By Assumption 1, a HS cannot include an invalid vote in the list of encrypted votes posted on a voter's area. By Assumption 2, a voter's final vote must be a re-encryption of one of the encrypted votes in the list. Moreover

Table 2. Comparison of Features with Other Schemes

	[4]	[5]	[3]	*Ours*
receipt-freeness	○	△*	○	○
universal verifiability	○	○	×	○
use of TTP	×	○	○	○
physical assumption	authorities → voters	HVs ↔ voters	HRs ↔ voters	HSs → voters

* Must use a designated proof to provide receipt-freeness

→, ↔: denotes a one-way and bi-directional untappable channel, respectively.

anyone can verify the correctness of these proofs. Therefore, anyone can verify the validness of each individual vote. This also allows anyone to compute (X_T, Y_T) which is a product of all valid votes. Therefore, they can also verify the final tally announced by the authorities.

Theorem 2 (Receipt-Freeness). *Without a collusion between a voter and a HS, or between a vote-buyer and a HS, this scheme satisfies receipt-freeness.*

Proof. The order of the list from which a voter chooses his vote is proven using a designated verifier proof and these proofs are sent to the voter through a one-way untappable channel. By Definition 1, no one can eavesdrop on this channel. Therefore, a voter can lie about the order using the method shown in subsection 3.2. Therefore, a voter cannot convince a vote-buyer about his/her choice.

5.2   Comparison

In this subsection, we compare our scheme with others and discuss the pros and cons of our system. Table 2 shows that Hirt and Sako's [4], Lee and Kim's [5], as well as our scheme satisfy both receipt freeness and universal verifiability. Among these, Hirt and Sako's and ours use the weakest physical assumption. Table 3 shows that our system requires less computation load than Hirt and Sako's. Therefore, we can conclude that our system requires the least computational load among schemes using the weakest physical assumption. Even more, with respect to a voter's computation load, our scheme requires the same load as that of Lee and Kim's and Hirt's [3].

Table 3. Comparison of Computational Load with Other Schemes

		[4]	[5]	[3]	*Ours*
Voter	*Proving K-out-of-1 proof*	0	1	1	1
	Verifying DV proof	NK	1	1	1*
HV, HR, HS,	*Proving 1-out-of-K proof*	NK	1	0	K
or Authority	*Proving DV proof*	NK	1	1	K

* Although K proofs are sent to a voter, voter only has to verify one of these proofs.

6   Conclusion

The ultimate goal of electronic voting is replacing the current offline voting. Therefore, all the basic requirements plus vote duplication, robustness, receipt-freeness, and universal verifiability must be met by the electronic voting schemes. To date, most electronic voting schemes do not provide both receipt-freeness and universal verifiability and those few which provide both properties are not practical due to heavy computational requirements. In this paper, we have presented a new electronic voting scheme based on homomorphic encryption that uses a trusted third party called HS. This scheme uses the weakest physical assumption while satisfying all the requirements. Among the schemes which use the same physical assumption, our scheme requires the least computational load.

Although our scheme is an improvement over Hirt and Sako's [4] scheme with respect to computational load, and an improvement over Lee and Kim's [5] with respect to physical assumption, it still requires physical channel assumption. Currently, smart cards are being considered as a tool to remove this assumption [8]. Furthermore, the tallying procedure needs to be improved in order for our scheme to be used in large scale elections with many candidates. Therefore, work on these areas are needed in the future.

References

1. Sako, K., Kilian, J.: Receipt-free Mix-Type Voting Scheme: A Practical Solution to the Implementation of a Voting Booth. In: Guillou, L.C., Quisquater, J. (eds.): Advances in Cryptology, Eurocrypt 1995, Lecture Notes in Computer Science, Vol. 921. Springer-Verlag (1995) 393–403
2. Okamoto, T.: Receipt-Free Electronic Voting Schemes for Large Scale Elections. In: Christianson, B., Crispo, B., Lomas, T., Roe, M. (eds.): Proc. of 5th Int. Workshop on Security Protocols. Lecture Notes in Computer Science, Vol. 1361. Springer-Verlag (1997) 25–35
3. Hirt, H.: Receipt-free Voting with Randomizers. Presentated at the Workshop on Trustworthy Elections. (2001) http://www.vote.caltech.edu/wote01/
4. Hirt, M., Sako, K.: Efficient Receipt-Free Voting Based on Homomorphic Encryption. In: Preneel, B. (ed.): Advances in Cryptology, Eurocrypt 2000. Lecture Notes in Computer Science, Vol. 1807. Springer-Verlag (2000) 539–556
5. Lee, B., Kim, K.: Receipt-free Electronic Voting through Collaboration of Voter and Honest Verifier. In: Proc. of the JWISC 2000. 101–108
6. Furukawa, J., Sako, K.: An Efficient Scheme for Proving a Shuffle. In: Kilian, J. (ed.): Advances in Cryptology, Crypto 2001. Lecture Notes in Computer Science, Vol. 2139. Springer-Verlag (2001) 368–387
7. Cramer, R., Franklin, M.K., Schoenmakers, B., Yung, M.: Multi-Authority Secret-Ballot Elections with Linear Work. In: Maurer, U.M., (ed.): Advances in Cryptology, Eurocrypt 1996. Lecture Notes in Computer Science, Vol. 1070. Springer-Verlag (1996) 72–83
8. Lee, B., Kim, K.: Receipt-Free Electronic Voting Scheme with a Tamper-Resistant Randomizer. In: Lee, P., Lim, C. (eds.): 5th Int. Conf. on Information Security and Cryptology. Lecture Notes in Computer Science, Vol. 2587. Springer-Verlag (2002) 389–406

Ontology-Based Conceptual Modeling
of Policy-Driven Control Framework: Oriented
to Multi-agent System for Web Services Management

Beishui Liao, Ji Gao, Jun Hu, and Jiujun Chen

College of Computer Science, Zhejiang University, Hangzhou 310027, China
{baiseliao,hujun111}@zju.edu.cn, gaoji@mail.hz.zj.cn,
rackycjj@163.com

Abstract. The integration of web services and intelligent agents is promising
for automated service discovery, negotiation, and cooperation. But due to the
dynamic and heterogeneous nature of web services and agents, it is challenging
to guide the behaviors of underlying agents to meet the high-level business
(changeful) requirements. Traditional Policy-driven methods (Ponder, Rei,
KAoS, etc) are not adaptable to direct the discovery, negotiation and cooperation of dynamic agents who may join in or leave out of a specific community or
organization (virtual organization) at run time. The purpose of this paper is to
model an ontology-based, policy-driven control framework that is suitable to
supervise the dynamic agents according to high-level policies. On the basis of
federated multi-agents infrastructure and ontologies of policies, domain concepts, and agent federations, a model of role-based policy specification framework is presented in this paper.

1 Introduction

In recent years, web services [1] facilitate the interaction and sharing of distributed
applications that are across the enterprise boundaries, while intelligent agents [2]
offer strong supports for automated discovery, transaction, cooperation and coordination, of web services. In order to fulfill a specific task, several agents who govern
various web services may dynamically gather and form a virtual organization (VO).
The members of a VO can join or leave at run time. In realizing this objective, we
will come across two main challenges.

✧ How to express the high-level business requirements of a VO and transform them
   into implementable strategies that guide the behaviors of agents
✧ How to control the behaviors of these dynamic agents without modifying their
   implementation

Policy-based management [3,4,5] provides effective means for these purposes.
Policies are a means to dynamically regulate the behavior of system components
without changing code and without requiring the consent or cooperation of the components being governed [6]. Currently, typical policy-based solutions are Ponder [3],
Rei [4], and KAoS [5]. Among them, Ponder is a declarative object-oriented language
that supports the specification of several types of management policies for distributed
object systems and provides structuring techniques for policies to cater for the complexity of policy administration in large enterprise information system, but the lack of

C.-H. Chi and K.-Y. Lam (Eds.): AWCC 2004, LNCS 3309, pp. 346–356, 2004.
© Springer-Verlag Berlin Heidelberg 2004

an ontology limits its ability to deal with semantic inconsistency of concepts in dynamic, heterogeneous VO environment. Rei is a policy framework that integrates support for policy specification, analysis and reasoning in pervasive computing applications, but it does not provide an enforcement model. KAoS policy services allow for the specification, management, conflict resolution, and enforcement of policies within domains, but like Ponder and Rei, it does not offer a policy-driven method for the control of discovery, negotiation, cooperation, and coordination, of agents.

On the basis of our earlier research on agent federation [7, 8, 9], we propose a model of policy-driven control framework. This paper is structured as follows. Section 2 introduces related work. Section 3 explains architecture of policy-driven control framework. Section 4 describes the modeling process. Finally, breakthrough and conclusions are given in Section 5.

2   Related Work

In recent years, we have developed a federated multi-agent system that can be used to manage and control the underlying web services [7,8,9].

As shown in the federated agents layer of figure 1, Web services are encapsulated as agents' skills (atomic activities of agents). Each agent has one or more skills. Agents as providers or consumers of Web services can join into one or more agent federations for services transaction, interoperation or cooperation according to federation goals, rules, and policies. These participating agents are called member agents (M_i) of specific agent federations. Each agent federation has one management agent (MA) that takes charge of recruiting member agents (M1~Mn), organizing cooperation of member agents according to recipes (plans) defined in advance. MA or individual member agents locally enforce the policies from policy distributor. The distributor distributes policies according to subjects or targets of policies, with the support of federation information service (FIS). FIS manages the information of agents, including role assignment information, agents' ID, agents' potential activities, properties, locations, etc. Each agent (including MA and member agents) has a local policy depository, a policy engine, and an agent mental state monitor.

In this system, agents who govern the web services participate in various social activities within a VO, including discovery, negotiation, cooperation and transaction with other agents. The granularity of agents fits in with high-level control according to business policies, while individual web services are too fine-grained to be controlled between different business parties. So, federated agent system lays concrete foundation for web services management according to the high-level policies. The detailed description of agent federation is out of the range of this paper (reader is referred to [8,10] for details). In the following sections, we will focus on modeling of policy specification and deployment.

3   Architecture of Policy-Driven Control Framework

On top of federated agent layer, there is a policy specification and deployment layer, as shown in figure 1. This layer mainly treats with representing high-level business policies, transforming them into low-level implementable policies, and distributing these policies to underlying agents who are in charge of enforcing policies. Since roles of agent federation and their rights and responsibilities are comparatively static and the agents who undertake the roles are dynamic, the policy specification is role-oriented. Before policy distributor distributes policies, role-based policies are transformed to specific implementable policies through role assignment.

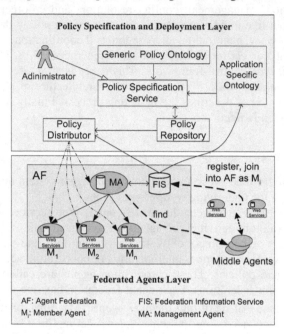

Fig. 1. Architecture of policy-driven control framework

There are five components in policy specification and deployment layer, including generic policy ontology (GPO), application specific ontology (ASO), policy specification service (PSS), policy repository (PR), and policy distributor (PD). The GPO defines the common ontology about subject, target, behavior, constraint, and policy (Section 4.1). ASO is ontology about agent federation and domain concepts (Section 4.1). With these two ontologies, human administrator establishes policies through PSS. According to the role assignment information from FIS, Policy Distributor takes change of policy distribution.

4 Modeling Process

The modeling process of policy is illustrated in figure 2. There are three level policies: high-level policies that directly reflect the business requirements, low-level policy templates that are based on roles, domain concepts and agent federation model, and implementable policies whose subjects and targets are agents who undertake the roles specified in low-level policy templates.

In order to concretely explain the modeling process, we use a scenario as shown in Fig.3. Suppose that there is a market research virtual organization, which is composed of several roles such as Raw Data Collector, Data Analyzer, Data Storer, and Data Mining Server. The rights and responsibilities of these roles are defined statically at design-time. On the other hand, there are many agents (service-providing agents) who are capable of fulfilling these roles in the open environment. Through the mechanism of service advertisement, discovery, and negotiation, service-providing agents will be recruited and joined into the VO by the management agent dynamically. Now, the question is how to use policy-based mechanism to manage and control the behaviors of these agents. In the following sections, we will describe the modeling of policy-driven control framework based on this example.

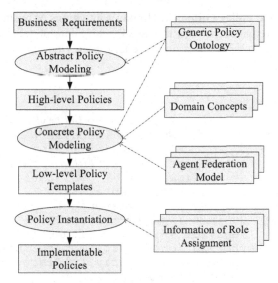

Fig. 2. The Modeling Process of Policy

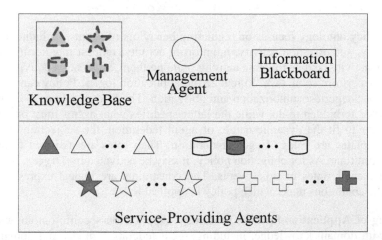

Fig. 3. Triangle, Column, Star and Cross denote DataCollectingAgents, DataStoringAgents, DataAnalyzingAgents, DataMiningAgents respectively. The green ones in the Knowledge Base denote roles of federation that will be fulfilled by agents. The blue shapes denote those agents who have joined the federation and been assigned to fulfilled specific roles. The role assignment is done by Management Agent according to the information provided by Information Blackboard

4.1 Ontology Modeling

Policy specification is based on ontology. In our policy-driven control framework, ontology mainly consists of generic policy ontology (GPO) and application-specific ontology (ASO). The ASO is composed of agent federation model and domain concepts. The use of ontology makes policy definition and concepts sharing in the distributed, heterogeneous environment a reality.

Modeling of Generic Policy Ontology. Human's intentions or business requirements are represented as semantic policies that are machine-interpretable in open, distributed environment. The current version of generic policy ontology can be defined in the form of EBNF as follows.

Definition 1:

```
Policy     ::= 'Policy(' PolicyID Modality {Trigger}
                          Subject {Behavior} [Target]
                          {Constraint } ')'
Modality ::= 'Authorization+' | 'Authorization-'
                  | 'Obligation+' | 'Obligation-'
Trigger    ::= 'Trigger('AgentMentalState
                          | TimeEvent ')'
Subject  ::= 'Subject (' Role | AgentID ')'
Behavior ::= 'Behavior (' ApplicationActivity
              | AuthorizationActivity|MonitoringActivity
                | RequestMonitorActivity|DiscoveryActivity
                | NegotiationActivity ')'
Target    ::= 'Target (' Role | AgentID ')'
Constraint ::= 'Constraint('LogicalExpression ')'
```

This policy ontology focuses on regulating behaviors of agents, including application activity, authorization activity, monitoring activity, request monitoring activity, discovery activity, and negotiation activity. Among them, application activity denotes that agents perform some tasks to realize the application logics. Policy can be classified as two categories: authorization and obligation. The former defines what agent is permitted or forbidden to do, while the latter specifies what agents must or must not do. In order to fit the dynamic nature of agent federation, the subject and target of policy templates are roles of agent federation. Then roles are assigned to specific agents at run time. As for obligation policy, it may be activated by *Trigger*, which can be agent mental states or time events. The constraints are logical expressions that specify the conditions under which policy is applicable.

Modeling of Application-Specific Ontology. Application-specific ontology is concerned with domain knowledge, including agent federation model and domain concepts.

Modeling of Agent Federation. With respect to a specific agent federation, the roles are statically defined. But the undertakers of roles may be dynamic. The model of agent federation is defined as 6-tuple:

Definition 2:

(ROLE, GOAL, DECOMPOSITION, RECIPE, ASSIGNMENT, AGENT)
DECOMPOSITION: (GOAL ↛ GOAL) ↛ ℙROLE
ASSIGNMENT: ROLE ↛ AGENT

ROLE is a set of roles that are in charge of realizing some goals. GOAL is a set of goals and sub-goals of agent federation. DECOMPOSITION decomposes goal to sub-goals and designates these sub-goals to corresponding roles (Symbols "↛"(partial function), and symbols "ℙ" (power set) are symbols of Z language). RECIPE is static plan that specifies the execution manner of sub-goals decomposed from a certain goal. ASSIGNMENT is a mapping mechanism that assigns roles to agents who are capable of undertaken them. AGENT is a set of agents including management agent (MA) of federation and member agents (M1~Mn) who join into federation and take on specific roles.

RECIPE can be viewed as a scheduling plan of sub-goals established statically at design-time, which defines possible plans, plan steps and sub-goals in these plan steps. A Recipe is defined in the form of BNF as follows.

Definition 3:

```
<Scheduling-Plan>::= {<Plan-Steps>| (Loop<Plan-Steps>) }
<Plan-Steps>      ::= { (← Return <Condition>)
                      | (←<Goal-Set>[<Condition>])
                      | (or{ (←<Goal-Set>[<Condition>]) })}
<Goal-Set>        ::= <Goal>| ((Sequence | Concurrence)
                      {(←<Goal> [<Condition>])})
<Condition>       ::= <Condition-Expression>
```

The condition-expression of RECIPE provides flexible approaches for MA to dynamically create the scheduling scheme of sub-goals according to current environment. In terms of this scheme, MA designates sub-Goals to roles of the federation.

As far as the market research virtual organization (figure 3) is concerned, the model of agent federation can be represented as figure 4.

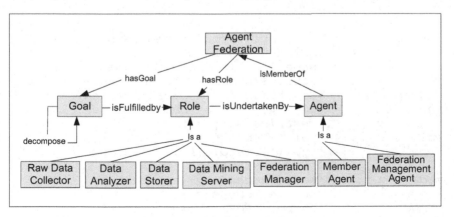

Fig. 4. A Model of Agent Federation

ASSIGNMENT dynamically binds roles to agents whose behaviors, inputs, outputs, pre-conditions, and post-conditions match the corresponding roles. Formally, the following definitions represent the model of ASSIGNMENT.

Definition 4: Member-Agent (Mem) is a set of agents who are intended to taken on specific roles of agent federation. ROLE is a set of roles that are in charge of realizing some goals of agent federation.

$$\text{Mem} = \{m1, m2, ..., mp\}, \quad p \in \mathbb{N}$$
$$\text{ROLE} = \{r_1, r_2, ..., r_q\}, \quad q \in \mathbb{N} \tag{1}$$

Definition 5: ASSIGNMENT is a binary relation between Mem and ROLE.

$$\text{ASSIGNMENT} = \text{ROLE}^T \times \text{Mem} = \begin{bmatrix} r_1 m_1 & r_1 m_2 & ... & r_1 m_p \\ r_2 m_1 & r_2 m_2 & ... & r_2 m_p \\ & ... & & \\ r_q m_1 & r_q m_2 & ... & r_q m_p \end{bmatrix} \tag{2}$$

In (2), $r_i m_j$ $(1 \le i \le q, 1 \le j \le p \quad q, p \in \mathbb{N})$ denotes that role r_i is bound to member m_j.

$$r_i m_j = \begin{cases} 1 & \text{role } r_i \text{ is bound to agent } m_j \\ 0 & \text{otherwise} \end{cases} \tag{3}$$

The Mem, ROLE, and ASSIGNMENT are stored in FIS, and updated by management agent of federation when it performs a planning based on a recipe.

Modeling of Domain Concept. In the open, distributed and heterogeneous VO environment, policy-associated entities, including roles, agents and their behaviors as well as context knowledge, are necessary to be represented at multiple levels of abstraction and to be shared by various agents VO-wide. Ontology of domain concepts is to meet these needs. Domain concepts include classes, properties and their instances. The frame-based ontology language for concept modeling (FOL4CM) is defined in the form of EBNF as follows.

Definition 6:

```
Concept      ::= 'Concept(' ConceptName [SuperClass]
                 {Slot}[Constraint] ')'
SuperClass ::= 'SuperClass(' {SuperClassName}  ')'
Slot         ::= 'Slot('SlotName{FacetName FacetValue}')'
Constraint ::= 'Constraint(' {LogicExpression} ')'
FacetName  ::= val |type |mode |number|derive
                 |restriction |unit
val          ::= 'val(' Constant ')
type         ::= 'type(' [ListOf] {PrimitiveType
                 | ConceptName}')'
mode         ::= 'mode('necessary |typical
                 |derive |converse ')'
number       ::= 'number(' PositiveInteger ')'
derive       ::= 'derive(' Formula | Rule| RuleGroup ')'
```

```
restriction::= 'restriction('Enumeration| Range
                | Limit ')'
unit        ::= 'unit(' MeasureName ')'
```

Take market research virtual organization as an example. Part of concept ontology of agent and management agent of VO (VO-MA) is shown in figure 5.

The domain ontology illustrated in figure 5 can be represented in the form of FOL4CM as follows.

```
Concept( Agent
            Slot(hasName   type   string)
            Slot(ableToPerform type Behavior
                              val ApplicationActivity)
Concept(VO MA         ،
            SuperClass(Agent)
            Slot(ableToPerform type Behavior
                              val NegotiationActivity))
Concept(NegotiationActivity
            SuperClass(Behavior)
            Slot(action type concept
                    val   setStrategy ))
```

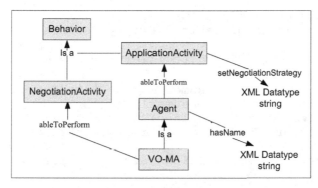

Fig. 5. An example of domain ontology

4.2   Modeling of Policy Specification and Deployment

On the basis of generic policy ontology and application-specific ontology, different levels of policies are established. According to the policy modeling process shown in figure 2, from business requirements to implementable policies, there are three steps: abstract policy modeling, concrete policy modeling and policy instantiation.

Abstract Policy Modeling. The high-level policies are directly derived from business requirements or goals. They are abstract and don't specify the concrete entities (specific subjects, targets of policies) and their properties.

Suppose that in the aforementioned Scenario, there is a business requirement described as follows:

Requirement1: Provide golden quality of service to trustful counterparts (successful transaction number is bigger than three).

This requirement (goal) can be decomposed into two sub-goals under the context of application.

◇ Take compromise negotiation strategy to trustful counterparts;
◇ Set highest precedence to trustful counterparts when assigning role.

These two sub-goals can be articulated as the following policies:

1) When a service consumer negotiates with a trustful service provider, the former sets its negotiation strategy as *compromise*.
2) When a service consumer assigns a role to the candidates (several service providers), it sets the highest precedence (Integer '1') to the service provider who is trustful.

Based on generic policy ontology, the previous policies are defined formally as follows.

```
Policy(P₁ Obligation+
      Triger (ServiceConsumer.MentalState(
                                  BeforeNegotiation))
      Subject (ServiceConsumer)
      Behavior(NegotiationActivity.SetStrategy(
                                  Compromise))
      Constraint (IsTrustful(ServiceProvider)))
Policy(P₂ Obligation+
      Triger(ServiceConsumer.MentalState(AssigningRole))
      Subject (ServiceConsumer)
      Target (ServiceProvider)
      Behavior (ApplicarionActivity.SetPrecedence(1,
                                  ServiceProvider))
      Constraint (IsTrustful(ServiceProvider)))
```

Concrete Policy Modeling. Abstract policy modeling directly reflects the high-level business requirements, but does not take underlying applications into consideration. Based on domain ontology and agent federation model, we can define the role-based concrete policies. The following policies P1-1 and P1-2 are the embodiment of P1.

```
Policy(P1-1 Obligation+
      Triger (VO-MA.MentalState(BeforeNegotiation))
      Subject (VO-MA)
      Behavior(NegotiationActivity.SetStrategy(
                                  Compromise))
      Constraint (IsTrustful(RawDataCollector)))
Policy(P1-2 Obligation+
      Triger (VO-MA.MentalState(BeforeNegotiation))
      Subject (VO-MA)
      Behavior(NegotiationActivity.SetStrategy(
                                  Compromise))
      Constraint (IsTrustful(DataAnalyzer)))
```

Policy Instantiation and Deployment. Before policy distributor distributes policies, it instantiates low-level policy templates (for example, P1-1, P1-2) into implementable policies according to the information of FIS (federation information service). The information includes Mem, ROLE, ASSIGNMENT defined in Section 4.1. Consider the aforementioned Scenario. The ROLE can be represented as:

```
ROLE = (RawDataCollector, DataAnalyzer, DataStorer,
        DataMiningServier, VO-MA)
```

Suppose that Mem and ASSIGNMENT are presented as follows:

$$\text{Mem} = (RDC_1, RDC_2, DA_1, DA_2, DS_1, DS_2, DMS_1, DMS_2, ma)$$

$$\text{ASSIGNMENT} = \begin{bmatrix} 1 & 0 & 0 & 0 & 0 & 0 & 0 & 0 & 0 \\ 0 & 0 & 0 & 1 & 0 & 0 & 0 & 0 & 0 \\ 0 & 0 & 0 & 0 & 1 & 0 & 0 & 0 & 0 \\ 0 & 0 & 0 & 0 & 0 & 0 & 1 & 0 & 0 \\ 0 & 0 & 0 & 0 & 0 & 0 & 0 & 0 & 1 \end{bmatrix}$$

This ASSIGNMENT is equal to the following binary relation set:

```
((RawDataCollector,RDC_1), (DataAnalyzer,DA_2),
 (DataStorer,DS_1), (DataMiningServier,DMS_1), (VO-MA,ma))
```

Therefore, P_{1-1} and P_{1-2} are instantiated as:

```
Policy(P_{1-1-Ins} Obligation+
      Triger (ma.MentalState(BeforeNegotiation))
      Subject (ma)
      Behavior(NegotiationActivity.SetStrategy(
                                    Compromise))
      Constraint (IsTrustful(RDC_1)))
Policy(P_{1-2-Ins} Obligation+
      Triger (ma.MentalState(BeforeNegotiation))
      Subject (ma)
      Behavior(NegotiationActivity.SetStrategy(
                                    Compromise))
      Constraint (IsTrustful(DA_2)))
```

The implementable policies $p_{1-1-Ins}$ and $P_{1-2-Ins}$ are distributed to specific agents who are enforcers of policies (i.e., ma). Generally speaking, obligation policies are distributed to subjects of policies, while authorization policies are distributed to targets of policies. The case study of authorization policies is not presented in this paper.

5   Breakthrough and Conclusions

The main contribution of this paper is: a model of ontology-based, policy-driven control framework is proposed to deal with the challenge about how to control the behaviors of agents who govern web services in the VO environment, according to the high-level business requirements. In this model, the role-based modeling and role assignment mechanism meet the dynamic nature of agent federation.

Like Rei and KAoS, this model is supported by ontology. The difference is that our method focuses on how to model high-level business requirements (goals) to implementable policies for regulating agents' behaviors, including discovery, negotiation, cooperation and coordination, etc., which is not treated with by Rei or KAoS.

There are many challenges to be coped with to make our framework more intelligent. One of them is how to automatically refine high-level abstract policies to low-level concrete policies. In current version, this part of work is done by human designers who model the policies. Our further objective is to make automated refinement of policies a reality based on domain ontology and policy refinement templates. This is one of our future research topics.

References

1. Francisco Curbera, Matthew Duftler, et al. Unraveling the Web Services Web: An Introduction to SOAP, WSDL, and UDDI. IEEE INTERNET COMPUTING, 86-93, March/April 2002.
2. Zambonelli, F., Jennings, N. R., et al, M. (2001) Agent-Oriented Software Engineering for Internet Applications, in Omicini, A., Zambonelli, F., Klush, M. and Tolksdorf, R., Eds. Co-ordination of Internet Agents, pages pp. 326-346. Springer Verlag.
3. N. Damianou, N. Dulay, E. Lupu, M. Sloman: The Ponder Policy Specification Language. In proceedings of Workshop on Policies for Distributed Systems and Networks (POLICY 2001). Springer-Verlag, LNCS 1995, Bristol, UK, (2001)
4. L. Kagal, et al: A Policy Language for Pervasive Computing Environment. In Proceedings of IEEE Fourth International Workshop on Policy (Policy 2003). Lake Como, Italy, 4-6 June, Los Alamitos, CA: IEEE Computer Society, pp. 63-76, (2003).
5. Uszok, J. Bradshaw et al., KAoS policy and domain services: Toward a description-logic approach to policy representation, deconfliction, and enforcement. In Proceedings of IEEE Fourth International Workshop on Policy (Policy 2003). Lake Como, Italy, 4-6 June, Los Alamitos, CA: IEEE Computer Society, pp. 93-98, (2003)
6. G. Tonti, J.M. Bradshaw, et al.Semantic Web Languages for Policy Representation and Reasoning: A Comparison of KAoS, Rei, and Ponder. Proc. Second International Semantic Web Conference (ISWC2003). October,2003.
7. Gao, Ji, et al., Agent cooperation based control integration by activity-sharing and joint intention. Journal of Computer Science and Technology, v 17, n 3, May, 2002, p 331-339.
8. HU Jun, GAO Ji, LIAO Bei-shui, CHEN Jiu-jun. An Infrastructure for Managing and Controlling Agent Cooperation. To appear in Proceedings of The Eighth International Conference on CSCW in Design, May 26-28, 2004, Xiamen, PR China.
9. GAO Ji, WANG Jin.ABFSC:AN AGENTS-BASED FRAMEWORK FOR SOFTWARE COMPOSITION.Chinese Journal of Computers, 1999, l22(10):1050-1058.
10. Zhou Bin. The Systematism of Assistant Service for Agents (pp.9-24) [Thesis of Master degree].Hangzhou:Zhejiang University, 2004.

An Approach to Dynamically Reconfiguring Service-Oriented Applications from a Business Perspective*

Jianwu Wang[1,2], Yanbo Han[1], Jing Wang[1], and Gang Li[1]

[1] Institute of Computing Technology, Chinese Academy of Sciences, 100080, Beijing, China
[2] Graduate School of the Chinese Academy of Sciences, 100080, Beijing, China
{wjw,yhan,wangjing,gangli}@software.ict.ac.cn

Abstract. This paper proposes an approach to dynamically reconfiguring service-oriented applications from a business perspective: CAFISE$_{adapt}$, which defines both business-level and software-level change operations to respectively express changes in the business domain and the software domain. Utilizing the convergence of these two level change operations, the approach expects application changes can be automatically coherent with business changes. Through hiding software-level technical details of applications that are necessary for traditional change operations, the business-level change operations can be used by business users to dynamically modify service-oriented application instances, which can realize the dynamic reconfiguration of service-oriented applications in a straightforward way to timely adapt to business requirement changes. This approach has been applied and validated in the project FLAME2008.

1 Introduction

Service-oriented applications are constructed by composing needed Web services to meet different business requirements. During the execution of a service-oriented application, new business requirements may be presented, which would cause the application impracticable [1]. So, dynamic reconfiguration of service-oriented applications is necessary to realize that application changes are coherent with business.

The traditional dynamic reconfiguration approaches are mainly from the software perspective: Business users need to report the business requirements changes to IT professionals, ask them to specify which application changes should be made to respond to the business requirement changes and modify application instances using pre-offered change operations. This kind of reconfiguration approaches need the communications between business users and IT professionals, which usually causes that application changes lag behind the rapid business requirement changes. Moreover, the abundance and dynamism of resources in the service environment make it difficult for the modifiers to know the exact information of the whole candidate Web services during the course of dynamic reconfiguration.

To solve the above problems, we present an approach to dynamically reconfiguring service-oriented applications from a business perspective: CAFISE$_{adapt}$, which defines software-level and business-level change operations, and these two-level change operations are correlated by convergent relations. Utilizing the approach, business users

---

* The research work is supported by the National Natural Science Foundation of China under Grant No. 60173018, the Key Scientific and Technological Program for the Tenth Five-Year Plan of China under Grant No. 2001BA904B07.

C.-H. Chi and K.-Y. Lam (Eds.): AWCC 2004, LNCS 3309, pp. 357–368, 2004.

can use business-level change operations to express changes in the business domain, the relevant software-level change operations expressing corresponding changes in the software domain can be automatically got according to the convergent relations. After the execution of software-level change operations, corresponding changes in the software domain will be realized. Besides, this approach can automatically specify needed Web services through the convergent relations, which reduces the difficulty of modification comparing with traditional approaches.

The rest of the paper is organized as follows: Section 2 introduces some concepts of CAFISE approach which is the foundation of CAFISE$_{adapt}$ approach. The CAFISE$_{adapt}$ approach is detailedly illustrated in section 3 and its implement in project FLAME2008 is presented in section 4. Section 5 discusses the related work. At last, the conclusion and further work are presented.

2   CAFISE Approach

The CAFISE$_{adapt}$ approach is part of our CAFISE (Convergent Approach for Information Systems Evolution) approach [2]. The core idea of CAFISE approach is the convergence of the business domain and the software domain, expecting user's requirements can be coherent with service-oriented applications during the course of application's construction and execution through the convergence, which can support just-in-time construction and dynamic reconfiguration of service-oriented applications from the business perspective. Just-in-time construction and dynamic reconfiguration are two aspects of CAFISE approach, and respectively denoted as CAFISE$_{jit}$ and CAFISE$_{adapt}$: CAFISE$_{jit}$ represents the approach supporting just-in-time construction of service-oriented applications and enables business users to rapidly construct new applications in a business-end programming way [3], which corresponds to new business requirements at the phase of application construction; CAFISE$_{adapt}$ represents the approach supporting dynamic reconfiguration of service-oriented applications and enables business users to dynamically reconfigure applications to adapt to business requirements changes, which corresponds to business requirement changes at the phase of application execution.

In CAFISE approach, a service-oriented application consists of three parts: business-level VINCA application [3] constructed through composing needed *business services* [4], software-level Darnel application [5] constructed through composing needed Web services, and convergent relations that correlate the two level applications organically (Fig. 1). Business services are defined by business domain experts according to different industry standards, and each service can fulfill a certain business function. Comparing Web services, business services comprise semantic information which is described with DAML-S [6] and are aggregations of Web services which have the same functionality and behavior semantics. Through hiding the technical details of Web services and encapsulating semantic information, business services can be regarded as business-level representation of service resources and be understood and operated by business users. Let's take an example of a business service and its corresponding Web services: *WeatherForecast* is a business service that can forecast weather, whose information is listed in table1, and related Web services are listed in table2.

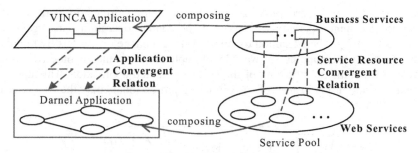

Fig. 1. Illustration of Two-level Applications in CAFISE Approach

Table 1. *WeatherForecast* Business Service

Basic Information		PublicService.WeatherForecast	
Business operation	Input	date	http://flame/KgBase/Weather.daml#Date
		city	http://flame/KgBase/Weather.daml#City
	Output	maxTemperature	http://flame/KgBase/Weather.daml#HighTemperature
		minTemperature	http://flame/KgBase/Weather.daml#LowTemperature
Non-functional constraints	Cost	[0.1￥, 1￥]	
	Provider	Beijing weather forecast bureau/ China weather forecast bureau/...	

Table 2. Web Services Related with *WeatherForecast* Business Service

Invocation Information		http://xxx.com/weatherforecast.wsdl	http://xx.com/weatherforecast.wsdl	...
Non-functional constraints	Cost	0.6￥	0.9￥	
	Provider	Beijing weather forecast bureau	China weather forecast bureau	
	...			

3   CAFISE$_{adapt}$ Approach

In this section, we will firstly introduce the principle of CAFISE$_{adapt}$ approach. Then we will illustrate the three main parts of this approach: change operations at business-level, change operations at software-level and the convergent relations between above two level change operations. At last, the usage of this approach will be demonstrated.

3.1   Principle of CAFISE$_{adapt}$ Approach

The convergence concept is firstly presented by David Taylor at 1995 to bridge the gap between the business domain and the software domain, expecting to construct software system directly through business designing and enable software to adapt to ever-changing business [7]. But the previous researches [8, 9] are mainly focused on how to utilize convergence to construct application basing on business model. Seldom researches are done to study how to take advantage of convergence to improve the application's adaptability. CAFISE$_{adapt}$ approach can realize the coherence between business-level application changes and software-level application changes through the convergence of two level change operations, which expects to realize the coherence between business requirement changes and application changes (Fig. 2).

According to CAFISE$_{adapt}$ approach, a business user firstly modifies his business-level application instance using business-level change operations; secondly the used business-level change operations are automatically transformed to corresponding software-level change operations by parsing the change operation convergent relations. At last, through the execution of software-level change operations by modification engine, the corresponding software-level application instance is modified, which eventually realize the modification of the service-oriented application. This approach can make business users instead of traditional IT professionals play the role of application modifier.

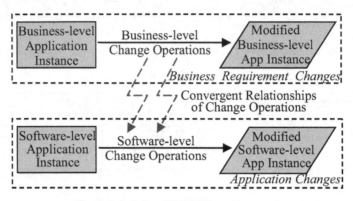

Fig. 2. Principle of CAFISE$_{adapt}$ Approach

3.2   Change Operations at Business-Level

The change operations at business-level are defined basing on the survey of business users' modification requirements, and each change operation corresponds directly to a certain typical business modification request. Besides, comparing with the software-level change operations, the objects of these business-level change operations are not concrete Web services but business encapsulation of them, for concrete Web services are too complex for business users to understand and manage directly. For example, it is difficult for business users to know which Web services in the current service environment can be added in a software-level application instance to meet their request changes. In this way, business-level change operations can conform to the business users' usage pattern and be easily understood and used by business users.

The business-level change operations on VINCA application instances are defined in interface format, which include two parts: change operation command (denoted as *OP*) and change operation parameter (denoted as *para*). The format of a change operation is like *Op(para1, para2,....)*, *Op* represents the semantic of an change operation and *para* represents the concrete target object of the change operation.

The change operations on VINCA application can be classified to following four types according to the different aspects of modification:

1. **Modification of business process's control structure:** including adding and deleting a certain business service, modifying a business service's location in business process, modifying a business process's control condition.
2. **Modification of business process's message associations:** including adding and deleting a message association between two business services.

3. **Modification of business service's properties:** including modifying a business service's non-functional properties, a business service's input values and a business service's output settings.

4. **Modification of application instance's execution state:** including pausing and resuming application instance's execution.

The above change operations can modify every aspects of business process and business service, through the composition use of different change operations we can realize the transformation from a certain valid VINCA application instance to another, therefore the completeness of these change operations can be guaranteed. As for the minimality of the change operation set, because we define these operations according to user-friendliness, a certain degree of redundancy can be permitted and user can do modification in his preferable manner.

3.3 Change Operations at Software-Level

Change operations at software-level are defined based on the characters of software-level application. Software-level change operations concern the software modification details which are normally too specialized for business users to master. Research results of [10, 11] can used to ensure the minimality of change operations and the correctness of new software-level applications.

The software-level change operations on Darnel application instances are also defined in interface format, mainly including the adding and deleting operations on the constituent elements of a Darnel application instance, such as Web services, the control and data associations between Web services. The modifications of application instance's execution state and the operation on Web service resources are also included. The detail information of these change operations can be found in [12].

3.4 Convergence of Two Level Change Operations

Utilizing above business-level and software-level change operations, we can realize the modification of VINCA application instances and Darnel application instances respectively. In order to transform the changes in the business domain to changes in the software domain automatically and correctly, XML-based convergent relations between these two level change operations are designed by IT professionals in advance to depict the correlations between these two change operation sets. Then the software-level change operations corresponding to the used business-level change operations by business users can be got according to the convergent relations.

Each business-level change operation can bring some business-level application instance changes. From these business-level application instance changes, corresponding software-level application instance changes can be got according to the application convergent relations defined in CAFISE model [2], and IT professionals can specify which software-level change operations are needed to bring the corresponding software-level application instance changes. Then these specified software-level change operations have convergent relations with the business-level change operation for they can bring the coherent changes of two-level application instances. After analyzing all the pre-defined business-level change operations in this way, the whole convergent relations can be got.

The convergent relations are described in XML through a set of convergent units (Fig. 3), and each convergent unit depicts which software-level change operations are corresponded to a business-level change operation. These convergent units can be classified into two categories: simple convergent unit expressing one-to-one relation, complex convergent unit expressing one-to-many relationship between business-level and software-level change operations. A complex convergent unit is composed of a set of simple convergent units whose business-level change operations should be the same. Each simple convergent unit comprises two parts: convergent relations between change operation command and convergent relations between corresponding parameters. These convergent relations of change operation command (parameters) are minimal constituents, comprising two parts: business-level change operation command (parameters), software-level change operation command (parameters).

The above convergent relationships only denote the mapping relations of two level change operations' meta-information. When using these change operations, concrete value are assigned to the parameters (we call the change operations with concrete parameter *change operation instances*). Special programs should be designed to get software-level concrete parameters from business-level concrete parameters, for example, to get corresponding Web service set from a concrete business service ID.

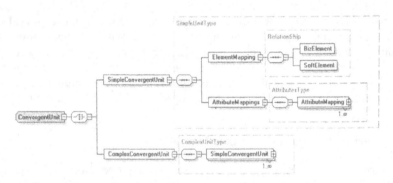

Fig. 3. XML Annotation of Convergent Relations between Two Level Change Operations

3.5   Usage of CAFISE$_{adapt}$ Approach

The usage of CAFISE$_{adapt}$ approach consists of two periods (Fig.4): preparation period and application period. In preparation period, IT professionals firstly define business-level change operations according to typical business modification requirements; secondly define software-level change operations according to the characteristics of software-level applications; lastly specify each business-level change operation's corresponding software-level change operations, which eventually result in these two level change operations' convergent relations. In application period, a business user modifies his VINCA application instance through selecting needed business-level change operations, and then the selected business-level change operation instances with concrete parameters can be recorded. By parsing change operations' convergent relations, these business-level change operation instances can be transformed into corresponding software-level change operation instances. With the modification engine executing each software-level change operation instances, corresponding Darnel application instance can be modified.

Once finishing the definition of change operations and their convergent relations in preparation period by IT professionals, these general change operations can always be used to dynamically modify different VINCA application instances. So we can see that through the prior work of IT professionals, the difficulty of subsequent modification is reduced and can be handled by common business users.

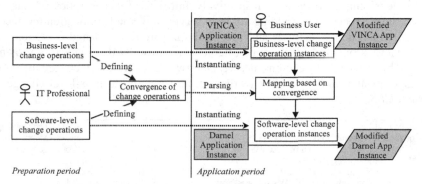

Fig. 4. Different Periods of the Usage of CAFISE$_{adapt}$ Approach

4 Implementation

The CAFISE$_{adapt}$ approach has been implemented in project FLAME2008 [13], expecting to develop service-oriented applications that provide integrated and personalized information services to the public during the Olympic Games 2008. We will validate the feasibility and features of CAFISE$_{adapt}$ approach by respectively explaining how to prepare and apply the approach in the following subsections.

4.1 Preparation of CAFISE$_{adapt}$ Approach

In this subsection, we will illustrate how to define the change operations and the convergent relations through a concrete change operation.

New business requirements may be usually brought forward during the execution of business-level application and request add proper service resources to application instance to meet the business requirement change, so adding service to application instance is a typical modification request. As a business service represents a common business functionality, different business users need set constraints to business service to express their different personalized requests, for example some business users may prefer 'China Weather Bureau' as the *WeatherForast* business service's provider, yet some other business users may prefer 'Beijing Weather Bureau'. Therefore we define the change operation *AddBS(BSID, BSCons, LocAtVINCA)*. This operation's command is *AddBS* and has three parameters: *BSID, BSCons* and *LocAtVINCA*, respectively representing the business service to be added, the constraints set by business users and location at VINCA application.

The VINCA application instance's change that *AddBS* can bring is a new business service inserted at a position that still not executed in the VINCA application instance's control flow. According to the two-level application convergent relations defined in CAFISE model, coherent change of Darnel application instance can be got, namely a corresponding new Web service inserted at corresponding position. Through analyzing the pre-defined software-level change operations, we know that two software-level change operations can implement this change of Darnel application instance: *SelWSByCons(WSSet,WSCons)* and *AddWS(WSUrl, LocAtDarenl)*. The two software-level change operations respectively fulfill the functionalities of selecting the suitable Web service and adding the Web service to Darnel application instance.

Based on the above analyses and specified software-level change operations, the convergent relations of *AddBS* can be established, whose XML fragment is shown in Fig. 5. The convergent relations depict that two software-level change operation *SelWSByCons* and *AddWS* have convergent relations with business-level change operation *AddBS*.

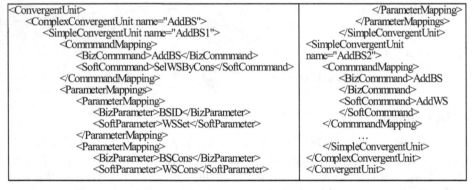

Fig. 5. XML Fragment of the Business-level Change Operation *AddBS*'s Convergent Relations

4.2   Application of CAFISE_adapt Approach

With defining the whole set of change operations and realizing them through programs, the CAFISE_adapt approach is implemented as a tool in the CAFISE framework (Fig. 6). Business-level change operations can be used through selecting proper menu items in graphical user interfaces. Now, we will illustrate how business users can achieve the dynamic reconfiguration of service-oriented application through a simplified scenario in the project FLAME2008 according to this approach.

Mr. George wants to travel Beijing during the Olympic Games 2008. Based on his travel schedule, he can construct his VINCA application by composing need business services in graphical interfaces. But during his traveling at Beijing, he hears that the recent weather in Beijing is often rainy, so he wants to add weather forecast functionality to his running traveling application in order to know the weather information timely. But as a business user, he doesn't have much knowledge about which Web services can provide the weather forecast functionality and how to invoke them, so he can't dynamically reconfigure his application by himself according to traditional approaches.

Utilizing CAFISE$_{adapt}$ approach, he needn't know the concrete information about Web services. After pausing his VINCA application instance, Mr. George can look up proper business service at Service Community in a graphical user interface. Supposing he finds business service *WeatherForecast* at the public service category, then he can add the business service to proper location in his VINCA application, and set some constraints to express his personalized requirements, for example, the provider should be 'Beijing Weather Bureau'. After the above operations, the work of Mr. George has finished and a business-level change operation instance is created: *AddBS(WeatherForecast, BSCons, LocAtVINCA)*.

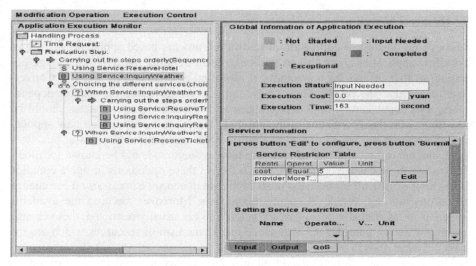

Fig. 6. Dynamic Reconfiguration Tool in the CAFISE Framework

The business-level change operation instance should be mapped to corresponding software-level change operation instances so that proper Web service can be selected and added to Darnel application instance. Fig. 5 depicts the convergent relations of the *AddBS* change operation which is designed by IT professionals in advance. The convergent relations are represented through a complex convergent unit which includes two simple convergent units, meaning that the *AddBS* operation is related with two software-level change operations. By parsing the convergent relations, corresponding software-level change operation instances can be gotten which are shown as follows:

- *SelWSByCons (WeatherForcastServiceSet, WSCons)*
  Select most suitable Web service according to user's constraints: the *WeatherForcastServiceSet* parameter depicts the set of Web services that can achieve weather forecast functionality; the *WSCons* parameter depicts the corresponding Web service constraints that the provider should be 'Beijing Weather Bureau'. The result is denoted as *WSUrl*.

- *AddWS(WSUrl, LocAtDarenl)*
  Add the selected Web service to the running Darnel application at the corresponding location.

After software-level modification engine executes the above software-level change operations respectively, the Web service is added to the running Darnel Application. Then the reconfiguration course is finished and Mr. Georges can resume his application and use the weather forecasting service in his application.

This modification scenario depicts that how business users can modify his VINCA application instance according to CAFISE$_{adapt}$ approach. The menu items in Fig. 6 depict the possible business-level change operations at the execution moment and business users can implement modification through selecting proper menu items that express his modification requirements, without seeking help from IT professionals.

5 Related Work

Research on dynamic modification of traditional process-based applications, such as workflow applications, emphasizes particularly on defining the minimal change operation set that ensures the correctness of modified application [10, 11, 14]. Correctness means that the information of new application including the control dependences, data dependences, time dependences and instance execution states should be consistent with the information of the old one. This is necessary for the new application's execution but not in direct association with requirement changes at business-level, and the technical details of software-level resources should be known for modifiers to use these change operations, which makes these operations' usage a complex labor. So it is difficult for business users to use them and we can classify these change operations into software-level change operations. Moreover, because the available resources in traditional process-based applications are usually restricted, these change operations do not consider the abundance and dynamism of resources which are the main characteristics in the service environment.

The related research on dynamic modification of service-oriented applications is still not much. The following paragraphs will discuss two representative works in this research field:

DY$_{flow}$ [15] supports the dynamic modification of service-oriented applications through dynamically modifying business rules according to the changes of business environment in order to invoke most suitable services at runtime. But this is only a part of modifiable contents and many other modifiable aspects are not supported.

In eFlow [16], the ad-hoc modification approach need the modifier firstly defines target process and verifies whether the target process is consistent with the source process. If it is consistent, the instant execution state of source process will be transferred to target process. This approach considers the dynamism characteristic of services and supports many aspects of modification. When users want to add e-services in eflow which are managed by e-services platforms to his application instance, he need to define service node through specifying needed service functionality and service selection rules by himself. Although having the similar dynamic service discovery functionality with the business services in CAFISE$_{adapt}$ approach, the service nodes in eflow should be defined by user himself from scratch during the course of dynamic modification, yet business services can be gotten directly from service community. So the request for modifier's ability of CAFISE$_{adapt}$ approach is reduced comparing the approach in eflow. Besides, the description of service in eflow is not based

based on a united semantic infrastructure which is used in CAFISE$_{adapt}$ approach, so service providers have to describe their services in their own ways, which will result in the difficulty of service selection for modifiers.

6 Conclusion and Future Work

As a part of CAFISE approach, CAFISE$_{adapt}$ approach defines user-friendly business-level change operations on the basis of correctness-ensuring software-level change operations, and these two-level change operations are correlated by convergent relations. Compared with change operations defined in traditional dynamic modification approaches, the objects of business-level change operations are not software-level resources but the business encapsulation of them. So the business-level change operations hide software technical details. This approach reduces the difficulties of modification and business users can modify his business application instances using the business-level change operations in a straightforward way to timely adapt to business requirement changes. This approach reflects a trend in software field: IT professionals concern the infrastructure and enabling techniques of dynamic and open Internet environment; while it is business professionals that concern the rapid (re)configuration of resources at business-level.

The approach is still an ongoing research whose goal is really making dynamic reconfiguration of service-oriented applications usable for business users. To achieve this goal, many aspects are to be improved in future, such as change operations that can modify the application's global constraints, the pre-condition and post-condition of each change operation and the change impact analysis at business-level.

References

1. L. Zeng, D. Flaxer, et al. PLM $_{flow}$-Dynamic Business Process Composition and Execution by Rule Inference. Technologies for E-Services: Third International Workshop (TES2002). Hong Kong, China, August 2002, pages 141-150.
2. Y. Han, Z. Zhao, et al. CAFISE: An Approach Enabling On-Demand Configuration of Service Grid Applications. Journal of Computer Science and Technology. Vol.18, No.4, 2003, pages 484-494.
3. Y. Han, H. Geng, et al. VINCA - A Visual and Personalized Business-level Composition Language for Chaining Web-based Services. The First International Conference on Service-Oriented Computing (ICSOC2003). Trento, Italy, 2003, pages 165-177.
4. Z. Zhao, Y. Han, et al. A Service Virtualization Mechanism supporting Business User Programming. Accepted by Journal of Computer Research and Development (in Chinese), 2004.
5. CAFISE group. Darnel Language Specification. Technical Report. Software Division, ICT, CAS, 2002.
6. DAML-S Coalition. DAML-S versions 0.9. Available at http://www.daml.org/services/daml-s/0.9/, 2003.
7. D. Taylor. Business Engineering with Object Technology. John Wiley & Sons. 1995.
8. R. Hubert. Convergent Architecture: Building Model-Driven J2EE Systems with UML. John Wiley & Sons. 2002.
9. J. Koehler, G. Tirenni, S. Kumaran. From Business Process Model to Consistent Implementation. The 6th IEEE International Enterprise Distributed Object Computing Conference. Lausanne, Switzerland, 2002, pages 96-106.

10. M. Reichert and P. Dadam. ADEPT$_{flex}$ – Supporting Dynamic Changes of Workflows without Losing Control. Journal of Intelligent Information Systems - Special Issue on Workflow Management. Vol.10, No.2, 1998, pages 93-129.
11. S. Sadiq and M. Orlowska. Architectural Considerations for Systems Supporting Dynamic Workflow Modification. Workshop of Software Architectures for Business Process management at the CaiSE'99, Heidelberg, June 1999.
12. G. Li, J. Wang, et al. MASON: A Model for Adapting Service-oriented Grid Applications. The Second International Workshop on Grid and Cooperative Computing (GCC2003). Shanghai, China, 2003, pages 99-107.
13. B. Holtkamp, R. Gartmann, and Y. Han. FLAME2008-Personalized Web Services for the Olympic Games 2008 in Beijing. Conference of eChallenges 2003. Bologna, Italy, Oct, 2003.
14. F. Casati. Models, Semantics, and Formal Methods for the design of Workflows and their Exceptions. Ph.D. Thesis. Dipartimento di Elettronicae Informazione, Politecnico di Milano, Milano, Italy, 1996-1998.
15. L. Zeng, B. Benatallah, et al. Flexible Composition of Enterprise Web Services. International Journal of Electronic Commerce and Business Media. Vol.13, No.2, 2003.
16. F. Casati and M. Shan. Dynamic and Adaptive Composition of E-services. Information Systems. Vol.26, No.3, 2001, pages 143-163.

Dynamically Reconfiguring Sitemaps Using RDF*

Huijae Lee and Sang Bong Yoo

School of Computer Science, Inha University, Incheon, Korea
Fax: 82-32-874-1435
cyberelf@islabs.inha.ac.kr, syoo@inha.ac.kr

Abstract. This paper presents extracting, storing, and applying the metadata and ontology of product data. In this paper, the design and tooling information included in STEP-NC files is focused as an example. By analyzing the relationship among the product data, the RDFS schema is designed first. Based on the schema, metadata is extracted and stored in RDF files. As an application of the stored metadata, we can reconfigure the sitemap of product data repositories. The users can select the view that he or she is interested in (e.g., the views from products, tools, persons, or a current location). The sitemaps also can be constructed from current location dynamically. With such various and dynamic views of product data repository, the users can access the specific data more effectively.

1 Introduction

As the Internet prevails all over the world, requirements to handle the data on the Web have been increased rapidly. The Semantic Web, which was initiated by W3C, is an effort to capture more meaning of the data on the Web [1, 2, 4, 6, 8, 9]. RDF (Resource Description Framework) and RDFS (RDF Schema) are the primary tools to serialize the metadata from the Web, which enable software agents or human can understand the contents. XML was introduced to enhance the syntax and semantics of Web data over HTML by using meaningful tags with structured schemata. For example, by using XML we can represent the same person as an employee in one place or as a customer in another place. However, XML has a limited capability to capture the interrelationship among objects. RDF and RDFS have been introduced in order to complement XML with rich semantics of the relationship among objects.

One issue in realizing the virtual enterprise is how to support the exchange of product information among application systems or personnel involved in the virtual activities. This is important to obtain the agility for improving the competitiveness of firms. There are two types of data that the enterprises need to properly manage, i.e., business data (e.g., accounting and personnel data) and product data (e.g., CAD and CAM data). Many modern enterprises have enough experience in dealing with business data, but it is not the case for product data, in particular when the product data need to be exchanged throughout the whole product life cycle with systems dealing with the business data. Product data used to be managed only by the design and production activities. However, for the virtual enterprises the product data need to be used in later stages of product life cycle (e.g., Web catalog and service manual) [7].

Differently from business data, product data have complex semantics and thus are not properly exchanged by different application programs [7]. Even though some

---

* This research was supported by Inha University.

C.-H. Chi and K.-Y. Lam (Eds.): AWCC 2004, LNCS 3309, pp. 369–373, 2004.

neutral formats of product data have been developed by standard organizations, translating them among various application programs still needs the comprehensive understanding of the complex semantics. Recently, it is widely recognized that capturing more knowledge is the next step to overcome the current difficulties on sharing product data [5].

This paper presents extracting, storing, and applying the metadata and ontology of product data. In this paper, the design and tooling information included in STEP-NC files is focused as an example. By analyzing the relationship among the product data, the RDFS schema is designed first. Based on the schema, metadata is extracted and stored in XML files. As an application of the stored ontology and metadata, we can reconfigure the sitemap of product data repositories. The users can select the view that he or she is interested in (e.g., the views from products, tools, persons, or a current location). With such various views of a product data repository, the users can access the specific data more effectively.

2 Reconfigurable Sitemaps

Sitemaps usually have hierarchical structures. However, as you can see the RDF schema, the structure of the schema for product data is a general graph that includes cycles. For drawing this graph as a sitemap, we have several choices to select a node to be the root node. According to the selection of the root node, different hierarchical structures result as in Fig. 1. There are 3 different structures in Fig. 1; each of them starts from nodes Model, Tool, and Person, respectively. Because different users may have different views of interests, it would be very useful to enable the users to select a particular node as the root in a sitemap.

The algorithm for reconfiguring sitemaps from RDF schema is basically same as the level search of graphs. The algorithm for reconfiguring sitemaps is as follows. Because the algorithm traverses each node only once, the complexity of the algorithm is O(n).

> **Algorithm** Reconfiguring Sitemaps
>   **Input**: RDF Schema, Starting node
>   **Output**: Hierarchical Sitemap
> **Procedure**
>   Initialize a queue and a sitemap
>   Insert the Starting node into the queue and the sitemap
>   While (queue is not empty)
>   Dequeue a node from the queue
>   Mark the node as visited and add it into the sitemap
>   For each properties of the node
>   If (it is not marked as visited)
>   Add it to the sitemap
>   Enqueue it into the queue

3 Prototype of Product Data Repository

A prototype of product data repository has been implemented and the reconfigurable sitemaps have been applied with example data. The overall architecture of the prototype is depicted in Fig. 2. Because the product data are usually specified in design files, we analyze standard design files (i.e., STEP files) and extract metadata from them. Extracted metadata are stored in RDF files and analyzed for reconfiguring sitemaps. The users can use Web browsers to navigate the product data repository.

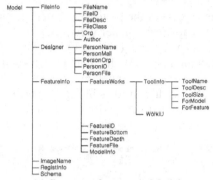

(a) Structure from node Model.

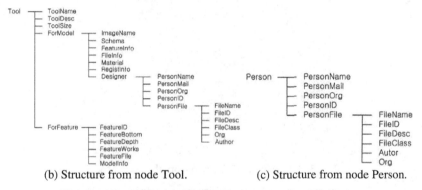

(b) Structure from node Tool.   (c) Structure from node Person.

Fig. 1. Different structures of RDF model from various nodes

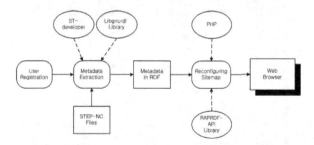

Fig. 2. Architecture of the prototype of a product data repository

In order to handle STEP and RDF files the following libraries are used in the prototype:

a) ST-Developer: A commercial tool from Steptools Inc. It analyzes STEP files and extracts metadata from them.

b) IsaViz: RDF generator and viewer from W3C. It verifies and tests RDF files.

c) libgnurdf: RDF tool from gnu. It supports C programming for generating RDF files and adding data to them.
d) RAPRDF-API: It generates and extracting data from RDF files with php programming.
e) Others: php 4.2.3 and VisualStudio

Fig. 3 depicts a screen capture of the prototype. After the user logged in, he or she can select the type of sitemaps (e.g., model view, tool view, and person view). The screen captured in Fig. 3 is an example of model view. When the user click the ImageName (i.e., 20021313oh.jpg in Fig. 3), the image file is on the browser as in Fig. 4. In Fig. 4, we can see a link named "From Here". When this link is clicked, the sitemap from the current location is displayed as in Fig. 4. This is an example of dynamic sitemap that draws a hierarchical structure of data from the current location. For dynamic sitemap the same algorithm can be applied as for reconfigurable sitemaps.

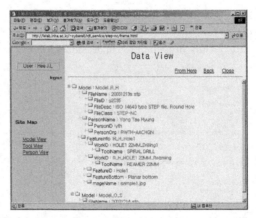

Fig. 3. An example of sitemap from the node Model

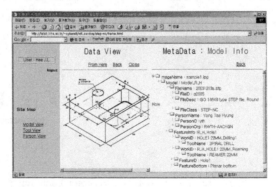

Fig. 4. An example of dynamic sitemap

4   Conclusion

As an application of metadata and ontology represented in RDF and RDFS, respectively, reconfigurable and dynamic sitemaps are presented in this paper. In virtual enterprise environments, there are mainly two types of data, i.e., business data and engineering data. As for the business data we have enough experience to organize and handle them effectively. However, because the structures of engineering data are usually general graphs including cycles, representing their structure hierarchically is not trivial. According to the interests of the users different views of sitemaps are more helpful.

A simple algorithm has been presented to provide different sitemaps to the users for product data repositories. The same algorithm can be applied for generating a dynamic sitemap that draws the structure form the current location dynamically. The reconfigurable and dynamic sitemaps enable the user can access the information more effectively that he or she is looking for. A prototype of product data repository that supports the reconfigurable and dynamic sitemaps has been implemented and presented. The contribution of this paper can be summarized as follows.

- Models the metadata and ontology in RDF and RDFS, respectively, for data repositories.
- Presents an algorithm that generates reconfigurable and dynamic sitemaps for data repositories.
- Implements and presents a prototype of data repositories that supports the reconfigurable and dynamic sitemaps.

Prospected application areas of the proposed system are almost all data repositories with complicated structures and relationship among stored data. Most engineering data repositories (e.g., CAD, CAM, e-manufacturing systems, GIS, LBS, real-time systems, monitoring systems, and tracking systems) have these characteristics. In order to be more powerful, it needs to be extended with various development tools. Novice users may have difficulties to model the metadata and ontology in RDF and RDFS, respectively. Some user-friendly designed GUI tools could make the system more effective.

References

1. Tim Berners-Lee, J. Hendler, and Ora Lassila, "The Semantic Web – A new form of Web content that is meaningful to computers will unleash a revolution of new possibilities," Scientific American, May 2001.
2. Stefan Decker et al., "The Semantic Web: The Roles of XML and RDF," IEEE Internet Computing, Vol 4(5), pp. 63-74, Sept/Oct 2000.
3. M. Hardwick, D. Spooner, T. Rando and K. C. Morris, "Sharing manufacturing information in virtual enterprises," Communications of the ACM 39(2), 46-54, 1996.
4. J. Kang and J. Naughton, "On Schema Matching with Opaque Column Names and Data Values," Proceedings of the ACM SIGMOD International Conference on Management of Data, pp. 205-216, June 2003.
5. J. Liebowitz, Knowledge management handbook (CRC Press, New York), 1999.
6. B. McBride, "Jena: a semantic Web toolkit," IEEE Internet Computing, Vol. 6, Issue 6, pp. 55-59, Nov/Dec 2002.
7. A. McKay, M. Bloor and A. de Pennington, "A framework for product data," IEEE Transactions on Knowledge and Data Engineering 8(5), 825-838, 1996.
8. A. Sheth, "Managing Semantic Content for the Web," IEEE Internet Computing, Vol. 6, Issue 4, pp. 80-87, July/Aug 2002.
9. Sang Bong Yoo, In Han Kim, "Application of Active Real-Time Objects and Rules in Semantic Web," Lecture Notes in Computer Science, Vol. 2822, September 2003.

A General Model
for Heterogeneous Web Services Integration

Wei Zhang[1,2], Shangfen Guo[3], and Dan Ma[1]

[1] Huazhong University of Science and Technology, 430074 Hubei, China
[2] Wuhan Ordnance N.C.O. Academy of PLA, 430074 Hubei, China
[3] Navy University of Engineering, 430033 HuBei, China
msj0810@21cn.com

Abstract. A General Integration Model of Web Services is presented in this paper to solve heterogeneous Web Services integration provided by different sellers. By use of transforming and coordinating mechanisms, services are presented to be a uniform general service for users, which efficiently provides a general mechanism to integrate a large number of heterogeneous Web Services.

1 Introduction

Web Service[1] proposes a service-oriented paradigm for computing in which distributed loosely coupled services. However, the actual Web Services technology does not present perfect solution for heterogeneous Web Services integration provided by different sellers. Researches as WSFL[2], XLANG[3].etc. mainly established XML-based standards, and defined primitive for Web Service integration which makes Web Service cooperating automatically. These researches do not directly solve services' heterogeneity problems and provide well transaction support for loose-couple Web Services integration as well. Aiming for this problem, a General Integration Model of Web Services (GIMWS) is presented in this paper. By use of transforming and coordinating Web Services in the model, Web Services are presented to be a uniform general Web Service for users, which efficiently provides a general mechanism to integrate a large number of heterogeneous Web Services.

This paper's organization is: the GIMWS model's structure is discussed in section 2. Section 3 shows an example. A conclusion is given in section 4.

2 General Integration Model of Web Services

GIMWS uses a multi-layers construction to implement Web Services integration, shown as Fig.1. A Composite Aggregation Service(CAS) is presented finally, called by application directly. A XML-based language – Web Service Description Language (WSDL) – is used in GIMWS to describe the interfaces of services. GIMWS model encapsulates several Web Services' message format, message content and transaction action, offering services in different layers.

2.1 Transition Layer

Web Services are separately provided by different enterprises with different operation rules. The heterogeneity of services is embraced in semantic difference among ser-

C.-H. Chi and K.-Y. Lam (Eds.): AWCC 2004, LNCS 3309, pp. 374–379, 2004.

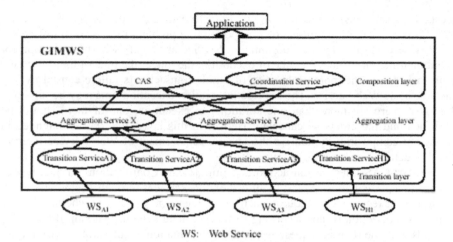

Fig. 1. Multi-layers Construction of GIMWS

vices providing same semantic function. So-called semantic difference means different understanding and definition of the same information. In Web Services integration, semantic difference is embodied in the definition of service interfaces.

In GIMWS, semantic differences are eliminated in transition layer by Transition Service. The Transition Service connects an Aggregation Service with a Web Service's PortType element, homogenizing heterogeneous Web Services. The transition mapping information is stored in Transition Service. The mapping information transforms heterogeneous Web Services to a semantic equivalence Aggregation Service with uniform semantic and format, eliminating the semantic and message format differences. Semantic equivalence means providing same semantic function with different WSDL descriptive interface.

2.2 Aggregation Layer

The function of aggregation layer is to eliminate the range difference, because Web Services with same semantic function may act on different range. For example, one Web Service(denoted by WS_{A1})and the other Web Service(WS_{A2}) can all offer domestic flight reservation, besides, WS_{A1} offer international flight reservation. In aggregation layer, Aggregation Service stores the range difference of Services and hides the heterogeneity of them. The services after being homogenized are aggregated to be a uniform access interface in this layer. When Aggregation Service receives a certain request message, it may call for corresponding Transition Service to operate.

Aggregation Service also ensures a certain Quality of Service, for that, Aggregation Service aggregates several Web Services with same semantic function. If one of them fails, the others work well, and the integration service may not collapse.

2.3 Composition Layer

CAS is obtained in composition layer, called by application directly. During the execution process, CAS may calls for multi-geography distributed basic Web Services(sub-transactions). 2-Phase Commitment Protocol(2-PC) can be used. However, if 2PC is directly used in transaction composition, a problem may occur. 2PC execution may be controlled by the Coordination Service absolutely with no limitation for execution time. The longer the time of execution, the longer the time of the resource's being locked, and the more probability of whole transaction's failure caused by any unusable basic Web Service. The Service integration execution time may be too long. Moreover, there are more than one solutions in execution, one of them should be confirmed and the others be canceled. Hence, in this layer, the 2PC is extended in transaction composition to address the special requirement of Web Service integration. The details are shown as follows:

1. Register: CAS issues a transaction and initiates the Coordination Service, broadcasting a participating request to all correlative services through Aggregation Service. After receiving the request, each service node may decide to whether register to this transaction or not according to its own load station. If it can, this service sends back the register request and relative information to enroll, otherwise it does not answer. By register phase, all unusable Web Services are filtered, decreasing the probability of transaction failures.

2. Ready: When register request sent back to Coordination Service, it knows what basic Services will enroll in such a transaction. CAS triggers a ready phase to begin. Coordination service executes a transaction, writes a "Begin Transaction" record in the log document and broadcasts a "ready" message(including transaction execution information) to all attending Web Services. If a certain Web Service gets ready to commit, Coordination Service writes this transaction in log and locks resource to be used by such transaction. Once resource has been getting ready, a "ready" message will be sent to Coordination Service.

3. Confirm: If the ready phase complements successfully, i.e. Coordination Service receives the "ready" messages of all enrolling Web Service, CAS will make the selection decision according to business logic. The Web Service receiving "confirm" message commits its own transaction, and unlocks the resource, in addition, sends a "confirmed" message to Coordination Service; The Web Service receiving "cancel" message rollbacks its own transaction, and unlocks the resource, in addition, sends a "canceled" message to Coordination Service. After receiving responsible messages(confirmed or canceled) of all enrolling Web Service, Coordination Service notifies CAS the transaction has been completed. Comparing with 2PC, the advantage of extending 2PC is, it is CAS to decide when prepare a subtransaction(a basic Web Service), and confirm (or cancel)such sub-transaction according to business logic(but not confirm or cancel all sub-transactions), realizing a fine grained control.

3   A Simple Example

This section introduces a simple example, shown as Fig2. In following description, we use B, C to denote a certain city, p airport, A airline, H hotel, WS Web Service. In this example, a tourist plans to travel in a city, need to book flight and a room in one hotel in that city. He uses explorer to access a travel agency's WS_T – a composition Web Service integrated with WS_{A1}, WS_{A2}, WS_{A3}, and WS_{H1}. User offers the demands to WS_T in explorer(source city, destination city, date, etc.). In contrast with traditional

Web application, WS_T calls for WS_{A1}, WS_{A2}, WS_{A3}, and WS_{H1} by use of SOAP protocol automatically to complete the all reservation operation, it is unnecessary for users to access WS_{A1}, WS_{A2}, WS_{A3}, and WS_{H1} one by one to compare and select.

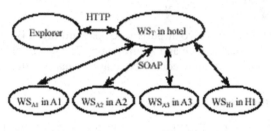

A:airplane company   H:hotel

Fig. 2. An Example of Web Service Integration

Supposing: (1)There are two airports in C, one airport in B. (2)semantic differences between WS_{A1} of A1 and WS_{A2} of A2 are: the input messages of WS_{A1} contain three elements: SourceCity,DestinationCity and Date. The output messages of WS_{A1} are all scheduled flight information from any airport in SourceCity to any airport in DestinationCity; the input messages of WS_{A2} contain three elements: Source Airport, DestinationAirport and Date. The output messages of WS_{A2} are all scheduled flight information from Source Airport to DestinationAirport. (3)There following range difference between WS_{A1} and WS_{A2}: WS_{A1} and WS_{A2} can all offer domestic flight reservation, besides, WS_{A1} offer international flight reservation.

3.1 Eliminating the Semantic Differences

Transition service stores the mapping information, transforms the messages between special semantic of each Web Service and uniform semantic of Aggregation Service. In order to eliminating the semantic difference between WS_{A1} and WS_{A2}, we prescribe they are unified to semantic of WS_{A1}, i.e. the input messages of Transition Service A1 and A2 all contain three elements: SourceCity, DestinationCity, Date. If A1and A2 all receive message(C,B,d) containing real data, according to WSDL description interface, the SOAP message request they send to WS_{A1} and WS_{A2} are followings respectively. (SOAP message header is missed).

WS_{A1}:
```
<SOAP-ENV:Body>
   <ScheduleRequestofA1>
      <SourceCity>C</SourceCity>
      <DestinationCity>B</DestinationCity>
      <Date>d</Date>
   </ScheduleRequestofA1>
</SOAP-ENV:Body>
```
WS_{A2}:
```
<SOAP-ENV:Body>
   <ScheduleRequestofA2>
```

```
      <SourceAirport>p1</SourceAirport>
      <DestinationAirport>p</DestinationAirport>
      <Date>d</Date>
   </ScheduleRequestofA2>
   <ScheduleRequestofA2>......
</SOAP-ENV:Body>
```

It is mapping information – two airports in C, one airport in B – realize the semantic transition between each service and Aggregation Service, homogenizing heterogeneous Web Services with semantic equivalence and semantic differences

3.2 Eliminating the Range Differences

Aggregation service X stores the range differences, and aggregates homogenized Web Services of airplane companies. WS_{A1} and WS_{A2} offer domestic flight reservation, while WS_{A2} offers international flight reservation. If Aggregation Service receives an international flight reservation request, it will only call for Transition Service A1, just because that it knows A2 cannot offer the international flight reservation service according to range difference information stored.

3.3 Composing the Transactions

In transaction composition, flight reservation and hotel room reservation are subtransactions in the whole transaction. After comparing tickets' prices of the every airline, CAS selects a scheduled flight in one airline. The interaction among CAS, Coordination Service and each basic Web Services are shown as Fig3.(In Fig3, the transition process in aggregation layers and transition layers are missed)

1. Register: CAS sends a service request to WS_{A1}, WS_{A2}, WS_{A3} and WS_{H1}. WS_{A1}, WS_{A2}, WS_{H1} all agree to enroll in this transaction, sending back the register information, price information. WS_{A3} is unusable, it doesn't answer.
2. Ready: CAS triggers a ready phase to begin. Coordination service executes a real transaction, sending a prepare message(including transaction execution information) to all attend Web Services, WS_{A1},WS_{A2},WS_{H1}. WS_{A1}, WS_{A2}, WS_{H1} get ready to commit, sending back a "Ready" message to Coordination Service.
3. Confirm: CAS judges and selects scheduled flight of A1 and hotel room in H1, according to backing prices and business rules(selecting scheduled flight with lower price, for example), canceling the sub-transaction of WS_{A2}. The cancel of WS_{A2} does not affect the whole transaction normal executing.

In transaction composition, unusable WS_{A3} was filtered in register phase. In transaction execution, CAS confirms WS_{A1} and cancels WS_{A2} for WS_{A1}'s lower price.

4 Conclusion

A General Integration Model of Web Services is presented in this paper. This model separates the task of homogenizing heterogeneous Web Services from the task of transaction composition, solves the heterogeneous problem of Web Services effec-

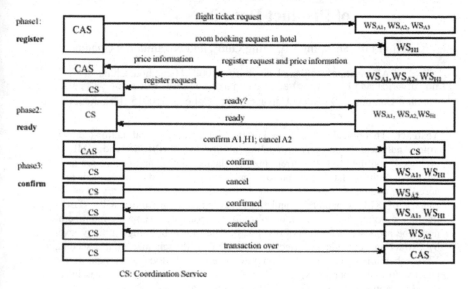

Fig. 3. The Interaction of CAS, Coordination Service and all Basic Web Services

tively. 2PC of distributed transaction management is extended to enhance the robustness and the adaptation of Web Services obtained from integration.

References

1. Web service concepts – a technical overviews, HP Web Services Platform: http://www.hp.com/go/webservices, 2001
2. Building the Mass Storage System at Jefferson Lab Proceedings of the 18th IEEE Symposium on Mass Storage Systems (2001)
3. Michael J. Lewis, Andrew Grimshaw. The Core Legion Object Model Proceedings of the Fifth IEEE International Symposium on High Performance Distributed Computing, August 1996
4. http://www-3.ibm.com/software/solutions/webservices/pdf/WSFL.pdf

Methodology for Semantic Representing
of Product Data in XML*

Xiangjun Fu[1], Shanping Li[1], Ming Guo[2], and Nizamuddin Channa[1]

[1] AI. Institute, Zhejiang University, 310027 Hangzhou, China
fuxiangjun@hotmail.com, shan@cs.zju.edu.cn, nchanna68@yahoo.com
[2] School of Computing, Zhejiang University City College, 310015 Hangzhou, China

Abstract. Theoretically based on highly general ontological notions drawn from Analytical Philosophy, Modeling ability for EXPRESS and XML is evaluated, and the limits of current product data modeling approaches are indicated. An ontology based method for representing product data by XML is proposed. Compared with those existed solutions, this approach not only takes advantage of XML's popularity and flexibility, and compatibility with STEP's rigorous description of product, but also aims at consistent semantic interoperation. The proposed method is of two levels: The first is building ontology level by extracting semantic knowledge from EXPRESS schema; in the second, XML schema is derived from ontology to access XML documents. And in this paper a formal semantic expression mechanism in description logics is introduced to capture the semantic of EXPRESS schema.

1 Introduction

Product data models in STEP are specified in EXPRESS (ISO 10303-11), a modeling language combing ideas from the entity-attribute-relationship family of modeling languages with object modeling concepts [1] [2]. To satisfy the a large number of sophisticated and complex requirements put forwards by large scale industry, the EXPRESS language has powerful expressing constructs to describe complicated product information, and had been used to built up a family of robust and time-tested standard application protocols which had been implemented in most CAX and PDM systems. But the lack of a formal semantic model for EXPRESS schema and the complexity of EXPRESS itself impose challenges on the serialization of product instance and data exchange [3] [4]. Sufficient interoperability between different applications in distributed and heterogeneous computing environment needs not only instance data exchanged but also high-level semantic information exchanged and conciliated. STEP Part 21 [5], Part 25 [7] and Part 28 [6], the solutions of product instance serialization, mostly take focus on the exchange of product instance data, cannot satisfy this requirement. STEP Part 21, which defines character-based serialization syntax, lacks extensibility, is hard for humans to read and perhaps most limiting – is computer-interpretable only by software supporting STEP. Unlike the Part 21 syntax, XML is easily extensible and is supported by inexpensive and widely used software tools. Part 25 and Part 28 use XML documents to encode product data. However, the biggest advantage of XML (its extensibility and flexible) is at the same time its biggest handicap to consistently express semantic information of product data in different application area [8].

---

* This project is supported by the Natural Science Foundation of China (Grant No. 60174053)

C.-H. Chi and K.-Y. Lam (Eds.): AWCC 2004, LNCS 3309, pp. 380–387, 2004.
© Springer-Verlag Berlin Heidelberg 2004

To take advantage of XML's popularity and flexibility, and to be compatible with STEP's rigorous description of product, we propose an ontology-based method for encoding STEP in XML. Compared with those past solutions, our method aims at consistent semantic interoperation. We argue that it is necessary to use ontology to model real-world data semantic and their relationship in a formal way. The proposed method is comprised of two steps: building ontology by extracting semantic knowledge from EXPRESS schema, deriving XML schema from ontology for access to XML documents.

Based on ontological evaluation of modeling ability for EXPRESS and XML, the remainder of this paper presents a formal ontology model for EXPRESS schema, and describes our approach of semantic information extracting rule for building ontology from EXPRESS schema.

2 Evaluation for STEP's Approaches

ISO group responsible for STEP is considering two approaches. One approach is the direct mapping from EXPRESS schema to XML Schema: STEP Part28 specifies how to directly map any EXPRESS schema to an XML schema. The other approach is the mapping indirectly by way of UML: Another proposed STEP standard, Part 25, defines a mapping from EXPRESS to static structure diagrams specified using the Unified Modeling Language (UML). Both approaches only satisfy the primary requirements as stated in the ISO10303, but once outside that scope, these approaches present the following problems for the XML representation of EXPRESS.

One problem is that XML itself is purely syntax standard. It provides no facilities for defining the semantics of elements. While document type declarations can impose some syntactic constraints, these are relatively limited, certainly in comparison to the full constraint language of EXPRESS. Thus, while XML has the quality that XML documents are easy to parse, it cannot be automatically provided with an underlying semantics, except the hierarchical information that is encoded in the mark-up tags. It is necessary to enforce XML semantic modeling power, making it easier to support semantic based product information integration.

The other one problem for XML representation of product data stems from EXPRESS language and complexity of the requirements, which is put forward by large-scale industry. Like the STEP standard, the EXPRESS language is correspondingly sophisticated and complex. In ISO 10303 whose original intention is only for data exchange, not for semantic exchange, so rigorous abstract model definition of EXPRESS constructs and EXPRESS model is missing. Powerful and flexible modeling constructs often misused to capture the meaning of an application domain. These deficiencies in using with EXPRESS language were called ontological deficiencies [10]. We employ an ontological framework of BWW [11] [12] to describe the real semantic implicated in and clearly describe by EXPRESS schema. This model articulates a set of high-level abstract constructs that intended to provide a precise meaning for concept modeling languages. According to [11], consistent semantic modeling should keep the one by one mapping between constructs of the general abstract model and specified language constructs. Thus BWW model provides a reference for ontological evolution, which reveals that, usually, the mapping from EXPRESS schema to semantic model is either ambiguous or partial. We clarify two major kinds of deficiencies in practical modeling activity according to the BWW model:

- The same ontological construct is represented by more than one kind of modeling language constructs, In the EXPRESS Schema, except entity declaration, data type declaration, also can be employed to represent objects class.
- Different ontological constructs are represented only by one kind of language constructs.

All these shortages not only stem from EXPRESS language itself, but also from the cognition confusing in modeling activity. Thus we argue that there are two ways to realize normative model in EXPRESS language. One is building the rules for using EXPRESS language; the other one is evolution for EXPRESS Schemas existed. But in practical usage, domain experts employ EXPRESS language not only to represent semantic information but also to build an interchangeable and operable data model for product engineering. Most EXPRESS Schemas cover semantic level and data level in product data representation. So demanding experts obey rules for normatively semantic information representation is unwieldy. In the following, we mainly describe the second approach: EXPRESS Schema evolution way to get semantic model: ontology.

3   Ontology Based Method for STEP Data Serialization

We propose that the ontology, which is extracted from EXPRESS Schema, can represent the semantic model both for EXPRESS schema and its serialization of XML documents. As figure 1 show, in ontology population approach for modeling product knowledge, ontology building through semantic information extracting from EXPRESS Schema is the first step. Then a XML schema is created, from ontology knowledge base represented by the above modeling units. In the following, we first introduce the definition of ontology, and explain why we need it.

3.1   Ontology Based Architecture for Modeling Product Knowledge

According to [13], an ontology is an explicit account or representation of (some part of) a conceptualization with a conceptualization being a world view with respect to a given domain, which is often conceived as a set of concepts (e.g. entities, attributes, processes), their definitions and their inter-relationships. Ontology describes information based on its semantic context, rather than describing it at the syntactic, or implementation level. The elementary modeling primitives in an ontology include atomic classes, basic classes, complex classes, attributes, relationships, and some basic axioms for the domain, i.e., class equivalent, class including, class relationship inverse, and classes disjointing.

Due to the complexity of EXPRESS language, automatic extracting complete semantic information from EXPRESS Schema is impossible. We commit ourselves to one specific ontology representation framework: description logics (DLs) with concrete domain [14]. The basic production rules for extracting semantic information are outlined, which consider first the core components of ontology to model common static semantic reserved in EXPRESS schema. In a modular way, which is supported by representation pattern of description logics, a more enriched ontology can be building up step by step to capture more semantic of EXPRESS schema.

The choice of description logics for representing ontology of product has the following advantages [14] : Instance can be classified automatically depending on their properties; Classes/concepts can be organized automatically, so that introduction of a new class would position it at the right place in the class hierarchy; It is possible to define instances and classes only partially because of the open world semantics of description logics; Instances can change their membership to classes during their existence and classes can change their definition during time; Description logics have much broader possibilities for representing and checking axioms or integrity constraints. Except these advantages, description logics are theory foundation for the prevalent ontology modeling Languages in the Semantic Web community. It can be translated into OWL language and migrated onto Semantic Web platform easily [15]. Utilizing current Semantic Web technology, product knowledge can be embedded inside Web resources. This may enable improved communication and resource utilization between potentially distributed work groups.

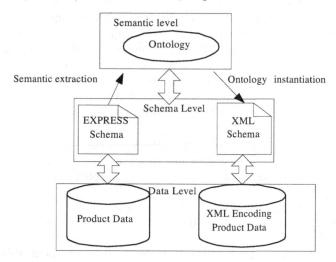

Fig. 1. Ontology based Methodology for Semantic Encoding Product Data in XML

3.2 Building the Product Ontology from EXPRESS Schema

The EXPRESS language is a completely generic facility for the definition of entity-attribute (or entity-relationship) models. EXPRESS is used to define data models or schemas through the definition of entity types and the allowed relationships among them. It uses a fairly classic entity-attribute paradigm in which entities are simply collections of attributes.

Data Type in EXPRESS
As the kernel of an information modeling language, data types determine the modeling ability of the language itself. Based on the data types of traditional programming languages, EXPRESS language absorbs those mechanisms used in Object-Oriented technology such as inheritance mechanism to describe the product data using abundant data types. These data types include simple data type, aggregate data type, named data type, constructed data type and generalized data type. We extract the ontology component from these data type declarations through different rules respectively.

Rule 1: Simple data types which are inherent in EXPRESS language are extracted as atomic classes in ontology, including INTEGER, REAL, etc.

Rule 2: Aggregate data types are atomic classes in ontology.

Rule 3: Among named data types, those whose member types are simple data are atomic classes; those whose member types are entity types are complex classes.

Rule 4: Among constructed data types, ENUMERATION types are atomic classes; for SELECT type, those whose composing members type are entity type are treat as complex classes in ontology, and need a class including axiom to describe that it is the super class of the member entities in the ENUMERATION type declaration.

Entity Declaration in EXPRESS

Entity declaration describes a class of objects in the real world which possess a same set of properties. Representation for properties includes the attributes/relations and constraints representations. To make terms not be confused, we use properties to denote the attributes declaration in EXPRESS, which will further be differentiated between attributes and relationships in ontology. The structure of an entity's definition is consisted of the id of entity, explicit property declarations, derived property declarations, inverse property declarations, unique property declaration, constraint property declarations, and super class or sub class declaration. Mapping rules are outlined as follows.

Rule 5: For every entity declaration in EXPRESS schema, there exists a corresponding class mapping to it, which takes the id of the entity as the name of the class. The class further is classified as basic class or complex class according to their property declarations.

Rule 6: Among explicit property declarations, those whose value types are atomic classes are attributes in ontology; those whose value types are basic classes are relationships in ontology.

Rule 7: Inverse properties can be directly represented by an axiom of Inverse relationships in ontology.

Rule 8: A derived property declaration is divided into two parts: a data type declaration and an explicit property declaration, which extracting semantic information into ontology according predefined in point rules respectively.

Unique property declaration denotes that value of the property must keep unique among all the instances, which provide an index for the implement of entity instantiation. Here we simply consider unique property same as explicit property. Constraints declarations have not been treated, because they very often include complete function calls which can not be transformed automatically. And the super class and sub class are treated as the inheritance mechanism in the following.

Inheritance Mechanism in EXPRESS

The most powerful feature that EXPRESS language embodies is an object-oriented inheritance mechanism which is much closer to the natural inheritance mechanism and much more facile to describe all complex relations between all objects, compared with those of other object-oriented languages. EXPRESS language introduces three additional relational operators: ONEOF, AND, and ANDOR. ONEOF means that all the components on the ONEOF list are mutually exclusive and the instances of super class must is the instance of subclasses in the list; ANDOR indicates that an instance of a certain super class can be the instance of its several subclasses; AND is only used in that a super class has more than one classification ways that divide the super class into subclasses, which refers to the fact that following set of SUBTYPE are always included in all instances of the SUPERTYPE.

Rule 9: For ONEOF operator, paradigms as "C SUPERTYPE OF ONEOF: $(C_1, C_2,...C_n)$" can be represented as: $C_i \subseteq C_n$, $C_i \subseteq \cap \neg C_j$, where $n \geq j \geq i$, $C \equiv C_1 \cup C_2...\cup C_n$.

Rule 10: For ANDOR operator, paradigms as "C SUPERTYPE OF ANDOR: $(C_1, C_2, ...$ Cn)" can be represented as: $C_i \subseteq C$, where $i \in \{1,2,...n\}$.

Rule 11: For AND operator, paradigms as "C SUPERTYPE OF:(ONEOF(C_1, C_2,... C_n) AND ONEOF (C_1', C_2',... C_m'))" is equal to "C SUPERTYPE OF ONEOF (C_1, C_2,... C_n)" and "C SUPERTYPE OF ONEOF (C_1', C_2',... C_m')". Further, it can be mapped into axioms in ontology through the 9th rule.

3.3 Mapping from Ontology to XML Schema

XML schema is mainly concerned with element/attribute declarations and simple/complex type definitions. Atomic classes can be defined only as simple types; basic class in ontology can be mapped to either an elements or an attribute, both of which are of simple type. Each complex class can be transformed to an element of complex type, whose content may include embedded sub elements. Father definitions of these XML simple/complex types and their association are dictated by various semantic relationship and constraints in the extracted ontology.

Declaring XML Simple Type for Atomic Classes and Basic Classes
An atomic class has simple content, which can be atomic value of an inherited data type or a constructional value, comprised of a collection of contents of atomic classes. We use stepwise mapping approach from atomic classes from ontology to data type declaration in XML Schema. First, for an atomic class, which directly corresponds to an inherited data type in XML Schema, XML Schema provides a rich set of simple data types, including integer, float, string, Boolean, date, time, and so on. We can easily map it to a build-in simple type from ontology to XML Schema. The second step, for those atomic classes whose definitions are based on other existed atomic classes, we can recursively derive a new class by restricting an existing atomic class through various facets.

Declaring XML Complex Type for Complex Class
As definite in section 4.1, the content of a basic class in ontology is only a set of attributes, whose value types are atomic class. At the XML Schema, each basic class corresponds to a complex type, describing its attributes. The content of a complex class in ontology include at least one relationship which describes association between entities in the refereed domain. In XML Schema, we use element definitions contained in complex type declaration to represent relationship. The name of the element is the name of element, element type is the opposite class directed by the relationship.

Declaring XML Complex Type for Descended Class

In ontology, classes hierarchy organizes entities on taxonomies by their similarities and differences, thus structures the description of entities. An ancestor objector holds common information, whereas the descendants can inherit this information and add specific contents. The inherited information can be reused or overridden in the descendant entities. The hierarchy mechanism in the ontology can be translated to XML complex type declarations through the flexible and powerful type creation facilities offered by XML Schema. Basically, there are three ways to construct a descendant class from existed one: deriving types by extension, deriving complex types by restriction and redefining types.

4   Conclusions

The proposed approach integrate EXPRESS Schema, ontology and XML Schema, which enlarge the range of possible applications using product data represented with STEP. There are earlier approaches on relating ontology language and XML [16] [17]. However, these approaches did not deal with XML Schema but with its predecessor, i.e. with DTDs, and focused on translation of attribute inheritance in tag nesting. But we think that relating ontologies to DTDs is less interesting, because DTDs provide very expressiveness compared to ontologies and XML Schema. For further work, we need to enrich the extracting rules to model more general application-specific integrity constrains. And dynamic knowledge---the process and function definition in EXPRESS schema also need to considered.

References

1. Mike Pratt, "Introduction to ISO 10303 - The STEP Standard for Product Data Exchange", *ASME Journal of Computing and Information Science in Engineering*, November, 2000.
2. Schenk, D.A., and Wilson, P.R., "Information Modeling: The EXPRESS Way", Oxford University Press, New York, NY, 1994 (ISBN 0-19-508714-3).
3. Felix Metzger, "The challenge of capturing the semantics of STEP data models precisely", *Workshop on Product Knowledge Sharing for Integrated Enterprises (ProKSI'96)*, 1996.
4. Matthew West, "Integration and sharing of industrial data", European PDT Days, 1997, pp. 145-154.
5. Industrial automation systems and integration – Product data representation and exchange - Part 21: Clear text encoding of the exchange structure. ISO 10303-21, 1994.
6. Industrial automation systems and integration – Product data representation and exchange – Part 28: Implementation methods: XML representations of EXPRESS schemas and data, ISO 10303-28, 1998.
7. Industrial automation systems and integration – Product data representation and exchange – Part 25: Implementation methods: EXPRESS to XMI Binding. ISO 10303-25, 2002.
8. W. Eliot Kimber, "XML Representation Methods for EXPRESS-Driven Data", National Institute of Standards and Technology, GCR 99-781, Novemeber 1999.
9. Object Management Group, "OMG Unified Modeling Language Specification, Version 1.4", September 2001.
10. Fettke P.; Loos, P., "Ontological evaluation of reference models using the Bunge-Wand-Weber-model", I*n: Proceedings of the Ninth Americas Conference on Information Systems 2003*. Tampa, FL, USA 2003, pp. 2944-2955.
11. M. Bunge, "Treatise on Basic Philosophy: Volume3 Ontology: The Furniture of the World", Reidel, Boston, 1977.

12. Parsons, J. and Wand, Y., "Choosing Classes in Conceptual Modeling", *Communications of the ACM*, 1997, 40(6), pp. 63-69.
13. T.R. Gruber, "A translation approach to portable ontology specifications", *Knowledge Acquisition*, 1998, 5(2), pp. 21--66.
14. Volker Haarslev, Carsten Lutz, Ralf Möller, "A Description Logic with Concrete Domains and a Role-froming Predicate Operator", *Journal of Logic and Computation*, 1999, 9(3).
15. Ian Horrocks, Peter F. Patel-Schneider, "Reducing OWL Entailment to Description Logic Satisfiability". *International Semantic Web Conference 2003*, pp. 17-29.
16. Klein, M., Fensel, D., van Harmelen, F., and Horrocks, I., "The Relation between Ontologies and XML Schemas", *Linköping Electronic Articles in Computer and Information Science*, 2001, 6(4).
17. M. Erdmann, R. Studer, "How to Sructure and Acess XML Documents With Ontologies", *Data & Knowledge Engineering*, 2001, 36(3), pp. 317-335.

Semantic Based Web Services Discovery

Jianjun Xu, Qian Zhu, Juanzi Li, Jie Tang, Po Zhang, and Kehong Wang

Computer Sciences Dept. Tsinghua University
xjj@263.net

Abstract. This paper presents a novel approach for Web Services discovery on
the envisioned Semantic Web. At first it proposes ontology based four-layer
Web Services description model which is helpful for data-independence and
concept-sharing. And then a users' services preferences and constrains model
upon the description is described. SBWSDF ("Semantic Based Web Services
Discovery Framework") is a framework to implement Web Services discovery
using these models. Using the prototype of this framework, we set up a services
ontology base and a rules base about flight booking. This prototype integrates
the services description, the preferences and constrains rules and the request information to select proper services by using an inference engine. The result
proves it's a new approach of Web Services discovery with intelligence.

1 Introduction

Now, the main impediment of web has been the lack of semantics to enable machines
to "understand" and automatically process the data. The Semantic Web is an emerging paradigm shift to fulfill this goal. It is defined as an extension of the existing Web,
in which information is given a well-defined meaning. A major player in enabling the
Semantic Web is the concept of Web Services. Web Services are networked applications that are able to interact using standard application-to-application Web protocols
over well-defined interfaces. But now UDDI, WSDL and SOAP, which are three most
important technologies of Web Services, provide limited support in mechanizing
service recognition, discovery, configuration and composition.

Service discovery is important for Web Services applications. And it is currently
done by name/key/category of the information model in UDDI which roughly defines
attributes that describe the service provider, the relationships with other providers and
how to access the service instance. The fixed set of attributes in UDDI limits the way
queries can be composed. Although UDDI can find more information of the service in
its WSDL, the WSDL only describes the service in a low-level form of interface signature and communication protocol and can't provide enough semantic description
for locating the service intelligently. So bringing web services application to their full
potential requires their combination with semantic web technology. It will provide
mechanization in service discovery, configuration, comparison, and composition.

Our research adopts the idea of Semantic Web to support discovery of Web Services. Section 2 introduces our four-layer ontology based Web Services description
model and Section 3 explains how we use F-Logic [6], a deductive database language
to define the logic rules about the users' preferences and constrains. Upon these models, a framework of discovering Web Services named as SBWSDF is introduced in
Section 4. Section 4 also presents a prototype of the SBWSDF about flight booking

C.-H. Chi and K.-Y. Lam (Eds.): AWCC 2004, LNCS 3309, pp. 388–393, 2004.
© Springer-Verlag Berlin Heidelberg 2004

services discovery. Section 5 discusses other work on discovering Web Services and makes the comparison and conclusion.

2 Ontology Based Web Services Description Model

We use a four layers model to make the semantic web services description.

M:={UO(L1), SUO(L2), DO(L2), SDO(L3), SD(L4)}
M: Ontology Base Web Services Description Model.
UO: Upper Ontology.
SUO: Upper Ontology for Web Services.
DO: Domain Ontology.
SDO: Domain Ontology for Web Services.
SD: Ontology Based Description for Service XXX.

Fig.1 shows the four-layer ontology based web description model and users' preferences and constrains model based on this description model.

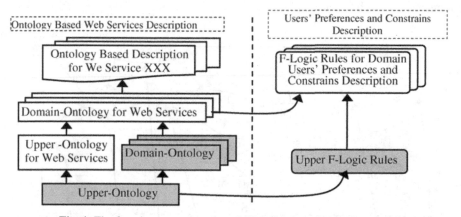

Fig. 1. The four-layer ontology based Web Services description model

Upper ontology (UO) contains universal concepts and their relationship, such as person, company and their relationship. Some common ontology base such as Word-Net, SUMO, etc. can be used as upper ontology and can help to share concept with other systems. Domain ontology (DO) is the common concept and their relationship in a specific domain. Upper ontology for Web Services (SUO) focuses on the architecture of Web Services and its relationship with customer (Fig.2). It refers to the classes of concepts that are related to a service including ServiceItem and ServiceMessage. ServiceItem is the operation unit of the service. The "Condition" to use the "ServiceItem" and the "Result" of it is subclass of the "ServiceMessage".

Semantic information specific to a particular service and common for service providers can be defined as SDO ("Domain Ontology for Web Services"). Service providers of the same service domain can refer to SDO when creating their own web service descriptions. A SDO may be proposed by a group of service providers and built upon the DO and SUO. To present what's SDO, we bring forward an example about flight booking in Fig.3.

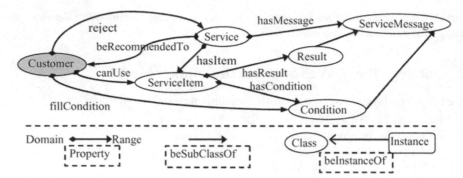

Fig. 2. Upper ontology for Web Services

Upon SDO, a lot of services in the domain can be defined. Fig.3 shows an example about LuoPan's flight booking Web Service description. LuoPan is an e-business platform for traveling (http://www.luopan.com) developed by us, and we have implemented the Web Service on it.

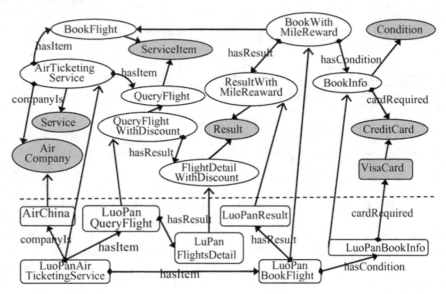

Fig. 3. Domain ontology for Web Services and the LuoPan service description

3   Users' Preferences and Constrains Model

To discover web services intelligently, we need to present users' preferences and constrains information. Fig.1 shows our two-layer users' preferences and constrains model named as UPCM ("Users' Preferences and Constrains Model"). We choice F-Logic as the rules language for UPCM because F-Logic combines the advantages of conceptual high-level approaches typical for frame-based language and the expressiveness, the compact syntax, and the well defined semantics from logics. F-Logic consists three parts: the fact, the logic rules and the query statement.

In UPCM, the fist layer is Upper F-Logic Rules, which defined the universal rules about UO and DO. Following is an example:

Table 1. Upper F-Logic rules example

Make the system now what is the meaning of "employee"	FORALL isEmployeeOf (X,Y) <- X:person(companyIs->Y)

The second layer of UPCM is F-Logic rules for domain users' preferences and constrains description upon SDO. It explains common rules about the domain when discovering service. This is an example about flight booking:

Table 2. Flight booking F-Logic Rules examples

If a customer wants to get the mile-reward, she or he must have the same type of credit card as requirement of the service provide.	FORALL canUse (X, Y) <- X:customer (hasCreditCard->Z) AND Y:ResultWithMileReward (hasCreditCard->Z)
AirChina company forbid its employee choice other air company's services for business trip.	FORALL reject(X,Y) <- X:customer (isEmployeeOf->Z) AND Y:AirTicketService (supportCompany->Z)
If a customer is female, she always likes to query discount of air-ticket before buying it.	FORALL beRecommendedTo(X,Y)<- Y:customer (sex->female) AND X:AirService (hasItem->QueryFlightWithDiscound)

4   A Framework of Semantic Based Web Services Discovery

SBWSDF ("Semantic Based Web Services Discovery Framework") consists of several components that cooperate in discovery procedure (as in Fig.4). To discover web services, we need set up a services database based on the ontology system created by the administrator. The discovery procedure will begin if a customer agent gives a request. This request includes user's profile which includes the information about the customer. Then this profile will be translated to the F-Logic's fact by Onto2F-Logic converter. The Onto2F-Logic converter also translates all ontology of four layers into the F-Logic's fact. As getting the fact, the F-Logic reasoner also gets the preferences and constrains rules from the rules DB. As the result of F-Logic reasoner, a list of services, which are recommended to customer and are not reject by the rules, are brought forward to customer agent.

To test what the prototype of SBWSDF can do, we make a small examination about flight booking. In this prototype, we import description about flight booking services described in Fig.2 and Fig.3 into the ontology base and import the rules showed in Table.1 and Table.2 as preferences and constrains rules into the rules base. And then a customer's request for discovering services is inputted with the customer's information is customer (isCompany->airChina, sex->female, hasCreditCard->visa). At last, after executing, the result is: "Recommended: LuoPanAirTicketingServices". Investigating the content of Fig.2 and Fig.3, Table1 and Table2, we can find it's the right result. This example presents a new way of intelligent web services discovery.

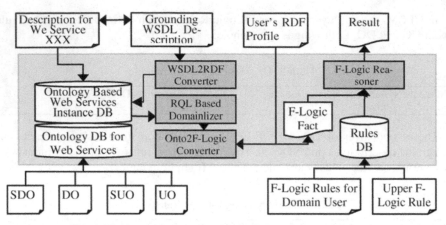

Fig. 4. The semantic based Web Services discovery framework

5   The Comparison and Conclusion

Table3 shows the comparison between SBWSDF and other projects.

Table 3. Comparison with other projects

	Services Description	Preference and Constrains	Key Characteristic
WSMO [8]	WSML	Constrains F-Logic rules based on services effect and condition	General "platform" for different services operations including discovery, mapping, composition etc.
the approach proposed in [3]	RDF and Extended WSDL	Generate constrains information as the rules form the relationship between effect and condition	Constrains rules is generated automatically from relationship between effect and condition of services
SBWSDF	For layers model	Preference and constrains F-Logics rules based on domain ontology as well as services effect and condition	Cooperates with other systems easily. Service is marched not only by service effect and condition, but also by references and constrain rules

Now, how to bring up a practical application is concerned much in semantic web research. Considering the intelligent web services discovery is likely to be one of the "kick-off" practical applications of semantic web, this paper proposes the four-layer services description model and the F-Logic users' preferences and constrains model and design the SBWSDF. They can work well in the prototype. Compared with other projects, there are two characteristics in this paper.

The first is the four-layer model services description. We think it's very useful for data-independence and concept-sharing. In application of SBWSDF, it's possible that SDO and SD need be changed frequently and in this case the UO, SUO and DO need not be modified because the data-independence of description model. And when application of SBWSDF needs to cooperate with other applications based on concept-sharing, UO, SUO and DO can be shared with other applications solely and easily.

The second characteristic is to use F-Logic based users' preferences and constrains model as well as services description model. Other project introduced in Table3 can generate constrains information form the relationship between effect and condition of services operation in the discovery procedure. It is a smart idea, but we think this way to generate rules limits the ability to describe the users' preferences and constrains. For examples, the rule "AirChina company forbid its employee choice other air company's services for business trip" is difficult to be generated in this way. But it's easy to be defined in our UPCM.

References

1. Oscar Corcho, Asuncion Gomez-Perez, and Mariano Fernandez-Lopez, Manuel Lama: ODE-SWS: A Semantic Web Service Development Environment. Proceedings of SWDB'03. The first International Workshop on Semantic Web and Databases, Humboldt-Universität, Germany, (2003) 203-216.
2. Alun Preece and Stefan Decker: Intelligent Web Service. IEEE Intelligent Systems, January/February 2002, 15-17.
3. Natenapa Sriharee and Twittie Senivongse: Discovering Web Services Using Behavioral Constraints and Ontology. Distributed Applications and Interoperable Systems, 4th IFIP WG6.1 International Conference, DAIS 2003, Proceedings, Springer, Paris, (2003) 248-259.
4. D. Fensel and C. Bussler: The Web Service Modeling Framework WSMF. Proceedings of the NSF-EU Workshop on Database and Information Systems Research for Semantic Web and Enterprises, Georgia, USA (2002) 15-20.
5. Trastour.D., Bartolini, C., Gonzalez-Castillo, J.: A Semantic Web Approach to Service Description for Matchmaking of Services. Proceedings of the International Semantic Web. Working Symposium (SWWS'01) (2001)
6. Michael Kifer, Georg Lausen, and James Wu: Logical foundations of objectoriented and frame-based languages. Journal of the ACM, 42(4) (1995). 741-843.
7. http://www.daml.org/services/owl-s/
8. http://www.wsmo.org/

What Are People Looking for in Your Web Page?

Chen Ding[1] and Chi-Hung Chi[2]

[1] School of Computer Science, Ryerson University, 350 Victoria Street,
Toronto, Ontario, Canada M5B 2K3
cding@scs.ryerson.ca
[2] School of Computing, National University of Singapore
10 Kent Ridge Crescent, Singapore 119260
chich@comp.nus.edu.sg

Abstract. Web server log analyses usually analyze the pattern of the access. We believe that it is also very important to understand the goal of the access. In this paper, we propose to combine the log analysis with content analysis to identify information goals on individual accessed pages. We analyze the web server log to extract information goals on entry pages from anchor texts and query terms, and propagate them along users' access paths to other linked pages. The experiment shows that our approach could find popular terms on web pages, temporal changes in these terms could reflect users' interest shifts, and unexpected terms could sometimes indicate a design problem.

1 Introduction

With the exponential growth of the World Wide Web, the web site plays a significant role in a company's business. It is not only the platform to deliver the content, but also the platform of the online transaction. Web site owners are always eager to understand people's visiting behaviors and what they are looking for. This kind of information could help them to optimize the web site design and make good business decisions.

There are many commercial log analysis tools [11] [13] available. They analyze the traffic data or server logs to generate some reports. Usually they don't have the detailed analysis on web page's content. Without the content analysis, web site owners could not know what users are looking for in each individual web page. Since every web page is designed for a purpose, to present content, to provide links, or to assist a transaction, it is very important for site owners to know the actual users' information needs on all pages. Thus, they could optimize individual web page design and make a better business decision with more knowledge on users. In this paper, we propose to combine the server log analysis with page level content analysis to find out what people are looking for in each web page.

Based on the observation that queries and anchor texts represent user's information need on the target page, we first analyze the web server log, to extract terms from actual user queries and anchor texts for entry pages, and then these terms are propagated to other pages along access paths, trying to cover as many pages as possible. In our approach, the information goal on a web page is represented with a group of terms ordered by their associated weights, and is determined by the content similarity between pages and between these terms and pages. A term in higher rank (i.e. with higher weight) is a term that more users look for on that page. In this paper, we use "goal term" to define the term which represents user's information goal.

C.-H. Chi and K.-Y. Lam (Eds.): AWCC 2004, LNCS 3309, pp. 394–402, 2004.

There are several potential uses of goal terms. First, web site owners could know what popular topics on individual pages are, and they could propose customized advertisements based on popularity, or make a better business decision. Second, the temporal changes on those topics could reflect users' interest shifts, which again could promote a better business decision. Third, terms which are different from web site owners' expectation sometimes could indicate a design problem, and thus, related pages are able to be reorganized to better meet users' needs. Fourth, goal terms from previous user accesses could be used to provide the browsing assistance for new users. For instance, a text box containing goal terms could appear besides a link, and then the new user could have a rough idea about what other people are interested on the linked page. Usually anchor texts on hyperlinks could only provide limited information, and goal terms extracted contain more information.

The remaining sections are organized as follows. Section 2 discusses several related works. Section 3 provides a detailed description of our approach, including preprocessing steps on web server logs, how to extract goal terms for entry pages, and how to spread to other pages on access paths. We discuss experiment results in section 4. And section 5 concludes the paper and specifies our future works.

2 Related Works

As we mentioned before, there are many commercial server log analysis tools available. In research arena, server logs have also been well studied in different areas, especially in web usage mining [10]. Here we only review the work closely related to ours.

Many log analysis tools [11] [12] [13] apply the statistical analyses on the usage data, and produce the useful information such as number of visitors per page, number of pages in a visit, page view duration, etc. Although this kind of information cannot give the direct instruction or the obvious indication of how to improve the site design, it does identify some usability problems and provide clues for designers to look into actual design improvement.

Chi et al. [1] tried to predict the usability of the alternative web site design by simulating user navigation patterns. Their approach used web mining techniques to find the information scent (a list of weighted keywords to represent information goal on a well-traveled path). Given starting pages, the information scent is used to make navigation decisions.

Kato et al. [5] developed a tool to extract web site designers' expectations by measuring the inter-page conceptual relevance and link connectivity, and users' behaviors by measuring the inter-page access co-occurrence. By evaluating the correlation between them, it could discover the gap and provide suggestions for site design improvement.

Based on the observation that when users could not find a page in an expected location, they would backtrack, Srikant et al. [9] proposed an algorithm to discover these pages, recommend the backtrack point where users actually found the page as the new location to site designers, and add navigation links appropriately.

Other related works include the following: Garofalakis et al. [4] examined the popularity of each web page, and developed a link-editing algorithm to rearrange the web site based on page popularity. Perkowitz et al. [7] used a cluster mining algorithm to find collections of web pages that tended to co-occur in user visits and put them under one topic, and then generated synthesized index pages consisting of links to pages on a particular topic.

There are a number of research works [1] [2] which combine the web usage mining with content analysis, for purposes such as web page clustering, personalization, finding information scent of a frequently visited path, etc. However, to our knowledge, there is little effort on using them to find information goal on individual web pages.

Anchor texts have been known to be able to improve web search, site finding and web site summarization. The study in [3] examined several aspects of anchor texts in a large intranet. They showed evidence that anchor text summaries, on a statistical basis at least, looked very much like real user queries. This was because most anchor texts were succinct descriptions of the destination page. Scholer et al. [8] also observed that a query which was highly similar to a page was a good descriptor of that page. Based on this notion, they developed query association technique which was an excellent way for describing a page. As declared in these studies, anchor texts as well as queries are all summaries of target pages, from people who are consumers of the content. Therefore, we believe that they could represent information goals on entry pages.

3   Finding Goal Terms for Web Site Pages

Following search engine results and links from other web sites are two major ways to enter a web site. People always have a certain information goal in mind when they access a web site, no matter informational or transactional. So query terms or anchor texts could be considered as goal terms of the entry page, which could be easily extracted from web server logs. Normally only a small portion of pages in a web site are entry pages. In order to find goal terms for as many pages as possible, we should further investigate server logs.

Based on works in usage mining area [1], we believe that user's access path could pass the initial information goal from entry page to subsequent linked pages. For instance, page A is a result from a user query, and if a user follows a link from to page B, it indicates a prolonged search on the original query. So, this query is related to both page A and page B, with different degrees of relevance. The similar statement could be made on anchor texts.

In this work, after we determine goal terms for entry pages, as long as users still focus on the initial information goal, all pages along the access path should also have these goal terms. But because of the possible distraction or deviation from the initial goal, goal terms on non-entry pages should have a faded weight.

If a user enters a web site just by directly typing the URL address in browser window or by following shortcuts such as a bookmark, there are no queries or anchor texts for entry pages. In this case, we cannot know exactly what people are looking for in the entry page. We considered the solution of extracting top terms from entry pages to approximate user's information goal, but it was merely designers' expected terms, which may not be the same as users' goal terms. Actually one of our purposes of finding goal terms is to identify the gap between the two. So in the current stage, we will not consider the situation where entry information is incomplete.

3.1   Session Identification in Server Log Analysis

In this study, the main purpose of the server log analysis is to get query terms and anchor texts linking to entry pages, and find access paths starting from these entry pages. Since query terms and anchor texts could only be extracted from referrers of entry pages, our basic data element is defined as the "referrer session". A referrer session is a consecutive sequence of web page accesses in a single user visit, in which the referrer field of the entry page is not empty. By "consecutive", we mean that each access after the entry page is referred from a previous page which is already in the access path, that is to say, it could always be traced back within the current session.

Considering the privacy issues, we first distort the IP address and use a number to represent a unique IP. Since we only care about HTML pages, we filter out user requests by file types and keep only HTML pages (e.g. .html, .php, .cgi). The data fields in a referrer session include a user ID (i.e. a number to represent a unique IP address), a session ID, the start time, the end time, the entry URL, the entry referrer, goal terms (i.e. anchor texts or query terms extracted from entry referrer), a list of URLs in the current session (i.e. access path), and a list of referrers (one referrer for one URL). There are several heuristics to decide when a new session starts and when a session should be discarded.

<u>Heuristic 1</u>: A new user ID starts a new session.

<u>Heuristic 2</u>: If the duration of a session is larger than a pre-defined threshold (e.g. 20 minutes), it means a new session starts.

<u>Heuristic 3</u>: If the referrer does not appear in accessed URLs of the current session, a new session starts.

<u>Heuristic 4</u>: If the referrer of the entry page is empty, or there is only one HTML access in the current session, this session is discarded.

3.2   Finding Goal Terms for Entry Pages and Propagating Along Access Paths

From referrer sessions identified from server logs, it is easy to extract goal terms. If the referrer is a search engine result page, it is quite straightforward to get query terms from the referrer URL. Otherwise, goal terms would be extracted from anchor texts. In the second situation, there are two things we should be especially aware of. First, there are a few very common terms such as "next", "previous" and "click here", which always appear in anchor texts. They are not content words. If we take them as goal terms, it is not accurate. Second, usually anchor text is not a long phrase, and thus, it might not include enough content words. In order to solve these two problems, we use anchor window [6] instead of anchor text, and we filter out those non-content terms before going into any further processing.

After goal terms are extracted for the entry page, they could be propagated along the access path within the same referrer session. The weight of goal terms in entry page is defined as 1. The weight of goal terms in other pages is determined by the degree of association between two linked pages, and the decay factor. In order to avoid that one user's information goal dominates the final result, multiple occurrences of a path followed by the same user are considered only once in server log analysis.

The association between two linked pages along an access path is determined by whether the anchor text is on the initial topic (i.e. goal terms of entry page in this path), the content similarity between two pages, the session duration, and the user access recency. The strength of association is specified by,

$$a_{ijk} = \frac{r_{dur}}{r_{rec}} \times r_{on-topic} \tag{1}$$

$$r_{on-topic} = (sim(T_0, T_{anchor}), sim(D_{entry}, D_j))/2 \tag{2}$$

Where a_{ijk} is the association from page i to j on path k, r_{dur} is the normalized access duration on path k, r_{rec} is the normalized access recency of path k, $r_{on-topic}$ is to measure whether the link is on initial topic, $sim()$ is to calculate the similarity between two term vectors, T_0 is the term vector representing the initial topic, T_{achnor} is the term vector of anchor texts on link i to j, D_{entry} is the term vector of the entry page, and D_j is the term vector of page j.

r_{dur} is normalized to (0, 1) range, in the following formula, dur_k is the actual access duration (in seconds) on path k, and max_k is the maximization operation on all paths identified in server log. r_{rec} is also normalized to (0, 1) range, t_{cur} refers to the current system time, t_k refers to the starting time of path k, and t_{start} refers to the starting time of server log.

$$r_{dur} = \ln(dur_k) / \ln(\max_k dur_k) \tag{3}$$

$$r_{rec} = \ln(1 + (t_{cur} - t_k)) / \ln(t_{cur} - t_{start}) \tag{4}$$

To measure the similarity between two pages, we use the popular TFIDF formula. To measure the similarity between two term vector T_0 and T_{anchor}, we simply calculate the number of common words in two vectors, and then normalize the value based on the total number of unique words in vectors.

The basic idea of above calculations is that if the access duration is long, it means users are more serious of this search task, if it is recently accessed, it could reflect the new content and current pattern more, and the reason we take the average similarity value to measure on-topic anchor texts is that the term similarity may not be accurate considering the complicated case of synonym, polymorphism, acronym, sub-topic terms, etc., and the document similarity calculation does not consider the initial topics on entry pages.

The term weight of linked page would be measured by,

$$w_{jk} = \alpha_{decay} \cdot a_{ijk} \cdot w_{ik} \tag{5}$$

Where w_{jk} is the goal term weight of page j on path k, w_{ik} is the goal term weight of page i on path k, and α_{decay} is the fading factor and set as 0.8.

There are several constraints in the propagation procedure. 1) If the term weight on any path is less than a threshold, the further propagation of the term along this path would be stopped. 2) If the level of propagation is over a certain distance, it would be stopped. 3) The propagation would be specially considered for page with a lot of out-links (i.e. fan-out page). Since for those pages, $r_{on-topic}$ may be very low, but as long as subsequent links are still on topic, we still continue the propagation. Currently we only look at the immediate link after the fan-out page. If it is still on topic, we move on, otherwise, we simply stop propagation. If the fan-out page is the entry page, the initial topic may be general, while after browsing all links, users decide to move on to a more specific topic. In this case, anchor texts of link to the first non-fan-out page would be set as the initial topic.

After propagation, each page has a vector of weighted goal terms. Since the same term could be propagated along different paths, there could be repeated terms in the vector. They would be combined, and each term would have a new combined weight in the final vector.

4   Experiments

In this study, we collected data from monthly server logs in school of computer science of Ryerson University, from January 1, 2004 through April 30, 2004. In average, there are 1.5 million requests per month, among which 453,838 are HTML requests. After session identification, there are about 209,074 sessions, in which only 15,022 sessions are valid. We further analyzed the data to check why the percentage of valid sessions is so low, and found that 165,774 sessions have only one HTML request, and in the remaining 43,300 sessions, about 35% have the referrer field available. Since the session definition is different in our system, every page access is intra-referred, while traditional session boundary doesn't check the referrer information, it could help explain why there is a huge drop in number of sessions after our processing.

```
        34100 - - [23/Jan/2004:13:32:07 -0500] "GET /~cding/ HTTP/1.1" 200
1048 http://www.google.ca/search?hl=en&lr=&ie=UTF-8&q=cherie+ding
        34100 - - [23/Jan/2004:13:32:10 -0500] "GET /~cding/teaching.htm
HTTP/1.1" 200 504 http://www.scs.ryerson.ca/~cding/
```

Fig. 1. A sample fragment of server log

```
    session_id: 1335
    user_id: 34100
    start_time: 23/Jan/2004:13:32:07
    end_time: 23/Jan/2004:13:32:10
    entry_url: http://www.scs.ryerson.ca/~cding/
    entry_referrer:
http://www.google.ca/search?hl=en&lr=&ie=UTF-8&q=cherie+ding
    goal_terms: cherie, ding
    urls: http://www.scs.ryerson.ca/~cding/,
http://www.scs.ryerson.ca/~cding/teaching.htm
    referrers:
http://www.google.ca/search?hl=en&lr=&ie=UTF-8&q=cherie+ding,
            http://www.scs.ryerson.ca/~cding/
```

Fig. 2. A sample referrer session

Figure 1 presents a small fragment of server log, which consists of a valid referrer session. And Figure 2 shows the actual referrer session extracted from log fragment in Figure 1. If the referrer field is http://www.scs.ryerson.ca/scs/fs.shtml, it is also a valid referrer session. But if this field is empty (i.e. "-"), it is an invalid session. If the subsequent request is /~cding/CPS125/cps125-index.htm, based on Heuristic 3, it starts a new session. But if the request is /~cding/research.htm, it is still in the current session since the referrer is /~cding/, which could be found in previous accesses.

In Table 1, we show a list of web pages and their goal terms in decreasing order based on their weights for January log. In a typical university department web site, besides the pages related to departmental information, a high percentage of pages are personal homepages. Here, we choose several top-level pages with the departmental information, and some well-accessed faculty homepages and student homepages.

Generally speaking, users' information goals could match the design expectation. Most of topic terms appear in goal terms. The propagation is able to add more context terms to describe information goals. For instance, in page /scs/fs.shtml, term "ryerson", "scs" and "people" are propagated from its parent pages, and it makes the list of goal terms for this page more complete. Another interesting finding in this page is that one professor's name is also among goal terms, e.g. term "sadeghian" appears as one of the goal terms. We checked the actual server log, and found that there were quite a number of search requests on this professor, while users clicked this page (/scs/fs.shtml) from the search result instead of his homepage. Possibly, the design of his homepage could be improved to promote the ranking of his homepage. So this term actually indicates a possible design problem.

Table 1. Sample web pages and their ranked goal terms

	Web Page	Ranked Goal Terms
1	/scs/	computer science ryerson university scs toronto canada engineering
2	/scs/fs.shtml	faculty information scs people ryerson staff sadeghian
3	/scs/news.shtml	ryerson university tony cellini what new scs
4	/~eharley/	harley eric eharley timetable course management form cps209
5	/~aabhari/	cps801 abhari abdolreza
6	/~mkolios/	kolios pcs213 ryerson mkolios pcs125
7	/~bhung/	
8	/~ajenkins/	adam jenkins freedom sweet

As we expected, goal terms could identify the current user interest on the page content. For instance, in page /scs/news.shtml, besides the expected topic terms, two other popular terms of the month are "tony" and "cellini". They appear in short news in that page, and it shows that many people are quite interested in this news. In faculty homepages, goal terms could identify their full names, and courses they are teaching. For student homepages, goal terms could identify their names, and also some hot topics on their pages. For instance, in page /~ajenkins/, "freedom" and "sweet" are popular topics. There is no goal term for page /~bhung/ since it was not accessed that month.

In Table 2, we show the ranked goal terms for the same list of web pages in the remaining three months. As we expected, it is able to capture the temporal changes in information goals. For instance, in /scs/news.shtml page, two terms – "tony" and "cellini", are not goal terms any more in these three months, which reflects users' interest shifts. In page /~aabhari/, the term "abdy" appears in all these three months, while not in the first month. The reason is that Abdy is a short name for this professor, only after first month's class, students knew that. The changes in goal terms related to courses also indicate students' interest shifts during months. Among goal terms in April for page /~bhung/, "dominion", "pizza" and "store" are new terms, and they seem to be quite irrelevant of a personal homepage. When we checked the page source, we found that these terms were in the title of the page, which was a project the student was doing during that month.

Table 2. Sample web pages and their ranked goal terms in different months

	February	March	April
1	computer science ryerson university toronto scs faculty staff	computer science ryerson university scs toronto canada school	computer science ryerson university scs school toronto applied
2	faculty information scs people ryerson computer science staff	faculty information scs people ryerson phd alex ferworn	faculty information scs people ryerson phd alex ferworn
3	what new scs paramedics ryerson building	computer what new scs ryerson university	ryerson computer science dean
4	harley eric ryerson eharley homepage cps 125 209	eharley harley eric ryerson timetable cps 209 scs	harley cps eric 125 ryerson 888 109 computer science
5	abhari abdy abdolreza ryerson	abhari abdy ryerson university	abhari abdy ryerson abdolreza carleton university
6	kolios pcs213 ryerson michael physics bioheat transfer thermal therapy	kolios michael pcs213 ryerson	kolios michael pcs213 ryerson university physics
7	brian hung	bhung	dominion pizza store brian hung
8	freedom adam jenkins student information	adam jenkins freedom	adam jenkins ryerson

As we expected, goal terms found by our system could identify popular topics, unexpected terms, and temporal changes in users' interest, which could help web site owners better understand users. As we illustrated, it could help improve the web page design. If we could show these goal terms besides the hyperlink, e.g. courses professors are teaching in the faculty homepage, it could also help improve new users' browsing experiences.

5   Conclusions and Future Works

We have proposed an approach to identify the information goals on web pages by analyzing web server logs, which is based on the observation that anchor texts and query terms could represent users' information goals on the linked web page. If the access path user follows has a consistent theme, goal terms on the entry page could be propagated along the path. We have had an initial run of the algorithm on a departmental web site. We have shown the actual goal terms we extracted for a sample set of web pages and ranked them in their weights. We find that changes in users' information needs in a web site could actually be reflected in goal terms, and sometimes it is able to identify design problems.

There are several directions in our future work. First, since our sample experiment data is quite small-scaled, we would like to run the experiment on a larger-scaled web site, and since the access patterns and web site structures are quite different in commercial sites from academic sites, we would like to run the experiment on a commercial web site. Then we could study how we can use the detailed knowledge on users' information goals on individual web pages to improve the web site design and make the smart business design. Second, in current stage, we only consider sessions with referrer information, which is only 35% as shown in our experiment. We will try to find a way to approximate information goals on the non-referrer sessions.

Acknowledgement

This work was carried out within a project sponsored by Natural Science & Engineering Research Council (NSERC) of Canada (grant 299021-04). We are grateful to Grace He in helping us access the server logs of School of Computer Science in Ryerson University.

Reference

1. E. H. Chi, P. Pirolli, K. Chen, and J. Pitkow, Using information scent to model user information needs and actions on the web, In *Proceedings of the ACM CHI Conference on Human Factors in Computing Systems (SIGCHI)*, 2001.
2. H. Dai, and B. Mobasher, Integrating semantic knowledge with web usage mining for personalization, Draft Chapter in *Web Mining: Applications and Techniques*, Anthony Scime (ed.), IRM Press, Idea Group Publishing, 2004.
3. N. Eiron, and K. S. McCurley, Analysis of anchor text for web search, In Proceedings of the 26th Annual International ACM SIGIR Conference on Research and Development in Information Retrieval (SIGIR), 2003.
4. J. Garofalakis, P. Kappos, and D. Mourloukos, Web site optimization using page popularity, In IEEE Internet Computing, pp 22-29, July/August, 1999.
5. H. Kato, T. Nakayama, and Y. Yamane, Navigation analysis tool based on the correlation between contents distribution and access patterns, In *Workshop on Web Mining for E-Commerce – Challenges and Opportunities at the 6th ACM SIGKDD International Conference on Knowledge Discovery and Data Mining*, 2000.
6. J. M. Kleinberg, Authoritative sources in a hyperlinked environment, In *Proceedings of the 9th ACM-SIAM Symposium on Discrete Algorithms*, 1998.
7. M. Perkowitz, and O. Etzioni, Towards adaptive web sites: Conceptual framework and case study, in *Artificial Intelligence*, 118:245-275, 2000.
8. F. Scholer, and H. E. Williams, Query association for effective retrieval, In *Proceedings of the 11th ACM Conference on Information and Knowledge Management (CIKM)*, 2002.
9. R. Srikant, and Y. H. Yang, Mining Web Logs to Improve Website Organization, In *Proceeding of the 10th World Wide Web Conference (WWW10)*, 2001.
10. J. Srivastava, R. Cooley, M. Deshpande, and P. Tan, Web usage mining: Discovery and applications of usage patterns from web data, In *SIGKDD Explorations*, 1(2):12-23, 2000.
11. SurfAid, http://surfaid.dfw.ibm.com/.
12. Webalizer, http://www.webalizer.com/.
13. WebTrends, http://www.netiq.com/webtrends/.

The Impact of OCR Accuracy
on Automatic Text Classification

Guowei Zu[1,2], Mayo Murata[1], Wataru Ohyama[1],
Tetsushi Wakabayashi[1], and Fumitaka Kimura[1]

[1] Mie University, Faculty of Engineering, 1515 Kamihama-cho, Tsu-shi, Mie, 5148507, Japan
http://www.hi.info.mie-u.ac.jp/
[2] Toshiba Solutions Corporation, Systems Integration Technology Center, Toshiba Building,
1-1, Shibaura 1-chome, Minato-ku, Tokyo 105-6691, Japan

Abstract. Current general digitization approach of paper media is converting them into the digital images by a scanner, and then reading them by an OCR to generate ASCII text for full-text retrieval. However, it is impossible to recognize all characters with 100% accuracy by the present OCR technology. Therefore, it is important to know the impact of OCR accuracy on automatic text classification to reveal its technical feasibility. In this research we perform automatic text classification experiments for English newswire articles to study on the relationships between the accuracies of OCR and the text classification employing the statistical classification techniques.

1 Introduction

With the development of internet and the information processing technology in these ten years, the main ways and means of information exchange has been shifted from the traditional paper to the digital data. Because the digital data, e.g. text, image, audio and so on, is transferred and retrieved much more quickly and easily, the digital publishing and the digital library will become the main resources of information in the twenty first century. Therefore, the traditional library should consider converting a great deal of paper media to the digital data in order to provide them on the internet. Current general digitization approach is converting paper media into the digital images by a scanner, and then reading them by an OCR to generate ASCII text for full-text retrieval. However, it is impossible to recognize all characters with 100% accuracy by the present OCR technology. Especially, the recognition accuracy can be quite low for classic books with special character font and handwritings. Therefore, it is important to know the impact of OCR accuracy on automatic text classification to reveal its technical feasibility.

In this research we perform automatic text classification experiments for English newswire articles to study on the relationships between the accuracies of OCR and the text classification employing the statistical classification. While the impact of OCR accuracy on information retrieval has been studied and reported in [1], [2], the impact on text classification has not been reported, to the best knowledge of the authors.

2 The Basic Classification Technology

In this research we employed the statistical classification technique for classifying a feature vector composed of frequencies of lexicon words that appear in a text. The

C.-H. Chi and K.-Y. Lam (Eds.): AWCC 2004, LNCS 3309, pp. 403–409, 2004.
© Springer-Verlag Berlin Heidelberg 2004

approach is learning a classification scheme from labeled training examples then using it to classify unseen textual documents [3]. Several classification techniques based on the Euclidean distance, Fisher's linear discrimination function, projection distances [4], and the support vector machine (SVM) are employed in the classification test for the English text collection (the reuters-21578).

A drawback of the statistical classification technique is that the dimensionality of the feature vector can increase together with the lexicon size. For example, the lexicon size and the feature dimensionality grow to 34,868 for Reuters-21578 articles, which requires enormous computational time and storage for the text classification. To solve this problem we need to employ a statistical feature extraction technique which extracts small number of features with high separability to reduce the feature dimensionality without sacrificing the classification accuracy. In this research the dimension reduction based on the principal component analysis (PCA) was employed.[5]

3   The Classification Experiment

3.1   Used Data

To study the impact of OCR accuracy on the automatic text classification, a set of texts that are pre-classified to their true category is required. The Reuters-21578 test collection is frequently used by many researchers as a typical test collection for English text classification. The Reuters-21578 is composed of 21578 articles manually classified to 135 categories. The Reuters-21578 data is a set of ASCII texts in which the predefined marks are embedded according to the SGML format to indicate the structural elements of the text. In this experiment total of 750 articles, 150 articles/category randomly selected from five categories (acq, crude, earn, grain, trade), were used. Since the sample size is not enough large, the sample is divided into three subsets each of which includes 50 articles/category. When a subset is tested, the rest of the two subsets are used as learning sample in order to keep the learning sample size as large as possible while keeping the independency between the samples for learning and test. Classification tests are repeated for three subsets and the correct classification rates are averaged to evaluate the classification accuracy.

3.2   The Procedure of the Experiment

The procedure of the experiment consists of three general steps for (1) text image generation, (2) ASCII text generation by OCR and (3) the automatic text classification.

Text Image Generation
Each ASCII text of the Reuters collection is printed out by a LBP with the character size of times11 point. The text on paper is converted to a digitized image of 300 dpi by a scanner. In order to obtain the digitized text images of different OCR accuracies, Photoshop 6.0 software was used to intentionally reduce the dpi of the images to 240, 200, 150, 145, and 140. Figure 1(a)-(c) show the example of the text images of 300dpi, 150dpi and 140dpi respectively.

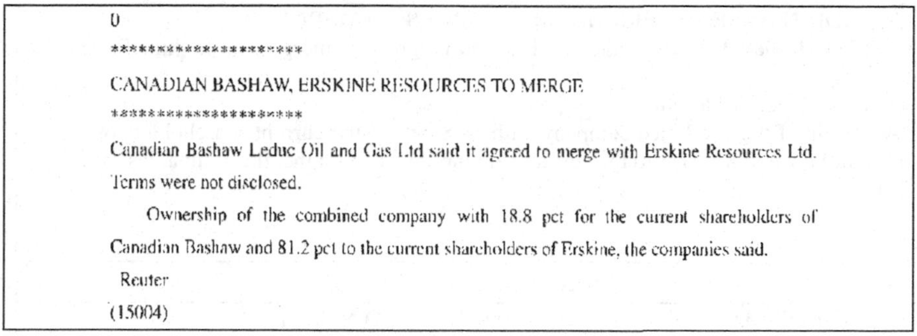

U

****

CANADIAN BASHAW, ERSKINE RESOURCES TO MERGE

****

Canadian Bashaw Leduc Oil and Gas Ltd said it agreed to merge with Erskine Resources Ltd. Terms were not disclosed.

Ownership of the combined company with 18.8 pct for the current shareholders of Canadian Bashaw and 81.2 pct to the current shareholders of Erskine, the companies said.

Reuter

(15004)

(a) 300 dpi

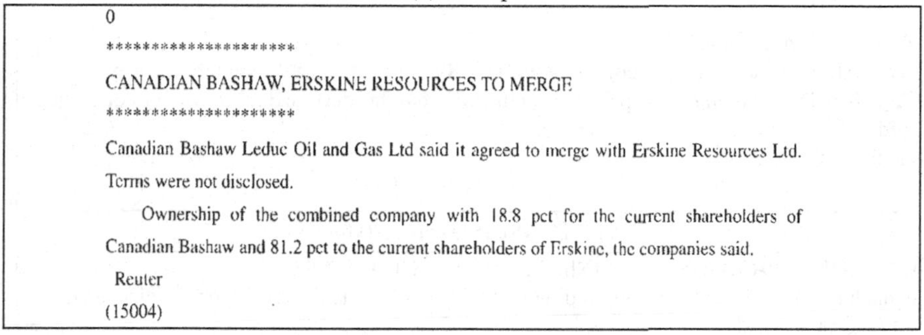

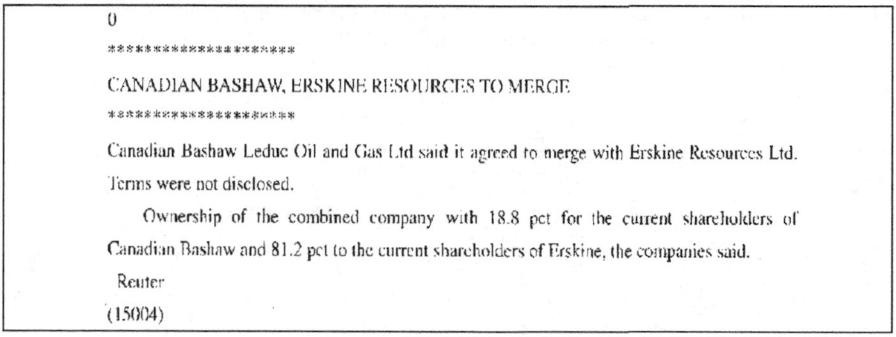

0

****

CANADIAN BASHAW, ERSKINE RESOURCES TO MERGE

****

Canadian Bashaw Leduc Oil and Gas Ltd said it agreed to merge with Erskine Resources Ltd. Terms were not disclosed.

Ownership of the combined company with 18.8 pct for the current shareholders of Canadian Bashaw and 81.2 pct to the current shareholders of Erskine, the companies said.

Reuter

(15004)

(b) 200 dpi

U

****

CANADIAN BASHAW, ERSKINE RESOURCES TO MERGE

****

Canadian Bashaw Leduc Oil and Gas Ltd said it agreed to merge with Erskine Resources Ltd. Terms were not disclosed.

Ownership of the combined company with 18.8 pct for the current shareholders of Canadian Bashaw and 81.2 pct to the current shareholders of Erskine, the companies said.

Reuter

(15004)

(c) 140 dpi

Fig. 1. Examples of the text images

ASCII Text Generation by OCR

The text images generated in above are converted to the ASCII texts by OCR software "OKREADER2000" (Figure 2(a)-(c)).

The obtained ASCII text is compared with the original ASCII text in the Reuters collection to calculate the average character recognition rate and the average word recognition rate for each dpi. The average character recognition rate is defined by

$$c = \frac{(s-t)}{s} \times 100 ,\tag{1}$$

where s and t is the number of total characters and the number of mis-recognized characters, respectively. The average word recognition rate is defined by

---

CANADIAN BASHAW, ERSKINE RESOURCES TO MERGE
Canadian Bashaw Leduc Oil and Gas Ltd said it agreed to merge with Erskine Resources Ltd.
Terms were not disclosed.
Ownership of the combined company with 18.8 pet for the current shareholders of Canadian Bashaw and 81.2 pet to the current shareholders of Erskine, the companies said.
Reuter

(a) The ASCII text of 300dpi

CANADIAN BASHAW, ERSKINR RESOURCES TO MERGE
Canadian Bashaw Leduc Oil and Gas Ltd said it agreed lu merge with Rrskme Resources Lid.
Terms were not disclosed.
Ownership of the combined company with 18.8 pet tor the current shareholders of
Canadian Bashaw and 81.2 pel to the current. shareholders ofF.rskinc, I he companies said.
Keuler

(b) The ASCII text of 200dpi

CANADIAN yASHAW. HR^KJNh kI';SOlJRCn,S TO V1HRGR
Canadian Bashaw Leduc Oil and Gas I.Id s;ilii IT agreed ro merge wirii Hnkine RL^OUI-CCS Ltd.
Forms were not disclosed.
Ownership of ihe combined company with 1^.8 pet for the cuncnt shareholders of
C,m;idi,in B^sbaw and 81.2 pel to ihc eiirrL'nt sbaicholLlcrs cifF.rskrne, die companies said.
Rt-'uter

(c) The ASCII text of 140dpi

Fig. 2. Examples of the ASCII texts converted by OCR software

$$v = \frac{(w-u)}{w} \times 100 \quad , \tag{2}$$

where w and u is the number of total words and the number of mis-recognized words, respectively.

Text Classification

Feature Vector Generation
A lexicon is generated from the learning sample by picking up all words in the sample. Then the feature vector for each text is composed of the frequencies of the lexicon words in the text. The dimensionality of the feature vector is equal to the lexicon size and is denoted by n.

Dimension Reduction
At first the total covariance matrix of the learning sample is calculated to find the eigenvalues and eigenvectors. Each feature vector is transformed to the principal

components in terms of the orthonormal transformation with the eigenvectors as the basis vectors. To reduce the dimensionality of the feature vector the principal components which correspond to the m largest eigenvalues are selected to compose the feature vector of dimensionality m $(< n)$.

Learning
Parameters of each classification technique are determined in the training process using the learning sample. The Euclidean distance classifier employs the mean vector of each class. The linear discriminant function employs the weight vector determined by the mean vector of each class and the pooled within covariance matrix of entire classes. The projection distance and the modified projection distance employ the eigenvectors (and the eigenvalues) of the individual covariance matrix. As a support vector machine (SVM), C-support vector classification method (C-SVC) of linear type and of RBF type (with radial basis function) were employed for the classification tests. We used the SVM library (LIBSVM Version 2.33) developed by Chang and Lin (2002) [6].

Classification
The feature vector of reduced dimensionality is classified to the class the distance (or the discriminant function) of which is minimized. Referring to the subject field manually given to each article in Reuters-21578, the classification rate R is calculated by

$$R = \frac{x}{(x+y)} \times 100 \quad , \tag{3}$$

where x and y is the number of articles correctly classified and incorrectly classified, respectively.

4   The Experiment Results

Table1 shows the character recognition rates and the word recognition rates for different dpi's. Table 2 shows the text classification rates of each classification technique for different character recognition rates, and for different word recognition rates. Figure3 shows the relationship between the text classification rate and the word recognition rate, and Figure 4 shows the relationship between the text classification rate and the character recognition rate.

Table 1. The character recognition rates vs. the word recognition rates

Resolution (dpi)	300	240	200	150	145	140
Word recognition rate (%)	97.54	94.84	92.69	82.77	66.40	63.33
character recognition rate (%)	99.28	98.72	98.14	95.35	91.14	90.04

The results of experiment are summarized as follows:
1. The text classification rates of all classification techniques were not deteriorated significantly until the character recognition rate or the word recognition rate was deteriorated to 95% or 80%, respectively.

2. The text classification rate for the modified projection distance and the SVM-linear was kept over 90% even when the character recognition rate or the word recognition rate was further deteriorated to 90% or 60%, respectively.
3. The text classification rates for the linear discriminant function and the Euclidian distance were more rapidly deteriorated than other techniques.
4. The SVM-linear outperformed the others in the accuracy and the robustness of the text classification in this experiment.

Table 2. The text classification rates vs. character recognition rates and word recognition rates

Word recognition rate	100	97.54	94.84	92.69	82.77	66.40	63.33
character recognition rate	100	99.28	98.72	98.14	95.35	91.14	90.04
Euclidean distance	83.6	83.2	82.4	81.2	78.4	71.2	66.0
Linear discrimination function	95.2	95.2	93.6	94.0	93.2	86.8	86.4
projection distance	93.2	93.2	92.4	92.8	90.4	89.2	88.6
modified projection distance	95.2	95.2	95.2	94.0	93.2	92.8	91.2
SVM-Linear	95.6	95.6	95.6	95.2	95.2	93.6	93.2
SVM- RBF	93.6	93.6	93.2	92.4	92.4	92.0	89.6

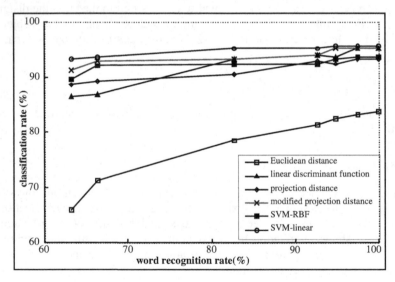

Fig. 3. The text classification rate vs. the word recognition rate

5   The Future Study

In the experiment we dealt with five category case and obtained encouraging result, however, we need to deal with more categories in real world application of text classification. We will perform similar experiment with more categories to reveal the feasibility of the OCR input text classification.

Error correction of words by spelling check is also remaining as a future study to improve the text classification accuracy.

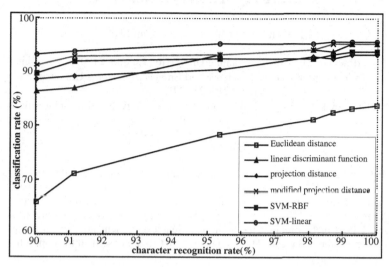

Fig. 4. The text classification rate vs. the character recognition rate

References

1. Ohta,M., Takasu,A., Adachi,J.: "Retrieval Methods for English-Text with Missrecognized OCR Characters", *Proceedings* of the Fourth International Conference on Document Analysis and Recognition (ICDAR), pp.950-956, August 18-20, 1997,Ulm, Germany.
2. Myka, A., Guntzer. U.: "Measuring the Effects of OCR Errors on Similarity Linking", *Proceedings* of the Fourth International Conference on Document Analysis and Recognition (ICDAR), pp.968-973, August 18-20, 1997, Ulm, Germany.
3. Sebastiani, F.: "Machine Learning in Automated Text Categorization", *ACM Computing Surveys,* Vol. 34, No. 1, 1-47, March 2002.
4. Fukumoto,T., Wakabayashi,T. Kimura,F. and Miyake,Y.: "Accuracy Improvement of Handwritten Character Recognition By GLVQ", *Proceedings* of the Seventh International Workshop on Frontiers in Handwriting Recognition Proceedings(IWFHR VII), 271-280 September 2000.
5. Guowei Zu, Wataru Ohyama, Tetsushi Wakabayashi, Fumitaka Kimura,: "Accuracy improvement of automatic text classification based on feature transformation" *DocEng'03* (ACM Symposium on Document Engineering 2003), pp.118-120, November 20–22, 2003, Grenoble, France
6. C.C. Chang, and C.J. Lin : "LIBSVM – A Library for Support Vector Machines (Version 2.33)", *http://www.csie.ntu.edu.tw/~cjlin/libsvm/index.html,* (2002.4)

TSS: A Hybrid Web Searches

Li-Xin Han[1,2,3], Gui-Hai Chen[3], and Li Xie[3]

[1] Department of Mathematics, Nanjing University, Nanjing 210093, P.R. China
[2] Department of Computer Science and Engineering, Hohai University,
Nanjing 210024, P.R. China
[3] State Key Laboratory of Novel Software Technology, Nanjing University,
Nanjing 210093, P.R. China
lixinhan2002@yahoo.com.cn

Abstract. Because of emergence of Semantic Web, It make possible for machines to understand the meaning of resources on the Web. The widespread availability of machine understandable information will impact on Information retrieval on the web. In this paper, we propose a hybrid web searches architecture, TSS, which combines the traditional search with semantic search to improve precision and recall. The components in TSS are described to support the hybrid web searches.

1 Introduction

Nowadays the amount of information on the Web is increasing dramatically. The ability of facilitating users to achieve useful information is more and more important for information retrieval systems. Information retrieval technology has improved, however, users are not satisfied with low precision and recall. With emergence of Semantic Web, this situation can be remarkably improved if machines could "understand" the content of web pages.

The existing information retrieval technology can be classified mainly into three classes.

(1) Traditional information retrieval technology [1] is based almost purely on the occurrence of words in documents. It is mainly limit to string matching. However, it is of no use when a search is based on the words themselves, rather than the meaning of words.

(2) Search engines are limit to string matching and link analysis. The most widely used algorithms are the PageRank algorithm [2] and the HITS algorithm [3]. The PageRank algorithm is based on how many other pages point to the Web page and the value of the pages pointing to it. Search engines like Google combine IR techniques with PageRank. In contrast to the PageRank algorithm, the HITS algorithm employs a query dependent ranking technique. In addition, the HITS algorithm produces the authority and the hub score.

(3) The widespread availability of machine understandable information on the Semantic Web offers some opportunities for improving on traditional search. If machines could "understand" the content of web pages, searches with high precision and recall would be possible. Although traditional search technology such as Latent Semantic Indexing [4] has explored the use of semantics for information retrieval, their work still focus on generating the semantic structures from text. Some semantic search methods [5], [6] have been proposed to improve traditional

C.-H. Chi and K.-Y. Lam (Eds.): AWCC 2004, LNCS 3309, pp. 410–415, 2004.
© Springer-Verlag Berlin Heidelberg 2004

search technology. The major difficulty in implementation of these methods is more time consuming to add annotations to web pages. It is possible that all of the relevant web pages are not described by markup, only partial answers can be returned. Therefore, there is not sufficient page volume become available. Moreover, in contrast to a typical web search interface for typing keywords, the search systems are more complicated. It has to have a way to choice detailed information such as ontology, category etc.

We propose a hybrid web searches architecture, TSS (Traditional Semantic Search), which combines the traditional search with semantic search to improve the above classes of methods.

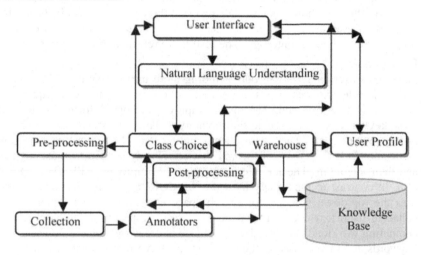

Fig. 1. The TSS Architecture

2   Overview of the TSS Architecture

The architecture of TSS system consists of user interface, natural language understanding, class choice, pre-processing, collection, annotators, post-processing, user profile. This architecture is shown in Fig 1.

(1) User Interface
The agent allows a user to enter a natural language question instead of some keywords in order that users are convenient to use the system. The results are returned in the two approaches. One approach is that the users browse the results in extended class hierarchy mode. The other approach is that the agent pushes useful information to the users according to different users' needs. The users browse information through their favorable interface based on their own ontologies.

(2) Natural Language Understanding
The agent is used to process the natural language questions. The agent employs LR algorithm [7] to complete grammar parse for a given question. A given question is parsed to create a grammar tree and submitted to slot-filling. In contrast to the slot-filling of some nature languages, the agent employs slot-

filling with grammar structure. Thus, besides patterns match, a given question can be processed based grammar parser. The agent then employs Brill's part-of-speech tagger [8] to analyse the words in a given question. The agent deletes certain frequent words, acquired from the widely used WordNet [9], such as punctuation, preposition, article, or conjunction. It treats the rest of the question as keywords. In the mean time, the agent also employs WordNet to identify phrases as keywords.

(3) Class Choice

The agent acquires the keywords from natural language understanding agent. According to Cosine similarity formula, similarity between the keywords and the classes in the Warehouse is calculated to find the related classes if its similarity is above threshold. According to class hierarchy, the related classes can be organized into the user ontology. The results are returned to user interface.

(4) Pre-processing

Sometimes users may have trouble finding more useful results. This is because all of the relevant web pages are not described by markup. Consequently, all answers can't be returned. The agent employs ontology information to extend these keywords so as to create their synonym. Thus, it extends to search scope and improve recall. The agent then employs our RK algorithm for mining association rules to create the words that are closely related to these keywords and their synonym. The RK algorithm uses the improved APRIORI algorithm [10]. In contrast to the widely used the APRIORI algorithm, the RK algorithm uses the top-down strategy for search space and some typical documents are collected from text corpus to reduce the size of transaction database. Thus the computing workload is reduced in the course of creating frequent itemsets. These keywords and their synonym then are restricted by these relevant words so as to reduce ambiguity and improve precision.

(5) Collection

The agent sends these queries to some search engines such as Alta Vista, Infoseek. Because different search engines have different input interfaces, the agent must convert query into the formats suitable for these input interfaces. When the query results were returned, it is possible to find duplicates web pages. Thus, the agent eliminates duplicates web pages and combines and ranks the returned results from the different search engines. The final results return to the annotators.

(6) Annotators

Annotation plays an important role on the semantic search. The key feature of our annotators can automatically discover associate annotations than some current semi-automatic annotation tools in [11]. The Annotators employ our AANN algorithm to discover semantic relationships. In the AANN algorithm, based on the existed association instances acquired from our association rules algorithm, the new meaningful relationships can be discovered through an inferential process. According to the semantics of these annotations, the agent automatically categorized these web pages and put them into the warehouse. The agent creates mapping rules from these annotations that are later employed by an inference engine.

(7) Post-processing
The agent post-processes the returned results from annotators. The agent provides several kinds of inference in order to make search more powerful. The agent generalizes or specializes terms and their relations from the results in order to return more useful results to the user.

(8) User Profile
Because large amount of user interaction information recorded in the web query logs has the potential to be available, the agent employs our BUP algorithm in order to create user profiles. In contrast to the other algorithms of building user profile, our algorithm employs ontology to express user profile in order that a user may own several interests. The user profile consists of a few keywords sets. Every keywords set expresses certain interest. Every ontology class expresses one interest. Our algorithm employs some heuristic rules to build keywords sets in order to reduce the computing workload. Our algorithm modifies user profile by adding and deleting keywords set in order to dynamically meet users' demand. Thus the algorithm can make a user profile more self-adaptive. Compared with the other method such as machine learning and typing users' demand, our algorithm can make a user profile less manually interfered. In addition, the agent employs push technology in order to actively send useful information to the users according to different users' user profiles.

3 Related Work

The SHOE Search tool [6] is unique in that it allows the user to specify a context for search, and provides the user with options which are relevant to that context. It is essentially a frame-based query by example interface, but includes features that allow the user to discover the content of the knowledge base and to extend the search beyond the knowledge base by translating the query into a format that can be issued to standard search engines. Since the user has been prompted to enter values for defining characteristics of the object in question, search engine queries created by SHOE Search are more likely to return relevant results. In contrast to the SHOE Search tool, TSS allows a user to enter a natural language question instead of some keywords in order that users are convenient to use the system. On the other hand, TSS sends actively useful information to the users according to different users' needs. TSS instead of the user chooses the related context. TSS employs ontology information to extend these keywords so as to create their synonym. It then employs association rules to create the words that are closely related to these keywords and their synonym. These keywords and their synonym are restricted by these relevant words so as to reduce ambiguity and improve precision. TSS generalizes or specializes terms and their relations from the returned results in order to return more useful results. TSS can automatically discover associate annotations. TSS employs ontology to express user profile in order that a user may own several interests.

Semantic Search [5] attempts to improve the results of research searches in 2 ways. (1) It augments this list of documents with relevant data pulled out from Semantic Web. The Semantic Web based results are independent of and augment the results obtained via traditional IR techniques. (2) Understanding the denotation can help understand the context of the search. However, it is more time consuming to add annotations to web pages. In the result, there is not sufficient page volume become available. Thus, only partial relevant answers can be returned. TSS is the hybrid web searches method of combined the traditional search with semantic search to solve such problems. If only part of answers can be acquire from the relevant annotated web pages, search engines must be employed to find more relevant answers.

4   Conclusion

The widespread availability of machine understandable information on the Semantic Web offers some opportunities for improving on traditional search. In this paper, a hybrid web search architecture called TSS is proposed, which combines the traditional search with semantic search in order to improve precision and recall. The components in TSS are described to support the hybrid web searches.

Acknowledgements

This work is supported by the State Key Laboratory Foundation of Novel Software Technology at Nanjing University under grant A200308, the National Grand Fundamental Research 973 Program of China under No. 2002CB312002 and the Key Natural Science Foundation of Jiangsu Province of China under grant BK2003001.

References

1. Mei Kobayashi and Koichi Takeda. Information Retrieval on the Web. ACM Computing Surveys, 2000, 32(2): 144 – 173.
2. S. Brin and L. Page. The Anatomy of a Large-Scale Hypertextual Web Search Engine. In the Proceedings of the Seventh International World Wide Web Conference. Brisbane, April 1998.
3. Soumen Chakrabarti, Byron E. Dom, S. Ravi Kumar, etc. Mining the Web's Link Structure. IEEE Computer, 1999(8): 60-67.
4. Deerwester, S., Dumai, S. T., Furnas, G. W., Landauer, T. K., and Harshman, R.. Indexing by latent semantic analysis. J. Am. Soc. Inf. Sci., 1990.41(6,): 391–407.
5. R. Guha, Rob McCool, and Eric Miller. Semantic Search. In the Proceedings of the Twelfth International World Wide Web Conference. Budapest, Hungary, May 20-24, 2003.
6. Jeff Heflin and James Hendler. Searching the Web with SHOE. In AAAI-2000 Workshop on AI for Web Search. 2000.
7. Tomita, M. Efficient Parsing for Natural Language: A Fast Algorithm for Practical Systems. Kluwer Academic, 1985.
8. E. Brill. A simple rule-based part of speech tagger. In Third Conference on Applied Natural Language Processing (ANLP-92), 1992.
9. G.Miller. WordNet: A Lexical Database for English. Communications of the ACM, 38(11): 39-41. 1995.
10. R. Agrawal and R. Srikant. Fast Algorithms for Mining Association Rules. In Proc. of the 20th Int. Conf. on Very Large Databases (VLDB' 94), pages 478-499, Santiago, Chile, Sep. 1994. Expanded version available as IBM Research Report RJ9839, June 1994.
11. S. Handschuh and S. Staab, Authoring and Annotation of Web Pages in CREAM, WWW2002, May 7-11, 2002, Honolulu, Hawaii, USA.

12. D. Brickley and R.V. Guha, Resource Description Framework (RDF) Schema Specification. W3C Candidate Recommendation 27 March 2000, www.w3.org/TR/2000/CR-rdf-schema-20000327.

13. D. Box, D. Ehnebuske, G. Kakivaya, A. Layman, N. Mendelsohn, H. F. Nielsen, S. Thatte, and D. Winder. Simple Object Access Protocol. http://www.w3.org/TR/SOAP/, May 2000.

14. T. Berners-Lee, J. Hendler, and O. Lassila. Semantic web. *Scientific American*, 1(1):68-88, 2000.

15. Siegfried Handschuh, Steffen Staab, and Raphael Volz. On Deep Annotation. In the Proceedings of the Twelfth International World Wide Web Conference. Budapest, Hungary, May 20-24, 2003.

16. Boanerges Aleman-Meza, Chris Halaschek, I. Budak Arpinar, and Amit Sheth. Context-Aware Semantic Association Ranking. Semantic Web and Databases Workshop Proceedings. Belin, September 7,8 2003.

17. M. Rodriguez and M. Egenhofer, Determining Semantic Similarity among Entity Classes from Different Ontologies, IEEE Transactions on Knowledge and Data Engineering, Vol. 15, No. 2, March/April 2003.

Determining the Number of Probability-Based Clustering: A Hybrid Approach

Tao Dai, Chunping Li, and Jia-Guang Sun

School of Software
Tsinghua University, Beijing, China
{Daitao02@tsinghua.org.cn}

Abstract. While analyzing the previous methods for determining the number of probability-based clustering, this paper introduces an improved Monte Carlo Cross-Validation algorithm (iMCCV) and attempts to solve the posterior probabilities spread problem, which cannot be resolved by the Monte Carlo Cross-Validation algorithm. Furthermore, we present a hybrid approach to determine the number of probability-based clustering by combining the iMCCV algorithm and the parallel coordinates visual technology. The efficiency of our approach is discussed with experimental results.

1 Introduction

Cluster analysis is one of the main functions in Data Mining and Knowledge Discovery, which groups data sets into classes by nature and gives a character depiction for every class. Under the assumption that we have known the number of clusters, i.e. K, we often use probability-based clustering algorithms to partition data into classes, making the similarity as small as feasible in the same class, and as big as possible between classes. However, probability-based clustering algorithms do not directly answer the question, how many clusters in a given data set?

We need probability-based clustering algorithms not only to discover the structure of a data set, but also to find the number of clusters. Obviously, letting the data set tell us the cluster structure as much as possible is a good method. In this paper, we introduce a novel approach to determine the number of probability-based clustering. Our approach is based on Gaussian mixture model. But actually, if a likelihood function is defined, then any other probabilistic clustering could apply this approach.

The organization of the rest of the paper is as follows. In Section 2, mixture models clustering algorithm and related works on determining the number of clusters are introduced. In Section 3, an approach to determine clustering number is presented. In Section 4, we give an evaluation of our approach with experimental results. Conclusions are drawn in Section 5.

C.-H. Chi and K.-Y. Lam (Eds.): AWCC 2004, LNCS 3309, pp. 416–421, 2004.

2   Related Works

2.1   Mixture Models

A probability-based clustering algorithm is mixture models, which assumes that the data sets are generated by a linear combination of component density functions and results in a mixture probability density function of the form:

$$p(x|\Theta) = \sum_{k=1}^{K} \alpha_k p_k(x|\theta_k)$$

where x is a given value of a d-dimensional feature vector, K is the number of components in the model. The α_k are the weights for each component k, and $\Theta = \{\alpha_1, \ldots, \alpha_k, \theta_1, \ldots, \theta_k\}$ denotes the data set of the parameter for the whole model, where θ_k is the d-dimensional component model parameter. The EM(Expectation-Maximization) algorithm [3] is a general method of finding the maximum-likelihood estimate of the parameters of mixture model.

2.2   Some Approaches to Determine K

In general, there are four different kinds of approaches to determine the number of clusters in an automatic form.

The first approach of hypothesis testing cannot be used to determine the number of mixture model clustering [5, 7].

The second approach is full Bayesian method. It is difficult in integrating over the parameter space to get posterior probabilities on K. Cheeseman and Stutz present the AutoClass algorithm to get posterior probabilities on K by mathematic analytic solution [2].

The third approach is the penalized likelihood, which gets K by subtracting a penalty term from the maximizing value of the likelihood. Bayesian Information Criterion (BIC) is a more reliable approximation [4], which is defined as follows:

$$BIC \equiv 2log\ p(X|M) + const. \approx 2L_M(\Theta|X) - m_M log(N) \qquad (1)$$

where $p(X|M)$ is the likelihood of the data X for the model M, $L_M(\Theta|X)$ is the maximized mixture log-likelihood for the model, Θ is the parameters of M, m_M is the number of independent parameters to be estimated in the model.

The four approach is cross-validated. The approach requires more computations than BIC, but it can get the estimation directly, while BIC cannot [5].

There are some different cross-validated methods. The most common one is v-fold Cross-Validation (vCV). Smyth presented a Monte Carlo Cross-Validation (MCCV) algorithm [7] and proved that the MCCV algorithm could get more accurate estimation than vCV. The MCCV algorithm partitions the data set M times into disjoint training data and testing data where the testing subset is a fraction β of the whole data. Typically the M is 20 and the β large than 0.5.

The time complexity of MCCV is $O(LNdMK_{max}^2)$, where L is the number of iteration, N is the count of data instances, d is the dimension of data, K_{max} is the probably maximum number of clusters. The algorithm is as follows:

- Input: data set D
- Output: Cluster number K
- Steps:
    1. FOR i $\leftarrow$ 1 TO M
        (a) Randomize D
        (b) $D_{Testing} \leftarrow \beta$ fraction of D, $D_{Training} \leftarrow D - D_{Testing}$
        (c) FOR k $\leftarrow$ 1 TO K_{max}
            i. $EM(D_{Training}, k)$, estimate parameter
            ii. $loglk[k] \leftarrow E(D_{Testing}, k)$
    2. $K = \{k | p(k|D)$ approximates to 1, $1 \leq k \leq K_{max}\}$

where $p(k|D)$ is the posterior probabilities, which is defined as follows:

$$p(k|D) \approx \frac{exp(loglk[k])}{\sum_{k=1}^{K_{max}} exp(loglk[k])},   1 \leq k \leq K_{max}$$

3   A Hybrid Approach to Determine the Cluster Number

3.1   Improved Monte Carlo Cross-Validation Algorithm

MCCV algorithm estimate the K by roughly calculating the posterior probabilities for each k $(1 \leq k \leq K_{max})$, where K_{max} is the probably maximum number of clusters. However, if the values of posterior probabilities are more spread out, the MCCV algorithm cannot get the number of clusters [7]. We present an improved Monte Carlo Cross-Validation algorithm (iMCCV) to resolve the problem mentioned above. The main idea is to avoid calculating posterior probabilities. We estimate K according to the M times local maximum of log-likelihood. The iMCCV algorithm is described as follows:

- Input: data set D
- Output: Cluster number K
- Steps:
    1. FOR i $\leftarrow$ 1 TO M
        (a) Randomize D
        (b) $D_{Testing} \leftarrow \beta$ fraction of D, $D_{Training} \leftarrow D - D_{Testing}$
        (c) FOR k $\leftarrow$ 1 TO K_{max}
            i. $EM(D_{Training}, k)$, estimate parameter
            ii. $loglk[k] \leftarrow E(D_{Testing}, k)$
            iii. IF $loglk[k]$ is local maximum THEN $\{C[i] \leftarrow k$ and break FOR$\}$
    2. $K = \frac{\sum_{i=1}^{M} C[i]}{M}$

where $C[i]$ records the local maximum location of the ith repeat, $loglk$ is the log-likelihood calculated from EM algorithm's E-Step, and K is the means of M times local maximum location.

The time complexity of the iMCCV algorithm is $O(LNdMK^2)$, comparing the MCCV algorithm's $O(LNdMK_{max}^2)$. Typically, $K \ll K_{max}$, the computing efficiency of the iMCCV algorithm is improved to a great extent compared with the MCCV algorithm.

3.2 Combining with the Visual Technology of the Parallel Coordinates

However, the K estimated from iMCCV may be not an integer. If the $K = 3.1$, we have a large probability to consider that the truth K is 3; if the $K = 3.9$, then truth K is 4 with more probably preferable. However, if the $K = 3.5$, then how shall we determine the truth K in such cases?

Because of the power of human eye to detect structures, we attempt to utilize the human-machine interaction to assist us to determine the truth K. We present a novel approach to determine the number of probability-based clustering. Firstly, we use iMCCV algorithm to estimate possibly number of clusters automatically. Secondly, We choose a most probably integer as the truth K by comparing some integer values cluster number in parallel coordinates [6]. The hybrid approach combines the iMCCV automatic method and the visual technology.

4 Experimental Results

The iMCCV algorithm has been evaluated on both simulated and real data sets (with $M = 20$, and $\beta = 0.62$). We have compared our algorithm to AutoClass v3.3.4 [1] and BIC (with equation (1)). We use the same EM algorithm component in both BIC and iMCCV algorithms.

The simulated data sets include four categories. Each category has three kinds of size data. The simulated data sets come from [7]. The real data sets are selected from UCI data sets [1]: Iris; Wine; Liver-disorders(Liver); Glass; Ecoli and Pima-diabetes(Diab).

4.1 Simulated Data and Real Data Sets

Table 1 contains a brief summary of the experiment results on simulated data sets and the real data sets.

From the experimental results with the simulated data sets, we can conclude that AutoClass and iMCCV perform better than BIC. AutoClass and iMCCV have the similar results on Iris, Glass, Wine, Diab and Liver. Moreover the K evaluated from iMCCV is close to the truth K. All the three algorithms get a bad result on Ecoli. However, AutoClass and iMCCV perform better than BIC obviously.

4.2 Using the Visual Technology of the Parallel Coordinates

From Table 1, we can see that $K = 3.4$ when the iMCCV algorithm is performed on Iris. We might use parallel coordinates to determine the truth K.

---
[1] http://ic-www.arc.nasa.gov/ic/projects/bayes-group/autoclass/autoclass-c-program.html#Obtaining.

Table 1. Experimental Results on Simulated Data and Real Data Sets

Data set	Data Size	BIC	AC	iMCCV	Truth K
1-Class	50	2	1	1.0	1
	200	1	2	1.0	1
	800	1	2	1.4	1
2-Class	100	2	2	2.1	2
	600	3	3	2.1	2
	1200	2	2	2.3	2
3-Class	100	3	2	2.7	3
	600	3	3	3.3	3
	1200	3	2	3.4	3
4-Class	100	4	2	2.7	4
	600	6	3	4.0	4
	1200	3	5	3.9	4
Iris	150	6	3	3.4	3
Wine	178	5	2	3.5	3
Liver	345	6	3	3.4	2
Glass	214	4	5	4.5	6
Ecoli	336	1	3	1.7	8
Diab	768	4	3	3.0	2

For the clustering result of the data set Iris, Figure 1 shows $K = 3$. Figure 2 shows $K = 4$. Comparing the Figure 1 with Figure 2, we can have a conclusion that $K = 4$ cannot bring more distinct data information than $K = 3$. As a result, we choose the $K = 3$ as the truth K.

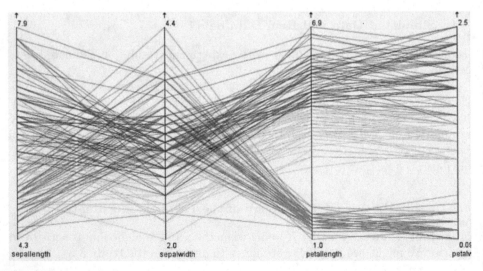

Fig. 1. Parallel coordinates shows the $K = 3$ Iris data, where the red, blue and green cluster sizes are 50, 45, 55, respectively

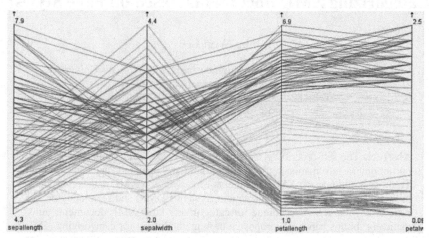

Fig. 2. Parallel coordinates shows the $K = 4$ Iris data, where the red, blue, yellow and green cluster sizes are 50, 48, 42, 10, respectively

5   Conclusions

The MCCV algorithm is a useful method to determine the number of clusters but it cannot solve the problem of posterior probabilities spread. We introduce the iMCCV algorithm to solve this problem by avoiding calculating posterior probabilities. However, the K estimated from iMCCV may be not an integer. We choose the truth K by the parallel coordinates visual technology. The efficiency of the hybrid approach which combines the iMCCV algorithm and the parallel coordinates visual technology has been proved by experimental results.

References

1. Blake, C.L. and Merz, C.J. UCI repository of machine learning databases, University of California, Irvine, Dept. of Information and Computer Sciences. *http://www.ics.uci.edu/~mlearn/MLRepository.html*, 1998.
2. Cheeseman, P. and Stutz, J., Bayesian Classification (AutoClass): Theory and Results. In *Advances in Knowledge Discovery and Data Mining*, (1995), AAAI Press/MIT Press, 153-180.
3. Dempster, A.P., Laird, N.M. and Rubin, D.B. Maximum Likelihood from Incomplete Data via the EM Algorithm. *Journal of the Royal Statistical Society, Series B(Methodological)*, 39 (1). 1-38.
4. Fraley, C. and Raftery, A.E. How Many Clusters? Which Clustering Method? Answers Via Model-Based Cluster Analysis. *Computer Journal*, 41. 578-588. 1998.
5. Hand, D., Mannila, H. and Smyth, P. *Principles of Data Mining.* Massachusetts Institute of Technology, 2001.
6. Inselberg, A. and Dimsdale, B., Parallel Coordinates : A Tool for Visualizing Multidimensional Geometry. In *Proceedings of the First conference on Visualization*, (San Francisco, California, 1990), 361 - 378.
7. Smyth, P., Clustering using Monte Carlo Cross-Validation. In *Proceedings of the 2nd International Conference on Knowledge Discovery and Data Mining (KDD'96)*, (1996), AAAI Press, 126-133.

Categorizing XML Documents Based on Page Styles*

Jung-Won Lee

Dept. of Computer Science and Engineering, Ewha Womans University,
11-1 Daehyun-dong, Sudaemun-ku, Seoul, Korea
Tel: +82-2-3277-3480, Fax: +82-2-3277-2306
jungwony@ewha.ac.kr

Abstract. The self-describing feature of XML offers both challenges and opportunities in information retrieval, document management, and data mining.
To process and manage XML documents effectively on XML data server, database, Electronic Document Management System(EDMS) and search engine, we
have to develop a new technique for categorizing large XML documents automatically. In this paper, we propose a new methodology for categorizing XML
documents based on page style by taking account of meanings of the elements
and nested structures of XML. Accurate categorization of XML documents by
page styles provides an important basis for a variety of applications of managing and processing XML. Experiments with Yahoo! pages show that our methodology provides almost 100% accuracy in categorizing XML documents by
page styles.

1 Introduction

Many applications using a database and EDMS as well as XML Data Server have
employed XML as a representative document format[11]. These all systems require
techniques for exchanging data using metadata, converting A format to B format
automatically, XML query processing, indexing, storing and so on. They also need
methods for categorizing and filtering XML documents. By categorizing documents,
it is possible to reduce the scope of candidate documents, which may be target documents that user requests.

An XML element may have meanings beyond the same words used in a flat or unstructured document. It can provide an important hint for building an index structure
for information retrieval(IR) or determining a schema for transferring data from the
Web to a database. Although XML has lots of benefits, there is no specialized IR
model to be able to quantify the meanings of the elements and nested structures of an
XML document, because traditional IR models are designed to deal with flat texts or
unstructured documents.

In this paper, we propose a new methodology for categorizing XML documents by
considering the meanings of the elements and nested structures of XML documents.
We analyze an XML document by considering XML features, extract common features between XMLs, and then quantify similarity based on common features. Experiments with Yahoo! pages, we got almost 100% accuracy in categorizing XML
documents based on page styles. Our methodology has broad applicability. If it is
combined with traditional search methods, it makes possible to query such as "find

---

* This Work was supported by the Ewha Womans University Research Grant of 2004.

C.-H. Chi and K.-Y. Lam (Eds.): AWCC 2004, LNCS 3309, pp. 422–429, 2004.

XML documents, which have stock information of Oracle and describe information as a graph of broken line or a pie chart", or "find XML documents including a bulletin board to communicate with each other about stock information". It can be also used widely for classifying and managing XML documents for EDMS and data warehousing, for building a knowledge base of a search engine, and for collecting focused documents using crawler[13] as well.

2 Background

The traditional methods for classifying or clustering documents use methods considering only term-frequency[4]. They cannot consider XML semantics–the meanings of the elements and nested structures. Some research has been done to develop text mining methods specialized for structured or semi-structured documents including XML[5,6,8,12]. [8] focuses on finding frequent tree patterns of semistructured data but does not present measure for document similarity. In other words, it deals with only the step of feature extraction. [5] and [12] propose measure for computing similarity considering structures of Web documents. However, it cannot consider the meanings of the elements composed of a structure. Therefore, it is difficult to compare with structures between XML documents obtained from different sites because they have synonyms, compound words, abbreviations, and so on. And [6] deals with only tag frequency without structural information.

The method for extracting common features between XML documents may be related to the problem of finding overlapped codes for the reuse of software. That problem has been researched for reducing the cost for software maintenance or for finding plagiarism of software. [7] uses the abstract syntax tree for finding duplicated parts of trees. However, it is dependent of parser of each programming language. Our target, XML, is a markup language, which does not have variable names and any specific syntax or defined grammar.

There are some research[2,3,9] for extracting an implicit structure from semistructured data but they are focused on fixed schema discovery for storing semistructured documents into a database. They try to optimize the schema regardless of losing a part of structural information. However, we have to discover a structure of XML without the loss of information.

3 The Process

For categorizing XML based on page styles, we have to quantify similarity between a sample XML document with a specific style and a query document. Therefore, it is essential to extract XML features exactly for accurate quantification of similarity. It is also important to determine which features are common between a sample and a query document and how much they are similar. In this section, we briefly describe the process for computing similarity between a sample document and query documents. The following figure 1 shows the process for determining which query document is similar or not.

The process is divided into three steps. The first step is for discovering XML structures. We discover and minimize the hierarchical structures of a sample document and query documents. We can get path expressions by connecting elements from a root to

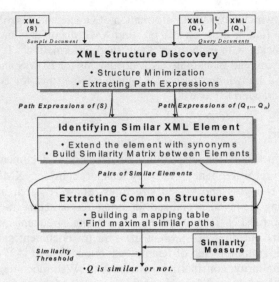

Fig. 1. The Process for Categorizing XML Documents

terminal of a minimized structure. In the second, we extend elements of path expressions to extended-element vectors, which have synonyms, abbreviations, or compound words for the approximate matching between elements. We have to build similarity matrix for measuring similarity between elements. Path expressions obtained from the first step and pairs of similar elements from the second are inputs of the third step for extracting common structures. We first transform path expressions to paths renamed by integers. We then find similar paths among renamed paths using an adapted sequential patterns mining algorithm and get maximal similar path by reducing duplicated paths. Based on maximal similar paths, we propose our new metric for quantifying similarity between a sample and a query document as percentage (%).

3.1 Feature Extraction

For extracting XML feature, we have to analyze both structures and elements of XML as the following.

- *XML Structure Discovery:* We have chosen to formalize the structure of an XML document using automata[1]. We can also get a Document Object Model(DOM) tree by XML parser. However, we cannot use DOM tree as it is because it has many duplicated paths. Our goal for discovering XML structures is to extract unique and minimized structures of each XML document. Therefore, we formalize XML structures using finite automata for applying state-minimization algorithm[1] of automata to minimize them.
- *Identifying Similar XML Elements*: Synonyms, compound words, or abbreviations may be used for defining XML elements in multiple documents (e.g., 'products' and 'goods', 'author' and 'writer', 'publisher' and 'publishing_company', 'book' and 'bib' as a abbreviation of 'bibliography'). To identify similar elements between XML documents, we create an extended-element vector for each element using thesaurus and user-defined library and a similarity matrix for comparing ex-

tended-element vectors. An extended-element vector is a list of synonyms, compound words, and abbreviations that are related to a given element. For example, the extended-element vector for a 'subject' is <subject> → [topic, theme, issue, matter, discipline, subject_area, subject_field, field, field_of_study, study, branch_of_knowledg, content, depicted_object, case, guinea_pig, national, subj]. It forms a normalized basis for measuring similarity between elements belonging to different XML documents.

3.2 Extracting Common Structures

We obtained paths from minimized XML structures and with synonym information. We first rename path expressions with integers for fast computing. We have to build a mapping table with synonym information (i.e. pairs of similar elements) between two path expressions and transform similar elements to the same integer. For example, <author> of a sample document and <writer> of a query document have the same number. It we have two paths, bib.book.author.name.nil and bib.book.writer.lastname. nil, we rename these paths as 1.2.3.4.nil and 1.2.3.5.nil. Then we find common path using an adapted sequential pattern mining algorithm, which will be explained the next section.

From now on, we compute document similarity using sequential pattern mining algorithm for finding maximal similar paths between XML structures. Original sequential pattern mining algorithm finds maximal sequences among transaction sequences that satisfy user-defined minimum support[10]. Transaction sequences, which the original sequential pattern mining algorithms deal with, are random sequences of goods purchased by customers, such as 'beer', 'diaper' and 'milk'. Maximal sequences that satisfy some minimum support among large transaction sequences are found. Similar paths between XML documents have semantic relationships among transactions, namely, nested XML elements on a path. Therefore it is reasonable to presume that XML documents are more similar when they have more identical paths in their structures.

The following figure 2 shows the algorithm for finding maximal similar paths between two sets of path expressions. This algorithm is revised by extending original sequential pattern mining algorithm for XML. Input and output of the algorithm are as follows. (For the purpose of comparing multiple documents, we denote the sample document as S and query documents as $Q_{1..n}$.)

- $L_1^{S \bullet Q1..n}$ (frequent path with length = 1): elements identified as similar in the mapping table between a sample and a query document
- PE_S: set of path expressions of a sample document
- $PE_{Q1..n}$: set of path expressions of each $Q_{1..n}$;
- $ML^{S \bullet Q1..n}$: all maximal large similar paths between PE_S and $PE_{Q1..n}$

The algorithm involves multiple passes over the path expressions. In the first path, we use L_1 as the seed set and generate new potential large paths, called candidate paths C_2 using a candidate-generation function. We use AprioriAll algorithm[10] among sequential pattern mining algorithms to find $L_2, ... L_n$. In the maximal phase, we remove non-maximal paths from all large paths. Finally, we get $ML^{S \bullet Qi}$ (i.e., maximal similar paths between a sample and i^{th} query document) and consider these remained paths as common features between two documents.

procedure Sequence&Maximal ($\mathbf{L_1}^{S \bullet Q1..n}$: all large 1-path expressions between a sample
document S and each query document, **PE$_S$**: path expressions of a sample document,
PE$_{Q1..n}$: path expressions of query documents)
returns ML $^{S \bullet Q1..n}$; // *all maximal large similar paths between PE$_S$ and PE$_{Q1..n}$*
  begin
    for (i=1; i <= n; i++) **do**
    begin
        for (k=2; $L_{k-1}^{S \bullet Qi} \neq \varnothing$; k++) **do**
        begin   // *same as apriori-generate function of sequential patterns*
            C_k=New candidate-paths generated from $L_{k-1}^{S \bullet Qi}$;
            foreach path expressions in PE$_S$ and PE$_{Qi}$ **do**
                    //*pruning minimum support 100%*
                if ($C_k \in$ PE$_S$ and $C_k \in$ PE$_{Qk}$)
                  then $L_k^{S \bullet Qi} = C_k$;
        end
        length = k; // *longest length of large paths $L_k^{S \bullet Qi}$*
        end
        for (j = length; j >= 1; j--) **do**   // *maximal phase*
            foreach j-large paths, $L_j^{S \bullet Qi}$ **do**
            delete all sub-paths of $L_j^{S \bullet Qi}$;
        end
        ML$^{S \bullet Qi}$ = { remained large paths in L$^{S \bullet Qi}$ }
    end
  end

Fig. 2. Algorithm for Finding Maximal Similar Paths

4   Quantifying Similarity Between XML Documents

We can obtain all maximal large paths between the sample document and query
documents from previous step. To quantify similarity between XML structures, we
have to define new metric. The key concept of the metric is to assign different
weights to each path. The more similar child elements the parent has, the more
weights it may be assigned. The following is our similarity metric.

$$\text{Similarity} = \frac{1}{T} \sum_{i=1}^{T} \frac{1}{2 \times L(PE_i) - 1} \sum_{k=1}^{L(PE_k)} V(E_k)$$

Here, T is a number of total paths of a sample document, PE is a path expression,
L(PE) is the total number of elements on PE, and E_k is k^{th} element of PE. $V(E_k)$ may
have one value among 0, 1, or 2 according to the degree of match between elements
of two documents. Consider the following example in Table 1. Let's assume that there
are four paths in a sample document and A.B.E.nil and A.G.nil, as maximal similar
paths between the sample and a query. We filled the columns with gray color according to maximal similar paths and computed their ratio.

We can partially consider the context problem as the mentioned in section 4.2.
Suppose that there are two paths, book.author.title.nil of a sample document and
book.title.nil of a query. Here, 'title' of the sample means author's title and another
'title' of a query means a title of a book. Even if 'title' and 'book' are completely
matched between two paths, similarity using our metric is 5/7 because parents of two
'title' are different.

Table 1. Computing Similarity

PE	Match							Ratio
A.B.E.nil	A	•	B	•	E	•	nil	1/7 * (2+2+2+1)
A.B.F.nil	A	•	B	•	F	•	nil	1/7 * (2+1+0+0)
A.C.G.nil	A	•	C	•	G	•	nil	1/7 * (2+0+2+1)
A.D.nil	A	•	D	•	nil			1/5 * (1+0+1)
Similarity	63.57%							

5 Experimental Results

We've implemented our methodology using Java, XML SAX parser, and WordNet. The system operates as follows. User has a sample document, which describes stock information of Oracle with a specific style including charts. He wants to categorize XML documents that contain stock information of other companies with similar style. He just puts the sample document into our system and sets the threshold of similarity. It computes similarity between the sample and other query documents and categorizes query documents over the threshold. The traditional method, which considers only term frequency, examines statistics of all terms used in documents. However, our methodology can categorize XML documents based on specific styles because it can consider the meaning of the element and nested structure of an XML.

Due to difficulty in obtaining large XML documents with various structures, we chose to translate HTML documents to equivalent XML documents. In translation, we extracted terms that exist in real HTML pages and defined XML elements using them. We have some experimental results but the following figure 3 shows only the case of Yahoo!(business.yahoo.com). There are four categories–chart(stock information during the specific dates), message(user's bulletin board about stock information), news(news of a company during the specific date), and profile (company information).

We did an experiment with one hundred of XML documents, which are randomly chosen among 783 files(18.3Mb). We assumed that sample documents of each category were Doc.0 for charts, Doc.1 for messages, Doc. 2 for news, and Doc.23 for profiles.

In this experiment, we set the threshold of similarity as 80%. XML documents that have similarity over 80% are over the line. We confirmed their categories of these documents were identified 100% correctly. If we set the threshold as 60%, documents belonging to 'news' category are very similar to all documents because structures of documents in news are very simple.

6 Conclusions

In this paper, we propose a new methodology for categorizing XML documents similar to a given document style by considering the meanings of the elements and nested structures of an XML. We analyze an XML document by considering XML features, extract common features between XMLs, and then quantify similarity based on common features. Experiments showed that our methodology provides 100% accuracy in categorizing XML documents by page styles. If this methodology is combined with

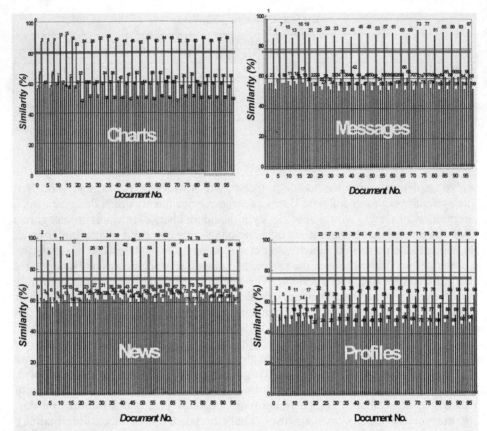

Fig. 3. The 'x' axis indicates the document number and the 'y' axis does similarity between a sample and the query document

traditional classifier, we can search target documents not only by keywords but also by a specific page style on the Web.

We need to do more experiments with various document sets and then revise our metric for computing similarity. We then extend our methodology to combine structural information with contents.

References

1. A.V.Aho, R.Sethi and J.D.Ullman. *Compilers:Principles, Techniques, and Tools*, Addison Wesley, 1986.
2. Brad Adelberg. "NoDoSE - A Tool for Semi-Automatically Extracting Structured and Semistructured Data from Text Documents", In *Proc. of SIGMOD*, pages 283-294, 1998.
3. Deutsch, Fernandez and Suciu. "Storing Semistructured Data with STORED", *In Proc. of SIGMOD*, pages 431-442, 1999.
4. Gerard Salton and Michael J. McGill. *Introduction to Modern Information Retrieval*, McGraw-Hill, New York, 1983.
5. Ho-pong Leung et al., "A New Sequential Mining Approach to XML Document Similarity Computation", in *Proc. of PAKDD*, pages 356~362, 2003.

6. Isabel F. Cruz, et al., "Measuring Structural Similarity Among Web Documents: Preliminary Results", *Lecture Notes in Computer Science*, 1375, 1998.

7. Ira D.Baxter, Andrew Yahin, Leonardo Moura, Marcelo Sant'Anna, and Lorraine Bier. "Clone Detection using Abstract Syntax Tree", In *Proc. of the ICSM'98*, Nov. 1998

8. Mohammed J. Zaki, "Efficiently Frequent Trees in a Forest", in *Proc. of SIGKDD*, page 71~80, 2002.

9. Nestorov, Abiteboul, Motwani. "Extracting Schema from Semistructured Data", *In Proc. of SIGMOD*, pages 295-306, 1998

10. R. Srikant and R. Agrawal. "Mining Sequential Patterns:Generalizations and Performance Improvements", In *Proc. of the Fifth Int'l Conf. on Extending Database Technology (EDBT)*, Avignon, France, March 1996.

11. Sutton, Michael J.D., "Document Management for the Enterprise: Principles, Techniques and Applications", *JASIS 49(1)*, pages 54-57, Jan. 1998.

12. Sachindra Joshi et al., "A Bag of Paths Model for Measuring Structural Similarity in Web Documents", in *Proc. of SIGKDD*, pages 577~582, 2003.

13. Soumen Chakrabarti et al, "Focused crawling: A new approach to topic-specific Web resource discovery.", *WWW8*, Toronto, May 1999.

Generating Different Semantic Spaces
for Document Classification[*]

Jianjiang Lu[1,2,3], Baowen Xu[1,2], and Jixiang Jiang[1]

[1] Department of Computer Science and Engineering, Southeast University,
Nanjing 210096, China
[2] Jiangsu Institute of Software Quality, Nanjing 210096, China
[3] PLA University of Science and Technology, Nanjing, 210007, China
jjlu@seu.edu.cn

Abstract. Document classification is an important technique in the field of digital library, WWW pages etc. Due to the problems of synonymy and polysemy, it is better to classify documents based on latent semantics. The local semantic basis, which contains the features of documents within a particular category, has more discriminate power and is more effective in classification than global semantic basis which contains the common features of all documents available. Because the semantic basis obtained by Nonnegative matrix factorization has a straightforward correspondence with samples while the semantic basis obtained by Singular value decomposition doesn't, NMF is suitable to obtain the local semantic basis. In this paper, global and local semantic bases obtained by SVD and NMF are compared. The experimental results show that the best classification accuracy is achieved by local semantic basis obtained by NMF.

1   Introduction

Recently, the amount of digital information has been sharply increased particularly in the digital library, knowledge databases, WWW pages etc. Document classification is an efficient technique frequently used to find valuable information in these data.

Usually the document classification system is based on vector space model [1]. A word-document matrix $X = (x_{ij})_{m \times n}$ is formed to represent a collection of n documents, where m is the number of words in these documents. Each column vector of X represents a document, and each element x_{ij}, defined by the *tfidf* weighting function [1], is the weight of the importance of the ith word to the jth document.

In the word space, the dimensionality is always high, and this may be problematic [2]. So techniques for dimension reduction is needed to reduce the dimensionality of the vector space from m to r, where $r \ll m$. One way to reduce the dimensionality is by word selection, which purports to select a smaller set of words to present the documents based on probability and frequency. Though this way is efficient, it couldn't solve the classical nasty problems of synonymy and polysemy. To solve these two and other similar problems, we would ideally like to represent documents not by words, but by the latent semantic relations.

---

[*] This work was supported in part by the NSFC (60373066, 60303024), National Grand Fundamental Research 973 Program of China (2002CB312000), and National Research Foundation for the Doctoral Program of Higher Education of China (20020286004).

C.-H. Chi and K.-Y. Lam (Eds.): AWCC 2004, LNCS 3309, pp. 430–436, 2004.

In this paper we mainly discuss the classification accuracy on different semantic basis. Most work has focus on global semantic basis, which contains the common features of all documents available. But the local semantic basis, which contains the features of documents within a particular category, has more discriminate power and is more effective in classification [3,8].

Singular value decomposition (SVD) [4,5] and non-negative matrix factorization (NMF) [6] are two techniques to capture the latent semantics of documents. The semantic basis obtained by SVD is orthogonal, and reflects the major associative patterns in the data. NMF is distinguished from SVD by its non-negativity constraints. These constraints lead to a parts-based representation, and the semantic basis obtained by NMF has a much more straightforward correspondence with training documents than the semantic bases obtained by the SVD [7]. Due to these characteristics, although both of them can be used to capture global semantic basis, only NMF is suitable in capturing local semantic basis. The experimental results show that the classification result based on the local semantic bases obtained by NMF is best.

The rest of the paper is organized as follows: Section 2 presents the methods to obtain global and local semantic basis by SVD and NMF, while in section 3 we discuss how to generate the projecting vectors based on different semantic basis. In Section 4, we introduce a classification method. Experimental results are presented and discussed in Section 5, and the conclusions are briefed in Section 6.

2   Obtaining the Semantic Basis

In the vector space model, documents are represented by vectors, called document vectors. Mathematically, to reduce the dimension of the document vectors, we first found a basis matrix $B = (b_{ij})_{m \times r}$, where $r<<m$ is the predefined number of dimensionality the document vectors reduce to. Then for any document vector $q=(q_1,q_2,...,q_m)^T$, we calculate a new column vector $v=(v_1,v_2,..,v_r)^T$ to satisfy that $q \approx Bv$, and v is the result of the dimension-reducing process for q.

Obviously information will lose during the dimension-reducing process. So the basis matrix B and vector v should be carefully chosen to retain important information for classification. In this section we discuss how to obtain the basis matrix B from training documents, and in the next section, we will discuss how to project each document vector to the new space spanned by semantic basis in matrix B, and get the projecting vector v.

2.1   Obtaining the Global Semantic Basis

Suppose in the training document corpus, there are k categories, we combine the document vectors in all categories together and form a word-document matrix $X = (x_{ij})_{m \times n}$, from which global semantic basis is obtained.

One way to obtain global semantic basis is by SVD. The SVD method decompose the matrix X into three matrix $U = (u_{ij})_{m \times m}$, $\Sigma = (\Sigma_{ij})_{m \times n}$, $V = (v_{ij})_{n \times n}$, where $X = U \Sigma V^T$, $U^T U = I_m$, $V^T V = I_n$, $\Sigma = diag(\sigma_1,\sigma_2,..,\sigma_p)$ with $p=min(m,n)$. The elements in matrix Σ are singular values and satisfies $\sigma_1 \geq \sigma_2 \geq ..\sigma_p \geq 0$. It is well known that good approximation can be achieved by choosing higher singular values and the corresponding vectors in U and V. So that we choose the first k column vectors in U and form the global semantic basis matrix B, $B = [u_1, u_2, .., u_k]$.

The other way to obtain global semantic basis is by NMF. For the word-document matrix $X = (x_{ij})_{m \times n}$, NMF finds non-negative matrices $U = (u_{ij})_{m \times r}$ and $V = (v_{ij})_{r \times n}$ such that $X \approx UV$. Here product UV can be regarded as a compressed form of the data in X , good approximation can only be achieved if the basis vectors in U discover the latent semantics of the vectors in X. So the matrix U can be taken directly as the global semantic basis matrix B.

Both SVD and NMF can be used to obtain the global semantic basis, but the semantic bases they obtain are different. The basis obtained by SVD is orthogonal, while the basis obtained by NMF is not. NMF guarantees that the basis it generates is non-negative, while SVD does not. Figure 1 shows the difference of them.

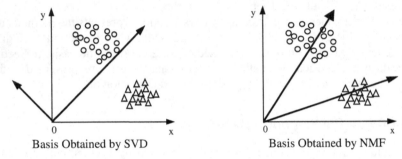

Basis Obtained by SVD   Basis Obtained by NMF

Fig. 1. The Semantic Basis Obtained by SVD and NMF

2.2 Obtaining the Local Semantic Basis

The global semantic basis contains the common features of all the documents, but may discard the local features of documents in particular category. These local features, which have more discriminate power [8], are more effective in the field of document classification. For better classification accuracy, we try to obtain the local semantic basis as follows:

Suppose in the training document corpus, there are k categories, we first combine the document vectors in the same category together and form k word-document matrices $X_1 = (x_{ij})_{m \times n_1}$, $X_2 = (x_{ij})_{m \times n_2}$,...., $X_k = (x_{ij})_{m \times n_k}$, where k is the number of categories and n_i denotes the number of documents in the ith category. Then we use the methods describe in section 2.1 to get the semantic bases of each category respectively from these k word-document matrices. To take the all categories equally, the numbers of basis vectors in each basis matrix are the same, and written as $\tilde{r}$. At last, we combine all the $m \times \tilde{r}$ basis matrix $B_1, B_2, ..., B_k$ together and form the local basis matrix $B=[B_1, B_2, .., B_k]$.

For obtaining local semantic basis, SVD is less effective. Because within a particular category, the semantic basis generated by SVD is more easily influenced by noises, here is an extreme example: there are three vectors $x_1=(0.5, 0.5, 1)^T$, $x_2=(0.51, 0.5, 1)^T$, $x_3=(0.5, 0.51, 1)^T$. Although they are almost the same except for a little noise, the basis matrix U_1 and U_2 generated from $A_1=[x_1,x_2]$ and $A_2=[x_1,x_3]$ by SVD are quite different. Figure 2 shows the decomposition results of them.

$$U_1 = \begin{bmatrix} -0.4116 & 0.9113 & -0.000 \\ -0.4076 & -0.1841 & -0.8944 \\ -0.8151 & -0.3682 & 0.4472 \end{bmatrix} U_2 = \begin{bmatrix} -0.4076 & 0.1841 & -0.8944 \\ -0.4116 & -0.9113 & 0.0000 \\ -0.8151 & 0.3682 & 0.4472 \end{bmatrix}$$

Fig. 2. Basis Matrix U_1 and U_2 Generated from A_1 and A_2

The semantic basis generated by SVD is easily influenced by noises and seem to be generated randomly, so the semantic information they contain is less important, and in most case they are not the local semantic basis we need.

Compare to SVD, the semantic basis obtained by NMF has a much more straight-forward correspondence with training documents and is less likely to be influenced by noises. So that NMF is more suitable than SVD to obtain the local semantic basis.

3   Dimension Reducing of Document Vector

After obtaining the basis matrix $B = (b_{ij})_{m \times r}$, we are now able to reduce the dimensionality of each document vector. For a given m-dimension document vector q, we try to find a r-dimension vector v, such that $q \approx Bv$. The vector v, called the projecting vector, can be gotten by minimizing the objective functions $E = \| q - Bv \|_2$, where $\|h\|_2$ is squared sum of all the elements in vector h.

If no additional condition needs to be considered, to minimize the objective function E is a typical least squares problem and the v can be generated by the following formula:

$$v = (B^T B)^{-1} (B^T q) \tag{1}$$

Furthermore, if the basis matrix B is an orthogonal matrix, the formula can be reduced to:

$$v = B^T q \tag{2}$$

The above two formulae are suitable for generating projecting vectors based on basis generated by SVD. But when we dealing with the basis generated by NMF, the situation changes. In the basis generated by NMF each non-negative vector represents a basic topic, and each document vector should be represented by an additive combination of these basic topics, i.e. all the elements in projecting vector v should be non-negative. So the formula (1) failed because it doesn't satisfy the non-negative constraints. Also the formula (2) failed because the basis matrix here is not an orthogonal matrix.

To solve this problem, we give an updating method for the objective function E to achieve a local minimum with the non-negative constraints. The method for its convergence proving is same as in [6]. For a given document vector q, the initial value of v is randomly picked and the updating rule is as follows:

$$v_i = v_i \frac{\sum\limits_{j=1}^{m} q_j B_{ij}}{\sum\limits_{j=1}^{r} v_j (B^T B)_{ji}} \tag{3}$$

Now, with three methods, we are able to get all the projecting vectors. Generally speaking, based on local semantic basis obtained by SVD, projecting vectors can be generated by formula (1); and based on global semantic basis obtained by SVD, projecting vectors can be generated by formula (2); and based on both local and global semantic basis obtained by NMF, the updating rule (3) is useful in generating non-negative projecting vectors.

4 Classification Approach

After dimension reducing, all the documents, both in training set and testing set, can be represented in new spaces with lower dimensionality. And typical classification method can be used to classify the documents in the new space. Here we briefly review the k-Nearest Neighbor (k-NN) method [9].

For a document in testing set, whose category is unknown, we find k nearest neighbor of it in the training set. The "closeness" between two documents is defined by Euclidean distance, or similarity with cosine measure etc., and the unknown sample is assigned to the most common category in its k neighborhoods.

5 Experimental Results

In our experiments, we use the document data set downloaded from http://www-2.cs.cmu.edu/afs/cs.cmu.edu/project/theo-20/www/data/, which contains WWW pages collected from computer science departments of various universities in January 1997. These pages were manually classified into 7 categories, including student, faculty, staff, department, course, project, and others. We choose 4000 pages of 6 categories; the numbers of pages we choose in every category are listed in table 1.

Table 1. Category and Number of the Pages

Category	Student	Faculty	Staff	Department	Course	Project
Number	1124	1124	136	182	930	504

The first step is to preprocess the pages, after stemming and eliminating the non-content-bearing words, including "stop words", "high-frequency" and "low-frequency" words; 6898 words are left to represent the pages.

Then we divided these pages into the training set and testing set. The numbers of pages are almost the same in the two sets with regard to all categories. So that both of two sets contain 2000 document.

Third we obtain the basis matrix using different methods describe in section 2, and for each method, we get several basis matrix with different dimension r.

At last, we generate the projecting vectors based on different basis matrices and use the k-NN method to classify the documents in different spaces.

If we classify the documents in original word space without performing dimension reduction to the 6898-dimension document vector, the classify accuracy is 58.3%. Tables 2-5 show the classification results in low dimension spaces, where P is the classification accuracy and r is the dimension of the new space. For simplicity, we do not discuss the influence of the parameter k and the similarity measure to the classification accuracy.

Table 2. Classification Accuracy in Global Semantic Spaces Obtained by SVD

r	10	20	30	40	50	60	70
P	68.3%	74.1%	72.1%	72.2%	71.1%	71.5%	70.5%

Table 3. Classification Accuracy in Global Semantic Spaces Obtained by NMF

r	10	20	30	40	50	60	70
P	46.8%	59.5%	64.5%	68.8%	69.8%	68.2%	68.5%

Table 4. Classification Accuracy in Local Semantic Spaces Obtained by SVD

r	12	18	24	30	48	60	96
P	31.1%	33.8%	35.2%	36.8%	40.3%	43.3%	46.7%

Table 5. Classification Accuracy in Local Semantic Spaces Obtained by NMF

r	12	18	24	30	36	42	48
P	76.4%	76.3%	76.8%	75.9%	74.9%	72.3%	73.4%

The differences among classification accuracy of all the method are more clearly showed in figure 3., where the line with no points (Line 1) shows the results in original space; the real line with star points (Line 2) and round points (Line 3) show the results in global space obtained by SVD and NMF respectively; the broken line with star points (Line 4) and round points (Line 5) show the results in local space obtained by SVD and NMF respectively. From the results we can see that:

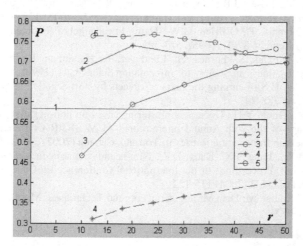

Fig. 3. Compare of the Classification Accuracy in all Spaces

1) With the dimension number increasing, the classification accuracy in global semantic spaces supervises that in original space. This shows that both NMF and SVD are suitable in obtaining global semantic space.
2) Due to the fact that the semantic basis obtained by NMF is not orthogonal, which cause information redundancy; the classification accuracy in global semantic space obtained by SVD is a little better than that of NMF.

3) SVD is not suitable in generating local semantic space, so the classification accuracy in the local semantic space generated by SVD is even worse than in original space.

4) The local semantic space obtained by NMF contain more common features within each particular category, which has more high discriminate power and is more effective for classification, so the classification accuracy in the local semantic space generated by NMF are the best.

6   Conclusion

In this paper several methods for dimension reducing based on SVD and NMF are proposed, and the classification accuracy in different semantic spaces are compared. The experimental results show that in the local semantic space generated by NMF, we can get best classification accuracy.

In the future more experiments will be done to confirm this conclusion. Also the impact of the requirement of the basis to be orthogonal will be further discussed.

References

1. Sebastiani, F.: Machine learning in automated text categorization. ACM Computing Surveys, 34(1) (2002) 1-47.
2. Yang, Y., Chute, C.G.: An example-based mapping method for text categorizationand retrieval. ACM Transactions on Information Systems, 12(3) (1994) 252–277.
3. Park, H., Jeon, M., Rosen, J.B.: Lower Dimensional Representation of Text Data Based on Centroids and Least Squares. Numerical Mathematics, 43(2) (2003) 427-448.
4. Berry, M.W., Dumais, T., O'Brien, G.W.: Using linear algebra for intelligent information retrieval. SIAM Review, 37(4) (1995), 573-595.
5. Deerwester, S., Dumais, S., Furnas, G., Landauer, T., Harshman, R.: Indexing by latent semantic analysis. American Society for Information Science, 41 (1990) 391-407.
6. Lee, D.D., Seung, H.S.: Learning the parts of objects by non-negative matrix factorization. Nature 401 (1999) 788-791
7. Xu, W., Liu, X., Gong, Y.H.: Document clustering based on non-negative matrix factorization. Proceedings of the 26th Annual International ACM SIGIR Conference on Research and Development in Information Retrieval, Toronto, Canada (2003) 267-273
8. Lu, J.J., Xu, B.W., Jiang, J.X., Kang, D.Z.: Non-negative matrix factorization for filtering Chinese document. Proceedings of the International Conference on Computational Science 2004. Krakow, Poland, 2 (2004) 115-122
9. Hanm. J., and Kamber. M: Data Mining: Concepts and Techniques. Morgan Kaufmann Publishers, August 2000.

A Component Retrieval Method
Based on Facet-Weight Self-learning

Xiaoqin Xie, Jie Tang, Juanzi Li, and Kehong Wang

Knowledge Engineering Group, Computer Science Department, Tsinghua University,
100084 Beijing, P.R.China
{xxq,tj,ljz,wkh}@keg.cs.tsinghua.edu.cn

Abstract. Component-based development method has been a new software development paradigm. How to get the needed components quickly and accurately is one of the basic problems about reusing software component automatically. In this paper, an intelligent component retrieval model – *FWRM*. is proposed. Facet presentation is used to model query and component. Multiple types of facets are defined which extends traditional keyword-based facet presentation. Genetic algorithm based facet weight self-learning algorithm can change the facet weight dynamically in order to improve retrieval accuracy. Corresponding similarity functions are defined also. In addition, risk minimization-based component sampling method is used to solve the insufficiency of training data. All these algorithms and methods are integrated into *FWRM*'s three main implementation parts: *Facet-Weight Optimize System, Component Retrieve System* and *Resource*. The experimental results prove that this method is feasible and can improve component retrieval effectively.

1 Introduction

Component-based development has great impact on each stage of software development. There is a growing interest in CBSD[1][2]. There are, however, many issues that must be addressed to achieve widespread acceptance of CBSD[3]. A major problem in software reuse is the lack of efficient means to search and retrieve reusable components from the repository [4], especially how to search for specific components to satisfy the users' requirements. Although there are rudimentary approaches available for searching component repositories [5], they have severe limitations. For example, when a user retrieves components, different user has different security requirements for a component that has the same functionality. So although the query is same, the results should differ from each other. Intelligent component retrieval system is the prerequisite for automatic reuse of software components. There are several component vendors (e.g.,flashline[6], componentsource[7], sourceforge[8]). In these on-line sites, components are cataloged with brief descriptions that can be searched through keywords. But keyword based searching is not efficient because it often results in too many or too few hits. Facet presentation is a popular presentation for software components, and the facet weight plays an important role in retrieval quality. Since various facets provide different contributions in retrieval and some component requesters' characteristics are embodied in the facets weights, considering each query as a facet representation, one problem in component retrieval is mapped to a problem of setting the weight of facet adaptively. Without setting the weight for each facet, the

C.-H. Chi and K.-Y. Lam (Eds.): AWCC 2004, LNCS 3309, pp. 437–448, 2004.
© Springer-Verlag Berlin Heidelberg 2004

retrieved components might cover either a great number of unrelated ones by Vector/Probability Model or only a minor part by Boolean model. Salton and Bukley [9] suggested that an appropriate term-weighting system is capable of enhancing retrieval effectiveness. So do facet-weighting system.

In this paper, a component is considered as an annotated semi-structure documents. A facet list is used to describe a component. Each facet in the list describes one characteristic of the represented component. Distance-based retrieval algorithm is adopted in this paper. The major contributions of the present research are:

- A facet-based indexing method is proposed to represent software components. It extends traditional facet item type from String to the multi-type involving plain text-based, enumerated and numerical type. Similarity calculation functions of components are defined based on multi-type facet items.
- A facet-weight self-learning algorithm is developed to weight the facet of software component adaptively. Risk minimization-based component sampling method is used to solve the insufficiency of training data.
- The above two techniques are integrated into an intelligent retrieval model namely Facet-Weight Self-Learning-based Intelligent Component Retrieval Model (*FWRM*). *FWRM* features in its personalization and adaptation

The structure of this paper is as following. Section 2 gives a facet-weight self-learning based intelligent retrieval model for software component. Section 3 depicts the detailed algorithm. The evaluation and experiment are given in Section 4. Finally, before conclude the paper with a discussion and future works, we gives the survey of the related work.

2   Facet-Weight Self-learning Intelligent Retrieval Model (FWRM) for Software Component

Component retrieval can be classified into three steps: index, search and represent. In this research facet-based presentation is used to represent query request and components in the library. Component facets each of which consists of basic terms reflect different identification characteristics of the component.

As depicted in figure 1, *FWRM* include three parts. The first part is *CRS* (Component Retrieval System). *CRS* is responsible for indexing, searching component and representing the results. In addition, reprocessing mixed type of facet and matching is done in *CRS*. The input and output of CRS are the query request and a list of ranked components respectively. The second part is *FWOS* (Facet Weight Optimize System). *FWOS* consists of two components. One is the Facet weight learner (*FWL*). The other is the risk minimization based sampler (*RMS*). Different facets have different impact on the component retrieval. By adapting the facet weight, some retrieval context such as user preference and feedback can be modeled into the retrieval model. Based on the training data, the learner will learn the optimal facet weights for a requester. GA-based facet weight self-learning algorithm (*GAFWLA*) is integrated into *FWL*. With the increasing use of component library, more and more usage knowledge can be obtained. Instead of making use of the selected component as new training data, the component with minimal risk is chosen as the new data. This is the goal of the *RMS*. By contract, active learning is a framework in which the learner has the freedom to select which data points are added to its training set [10]. An active learner may begin with a very small number of labeled examples, carefully select a few additional examples for which it requests labels, learn from the result of that request, and then using its newly-gained knowledge, carefully prepare for next query request. *RMS* assures that *FWL* can work under small number of training data. The third part of *FWRM* is retrieval resource. The most important resource is component repository.

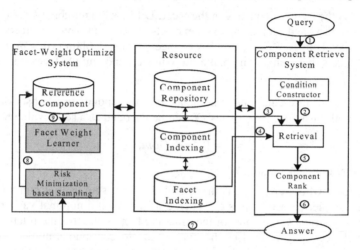

Fig. 1. The Structure of Intelligent Component Retrieval Model (*FWRM*)

3   Algorithms

The task of retrieval is divided into indexing and searching stages. Here indexing terms mean facets. Different weights are assigned to facets by a self-learning algorithm. The search stage has to do with evaluating the similarity between a component and a query.

3.1   CRS

The main work of data preprocessing in CRS is to index components.

3.1.1   Facet Indexing

The data type of facet can be classified into three types, plain text, enumeration and numerical value, and recorded as *FT, FE* and *FN* respectively. Following gives different encoding method for different type facets value.

- Facet of Plain Text (*FT*)

The value of facet *FT* is a paragraph of plain text. *FT* are filtered and represented as a vector of the candidate words/phrases called terms. This process includes word segmentation, stop-list removing, and stemming. Frequency of each term will be counted and the weight of each term is calculated. *FT* can be represented as a feature vector:

$$\overrightarrow{FT} = (w_1, w_2, ..., w_s) \tag{1}$$

Where w_i is the weight of the ith term t for *facet FT*. The calculation is defined as:

$$\omega_i(ft) = \frac{tf_i(ft)\log(\frac{N*R+1}{ComFreq_i+1})}{\sqrt{\sum_{i=1}^{n}(tf_i(ft))^2 * \log^2(\frac{N*R+1}{ComFreq_i+1})}} \tag{2}$$

Where tf is the term's frequency in the facet. Let N is the number of components in component library, and each component exhibits M facets in which R facets belong to plain text type. Thus $N*R$ is the number of facets which is plain text. *ComFreq* is the number of facets that contain t no matter in which component the facet is included.

- Facet of Enumeration (*FE*)

For the facet whose data type is nominal, *FE* corresponds to a subset of set *Dom* that includes all possible values. Thus *FE* can be encoded as a set of value S:

$$\overrightarrow{FE} = S = \{v \mid v \in Dom\} \tag{3}$$

- Facet of Numerical Value (*FN*)

For the facet whose data type is numerical, *FN* corresponds to a numerical value. For discrete numerical value, it is considered as an ordered nominal variable. As for continuous numerical value, most of the time, the fact is that it is the relative order of value that is necessary instead of the real value. So continuous numerical value is converted into discrete numerical value. Let variable g represents one numerical type of facet. After g is discretized, all possible values correspond to a sequence:$1, ..., M_g$. Let the detail value of the facet is x_{ig}. The x_{ig} can be replaced by r_{ig}, where $r_{ig} \in \{1,...,M_g\}$. The *FN* can be encoded as:

$$FN = z_{ig} = \frac{r_{ig}-1}{M_g-1} \tag{4}$$

3.1.2 Facet Matching

Distance-based algorithm is used to compare query and result component. Indeed, Similarity measure of query and result component is the similarity between facets. According to different facet type, different calculating functions for similarity metric are given as following. Assume a component has N facets, in which p facets is plain text type, q facets are enumerated, and r facets are numerical, Let C be C={(FT$_1$, FT$_2$, ...FT$_p$,), (FE$_1$, FE$_2$, ..FE$_q$), (FN$_1$, FN$_2$, ..FN$_r$)}, and C$_i$, C$_j$ are two components.

- Definition 1. *Text Similarity*. It is used to compute the similarity of plain text type of facets. With the cosine measure, the similarity function of *FT*s is as following:

$$SimT(FT_{ci}, FT_{cj}) = \frac{\sum_{k=1}^{S} w_{ci}^k w_{cj}^k}{\sqrt{(\sum_{k=1}^{S} w_{ci}^{k\,2})(\sum_{k=1}^{S} w_{cj}^{k\,2})}} \tag{5}$$

Where FT_{ci} means the feature vector of plain text facet of C_i component and w_{ci}^k is the kth value of feature vector, S is the dimension of the feature vector.

- Definition 2. *Enumeration Similarity*. It is used to compute the similarity between enumerated type of facets. Set operation is used to define the similarity.

$$SimE(FE_{ci}, FE_{cj}) = \frac{Num(FE_{ci} \cap FE_{cj})}{Num(FE_{ci} \cup FE_{cj})} \tag{6}$$

where $Num(.)$ is the number of elements in the set.

- Definition 3. *Numerical Similarity* It is used to compute the similarity of numerical type of facet.

$$SimN(FN_{ci}, FN_{cj}) = 1 - \frac{|value_{ci} - value_{cj}|}{|max - min|} \tag{7}$$

- Definition 4 Component Similarity

Facet of component may include different type of facets instead of single type. So how to compute similarity between components with the mixed type of facet is critical. The component similarity is defined as formulae 8.

$$Sim(C_i, C_j) = \frac{(\sum_{l=1}^{p} \delta_{ij}^{FT(l)} w_{tl} SimT^l + \sum_{l=1}^{q} \delta_{ij}^{FE(l)} w_{el} SimE^l + \sum_{l=1}^{r} \delta_{ij}^{FN(l)} w_{nl} SimN^l)}{\sum_{f=1}^{N} \delta_{ij}^{f}} \tag{8}$$

Where, if C_i (or C_j) does not have value in facet $FT_{c_i}^l$, namely $FT_{c_i}^l$ ($FT_{c_j}^l$)=0, then $\delta_{ij}^{FT(l)}$ =0, or $\delta_{ij}^{FT(l)}$ =1. SimT, SimE, SimN is computed as following:

$$SimT^l = SimT(FT_{c_i}^l, FT_{c_j}^l), SimE^l = SimE(FE_{c_i}^l, FE_{c_j}^l), SimN^l = SimN(FN_{c_i}^l, FN_{c_j}^l) \tag{9}$$

- Definition 5. *Facet weight vector*. The set of weights w in formula (8) is defined as $w = \{\{w_{tl}\}_{l=1}^{p}, \{w_{el}\}_{l=1}^{q}, \{w_{nl}\}_{l=1}^{r}\}$, where w_{tl}, w_{el}, w_{nl} is the weight assigned to feature: FT, FE, FN. The facet-weight vector is:

$$\overrightarrow{W} = (w_{t1}, w_{t2}, ..., w_{tp}, w_{e1}, w_{e2}, ..., w_{eq}, w_{n1}, w_{n2}, ..., w_{nr})^T \tag{10}$$

Retrieval problem is to find the component that has the largest similarity with query, while the similarity degree depends on the facet weight vector.

3.2 Risk Minimization-Based Sampling

In text retrieval, a retrieval action is thought as a decision involving selecting a subset of documents D from collection C and presenting them to the user who has issued query q according to some presentation strategy π. In [11], A general formulation of retrieval as a decision problem is as following.

$$a' = (D', \pi') = \arg\min_{D, \pi} R(D, \pi \mid U, q, \overrightarrow{S}, C) \tag{11}$$

By Bayes decision rule, retrieval is to choose the action a' with the least expected risk. Base on this theory, following gives the risk minimization based component sampling method.

Take the component x with facet presentation $\{f_1, f_2, ..., f_m\}$ as input, where m is the count of facet; and take component grade $y \in \{y_1, y_2, ..., y_n\}$ as output classes, where n is the count of grade (it is 6 in our experiments). Given a graded training set, C, the learner learns model parameters, θ. Then given an input x, produces an estimated output distribution $\hat{P}_C(y \mid x)$. Thus the expected risk can be written as:

$$R_{\hat{P}_C} = \int L(P(y \mid x), \hat{P}_C(y \mid x))P(x)d(x) \tag{12}$$

Where L is the loss function associated with estimation. $P(y \mid x)$ is the true predication, $\hat{P}_C(y \mid x)$ is the model's prediction. Loss function is $L = \sum_{y \in Y} P(y \mid x)\log(\hat{P}_C(y \mid x))$. The learning procedure is as following: in the retrieved candidate component list, a component x^*, which is grade as y^*, will be selected out and added to the training data set if and only if the model trained on the new data set $(C + (x^*, y^*))$ has minimal risk, i.e.

$$R_{\hat{P}_{D+(x^*,y^*)}} = \min_{(x,y) \in CCL} R_{\hat{P}_{D+(x,y)}} \tag{13}$$

Where CCL means the candidate component lists. In this way, the component x^* with minimal risk can be selected and added to the training set.

3.3 Active Facet Weight Learning (AFWL) Algorithm

There are two methods to get the facet weight of a component. One is defined directly by component requester. But it will aggravate the requester's work and limit the generality of retrieve tool. Natural language-like description of query request is preferred. The other is to learn the facet weights actively. This section proposes an active facet-weight learning (AFWL) algorithm based on genetic algorithm (GA).

3.3.1 Fitter Function Model

Retrieval accuracy is used to evaluate the quality of facet weight vector. The optimal facet weight vector can result in a maximum value of fitter function. The mathematical model for fitter function is as following:

$$\max f(W) = \cfrac{1}{\alpha \cfrac{1}{P(W)} + (1-\alpha)\cfrac{1}{R(W)}} \tag{14}$$

$$P(W) = \frac{1}{N_Q} \sum_{i=1}^{N_Q} P_{Qi_i}(W) \tag{15}$$

$$R(W) = \frac{1}{N_Q} \sum_{i=1}^{N_Q} R_{Qi}(W) \tag{16}$$

Where P is precision and R is recall respectively with the set of weights W for searching, and $\alpha = 0.5$ is commonly used. N_Q is the number of query problem in test data. f can be also considered as the retrieval criterion. W is as defined in formula (10). P_{Qi} and R_{Qi} are the precision and recall respectively for ith query problem.

3.3.2 Active Facet Weight Learning (AFWL) Algorithm

The goal of the *AFWL* algorithm is to get the optimal facet weight vector. The input of AFWL is queries that are described in xml documents. The output is optimal facet weight vector. Training data set is classified into test data set (T) and reference data set (R). formula (18) defined a training pair *TP*. Each data in T or R is called a case. Each case consists of two parts, one is the query problem and the other is query result. Each data in them is written in tuple notation as (*query_no, component_id, score*). A sample data is looked as: (1 CG_16 1.28). Query result is a list of candidate components. Both of query request and results are expressed as a XML document. Before forward to the detailed algorithm, some concepts are defined as following.

Definition 6. Given some training components $cl \subset CL$ (CL means component library). A training pair *TP* is defined as: $TP = (C_T, C_R)$, where $C_T \in cl$ is the target component for a query and $C_R \in cl$ is the user defined best matched components.

Given a set of training pairs $TP = (C_T, C_R)$, according to formula (8), different w results in different function value $f(.)$. The problem is to find w such that $f(w)$ is maximized, namely $\arg\max_w f(W)$. This research uses genetic algorithm to find optimal weights. The details of our GA are as follows.

- Chromosome Representation

A chromosome is defined as the facet weight vector: $c = \{w_1, w_2, ..., w_n\}$, where w_i is the weight assigned to i^{th} facet. and n is the number of facets. n is the same as the number of genes in the chromosome. And a population P is defined as $P = \{c_1, c_2, ..., c_i, ..., c_{popsize}\}$, where *popsize* is the number of individuals in the population and c_i is a chromosome. Each weight is binary-encoded between [0,1024].

- Selection Function

A selection function selects individuals to reproduce successive generations. The selection probability P_i is define as:

$$P_i(c \text{ is chosen}) = \frac{f_i(c)}{\sum_{k=1}^{popsize} f_k(c)}$$

where f_k is equal to the fitness of individual k, the denominator is the sum of all individual fitnesses. Roulette wheel method is used in our implementation.

- Genetic Operators

Genetic operators provide the basic searching mechanism of the GA. *uniform crossover* is used in our implementation.

The step of learning algorithm is as following:

Step 1: the initial population is randomly generated, that is to automatically create M number of population $VGroup = \{V_1, V_2, ..., V_M\}$, where $V_i = \{w_{i1}, w_{i2}, ..., w_{iN}\}$, N is the number of facets of one component.

Step 2: for each facet weight vector, input the query in test data to component retrieval system and get a list of components, which are sorted according to the similarity to query. Facet matching as describe in section 3.1.2 is executed in this step.

Step 3: Compute the average precision/recall according to formula (15) and (16).

Step 4: Compute the retrieval quality over this facet weight vector according to formula (14).

Step 5: If all vectors in Step 1 have not been processed, go to Step 2.

Step 6: Evaluate the retrieval quality for different facet weight vectors.

Step 7: Judge if the stopping condition of GA has been met, then goes to 9. The stopping criterion is a predefined maximum number of generations.

Step 8: Execute such operations as selection, crossover and mutation on winning vector in Step 6, then output next generation facet-weight vector group. Go to Step 2.

Step 9: Output the optimal facet weight vector.

4 Retrieval Experiment

A retrieval experiment based on *FWRM* was performed. Retrieval queries were described in a XML document, in which element value can be plain text, enumeration value or numerical value. The descriptions were transformed into facet presentation by facet encoding as described in section 3.1.

Queries used in this experiment were obtained from the *sourceforge.com* component library, which is the world's largest open source software development website with the largest repository of Open Source code and applications. At present, there are 83461 hosted projects. We take more than 300 components from the library involving *Build Tools*, *Code Generators* and *Object brokering* topics. The original component description format is HTML, so a wrapper will automatically convert the HTML files to the XML format that is as depicted in table 1. Thirteen xml elements are defined to represent the facets. Two belong to numerical type, three belong to plain text type, and the others belong to enumerative type. While specifying the query, user uses these xml elements. Table 2 gives a query description.

Table 1. XML Formatted Component Description File

```
<component>
    <id>1</id>
    <name>Compiere ERP + CRM Business Solution</name>
    <description> - Smart ERP+CRM solution.... </description>
    <topic>Front-Ends,Dynamic Content,Accounting,Point-Of-Sale,Build Tools</topic>
    <natural_language>Chinese,English,French,German, </natural_language>
    ...
    <activity_ranking>10</activity_ranking>
</component>
```

Table 2. Description of Query Problem

```
<set queryno="1"> <condition> <part>
                  <name>description</name>
                  <value>Eclipse IDE plug-in, ....</value>
                  <weight>0.1</weight>
            </part>
      </condition>
</set>
```

The proposed AFWL algorithm was tested with the following setup. The maximum number of iterations was set to 15. *TP* is classified into test data set and reference data set expressed in two text files respectively as depicted in section 3.3.2. Ten query requests were gathered from ten graduate students. And three teachers in computer science defined the reference data set. The size of the training database, *cl*, was 300. The values of the weights were bounded between 0 and 1.

After the AFWL training has been terminated, the chromosome with the highest $f(w)$ is selected as the final weights for retrieval. The found weights were tested with a database of 300 components on pc586. The system was developed using Java under windows2000 system. Figure 2 depicts the curve of recall vs. number of selected candidates. This means that the active facet-weight learning (*AFWL*) algorithm improves the recall of the retrievals by learning the weights. We choose $\alpha = 0.5$. But we can change α to get more desirable results. Figure 3 gives the precision versus selected number curve. Figure 4 depicts the precision vs. recall curve. When selected number is less than 25, the precision with optimal weights super-exceeds the precision with other weights.

In addition, those queries with different facet type are tested. In our implementation, the two group data $(p=10,q=0,r=2)$ $(p=8,q=2,r=2)$ are tested. We found that the result is undesirable. One of the reason for that is because in enumeration type facet, we only process the *or* relation. For example, as for programming-language facet, the possible value can be Linux, WindowsXP, Win98. Then the expression can be ((Linux *and* WinXP) *or* Win98), or (Linux and WinXP and Win98) etc. But at present we just process Linux *or* WinXP *or* Win98. We will add more condition expressions. Another reason is the different processing method about different facet type. For efficient retrieval, in the implementation, the two types of facet including enumerated and numerical one act as a filter. And the filter only functions on the retrieval results based on plain text type of facet. After we change the filter mode, the results are better.

5 Related Works

Currently there are four major categories of methods to represent components. These are the library science approach, the AI-based approach, the formal method approach and the hypertext approach. The facet representation, which belongs to the first one category, was first studied by Prioto-Diaz[12]. Now the facet description of software component is increasing. With the popular use of xml, facet description based on xml format is also promising. But at present, most of the facet-based component retrieval is based on traditional database retrieval technology, with the help of hierarchy

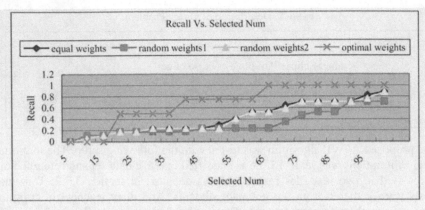

Fig. 2. Recall versus the number of selected candidates

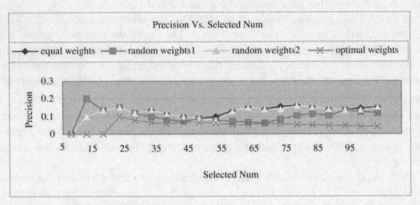

Fig. 3. Precision versus the number of selected candidates

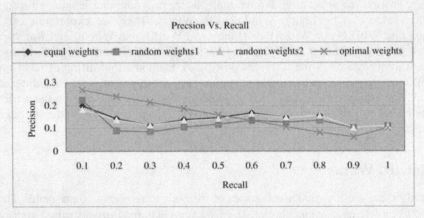

Fig. 4. Precision versus recall for AFWL and random sampling

structure of facet terms and synonym thesaurus [13][14]. In addition, many research-ers apply AI technology to component retrieval. For example, [15] made use of neural network technology to retrieve relevant components. In our research, GA is used to improve retrieval efficiency.

Most proposed component retrieval schemes can be classified into five types: keyword search, faceted classification, signature matching [16], behavioral matching [17] and semantic-based method [3][18]. In [13], A method based on tree inclusion was proposed to retrieve reusable components classified in faceted scheme, which combined the theory of tree matching and the feature of faceted classification scheme. In our implementation, for simplicity, we use vector and hastable as inverting index table of facet and component. In the future, we will change vector to tree structure. David etc. proposed a weight assignment in dissimilarity function in trademark retrieval [19]. It is similar to our idea.

At present, there exist many online component libraries, such as flashline, componentsource and sourceforge. But their supported search capability is limited. For example, the sourceforge.com site just provides the keyword-based searching. It provides two matching method. One is all word matching (or exact match). The other is partial word matching. This results in that the search results are either large number or only few. This is undesirable. *FWRM* can be integrated into these web component libraries in order to improve their search capabilities.

6   Conclusions and Future Work

This paper proposes a facet-weight self-learning based intelligent component retrieval model. A method for finding the optimal weighting factors using similarity metric based on GA has been proposed. During accessing the component library, personalized facet-weights can be learned in terms of different users or organizations characteristic. The experimental results show that the weighting factors found by the GA improves the accuracy of software component retrieval. At the same time, risk-minimization based updating of training data set solve the problem issued by little training data during the initial stage of component library. All these method or model can be served for a personalized component recommending system, and provide the supporting tools for popularizing the CBSD. Besides, this model can be applied to the description and discovery of semantic web service. During the period of data preprocessing in our model, although having extended the simple string facet type to multiple types, only three types of facets including plain text, enumerate and numerical are supported. The future works will consider to using more semantic facets, such as the ontology annotation, context etc. to further improve the accuracy of retrieval. In addition, current facet does not have the capability of providing the semantic relationships between software components. This is also the future works.

References

1. Brown, A.W. Large-scale component-based Development, Upper Saddle River, NJ, Prentice Hall. 2000
2. Herzum, P., and Sims, O. Business Component Factory: A Comprehensive Overview of Component-Based Development for the Enterprise, John Wiley, New York. 2000
3. Vijayan Sugumaran and Veda C.Storey. A semantic-based approach to component retrieval. ACM SIGMIS Database. 2003, 34[3], 8-24.

4. Spinellis, D and Raptis, K. Component mining: a precess and its pattern language. Information and Software Technology, 2000, Vol. 42, No. 9, Jun 1, pp609-617.
5. Mili, H., Valtchev, P., Di-Sciullo, A., and Gabrini, P. Automating the Indexing and Retrieval of Reusable Software Components. Proceedings of the 6th International Workshop NLDB'01, June 28-29, 2001, Madrid, Spain, pp 75-86
6. http://www.flashline.com
7. http:// www.componentsource.com
8. http:// www.sourceforge.net
9. Salton,G., and Buckley, C. "Term-weighting approaches in automatic text retrieval". Info. Proc. Manage., 1988, 24,(5), pp513-523
10. Nicholas Roy, Andrew McCallum. Toward Optimal Active Learning through Sampling Estimation of Error Reduction. Proceedings of the Eighteenth International Conference on Machine Learning 2001.pp. 441-448
11. Cheng Xiang Zhai. Risk minimization and language modeling in text retrieval. Phd dissertation. School of Computer Science, Carnegie Mellon University. 2002.
12. R. Prieto-Diaz. Implementing Faceted Classification for software reust. Communication of ACM, 1991, Vol.35, No. 5. pp. 89-97
13. Wang Yuanfeng Zhang Yong, Ben Hongmin,Zhu Sanyuan, Qian Leqiu. Retrieving Components based on Faceted Classification. Journal of Software. 2002, 13(8) p1546-1551
14. Sorumgard, L.S., Sindre, G., Slokke, F. Experiences from application of a faceted classification scheme. In: Proceedings of the 2nd international conference on software reuse, IEEE Computer Society Press, 1993, pp 24-26
15. Wang Zhiyuan. Component based software engineering. Phd dissertation, Depart of Computer and Information Science. New Jersey Institute of Technology. 2000.
16. Ma Liang, Sun Jiasu. Component Retrieval Based on Specification Matching. Mini-Micro System, 23(10),pp.1153-1157
17. AMY Moormann Zaremski; Jeannette M.Wing. Specification Matching of Software Components. ACM Transactions on Software Engineering and Methodology 10 1997 6[4], 333-369
18. Paolucci, M., Kawamura, T., Payne, T. R., and Sycara, K., *Semantic matching of Web services capabilities*, SPRINGER-VERLAG BERLIN, BERLIN, 2002, pp. 333-347
19. David Yuk-Ming Chan. King, I. Genetic algorithm for weights assignment in dissimilarity function for trademark retrieval. Visual Information and Information Systems. Third International Conference, VISUAL'99. Proceedings (Lecture Notes in Computer Science Vol.1614), 1999, p 557-65

The Algorithm About Division
and Reducts of Information System
Based on Discernibility Index of Attribute*

Jun Li[1,2,3], Xiongfei Li[1,2], Hui Liu[1,2], and Xinying Chen[1,2]

[1] College of Computer Sci. & Tech., Jilin University, Changchun 130025, China
[2] Key Laboratory of Symbolic Computation & Knowledge Engineering in JLU
[3] Changchun University of Science and Technology, Changchun, China

Abstract. The effective reduct algorithm is the foundation to use the rough set theory in data mining and knowledge discovery in database. In this paper, we discuss the well-known reduct algorithms, and propose the conception of discernibility index of attribute. We also propose the algorithm about division and reducts of information system based on discernibility index of attribute. We analyze the completeness and validity of the algorithm. The experiments indicate that our algorithm is efficient and practical.

Keywords: rough set, reduct, discernibility index, data mining

1 Introduction

Rough Set theory is founded by a Polish mathematician – Z. Pawlak in 1982. It is a new kind of mathematical tool to deal with Vagueness and Uncertainty problems [1][2]. The high efficient reduct algorithm is the foundation of applying Rough Set theory in Data Mining and Knowledge Discovery. However, seeking all reducts or minimal reduct is a NP-hard question [3]. So finding the high efficient reduct algorithm is still a crucial task to rough set applications in data mining.

In this paper, the discernibility index of attribute $I(a)$ is defined, and several characters of $I(a)$ are given. We also propose a reduct algorithm that adopts Divide and Conquer strategy. The algorithm divides information system into sub-tables in virtue of the attribute which has the maximal discernibility index and extracts the reducts of original system after founding the reducts of sub-tables. In this paper, we will discuss the integrity and practicality of our algorithm.

The rest of the paper is organized as follows. The definition of reduct of information system is introduced in section 2. In section 3, the great reduct algorithms are briefly summarized. In section 4, we define discernibility index of attribute, and give several characters of discernibility index of attribute. We also give the idea of reduct algorithm in section 4. In section 5, we propose the division of information system and reduct algorithm based on discernibility index of attribute, and then discuss the algorithm's completeness and validity. We analyze the results of experiments in section 6.

---

* This work was supported by the Natural Foundation of Jilin province under Grant No. 19990528.

C.-H. Chi and K.-Y. Lam (Eds.): AWCC 2004, LNCS 3309, pp. 449–456, 2004.

2 Information System and Reduct

The definition of information system and reduct are introduced in this section.

Definition 1: $S=(U, A, V, f)$ is a *information system*, where nonempty set U is the *universe* of *objects*; A is a nonempty set of *attributes*; $V = \cup V_a$, V_a is the *range* of attribute a; $f: U \times A \rightarrow V$ is a *information function*, $\forall x \in U$, $a \in A$, $f(x, a) \in V_a$, as x was concerned, $f(x, a)$ give the value of x about attribute a. We can also abbreviate information system to $S=(U, A)$, $a(x)$ means value of x about attribute a.

Information system can be expressed by table, where rows correspond to objects in universe, and columns correspond to attributes of objects. All information of an object is shown in a row.

Table 1. Information System

U	a	b	c	d	e
u_1	1	1	1	1	1
u_2	2	1	2	3	2
u_3	1	2	1	1	2
u_4	2	3	2	1	1
u_5	2	2	1	2	1
u_6	3	3	1	2	2
u_7	4	1	1	3	1
u_8	3	1	2	2	1
u_9	3	2	2	3	2
u_{10}	4	2	1	3	2

Example 1: Information system $S=(U, A)$ as shown in Table 1, $S = \{ u_1, u_2, ..., u_{10} \}$, $A = \{ a, b, c, d, e \}$. Rows denote objects and columns denote attributes. The cross of row and column is the value of an attribute to an object.

Definition 2: Given an information system $S=(U, A)$, a set of attribute $P \subseteq A$, attribute $a \in P$, if $IND(P)=IND(P-\{a\})$, we call the attribute a is *dispensable attribute*, else we call the attribute a is *indispensable attribute*. If each attribute a in P is indispensable, then P is *independent*, else P is *dependent*.

Definition 3: Given a set of attribute $Q \subseteq P$, if Q is independent, and $IND(Q)=IND(P)$, then Q is a *reduct* of P. The *core* of attributes set P is all indispensable attributes in P, denoted by $CORE(P)$.

3 Summary of Reduct Algorithm

Algorithm based on discernibility matrix was proposed by Skowron in 1992[4]. First of all, the algorithm constructs discernibility matrix, seeks discernibility function, then transforms discernibility function into disjunction normal form. Each primer implication is a reduct.

Reduct algorithm based on attribute significance was first proposed by Xiaohua Hu in 1995 [5]. The algorithm used Core as computional basis of reduct, seeking the minimal reduct that user could accept. The algorithm's heuristic information is significance of attribute. According to the significant degree, the algorithm adds attribute one by one into the set of attribute until the set is a reduct. Then it examines each attribute in the set whether it can be removed. If the answer is yes, it will then be removed from the set. Attribute significance can also be defined by information entropy [6].

Keyun Hu proposed reduct algorithm based on attribute frequency [7]. The algorithm first computes weighted frequency of attribute. Then reduct is sought based on attribute frequency which is the heuristic information.

Bjorvand and Komorowski propound reduct algorithm based on the representative genetic algorithm [8]. The mainly difference of reduct algorithm based on genetic algorithm is that the selection of coding and fitness function is different.

Kryszkiewicz and Rybinski researched the relation between sub-table's reduct and complex system and discussed that if given sub-table's reducts, how reducts of complex system [9] should be sought.

Starzyk, Nelson and Sturtz put forward the definition of Strong Equivalence [10] [11] that further developed into expand rule of which can quickly transform the discernibility function.

Bazan proposed the definition of Dynamic Reduct [12]. After random sample in the original decision table, sub-table's reducts can be found. Bazan defined that Dynamic Reducts is the reducts that belong to decision table and exit in each set of sub-table's reducts. Dynamic Reduct can efficiently strengthen the reduct's noiseproof capability. Bazan discussed how to sample and how to seek dynamic rules by dynamic reduct. Keyun Hu also gave an approximate reduct algorithm based on sampling in his PhD thesis [7].

Xiaohua Hu, T.Y.Lin and Jianchao Han etc. put forward a rough set model [13] based on database system in 2003, and gave the corresponding reduct algorithm.

4 The Principle

The algorithm in this paper adopts Divide and Conquer strategy. Firstly, the system is divided into some sub-tables. Then, the reducts of original system is solved after the reducts of every sub-table is gotten. This section interprets the principle of the algorithm, and defines the concept of discernibility index of attribute and its several properties.

Suppose the number of equivalence classes corresponding to attribute a is l, i.e. $|U / a| = l$, and a_i expresses the ith value of a, then the ith of equivalence class is $U_i = \{u \mid a(u) = a_i\}$, and the number of U_i's objects is n_i, the discernibility function of sub-tables corresponding to U_i is f_i. According to the relation of discernibility matrix of original system and discernibility matrix of sub-table which is showed in figure 1 (the pane of f_i is a discernibility matrix of a sub-table), we can know that after $af_1 \wedge f_2 \wedge \cdots \wedge f_l$ is transformed to disjunction normal form, the attribute set of its primer implication is original system's reduct or its superset.

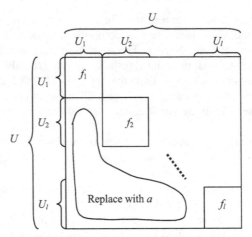

Fig. 1. The Principle of the Algorithm

In order to decrease the computational difficulty, we hope that the discernibility elements corresponding to f_1, f_2, $\cdots$, f_l in figure 1 are as lesser as possible. Moreover, the less $\sum_{i=1}^{l} n_i^2$ is, the less the discernibility elements in panes are.

Definition 4: Suppose the range of attribute a is V_a and $|V_a|=l$, the *discernibility index* of attribute a is defined as

$$I(a)=1-\sum_{i=1}^{l}\left(\frac{n_i}{n}\right)^2 \tag{1}$$

Obviously, $0 \le I(a) < 1$. For two different attributes a and b, if $I(a) \ge I(b)$ then $\sum_{i=1}^{l_a} n_i^2 \le \sum_{i=1}^{l_b} n_i^2$.

Thereby, $I(a)$ shows discernibility of attribute a. The bigger $I(a)$ is, the stronger the discernibility of a is. When there are less discernibility elements in panes corresponding to f_i, there is less computational difficulty of reducing Boolean function $a \wedge f_1 \wedge f_2 \wedge \cdots \wedge f_l$.

For the information system in example 1, the discernibility index of attribute a is:

$$I(a)=1-\frac{2^2+3^2+3^2+2^2}{10^2}=0.74 \tag{2}$$

Similarly, $I(b)=0.64$, $I(c)=0.52$, $I(d)=0.66$, $I(e)=0.50$.

Theorem 1: Suppose the number of attribute values of a is l, the less the sample variance $S^2 =\frac{1}{l-1}\sum_{i=1}^{l}\left(n_i -\frac{n}{l}\right)^2$ is, the bigger $I(a)=1-\sum_{i=1}^{l}\left(\frac{n_i}{n}\right)^2$ is. When $n_i =\frac{n}{l}$, $I(a)$ gets its maximum $1-\frac{1}{l}$.

Proof: The sample variance $\dfrac{1}{l-1}\sum\limits_{i=1}^{l}\left(n_i-\dfrac{n}{l}\right)^2$ describes the convergence degree of

n_i, because $\sum\limits_{i=1}^{l}n_i=n$, so

$$S^2=\frac{1}{l-1}\sum_{i=1}^{l}\left(n_i-\frac{n}{l}\right)^2=\frac{1}{l-1}\sum_{i=1}^{l}\left(n_i^2-2n_i\cdot\frac{n}{l}+\frac{n^2}{l^2}\right)$$

$$=\frac{1}{l-1}\left(\sum_i n_i^2-2\frac{n^2}{l}+\frac{n^2}{l}\right)=\frac{1}{l-1}\left(\sum_i n_i^2-\frac{n^2}{l}\right)$$

$$=\frac{n^2}{l-1}\left(\sum_i\left(\frac{n_i}{n}\right)^2-\frac{1}{l}\right)=\frac{n^2}{l-1}\left(\sum_i\left(\frac{n_i}{n}\right)^2-1+1-\frac{1}{l}\right)$$

$$=\frac{n^2}{l-1}\left(-I(a)+\frac{l-1}{l}\right)=\frac{n^2}{l}-\frac{n^2}{l-1}I(a)$$

Because n and l are constant, the less S^2 is, the bigger $I(a)$ is.

When the sample variance $S^2=0, n_i=\dfrac{n}{l}$, $I(a)$ gets its maximum $1-\dfrac{1}{l}$.

If the radix of attribute's range is l, Theorem 1 indicates that when objects get different attribute's values with equal probability, the attribute's discernibility is the strongest. Reflect in sketch map, the theorem's idea is that discernibility elements considered in panes corresponding to $f_1, f_2, \dots, f_l$ are least. When the probability that objects get different attribute's values is more closely equal, the bigger $I(a)$ is. Moreover, if the size of sub-tables is nearly equal, the parallel computation of sub-table's reduct is more reasonable.

Theorem 2: Suppose the sequence $n_1,n_2,\dots, n_{l-1}, n_l$ corresponding to attribute a, the sequence $n_1,n_2,\dots, n_{l-1}, n_{l1}, n_{l2}$ corresponding to attribute b, and $n_l= n_{l1}+n_{l2}$, then $I(b)\geq I(a)$.

Proof: Because $n_l^2=\left(n_{l1}+n_{l2}\right)^2\geq n_{l1}^2+n_{l2}^2$, according to the hypothesis of theorem 2, it is easy to testify $I(b)\geq I(a)$.

Theorem 2 shows that when attribute b is *thinning* of attribute a, the discernibility of attribute b is not less than that of attribute a.

5 Reduct Algorithm

The algorithm about division and reducts of information system based on discernibility index of attribute:

(1) Compute the discernibility index $I(a)$ of each attribute.
(2) Select attribute a with the biggest discernibility index, find the equivalence classes U_i of attribute a, then divide original system into sub-tables $(U_i, A$-$a)$, $i=1,2,\dots,l$, in which $l=|U/a|$.

(3) Solve the discernibility matrix of each sub-table, and compute discernibility function f_i.

(4) Reduce the discernibility function f_i to the form of disjunction normal form, and sort the result.

(5) Transform $a \wedge f_1 \wedge f_2 \wedge \ldots \wedge f_l$ into disjunction normal form, and solve the attribute sets corresponding to each primary implication of disjunction normal form.

(6) For each set that the 5th step gets, take into account whether the attribute a is indispensable attribute.

For instance, the following is the algorithm steps of the information system in example 1. The discernibility index of attribute a is the biggest, and it makes use of attribute a to divide the system into sub-tables. The number of equivalence classes corresponding to attribute a is 4, i.e. $l=4$, and each equivalence class is:

$$U_1 = \{u|a(u)=1\} = \{u_1, u_3\}, n_1 = 2.$$
$$U_2 = \{u|a(u)=2\} = \{u_2, u_4, u_5\}, n_2 = 3.$$
$$U_3 = \{u|a(u)=3\} = \{u_6, u_8, u_9\}, n_3 = 3.$$
$$U_4 = \{u|a(u)=4\} = \{u_7, u_{10}\}, n_4 = 2.$$

The relation of discernibility matrix of the information system and that of sub-table is shown in table 2.

Table 2. Relation of discernibility matrix of information system and that of sub-table

	u_1	u_3	u_2	u_4	u_5	u_6	u_8	u_9	u_7	u_{10}
u_1										
u_3	Be									
u_2	acde	abcde								
u_4	Abc	abc	bde							
u_5	Abd	ad	bcde	bcd						
u_6	abde	abde	abcd	acde	abe					
u_8	Acd	abcd	ace	abd	abc	bce				
u_9	abcde	acde	ab	abde	acde	bcd	bde			
u_7	Ad	abd	ace	abcd	abd	abde	acd	abce		
u_{10}	abde	ade	abc	abcde	abc	abd	abcde	ac	be	

A pane in table 2 corresponds to a sub-table's discernibility matrix and discernibility function f_i.

$$f_1 = b \vee e$$
$$f_2 = (b \vee d \vee e) \wedge (b \vee c \vee d \vee e) \wedge (b \vee c \vee d) = b \vee d \vee (c \wedge e)$$
$$f_3 = (b \vee c \vee e) \wedge (b \vee c \vee d) \wedge (b \vee d \vee e) = b \vee (c \wedge d) \vee (c \wedge e) \vee (d \wedge e)$$
$$f_4 = b \vee e$$

The principle of the algorithm in this article is that we can replace the shadow partition in table 2 by attribute a with the biggest discernibility index, and get original system's some reducts after reducing $a \wedge f_1 \wedge f_2 \wedge \ldots \wedge f_l$.

According to the algorithm, we can get the attribute reducts, such as $\{a, b\}$, $\{a, c, e\}$, and $\{a, d, e\}$.

Theorem 3: The sets that the algorithm gets are original system's reducts, and this algorithm is incomplete, i.e. this algorithm does not ensure that it can get all of the reducts and the minimal reduct.

Proof: Firstly, we have to prove the sets that the algorithm can get are original system's reducts. In the following proof, $(a \wedge m_i)^*$ denotes all of the attribute sets in this primary implication.

In the 5th step, the procedure that transforms $a \wedge f_1 \wedge f_2 \wedge \cdots \wedge f_l$ to disjunction normal form is divided into two steps. The first step is to transform $f_1 \wedge f_2 \wedge \cdots \wedge f_l$ to disjunction normal form $m_1 \vee m_2 \vee \cdots \vee m_K$, m_k is the primary implication of the disjunction normal form($k=1, 2, \cdots, K, K$ is the count of primary implication). Then the second step is to transform $a \wedge (m_1 \vee m_2 \vee \cdots \vee m_K)$ into disjunction normal form $(a \wedge m_1) \vee (a \wedge m_2) \vee \cdots \vee (a \wedge m_K)$, and get the result of the 5th step, i.e. $(a \wedge m_1)^*$, $(a \wedge m_2)^*$, $\cdots$, $(a \wedge m_K)^*$.

For any k, m_k is a primary implication of disjunction normal form $f_1 \wedge f_2 \wedge \cdots \wedge f_l$, Since $(m_k)^*$ can distinguish the object pairs in sub-tables, a can distinguish any two objects that come from different sub-tables, $(a \wedge m_k)^*$ can distinguish all objects of original system, $(a \wedge m_k)^*$ is some reduct of original system or some reduct's super-set.

In the 6th step, check whether a is dispensable. If a is dispensable, it shows that $(m_k)^*$ can distinguish all of objects, and the algorithm's output is $(m_k)^*$. If a is indispensable, the algorithm's output is $(a \wedge m_k)^*$.

$(m_k)^*$ is sub-table's a reduct, so attribute in $(m_k)^*$ is indispensable attribute. It proves that the attribute set which the algorithm's output is reduct.

The algorithm makes use of the attribute a replacing all of discernibility elements in corresponding area, so it is possible that some reducts would be lost. For example, the information system attribute reducts are $\{a, b\}$,$\{a, c, e\}$,$\{a, d, e\}$,$\{b, c, d\}$ in example 1, but the algorithm does not get $\{b, c, d\}$.

6 Conclusion and Future Work

The algorithm is implemented by standard C++ language. We test this algorithm on 16 data sets, and compare with the result by "discernibility matrix" method.

The results show that our algorithm is efficient and practical. Our algorithm can achieve large numbers of reducts on numerous data sets. However the algorithm can only get the reducts of a data set partly when the count of the data set's reducts is great. But to classifying task, the part of reducts is good enough.

Our algorithm adopts Divide and Conquer strategy. Some topics, such as the parallel problem of sub-tables' reducts and the idea how to use some attributes instead of one attribute when dividing a information system, need more research and experiments.

References

1. Pawlak Z., Rough sets, International Journal of Computer and Information Sciences,11(1982),341-356.
2. Pawlak Z. et al., Rough Sets, Communication of the ACM,38(1995),189-195.
3. Wong S.K.M, Ziarko W., Optimal Decision Rules in Decision Table, Bulletin of Polish Academy of Sciences, 1985,33(11-12), 693-696.
4. Skowron A, Rauszer C,The Discernibility Matrices and Functions in Information Systems, Intelligent Decision Support: Handbook of Applications and Advances of the Rough Sets Theory, 1992,331-362.
5. Xiaohua Hu and Cercone N.,Learning in Relational Database: a Rough Sets Approach, Computational Intelligence,11(1995),323-355.
6. Miao D Q.,Wang J. An Information Based Algorithm for Reduction of Knowledge. Technical Report, Institute of Automation, Chinese Academy of Sciences, March, 1996.
7. Hu Keyun, Research on Concept Lattice and Rough Set Based Data Mining Methods, Ph.D thesis, Tsinghua University, 2001.
8. Bjorvand A T. (1998). 'Rough Enough' – A System Supporting the Rough Sets Approach. http://home.sn.no/~torvill.
9. Kryszkiewicz M, Rybinski H. (1993). Finding Reducts in Composed Information Systems. In: Ziarko W P(Ed.). Proceedings of RSKD'93. London: Springer-Verlag, 261-273.
10. Starzyk J, Nelson D E, Sturtz K., A Mathematical Foundation for Improved Reduct Generation in Information Systems, Knowledge and Information Systems(2000)2, 2000, 131-146.
11. Starzyk J, Nelson D E, Sturtz K. (1999). Reduct Generation in Information System. Bulletin of international rough set society, 3(1/2):19-22.
12. Bazan J., Skowron A, Synak P. Dynamic Reducts as a Tool for Extracting Laws from Decisions Tables. In: Ras Z W, Zemankiva M(Eds.). Methodologies for Intelligent Systems. 1994. Berlin: Springer-Verlag, 346-355.
13. Xiaohua Tony Hu, T.Y.Lin,and Jiaochao Han, A New Rough Sets Model Based on Database Systems, G. Wang et al.(Eds):RSFDGrC 2003, LNAI 2639, 2003, 114-121.

An Effective Document Classification System Based on Concept Probability Vector

Hyun-Kyu Kang[1], Yi-Gyu Hwang[2], and Pum-Mo Ryu[3]

[1] Dept. of Computer Science, Konkuk University,
322 Danwol-dong, Chungju-city, Chungbuk, 380-701, Korea
hkkang@kku.ac.kr
[2] Knowledge Mining Team, ETRI,
161 Gajeong-dong, Yuseong-gu Daejeon, 305-350, Korea
yghwang@etri.re.kr
[3] K4M Inc., Segi-Bldg. 2nd Fl. 66-2 Bangidong Songpagu, Seoul, 138-050, Korea
pmryu@k4m.com

Abstract. This paper presents an effective concept-based document classification system, which can efficiently classify Korean documents through the thesaurus tool. The thesaurus tool is the information extractor that acquires the meanings of document terms from the thesaurus. It supports effective document classification with the acquired meanings. The system uses the concept-probability vector to represent the meanings of the terms. Because the category of the document depends on the meanings than the terms, even though the size of the vector is small, the system can classify the document without degradation of the performance. The system uses the small concept-probability vector so that it can save the time and space for document classification. The experimental results suggest that the presented system with the thesaurus tool can effectively classify the documents.

1 Introduction

This paper presents such an effective system with the thesaurus tool. It is a concept-based document categorization system (C-DCS) that classifies Korean documents using the thesaurus tool. We present a thesaurus tool for Korean to use in Korean document classification. In order to look for the categories of the documents, we must firstly represent the documents. The thesaurus tool provides the meanings and upper meanings of the document words so that the system can represent the document with not the terms but the concepts. In general, the concepts are more closely associated with the category of the document than words. For this reason, we can do the good document classification even if we represent the document with a small number of concepts. Then, we present a concept-based document classification system that classifies the documents with the thesaurus tool so that it can be useful to application that need speedy response or not much space.

The probability-based method classifies the documents with the probability acquired from training data. [5,8,12] determine the category of the document by inferring the Bayes association estimate between keywords and category. [1,9,11] classify the category of the document by measuring the similarity between the probability of the document and categories. Here, the probability means the frequency of keywords in the document. In this model, as the knowledge acquired in classifying the documents is added to the system, it is possible to incrementally learn. The neural network

C.-H. Chi and K.-Y. Lam (Eds.): AWCC 2004, LNCS 3309, pp. 457–462, 2004.
© Springer-Verlag Berlin Heidelberg 2004

method constructs the neural network to classify the document from training data. It determines the category of the document with the constructed network. This method is also possible to incrementally learn, however, it needs much learning time.

In this paper, we adopt the probability-based method that has no similarity measure overhead to all training documents for effective system. This system is easy to expand for incremental learning capability. In the following section, we briefly explain C-DCS for effective document classification. In section 3, we describe the experiments and results of this system. Finally, in section 4, we describe the conclusion.

2   An Effective Document Classification System

The C-DCS consists of the Korean morphological analyzer [4], the thesaurus tool, and the similarity measurer. The Korean morphological analyzer transforms the input document into the list of terms. The thesaurus tool gets the terms from the Korean morphological analyzer and draws the concepts included in the terms. Finally, the similarity measurer finds the category code by measuring the similarity between the input document and the categories.

2.1   Thesaurus Tool

Since this system classifies the document with the concepts provided by the thesaurus tool, the performance of the system depends on the thesaurus tool. Even though there have been researches on the thesaurus tool [3,7,10], they are not adequate to represent the concepts of Korean terms. So, we make the thesaurus tool to provide the concepts of Korean terms.

The thesaurus generally contains the meaning of words with the noun, verb, adjective, and adverb, but the thesaurus in C-DCS includes only the concepts on the noun important on document classification. However, this thesaurus has the event concept since the concept on noun also includes the action or event concept. The structure of the concept taxonomy is the tree structure. In the structure, the higher the concept is, the more abstract it is.

C-DCS uses the 150 concepts to classify the document. To get the better classification quality, we may use the more many concepts than 150. If we use too many concepts, the system may not be efficiently operated. As there is usually a tradeoff between the number of the concepts and effectiveness of the system, the concepts should be carefully selected. In this system, we examine and review the thesaurus with the 150 concepts. In the meantime, the thesaurus tool should get the concepts on all words appeared in the document. However, it is time-consuming and expensive to develop such thesaurus tool. In this paper, we firstly construct the thesaurus tool that can get the concepts on the 3990 words that are frequently used in the documents. In future, we will increase the number of the words what the thesaurus tool can get the concepts.

2.2   Similarity Measurer

This system adopts the probability-based method to categorize the document. As this system uses the probability of the concepts, we should represent the document with the concept-probability vector. The similarity measurer compares the concept-probability vectors of an input document and categories.

Firstly, we construct the concept-probability vectors from training documents to every category. Then, the thesaurus tool transforms the terms of the documents into concepts so that we can represent the documents with the concept-probability vectors. In this system, we use the 76 category codes and 12 category codes to identify the category. If we use the 76 category codes, the number of the concept-probability vectors for each category will be 76. Secondly, we transform the input document into the concept-probability vector for input document with the thesaurus tool. Finally, the similarity measurer compares the input vector with the vectors for categories. In the following, we describe the estimate function of the similarity measurer.

We represent the category C_i with the concept-probability vector $C_i = (WC_{i1}, WC_{i2}, \ldots, WC_{in})$. In this expression, WC_{ij} means the probability of the j-th concept appeared in the document set on the category C_i. So, $0 \leq WC_{ij} \leq 1$, $\Sigma j\, WC_{ij} = 1$. The input document is represented with the concept-probability vector $D = (WD_1, WD_2, \ldots, WD_n)$. In this expression, WD_j means also the probability of the j-th concept appeared in the document D. So, $0 \leq WD_j \leq 1$, $\Sigma j\, WD_j = 1$. The similarity between the document $D = (WD_1, WD_2, \ldots, WD_n)$ and the category $C_i = (WC_{i1}, WC_{i2}, \ldots, WC_{in})$ is measured by the measuring function $SIM(D, C_i)$.

$$SIM(D, C_i) = 1 - H[(D + C_i)/2] + [\,H(D) + H(C_i)\,]/2$$

$H(P)$ is the entropy which represents the uncertainty of the probability vector $P = (W_1, W_2, \ldots, W_n)$ and is calculated as $H(P) = -\Sigma i\, W_i * log_2\, W_i$ [1]. The similarity measuring function $SIM(D, C_i)$ has the maximum value 1 when both probability vectors are same, the minimum value 0 when the vectors is completely not same.

3   Experiments and Results of C-DCS

We examined C-DCS with the factors that effect the performance of the system. They are the number of training documents, the size of the concept vector, and the number of words that the thesaurus tool can get the concepts. The training documents are extracted in the Kemongsa's encyclopedia [2]. The total number of training documents is 21558. Firstly, we describe the experimental results according to the number of training documents.

3.1   Experiment of C-DCS According to the Number of Training Documents

We constructed the systems with 3593 training documents, 7186 documents, 10779 documents, 14372 documents, and 17965 documents. We called the systems as C-DCS-1, C-DCS-2, C-DCS-3, C-DCS-4, and C-DCS-5. Table 1 describes the success rates on the five systems on the test documents. The number of the test documents is 3593.

3.2   Experiment of C-DCS to Each Concept Vector

C-DCS uses the concept-probability vector to represent the document. As the size of the concept-probability vector is smaller than term-probability vector, it can support effective concept-based document classification. Since the performance of the system depends on the designed concepts, we carefully designed the concepts. In this paper, we use the 87 concept vector, 150 concept vector, and 768 concept vector. The former two vectors are carefully designed, but the third 768 vector is defined by adding 5-6 words related per 150 concepts for experiment of the vectors. Table 2 shows the experimental result on these vectors.

Table 1. Success rates on the five systems

Kinds of system	Best success rate		Secondary success rate	
	Category 76	Category 12	Category 76	Category 12
C-DCS-1	0.524	0.645	0.674	0.841
C-DCS-2	0.535	0.647	0.686	0.837
C-DCS-3	0.543	0.652	0.689	0.839
C-DCS-4	0.543	0.650	0.694	0.840
C-DCS-5	0.547	0.650	0.692	0.840

Table 2. Experiment result per each concept vector

	Category 76/ best	Category 12/ best	Category 76/ secondary	Category 12/ secondary
Vector 87	0.332	0.465	0.452	0.673
Vector 150	0.502	0.634	0.651	0.830
Vector 768	0.547	0.650	0.692	0.840

The result shows that the more the size of vector is increased, the higher the success rate becomes. But the improvement of success rate to the vector 768 is not good. It seems the vector 768 is not carefully designed. If we design the vector 768 with deep study, we can expect the better success rate. If improvement rate is linear, the success rate to the carefully designed 768 vector will be 65%(category 76) and 80%(category 12). As stated above, when we design the concept vector, we must think tradeoff between the number of the concepts and effectiveness of the system.

3.3 Experiment of C-DCS to Each Word Set That the Thesaurus Tool Can Get the Concept

In this section, we tested the system to each word set that the thesaurus tool can get the concept. In this system, we firstly select 3990 words that the thesaurus tool can get the concept. For the experiment on the performance of the thesaurus tool, we divided the 3990 words into three sets. Table 3 shows the experimental results on the defined word sets.

Table 3. Experiment result per each word set

Kind of word set	1330 words	2660 words	3990 words
Category 76/best	0.364	0.472	0.547
Category 12/best	0.517	0.620	0.650
Category 76/seco.	0.488	0.616	0.692
Category 12/seco.	0.682	0.791	0.840

The result shows that the more the size of the word set is increased, the success rate is increased linearly. Hence, in order to get the better success rate, we should firstly increase the size of word set used in the thesaurus tool.

The performance of the document classification system, in general, is measured by recall, precision, and breakeven point [5,6]. The recall is the proportion of all the relevant documents that are retrieved. The precision is the proportion of retrieved documents that are relevant to the query. The breakeven point is the point at which recall equals precision. In this system, we evaluate the system with the thesaurus tool of each word set. We can get the 0.65 breakeven point with the final thesaurus tool. The result shows that the more the size of the word set is increased, the more the breakeven point is increased. Then, this result says that we can effectively classify the documents with the thesaurus tool to expanded word set.

3.4 Review on the Experiment Results

In above sections, we reviewed the experiments on C-DCS. As a result of the review, we must firstly improve the word set used in the thesaurus tool. In next, we have to redefine the 768 concept vector to get the correct and general concept set. We carefully reviewed the failed cases for the test documents and found the following reasons.

(1) Low performance of the thesaurus tool. As stated above experiments, in order to get the better performance, we must improve the thesaurus tool.
(2) Frequent appearance of unrelated words to category of the document. It needs the definition of the weight to each word in the document. To do so, we must use the linguistic analysis technique.
(3) Polysemy problem. To resolve this problem, we must disambiguate the meaning of the words.
(4) Ambiguous category of the document. The problem is due to selecting the best category. If necessary, we can select two or more categories.

4 Conclusion

In this paper, we designed and constructed the effective concept-based document classification system C-DCS. It uses the thesaurus tool so that we can effectively classify the document. Then, the thesaurus tool finds the concepts of terms in the document to represent the document with the concept-probability vector. C-DCS got 65% success rate for the best category and 84% rate including the secondary category. It is encouraging for the restrained thesaurus tool. According to the experimental results, it seems that the system with thesaurus tool is necessary in effective document classification.

In future, we will improve the thesaurus tool to get the better classification result. After the improvement, C-DCS will be more valuable to document classification and other application domains. To get the better result, we need the research on defining the weight on the valuable word.

References

1. Wong, K.M., Yao, Y.Y.: A Statistical Similarity Measure, In Proc. Intl. Conf. on Research and Development in Information Retrieval, ACM SIGIR (1987) 3-12
2. ETRI Natural Language Processing Lab.: ETRIKEMONG SET, ETRI (1997)
3. EDR Technical Report: Concept Dictionary, Japan Electronic Dictionary Research Institute (1988)
4. Kang, W.S.: Semantic Analysis of Prepositional Phrases in English-to-Korean Machine Translation, KAIST Ph.D. Thesis (1995)
5. Lewis, D.D.: An Evaluation of Phrasal and Clustered Representations on a Text Categorization Task, ACM SIGIR'92 (1992)
6. Apte, C., Famerau, F., Weiss, S.M.: Automated Learning of Decision Rules for Text Categorization, ACM Tr. on Information Systems, Vol.12, No.3 (1994)
7. Miller, G.A., Beckwith, R., Fellbaum, C., Gross, D., Miller, K.: Introduction to Word-Net:An On-line Lexical Database, Report of WordNet, Princeton University (1990)
8. Sebstiani, F.: Machine Learning in Automated Text Categorization, ACM Computing Surveys, Vol.34, No.1, (2002) 1-47
9. Yang, Y., Zhang, J., Kisiel, B.: A Scalability Analysis of Classifiers in Text Categorization, In Proceedings of SIGIR-03, 26th ACM International Conference (2003) 96–103
10. Linoff, M.D., Waltz, D.: Classifying News Stories using Memory Based Reasoning, In Proc. Intl. Conf. on Research and Development in Information Retrieval, ACM SIGIR (1992) 59-65
11. Hayes, J.: Intelligent High-Volume Text Processing Using Shallow, Domain-Specific Technique, In Paul S. Jacobs, editor, Text-Based Intelligent Systems: Current Research and Practice in Information Extraction and Retrieval, Hillsdale, New Jersey (1992) 227-241
12. Yang, Y.: Expert Network: Effective and Efficient Learning from Human Decision in Text Categorization and Retrieval, In Proc. Intl. Conf. on Research and Development in Information Retrieval, ACM SIGIR (1994) 13-22

Accuracy Improvement of Automatic Text Classification Based on Feature Transformation and Multi-classifier Combination

Xuexian Han[1], Guowei Zu[1,2], Wataru Ohyama[1],
Tetsushi Wakabayashi[1], and Fumitaka Kimura[1]

[1] Faculty of Engineering, Mie University,
1515 Kamihama-cho, Tsu-Shi, Mie, 514-8507, Japan
http://www.hi.info.mie-u.ac.jp/en/top.html
[2] Toshiba Solutions Corporation, Systems Integration Technology Center
Toshiba Building, 1-1, Shibaura 1 chome, Minato-ku, Tokyo 105-6691, Japan

Abstract. In this paper, we describe a comparative study on techniques of feature transformation and classification to improve the accuracy of automatic text classification. The normalization to the relative word frequency, the principal component analysis (K-L transformation) and the power transformation were applied to the feature vectors, which were classified by the Euclidean distance, the linear discriminant function, the projection distance, the modified projection distance and the SVM. In order to improve the classification accuracy, the multi-classifier combination by majority vote was employed.

1 Introduction

The basic process of automatic text classification is learning a classification scheme from training examples then using it to classify unseen textual documents[1][2]. In this paper, we focus on techniques of feature transformation such as the normalization to the relative word frequency, the principal component analysis and the power transformation to improve the accuracy and the speed of automatic text classification.

1.1 Normalization to Relative Word Frequency

The word frequency is widely used as the basic feature in the statistical text classification approach. Since the absolute frequency depends on the length of the text, the relative frequency:

$$y_i = \frac{x_i}{\sum_{i=1}^{n} x_i} \tag{1}$$

which does not depend on the length is also employed, where x_i is the absolute frequency of word i and n is the number of different words. Because the relative frequency does not depend on the text length, the within-class variance of the relative frequency is smaller than the absolute frequency. Therefore we can expect that separability in the feature space and the classification rate is improved when the relative frequency is employed.

C.-H. Chi and K.-Y. Lam (Eds.): AWCC 2004, LNCS 3309, pp. 463–468, 2004.

1.2 Power Transformation

Another variable transformation, the power transformation [3]:

$$z_i = x_i^v \quad (0 < v < 1) \tag{2}$$

is employed to improve the classification accuracy. This transformation improves the symmetry of the distribution of the frequency $x_i \geq 0$ which is noticeably asymmetric near the origin.

1.3 Dimension Reduction by the Principal Component Analysis

Furthermore, it is a critical problem for the statistical classification techniques that the dimensionality of the feature vector can increase together with the lexicon size. To solve the problem we need to employ a statistical feature extraction technique which extracts small number of features with high separability to reduce the feature dimension without sacrificing the classification accuracy. In this paper the effect of the dimension reduction by the principal component analysis on the classification accuracy is experimentally studied.

1.4 Comparative Study on Statistical Classification Techniques

In order to evaluate the efficiency of the variable transformation and the principal component analysis, five classification techniques based on the Euclidean distance, Fisher's linear discrimination function, projection distance, modified projection distance[4] and the support vector machine (SVM) are employed in the classification test for the English text collection (the reuters-21578 [5][6]).

2 Procedure of Classification

The procedure of the automatic text classification consists of four general steps for feature vector generation, dimension reduction, learning and classification.

2.1 Feature Vector Generation

A feature vector for a text is composed of n feature elements each of which represents the frequency of a specific word in the text. At first a lexicon consisting of the all different words in a learning text set is generated. Then the feature vector for a text is composed of the frequencies of the lexicon words in the text. The dimensionality of the feature vector is equal to the lexicon size and is denoted by n. The normalization to the relative frequency is easily performed by (1), and the power transformation by (2).

2.2 Dimension Reduction

At first the total covariance matrix of the learning sample is calculated to find the eigenvalues and eigenvectors. Each featurevector is transformed to the principal components in terms of the orthonormal transformation with the eigenvectors as the basis vectors. To reduce the dimensionality of the feature vector the principal components

nents which correspond to the m largest eigenvalues are selected to compose the feature vector of dimensionality m ($< n$).

2.3 Learning

Parameters of each classification technique are determined in the training process using the learning sample. The Euclidean distance classifier employs the mean vector of each class. The linear discriminant function employs the weight vector determined by the mean vector of each class and the pooled within covariance matrix of entire classes. The projection distance (and the modified projection distance)employ the eigenvectors (and the eigenvalues) of the individual covariance matrix. As a support vector machine (SVM), C-support vector classification method (C-SVC) of linear type and of RBF type (with radial basis function) [7] were employed for the classification tests. We used the SVM library (LIBSVM Version 2.33) developed by Chang and Lin (2002) [8].

2.4 Classification

The feature vector of reduced dimensionality is classified to the class the distance (or the discriminant function) of which is minimized. Referring to the subject field manually given to each article in Reuters-21578, the classification rate R is calculated by

$$R = \frac{x}{(x+y)} \times 100 \tag{3}$$

where x is the number of articles correctly classified, and y is incorrectly classified respectively.

3 Classification Experiments

Classification experiments were performed to comparatively evaluate the feature extraction and classification techniques using the data collection Reuters-21578, which is composed of 21578 articles manually classified to 135 categories. In the experiments total of 750 articles, 150 articles/category randomly selected from five categories (acq, crude, earn, grain, trade), were used.

Table 1. Classification rate (%) at the optimal feature dimensionality

Classifier	Absolute frequency		Relative frequency	
	Without power transformation	With power transformation	Without power transformation	With power transformation
Euclidean distance	73.7	87.9	87.5	90.9
Linear discriminant function	90.5	94.9	93.3	95.3
projection distance	90.1	92.0	94.1	95.3
Modified projection distance	92.1	93.1	94.9	95.2
SVM-Linear	90.3	94.0	92.9	94.3
SVM- RBF	92.3	92.1	94.3	94.3

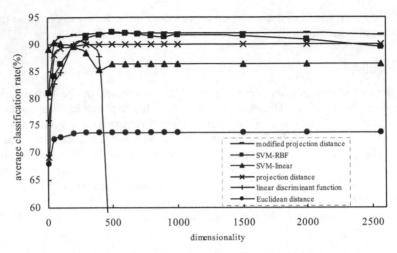

Fig. 1. Classification rate vs. dimensionality (absolute frequency)

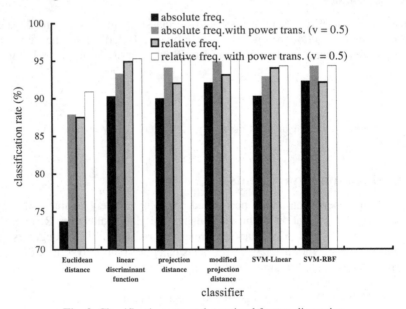

Fig. 2. Classification rate at the optimal feature dimension

Fig.1 shows the relationship between the average classification rate and the dimensionality of the feature vector composed of the absolute word frequencies. Table 1 and Fig.2 shows the classification rate at the optimal feature dimensionality.

The results are summarized as follows.

1. The classification rate was not sacrificed by the dimension reduction when the dimensionality was reduced to 15% (300-400 dim.) by the principal component analysis. Except for the linear discriminant function and the SVM-RBF the classification rate was not deteriorated significantly even when the dimensionality was further reduced to 5% (100 dim.).

2. The best classification rate was achieved by the linear discriminant function for small dimensionality (less than 50) and was achieved by the SVM-RBF for dimensionality from 450 to 600. The classification rate of the modified projection distance was totally the best for different dimensionality.
3. The classification rate was significantly improved by employing the relative frequency instead of the absolute frequency. The classification rate of the Euclidean distance classifier was most significantly improved from 73.7% to 87.5%.
4. The power transformation further improved the performance of each classification technique. When the power transformed relative frequency was employed the classification rate was over 94% for all classification techniques except for the Euclidean distance classifier.

4 Multi-classifier Combination

Multi-classifiers were combined by majority vote to improve the classification accuracy. In this experiment the projection distance, the linear discriminant function and the SVM-linear were used to classify the feature vector, the component of which is the power transformed relative frequency. The final classification was performed by the majority vote of these three classifiers.

Table2 and Fig.3 show the result of classification test.

Table 2. Classification rate(%) of individual and combined classifiers

	Group1	Group2	Group3	average
linear discriminant function	93.6	96.4	96.0	95.3
projection distance	93.6	96.8	95.6	95.3
SVM-linear	92.4	96.4	95.2	94.6
Multi-classifier combination	93.2	97.6	96.4	95.7

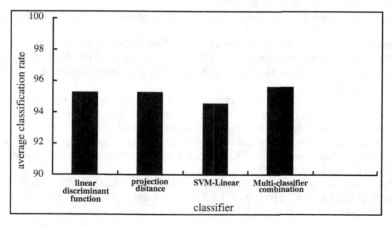

Fig. 3. Classification rate of individual and combined classifiers

Based on these results it is know that the classification rate was improved 0.4% using the multi-classifier combination.

5 Conclusions

This paper described a comparative study on techniques of feature transformation and classification to improve the accuracy of automatic text classification. The normalization to the relative word frequency, the principal component analysis (K-L transformation) and the power transformation were applied to the feature vectors, which were classified by the Euclidean distance, the linear discriminant function, the projection distance, the modified projection distance and the SVM.

The result of the experiments showed that

1. the principal component analysis drastically reduced the feature dimensionality without sacrificing the classification performance,
2. the normalization to the relative frequency followed by the power transformation improved the classifier performance significantly, and
3. considerably high classification rate for the transformed features was achieved by the linear discriminant function with less computational cost.
4. The classification rate can be improved using the multi-classifiers combination.

Intensive experimental evaluation employing more text samples of more categories is remaining as a future study. In order to simplify and clarify the performance evaluation, it was assumed that each article belonged to one category indicated by the first label in the subject list. The classification problem of multiply labeled articles is also remaining as a future study.

References

1. Sebastiani, F.: Machine Learning in Automated Text Categorization. ACM Computing Surveys, Vol. 34, No. 1, 1-47, March 2002.
2. Lam,W., Han,Y.: Automatic Textual Document Categorization Based on Generalized Instance Sets and a Metamodel. IEEE Transactions on Pattern Analysis and Machine Intelligence, Vol.25, No.5, 628-633, May 2003.
3. Fukunaga,K.: Introduction to Statistical Pattern Recognition, 76-77, Academic Press, Inc, 1990.
4. Fukumoto,T., Wakabayashi,T. Kimura,F. and Miyake,Y.: Accuracy Improvement of Handwritten Character Recognition By GLVQ, Proceedings of the Seventh International Workshop on Frontiers in Handwriting Recognition Proceedings(IWFHR VII), 271-280 September 2000.
5. Sebastiani,R. Sperduti,A. and Valdambrini,N.: An Improved boosting algorithm and its application to text categorization, Proceedings of the Ninth International Conference on Information and Knowledge Management (CIKM 2000), 78-85 ,2000
6. Yang,Y. and Liu.X. :A re-examination of text categorization methods, Proceedings of the Twenty-First International ACM SIGIR Conference on Research and Development in Information Retrieval, 42-49 ,1999
7. Cortes,C. and Vapnik,V. : Support-vector network, Machine Learning 20, 273-297 ,1995.
8. Chang,C.C. and Lin,C.J. : LIBSVM – A Library for Support Vector Machines Version 2.33, http://www.csie.ntu.edu.tw/~cjlin/libsvm/index.html

Risk Minimization Based Ontology Mapping*

Jie Tang, Bang-Yong Liang, Juanzi Li, and Kehong Wang

Knowledge Engineering Group, Department of Computer,
Tsinghua University, 100084, P.R. China
j-tang02@mails.tsinghua.edu.cn

Abstract. The key point to reach interoperability over distributed ontologies is the mediation between them, called ontology mapping. Absolutely manually specified mapping is tedious and time consumption. Additional, how to ensure the consistency and deal with error prone in manual process, further how to maintain the mapping with the evolution of ontologies are all beyond manual work. Therefore, it is indeed necessary to automatically discover the mapping between ontologies so that mergence and translation of different ontology-based annotations become possible. Existing (semi-)automatic processing system are restricted to limited information, which depress the performance especially when the taxonomy structures have little overlapping or the instances have few commons. In this paper, based on Bayesian decision theory, we propose an approach called RiMOM to automatically discover mapping between ontologies. RiMOM treats the entire mapping problem as a decision problem instead of similarity problem in previous work. It explicitly and formally gives a complete decision model for ontology mapping. Based on shallow NLP, this paper also introduces a method to deal with instances heterogeneity, which is a long-standing problem for information processing. Experiments on real world data show that RiMOM is promising.

1 Introduction

Semantic Web, suggests means for annotation of Web resources with machine-processable metadata providing them with background knowledge and meaning [Tim Berners-Lee, 1999]. Ontologies, as means for conceptualizing and structuring domain knowledge, can be seen as metadata that explicitly represents semantics of data in machine processable way and have become the backbone to enabling the fulfillment of the Semantic Web vision. Several domain ontologies have been constructed such as in the bibliographical, medical, and chemical fields. However, the distributed nature of the Web makes it indeed inevitable that communities will describe their data with their own ontologies. In this vision, ontologies themselves are heterogenous, therefore the key point is the mediation over distributed data using mappings between ontologies, namely interoperability based on ontology mapping.

Most previous research efforts on ontology integration have used ad-hoc mapping rules between ontologies (as surveyed in [Wache et al. 2001]). This approach allows flexibility in ontology integration, but none of them provides semantics for the mapping rules. Some other research proposes semantic bridge [Maedche. 2002, Nuno Silva and Joao Rocha, 2003] or semantic definition for mapping rules [Calvanese, D.

---

* Supported by the National Natural Science Foundation of China under Grant No. 60443002.

C.-H. Chi and K.-Y. Lam (Eds.): AWCC 2004, LNCS 3309, pp. 469–480, 2004.
© Springer-Verlag Berlin Heidelberg 2004

et al. 2002, Park, J. Y. 1998, Omelayenko, B. 2002], which partly resolve this problem. So far, however, there still exist two problems.

(1) Manually mapping is tedious and time consumable. In addition, how to ensure the consistency and deal with error prone in the manual process, further how to maintain the mapping with the evolution of ontologies are also beyond manual works. Therefore, it is indeed necessary to automate the discovery in ontology mapping.

(2) Existing (semi-)automatic processing system are all restricted to limited information, which depress the performance especially when the taxonomy structures have little overlapping or the instances have few commons.

This paper proposes an approach RiMOM (Risk Minimization based Ontology Mapping) to discover mapping between ontologies. In term of Bayesian decision theory, the discovery task can be cast as a problem of risk minimization. Based on the instances normalization and shallow NLP, RiMOM improves the feasibility of machine learning in ontology mapping. The other contribution of this paper is proposing a framework to flexibly integrate new theoretical approaches to ontologies mapping with potential of going beyond the traditional notion of similarity. Content of this paper is structured as following. Section 2 describes our method RiMOM. Section 3 depicts related algorithm. The evaluation and experiment are given in Section 4. Finally, before conclude the paper, we gives the survey of the related work.

2   Ontology Mapping Modeling

Bayesian decision theory can be described as: Assume that x is made on a random variable X whose distribution depends on the parameter θ. Let $A = \{a_1, a_2, \cdots, a_n\}$ be all the possible actions. Further assume that a loss function $L(a_i, \theta)$ is associated with each action and each θ. The task is to make a decision on which action to take [Berger, 1985]. In order to evaluate each action, consider the Bayesian expected risk associated with action a_i given a specified x:

$$R(a_i \mid x) = \int_{\theta} L(a_i, \theta) p(\theta \mid x) d\theta$$

$p(\theta \mid x)$ is the posterior distribution of x. Bayesian decision theory states that given x, the optimal decision is to choose the action with minimal expected risk:

$$a^* = \arg_a \min R(a \mid x)$$

2.1   RiMOM (Risk Minimization Based Ontology Mapping)

RiMOM is a general framework. It explicitly and formally gives a complete decision-theoretic model for ontology mapping. We firstly introduce the definition of ontology.

Ontology can be defined by a five tupel $O = \{Cs, Attrs, H^C s, rels, A^O s\}$ [A. Maedche et al. 2001].

Where: Cs is a set of concepts C; $Attrs$ is a set of attribute $Attr$; $H^C \in C \times C$ is a directed relation which is called concept hierarchy or taxonomy, e.g.

$H^C(C_i, C_j)$ means that C_i is the sub-concept of C_j; $rel \in C \times C$ is a function that relates concepts non-taxonomically; $A^O s$ is a set of axioms A^O.

As for ontology mapping, we mainly care about how to map concepts/attributes/relations from one ontology to another ontology. That is, to select the most possible element(s) in ontology O_i for element(s) in the ontology O_j, vice versa. Let I denote the instance of ontology, *name* denote the textual name, *ct* denote the constraints in ontology. According to the Bayesian decision theory, our observation are O_j, O_i and instances I_i, I_j of them respectively. The action corresponds to a possible mapping χ from O_i to O_j. There are five mapping cardinalities between ontologies, i.e. 1:1, 1:n, n:1, 1:null and n:m. Table 1 shows these five cardinalities.

Table 1. Mapping cardinalities between two ontologies

cardinality	O_1	O_2	Mapping expression
1:1	Faculty	Academic staff	O_1.Faculty= O_2.academic staff
1:n	Name	first name, last name	O_1.name= O_2.first name+O_2.last name
n:1	cost, tax ratio	Price	O_1.cost*(1+ O_1.tax ratio)= O_2.price
1:null	AI		
n:m	Title, name	book, author	O_1.title+ O_1.name= O_2.book+ O_2.author

Generally, we can think of a compound decision involving selecting element(s) in O_i for element(s) in O_j. Additional, for each mapping, there should be an expression strategy κ as shown in table 1. Therefore, we can represent action by $A = \{(\chi, \kappa)\}$. Based on Bayesian decision theory, to each action $a_i = \{(\chi_i, \kappa_i)\}$ there is associated a loss function $L(a_i, \theta, F(O_i), F(O_j), F(I_i), F(I_j), ct)$. Therefore, the expected risk of action a_i is given by

$$R(a_i \mid O_i, O_j, I_i, I_j) = \int_\Theta L(a_i, \theta, F(O_i), F(O_j), F(I_i), F(I_j), ct) p(\theta \mid O_i, O_j, I_i, I_j) d\theta$$

Where: $\theta \equiv (\{\theta_{C_i} \mid C_i \in Cs\}, \{\theta_{Attr_i} \mid Attr_i \in Attrs\}, \{\theta_{rel_i} \mid rel_i \in rels\})$ is the model for concept, attribute and relation. The posterior distribution is given by

$$p(\theta \mid O_i, O_j, I_i, I_j) \propto p(\theta_C \mid O_i, I_i) p(\theta_{Attr} \mid O_i, I_i) p(\theta_{rel} \mid O_i, I_i)$$

In this case, the risk minimization framework leads to the following form:

$$a^* = (\chi^*, \kappa^*) = \arg\min_{\chi, \kappa} R(a_i \mid O_i, O_j, I_i, I_j) \tag{1}$$

That is, to select χ^* as mapping rules and express χ^* with κ^*.

2.2   A Practical Case on RiMOM

Equation (1) is a general formula when view ontology mapping as a decision problem. In practical we need to be able to quantify the loss associated with a specified expression strategy. There are many different methods to estimate equation (1). To determine whether a mapping χ^* and its expression strategy κ^* are optimal can depend on four types of information: textual name, annotated instances I, taxonomy structure ts and constraints ct. In this section, we derive a practical formula based on these four features.

1. Annotated Instances

Firstly, instances of O_j can be exploited as training samples for Bayesian decision, then decision is made based on the instances of O_i. It is defined as:

$$p(e_{jl} \mid I_{iek}) = \frac{p(I_{jel} \mid e_{jl})p(e_{jl})}{p(I_{iek})} \tag{2}$$

Where $e_{ik} \in O_{ie}$, O_{ie} is the collection of all elements. Elements include concepts, attributes and relations. I_{iek} is the collection of annotated text by e_{ik}. $p(I_{jel} \mid e_{jl})$ is the probability distribution for instances of e_{jl}, e.g. let $I_{jel} = i_1 i_2 ... i_n$ denote an instance for C_{ik}, $p(I_{jel} \mid C_{jl})$ can be computed by

$$p(I_{jel} \mid e_{jl}) = \prod_{i=1}^{n} p(i_i \mid e_{jl}).$$ $p(e_{jl})$ is the distribution for e_{jl} in instance space.

$p(I_{iek})$ is independent with each other, therefore let it $p(I_{iek}) = 1$.

2. Textual Name

As for textual name, we mainly focus on its similarity. Therefore, we define a similar measurement for pairwise words as:

$$sim(w_1, w_2) = (Sense(w_1, w_2) + relatedness(w_1, w_2))/2$$

Where: $Sense(w_1, w_2)$ denotes the meaningful similarity between w_1 and w_2. $relatedness(w_1, w_2)$ is the relatedness measurement of them. $Sense(w_1, w_2)$ is defined using Wordnet.

$$Sense(s_1, s_2) = \frac{2 \times \log p(s)}{\log p(s_1) + \log p(s_2)}$$

Where $p(s) = \dfrac{count(s)}{total}$, $w_1 \in s_1, w_2 \in s_2$. s is a sense node in Wordnet, it is the common hypernym for s_1 and s_2.

Dekang Lin proposed a method to automatically construct thesaurus based on words' context and dependency extracted from a parsed corpus [Patrick. P, Dekang. L. 2002]. In this thesaurus, similar/related words are discovered for each word with a relatedness value. Therefore, *relatedness* for every pairwire words can obtained by look up in the thesaurus. To sum up, textual name similar measurement is defined as:

$$Sim(name_1, name_2) = \frac{\sum_{i=1}^{n} \sum_{j=1}^{m} sim(w_{1i}, w_{2j})}{n \times m}$$

Where n is the word count in *name*$_1$ while m is the word count in *name*$_2$.

3. Taxonomy Structure

Taxonomy structure denotes the taxonomy context for the element. For a concept, taxonomy structure includes its super class, subclasses, attributes and relations. The structural overlapping of two elements is defined as

$$Ol(e_1, e_2) = \alpha(p.)_h + \beta(p.)_s + \lambda(p.)_a + v(p.)_r$$

Where $p. = \dfrac{p(e_1 \cap e_2)}{p(e_1 \cup e_2)}$, $p(e_1 \cap e_2)$ denotes the common taxonomy context for element e_1 and e_2. $(p.)_h$ is the hypernym overlapping for e_1 and e_2, $(p.)_s$ is the hyponym overlapping, $(p.)_a$ is the property overlapping and $(p.)_r$ is the relation overlapping. α, β, λ, v are the weight for them respectively, satisfying $\alpha + \beta + \lambda + v = 1$. In the experiment, they are all assigned as 0.25.

4. Constraints

Constraints are used to define data types or relation in ontology, such as value ranges, uniqueness, optionality, relationship types and cardinalities, which also provides useful information for mapping. However it is not so meaningful to use alone. Together with other parameters, it can be used to increases the reliability. Examples of constraint are: "property with *range* 'Date' can only be mapped to the *datatypeproperty* with *range* 'Date'->confidence: 1.0".

Combining the annotated instances, textual name and taxonomy structure, Bayesian decision for each element becomes

$$p(e_{jl} \mid I_{iek}, I_{jel}, O_i, O_j) \propto p(e_{jl} \mid I_{iek}, I_{jel}) sim(e_{ik}, e_{jl}) overlapping(e_{ik}, e_{jl})$$

Then, based on the constraint rules, we define a loss function for each decision

$$L_{ik}(e_{ik} \rightarrow e_{jl}, ct, O_i, O_j, I_i, I_j) = \begin{cases} 0, ct_{ik \rightarrow jl} < \alpha \\ -conf, \alpha \le ct_{ik \rightarrow jl} \le \beta \\ -1, ct_{ik \rightarrow jl} \ge \beta \end{cases}$$

Where: *conf* is the confidence for constraint $e_{ik} \rightarrow e_{jl}$. α and β are two thresholds. Empirical values for them are 0.3 and 0.9 respectively.

Accordingly, the risk minimization formula becomes

$$R_{ik} = \sum_{k=1}^{N} L_{ik}(e_{ik} \rightarrow e_{jl}) p(e_{jl} \mid I_{iek}, I_{jel}, O_i, O_j)$$

In this way, how to decide the mapping for each element is up to R_{ik}. To simplify the description, let $p(e_{jl} \mid \cdot)$ denote $p(e_{jl} \mid I_{iek}, I_{jel}, O_i, O_j)$ and $L_{ik}(\cdot)$ denote $L_{ik}(e_{ik} \rightarrow e_{jl})$. Then Bayesian decision for all elements becomes

$$R = \int_\theta \sum_{k=1}^{N} L_{ik}(\cdot) p(e_{ik} \mid \cdot)$$

5. Shallow NLP

Information processing on plain text always meets problem of data sparseness. Sparse data cause the learned model to be applicable to a limited number of cases, over fitting the training examples, therefore affecting effectiveness on unseen cases.

In the mapping scene, we also found such problem: lack of common instances, for example: instances of concept *telephone* in O_i and instances of concept *phone* in O_j might have few common ones, which depress the performance of machine learning. Therefore, we optimize RiMOM by shallow NLP.

Shallow Natural Language Processing is used to associate additional knowledge to each word in the instances via a morphological analyzer, a POS tagger (lexical category) and user-defined dictionary (or gazetteer, if available). Table 2 gives an example to describe how shallow NLP is exploited in this scene.

Table 2. An instance of Concept *Address* with NLP knowledge

Instance with NLP knowledge				Concept
Index	Word	POS	SemCat	
1	Knowledge	Noun		
2	Engineering	Noun	Organization	
3	Group	Noun		
4	Tsinghua	Noun	University	Address
5	University	Noun		
6	China. P.R	Noun	Country	
7	100084	Digit	Zipcode	

In this way, instance-based Bayesian decision is relaxed by substituted constraints on words with constraints on some parts of the NLP knowledge.

3 Algorithm

There are four dimensions in ontology mapping: Preprocessing, Discovery, Representation and Translation. Representation is the expression of the mapping. In our experiments, we adopt Semantic Bridging Ontology (SBO) to represent the mapping [A. Maedche et al. 2002, Nuno Silva and Joao Rocha, 2003]. Translation is the application of mapping, viz. translate instances of source ontology into instances of target ontology. In this section, we will focus on the procedure of Discovery.

Discovery process has three steps: concept mapping, attribute/relation mapping and mapping pruning. Concept mapping is constructed according to the risk minimization decision as described above. Secondly, according to each concept bridge, RiMOM searches the optimal mapping for their properties. Then, the relation bridges are generated based on the concept and attribute mapping. In the finally step, pruning algorithm uses some predefined inferring rules to refine the generated mapping. The inferring rules are defined manually. The inferring step focuses on pruning the mapping of inaccuracy. For instance, c_{i1} has a concept bridge to c_{j1}, and its super concept c_{i2} has a concept bridge to the super concept c_{j2} of c_{j1}, while its sub concept c_{i3} also has a concept bridge to c_{j2}. Then it leads to a contradiction, which means that there exists an error bridge. With the context information, we induce that the bridge c_{i3} to c_{j2} is a error bridge, which should be removed.

According to the constraints, RiMOM computes loss for each decision, and then searches the whole space to find the minimal risk of the decision in all possible mapping. Currently we don't support automatically mapping for complicated function among elements, e.g. the sample *cost*(1+tax ratio)=price* in table 1. We mainly address the three main mapping cardinality, i.e. 1:n, n:1, 1:1.

1. 1:1 mapping

1:1 mapping is the simplest and most common mode. Only considering one element e_{ik}, the task is to select the element e_{jl} with minimal risk R_{ik}. When all comes to all, the task becomes to select the possible mapping for all elements with minimal risk R.

2. n:1 and 1:n mapping

n:1 exists when multiple elements in O_i are mapped to the one element in O_j, when this case occurs, RiMOM triggers a combination process, which automatically search the optimal composition. For example, RiMOM finds that concepts: *Address, Zipcode, telephone* are mapped to concept *contract_infomation*, then a special processing called *Composition_Optimal*, is triggered to search all possible composition, formal description is

$$F(f(C_{Address}), f(C_{Zipcode}), f(C_{telephone})) = f(C_{contract\_information})$$

Where $f(C_i)$ is a function for C_i, which means that in the mapping process, there might be a functional mapping for C_i, such as $left(C_i, n)$, $lower(C_i)$, $mid(C_i, n_1, n_2)$, etc. $F(.)$ is an optimal operator for its input parameters.

1:n is the inverted discovery process for n:1. Same as n:1 mapping, this processing is to find elements in O_j are mapped to the same element in O_i.

4 Experiments and Evaluation

In order to evaluate RiMOM, we have conducted experiments on two test collection: Employee Ontologies and Sales Ontologies. For each data set, instances only, Ri-MOM, and RiMOM with initial points are tested respectively. Initial points are some elements mapping assigned manually before learning processing.

Employee ontologies are constructed from real world database, which contains 27 tables, records of which have few duplicate ones. Two heterogeneous ontologies are constructed according to the schema of database while instances are collected from the records random for them respectively. Ontology O_1 has 51 concepts, 218 attributes and 240 relations. Ontology O_2 has 45 concepts, 186 attributes and 194 relations. Table 3 shows the experiment results based on only instances.

Table 3. Mapping evaluation based on only instances

Test	instances in O_2	instances in O_1	1:1(%)		n:1(%)	
			Precision	Recall	Precision	Recall
1	505	509	62.5	70	50	63.5
2	506	495	25	37.5	20	30
3	501	492	37.5	50	25	32.5
4	498	497	62.5	75	42.5	25
5	702	702	87.5	100	80	85.5
Avg	542.4	539	55	66.5	43.5	45.7

Table 4. Mapping evaluation for RiMOM

Test	instances in O_2	instances in O_1	1:1(%)		n:1(%)	
			Precision	Recall	Precision	Recall
1	505	509	87.5	98	80	87.5
2	506	495	80	94	75	85
3	501	492	85	95	83.3	90
4	498	497	83.3	90	82.5	92
5	702	702	92	100	87.5	100
Avg	542.4	539	85.56	95.4	81.66	90.9

Table 5. Mapping evaluation for RiMOM with several initial points

Test	instances in O_2	instances in O_1	1:1(%)		n:1(%)	
			Precision	Recall	Precision	Recall
1	505	509	92	94	82	90
2	506	495	82	96	86.5	93
3	501	492	85.5	94.5	84	92
4	498	497	85	92	87.5	95
5	702	702	98	100	92.5	100
Avg	542.4	539	88.5	95.3	86.5	94

Sales ontologies are also derived from a real world database, which contains 41 tables. Different from the employer database, sales database have definite duplicate data. Two heterogeneous ontologies are constructed according to the schema of database while instances are collected from the records random for them respectively. Ontology O_1 has 102 concepts, 310 attributes and 387 relations. Ontology O_2 has 135 concepts, 353 attributes and 406 relations. Three groups of experiments are conducted for cardinality of 1:1(only), n:1(only) and mixed respectively. For each group, we evaluate the performance with 80%, 50% and 30% instances for training respectively, and then average their precision. Also, in each group of experiments, perform-ance of concept mapping, attribute/relation mapping, and overall are compared. Fig-ure 1 shows the experiment results based on only instances with 50% instances to train and 50% to test.

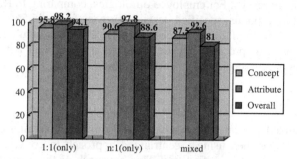

Fig. 1. Average precision for concept/attribute/overall on Sales Ontologies

Other two tests on sales ontologies are based on RiMOM and RiMOM with initial points. Figure 2 shows the comparison of the three tests. The four points in the x-axis, i.e. 1(40%), 2(50%), etc., indicate the proportion of instances used to train.

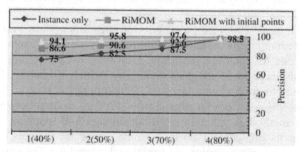

Fig. 2. Comparison of instance/RiMOM/RiMOM with initial points on Sales Ontologies

Experiments results show that:

(1) Annotated instances contribute a lot to the performance of mapping, however when the instances have little overlapping data, the performance will be de-pressed. This can be obtained from comparison between experiments on the two test collection. Average precision on employee data is only 55% for of cardinality 1:1 while it is 86.6% on sales data. In the same way, the value of cardinality n:1 is 43.5% against 82.6%. With the instances for training increasing, the difference reduces.

(2) Compared to the mapping on instances only, RiMOM improves the performance greatly. And with the help of NLP and preprocessing, the mapping results are closing to the practice. Comparison between table 3 and table 4 shows this point. Traditional instance based method's precision results in only 55% and 43.5% of 1:1 and n:1 respectively while RiMOM improves the performance up to 85.56% and 81.66% on employee ontologies. As for the sales ontologies, RiMOM also has a clear improvement comparing to that on instance only. From Figure 3, we can see that the result of RiMOM against instance only is 90.6% to 82.5%.

(3) Since ontology is the foundation of the semantic web, quality of ontology mapping is very important for interoperability. Therefore, targeted interaction with users is also necessary. This point is concluded it by comparing table 4 and table 5 and figure 3. In both ontologies, the tests of customer-specified initial points show promising results. For employee ontologies, comparing to RiMOM, the precision of initial points specified tests improves from 85.56% to 88.5% and 81.66% to 86.5% for 1:1 and n:1 respectively. For sales ontologies, the average improvement of the precision for the four tests is about 4.55% by comparing the test of initial points specified to that of non-initial points.

5   Related Works

Both the centralized mediated data schema and ontology merging define a unified schema/ontology, and then using a centralized approach to convert all data source schemas/ontologies into the unified one. This approach of the mediation is probably not flexible enough to be scaled up to the Semantic Web. On the contrary, ontology mapping is a more dynamic knowledge sharing problem.

Most previous research efforts on ontology integration have used ad-hoc mapping rules between ontologies (as surveyed in [Wache et al. 2001]). This approach allows flexibility in ontology integration, but most works do not provide semantics for the mapping rules.

[Calvanese, D. et al. 2002] proposed an Ontology Integration Framework, which provides clear semantics for ontology integration by defining sound and complete semantic conditions for each mapping rule. However, each mapping rule and its semantic conditions have to be assigned manually, which, therefore, lead to tedious work and difficulty to ensure consistency of the mapping rules.

[Park, J. Y. 1998] describes an extension to Protégé to map between domain ontologies. In this method, a valuable set of desiderata and mapping dimensions are defined, however its implementation lacks some important features especially in allowing multiple concepts mapping or functional mapping. The other approach is RDFT [Omelayenko, B. 2002], a meta-ontology that describes Equivalence and Versioning relations between either an XML DTD or RDFS document and another XML DTD or RDFS document. An RDFT instantiation describes the semantic relations between source and target ontologies, which will be further applied in the transformation of documents. Thirdly, the Buster project [Stuckenschmidt, H. et al. 2000] applies information integration to the GIS domain. Two distinct approaches are proposed: rule-based transformation and re-classification. The rule-based approach applies a procedural transformation to instance properties, while classification applies class membership conditions to infer target classification through description-logic tools. However, these two approaches are not integrated, yet they don't provide practical (semi-)automatic ability, which greatly limits their mapping capabilities.

Also some researchers are working on automatic method of mapping. [N. F. Noy and M. A. Musen. 2000] exploits information structures to induce the mapping rules, which [A. Doan. 2002] uses joint distribution of the annotated instances to learn the mapping rules. Chimaera [McGuinness, 2000] and PROMPT [N. F. Noy and M. A. Musen. 2000] both support the automatic merging of ontological terms i.e. class and attribute names from various sources. The matching algorithms exploit taxonomy structures and textual names to looks for an exact match in class names or a match on prefixes, suffixes, and word root of class names. They are both restricted to limited information, which depress the results especially when the structures have little overlapping or the instances have few common ones.

6 Conclusions

This paper proposes a novel approach RiMOM to deal with the interoperability over various ontologies. A specific focus has been set on mapping discovering phase where we have provided a detailed description of mapping rules inducing in term of Bayesian decision theory. Experiments show preferable results in precision. Main contributions of this paper include three aspects:

RiMOM treats the entire mapping problem as a decision problem and incorporates several existing mapping methods while previous work has treated this problem as similarity problem. This is the first time to explicitly and formally give a complete decision-theoretic model for ontology mapping.

Instances heterogeneity is always a difficult problem for information processing community. Based on instances normalization and shallow NLP, this paper improves the feasibility of machine learning in ontology mapping.

The other contribution of this paper is RiMOM makes it possible to systematically and formally study general optimal mapping strategies. With different assumptions about the loss function, we can compare various strategies and derive the optimal one. Also RiMOM provides the flexibility to integrate new principled approaches to ontologies mapping with potential of go beyond the traditional notion of similarity.

In the further work, we will continue our work to provide a more practicable system. Based on this paper, we will improve on these aspects:

(1) Mapping representation. Current work on representation gives semantics to mapping rules in certain extent, however there still lacks a standard language to express the complex relation, such as functional relation and set-based operation.
(2) A practical system. There is really lack of a practical system to implement the interoperability over ontologies, including ontology mapping, translation, reasoning over ontologies etc.

References

[A. Maedche et al. 2001] Alexander Maedche, Steffen Staab: Ontology Learning for the Semantic Web. IEEE Intelligent Systems 16(2): 72-79 (2001)
[Berger, 1985] Berger, J. Statistical decision theory and Bayesian analysis. Springer-Verlag. 1985
[Calvanese, D. et al. 2002] Calvanese, D.; De Giacomo, G.; and Lenzerini, M. 2002. A framework for ontology integration. In Cruz, I.; Decker, S.; Euzenat, J.; and McGuinness, D., eds., The Emerging Semantic Web. IOS Press. 201–214.
[H. Cunningham. 2002] H. Cunningham, D. Maynard, K. Bontcheva, and V. Tablan. GATE: A Framework and Graphical Development Environment for Robust NLP Tools and Applications. In Proceedings of the 40th Anniversary Meeting of the Association for Computational Linguistics, 2002.

[A. Doan. 2002] A. Doan, J. Madhavan, P. Domingos, and A. Halevy. Learning to map between ontologies on the semantic web. In Proceedings of the World-Wide Web Conference (WWW-2002), pages 662–673. ACM Press, 2002.

[A. Maedche et al. 2002] A. Maedche, B. Moltik, N. Silva and R. Volz. MAFRA —An Ontology MApping FRAmework in the Context of the Semantic Web. In Proceeding of the EKAW'2002, Siguenza, Spain. 2002.

[Maedche. 2002] A. Maedche, B. Motik, N. Silva, and R. Volz. MAFRA - A Mapping Framework for Distributed Ontologies. In Proceedings of EKAW 2002, LNCS 2473, pages 235–250. Springer, 2002.

[McGuinness. 2000] McGuinness D., Fikes R., Rice J., and Wilder S. :An environment for merging and testing large ontologies. Proceedings of the 7th International Conference on Principles of Knowledge Representation and Reasoning. Colorado, USA.

[N. F. Noy and M. A. Musen. 2000] N. F. Noy and M. A. Musen. PROMPT: Algorithm and Tool for Automated Ontology Merging and Alignment. In Proc. of AAAI-2000, pages 450–455, 2000.

[Nuno Silva and Joao Rocha, 2003] Nuno Silva and Joao Rocha. Semantic Web Complex Ontology Mapping. IEEE/WIC International Conference on Web Intelligence (WI'03) October 13-17, 2003 Halifax, Canada:82-100

[Omelayenko, B. 2002] Omelayenko, B. RDFT: A Mapping Meta-Ontology for Business Integration; Workshop on Knowledge Transformation for the Semantic Web (KTSW 2002) at ECAI'2002. Lyon, France; 2002:76-83

[Park, J. Y. 1998] Park, J. Y., Gennari, J. H. and Musen, M. A.; "Mappings for Reuse in Knowledge-based Systems"; 11th Workshop on Knowledge Acquisition, Modelling and Management (KAW 98); Banff, Canada; 1998.

[Patrick. P, Dekang. L. 2002] Patrick. P, Dekang. L. Discovering Word Senses from Text. In Proceedings of ACM SIGKDD Conference on Knowledge Discovery and Data Mining 2002:613-619.

[Stuckenschmidt, H. et al. 2000] Stuckenschmidt, H. and Wache, H. Context Modeling and Transformation for Semantic Interoperability. Workshop of Knowledge Representation meets Databases (KRDB 2000) at ECAI'2000. Berlin, Germany; 2000:115-126

[Tim Berners-Lee, 1999] Tim Berners-Lee, Mark Fischetti (Contributor), Michael L. Dertouzos; "Weaving the Web: The Original Design and Ultimate Destiny of the World Wide Web"; 1999.

[Wache, H. et al. 2001] Wache, H.; Voegele, T.; Visser, U.; Stuckenschmidt, et al. 2001. Ontology-based integration of information – a survey of existing approaches. In Proc. of IJCAI 2001 Workshop on Ontologies and Information Sharing.

Evolutionary Parameter Estimation Algorithm for Combined Kernel Function in Support Vector Machine*

Syng-Yup Ohn, Ha-Nam Nguyen, and Sung-Do Chi

Department of Computer Engineering, Hankuk Aviation University, Seoul, Korea
{syohn,nghanam,sdchi}@hau.ac.kr

Abstract. This paper proposes a new kernel function for support vector machine and its learning method with fast convergence and good classification performance. A set of kernel functions are combined to create a new kernel function, which is trained by a learning method based on evolution algorithm. The learning method results in the optimal decision model consisting of a set of features as well as a set of the parameters for combined kernel function. The combined kernel function and the learning method were applied to obtain the optimal decision model for the classification of clinical proteome patterns, and the combined kernel function showed faster convergence in learning phase and resulted in the optimal decision model with better classification performance than other kernel functions. Therefore, the combined kernel function has the greater flexibility in representing a problem space than single kernel functions.

1 Introduction

Support vector machine [1-5] (SVM) is learning method that uses a hypothesis space of linear functions in a high dimensional feature space. This learning strategy, introduced by Vapnik [2], is a principled and powerful method. In the simplest and linear form, a SVM is the hyperplane that separates a set of positive samples from a set of negative samples with the largest margin. The margin is defined by the distance between the hyperplanes supporting the nearest positive and negative samples. The equation for decision in the linear case is

$$y = \mathbf{w} \cdot \mathbf{x} - \mathbf{b},$$

(1)

where $\mathbf{w}$ is a normal vector to the hyperplane and $\mathbf{x}$ is an input vector. The separating hyperplane is the plane $\mathbf{y} = 0$ and two supporting hyperplanes parallel to it with equal distances are

$$H_1 : \mathbf{y} = \mathbf{w} \cdot \mathbf{x} - \mathbf{b} = +1$$
$$H_2 : \mathbf{y} = \mathbf{w} \cdot \mathbf{x} - \mathbf{b} = -1$$

(2)

In order to find the optimal separating hyperplane having maximal margin, $\|\mathbf{w}\|$ should be minimized subject to inequality constraints. This is a classic nonlinear optimization problem with inequality constraints. The optimization problem can be solved by finding the saddle point of the Lagrange function in the following.

---

* This research was supported by IRC (Internet Information Retrieval Research Center) in Hankuk Aviation University. IRC is a Kyounggi-Province Regional Research Center designated by Korea Science and Engineering Foundation and Ministry of Science & Technology.

C.-H. Chi and K.-Y. Lam (Eds.): AWCC 2004, LNCS 3309, pp. 481–486, 2004.

$$L(\mathbf{w},\mathbf{b},\alpha) = \frac{1}{2}\mathbf{w}^T\mathbf{w} - \sum_{i=1}^{N}\alpha_i\mathbf{y}_i([\mathbf{w}^T\mathbf{x}+b]-1) \tag{3}$$

where $\alpha_i \geq 0$,$i = 0,\dots, N$, are Lagrange multipliers. However, the limitation of computational power of linear learning machines was highlighted in the 1960s by Minsky and Papert [6]. It can be easily recognized that real-world applications require more extensive and flexible hypothesis space than linear functions. Such a limitation can be overcome by *multilayer neural networks* proposed by Rumelhart, Hinton and William [3]. Kernel function also offers an alternative solution by projecting the data into high dimensional feature space to increase the computational power of linear learning machines. Non-linear mapping from input space to high dimensional feature space can be implicitly performed by an appropriate kernel function (see Fig. 1). One of the interesting characteristics on kernel functions is that a new kernel function can be created by combining a set of kernel functions with the operators such as addition or multiplication operators [1].

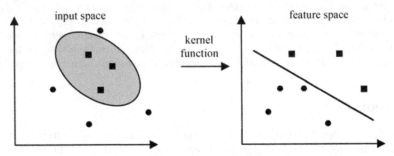

Fig. 1. An input space can be transformed into a linearly separable feature space by an appropriate kernel function

Evolutionary algorithm (EA)[7-9] is an optimization algorithm based on the mechanism of natural evolution procedure. Most of evolution algorithms share a common conceptual base of simulating the evolution of individual structures via the processes of selection, mutation, and reproduction. EA performs a multi-directional search by maintaining a population of potential solutions and encourages the formation and the exchange of information among different directions. EAs are generally applied to the problems with a large search space. They are different from random algorithms since they combine the elements of directed and stochastic search. Furthermore, EA is also known to be more robust than directed search methods.

In this paper, we propose a new kernel function combining a set of simple kernel functions for SVM and a method to train the combined kernel function. In the new learning method, EA is exploited to derive the optimal *decision model* for the classification of patterns, which consists of the optimal set of features and parameters of combined kernel function. The new method was applied to the classification of proteome patterns for the identification of stomach cancer, which are extracted from actual clinical samples. The combined kernel function and the learning method showed faster convergence and better classification rate than single kernel functions.

This paper is organized as follows. In section 2, our new combined kernel and its learning method are presented in detail. In section 3, we compare the performances of combined kernel functions and single kernel functions based on case study on the classification of proteome pattern samples. Finally, section 4 is our conclusion.

2 Proposed Learning Method

The framework of our learning method is illustrated in Fig. 2. EA creates new chromosomes and searches the *optimal decision model* based on the fitness values obtained from SVM[1] classifier.

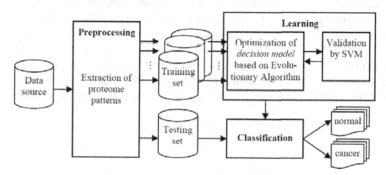

Fig. 2. EA-SVM learning method for combined kernel function

A kernel function provides a flexible and effective learning mechanism in SVM, and the choice of a kernel function should reflect prior knowledge about the problem at hand. However, it is often difficult for us to exploit the prior knowledge on patterns to choose a kernel function, and it is an open question how to choose the best kernel function for a given data set. According to *no free lunch theorem* [4] on machine learning, there is no superior kernel function in general, and the performance of a kernel function rather depends on applications. In our case, a new kernel function is created by combining the set of kernel functions. The combined kernel function has the form of

$$K_{Combined} = (K_1)^{e_1} \circ \cdots \circ (K_m)^{e_m} \qquad (4)$$

where $\{K_i \mid i = 1, \ldots, m\}$ is the set of kernel functions to be combined, e_i is the exponent of i-th kernel function, and $\square$ denotes an operator between two kernel functions. In our case, three types of the kernel functions listed in Table 1 are combined, and multiplication or addition operators are used to combine kernel functions. The parameters in a kernel function play the important role of representing the structure of a sample space. The set of the parameters of a combined kernel function consists of three part - i) exponents of individual kernel functions, ii) operators between kernel functions, iii) coefficient in each kernel function.

The optimal set of the parameters maximizing the classification performance can be selected by a machine learning method. In a learning phase, the structure of a sample space is learned by a kernel function, and the knowledge of a sample space is contained in the set of parameters of the kernel function. Furthermore, the optimal set

---

[1] mySVM was used for the implementation of the proposed method in this paper. (Available at: http://www-ai.cs.uni-dortmund.de/SOFTWARE/MYSVM/)

of features also should be chosen in the learning phase. EA technique is exploited to obtain the optimal set of features as well as the optimal combined kernel function. The challenging issue of EA is how to map a real problem into a *chromosome*. In our learning method, we need to map feature space, the set of the parameters for kernels, and the set of operators combining kernels. Firstly, the set of features is encoded into a n-bit binary string to represent an active or non-active state of n features. Then the exponents of m individual kernel functions, the operators between individual kernel functions, and the coefficients in each individual kernel function are encoded into a multi-valued gene string. The combination of the two gene string forms a chromosome in EA procedure which in turn serves as a *decision model* (see Fig. 3). In learning phase, simulating a genetic procedure, EA improves decision models containing a combined kernel function and a set of features by the iterative process of reproduction, evaluation, and selection process. At the end of learning stage, the optimal decision model consisting of a combined kernel function and the set of features is obtained, and this optimal decision model is used to classify new pattern samples.

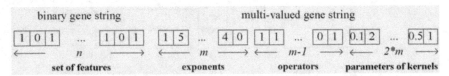

Fig. 3. Structure of a chromosome used in EA procedure

Table 1. Kernel functions are used to construct combined kernel function

Kernel function	Formula
Inverse Multi-Quadric	$1/\sqrt{\|x - y\|^2 + c^2}$
Radial	$e^{\left(-\gamma\|x-y\|^2\right)}$
Neural	$\tanh(s \cdot \langle x, y \rangle - c)$

3   Experiments

In this section, we apply the new kernel function and the learning method to obtain the optimal decision model to classify proteome patterns for the identification of stomach cancer. Furthermore, the performances of the combined kernel function and single kernel functions are compared. A proteome pattern sample consists of a set of the values representing the amount of the different types of proteins in a material. A proteome pattern from human serum represents the status of the cells in human organs, and the anomalies or the disease in organs such as cancer can be detected by the analysis of proteome patterns. The proteome pattern samples used in the case study were provided by Cancer Research Center at Seoul National University in Seoul, Korea.

3.1   Comparison of Learning of Kernel Functions

Our combined kernel function and three single kernel functions (see Table 1) were trained by EA, and their convergence rates were compared. Furthermore, the classifiers based on the optimal decision models resulted from learning phase were evaluated by their classification rates. Fig. 4 depicts the maximum hit rates achieved at each generation during learning phase. While EA was executed for 30 generations, the combined kernel function showed the fastest convergence and achieved the highest hit rate among the kernel functions compared. Thus, our combined kernel function has greater flexibility in representing the structure of a sample space than single kernel functions. The combined kernel function reached hit rate of 91.25% after 30 generations, and the optimal kernel function obtained at this point is

$$K_{Combined} = (K_{Inverse\ multi-quadric})^2 + (K_{Radial})^0 + (K_{Neural})^1 .$$

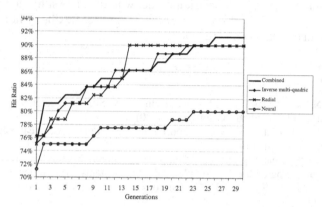

Fig. 4. Classification rates of 4 kernel functions in learning phase

3.2 Comparison of Classification by Optimal Decision Models

The *testing on training set* methodology shows that the training error rate decreases monotonically during training for most problems. However, the error rate on the validation set decreases first and then increases. It means the classification model may be overfitting the training data. To prevent the overfitting problem, it was suggested that learning phase should stop at the first local minimum of validation error rate to obtain the optimal decision model [4]. Also, in our case, the optimal decision models from the case of the combined and the three single kernel functions were obtained at the point of the first local minimum of validation error rate, and the models are used to classify an independent test set. The classification performances by the optimal decision models are shown in Table 2. The combined kernel function achieved better classification rate than single kernel functions.

Table 2. Classification rates by the optimal decision models obtained at the point of local minimum of validation error rate

	Combination	Radial	Neural	Inverse Multi-Quadric
Generation	25	15	25	15
Hit Rate	84.26%	83.33%	74.17%	81.48%

4 Conclusion

In this paper, we proposed a new kernel function combining a set of kernel functions for SVM and its learning method exploiting EA technique to obtain the optimal decision model for classification. A kernel function plays the important role of mapping the problem feature space into a new feature space so that the performance of a linear classifier is improved. The combined kernel function and the learning method were applied to classify the clinical proteome patterns to identify stomach cancer. In the comparison of the classifications by combined kernel and single three kernel functions, the combined kernel function achieved the fastest convergence in learning phase and results in the optimal decision model with the highest hit rate in classification phase. Thus our combined kernel function has greater flexibility in representing a problem space than single kernel functions.

References

1. Cristianini, N. and Shawe-Taylor, J.: An introduction to Support Vector Machines and other kernel-based learning methods. Cambridge (2000)
2. Vapnik, V.N. and et. al.: Theory of Support Vector Machines, Technical Report CSD TR-96-17. Univ. of London (1996)
3. Vojislav Kecman: Learning and Soft Computing: Support Vector Machines, Neural Networks, and Fuzzy Logic Models (Complex Adaptive Systems). The MIT press (2001)
4. Duda, R. O., Hart, P. E., Stork, D. G.: Pattern Classification (2nd Edition). John Wiley & Sons Inc. (2001)
5. Joachims, Thorsten: Making large-Scale SVM Learning Practical. In Advances in Kernel Methods - Support Vector Learning, chapter 11. MIT Press (1999)
6. M.L. Minsky and S.A.Papert, Perceptrons, MIT Press, 1969.
7. Michalewicz, Z.: Genetic Algorithms + Data structures = Evolution Programs. 3rd rev. and extended edn, Springer-Verlag (1996)
8. Goldberg, D. E.: Genetic Algorithms in Search, Optimization & Machine Learning. Adison Wesley (1989)
9. Mitchell, M.: Introduction to genetic Algorithms. Fifth printing. MIT press (1999)

Enriching Domain Ontology
from Domain-Specific Documents with HowNet

Yong Cheng[1,2] and Zhongzhi Shi[1]

[1] Institute of Computing Technology, Chinese Academy of Sciences, 100080 Beijing, China
{chengyong,shizz}@ics.ict.ac.cn
http://www.intsci.ac.cn
[2] Graduate School of Chinese Academy of Sciences, 100039 Beijing, China

Abstract. Constructing domain ontology by hand is still a hard and time-consuming job. So, developing methods and techniques to acquire ontology from a large amount of documents in a semi-automatic manner is indispensable. In this paper, we present a technique of how to enrich existing ontology from domain-specific documents with online knowledge system like HowNet. HowNet is a bilingual general knowledge base that encodes inter-concept semantic relations and the inter-attribute semantic relations that can provide a hint to enrich existing ontology. We present the enrichment algorithms in detail. The preliminary experiment in physical education domain is taken and useful conclusions is made and presented through the paper.

1 Introduction

Incorporating semantic information into electronic resources available in current WWW has been proved to be important for the communication and cooperation among people. Ontology from knowledge engineering community provides a right alternative for embodying the semantics. However, constructing domain ontology is still hard and time-consuming job. It's imperative to develop methods and techniques to learn ontology from a large amount of documents in a semi-automatic way. This paper addresses the problem of how to enrich existing ontology from domain-specific documents with online knowledge system like HowNet[1]. HowNet is a bilingual general knowledge base that encodes inter-concept semantic relations and the inter-attribute semantic relations. Contrary to WordNet[2], HowNet is a general knowledge base but not a semantic dictionary. We present the concept and relation enrichment algorithms that deal with enrichment of concept and relation respectively. The preliminary experiment in physical education domain is presented and evaluated.

The remainder of this paper is organized as follows: In Section 2, we outline the technology underlying our approach, relevant work and give a brief introduction to HowNet. Then we introduce the concept and relation enrichment algorithms. In section 3, a preliminary experiment result is presented and evaluated. Followed the conclusion section.

2 Enriching Existing Ontolgy with HowNet

Ontologies offer a shared vocabulary for communication among software or human agents. In usual life, written documents like book, newspaper and letter are the most important means for people to communicate with each other. So, it has good reasons

C.-H. Chi and K.-Y. Lam (Eds.): AWCC 2004, LNCS 3309, pp. 487–492, 2004.
© Springer-Verlag Berlin Heidelberg 2004

to develop techniques and methods and learn ontology from these various sources. But the initial ontology learned is often redundant and ill-defined in semantics. Therefore, The issue of how to enrich and validate ontology is proposed. Missikoff proposes a method to build a core domain ontology using WordNet as a source of prior knowledge[3]. In his method, WordNet is as a semantic and linguistic resource to interpret the terms. The senses of each word are defined as a synset of synonyms. In [4], A work to annotate Chinese texts with information derived from HowNet is reported. Papatheodorou also presents a method to build taxonomies using clustering mining techniques from XML-based corpus[5]. The key is to select appropriate words to describe the documents and calculate their similarity, during the process, WordNet can be used to extract the word roots. The work closed to our approach is Gupta et al's work[6]. They present a method to maintain sublanguage WordNet using domain-specific documents. There are two differences between Gupta's work and ours. One is that we expect to enrich domain-specific ontology. The other is that we use HowNet to perform the work that is more appropriate to Chinese environment.

2.1   An Introduction to HowNet

HowNet, introduced by Prof. Zhenqiang Dong, is an online common sense knowledge base describing relations between concepts and the relations between the attributes of concepts. From HowNet's points of view, all matters in objective world are in constant motion and are changing in a special time and space. The motion and change are reflected by changes in values of attributes of a concept. The structure of HowNet is a graph that provides more conveniences to deal with general and specific properties of concepts than tree. In the 2004 version of HowNet, about 75524 concepts in Chinese and 73127 English equivalents are covered. At the up-most level, these concepts are classified into entity, event, attribute and attribute value. Event can be further classified as static and dynamic. Apart from the concepts, a variety of relation types are addressed explicitly in HowNet, including: Hypernym-Hyponym, Hypernym-Hyponym, synonym, antonym, converse, part-whole, attribute-host, material-product, agent-event, patient-event, instrument-event, location-event, time-event, value-attribute, entity-value, event-role, concepts co-relation and so on. The relations are the core of HowNet as a knowledge system, but not a semantic dictionary. An important concept used in HowNet is sememe. Sememes refer to some basic unit of senses and are used to describe all the entries in HowNet. Currently, a total of over 1,500 sememes are found in HowNet and organized hierarchically. These sememes are extracted from Chinese characters and further classified, refined and examined.

2.2   Concept Enrichment

Given raw documents, it is necessary to do a previous preprocessing on them. As a result of this activity, we obtain some terms including words, multi-word phrases that are the lexical terms of candidate concepts. As we all know, the meaning of a term is highly correlated to the contexts in which it appears. If we can get the relations of these lexical terms quantitatively with the help of HowNet, we would group similar words together to form new concepts and add to the existing ontology. For this purpose, we first define sememe set.

Definition 1. The sememe set refers to the set of sense item of a word. Suppose a word W has n sense items in HowNet: s1, s2, ... , s3 then the sememe set is defined as {s1, s2, s3}.

Example 1: Let us consider the sememe set of word excitant (兴奋剂) and judgement(裁判). According to HowNet, the corresponding sememe sets are illustrated as follows:

Sememe set of excitant is {药物(Medicine), 使动(CauseToDO), 激动(excited), 体育(sport), 莠(undesired)}, while the sememe set of judgement is {{人(human), 职位 (occupation), 锻练 (exercise), 裁定 (judge), 体育 (sport)}{裁定 (judge), 体育(sport)} {结果(result), 裁定(judge),体育(sport)}}

With Sememe set, we can calculate the similarity more exactly. The algorithm of discovering new concept can be presented in the following:

Algorithm 1: Discovering new concept from document with HowNet.
Input: The set of words, multi-word phrases from preprocessed documents.
Output: Set of similar words as new concept.
Step1: Get the frequency of each term in each document in some domain.
Step2: Calculate the similarity of term using Cosine distance or Euclidean distance: $Sim_{orgin} = \dfrac{V(term1) \cdot V(term2)}{V(term1) \times V(term2)}$.

Step3: For each term in training corpus, obtain the sememe set according to HowNet and calculate similarity $Sim_{KL}(term1, term2)$ using KL divergence.
Step4: combine the similarity value based on different weight factor.

$$Sim = \alpha \cdot Sim_{orgin} + (1 - \alpha) \cdot Sim_{KL}(term1, term2)$$

α is the weight factor.
Step5: Calculate the similarity matrix of terms.
Step6: Group the terms with high value of similarity together using clustering method and return the set of terms as new concept.

End

From above algorithm, we notice that the last similarity consists of two parts: the first is vector similarity, the second is sememe set similarity. With HowNet, we get the better result. Other similarity measures such as mutual information (MI), Information Gain (IG) and chi-square can be used according to different document types.

2.3 Relationship Enrichment

As stated before, relation is the core of HowNet knowledge system. There are nine relations identified in HowNet that can be used to enrich existing ontology. At first we investigate several most important relations and present our relation enrichment algorithm.

2.3.1 Dynamic Role

HowNet uses dynamic role to specify the attributes what a concept has. This kind of relation is expressed by "*" pointer. An example is give in the following:

NO.=043517
W_C=剑 G_C=N E_C= W_E=falchion G_E=N E_E= DEF=weapon|武器,*stab|扎

The concept being defined 剑(falchion) is the instrument of the event type "扎"(stab).

2.3.2 Hyponymy Relation

In HowNet, the hyponymy are organized in a hierarchical structure. For example, event, entity, attribute and quantity are top-level classes. Event can be further classified into static and dynamic. Entity class is classified into thing, time, space and component.

2.3.3 Meronymy Relation

In HowNet, meronymy relation is described by "%" pointer. See following example:

NO.=061449
W_C=南方 G_C=N E_C= W_E=the southern part of the country G_E=N E_E=
DEF=part|部件,%place|地方,#south|南,#country|国家
"南方"(south) is a part of the class of "地方"(place).

In HowNet, there have other classes of relations, such as material-product relation, attribute-host relation, concept-coourrence relation and on so, which are described in "?", "&", "#" respectively. Because of the limit of space, details of these relations are omitted and available from the website[1].

Algorithm 2: Enriching new relation from document with HowNet.
Input: Concept extracted from documents using Algorithm 1.
Output: Set of new relation.
Step1: Set the depth of search in HowNet, the depth value can be 1, 2, 3 or more.
Step2: Identify all concepts that are similar semantically to the concepts in existing ontology.
Step3: Identify various relations between the concepts to be added and the concepts in existing ontology.
   Step3.1: Identify hyponymy relation as taxonomic relation.
   Step3.2: Identify dynamic role, meronymy relation and other relation as non- taxonomic relation.

End

These relations should be validated by domain experts and exported in machine-readable form.

3 Preliminary Experiment

Ontology learning from texts is becoming one of hot topics in current knowledge engineering community. We develop an ontology engineering environment called OntoSphere in which ontology editing, learning, evaluation are supported. To experiment the enrichment algorithm, we choose a corpus that contains 500 articles in sports column of 1997 People Daily. After segmenting and key phrase extraction, we get a set of terms. The similarity measure we use is calculated by algorithm 1. When $\alpha = 0.25$, the numbers of concepts and relations newly discovered are shown in figure 1 and figure 2 when numbers of document are 50, 100, 150, 200, 250, 300.

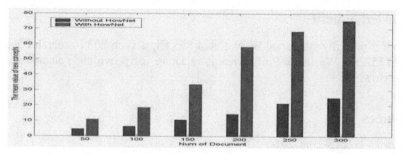

Fig. 1. New Discovered Concepts

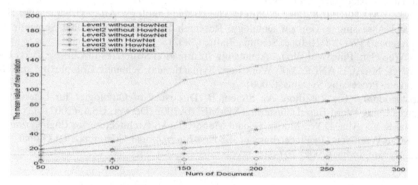

Fig. 2. New Enriched Relations

We notice that in the two figures above, the performance with HowNet gets better results than the performance without HowNet. We observe that when the number of document equals 50, 100, 150, 200, 250, 300, the number of new concepts averagely increases by 137%, 193%, 220.9%, 304.2%, 219.2%, 200% respectively. In this experiment, effect of search depth in HowNet is also explored. If we increase the depth of search, more new relations will be discovered and vice versa some relations will be missed.

4 Conclusions and Future Work

In this paper, we present a technique of how to enrich the existing ontology using the relations contained in HowNet. The work reported here makes the following contributions: (1) Presenting an introduction to HowNet. (2) Introducing algorithms to enrich existing ontology from domain-specific documents using HowNet and reporting preliminary experiment results.

The work provides us a good beginning for future work. The following several issues should be addressed: firstly, strategies and guidelines should be developed to choose appropriate documents to add the corpus, which is an important factor to affect the quality of ontology. Secondly, in different domains, the similarity measure between the concept in existing ontology and concept extracted from documents should be further refined. At last, other important knowledge sources like domain dictionary and glossary should be considered.

Acknowledgement

This work is partially supported By National 863 High-Tech 863 Research Plan. (No: 2003AA115220). We thank Prof. Zhenqiang Dong for providing valuable research resource HowNet.

References

1. http://www.keenage.com, 2004
2. Miller, George A. WordNet: An Online Lexical Database. Special Issue of International Journal of Lexicography. 4 (1990)
3. Missikoff M., Navigli R., and Velardi P. The Usable Ontology: An Environment for Building and Assessing a Domain Ontology. Research Paper at International Semantic Web Conference(ISWC2002), June, Sardinia, Italia, (2002)
4. Kok Wee Gan, Ping Wai Wong. Annotating Information Structures in Chinese Texts Using HowNet. NAACL-ANLP 2000 Workshop: Syntactic and Semantic Complexity in Natural Language Processing Systems. (2000)
5. Papatheodorou, C., Vassiliou, A., Simon, B. Discovery of Ontologies for Learning Resources Using Word-Based Clustering. ED-MEDIA2002, Denver, USA, (2002)
6. Gupta, K.M., Aha, D.W., Marsh, E., and Maney, T. An Architecture for Engineering Sublanguage WordNets. In Preceedings of the first International Conference on Global WordNet. Mysore, India, (2002) 207-215

A Framework of Extracting Sub-ontology[*]

Baowen Xu[1, 2], Dazhou Kang[1], and Jianjiang Lu[1, 2,3]

[1] Department of Computer Science and Engineering, Southeast University,
Nanjing 210096, China
[2] Jiangsu Institute of Software Quality, Nanjing 210096, China
[3] PLA University of Science and Technology, Nanjing, 210007, China
Bwxu@seu.edu.cn

Abstract. It often needs to extract sub-ontology from large-scale ontology for application. Current approaches mainly focus on extraction in single ontology. However, an application may require several large-scale ontologies in different domains; it needs approaches of extracting sub-ontology from multiple ontologies. This paper proposes a framework of extracting sub-ontology from multiple ontologies. In the framework, a unified visualized ontology model is proposed; different Ontology language codes are translated into the unified model firstly. Then we divide the user requirements to extract sub-ontology from each ontology; the extraction is in an iterative and incremental process. Finally, we integrate these sub-ontologies into the sub-ontology that the user demands, and translate the result back to the Ontology language the user uses. This framework avoids doing integration and extraction processes with large-scale ontologies, which are the most difficult processes in current approaches.

1 Introduction

The Semantic Web [1] is a promising extension of the current Web, and the key technology in the Semantic Web is Ontology [2]. Ontology is shared conceptualization of some domain that formally defines concepts, relations and axioms. It is the basic of sharing and reusing knowledge on the Web.

There are many large-scale ontologies on the Web. For example, the Unified Medical Language System [3] ontology has more than 800,000 concepts and 9,000,000 relationships. Large-scale ontologies are hard to maintain and use. However, Ontology creators often attempt to model certain domains accurately and completely; this leads to more and more large-scale ontologies.

An application may only need a small part of a large-scale ontology [4]. Extracted form the original ontology, a smaller and simpler sub-ontology can make the application more efficient [5]. The sub-ontology only contains the particular parts of the whole ontology required by the application, and other outlying information has been removed.

Sub-ontology extraction is a new research area. Early researches only study generating application-focused databases from large ontologies [4]. Materialized Ontology View Extraction (MOVE) [5] is a sequential extraction process of extracting sub-

---

[*] This work was supported in part by NSFC (60373066, 60303024), National Grand Fundamental Research 973 Program of China (2002CB312000), and National Research Foundation for the Doctoral Program of Higher Education of China (20020286004).

C.-H. Chi and K.-Y. Lam (Eds.): AWCC 2004, LNCS 3309, pp. 493–498, 2004.

ontology. Under application requirements, MOVE supports optimization schemes to guarantee sub-ontology with high quality [6]. *Subsequent researchers* proposed a distributed approach [7] to decrease cost of sub-ontology extraction from large complex ontology. They also analyze the semantic completeness issue [8]. GoPubmed system [9] presents the relevant sub-ontology for browsing GeneOntology; it shows the extraction of sub-ontology is profitable.

Current methods only focus on extracting sub-ontology from single ontology. However, in many practical cases, especially in the web environments, we often face multiple ontologies in one application [10]. Nevertheless, there are no existing methods to extracting sub-ontology from multiple ontologies. The methods for single ontology are not able to solve many new problems with multiple ontologies.

This paper proposes a framework of extracting sub-ontologies from multiple ontologies, and suggests some first step notions. Section 2 introduces our framework of extracting sub-ontology from multiple ontologies. Section 3 discusses the extracting process in detail. Section 4 gives the conclusion.

2   Proposed Framework

There are two approaches to extract sub-ontology from multiple ontologies:

1. Integrate all the original ontologies, and then extract the demanded sub-ontology from the integrated one. It can use the current methods of extracting sub-ontology from single ontology. However, there are two disadvantages: the ontology integration [11] is difficult, especially for large ontologies; the current methods is computationally expensive [7] to extract sub-ontology from the integrated ontology, which is often very large.
2. Extract sub-ontology form each ontology separately, and then integrate them into the demanded one. It wipes off the outlying information at first, so the sub-ontologies to be integrated are much smaller than original ones. It is better than the former approach at least in aspect of efficiency.

We adopt the approach in our framework. An example of applying the framework is showed in Fig.1. The squares are processes; the real line arrows are inputs and outputs of the processes, and the dashed arrows shows the requirements guiding the processes. The ontologies are all in the unified Ontology model. The bridge ontology [10] contains information to help the integration process. The framework contains mainly four processes:

1. convert all the ontologies into a unified ontology model;
2. divide the requirements into sub-requirements;
3. extract sub-ontologies based on the sub-requirements respectively;
4. integrate the sub-ontologies.

2.1   Unified Ontology Model

There are many different Ontology languages on the Web, such as OWL, DAML-OIL and Ontolingua. We have to translate them into a unified internal representation, i.e. a unified Ontology model. The unified model must involve most of the features in typical Ontology languages.

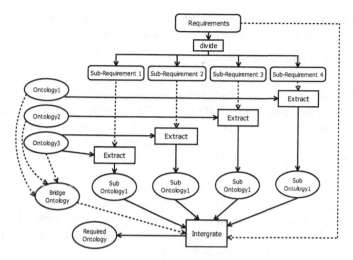

Fig. 1. The flow chart of the framework

Definition 1. In the framework, we consider an ontology as a eight-tuple

$$O = (C, A^C, R, A^R, S(C), E(C), H, X) \tag{1}$$

C is the set of concepts. A^c is the set of attributes about concept $c \in C$. R is the set of relations. A^r is the set of attributes about relation $r \in R$. $S(c)$ is the set of relations $\{r \mid r \in R \wedge \exists a, b(a \in c \wedge (a,b) \in r)\}$, $E(c)$ is the set of relations $\{r \mid r \in R \wedge \exists a, b(b \in c \wedge (a,b) \in r)\}$, where a, b are individuals. The concept hierarchy H is the set of two-tuples of concepts that have subsumption relations. X is the set of axioms. The meaning of these elements in Ontology can be found in OWL standards of W3C [12]. This model is expressive enough to represent ontologies in most Ontology languages. It is possible to translate ontologies in other languages into this model and vice versa.

In our framework, the information about individuals is not concerned. Concept is the only fundamental element. Relations need to depend on certain concepts by $S(c)$ and $E(c)$. Attributes are depending on certain concept or relation. Axioms are restrictions about the concepts, relations and attributes, and of course depend on them. Therefore, the Ontology is organized into a modularized model, it makes the extraction easier.

Visualization of this model is realizable. It can be viewed as a tree-like hierarchy. Users can browse through an ontology in order to understand its scope, structure and content, and rapidly search it for terms of interest and related terms.

2.2   Requirements Division and Sub-ontology Integration

When extracting sub-ontology from single ontology, user requirements can directly conduct the extraction. Nevertheless, it is hard to decide requirements to extracting sub-ontology from a certain ontology in multiple ontologies.

User requirements are often in inexplicit natural language. Requirement analyzers have to understand the user requirements, and convert them to formal functional requirements. Then for each function requirement, they analyze what concepts or relations are needed, and get sub-requirement for each ontology.

Definition 2. A sub-requirements is a seven-tuple

$$Re = (SC, SR, SA, UC, UR, UA, EX) \tag{2}$$

where they are sets of concepts, relations and attributes in the select ontology, and are short for Select Concepts, Select Relations, Select Attributes, Unselect Concepts, Unselect Relations, Unselect Attributes, and *EX* is the set of extra requirements.

The sub-requirements can be showed in visualized ontology model marking selected and unselected elements differently. Analyzers can browse the visual model, and change the requirements.

The extraction process will be discussed in detail in the next section.

After the extraction process, it has to integrate the sub-ontologies into one. The Ontology integration is a difficult task. However, some existing methods are able to integrate simple ontologies [11]. Sub-ontologies are often small and simple; these methods can integrate them with acceptable results.

Bridge ontology [10] is used to keep information about the relations between different original ontologies, which is needed in integration. The bridge ontology has the advantages of low-cost, scalable, robust in the web circumstance, avoiding the unnecessary ontology extending and integration, and promoting ontology reuse.

3   Extraction

Extracting sub-ontology from original ontology is the key process of the framework. The input of this process is a ontology and a sub-requirement, the output is the sub-ontology extracted from the original ontology according to the sub-requirement. The extraction contains mainly six steps showed in Fig.2. The six steps are iterative; the process will continue until the sub-ontology satisfies the sub-requirement.

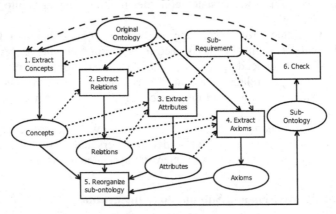

Fig. 2. The steps in extraction process

The extraction of concepts is the base of all following works. There are mainly three methods. A sophisticated method is to include all the concepts on the path from the selected concepts to the root of the concept hierarchy except the unselected ones

[9]. Another method is to extract concepts that are the smallest parent of any pair of the selected concepts; it greatly reduced the number of concepts extracted but may lose many related concepts. The above two methods focus the structure of concept hierarchy. The semantic of concepts can also be used in extraction. For example, if one selected concept is defined in terms of another concept, the latter should be extracted [8]. However, it is more difficult to be implemented.

Relations are depending on the concepts they linked. Let the extracted concepts in the previous step be EC. We can consider extracting relations based on both SR and EC: $\{r \mid r \in SR \land \exists(c_1, c_2 \in EC)(r \in S(c_1) \land r \in E(c_2))\}$ and specific relations between the extracted concepts: $\{r \mid r \notin UR \land \exists(c_1, c_2 \in EC)(r \in S(c_1) \land \forall c(c \subset c_1 \rightarrow r \notin S(c))$ $\land r \in E(c_2) \land \forall c(c \subset c_2 \rightarrow r \notin E(c)))\}$.

Attributes are depending on certain concepts and relations. Let the extracted relations be ER. The extraction of attributes is based on SA, EC and ER: $\{a \mid a \in SA \land (\exists c(c \in EC \land a \in A^c) \lor \exists r(r \in ER \land a \in A^r))\}$. Let it be EA.

Axioms are not in sub-requirements except extra requirements. The extraction of axioms is based on EC, ER and EA. If all the elements that an axiom describes are in them, the axiom is extracted.

These steps are based on the results of the previous steps, and they extract different kinds of elements in ontology separately. Moreover, user can have a visual tool to browse the ontology, and select or unselect select and unselect any elements manually.

Reorganizing sub-ontology is a simple work, for no new information is introduced and all the extracted elements are in the original ontology. It is important to check the sub-ontology. The checking step adjusts sub-ontology and the sub-requirements, and decides whether to end the extraction or repeat it.

Our extraction process is iterative and incremental. If the checking fails, it repeats the extracting process but the previous results can be reused. Moreover, it corrects the sub-requirements to make the next result more appropriate. If the dependent concept of a selected attribute is not extracted, the concept should be added to sub-requirements. If a selected relation is not extracted because it starts or ends with no extracted concepts, certain concepts need to be selected; but if it starts and ends both with no extracted concepts, the relation may not be selected. If the dependent relation of a selected attribute is not extracted nor selected, the relation should be selected.

4 Conclusion and Future Work

We propose a framework of extracting sub-ontologies from multiple ontologies, and suggest some first step notions. We first translate different Ontology language code into a unified visualized model representing ontologies, and then divide the user demand to extract sub-ontology from each single ontology. We carry out the sub-ontology extraction based on the unified model in an iterative and incremental way. Finally, we integrate these smaller sub-ontologies into the ontology of the user demand. The result can be translated back to the Ontology language the user uses. The high efficient methods of extraction and integration aim at the framework and the visualized tools implementing the framework are the future work.

References

1. Berners-Lee, T., Hendler, J., and Lassila, O.: The Semantic Web. Scientific American, 284(5) (2001) 34-43
2. Stuckenschmidt, H.: Ontology-Based Information Sharing in Weakly Structured Environments. PhD thesis, AI Department, Vrije Universiteit Amsterdam (2002)
3. Unified medical language system. http://www.nlm.nih.gov/research/umls/
4. Peterson, B.J., Andersen, W.A., and Engel, J.: Knowledge Bus: Generating Application-Focused Databases from Large Ontologies. Proceedings of the 5th Knowledge Representation Meets Databases (KRDB) Workshop, Seattle, WA (1998) 2.1-2.10
5. Wouters, C., Dillon, T., Rahayu, W., and Chang, E.: A practical walkthrough of the ontology derivation rules. In Proceedings of DEXA 2002, Aix-en (2002) 259-268
6. Wouters, C., Dillon, T., Rahayu, W., Chang, E., and Meersman, R.: A practical approach to the derivation of materialized ontology view. Web Information Systems, Idea Group Publishing (2004) 191-226
7. Bhatt, M., Flahive, A., Wouters, C., Rahayu, W., and Taniar, D.: A distributed approach to sub-ontology extraction. Proceedings of the 18th International Conference on Advanced Information Networking and Application (2004) 636-641
8. Bhatt, M., Wouters, C., Flahive, A., Rahayu, W., and Taniar, D.: Semantic Completeness in Sub-ontology Extraction Using Distributed Methods. ICCSA (3) (2004) 508-517
9. Delfs, R., Doms, A., Kozlenkov, A., and Schroeder, M.: GoPubMed: ontology-based literature search applied to Gene Ontology and PubMed. German Conference on Bioinformatics (2004) 1-9
10. Peng, W., Baowen, X., Jianjiang, L., Dazhou, K., and Yanhui, L.: A Novel Approach to Semantic Annotation Based on Multi-ontologies. Proceedings of the Third International Conference on Machine Learning and Cybernetics, Shanghai (2004)
11. Keet, C.M.: Aspects of Ontology Integration. Internal report to the PhD proposal (2004)
12. W3C Web-Ontology (WebOnt) Working Group. http://www.w3.org/2001/sw/WebOnt/

Ontology Based Sports Video Annotation and Summary

Jian-quan Ouyang[1,2,3], Jin-tao Li[1], and Yong-dong Zhang[1]

[1] Institute of Computing Technology, Chinese Academy of Sciences, Beijing 100080, China
{oyjq,jtli,zhyd}@ict.ac.cn
[2] College of Information Engineering, Xiangtan University, Xiangtan 411105, China
[3] Graduate School of the Chinese Academy of Sciences, Beijing 100039, China

Abstract. With digital sports video increasing everyday, effective analyzing sports video content becomes more and more important. Effective and efficient representation of video for searching, retrieval, inference and mining is a key problem in knowledge engineering. To describe sports video content efficiently, sports video ontology for video annotation is represented in OWL, a description logic based Web Ontology Language. We describe a user-friendly platform for sports video annotation. Ontology based sports video annotation can facilitate video indexing, retrieval and reasoning in a broad range of applications including Digital Olympic Project in China. Moreover, we present a hierarchical sports video summarization strategy to browse the sports video in a progressive way. In sports video, replay scenes often represent the highlight or interesting event of the video. Hence, our representative scene selection is based on the replay detection algorithm and identical events detection. The basic experimental results show our strategy is effective.

1 Introduction

As digital multimedia works become more and more prevalent, it drives the need for indexing searching and summarization of multimedia content. Effective and efficient representation of multimedia video data for searching, retrieval, inference and video mining is an important task in knowledge engineering. Sports video is one of the most desirable video that is enjoyed by lots of funs in the world. Hence, broadcasters and sports experts are strongly interested the method that can log the key events with annotations. Annotations should include the descriptions of the most relevant highlights and interesting events.

There have been several approaches for description of multimedia metadata, Such as the advent of the MPEG-7 (formally called Multimedia Content Description Interface)[1]. MPEG-7 definitions (description schemas and descriptors) are expressed in XML schema. While XML is useful for representation of hierarchically structured documents, but imposes no semantic constraints on the meaning of multimedia documents.

Multimedia ontology provides a way of a shared understanding of media that can be useful for information exchange. Multimedia ontology can be applied to the following areas.

- Multimedia indexing: to improve the efficiency of multimedia database.
- Multimedia mining: to mine the information not explicit in the multimedia data.

C.-H. Chi and K.-Y. Lam (Eds.): AWCC 2004, LNCS 3309, pp. 499–508, 2004.
© Springer-Verlag Berlin Heidelberg 2004

- Knowledge sharing: to provide a suitable format and a common-shared terminology for describing the multimedia content.
- Multimedia visualization: table of content and browsing.

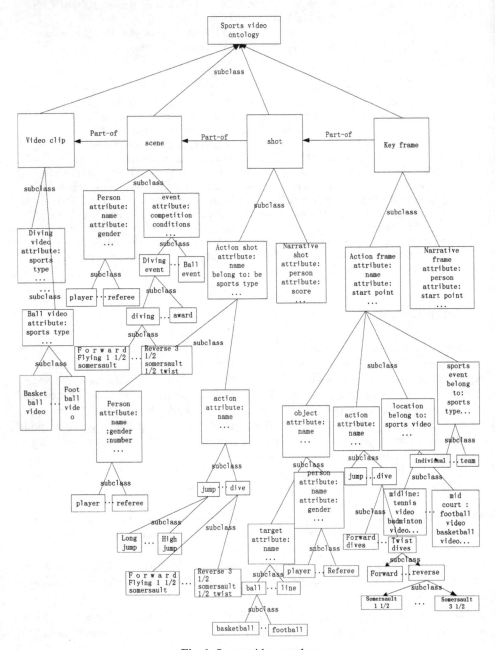

Fig. 1. Sports video ontology

Multimedia ontology has been used for photo annotation [2], video summary [3] and Colonoscopy video annotation [5]. But in Zhu [3], there is no further description of the category of medical video, and there is no reasoning schema. Moreover, paper [5] only introduced the integration of domain-specific and video ontology.

Due to the fact that different users have various perceptions and preferences of the same video, and the ambiguity and equivocalness of natural language can cause annotators to use different keywords to label the same object or event. The ontology-based annotation is proposed in this paper.

Ontology can provide a formal format and a shared terminology for describing the content of knowledge. Our ontology facilitates: metadata acquisition of video and improvement of query performance. Our Ontology also provides a flexible way to query the sports video database, which cannot be achieved by simple keyword search.

The rest of this paper is organized as follows. In section 2, the sports video ontology is proposed. The video content annotation scheme based on the ontology is presented in section 3. The sports video summarization scheme is addressed in section 4. In section 5 the effectiveness of our strategy is validated by experiments over sports video clip. Finally, conclusions are given in the section 6.

2 Sports Video Ontology

2.1 Class Taxonomy

OWL [4] is a new ontology language for the Semantic Web, developed by the World Wide Web Consortium (W3C) Web Ontology Working Group. While ontology is a term borrowed from philosophy that refers to the science of describing the kinds of entities in the world and how they are related. As there were already several ontology languages designed for use in the Web, OWL had to maintain as much compatibility as possible with these existing languages, including SHOE, OIL, and DAML+OIL. MPEG-7 standard does not contain semantic information in sports video. While OWL adds more vocabulary for describing properties and classes: among others, relations between classes, cardinality, equality, richer typing of properties, characteristics of properties, and enumerated classes [4]. Hence we use OWL language to describe operation of the sports video. The proposed sports video ontology is shown in Fig.1.

In popular view, the video content is organized into a four level hierarchy (video, scene, shot, frame). Thereby, in the proposed ontology, the lowest class is "key frame" instead of frame because key frame can concisely represent the content of the shot and there is often indistinctive difference between the consecutive frames.

Note that all concepts are group as subclass of "sports video ontology". Moreover, we use "part of" relations to model the hierarchical structure of sports video, so the top-level class "sports video ontology" is the super class of all concepts related to sports video descriptors, such as "video clip", "scene", "shot" and "key frame". For example, "key frame" is "part of" of "shot", the definition of class "part of" is follows.

```
<owl:TransitiveProperty rdf: ID="part of">
```
The definition of class "key frame" is follows.
```
<owl:Class rdf: ID="key frame">
  <rdfs: comment> key frame is a part of shot</rdfs: comment>
```

```
<rdfs:subClassOf>
    <owl:Restriction>
        <owl:onProperty rdf: resource="#part of">
        <owl:allValuesFrom rdf: resource="#shot"/>
    </owl:Restriction>
</rdfs:subClassOf>
</owl:Class>
```

2.2 Properties

In OWL there are two kinds of properties:

- Object properties, which relate objects to other objects.
- Datatype properties, which relate objects to datatype values.

Here, "id", "start point" and "end point" are the Datatype property. The definition of id in OWL is shown is follows.

```
<owl:DatatypeProperty rdf: ID= "start point">
  <owl:domain rdf:resource="#video clip"/>
  <owl: range rdf: about= "http://www.w3.org/2001/XLMSchema #nonNegativeInteger"/>
</owl:DatatypeProperty>
```

The object property means a relationship between two entities. There are two important classes of properties: class "attribute" means the sets of active relations, while class "belong to" means the sets of inverse properties of "attribute".

For example, "sports type" is a part of "attribute", the definition of "sports type" in OWL is shown is follows.

```
<owl: ObjectProperty rdf:ID="sports type">
  <owl:domain rdf:resource="#video clip"/>
</owl: ObjectProperty >
```

Similarly, "be sports type" is a part of "belong to", the definition of "be sports type" in OWL is shown is follows.

```
<owl: ObjectProperty rdf: ID=" be sports type">
  <owl:inverseOf rdf:resource="#sports type"/>
</owl: ObjectProperty >
```

2.3 Properties Restrictions

Because there are four level classes (video clip, scene, shot, key frame), their domain and range constraints are different at each level. Hence, lower-level class cannot inherit all properties of higher-level class; for example, the "attribute" of "shot" may not exist in the properties of the "video clip". However, All the class shares the same common properties "start point" and "end point", which represent the corresponding physical location and id. Similar to [4], the range of "start point" and "end point" of class scene is restricted to shot while that of shot is restricted to key frame. The definition of the restriction of scene is shown is follows.

```
<owl:Class rdf:ID="scene">
  <rdfs:subClassOf>
      <owl:Class rdf:about="#VideoClip"/>
```

```
    </rdfs:subClassOf>
    <rdfs:subClassOf>
        <owl:Restriction>
            <owl:onProperty>
                <owl:FunctionalProperty rdf:about="#start point"/>
            </owl:onProperty>
            <owl:allValuesFrom>
                <owl:Class rdf:about="#shot"/>
            </owl:allValuesFrom>
        </owl:Restriction>
    </rdfs:subClassOf>
</owl:Class>
```

3   Video Content Annotations

Video annotation with domain-specific controlled vocabularies or ontology for spe-cific domains can describe the structure of the video within a single unified frame-work. Some semi-automatic annotation schemes have been in video database[3] with relevance feedback to assist the annotator to refine the annotation. The shot and key frame annotation interface is as shown in Fig. 2. The annotator can both assign "shot" description and "key frame" description keywords related to the shot. In this paper, "key frame" description can describe more details of action frame than that of action shot in the "shot" description. For instance, we can only use the keyword "107(b) Forward 3 1/2somersault" to annotate the shot whose action is "107(b) Forward 3 1/2 somersault" in diving video, while we use the keyword "forward" in former key frame and keyword "3 1/2 somersault" in the latter key frame. The definition of union relation of "107(b) Forward 3 1/2 somersault" is shown is follows.

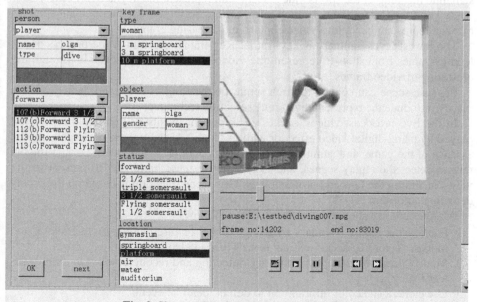

Fig. 2. Shot and key frame annotation interface

```
<owl:Class rdf:ID="dive">
<owl:unionof rdf:parseType="#107(b) Forward 3 1/2 somersault" />
<owl:Class rdf:about="#forward">
<owl:Class rdf:about="#3 1/2 somersault">
</owl:unionof>
</owl:Class>
```

After finishing the shot and key frame annotation, because lower-level class can inherit the properties of higher-level class, the video and scene description can get from the description of the shot. For instance, the "name" property of the scene can be assigned the shot description key words "107(b) Forward 3 1/2 somersault".

So using our strategy, a more reliable and effective video content annotation can be achieved:

1. The categories and details information about the sports video are presented in different level.
2. The annotated video content can be visualized and the user interface is user-friendly.

4 Video Summaries

After the video content annotation has been acquired, the video content is organized into a three level hierarchy summarization (video clip, scene, key frame). Video clip summary is based on the representative scene, and the representative shot organizes the scene summary, while the lowest level is the key frame. The first three types are moving-image abstracts, while the last is a pictorial summary. To present and visualize the sports content for summarization, the representative scene, representative shot and representative frame can express the video abstraction in various granularity. Among the three-hierarchy summarization, video clip can convey the comprehensive semantic meaning of the sports video, scene can represent the key action in the video, while key frame address the detailed information. So these three hierarchical summaries can represent the various video content in increasing granularity.

The lowest level summary is key frame. Key frame selection is the process of selecting frames from shots to represent the video content. The approach is through the clustering of video frames.

Because scene can convey the rich semantic meaning of the video, hence we primarily introduce the representative scene selection technique.

In the live broadcast videos, scenes of important events or highlights repeatedly played by using digital video effect or adding "logo". Usually these highlights are the essence of the game, and summarize the exciting actions of the video. So it is important to detect the replay scenes, and to reorganize these highlights to present to the views including the fans and professionals. Our scene selection is based on the replay detection algorithm [6].

A representative shot selection method is as follows.

1. Identify the replay boundary by using MPEG feature including macroblock and motion vector that is easy extract from MPEG video [6].
2. Modify the result of replay boundary detection and recongize slow motion to detect replay scene.
3. Use camera and color inforamtion to detect identical events.
4. Combine the replay scene and live scene as the representative shot.

After detecting the replay scenes and linking up live and replay scenes, the highest summary, video clip summary, can bulid on the highlights correspond to replay scene and live scene.A representative scene selection technique is described below.

The representative scene selection for video level summary construction is executed based on representative shot selection method, and then assembles those live and replay scenes to form the summary at the highest level.

The survey of representative scene selection strategy is adopted:

1. Detect the replay scenes and the identical live scenes.
2. Clustering operation is applied to assemble all detected replay and live scenes.
3. Organize the clustered scene structure and display.

5   Experiments Results and Applications

5.1   Video Summarization Results

In the experiments, we take MPEG-1 compressed video as the input. The test data is a set of sports video clip from the live broadcasted TV. They are "The 9th FINA Swiming Champsionships Fukuoka 2001" including the "3m Synchronised Diving Man (A1)" , "3m Synchronised Diving Women (A6)". That is, we mainly focus on diving videos in the experiments.

Total length of the test MPEG-1 video clip is 9:22:48, each frame is 352x288 pixels in size, and the frame rate is 25 frame/s. Videos are parsed into shots first.

Here, we only list the experimental results of A1 and A6. Table 1 lists the experimental results of replay scene dectection, and the accuracy and precise of identical events detection is shown in table 2. The recall and precision is used for replay scene dectection performance evaluation.

$$Precision = \frac{Dectected}{Dectected + False}, \quad recall = \frac{Dectected}{Dectected + Missed} \tag{1}$$

Table 1. The experimental results of replay scene dectection

	A1	A6
Video length	46:54	49:3
Total replay scenes	40	40
Dectected	40	40
False alarm	0	0
Miss	0	0
Recall	100%	100%
Precise	100%	100%

Table 2. The experimental results of identical events detection

	A1	A6
Video length	46:54	49:3
Total live scenes	40	40
Dectected	37	31
False alarm	3	9
Miss	0	0
Recall	100%	100%
Precise	92.5 %	77.5 %

As shown in Table1 and Table2, the accuracy and prcise of replay scene detection is fairly good, and the recall olf identical events detection is also 100%. But there are

12 error identical events detection. The main reason of false alarm and miss identical events detection is due to the approximate error of the camera motion estimation.

Moreover, hierarchical sports video summary at the scene layer is as shown in Fig.3. And corresponding video player window is as shown in Fig.4.

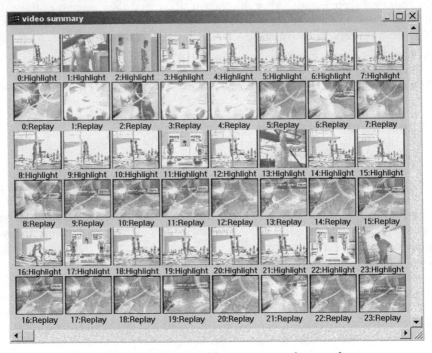

Fig. 3. Hierarchical sports video summary at the scene layer

Fig. 4. Video player window

From the Fig.3 and Fig.4, the sports video summary at the scene layer can contain the meaningful actions of the diving game. And it also present compact and time-compressed summary of the original video. In addition, for directly working in the compress domain, the hierarchical summaries can be generated in real-time.

5.2 Comparison with Current Methods

The main limitation of Zhu [3] is that the class taxonomy is not as expressive as the ontology. For instance, Zhu [3] given the example of the instance for both video category and a specialty category of medical video, but it did not further formalize the relationship between the video category and specialty category. Comparing with the method of Zhu [3], there are two advantages in building ontology. At first, we not only present the class taxonomy of sports video properties but also describe their relationships and restrictions. Secondly, our strategy can express the inherence relation between the four level hierarchy video content descriptions.

5.3 Potential Application

With proposed strategies, ontology based sports video annotation can facilitate video indexing, retrieval and reasoning in a broad range of applications including Digital Olympic Project in China.

"Digital Olympics" is one of the Beijing Olympic Action Plans fro 2008 Beijing Olympics. "Digital Olympics" refers to building all sorts of information and communications basic infrastructures and systems as required by the Olympic games. Our proposed strategies provide a solution to acquire effective and accurate sports video descriptions. Moreover, it can improve the retrieval performance of Olympic video database. In addition, we provide a solution from video summarization to comprehensive video browsing to facilitate Olympic video database indexing, retrieval and browse.

6 Conclusions

In this paper, we have addressed a strategy of sports video ontology to describe the video content. We introduced OWL to build the ontology. Based on this ontology, we describe a user-friendly platform for sports video annotation. Moreover, we present a hierarchical sports video summarization. In sports video, replay scene often represents the highlight or interesting event of the video. Hence, our representative scene selection is based on the replay detection algorithm and identical events detection. Due to the hierarchical video summary can convey the semantic information in various level, our summarization can achieves a more reliable result.

In the future, we will focus on using relevance feedback in the process of video annotation to refine annotation results. In the mean time, we will use video context rules in a reasoning framework for video mining and video reasoning. Our goals is enhancing the effective content-based sports video query and apply the strategy to the Digital Olympic Project in China.

Acknowledgements

This research is very grateful for discussing with Jiang Yunchen and Zhangchunxia. In addition, this work has been supported by Digital Olympic Project in China (2001BA904B07) and Scientific Research Fund of Hunan Provincial Education Department (03C484).

References

1. Jos M.Martnez:(UPM-GTI, ES), Overview of the MPEG-Standard(version 8) ISO/IEC JTC1/SC29/WG11 N4980, Klangenfurt, July 2002.
2. A.Th. Schreiber, et al.: Ontology-Based Photo Annotation, IEEE Intelligent Systems,May-June 2001.
3. X.Q Zhu, J. Fan, A. Elmagarmid: Hierarchical Video Content Description and Summarization Using Unified Semantic and Visual Similarity. Multimedia Systems.Vol.9 , Issue 1 (2003) 31 - 53.
4. M.Dean, G.Schreiber(Eds.):OWL Web Ontology Language Reference, W3C Recommendation, 10 Feb.(2004), http://www.w3.org/TR/owl-ref/ .
5. J. Bao, Y. Cao, W.Tavanapong: Integration of Domain-Specific and Domain-Independent Ontologies for Colonoscopy Video Database Annotation, Proceedings of 2004 International Conference on Information and Knowledge Engineering, Las Vegas, Nevada (2004).
6. J.Q OUYANG,LI J.T,ZHANG Y.D:Replay Boundary Detection in MPEG Compressed Video, IEEE The Second International Conference on Machine Learning and Cybernetics, Xi'an China, (2003)2800-2803.

Author Index

Lecture Notes in Computer Science

For information about Vols. 1–3209

please contact your bookseller or Springer